Further praise for

LAST TRAIN TO MEMPHIS

'Guralnick is the paramount historian of American vernacular music; he writes about blues, country, R. & B., soul, and rockabilly with the curiosity and delight of a teenager tearing the shrink-wrap off a new record . . . It is impossible to imagine a finer book [on Presley], as the familiar course from Tupelo to Graceland is plotted with observant social and cultural history, keen musicology, and good humour'
The New Yorker

'An absorbing biography that is also a slice of social history'
Sunday Times Books of the Year

'Surely the very last word on the King's beginnings'
Q magazine

'It's hard to reclaim Elvis from the weight of history and slander, but Guralnick – as you might expect from his great book about the soul '60s, *Sweet Soul Music* – does it beautifully'
Jon Savage in *Mojo*

'Allow yourself the luxury of sitting and reading Guralnick's book. Not only exhaustive but also excellent on placing the Memphis Flash in his cultural and critical context'
Vox

Also by Peter Guralnick

FEEL LIKE GOING HOME:
Portraits in Blues and Rock 'n' Roll

LOST HIGHWAY:
Journeys and Arrivals of American Musicians

NIGHTHAWK BLUES

SWEET SOUL MUSIC:
Rhythm and Blues and the Southern Dream of Freedom

SEARCHING FOR ROBERT JOHNSON

Last Train to Memphis

Last Train to Memphis

The Rise of Elvis Presley

PETER GURALNICK

An *Abacus* Book

First published in Great Britain in 1994
by Little, Brown and Company
This edition published by Abacus in 1995

A CIP catalogue record for this book
is available from the British Library.

ISBN 0 349 10651 7

FRONTISPIECE:
KATZ DRUG STORE OPENING, SEPTEMBER 8, 1954. (OPAL WALKER)

DESIGNED BY SUSAN MARSH

Printed and bound in Great Britain by
Clays Ltd, St Ives plc

Abacus
A Division of
Little, Brown and Company (UK)
Brettenham House
Lancaster Place
London WC2E 7EN

For my mother and father
and for Alexandra

Contents

Author's Note

"Biography" meant a book about someone's life. Only, for me, it was to become a kind of pursuit, a tracking of the physical trail of someone's path through the past, a following of footsteps. You would never catch them; no, you would never quite catch them. But maybe, if you were lucky, you might write about the pursuit of that fleeting figure in such a way as to bring it alive in the present.

— Richard Holmes, *Footsteps: Adventures of a Romantic Biographer*

I FIRST WROTE about Elvis Presley in 1967. I did so because I loved his music and I felt that it had been unjustly ridiculed and neglected. I was not writing about movies, image, or popularity. I was writing about someone whom I thought of as a great blues singer (I might today amend the term to "heart" singer, in the sense that he sang all the songs he really cared about — blues and gospel and even otherwise inexplicably sentimental numbers — without barrier or affectation) and who I imagined must conceive of himself in the same way. In that same spirit of barrierlessness I sent Elvis a copy of the review at his address, 3764 Highway 51 South (later renamed Elvis Presley Boulevard) in Memphis, and I got a printed Christmas card in reply.

I wrote about him a number of times over the years, seeking in one way or another to rescue him from both his detractors and admirers. What I wrote was based on passionate listening, research, and interviewing, and, of course, the kind of speculation that we inevitably apply to anything, or anyone, whom we admire from a distant shore. I wouldn't altogether disown anything that I wrote, though in retrospect I might correct a good deal of its perspective. But I don't know if I ever thought about the real Elvis Presley until I was driving down McLemore Avenue in South Memphis one day in 1983, past the old Stax studio, with a friend named Rose Clayton. Rose, a native Memphian, pointed out a drugstore where Elvis' cousin used to work. Elvis used to hang out there, she said; he would sit at the soda fountain, drumming his fingers on the countertop. "Poor baby," said Rose, and something went off in my head. This wasn't *"Elvis Presley"*; this was a kid hanging out at a soda fountain in South Memphis, someone who could be observed, just like you or me, daydreaming, listening to the jukebox, drinking a milk shake, waiting for his cousin to get off work. "Poor baby."

I didn't come to the book itself for several years after that, but this was the vision that sustained it. When I finally decided to write the book, I had one simple aim in mind — at least it seemed simple to me at the start: to keep the story within "real" time, to allow the characters to freely breathe their own air, to avoid imposing the judgment of another age, or even the alarums that hindsight inevitably lends. That was what I wanted to do, both because I wanted to remain true to my "characters" — real-life figures whom I had come to know and like in the course of both my travels and research — and because I wanted to suggest the dimensions of a world, the world in which Elvis Presley had grown up, the world which had shaped him and which he in turn had unwittingly shaped, with all the homeliness and beauty that everyday life entails.

Discovering the reality of that world was something like stepping off the edge of my own. The British historian Richard Holmes describes the biographer as "a sort of tramp permanently knocking at the kitchen window and secretly hoping he might be invited in for supper." Holmes is presumably alluding to the researcher's attempt to penetrate the recesses of history, but he might as well be describing the literal truth. If one cannot recognize one's status as an outsider, if I were not able to laugh at the comic contretemps in which I have often found myself over the years, then I would be lacking in the humility necessary for the task. But if one were not vain enough, on the other hand, to think it possible to make sense of the mass of random detail that makes up a life, if one did not imagine oneself capable somehow of the most diverse explorations, divagations, and transcendental leaps, then one would never seek to tell the story. "The moment one begins to investigate the truth of the simplest facts which one has accepted as true," wrote Leonard Woolf in his autobiography, "it is as though one had stepped off a firm narrow path into a bog or a quicksand — every step one takes one steps deeper into the bog of uncertainty." And it is that uncertainty which must be taken as both an unavoidable given and the only real starting point.

For this book I interviewed hundreds of firsthand participants. To my great joy, and not incidental distraction, I discovered worlds within worlds: the world of quartet singing; the pioneering spirit of post–World War II radio; the many worlds of Memphis (which I might have thought I already knew); the carnival world of self-invention and self-promotion out of which Colonel Thomas A. Parker emerged; the small-time dreams of a music industry that had not yet defined itself; the larger dreams of an art form that had not yet been explored. I have tried to suggest these worlds, and the men and women who peopled them, with a respect for the intricacy, complexity, and integrity of their makeup, but, of course, one can only suggest. As for the central figure, I have tried to convey his complexity and irreducibility as well. This is an heroic story, I believe, and ultimately perhaps a tragic one, but — like any of our lives and characters — it is not all of one piece, it does not lend itself to one interpretation exclusively, nor do all its parts reflect anything that resembles an undifferentiated whole. To say this, I hope, is not to throw up one's hands at the impossibility of the task; it is, simply, to embrace the variousness, and uniqueness, of human experience.

I wanted to tell a true story. I wanted to rescue Elvis Presley from the dreary bondage of myth, from the oppressive aftershock of cultural significance. To the extent that I have succeeded, I suppose, I have merely opened up the subject to new aftershocks, new forms of encapsulation. Like any biographer, I am sure, I have worried over scenes, imagined and reimagined the way that things must have been, all too keenly aware of my own limitations of perspective and the distorting lens of history. I have sought to reconcile accounts that cannot be reconciled, and I have engaged in the kind of dialogue with my subject that Richard Holmes describes as leading to "a relationship of *trust*" between biographer and subject. As Holmes points out, trust is what one seeks, implicitly, to achieve, and yet there is always the possibility that trust is misplaced: "The possibility of error," he insists, "is constant in all biography."

That is why I would like to suggest that this work, like any other, is a beginning, not an end, an invitation to inquiry, not an attempt at foreclosure upon it. So much of what becomes a story, whether formally or merely in the relation of a dinner-table anecdote, is based upon verbal shorthand, metaphorical leaps of faith, *interpretation* of the facts at hand. It should be clearly understood: facts can change, and new interpretations can, at any moment, alter our interpretation of them. This is *my* story of Elvis Presley: it cannot be *the* story of Elvis Presley. There is no such thing; even autobiography, or perhaps autobiography most of all, represents an editing of the facts, a selection of detail, an attempt to make sense of the various, arbitrary developments of real life. In the end, there should be nothing shocking about human existence, because, in the end, whatever has occurred is simply human. If I have succeeded in my aim, I have given the reader the tools to create his or her own portrait of a young Elvis Presley, the opportunity to reinvent and reinterpret, within the broad context of a particular time and place, the early life of a remarkable American original.

Last Train to Memphis

WITH DEWEY PHILLIPS, BEALE STREET, 1956. (ROBERT WILLIAMS)

PROLOGUE: MEMPHIS, 1950

It is late May or early June, hot, steamy; a fetid breeze comes in off the river and wafts its way through the elegant lobby of the Hotel Peabody, where, it is said, the Mississippi Delta begins. There is a steady hum of conversation in the room — polite, understated, well bred, but never letting up: the room is redolent with the suggestion of business dealings transacted in grandiloquent style, amid cigar smoke and sips of whiskey, with the anticipation of a social evening to come. When the novelist William Faulkner is in town, he always stays at the Peabody; perhaps he is observing this very scene.

Out on the street men pass by, walking with deliberate speed. They are wearing Panama hats and straw boaters; some are in shirtsleeves and suspenders, wearing their pants high up on their waist; most are more formally dressed in summer-weight seersucker suits. The women generally look cool and elegant in broad, shadowing hats and light summer dresses. The Negroes whom you see all fulfill a function: they are maids, bootblacks, barbers, bellboys, each playing a familiar, muted role. But if you wanted to get another sense of the life of these accommodating, uncomplaining, almost invisible handmaidens and impersonal valets to white wealth and power, you would only have to go around the corner, to Beale Street, a lively, thriving, brightly colored metropolis of quite another sort.

In the Peabody Drugstore, on the corner of Union and Second, a well-dressed, elegant-looking young man of twenty-seven sits, nervously drumming his fingers on the countertop. His tie is carefully knotted, his luxuriant chestnut-brown hair is carefully sculpted in such a fashion that you know that this might be the feature of which he is most proud; he is smoking a Chesterfield in a slender cigarette holder and wearing a gold pocket chain. He is an arresting-looking young man in every way, but it is his eyes which truly compel attention. Set low under fairly prominent brows, they are neither small nor especially close together, but they give the impression in a photograph that they are squinting, in real life that their possessor is gazing into your very soul. Right now they are looking about, distracted, not focusing on anything in particular, until at last they catch sight of the very person they are looking for, as a tall, redheaded, loose-limbed, and rawboned young man, clearly from the country and not ashamed of it, bursts through the door. His mouth curls in a little smile that suggests neither the need for, nor the hint of, any apology; his brightly patterned shirt stands at odds with the elegance of the earlier arrival, whom he evidently does not know but greets with an expansive wave, an infectious bonhomie, and then a clap on the back and a loudly brayed "Dee-gaw!"

The newcomer, Dewey Phillips, is twenty-four years old and already a radio celebrity, with his own show on WHBQ broadcasting from the Gayoso Hotel just up the street. He is on the air from 10:00 P.M. to midnight every weekday, and until 1:00 A.M. on Saturday nights, while keeping his job in the record department at W. T. Grant's, on South Main. The music that he plays is some of the finest American vernacular music ever recorded: in the course of one fifteen-minute segment, you might hear Muddy Waters' latest hit, a gospel number by the Soul Stirrers (with their great singer, R. H. Harris), Larry Darnell's "For You, My Love," and Wynonie Harris' "Good Rockin' Tonight"—"boogies, blues, and spirituals," as the *Memphis Commercial Appeal* reports in a full-length feature. He mangles the names of his advertisers, plays 78s at the wrong speed, and appends to every commercial message the grace note "I don't care where you go or how you go, just tell 'em Phillips sent you." Only recently one of his listeners was taken to the hospital emergency ward and announced to a startled medical staff that Phillips had sent him. He has perhaps the most popular show on Memphis radio, with talk of Mutual broadcast syndication. Tastes being what they are, and the postwar world being as unpredictable and unconventionally wide open as it has become, there is only one thing that is truly startling about his success: the music that he plays, and the listeners that he reaches, are almost exclusively black.

That is why Sam Phillips has wanted so badly to meet him. Aside from the coincidence of their names, there is a coincidence of purpose which links these two very disparate-seeming young men. Just six months ago, Sam Phillips, with the assistance of Marion Keisker, a prominent Memphis radio personality best known for her *Kitty Kelly* show on WREC, launched his own studio, the Memphis Recording Service, at 706 Union Avenue, with the avowed purpose of recording "Negro artists in the South who wanted to make a record [and] just had no place to go. . . . I set up a studio just to make records with some of those great Negro artists." Phillips, an engineer and sometime disc jockey on WREC, the CBS affiliate whose offices were in the Peabody, had come to town in 1945. He had started in radio as a teenager in his native region of Muscle Shoals, Alabama, and at twenty-two was engineering the network broadcasts every night from the Peabody Skyway. And yet despite his abiding love for big band music — for the Dorsey brothers and Glenn Miller, Freddy Martin and Ted Weems — he had come to feel that it was all just too programmed, that "the girl singer just sat up there and looked pretty, the musicians might have played the damn song four thousand times, but they were *still* turning the pages!"

At the same time Sam believed wholeheartedly in the music that he had grown up with as a child, in the glorious spiritual offerings of the Negro church, in the tales and songs of Uncle Silas Payne, who had worked on his father's farm and told the little boy stories of Memphis' Beale Street, trips to the Molasses River, and the battercake trees which grew up next to the sausage trees in Africa. "I listened to that beautiful a cappella singing — the windows of the black Methodist church just half a block down from Highland Baptist would all be open, and I was just fascinated by the rhythms. Even when they hoed, they'd get a rhythm going, maybe more than one, and there was that beautiful rhythmic silence of the cotton fields, with a hoe hitting a rock every now and then just as it spaded through the dirt, and then the singing, especially if the wind happened to be from the right direction — believe me, all that said a lot to me."

Many children have been entranced by just such encounters, but they grow up, they put aside childish things, in Sam Phillips' words, they *conform*. Sam Phillips believed in something else. He believed — entirely and without reservation — in differentness, in independence, in individuation, he believed in himself, and he believed — even to the point of articulating it in public and private utterances from earliest adulthood on — in the scope and beauty of African-American culture. He wanted, he said, "genuine, untutored negro" music; he was looking for "Negroes with field mud on their boots and patches in their overalls . . . battered instruments and unfettered techniques." The music that he was attempting to record was the very music that Dewey Phillips was playing on the air.

The ostensible reason for his meeting with Dewey was that his uncle-in-law, Jimmy Connolly, who was general manager of the 250-watt station WJLD in Bessemer, Alabama, where he had gone after first hiring Sam in Muscle Shoals, had launched a program called *The Atomic Boogie Hour*. This was an afternoon program similar to the kind of show that Dewey had started in Memphis and that was springing up in one form or another all across the South: black music on a white radio station with a strong Negro audience and a growing, if for the most part unacknowledged, core of young white listeners with a growing, if for the most part unexamined, buying power. The owner of the station, a Mr. Johnson, didn't want Connolly doing the show anymore, because it was "low-brow," and Sam had told his uncle-in-law about "this cat that's on the air here that you wouldn't believe." Jimmy suggested that he talk to Dewey about coming to Bessemer, and Sam agreed, but his heart wasn't in it. "I just didn't want Dewey leaving Memphis. I even backed off a little on my recommendation afterwards: I told Jimmy, 'Well, your *Atomic Boogie Hour* is fantastic, but I'm just not sure if Dewey would fit in. This is a guy that somehow or another generates a night atmosphere. . . . What we need in Memphis is exactly what Dewey Phillips is doing.' I could have gotten Dewey a job just like that, but I told him, I said, 'Dewey, I'm going to try to get something going, in the way of making records.' "

Who knows what they did in the immediate aftermath of that initial meeting? Perhaps they wandered over to Beale Street, where Dewey, who has been described as "transracial" by more than one admirer, could go wherever he liked, where Dewey, Sam came to see with some ambivalence, was "a hero, everyone loved him." Perhaps they walked by the Hippodrome, where Roy Brown or Larry Darnell or Wynonie Harris could have been playing that very evening. They might have run into club owner–entrepreneur Andrew "Sunbeam" Mitchell or the Beale Street Blues Boy himself, B. B. King, whom Sam would start to record for the California-based RPM (Modern) label just around this time. One-man band Joe Hill Louis was probably playing in Handy Park. Or they might have just decided to go down to Johnny Mills' Barbecue at Fourth and Beale for a fish sandwich.

Wherever they went, Dewey would have been greeted with cries of delighted recognition, and he returned those greetings with unfeigned goodwill, unfettered enthusiasm, a delighted exclamation of his own. Sam, meanwhile, quieter, more reserved, more formal somehow, hung back, soaking up a scene that held long-standing reverberations for him as well. He had dreamt of Beale Street long before he ever saw it, from the stories that Uncle Silas had spun, and his first view of it, at sixteen, had not failed to live up to his expectations. He was on his way to Dallas with his older brother Jud and some friends to hear the Reverend George W. Truett preach, but he was drawn, it seemed, almost inexorably to Beale, because "to me Beale Street was the most famous place in the South. We got in at five or six o'clock in the morning and it was pouring down rain, but we just drove up and down, and it was so much more than I had even envisioned. I don't know if I can explain it to this day — my eyes had to be very big, because I saw everything, from winos to people dressed up fit to kill, young, old, city slickers and people straight out of the cotton fields, somehow or another you could tell: *every damn one of them was glad to be there*. Beale Street represented for me something that I hoped to see one day for all people, something that they could say, I'm a part of this somehow." This was Sam Phillips' vision, and he kept it with him when he moved to Memphis with his wife and infant son some six years later. Memphis had drawn him like a magnet, but not for the elegant appointments of the Hotel Peabody or the big band broadcasts from the Skyway. It was Beale Street that lured him in a way he would never be able to fully explain and Beale Street with which, as it was, he could never be fully comfortable.

Sam and Dewey Phillips went on to become closer than brothers; they propped each other up in times of trouble and undoubtedly dragged each other down on some occasions as well. They became business partners for the briefest of moments, within just a month or two of that initial meeting, when Sam launched a label called The Phillips, which put out one official release ("Boogie in the Park," by Joe Hill Louis, with three hundred copies pressed), and then dissolved it for reasons never fully specified. For all of their shared values, however, for all of their shared dreams and schemes and the fact that they were laboring in the same field (Sam continued to record blues singers like Howlin' Wolf and B. B. King for some time for various labels and then started up a label of his own; Daddy-O-Dewey just got bigger and bigger on the radio), they were not destined to come together in business or in the history books for another four years, one year after the unheralded and altogether unanticipated arrival of an eighteen-year-old Elvis Presley in Sam Phillips' Sun recording studio.

The Presleys were themselves relatively recent arrivals in Memphis in 1950, having picked up stakes in their native Tupelo, Mississippi, in the fall of 1948, when their only child was thirteen years old. Their adjustment to city life was difficult at first. Although the husband, Vernon, had worked in a munitions plant in Memphis for much of the war, good, steady peacetime work was not easy to come by, and the three of them were crammed into a single room in one boardinghouse or another for the first few months after their arrival. Wary, watchful, shy almost to the point of reclusiveness, the boy was obviously frightened by his new surroundings, and on his first day of school at sixteen-hundred-student Humes High (which went from seventh to twelfth grade) he was back at the rooming house almost before his father had finished dropping him off. Vernon found him "so nervous he was bug-eyed. When I asked what was the matter, he said he didn't know where the office was and classes had started and there were so many kids. He was afraid they'd laugh at him." His father, a taciturn, suspicious man, understood: in some ways the Presleys gave the impression to both relatives and neighbors that they lived in their own private world. "I thought about it a minute," said Vernon, "and I knew what he meant. So I said, 'Son, that's all right for today, but tomorrow you be there, nine o'clock, and no foolin'!' "

In February 1949, Vernon finally landed a regular job, at United Paint Company, just a few blocks away from the rooming house on Poplar they had moved into, and on June 17 he applied for admission to Lauderdale Courts, a neat public assistance housing project administered by the Memphis Housing Authority. In September their application was finally approved, and they moved to 185 Winchester, Apartment 328, just around the corner from where they were presently living. The rent was thirty-five dollars a month for a two-bedroom ground-floor apartment in a well-maintained neighborly complex. Everyone in Lauderdale Courts felt as if they were on their way somewhere. If only in terms of aspirations, for the Presley family it was a big step up.

TUPELO CIRCA 1942. (COURTESY OF THE ESTATE OF ELVIS PRESLEY)

TUPELO: ABOVE THE HIGHWAY

VERNON PRESLEY was never particularly well regarded in Tupelo. He was a man of few words and little ambition, and even in the separate municipality of East Tupelo, where he lived with his family "above the highway," a tiny warren of houses clustered together on five unpaved streets running off the Old Saltillo Road, he was seen as something of a vacant, if good-looking, even handsome, ne'er-do-well. East Tupelo itself was separated by more than just the geographical barrier of two small creeks, corn and cotton fields, and the Mobile & Ohio and St. Louis & San Francisco railroad tracks from the life of a parent city which was hailed in the 1938 WPA Guide as "perhaps Mississippi's best example of what contemporary commentators call the 'New South.' " East Tupelo, on the other hand, was a part of the New South that tended to get glossed over, the home of many of the "poor white" factory workers and sharecroppers who could fuel a vision of "industry rising in the midst of agriculture and agricultural customs" so long as the social particulars of that vision were not scrutinized too closely. "Over the years of its existence and even after its merger with Tupelo [in 1946]," wrote a local historian, "East Tupelo had the reputation of being an extremely rough town. Some citizens doubt that it was worse than other small towns, but others declare it to have been the roughest town in North Mississippi. The town had its red light district called 'Goosehollow.' . . . By 1940 the tiny community of East Tupelo was known to have at least nine bootleggers."

In 1936 the mayor of East Tupelo was Vernon Presley's uncle, Noah, who lived on Kelly Street above the highway, owned a small grocery store, and drove the school bus. Noah's brother, Jessie, Vernon's father, was relatively comfortable as well, if not as upstanding a member of the community. He owned his own home on Old Saltillo Road, just above Kelly Street, and he worked fairly steadily, even if he had a reputation as a hard drinker and a "rogue." Vernon, by way of contrast, showed little drive or direction. Though he worked through the Depression at a succession of odd jobs (milkman, sharecropper, WPA carpenter, day laborer), he never really seemed to make a go of it, and he never seemed to particularly care about making a go of it either. Closemouthed, recessive, almost brooding at times, "dry" in the description of his friends, Vernon did appear to care deeply about his little family: his wife, Gladys Smith, whom he married in 1933; his son, Elvis Aron Presley, who was born on January 8, 1935; the twin, Jesse Garon, whom they had lost. He built a home in preparation for the birth, a two-room shotgun shack next to his parents' four-room "big house," with the help of his father and his older brother, Vester (who in September 1935 would marry Gladys' sister Clettes). He took out what amounted to a mortgage of $180 from Orville Bean, on whose dairy farm he and his father occasionally worked, with the property remaining Bean's until the loan was paid off. There was a pump and an outhouse in the back, and although East Tupelo was one of the first beneficiaries of the TVA rural electrification program, the new home was lit with oil lamps when he and Gladys moved in in December 1934.

Gladys Presley, everyone agreed, was the spark of that marriage. Where Vernon was taciturn to the point of sullenness, she was voluble, lively, full of spunk. They had both dropped out of school at an early age, but Gladys — who had grown up on a succession of farms in the area with seven brothers and sisters — took a backseat to no one. When she was twenty, her father died, and she heard of a job at the Tupelo Garment Plant that paid two dollars a day for a twelve-hour workday. There was a bus to pick up the girls who lived out in the country, but not long after starting work she decided to move to town, and she settled herself and her family on Kelly Street in the little community above the highway, in East Tupelo, where her uncles Sims and Gains Mansell already lived and Gains co-pastored the tiny new First Assembly of God Church that had sprung up in a tent on a vacant lot. That was where she met Vernon Presley. She saw him on the street, and then she met him at a typically charismatic, "Holy Roller"–type church service. In June 1933 they ran off with another couple and got married in Pontotoc, Mississippi, where Vernon, still a minor, added five years to his age and claimed to be twenty-two, while Gladys reduced hers by two, to nineteen. They borrowed the three dollars for the license from their friends Marshall and Vona Mae Brown, with whom they moved in for a short time after the marriage.

Gladys had a difficult pregnancy and toward the end had to quit her job at the Garment Plant. When she came to term, Vernon's mother, Minnie, a midwife named Edna Martin, and one other woman attended her until the midwife called the doctor, sixty-eight-year-old William Robert Hunt. At about four in the morning of January 8, he delivered a baby, stillborn, then thirty-five minutes later another boy. The twins were named Jesse Garon and Elvis Aron, with the rhyming middle names intended to match. Aron (pronounced with a long *a* and the emphasis on the first syllable) was for Vernon's friend Aaron Kennedy, Elvis was Vernon's middle name, and Jesse, of course, was for his father. The dead twin was buried in an unmarked grave in Priceville Cemetery, just below Old Saltillo Road, and was never forgotten either in the legend that accompanied his celebrated younger brother or in family memory. As a child Elvis was said to have frequently visited his brother's grave; as an adult he referred to his twin again and again, reinforced by Gladys' belief that "when one twin died, the one that lived got all the strength of both." Shortly after the birth both mother and child were taken to the hospital, and Gladys was never able to have another baby. The physician's fifteen-dollar fee was paid by welfare.

Elvis grew up a loved and precious child. He was, everyone agreed, unusually close to his mother. Vernon spoke of it after his son became famous, almost as if it were a source of wonder that anyone could be that close. Throughout her life the son would call her by pet names, they would communicate by baby talk, "she worshiped him," said a neighbor, "from the day he was born." He was attached to his father as well. "When we went swimming, Elvis would have fits if he saw me dive," Vernon recalled. "He was so afraid something would happen to me." And Gladys told of a house fire in East Tupelo, when Vernon ran in and out of the burning building trying to salvage a neighbor's belongings. "Elvis was so sure that his daddy was going to get hurt that he screamed and cried. I had to hold him to keep him from running in after Vernon. I said right sharp, 'Elvis, you just stop that. Your daddy knows what he's doing.' " Elvis' own view of his growing up was more prosaic. "My mama never let me out of her sight. I couldn't go down to the creek with the other kids. Sometimes when I was little, I used to run off. Mama would whip me, and I thought she didn't love me."

In that respect, and in every other, there was not much out of the ordinary about the young Presley family. They were a little peculiar, perhaps, in their insularity, but they were active in church and community, and they had realistic hopes and expectations for their only child. Vernon was, in his own view, a "common laborer," but Gladys was determined that her son would graduate from high school.

In 1937 Gladys' uncle Gains became sole preacher at the Assembly of God Church, which was now housed in a modest wood-framed structure on Adams Street built primarily by Gains. Many in the tiny congregation later recalled a very young Elvis Presley throwing himself into the hymn singing with abandon, and Gladys liked to tell how "when Elvis was just a little fellow, not more than two years old, he would slide down off my lap, run into the aisle and scramble up to the platform. There he would stand looking at the choir and trying to sing with them. He was too little to know the words . . . but he could carry the tune and he would watch their faces and try to do as they did."

It was shortly thereafter that the life of the Presley family was forever changed, or at least diverted from what might have been a more predictable course. Vernon, Gladys' brother Travis, and a man named Lether Gable were charged on November 16, 1937, with "uttering a forged instrument" — altering, and then cashing, a four-dollar check of Orville Bean's made out to Vernon to pay for a hog. On May 25, 1938, Vernon and his two companions were sentenced to three years in Parchman Farm.

In fact, he remained in prison for only eight months, but this was a shaping event in the young family's life. In later years Elvis would often say of his father, "My daddy may seem hard, but you don't know what he's been through," and though it was never a secret, it was always a source of shame. "It was no big disgrace," said Corene Randle Smith, a childhood neighbor. "Everyone realized that Mr. Bean just made an example of him, and that he was on the up-and-up, except maybe that one little time." But it seemed to mark, forever, Vernon's view of himself: few enough saw him as a solid provider before this incident; he could no longer see himself in that role in its aftermath.

During the brief time that he was in prison, Gladys lost the house and moved in briefly with her in-laws next door. There was no love lost between Gladys and Jessie, though, and soon mother and child moved to Tupelo, where Gladys lived with her cousins Frank and Leona Richards on Maple Street and got a job at the Mid-South Laundry. The Richards' daughter, Corinne, retained vivid memories of the forlorn mother and son. When Elvis played ball with the other children out in the street, Corinne said, Gladys was "afraid that he would get run over. She didn't want him out of her sight. She had always been lively, but after [Vernon] went to prison she was awful nervous." To writer Elaine Dundy, Leona recalled Elvis sitting on the porch "crying his eyes out because his daddy was away." On weekends Gladys and her son frequently rode the Greyhound five hours each way to visit Vernon at Parchman.

Vernon, Travis, and Lether Gable were released from jail on February 6, 1939, in response to a community petition, and a letter from Orville Bean requesting sentence suspension. The Presleys continued to live with Gladys' cousins for a brief time, and all three experienced what Leona Richards called "action nightmares," sleepwalking episodes that none could recall in the morning. They soon moved back to East Tupelo, going from one small rented house to another.

In 1940 they moved briefly to Pascagoula, Mississippi, near Biloxi on the Gulf Coast, with Vernon's cousin Sales and his wife, Annie, and their children. Vernon and Sales had found work on a WPA project to expand the Pascagoula shipyards, and the two families stayed six or eight months until Sales and Annie announced that they were heading home. Vernon bravely declared that he thought he and his family would stay, but he caught up with Sales on the road before Sales and Annie had gotten very far, and both families headed back to Tupelo together. They moved in for a time with Vernon's brother, Vester, and his wife, Clettes (Gladys' sister), then continued the cycle of temporary jobs and even more temporary abodes, with the First Assembly Church serving increasingly as their social as well as moral focus. In the fall of 1941 Elvis started school at the seven-hundred-pupil East Tupelo Consolidated (grades 1 through 12), on Lake Street, across Highway 78, about half a mile away. Every day Gladys walked Elvis proudly to school, a small towheaded youngster accompanied by his dark-haired, flashing-eyed mother, the two of them clasping hands tightly when they got to the highway, a picture of apprehensive devotion.

"Though we had friends and relatives, including my parents," Vernon recalled, "the three of us formed our own private world." The little boy was as insular in his way as his parents. Apart from family, his few friends from that period have painted him as separate from any crowd — there are no recollections of a "gang," just isolated memories of making cars out of apple crates, playing out behind someone's house, going fishing once in a while with James Ausborn, who lived over by the school. "Mrs. Presley would say to be back at two, and he'd get worried, keep looking at the sun, say, 'I believe it's about two o'clock. We better go.' " He was a gentle boy, his father said; "[one time] I asked him to go hunting with me, but when he answered, 'Daddy, I don't want to kill birds,' I didn't try to persuade him to go against his feelings." Once he learned to read he loved comic books; they captured his imagination — he loved the brightly colored pages and the forceful images of power and success. "Elvis would hear us worrying about our debts, being out of work and sickness," his mother recollected proudly, "and he'd say, 'Don't you worry none, Baby. When I grow up, I'm going to buy you a fine house and pay everything you owe at the grocery store and get two Cadillacs — one for you and Daddy, and one for me.' " "I [just] didn't want him to have to steal one," said Vernon.

For the most part he failed to distinguish himself in any way. At school he was "an average student," "sweet and average," according to his teachers, and he himself rarely spoke of his childhood years, except to note that they had not been easy and, occasionally, to recall moments of rejection. With his father, toward the end of his life, he reminisced about the time Vernon had taken him to see his first movie, "and we couldn't let the church know anything about it." The picture that you see of him with his third-grade class shows a little boy standing apart, arms folded, hair neatly combed, his mouth inverted in that familiar pout. Everyone else — the Farrars, the Harrises, Odell Clark — seems connected somehow, grouped together, smiling, arms around each other's shoulders. Elvis stands apart — not shunned, just apart. That is not the way any of his classmates ever remembered it, but it is how the picture looks.

There are a multitude of semiapocryphal stories from these years, most based on the kind of homely memories of childhood that any of us is likely to possess: who focuses upon the classmate who is out of the picture, why should anyone have noticed Elvis Presley in particular or committed to memory his every utterance, noted his views on issues of the day, or even imagined that he would ever come to anything? The war was going on, but it seems never to have impinged upon memories of growing up in East Tupelo, except, perhaps, to have provided opportunities for employment. In 1942 Vernon worked on the construction of a POW camp in Como, Mississippi, forty miles from Memphis. The following year, like so many other men looking to help out their family, he actually moved to Memphis, to work in a munitions plant, and that is where he stayed throughout the war, coming home only on weekends. "I'd tramp all over town looking for so much as a single room. I'd find one, and first thing they would ask is, 'You got any children?' And I'd say I had a little boy. Then they'd shut . . . the door." On August 18, 1945, with the war barely over, Vernon used the savings that he had accumulated from his war work to make a down payment of two hundred dollars on a new home on Berry Street, once again owned by Orville Bean, and around the same time, with his cousin Sales' sponsorship, became a deacon in the church. This was undoubtedly the high point of the Presleys' life in East Tupelo.

Obviously this is not the whole picture, but in the absence of time travel, what collection of random snapshots could provide one? One of the most common stories to have made its way down through the years is that the Presleys formed a popular gospel trio who sang in church, traveled about to various revival meetings in the area, and generally stood out in people's memories as a foreshadowing of what was just over the horizon. It is not difficult to understand where the story would come from: the Presleys, like every other member of the small congregation, did sing in church; they did go to revival meetings; Vernon and Gladys most likely sang "quartet-style" with Sales and Annie in church and at home. But the story that they formed any kind of traveling trio is most likely not true. As Elvis himself said in a 1965 interview, "I sang some with my folks in the Assembly of God church choir [but] it was a small church, so you couldn't sing too loud," and he told Hollywood reporter Army Archerd that he "trioed" with his mother and father — but only as part of that same congregation. There is no mention on his part of anything resembling "professional" experience and no credible contemporary witness in the face of relatives (Corinne Richards), childhood friends and neighbors (Corene Randle Smith, whose mother was Elvis' Sunday school teacher), and the minister who taught him to play guitar (Frank Smith, Corene's husband) who recalled otherwise or found the suggestion highly implausible.

What is not only plausible but clearly the case is that Elvis himself, on his own and without reference to anyone else's dreams, plans, or imaginings, was drawn to music in a way that he couldn't fully express, found a kind of peace in the music, was able to imagine something that he could express only to his mother. Still, it must have come as a surprise even to Gladys when Elvis Presley, her shy, dreamy, oddly playful child, got up and sang in front of an audience of several hundred at the age of ten at the annual Mississippi-Alabama Fair and Dairy Show at the Fairgrounds in the middle of downtown Tupelo.

It came about, evidently (though here, too, the story is unavoidably muddled), after he sang "Old Shep," the Red Foley "weeper" about a boy and his dog, at the morning prayer program at school. His teacher, Mrs. Oleta Grimes, who had moved in two doors down from the Presleys on Old Saltillo Road in 1936 and was, not entirely coincidentally, the daughter of Orville Bean, was so impressed by his singing that she brought him to the principal, Mr. Cole, who in turn entered the fifth-grader in the radio talent contest sponsored by local station WELO on Children's Day (Wednesday, October 3, 1945) at the fair. All the local schools were let out, teachers and children were transported to town by school bus and then marched from the courthouse lawn down the hill to the Fairgrounds, where they were guests of the fair. A prize was given to the school with the greatest proportional representation, and there were individual prizes in the talent contest, from a $25 war bond down to $2.50 for rides. The five-day-long fair included a livestock show, cattle auctions, mule- and horse-pulling contests, and poultry competition, but the Duke of Paducah and a Grand Ole Opry Company which included Minnie Pearl and Pee Wee King were advertised as well. Annie Presley, Sales' wife, recalled the fair as the highlight of both Presley families' social year, when the two couples would share a baby-sitter and go out together for the fair's last night.

The newspaper did not cover the children's contest or even list the winner of the competition. Over the years there have been a number of claimants to the throne, but to Elvis Presley it mattered little who actually won. "They entered me in a talent show," he said in a 1972 interview. "I wore glasses, no music, and I won, I think it was fifth place in this state talent contest. I got a whipping the same day, my mother whipped me for something — I don't know, [going on] one of the rides. Destroyed my ego completely." Gladys gave a more vivid account in 1956, minus the whipping. "I'll never forget, the man at the gate just took it for granted I was Elvis' big sister and sold me a schoolkid's ticket same as him. Elvis had no way to make music, and the other kids wouldn't accompany him. He just climbed up on a chair so he could reach the microphone and he sang 'Old Shep.' " He probably had his picture taken in the western booth, too, just as he would two years later, complete with cowboy hat, chaps, and western backdrop. Although, somewhat surprisingly, there seems to have been little awareness of his triumph among friends and classmates, and he evidently did not sing at the fair again, Elvis always spoke of the event, without embroidery, as the first time he sang in public, and the whipping is a more convincing detail than the conventional story, which has Vernon listening in on the contest on his delivery-truck radio.

It was not long after the contest that he got his first guitar. The chronology can be argued any way you like (and has been), but it appears likely that he got the guitar for his eleventh birthday, since in all of Elvis' own accounts — and in most of the early publicity accounts as well — he sang unaccompanied at the fair simply because he did not have a guitar. In many of those same accounts he was supposed to have gotten the guitar as a birthday present, and the 1956 *TV Radio Mirror* biography has him getting his first guitar the day after a storm which frightened Gladys and him (the tornado of 1936 had been a traumatic event that literally flattened Tupelo, killing 201 people and injuring more than 1,000). In fact there was a small tornado on January 7, 1946, the day before his eleventh birthday. In any case Elvis wanted a bicycle, he said, and the only reason he ended up with the guitar was because his mother was worried that he might get run over, not to mention the fact that the guitar was considerably less expensive (he got the bicycle not long afterward anyway). "Son, wouldn't you rather have the guitar?" Gladys concluded. "It would help you with your singing, and everyone does enjoy hearing you sing."

His uncle Vester, who played frequently in honky-tonks and at country dances and had a great appreciation for country music, and Gladys' brother Johnny Smith taught him a few chords, but it was the new pastor, twenty-one-year-old Frank Smith, who provided the greatest influence. Smith, who had come to Tupelo from Meridian, Mississippi, for a revival in early 1944 and then returned to stay when he married the Presleys' fifteen-year-old neighbor Corene Randle later that year, distinctly recalled the little boy coming to him with the guitar he had just acquired. "I always played the guitar, and I guess he picked up some from that, because a couple of years [after Smith's arrival] he got a guitar and really applied himself. He bought a book that showed how to place your fingers in position, and I went over to his house a time or two, or he would come to where I was, and I would show him some runs and different chords from what he was learning out of his book. That was all: not enough to say I taught him how to play, but I helped him." From his newfound knowledge Elvis started playing for the "special singing" portion of the service, although Smith had to call him up to get him to perform. "I would have to insist on him [getting up there], he didn't push himself. At the special singings we might have someone do a Blackwood Brothers type of quartet number, different ones in the church would get up or maybe somebody visiting would sing, but there were no other kids to sing with him at that time. He sang quite a few times, and he was liked."

Smith put no particular stock in music other than to glorify the Lord and never found it anything but painful to have to dredge up the memory of teaching an eleven-year-old how to play the guitar when this was scarcely relevant to his life's work. Yet even to him Elvis' commitment to music was clear-cut, not just from his singing in church but from the trips that he, the Smiths, and many other East Tupeloans would make to town on Saturday afternoon to attend the WELO Jamboree, a kind of amateur hour which was broadcast from the courthouse. "A whole crowd went down, grown-ups and kids. You got in line to perform, it was just something to do on Saturday. And he would go to the radio station to play and sing — there was nothing to highlight him, really, he was just one of the kids."

WELO HAD BEGUN BROADCASTING on South Spring Street, above the Black and White dry goods store, on May 15, 1941. There were a number of local talents involved in starting up the station, including Charlie Boren, its colorful announcer, and Archie Mackey, a local bandleader and radio technician who had been instrumental in establishing Tupelo's first radio station, WDIX, some years earlier, but the hillbilly star of the station in 1946 was a twenty-three-year-old native of Smithville, some twenty miles to the southeast, Carvel Lee Ausborn, who went by the name of Mississippi Slim. Ausborn, who had taken up guitar at the age of thirteen to pursue a career in music, was inspired by Jimmie Rodgers, though Hank Williams and Ernest Tubb became almost equal influences in the forties. Probably his greatest influence, however, was his cousin Rod Brasfield, a prominent country comedian, also from Smithville, who joined the Opry in 1944 and toured with Hank Williams, while his brother, Uncle Cyp Brasfield, became a regular on the Ozark Jubilee and wrote material for Rod and his comedy partner, Minnie Pearl. Though Mississippi Slim never attained such heights, he traveled all over the country with Goober and His Kentuckians and the Bisbee's Comedians tent show and even played the Opry once or twice, largely on the strength of his cousin's connections. Just about every prominent musician who passed through Tupelo played with Slim at one time or another, from Merle "Red" Taylor (who furnished the fiddle melody for Bill Monroe's "Uncle Pen") to college-bound youths like Bill Mitchell (who in later life, after a career in politics, would win many national old-time fiddle contests), to weekend pickers like Slim's uncle Clinton. "He was a good entertainer," recalled Bill Mitchell, "put on a pretty good show, love songs with comedy (he came from a family of comedians) — it was a pretty lively show. The people really enjoyed it." In addition to a regular early-morning program on weekdays, Slim had a noontime show every Saturday called *Singin' and Pickin' Hillbilly* that served as a lead-in to the Jamboree, on which he also appeared. This was where Elvis first encountered the world of entertainment.

Archie Mackey's memory was of a young boy accompanied by his father. "Vernon said that his boy didn't know but two songs," said Mackey, another Jamboree regular, who claimed that he had Elvis sing both, with Slim accompanying him on guitar. Some have suggested that Slim was reluctant to play behind an "amateur" and that announcer Charlie Boren practically had to force him to do so, while others have sought credit for first carrying Elvis to the station. It's all somewhat academic. Like everyone else, he was drawn by the music and by the show. He was not the only child to perform, though according to Bill Mitchell most of the others were girls. And, it seemed, none of the others felt it like he did.

"He was crazy about music," said James Ausborn, Slim's kid brother and Elvis' schoolmate at East Tupelo Consolidated. "That's all he talked about. A lot of people didn't like my brother, they thought he was sort of corny, but, you know, they had to get a mail truck to bring all his cards and letters. Elvis would always say, 'Let's go to your brother's program today. Can you go up there with me? I want him to show me some more chords on the guitar.' We'd walk into town on Saturday, go down to the station on Spring Street [this was the broadcast before the Jamboree], a lot of times the studio would be full but my brother would always show him some chords. Sometimes he would say, 'I ain't got time to fool with you today,' but he'd always sit down and show him. Then maybe he'd sing him a couple of songs, and Elvis would try to sing them himself. I think gospel sort of inspirated him to be in music, but then my brother helped carry it on."

Music had become his consuming passion. With the exception of a couple of playmates who shared his interest, like James, or who might have looked up to him for it, no one really noticed. His uncle Vester, who said that his mother's people, the Hoods, were "musicians out of this world," never noticed the transformation. Frank Smith saw him as one of the crowd, not really "eager" for music — "he just liked it." Even his parents might have missed this development in their closely watched son: "He always knew," said Vernon, as if he and Gladys had ever doubted, "he was going to do something. When we didn't have a dime, he used to sit on the doorstep and say, 'One of these days it'll be different.' "

If you picture him, picture someone you might have missed: a wide-eyed, silent child scuffling his feet, wearing overalls. He stands in line in the courtroom, waiting his turn to tiptoe up to the mike. His small child's voice carries a quavering note of yearning — other children get up and do letter-perfect recitals, big burly men frail on their beat-up guitars, but Elvis cradles his like a bird. After the broadcast is over, as the crowd slowly dissipates, the little boy hangs around on the outskirts of the group, watching Mississippi Slim and the other musicians pack up. He walks out behind them onto the courthouse square, with the statue of the Confederate soldier facing the Lyric Theater, the movie house that he and his friends never go to because it costs fifteen cents, a nickel more than the Strand. He hangs around on the edge of the crowd, nervously shifting from one foot to the other, desperately sidestepping every offer of a ride back to East Tupelo. He is waiting for an invitation, and in his determination to wait he shows the kind of watchful perseverance that is the hallmark of his solitary style. Maybe his friend James will say something to his brother, will suggest that they go off and have a Nehi together. Meanwhile he hangs on every word that is spoken, every glance exchanged: talk of the music, talk of the Opry, what cousin Rod Brasfield had to say the last time he was in town.

He soaks it all in. While others allow themselves to be distracted, his nervous attention never wanders; his fingers are constantly drumming against his pants leg, but his gaze bores in on the singer and the scene. Does he hang around with Slim? It's hard to imagine where. He dreams of *being* Slim. He dreams of wearing a western shirt with fancy pockets and sparkles and a scarf around his neck. Slim knows all the Opry stars. He knows Tex Ritter — the boy has heard the story a dozen times, but he doesn't mind if he hears it one more time from James: how Tex Ritter was making a personal appearance over in Nettleton with one of his movies, and Slim said to his little brother, "You want to go? You talking all the time about Tex Ritter, I'll show you that me and him is friends." So they went over to Nettleton, where Tex played a few songs before they showed his film, and then he signed some autographs. He had his six-guns on. Then all of a sudden he looked out and said, "I'll be damned, there's old Mississippi Slim sitting out there in the front row," and he stopped everything he was doing and went out and shook his hand. Then he said, "You come on right up here, and why don't you do a song for us." When he shook James' hand, James thought his hand was going to break, that was the kind of grip old Tex Ritter had. That was exactly the way it happened.

"I took the guitar, and I watched people," Elvis recalled, "and I learned to play a little bit. But I would never sing in public. I was very shy about it, you know." Every Saturday night he would listen to the Opry. He and Gladys and Vernon, his cousin Harold (whose mother, Rhetha, has died and who lives with them part of the time), maybe Grandma Minnie, too, now that Grandpa has lit out and she is living with them mostly — you had just better not run down the battery before the Saturday-night broadcast. The adults laugh and exchange glances at some of the jokes and tell half-remembered stories about the performers: Roy Acuff and Ernest Tubb, the Willis Brothers and Bill Monroe, here's that Red Foley to do "Old Shep" that Elvis sung at the fair. The music can carry you off to faraway places. But no one really knows. Daddy loves him. Mama will take care of him. There is nothing in his life that they do not know except for this. It is his secret passion.

IN THE SUMMER of 1946 the Presleys moved from East Tupelo to town. Vernon was not able to keep up payments on the Berry Street house and sold it — or transferred the payments — to his friend Aaron Kennedy. They moved first to Commerce Street, and then to Mulberry Alley, virtually next to the Fairgrounds and opposite Tupelo's teeming black quarter, Shake Rag, which abutted the Leake and Goodlett Lumberyard, on East Main Street, where Vernon worked. The house was just a shack, one of three in the little alley, but it was moving into town that was the real comedown. In East Tupelo the Presleys had risen to a level of respectability that they might never have expected to attain. They were at ease among family and friends who shared the same background and experience. In Tupelo they were scorned, like virtually anyone from above the highway, as poor white trash. To Ernest Bowen, whose father's woodworking shop was just across the alley and who had only recently gone to work as city salesman for L. P. McCarty, a wholesale grocer, the Presleys were the kind of family who moved every time the rent came due. When Vernon went to work for L. P. McCarty delivering groceries to all the little corner stores in the surrounding region, Bowen's opinion was not improved any. "He had no ambition whatsoever. It didn't bother him if they threw him out of his little house — he's going to get another one. Many times the salespeople would get together and would give samples, canned food, to Vernon. He was a sorry sort, what we call a real ne'er-do-well." Bill Mitchell, on the other hand, who got his first real job around this time, also driving for L. P. McCarty, and who, like Bowen, had tangential musical connections with Elvis (Bowen became the longtime general manager at WELO within a few years of the Presleys' departure for Memphis, while Mitchell recalled playing fiddle behind the boy in Mississippi Slim's band on the Jamboree), remembered Vernon's kindness and taciturn nature as well as his blinding lack of ambition.

It's doubtful if either ever really knew Vernon or his family: certainly they would have had no way of imagining their hopes and dreams, and for all the pictures that we get of Vernon as an improvident loafer, there appears never to have been a time that he was not working or actively in pursuit of work. He supported his mother, after all, and he had taken in Gladys' sister's boy. When Elvis went to visit his cousin Willie Wileman (Willie's grandmother was Minnie's sister, and he was later to become a versatile and well-known musician in the Tupelo area), he was the sophisticated city cousin. From Willie's point of view: "All of us were country kids. We wore overalls, and he wore pants and a shirt. We would ride bicycles together — he would always get out and mix and mingle. But he was a city dude!"

In the fall of 1946 Elvis started a new school, Milam, which went from grades 5 through 9 and was about half a mile from Mulberry Alley. He failed to make much of an impression on any of his sixth-grade classmates, but that would hardly have been surprising, irrespective of social status, given Elvis' own cautious, watchful nature. Despite Willie Wileman's testimony, in the sixth-grade-class picture he is the only child in overalls, the only one visibly struggling to put on a happy postwar face, the only one whose expression gives any harbinger of a different kind of future. He looks curious, optimistic, at ease with himself — but no more a part of the group picture than he was in the earlier school snapshot. His seventh-grade classmate Roland Tindall moved to town himself from Dorsey, Mississippi, the year before and had encountered the same sort of dislocation. "It was unbelievable, the change, from leaving all my friends, the people I had grown up with and known from — well, you just knew everyone. Then, to come to Tupelo and have three classes of one grade, I mean in this time you can't really comprehend it. I wanted to go back to the country." To Elvis it was altogether bewildering and, at the same time, no more bewildering than anything else that was happening in his life. He was watching, he was waiting — but he didn't know for what.

The Presleys moved around some in the next year, and Gladys went back to work at the Mid-South Laundry. By the time Elvis started the seventh grade, they were living on North Green Street, closer to school and in a respectable enough neighborhood, but in a respectable *colored* neighborhood. Unlike Shake Rag, which had a Catfish Row kind of appearance and was destined to be obliterated in the first urban renewal project to be carried out in the state of Mississippi, in 1968, North Green Street ran right up against one of the "better," more exclusive, white sections of town and consisted, for the most part, of neatly kept one- and two-family homes. Although the house that they rented was designated as one of two or three "white" houses in the area, they were surrounded by black families, black churches, black social clubs, and black schools (the Lee County Training School, where Ben Branch taught music for years before moving to Memphis and joining the Stax horn section, was just down the hill). To friends and relatives this was a matter of some note — this was not South Tupelo, for example, where all the mill workers and factory hands lived — and not all of their old friends came to visit the Presleys in their new home, but it was nothing so shocking or out-of-the-way that it would prevent Gladys' sister Lillian and her family from occupying the same rental when Gladys and Vernon left.

It was in his seventh-grade year that Elvis started taking his guitar to school every day. Although teachers in later years would recall the early manifestations of a child prodigy, many students viewed his playing more dubiously, dismissing it with the same faint wrinkle of distaste with which they would greet déclassé fare of any sort ("hillbilly" music and "race" music probably fell into the same category in this regard). Others, like Roland Tindall, admired him for what they saw almost as a declaration of faith. "Elvis would bring his guitar to school, as far as I know, from the very beginning of the school year. At that time the basement of Milam was like a recess area, you went there during lunch hour — it was all open down there for the children to stay out of the wet and cold. Many times Elvis and a boy named Billy Welch would play and sing down there, and we would stay inside just to hear them. Once in a while Elvis might perform for an activity period in the classroom, but only occasionally, because those type of children didn't believe in country music and that was what he sang. He told us he was going to the Grand Ole Opry. Not bragging: he just made the statement." "He brought his guitar to school when it wasn't raining," said James Ausborn, Mississippi Slim's brother, who had recently moved to town himself. "He'd bring his guitar swung over his back and put it in his locker till lunchtime. Then everybody would set around, and he would sing and strum on that guitar. All he talked about was music — not the Opry so much as gospel music. That was what he sung mostly."

A classmate, Shirley Lumpkin, told Elaine Dundy, author of *Elvis and Gladys*, "The nicest thing I can say about him was that he was a loner," and another classmate, Kenneth Holditch, recalled him to Dundy as "a sad, shy, not especially attractive boy" whose guitar playing was not likely to win any prizes. Many of the other children made fun of him as a "trashy" kind of boy playing trashy "hillbilly" music, but Elvis stuck to his guns. Without ever confronting his denigrators or his critics, he continued to do the one thing that was important to him: he continued to make music.

Neither Roland nor James ever visited Elvis at his home on North Green Street, although James continued to go to the radio station with him and, occasionally, to the movies. Roland, by his own account, was not a social person. "All the socializing I did was at school, but we were very close friends there. At Christmastime in the seventh grade he gave me a little truck, and he gave Billy something of a similar sort — it was one of his own toys. I remember that impressed me, that he wanted to do something so badly that he would give us one of his toys when he couldn't afford anything else."

Frank and Corene Smith visited shortly before the Presleys left Tupelo for good, but by then they, too, had fallen somewhat out of touch with their old parishioners, and Vernon and Gladys were not attending church as regularly either. Because the house that they were renting was clearly reserved for white people, to the Smiths the Presleys "were not living in the black community," a distinction that Vernon and Gladys would certainly have made themselves, but a distinction that might have been lost in a real sense on their twelve-year-old son. Living across Main Street from the jumble of crooked alleyways and tumbledown shacks that made up Shake Rag, he would have to have sensed something of the life, he could not have missed the tumultuous bursts of song, the colorful street vendors' cries, he would have observed it all with intense curiosity, and he might have envied the sharp flashes of emotion, the bright splashes of color, the feelings so boldly on display. But he was forever sitting at the gate; there was no entry point for a stranger, there was no way in.

On North Green Street, "Elvis aron Presley" (as he signed his library card that year) was like the "Invisible Man" — he was the boy who lived in Dr. Green's house, he *belonged,* he had business there. For the first time he was truly in the midst of another world, a world so different that he might as well have stepped right onto the movie screen, and yet he was an unseen, and unsuspected, presence — like Superman or Captain Marvel, unprepossessing in their workaday disguises, but capable of more than anyone could ever imagine, he was just waiting for the opportunity to fulfill his destiny.

You walked by the Elks Club just off Green, where a small combo that patterned itself on Louis Jordan might be playing "Ain't Nobody Here But Us Chickens," or Jimmy Lunceford or Earl "Fatha" Hines might stop in after playing a dance at the Armory on the Fairgrounds downtown. You walked by a bar and barely heard the wailing of the jukebox over the noise of men and women drinking and gambling and signifying the sounds of love. On weekends the churches would be jumping, in a fashion not dissimilar to an Assembly of God congregation when it started speaking in tongues, but with a joyfulness and a sense of celebration, an expelling of emotion that was embarrassing for a closeted young boy to see at close hand — it seemed sometimes as if they were in the throes of a kind of passion that was not meant to be revealed in public.

Several times a year, in warm weather, a slightly moth-eaten, crudely patched tent would be erected on a vacant lot on the east side of Green for a revival: Friday night, Saturday night, all day Sunday, people would come from all over, dressed up in their finest regalia, the women in pink and yellow and hot fuchsia, wearing fantastic feathered boa hats and carrying their weight without apology, the preachers preaching without anything to hold them back, getting lost in their Bible, chanting, breathing, snorting rhythmically, gutturally, breathlessly, until their voices soared off into song. You didn't have to go inside to get the feeling—the sound, the sense, the allure, were all around you. You only had to walk up the street and the street was *rocking*. Well-to-do white college boys and their dates would come out for the show on Saturday night—there was really nothing like it, you had to hand it to the colored people, they really knew how to live. The college boys were strictly tourists, though. If you lived on North Green Street, you breathed it in, as natural as air—after a while you got used to it, it became yours, too, *it was almost like being in church.*

In the fall of 1948 Elvis started school again. Sometime in the first month or two, a few of the "rougher-type" boys took his guitar and cut the strings, but some of his eighth-grade classmates chipped in and bought him another set. When he announced in the first week of November that he and his family were leaving for Memphis, the other children were surprised but not shocked. People like the Presleys moved all the time. On his last day of school, Friday, November 5, a classmate named Leroy Green recalled to writer Vince Staten, he gave a little concert. The last song he sang was "A Leaf on a Tree" and, according to Green, "most people wouldn't believe this, but I went up to him and I told him, 'Elvis, one of these days you're gonna be famous.' And he smiled at me and said, 'I sure hope so.' "

They moved on a Saturday, Vernon explained, so that Elvis wouldn't miss a day of school. "We were broke, man, broke," Elvis declared in later years, "and we left Tupelo overnight. Dad packed all our belongings in boxes and put them in the trunk and on top of a 1939 Plymouth [actually a '37]. We just headed for Memphis. Things had to be better." According to Gladys: "We'd been talking about moving to Memphis. One day we just made up our minds. We sold off our furniture, loaded our clothes and things into this old car we had, and just set out." Elaine Dundy posited in *Elvis and Gladys* that Vernon Presley was fired by L. P. McCarty for using the company truck to deliver bootleg whiskey, but Gladys' cousin Corinne Richards recalled prior discussion of the move and saw it as part of a family migration, soon to be joined by other Presleys and other Smiths. In any event, Tupelo was a dead end. What they were looking for in Memphis might have been difficult to articulate, but what they were seeking to escape was perfectly clear. "I told Elvis," said Vernon, "that I'd work for him and buy him everything I could afford. If he had problems, he could come to me and I'd try to understand. I also said, 'But, son, if you see anything wrong going on, promise me you'll have no part of it. Just don't let anything happen so that I'd have to talk to you between bars. That's the only thing that would break my heart.' "

"There were times we had nothing to eat but corn bread and water," recalled Vernon not long before he died, "but we always had compassion for people. Poor we were, I'll never deny that. But trash we weren't. . . . We never had any prejudice. We never put anybody down. Neither did Elvis."

MEMPHIS CIRCA 1950. (COURTESY OF JIMMY DENSON)

MEMPHIS: THE COURTS

A SMALL, FAIR-HAIRED BOY, fourteen years old, sits on the front steps of the three-story brick building. It is twilight, and you would never notice him if you didn't know he was there. There is scarcely a word of greeting to any of the frequent passersby: men coming home from work, boys playing corkball, little girls dressed up in their Sunday best visiting a neighbor's apartment with their mama. A sailor from the nearby Millington base passes by on Third, while a jaunty teenager, wearing a neat Eisenhower jacket and wide, billowing pants, turns the corner from Market Mall, the tree-lined, grassy way that divides Lauderdale Courts, a trim collection of public-assisted garden apartments in the heart of downtown Memphis. Two blocks away is Ellis Auditorium, where they have boxing and musical events and the high schools all graduate in the spring. Ellis sits on the corner of Main, which, of course, in 1949 is the hub of Memphis city life. Movie theaters line Main Street: the Malco, Loew's State, the Strand, all on South Main "downtown," the Suzore No. 2, a second-run house on North Main just up the street, where you can gain admission for a dime. There are buses that run up and down Main, but if you don't have the money, all you have to do is walk. The Hotel Peabody is no more than three quarters of a mile away. Goldsmith's giant department store, which offers the latest in fashions and furnishings and can serve as readily for dreams as for purchases, sits on the west side of Main, with the corner of Beale, and the beginning of the colored section, just beyond. There is a world within a stone's throw of the Courts, but there is a world within it, too.

The young boy silently watches and observes: the black children playing in front of the two little ramshackle shacks just across the street from the well-maintained redbrick apartment buildings; the nurses changing shifts at St. Joseph's; the trolley cars on Jackson; the bigger boys coming back from playing football at the Triangle on the northeast end of the Courts. Finally he spots his father coming home from work just two blocks away. Vernon Presley is carrying his lunch pail. He turns in from Third and comes down the path, not hurrying but not lingering either. The towheaded little boy rises from the stoop, as if it were coincidence that he should be sitting out there. The two of them flash each other a quick half smile, the boy and the man; then they turn in, enter the door of 185 Winchester, go up the steps to the first-floor landing and in the door of Apartment 328, where dinner is waiting. Gladys looks at them both. Maybe she says "I was just beginning to worry." Does she give the man a quick kiss? Perhaps. The picture is blurred. But she hugs the boy as if he might have been gone for years.

When the Presleys arrived in Memphis on November 6, 1948, they moved first into a rooming house at 370 Washington Street, then into another one, at 572 Poplar, just around the corner from the Courts. Possibly they found it through a neighbor from Tupelo, Mrs. Tressie Miller, who lived upstairs; maybe Vernon had even stayed in one of the boardinghouses during the war. The house on Poplar, like many others in the area, was a big old Victorian-style edifice that had been cut up into sixteen single-room apartments, three or four to a floor, with a shared bathroom at the end of the hall. The Presleys paid $9.50 a week rent and cooked their meals on a hot plate. In the evening the whole family might cross the street to attend services at the Reverend J. J. Denson's Poplar Street Mission. The Reverend Denson had a fine voice. He played the guitar, and there was always lots of singing and shouting and carrying on as well as a communal supper to be shared. Some nights the family would have dinner with Mrs. Miller and reminisce about Tupelo. Gladys got a job as a sewing machine operator at Fashion Curtains, and then, after her brother Travis and his wife, Lorraine, had moved up within a few weeks of the Presleys' arrival, Vernon and Travis found work at Precision Tool, a munitions manufacturer—perhaps he had worked there during the war. It was over at Kansas and McLemore, about two miles away; in good weather Vernon and Travis could walk, in bad weather they might drive or take the bus up Third. Poplar Avenue was a busy commercial thoroughfare, but it was an isolating one as well. It was hard to get to know people in the city, and Gladys tried to persuade her other brothers and sisters and in-laws to join them. "The places that they moved in up there didn't seem much better than what they had down here," sniffed her cousin Corinne Richards Tate, but eventually most of the family moved up, forming a little enclave in the vicinity of Third and Poplar.

The Presleys lived there all through that winter and the following spring, and Vernon got a job as a loader at United Paint in February before they applied to get into public housing in June. He was making 85 cents an hour, $40.38 a week with overtime, when Jane Richardson, a home service adviser for the Memphis Housing Authority, interviewed Gladys Presley in the Poplar Avenue rooming house on June 17, 1949. She noted the poor conditions under which they were living, a prerequisite for consideration. Miss Richardson wrote: "Cook, eat, and sleep in one room. Share bath. No privacy. . . . Need housing. Persons interviewed are Mrs. Presley and son. Nice boy. They seem very nice and deserving. Lauderdale if possible, near husband's work."

They finally gained admission to the Courts on September 20, at the start of Elvis' freshman year at Humes. The rent was $35 a month, about what they had been paying on Poplar, but instead of a single room they got two bedrooms, a living room, a kitchen, and a bathroom of their own. There was a $2,500 ceiling on annual family income as a qualification for continued tenancy, and it was noted that the Presleys possessed no telephone and a car that barely ran, and that Vernon sent $10 every month to his mother in West Point, Mississippi. The repairs that the apartment needed were detailed on a Housing Authority form on the day they moved in: "Wall around bath tub needs repair . . . apartment in need of paint job . . . 1 shade will not roll in bed room . . . light in front hall will not stay on . . . oven door will not shut tight . . . one leg broke off cabinet . . . bathroom sink stopped up . . . faucet in kitchen sink needs repairs." But this marked the real beginning of the Presleys' arrival in Memphis.

I don't think anyone visiting the latter-day Courts could get a sense of what the Courts were like at that time: a humming, bustling little village, full of kids and ambition. Forty years later graduates of the Courts would include doctors, lawyers, judges, and successful businessmen, and many would have achieved the Housing Authority goal ("From slums to public housing to private ownership") in a single generation. The homes, 433 units in all, were inspected at frequent but unspecified intervals ("We always found Mrs. Presley to be an excellent housekeeper," Jane Richardson told Elvis biographer Jerry Hopkins, "and a very nice person. . . . She kept [the oak floors] waxed all the time"), and the grounds were immaculate. For many of the residents it was "like we'd come into the money." For some it was the first time they had ever had indoor plumbing or taken a real bath.

It would be easy to romanticize the sense of hope and striving that dominated the Courts, because this was still a hard, tough world in which many of the kids came from broken homes, the quickest way to resolve a problem was with your fists, and you would rather die (if you were male, anyway) than articulate your innermost hopes and dreams. But it would be wrong to ignore the sense of social aspiration, and of pride, too, because that was the dominant tone of the Courts. The prevailing attitude was that you didn't talk about it, you just did it. Yet it was an idyllic world, too. For a kid growing up there was a degree of comfort, a sense of place, and a reassuring sense that everyone was heading in the same direction, everyone was looking toward a bright new day. In many ways it mirrored the comfortable small-town environment of Tupelo. It was just the kind of thing that a wide-eyed boy from the country, too doubtful to know what he really felt, too fearful to express it even if he did, needed. It was home.

THE PRESLEYS themselves were not atypical Lauderdale residents: Mr. Presley dour and grave on the outside, a decent man, a good provider, a man whose taciturnity not infrequently conveyed a sense of suspiciousness, of mild disapproval; Mrs. Presley working part-time at Fashion Curtains, attending Stanley Products (Tupperware-like) parties with the other ladies, laughing, sociable, exchanging recipes and small confidences, but sometimes bringing her adolescent son along, too — he never said anything, just sat silently by her side — which caused some of the women to talk. Mrs. Presley was much more popular than Mr. Presley. Everyone spoke of her warmth and liveliness and spontaneous expressions of emotion, but there was also a sense of a family set apart, a sealed-off world that few outsiders ever penetrated. They didn't attend any one church regularly, for the most part they were not joiners, but as much as anything else the sense that others got of their separateness seemed to center on their son. "They treated him like he was two years old," said Mrs. Ruby Black, most of whose ten children had grown up in the Courts. But even to Gladys' sister Lillian, who, once she and her family had moved to Memphis, too, could look out her back door and practically see Gladys' living room window, there was something about Vernon and Gladys' focus on their only child that turned even family into outsiders. "He was particular about his funny books, Elvis — he wouldn't even let anyone look at them. Grandma Presley would tell my little boys, 'No, you can't look at them. Elvis will get mad at me.' He had his own dishes that he'd eat out of. A knife and fork and spoon. Mrs. Presley would say, 'I'm gonna set the table,' and she always washed his things and set them over there by their selves: his plate and his spoon and his bowl, whatever. She says, 'Don't you eat out of that.' I said, 'Why?' She said, 'That's Elvis'. He wouldn't eat a bite if he knowed anybody had eat out of them.' " "He never spent a night away from home until he was seventeen," Vernon told an interviewer, with only slight exaggeration, in 1978.

He went to school each day, walking the ten blocks down Jackson to Manassas, where Humes stood imposing and monolithic and the halls reverberated with the clatter of voices, locker doors slamming, students seemingly confident of their destination, whatever it might be. At first he was frightened — this was a school where the principal was not reluctant to enunciate or act upon his philosophy and could write as his message in the graduation yearbook, "If one has no scruples about embarrassing this institution, he would do well to withdraw because hereafter we shall oppose the readmittance of one who has knowingly and willingly defamed the school's good name." That was something to think about — probably every day — but after the first day he got used to it, it was a whole new world to study, and gradually he even came to feel at home.

At first Gladys walked him to the corner, until he made friends in the neighborhood. Outside of the Courts there was no one who really noticed much about him his first two years at Humes. "He was a gentle, obedient boy, and he always went out of his way to try to do what you asked him to do," said Susie Johnson, his ninth-grade homeroom teacher. "His English was atrocious . . . but he had a warm and sunny quality about him which made people respond." "He was during his first years in our school a shy boy. . . . At times he seemed to feel more at ease with [the teachers] than with his fellow students," wrote Mildred Scrivener, his twelfth-grade homeroom and history teacher, in 1957. "Thinking back now, I wonder if he wasn't overly conscious that he and his parents had just moved from Tupelo, that the other students were familiar with the place and knew each other. If so, it was a typical bit of teenaged near-sightedness."

His grades were decent. In the eighth grade he got an A in language and a C in music. In a rare moment of self-assertion, he challenged the contention of his music teacher, Miss Marmann, that he couldn't sing. Yes, he could, he said, she just didn't appreciate his type of singing, and he brought his guitar to class the next day and sang Fairley Holden and His Six Ice Cold Papas' 1947 hit, "Keep Them Cold Icy Fingers Off of Me." According to a classmate, Katie Mae Shook, Miss Marmann "agreed that Elvis was right when he said that she didn't appreciate his kind of singing." In the ninth grade he got Bs in English, science, and math. "My older brother went to school with him," recalled singer Barbara Pittman, "and he and some of the other boys used to hide behind buildings and throw things at him — rotten fruit and stuff — because he was different, because he was quiet and he stuttered and he was a mama's boy." Sophomore year he joined ROTC, became a library volunteer worker, and took wood shop, where he made projects for his mother. His grandmother was living with them part of the time, and Gladys was working at the coffee urn at Britling's Cafeteria downtown.

In pictures he does not look any different from his fellow students, neither humbler nor poorer nor more flamboyant. The only difference that one might detect is that he appears more diffident than his classmates. No one else appears to have any reservation about buying in — the pictured students are models of comportment and posture. But surely that is not fair either. What is so touching about this portrait of the American dream, circa 1950, is the conscious striving on everyone's face, not least that of the young cadet, Elvis Aron Presley, who wore his ROTC uniform proudly everywhere, his face stern, his posture erect, his demeanor, one senses, boundlessly optimistic. In retrospect he clearly felt the same pride in Humes that most of his classmates did: that it was tough, tough but fair, and that one of the proudest achievements of his life would be simply getting through.

In the Courts, meanwhile, his world was rapidly expanding. There were three other boys in his building — Buzzy Forbess, Paul Dougher, and Farley Guy — and Buzzy ran into him one day on his way to visit Paul. "Paul lived on the third floor (Farley lived on the second, right over Elvis), and Elvis was standing out on one of the little stairways out in front of the building, talking to some other people. And I went by and had some funny books in my hand rolled up. First time I ever saw him, I said, 'Hi, how ya doing?' and slapped him on the back of the head with the funny books, and he slapped me upside the head as I went by. We like to got in a scrape. But as soon as I looked at him, and he looked at me, we both grinned and shook hands and I went upstairs to see Paul. That was how we become friends." Soon the four of them were virtually inseparable. Together they formed a football team to play other neighborhoods, they rode their bikes, went to the movies, when it was warm enough they hung out at Malone Pool just a few blocks away, where they eyed the girls and made awkward stabs at actually swimming. It was nothing to brag about, said Buzzy, "just kids growing up together. If somebody moved into the Courts, they was going to get involved with *everybody*, one way or another. If you was going to have a party, everybody was going to get invited. We did all the things that you do. We lived two or three blocks from Main Street. We was right in the middle of everything. What we didn't do was crack the books and study a lot. We were close enough. We were good friends."

One time Buzzy got hurt in one of their football games against another neighborhood team. "I was bleeding and pretty bruised, and Mrs. Presley started crying. She was a softhearted lady. But Mr. Presley was a fine person, too. I was around him enough to know that a lot of Elvis' wit and abilities came from his dad. I loved Mrs. Presley to death, but as far as the humor, the dry humor — that's Mr. Presley. Most people smile with their lips, but he laughed with his eyes. Dry wit, dry smile — Elvis got an awful lot of that from him."

Elvis and Buzzy and Farley and Paul roamed all around the downtown area; they walked everywhere together in a jaunty group, passing kosher butcher shops and Italian fruit stands, exploring the dock area below Front Street, observing the bustling prosperity of the downtown shoppers, checking out the blues guitarist and washtub bass player who stood out in front of the Green Owl, on the corner of Market, when the weather was good. Sometimes they might travel as far as the corner of Beale and Main, or they might even venture a block down Beale to get their pictures taken at the Blue Light Studio, four for a quarter, but there was no need to wander very far, there was so much going on all around them, a riot of sounds, colors, hustle, and excitement, even for a kid who'd grown up in the city. The summer after his freshman year Vernon bought Elvis a push lawn mower, and the four of them would go around with the mower and a couple of hand sickles soliciting yard work at four dollars per yard. "The first evening he came in," said Vernon, "and sat there with a frown on his face and laid fifty cents out. Then all at once he broke out laughing and pulled a handful of change out of his pocket . . . and he had about seven dollars."

Elvis' musical interests remained something of a secret his first couple of years at Humes. He didn't bring his guitar to school, and he rarely carried it around the Courts with him. "With the three of us he played," said Buzzy. "He wasn't shy about it, but he wasn't the kind of kid you just turn him around and put him onstage, either. He got used to it right there with us." One time Farley's mother complained that he was making too much racket, and the Housing Authority got several other complaints from older tenants, but Miss Richardson would just "ask him to tune down a little bit," and he always would. He shared a tenth-grade biology class with Buzzy and was going to bring his guitar to school for the class's Christmas party. "He even practiced two or three songs," said Buzzy, "Christmas-type songs, but he chickened out — didn't even bring it." He doesn't seem to have told any of his friends about the Mississippi-Alabama Fair; he never spoke of Mississippi Slim.

And yet, one feels, he never lost sight of music for a moment. In fact, if he had never left the apartment, just listening to the radio would have been a big step toward completing his musical education. Memphis radio in 1950 was an Aladdin's lamp of musical vistas and styles. Late at night Elvis could have listened — along with most of the other kids in the Courts and half of Memphis, it seemed — to Daddy-O-Dewey, Dewey Phillips, broadcasting from the Gayoso on WHBQ. In one typical 1951 segment he would have heard Rosco Gordon's "Booted" (which had been recorded in Memphis, at Sam Phillips' studio), Muddy Waters' "She Moves Me," "Lonesome Christmas" by Lowell Fulson, and Elmore James' brand-new "Dust My Broom," all current hits, and all collector's classics some forty years later. "Rocket 88," which has frequently been tagged the first rock 'n' roll record, came out of Sam Phillips' studio in 1951, too, and merited a write-up in the paper that led with the somewhat arch suggestion, "If you have a song you can't get published, you might ask Sam Phillips for help." "Come on, good people," exhorted Dewey, telling his public to buy their threads at Lansky Brothers on Beale. "Do like me and pay for 'em while you wearing 'em out, or when they catch up with you, *dee-gawwwww!* And be sure and tell 'em Phillips sent you!" In the morning there was Bob Neal's wake-up show on WMPS, hillbilly music and cornpone humor in a relaxed Arthur Godfrey style of presentation, and at 12:30 P.M. Neal offered thirty minutes of gospel with the Blackwood Brothers, who had recently moved to Memphis and joined the First Assembly of God Church on McLemore Avenue. The first half of the *High Noon Round-Up* featured country singer Eddie Hill, who along with the Louvin Brothers, Gladys Presley's favorite country group (the Blackwoods were her favorite quartet, though Vernon and Elvis preferred the somewhat livelier Statesmen), was among Memphis' biggest hillbilly stars.

If you changed the dial to WDIA, which since its switchover in 1949 to an all-black programming policy had billed itself as "The Mother Station of the Negroes," you could hear not only local blues star B. B. King, deejaying and playing his own music live on the air, but also such genuine personalities as Professor Nat D. Williams, history teacher at Booker T. Washington High School, columnist for Memphis' Negro newspaper, the *World,* and longtime master of ceremonies at the Palace Theatre's Amateur Night; comedic genius A. C. "Moohah" Williams; and the cosmopolitan Maurice "Hot Rod" Hulbert, not to mention the Spirit of Memphis Quartet, who had their own fifteen-minute program and made even the Carnation Milk jingle reverberate with feeling. On Sunday night on WHBQ the sermons of the Reverend W. Herbert Brewster, author of such Negro spiritual classics as Mahalia Jackson's "Move On Up a Little Higher" and Clara Ward's "How I Got Over," were broadcast live from the East Trigg Baptist Church, with his famed soloist, Queen C. Anderson, leading the musical interludes.

There would have been no way for any but the most avid student to keep up with it all —and this doesn't even begin to take into account Howlin' Wolf and Sonny Boy Williamson's broadcasts from West Memphis, Arkansas, just across the river, Sleepy Eyed John's hillbilly parade on WHHM, all the regular showcases for popular tunes of the day, the big band broadcasts from the Peabody Skyway, and, of course, the Opry broadcasts on Saturday night. Here was an education of a sort, and of a quality, virtually unimaginable today and, in an age and a place that were strictly segregated in every respect, an education that was colorblind. "In one aspect of America's cultural life," wrote *Billboard*'s pioneering music editor Paul Ackerman, looking back in 1958 on the impact of the music that had first arrived in such profusion after the war, "integration has already taken place." This was as true in 1950 as it was in 1958 — but only in the privacy of the home, and only where music was truly in the air.

PERHAPS IT WAS at one of the ladies' Stanley Products parties that Gladys first asked Mrs. Mattie Denson, wife of the Reverend J. J. Denson, if her husband could possibly give her son guitar lessons. Mrs. Denson said her husband would be glad to help ("He has such a nice voice," said Mrs. Presley), but it was her son Jesse Lee who was the real talent in the family. Jesse Lee was not thrilled when she told him about the idea. At eighteen he was two and a half years older than Mrs. Presley's son in 1950 and possessed a well-deserved reputation as a school truant and something of a delinquent. He had run away from home for the first time at the age of nine, had started playing professionally when he was not much older, and had been in and out of one juvenile correctional facility or another for much of his young life. A superb athlete, he fought one of the most memorable Golden Gloves matches in Memphis history in 1952, when he lost the bantamweight championship to fellow Courts resident George Blancet and made the papers for performing Hank Snow's "Golden Rocket" and the semiclassical "Blue Prelude" in between bouts as well.

He didn't want to teach Elvis, he told his mother, because the other boy "was very shy, and kind of timid. 'He's scared of the other kids that I pal around with,' I said. 'They're tough kids, and I'm afraid they're going to tease me, and then I'll get my hands all broken up from having to defend myself . . . and I don't think I should do it!' Well, she turned around and walked away and said, 'Jesse Lee, remember: "Whatsoever you do for these the least of my brothers, that you would do unto me." ' I said, 'Send him over, Mama.'

"He showed up, he had a little itty-bitty, Gene Autry–type guitar that he really couldn't play. He couldn't press the strings down on it they was set so high, so I let him practice on mine — I had a little Martin. I just tried to show him basic chords. I would take his fingers and place them, say, 'You're pressing the wrong strings with the wrong fingers,' trying to straighten him out. He couldn't really complete a song for a long time, couldn't move his fingers and go with the flow of the music, but once I straightened him out he started to learn to do it right."

Every Saturday and Sunday, Elvis would show up with his guitar. Although Mrs. Denson was a champion of Christian fellowship, it didn't extend so far as to let the boys practice in her home, so they went down to the laundry room underneath the Presleys' apartment. Lee's friends Dorsey Burnette and his younger brother, Johnny, whose family had lived across from the Densons for thirteen years on Pontotoc Street, were frequently present and, as Lee had predicted, did give Elvis a hard time. Dorsey was another prominent Golden Gloves boxer, but as many of their friends remarked, he and Johnny just liked to fight, and the more pacific Elvis referred to them somewhat ruefully as the Daltons, after the famous outlaw gang.

Lee dazzled the other boys with his virtuosic execution of "Wildwood Flower" and "Under the Double Eagle," not to mention the tremolo yodel that he had developed for his vocal showpieces. With still another resident of the Courts, Johnny Black, whose older brother Bill was a sometime professional musician, the five boys became well known for their concerts on Market Mall, the cool, leafy path that ran down the middle of the Courts. Often in the evening the boys would sing, harmonizing on "Cool Water" and "Riders in the Sky," showcasing Lee's guitar and his vocals, too, on numbers like "I'm Movin' On," "Tennessee Waltz," or just about any Eddy Arnold song you could name. In the summertime there were informal dances on the lawn, while older residents sat on their porches and patted their hands and the sound carried all over the Courts. Lee Denson's older brother, Jimmy, recalled them as a group centering around his younger brother. "They walked single file, Indian-fashion, four or five teenage boys holding their guitars wherever they went." To Johnny Black it was more of a loose-knit association: "We would play under the trees, underneath those big magnolia trees — I've got pictures of us all. It was just whoever would come, whoever showed up. We'd have a mandolin maybe, three or four guitars, and the people would gather. We weren't trying to impress the world, we were just playing to have a good time."

No one has ever remembered Elvis Presley in the foreground of any of these pictures, but he clearly showed up in the back, hovering on the edges of the frame, tentatively forming his chords, joining in occasionally on the background vocals. When he missed a note, he threw up his hands in the air and then shrugged with a shy, self-deprecating grin that caused his audience to laugh. To the older boys he was a mush-mouthed little country boy, a mama's boy who deserved a certain amount of respect just for not letting himself be run off. To Buzzy and Farley and Paul he was something of a hero — their memories centered on their friend. Like younger boys of every generation they don't think much of the older boys, they see them as bullies and boors, if they ever get in that position themselves, they tell each other, they will never act that way.

Everyone reacts in predictable enough fashion, except for the dreamy boy at the edge of the picture. For Elvis it is as if he has been set down in a foreign land. Music both thrills and holds him in its hypnotic sway. With music he is transported to another place, he experiences a soft dreamy feeling, a sense of almost cushiony release, but at the same time it is as hard and concrete as desire. The older boys might be surprised that he knows the words to every song that they have sung (Lee Denson, for one, has no idea that he has not taught "Old Shep" to his bumbling pupil); he may well know the lyrics to every song that they might ever want to sing — the words imprint themselves on his memory, he has only to hear them once or twice, the chords, too, it is just his fingers which stubbornly resist. In his mind he hears the song differently; it is less florid at times, less like the Irish tenor John McCormack on the sentimental songs, more dramatic on the hillbilly ones. The only songs he would not change are the gospel numbers — those he would do just as they have been done, by the Statesmen, the Blackwood Brothers, the Sunshine Boys. It would seem like sacrilege almost to alter those songs.

He sits alone on the steps of the apartment house at night, fingering the chords softly in the dark. His voice barely rises above a murmur, but he is looking for attention, mostly from the girls, from Betty McMahan, his "first love," and from Billie Wardlaw, who lives next door to Betty on the third floor and took Betty's place when Betty started going with a boy from Arkansas. Betty had met Gladys before she met her son. "She used to come out and we had lawn chairs, or we'd sit on the steps. My mother and his mother started a conversation. Finally one night I guess she just forced him to come outside and sit with us and talk." Billie Wardlaw moved in with her mother at fourteen in 1950 — even before Betty broke up with him, he started courting Billie. "Elvis was a great kisser, and since we were always playing spin the bottle in the dark, he didn't let his shyness get in the way. . . . Lots of times when my mother and I would walk home, Elvis would be outside picking his guitar in the dark. His mother and dad would be sitting out there on quilts, listening. Elvis would do anything in the dark. . . . Once my mother told him, 'Elvis, you sing so good you ought to be singing on the radio.' He blushed and told my mother, 'Mrs. Rooker, I can't sing.' "

He likes the company of women, he loves to be around women, women of all ages, he feels more comfortable with them — it isn't something he would want to admit to his friends, or even perhaps to himself. His aunt Lillian notices it: "He'd get out there at night with the girls and he just sang his head off. He was different with the girls — I'm embarrassed to tell, but he'd rather have a whole bunch of girls around him than the boys — he didn't care a thing about the boys." The women seem to sense something coming out of him, something he himself may not even know he possesses: it is an aching kind of vulnerability, an unspecified yearning; when Sam Phillips meets him just two or three years later, in 1953, he senses much the same quality but calls it insecurity. "He tried not to show it, but he felt so *inferior*. He reminded me of a black man in that way; his insecurity was so *markedly* like that of a black person." Bathed in the soft glow of the streetlight, he appears almost handsome — the acne that embarrasses him doesn't show up so badly, and the adolescent features, which can appear coarse in the cold light of day, take on a kind of delicacy that is almost beautiful. He sings Eddy Arnold's "Molly Darling," a Kay Starr number, "Harbor Lights," Bing and Gary Crosby's "Moonlight Bay," all soft, sweet songs, in a soft, slightly quavering voice, and then, satisfied, takes his comb out of his back pocket and runs it through his hair in a practiced gesture clearly at odds with his hesitancy of manner. With the women, though, he can do no wrong: young girls or old ladies, they seem drawn to his quiet, hesitant approach, his decorous humility, his respectful scrutiny. The men may have their doubts, but to the women he is a nice boy, a kind boy, someone both thoughtful and attentive, someone who truly cares.

THE SUMMER BEFORE his junior year in high school Elvis went to work at Precision Tool, where his father had started when they first moved to Memphis and where his uncles Johnny and Travis Smith and Vester Presley all continued to work. He was making twenty-seven dollars a week, but it didn't last long, because an insurance inspector found out that he was underage, so he went back to his yard business with Buzzy, Farley, and Paul. Sophomore year he had worked as an usher at

Loew's State for much of the fall, giving the Presleys three breadwinners for a while and enabling them to purchase a television set and have Vernon's mother, Minnie, move in with them full-time.

Junior year was something of a watershed; even his teachers remarked upon the change. His hair was different — he was using more Rose Oil hair tonic and Vaseline to keep it down, and he had grown sideburns both to look older and to emulate the appearance of the kind of cross-country truck driver that he sometimes said he wanted to be ("Wild-looking guys, they had scars, I used to lay on the side of the road and watch [them] drive their big diesel trucks"). He seemed to have gained in self-confidence, and his appearance was more distinctive; without calling attention to himself in words he demanded it by his dress and demeanor ("It was just something I wanted to do, I wasn't trying to be better than anybody else"). He even went out for football, an ambition that he had harbored for some time but that proved to be the single, dramatic misstep in an otherwise carefully navigated high school career. By trying out for the team he made himself vulnerable to the very forces which most scorned him, and in perhaps the best-known story of his growing-up years some of the other players ganged up on him in the locker room and threatened to cut his hair, and the coach eventually kicked him off the team when he refused. Whether it happened exactly that way or not, there is little question that he had his pride hurt, and he frequently referred to the incident in later life with some ruefulness and anger.

He went back to work at Loew's State, on South Main, but that didn't last long either, after he got into a fight with another usher who he thought had been a stool pigeon and was fired by the manager. In November 1951, Gladys got a job at St. Joseph's Hospital as a nurse's aide at $4 a day, six days a week. St. Joseph's was just a couple of blocks from their home, and she was very proud of the job, but she had to quit the following February after the Memphis Housing Authority threatened to evict them because their combined family income exceeded the maximum allowed. "Illness in the family," Vernon wrote to the Housing Authority by way of explanation. He had hurt his back and been out of work for a while. "Wife is not working [now]. Trying to pay ourselves out of debt. Bills are pressing and don't want to be sued." In February they got a new lease at a reduced rent of $43 a month and a $3,000 ceiling on income. By June they had recovered enough financially to purchase a 1941 Lincoln coupe, which Elvis was encouraged to consider "his" car. "My daddy was something wonderful to me," said Elvis to a 1956 interviewer. One time, Vernon recalled, Elvis brought the car home and "came running up yelling, 'Hi, Dad, I put fifteen cents' worth of gasoline into the car.' Everyone laughed, and he like to have died of embarrassment."

He didn't need the car, though, for the majority of his common pursuits. He had seen the lights of Main Street, and as Bob Johnson of the *Memphis Press-Scimitar* wrote in 1956 in the first official fan biography: "Elvis saw the street late, with the signs glowing, and to this day it holds a spell over him. . . . Sometimes with his friends, sometimes alone, Elvis would head for Main Street, where the windows, the bustle of moving traffic, the hurrying crowd gave him something to watch and wonder about."

He started hanging out at Charlie's, a little record store, which was at first situated next to the Suzore No. 2 on North Main across the alley from the firehouse, then directly across the street. It had a jukebox and a little soda fountain and even sold "dirty" Redd Foxx comedy records under the counter — and within a short time Elvis became a regular there, sometimes alone, as Bob Johnson suggested, sometimes with friends. He might go to the movies, where you could still see a double feature for a dime, stop by the firehouse, where the firemen, who welcomed any diversion, were always happy to hear him sing a song, then sidle into Charlie's, not to buy anything, necessarily, just to listen, to handle the precious 78s, to put a nickel in the jukebox every once in a while. The proprietor, Charlie Hazelgrove, never kicked anyone out; the store was a hangout for teenagers who were passionate about music, which was why Buzzy Forbess, for example, never went in there at all. For while he and Elvis were the best of friends, that part of Elvis' life did not impinge on his own. "One time we were hanging around Charlie's," recalled Johnny Black, a more casual acquaintance but a *musician,* "and Elvis said to me, 'Johnny, someday I'm going to be driving Cadillacs.' It's so weird to think about — we're talking about an era when we probably couldn't have gotten the money together for a Coke between us."

He wandered down the street, past Loew's to the corner of Beale and Main, then headed down Beale to Lansky's clothing store. A lot of kids liked to go on Beale just to watch the colored acting up. One store a few doors down from Lansky's had its customers lie down on the floor to be measured, with the salesman drawing a chalk outline for a new suit with the gravest of faces; another displayed the tuxedo that local mobster Machine Gun Kelly was said to have been mowed down in, bullet holes intact. The political machine of Boss E. H. Crump took a benevolent attitude toward its Negro population — anything went on Beale Street, up to the point that it threatened the safety of whites — but city censor Lloyd Binford consistently bowdlerized Lena Horne's movies and banned the Hollywood comedy *Brewster's Millions,* because costar Eddie "Rochester" Anderson had "too familiar a way about him, and the picture presents too much racial mixture." In the late 1940s he banned the stage musical *Annie Get Your Gun,* because it had a Negro railroad conductor and "we don't have any Negro conductors in the South. Of course it can't show here. It's social equality in action."

For Elvis, though, it was the clothing, it was the styles, the bold fashions, that drew him in, as he gazed hungrily into Lansky's windows. He made a definite impression on Guy and Bernard Lansky, the brothers who owned and operated the store. "He came down and looked through the windows before he had any money — we knew him strictly by face," recalled Guy. "He was working at the theater at that time, holes in his shoes and socks, real shabbily dressed, but he stood out, his hair, sure, but it was his . . . what I'm trying to say, it was his, you know, manners. He was just a very nice person."

At noon — if it was a Saturday or a vacation day or maybe just a day when he cut school — he headed down to the WMPS studio on the corner of Union and Main for the *High Noon Round-Up,* where the Blackwood Brothers appeared live with WMPS DJ Bob Neal emceeing. "I suppose that was where I saw him for the first time," said Bob Neal, who would become his first manager several years later and who, like Guy Lansky, was struck more by his manner than his appearance. Even James Blackwood, leader of the Blackwood Brothers Quartet, who had a national hit on RCA in 1951 with "The Man Upstairs," remembered the hungry-looking young boy, as did his counterpart in the Statesmen, lead singer Jake Hess, who recalled meeting Elvis at this time not in Memphis but in Tupelo, when the Presleys were presumably back for a visit. How, Jake Hess was asked, could he remember the boy? Weren't there other fans equally ardent in their enthusiasm? To Hess, a spectacular singer with the kind of soaring tenor voice and controlled vibrato that Elvis would explicitly aspire to, it was not prescience that caused him to notice but, rather, something about the young man's fierce, burning desire. "I mean, we didn't know Elvis Presley from a sack of sand. He was just nice, a nice kid, this bright-eyed boy asking all kinds of questions, and asking in a way that you would really want to tell him. He wanted to know about the spiritual aspects of it — did you have to do this or that? He wanted to know if he would be handicapped because he couldn't read music. He was such a bright-eyed boy, you know, he just looked important, even as a kid."

He became a regular at the All-Night Gospel Singings, which had started at Ellis Auditorium up the street and all through the South in the previous two or three years, not with his friends from the Courts or even with musician friends like Lee Denson and the Burnette brothers, who had started playing the roadhouses by now, but by himself, with his mother and father, maybe with his cousin Junior or Gene, with whoever would go — but he rarely missed a show. Once a month Ellis was filled for what amounted to a marathon sing-off, into the early hours of the morning, among the top white gospel quartets of the day. He sat there mesmerized by what he later described as "the big heavy rhythm beats" of some of the spiritual numbers and the delicate beauty of others. There was probably no type of music that he didn't love, but quartet music was the center of his musical universe. Gospel music combined the spiritual force that he felt in all music with the sense of physical release and exaltation for which, it seemed, he was casting about. And the shows — the shows themselves were the broadest of panoplies, running the full spectrum of gospel styles, from the dignified "shape note"-influenced singing of older groups like the Speer Family and the Chuck Wagon Gang, to the flashy showmanship of the Sunshine Boys, to the stately harmonies of the Blackwoods, who adapted many of their hits from the new spiritual style of such Negro quartets as the Soul Stirrers and the Original Gospel Harmonettes of Birmingham. There were hints of the Ink Spots and the Golden Gate Quartet, and even of contemporary rhythm and blues singers like Clyde McPhatter and Roy Hamilton, in their beautifully arranged, precisely articulated stylings, but for all of his admiration for the Blackwoods' work, it was the Statesmen who really captured Elvis' imagination.

The Statesmen were an electric combination, anchored by the disarmingly conventional and unremittingly cheerful manner of their accompanist, leader, and founder, Hovie Lister, and featuring some of the most thrillingly emotive singing and daringly unconventional showmanship in the entertainment world. Sharply dressed in suits that might have come out of the window of Lansky's, they piled tenor on top of countertenor, and then falsetto on top of that, building to Jake Hess' virtuosic lead. Meanwhile bass singer Jim Wetherington, known universally as the Big Chief, maintained a steady bottom, ceaselessly jiggling first his left leg, then his right, with the material of the pants leg ballooning out and shimmering. "He went about as far as you could go in gospel music," said Jake Hess. "The women would jump up, just like they do for the pop shows." Preachers frequently objected to the lewd movements, racial fundamentalists decried the debt to Negro spirituals (particularly in the overt emotionalism of the delivery), but audiences reacted with screams and swoons. It was a different kind of spirituality, but spirituality nonetheless, as the group ran, not walked, out onto the stage, singers tossed the microphone back and forth, and Jake Hess at the audience's coaxing repeated the thrilling climax of his last song over and over again, as Chief maintained his tireless act.

Music, more and more, became the focus of his life. At parties in the Courts Elvis would always sing, sometimes to the point that his friends would groan, "Oh, no, not again!" He was still extremely shy, didn't know how to dance, and sometimes would play only with the lights out, even in as intimate a setting as his cousin Bobbie's birthday party, said his aunt Lillian. "I moved everything out of the living room, and Elvis come in, brought his guitar, but we had to put the lights out before he'd sing. We had a fire in the fireplace, but it wasn't enough light to show his face. He got way over yonder in the corner — that's just how shy he was." He sang quite a few of Kay Starr's songs, he was partial to Teresa Brewer, Joni James, Bing Crosby, Eddie Fisher, and Perry Como as well as Hank Williams and Eddy Arnold. Some evenings Vernon and Gladys would go to the movies so that he, Buzzy, Paul, and Farley could have a party in the apartment. Elvis would never play a slow song, Buzzy said, when Buzzy was dancing with Elvis' girlfriend, Billie Wardlaw, though Billie broke up with him not long afterward when she started going with a sailor she had met at the USO on Third Street. Elvis' reaction when he saw another boy's picture in her wallet surprised her. "He grabbed it out of my purse and began stomping and grinding it into the ground with the heel of his shoe." When she actually broke up with him, "he started crying. Until that night I had never seen a man, or a boy, cry."

Occasionally Buzzy and the other boys would arrange with Miss Richmond, the Lauderdale Courts supervisor, to use the basement under the main office on Lauderdale. She would give them the key, and they would set up tables and issue invitations, charging twenty-five cents per couple. They'd have Cokes and popcorn and a record player, and in the course of the evening Elvis would never fail to sing. One time he accompanied Buzzy and Paul, who had joined the Junior Order of the Oddfellows and made monthly trips to area hospitals as a kind of civic project, when they went to the Home for Incurables out on McLemore in South Memphis. Ordinarily they just passed out ice cream and cookies and spoke to the patients, but this time, to Buzzy's surprise, Elvis had brought his guitar with him and got up and sang, making it in Buzzy's view the first time he ever entertained in Memphis outside of the Courts.

Senior year he went to work for MARL Metal Products, a furniture-assembling plant on Georgia near the Memphis and Arkansas Bridge, where he worked from 3:00 to 11:30 P.M. each day, but the work took its toll. According to a teacher, Mildred Scrivener: "Elvis was working too hard. He was in my homeroom, and he also was in one of my history classes. One thing I have always been very strict about is the matter of sleeping in class. Nothing can spread yawns and boredom so fast from row to row. But the day came when Elvis fell asleep in class. . . . That day when the class bell shrilled, Elvis, like a little boy, raised his head, got to his feet, and wandered out like a sleepwalker." "It got so hard on him," said Gladys, "he was so beat all the time, we made him quit, and I went [back] to work at St. Joseph's Hospital."

That evidently got them thrown out of the Courts. Despite Vernon's back troubles, in November 1952 it was determined that the Presleys' projected annual income had risen to $4,133, well over Housing Authority limits, and on November 17 the Presley family got an eviction notice, requiring them to move out by February 28. In a sense their eviction could be seen as evidence of upward mobility, though it seems unlikely Vernon would have taken it that way at the time.

Elvis meanwhile was making a greater claim on his schoolmates' attention. It seemed as if he was determined to make a statement, he was intent upon setting himself apart, without ever raising his voice or changing from the polite, well-mannered boy that he knew he would always be. By his dress, his hair, his demeanor, though, he was making a ringing declaration of independence. More and more to his fellow schoolmates he was a "squirrel," a misfit, a freak, as he would later describe himself, but not a freak to himself. Photographs show an increasing self-confidence, an increasingly studied self-image, even as he was being increasingly rejected by others. He entered a citywide automobile-safety contest sponsored by the Junior Chamber of Commerce and was pictured in the paper changing a tire, expression pensive, dress immaculate: where others wore short-sleeved shirts and work pants and boots, Elvis is spectacularly attired in what could be a pink and black drape jacket, dress pants and loafers, and black shirt.

Red West, the All-Memphis football player who was reputed to have rescued Elvis in the football-team incident and thus laid the groundwork for a lifelong friendship, admired that he had the guts to be different, but "I really felt sorry for him. He seemed very lonely and had no real friends. He just didn't seem to be able to fit in." To Ronny Trout, who shared a workbench with him in wood shop though they were a couple of years apart in school, it was as if he were newly creating himself. "He would wear dress pants to school every day — everybody else wore jeans, but he wore dress pants. And he would wear a coat and fashion a scarf like an ascot tie, as if he were a movie star. Of course he got a lot of flak for this, because he stood out like a sore thumb. People thought, 'That's really weird.' It was like he was already portraying something that he wanted to be. One thing I noticed, and I never really knew what to make of this: when he walked, the way he carried himself, it almost looked as if he was getting ready to draw a gun, he would kind of spin around like a gunfighter. It was weird.

"The way I found out he could play the guitar — I never remember seeing him have it in school, but one of the projects we had in wood shop was to bring an article from home that needed to be repaired, and our wood shop instructor, Mr. Widdop, would look at it and evaluate what had to be done, and that would be our project for a six-week time period. Anyway, I brought something from home, and Elvis brought a guitar. And he fooled around with it, sanded it, used some rosin glue and fixed a crack in it, stained it, varnished it, then he took this real fine steel wool to get all the bubbles out of the lacquer and bring it down to a satin finish so it looked really good. Then he put the strings back on it and was tuning it just before the period ended. So, naturally, somebody came up and said, 'Hey, man, can you play that thing?' And he said, 'No, not really. I just know a few chords. My uncle's taught me a few chords.' So they said, 'Why don't you play something for us?' He said, 'Naw, I can't do that,' and he kept tuning it. Well, somebody grabbed him from behind and locked his arms behind him, and another guy got his car keys out of his pocket, and they said, 'If you play something, you'll get your car keys back.' He said, 'Well, okay, I'll try, but I really don't know that much.' And he started picking out the melody to a song that most people today probably wouldn't even know called 'Under the Double Eagle,' and he did it very expertly. And it just blew me away. I didn't even know he could play that guitar — I just thought he was fixing it for somebody else."

More and more, it seemed, his determination to be himself — his determination to be a *different* self — grew. He started wearing a black bolero jacket that he had bought at Lansky's and a pair of dress pants with a stripe down the side that made him look, some said, like a carhop. He was constantly fooling with his hair — combing it, mussing it up, training it, brushing the sides back, seemingly oblivious to the attention he was getting from teachers and fellow students alike ("We had grown accustomed to those sideburns," wrote Miss Scrivener in the nostalgic afterglow of success). One time he got a home permanent and came into school the next day asking if he didn't look like Tony Curtis.

He put a couple of gallons of gas in the Lincoln and cruised around town by himself or with his cousin Gene or Bobbie — to Leonard's Barbecue, to the drugstore where Gene worked as a soda jerk; every afternoon he stopped by St. Joseph's to visit his mother at work, and once or twice he and Gene drove down to Tupelo to visit old friends. Perhaps he attended the Midnight Rambles at the Handy Theater, on Park and Airways. Everyone else did. A whole gang would get together on Sunday night and go out to the colored district in Orange Mound for the late show, which was whites-only. There you could catch Eddie "Cleanhead" Vinson, Ivory Joe Hunter, Wynonie Harris, even Dizzy Gillespie, and local acts like Bobby "Blue" Bland, Little Junior Parker, and the comedy team of Rufus (Thomas) and Bones. Was Elvis there — or was he just at home, lying on his bed and listening to Dewey Phillips and dreaming of a world that the music alone could transport him to? By himself he would venture out east to Overton Park, the 330-acre expanse that housed the zoo he had first visited as a child (his uncle Noah had driven the East Tupelo schoolchildren in his school bus), "the same place," he later recalled, "that I did my first concert. I used to go there and listen to the concerts they had with big orchestras. I watched the conductor, listened to the music for hours by myself — I was fascinated by the fact that these guys could play for hours, you know, and most of the time the conductor wouldn't even look at his sheet. . . . I had records by Mario Lanza when I was seventeen, eighteen years old, I would listen to the Metropolitan Opera. I just loved music. Music period."

THE PRESLEYS moved out of the Courts on January 7, 1953. At first they moved to a rooming house at 698 Saffarans, just a couple of blocks from Humes, but then at the beginning of April they moved back to their old neighborhood at 462 Alabama, opposite the Blacks' house on the northeast end of the Courts. Johnny, like his older brother Bill, had by now taken up the bass, married, and moved out of his mother's home, but like all of his grown brothers and sisters he visited frequently and came back to play music with his friends from the Courts from time to time. "We just thought he was pretty," Bill's wife, Evelyn, said of the women's reaction to Elvis. "We'd sit out there under the tree in front of Mrs. Black's with him playing guitar: Bill's mama said he was her boyfriend! We knew he could play, but we didn't think it was any big deal."

The house on Alabama was a big Victorian set on a rise and divided up into two good-size apartments. The rent was fifty dollars a month, payable to a Mrs. Dubrovner, whose husband had been a kosher butcher and who lived down the street herself, and both Mrs. Dubrovner and the Presleys' upstairs neighbors, Rabbi Alfred Fruchter and his wife, Jeanette, showed a considerable amount of kindness, and financial consideration, toward the new tenants. Mrs. Presley visited with Mrs. Fruchter almost every afternoon after work, and the Fruchters were particularly fond of the boy, who would turn on the electricity or light the gas for them on the Sabbath when it was forbidden for Orthodox Jews to do so for themselves. "They never had much," said Mrs. Fruchter, but every Saturday morning Vernon and Elvis "would stand outside and polish that old Lincoln like it was a Cadillac."

On April 9, 1953, the Humes High Band presented its "Annual Minstrel" show in the Humes Auditorium at 8:00 P.M. It was a Thursday night, and much of the school had turned out to see the dancers, twirlers, xylophone trio, male quartets, band performances, and comic turns. On a printed program that listed twenty-two acts, the sixteenth entry captured a number of people's attention. "Guitarist. . . . Elvis Prestly," it read. He had told only one or two of his friends beforehand, and even they were not fully convinced he would go through with it. For the minstrel show he wore a red flannel shirt that he had borrowed from Buzzy, and he appeared neither visibly nervous nor particularly at ease either. Unlike some of the kids, who were practiced showmen (Gloria Trout, Ronny's sister, starred in virtually every show that was ever put on at Humes and was renowned for her dance technique), he didn't appear to know what to do when he stumbled out onstage, stood there for what seemed like a full minute, looked at the audience sidelong from under hooded eyes, and finally, as if an internal switch had somehow clicked on, began to sing.

"I wasn't popular in school, I wasn't dating anybody [there]. I failed music — only thing I ever failed. And then they entered me in this talent show, and I came out and did my [first number,] 'Till I Waltz Again with You' by Teresa Brewer, and when I came onstage I heard people kind of rumbling and whispering and so forth, 'cause nobody knew I even sang. It was amazing how popular I became after that. Then I went on through high school and I graduated."

He sang at the homeroom picnic at Overton Park. "While other students were dashing around . . . playing games," wrote Miss Scrivener, "Elvis sat by himself plunking softly at that guitar. The other students began gathering around. There was something about his quiet, plaintive singing which drew them like a magnet. It wasn't the rock 'n' roll for which he later became famous . . . more like [the ballad] 'Love Me Tender.' . . . He went on and on singing his young heart out."

Toward the end of the school year he took Regis Vaughan, a fourteen-year-old freshman at Holy Name School, to the senior prom, which was held at the Continental Ballroom in the Hotel Peabody. He had started going with Regis, whom he had met while she was living with her mother in the Courts the previous year, in February, and they went together all spring. Generally they would double-date with Elvis' cousin Gene and go to a movie or out to the "Teen Canteen" overlooking McKellar Lake at Riverside Park, a recreation spot in South Memphis that was very popular. He sang one song to her, "My Happiness," over and over, and when they went to the gospel All-Night Singings at Ellis, he embarrassed her by singing along with each of the groups, trying to hit the low notes with the bass singer, the high ones with the lead tenor. For the prom he borrowed a car and wore a shiny new blue suit, but they never danced once the whole evening because Elvis said he didn't know how. Afterward they were supposed to meet some friends of Elvis' at Leonard's Barbecue and go to a party, but the friends didn't show up. He never told Regis about the talent show at school, he never talked about becoming a singer, "he talked about finding a job so that he could afford to buy a house for his mama."

He graduated on June 3, 1953, in a program that took place at 8:00 P.M. in Ellis Auditorium's South Hall. The Senior Glee Club sang a selection by Rachmaninoff and "Nocturne" by the Czech composer Zdenko Fibich. Elvis was visibly proud that he had made it through, and Vernon and Gladys were no less elated. They had the diploma framed, and it was placed in an honored spot in their home. The 1953 yearbook, the *Herald*, announced in its "Class Prophecy" that "we are reminded at this time to not forget to invite you all out to the 'Silver Horse' on Onion [Union] Avenue to hear the singing hillbillies of the road. Elvis Presley, Albert Teague, Doris Wilburn, and Mary Ann Propst are doing a bit of picking and singing out that-away." Meanwhile, on the morning of his graduation Elvis had gone down to the Tennessee Employment Security Office, where he got a job, starting the next day, at M. B. Parker Machinists' Shop, not too far from Humes. He would be making thirty-three dollars a week. He was out in the world.

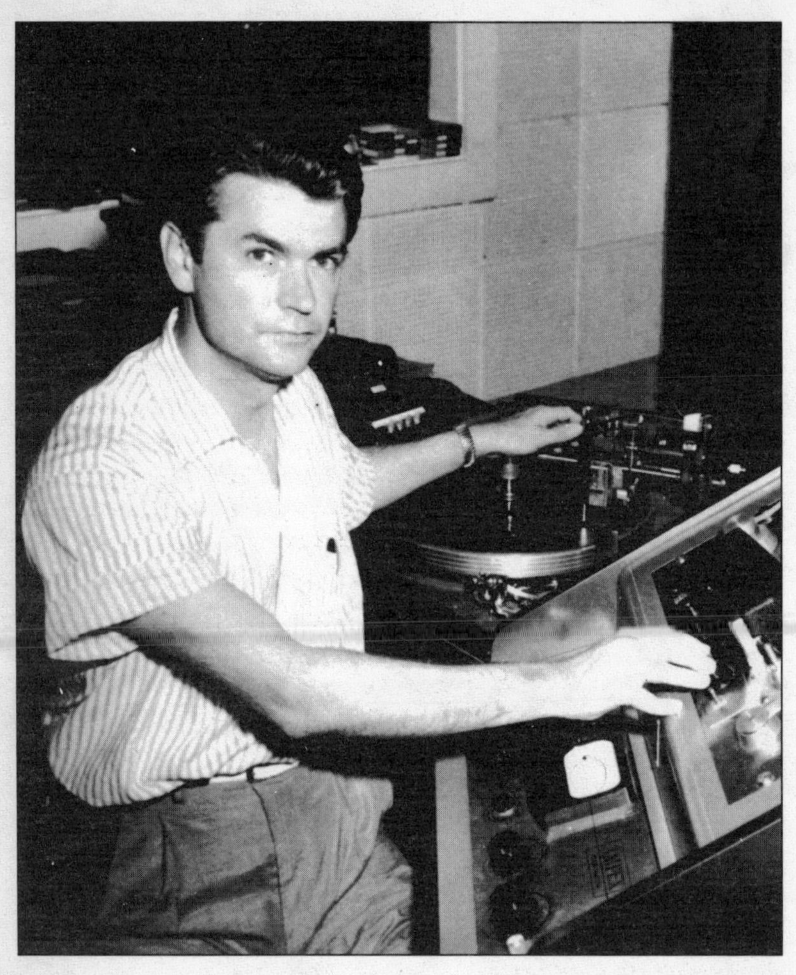

SAM PHILLIPS AT 706 UNION AVENUE. (COURTESY OF GARY HARDY, SUN STUDIO)

"MY HAPPINESS"

On July 15, 1953, an article appeared in the *Memphis Press-Scimitar* about a new group, which was making records for a label that had just started up locally. The Prisonaires were the group. They had begun their career inside the walls of the Tennessee State Penitentiary, in Nashville, where they had come to the attention of Red Wortham, a small-time Nashville song publisher. Wortham contacted Jim Bulleit, only recently the proprietor of his own self-named record company in Nashville (the Bullet label had had a number-one pop hit with Francis Craig's "Near You" in 1947 and had released B. B. King's first sides, in 1949) and a recent investor in the new Memphis label. Bulleit called his partner, Sam Phillips, reported the *Press-Scimitar* story, "and said he had something sensational. . . . Phillips, who has been operating [his studio, the Memphis Recording Service] since [January] 1950, and has established a reputation as an expert in recording negro talent, was skeptical — until he heard the tape. Then came the problem of how to get the prisoners for a record-cutting session." The newly appointed warden, James Edwards, however, was fully committed to the principle of prisoner rehabilitation, as was Governor Frank Clement, a close friend and fellow townsman of Edwards'. And so on June 1, "Bulleit drove the five singing prisoners to Memphis, the composer having to stay in prison. An armed guard and a trusty came along, the record company paying the expenses."

The Prisonaires arrived at 706 Union Avenue to make their first record for the fledgling Sun label, which, despite Sam Phillips' considerable experience in the record business (he had been leasing sides to the r&b labels Chess and RPM for three years now and had made an abortive start at his own label a year before), had put out fewer than a dozen releases to date. "They worked from 10:30 A.M. to 8:30 P.M.," the article noted, "until the records were cut just right to suit painstaking Mr. Phillips."

"Just Walkin' in the Rain" came out about the same time that the local story did. It went on to become a hit, as the reporter, Clark Porteous, had predicted it would, if nowhere near as big a hit as it would become when Johnnie Ray recorded it three years later, in 1956. It was the song that put Sun Records on the map, though, and, very likely, the item that captured the attention of Elvis Presley as he read about the studio, the label, and "painstaking" Sam Phillips, who had staked his reputation on a recording by an unknown singing group and a song whose plaintive notes Elvis heard reverberating over and over again in his mind and in his memory and on the air.

Why didn't everyone else come running to 706 Union Avenue at this point? Why didn't Lee Denson and Johnny Black and Johnny and Dorsey Burnette and the dozens of other aspiring young singers and players in and around the city flock to the doors of the Memphis Recording Service, just up the street from the newspaper and less than a mile away from the teeming downtown area? I don't know. It may have had something to do with the fact that Sun started out as a blues and "race" label, it may simply have been that none of the others was as innocent, or as open, as a young Elvis Presley, who could dream of success beyond the scope of his knowledge or experience. It's a question that I put to nearly every Memphis musician that I interviewed in the course of doing this book, but the closest that I got to an answer was that they simply didn't think of it — they were too caught up in other things, boxing or girls, playing the honky-tonks, some of them made recordings of their own voice in a booth at the five-and-dime for twenty-five cents, they may even have harbored the ambition to get on the radio and become a star, like Slim Rhodes or Eddie Hill — but it never seems to have occurred to any of them that there was even a possibility of making records, at least not here in Memphis. Did it occur to Elvis Presley? Perhaps. Perhaps, like so many things in his life, it was no more than inchoate desire, a vision he could scarcely make out, words that remained unformed. But it was a vision that he pursued.

He showed up at the office of the Memphis Recording Service sometime in mid to late summer 1953, two or three months after graduation. Sun Records, and the Memphis Recording Service, were a two-person operation set in a storefront next to Miss Taylor's restaurant and renting for $75 or $80 a month. Venetian blinds made it impossible to see through the plate glass window from the outside, but when you walked in the door into a shallow reception area that had been partitioned off from the studio directly behind it, you saw a blond woman of thirty-five or thirty-six behind a desk wedged into the far left corner of the room. Marion Keisker would have been a familiar voice to virtually anyone who listened to Memphis radio over the past twenty-five years. A native Memphian, she had made her radio debut on the weekly children's hour *Wynken, Blynken, and Nod* on WREC in 1929 at the age of twelve and had been appearing on one show or another ever since. A 1938 graduate of Memphis' Southwestern College, where she had majored in English and medieval French, she had been the host of the very popular *Meet Kitty Kelly* since 1946, a talk show on which as the eponymous hostess she interviewed visiting celebrities or simply discoursed on subjects of her own choosing if a guest didn't happen to be on hand. In addition to *Kitty Kelly,* which was on the air five days a week, as well as the nightly broadcasts of *Treasury Bandstand* from the Peabody Skyway, she wrote, produced, and directed as many as fourteen other programs at a time on WREC and was an industrious on- and off-air personality. It was at WREC, located in basement offices at the Hotel Peabody, that she first met Sam Phillips.

Phillips, a native of Florence, Alabama, had arrived in town at the age of twenty-two with four years of broadcast experience under his belt. The youngest of eight children, he had originally intended to become a criminal defense lawyer and help the downtrodden, like Clarence Darrow, but he had been forced to give up that ambition when his father died and he dropped out of high school in his senior year to help take care of his mother and deaf-mute aunt. As the captain, occasional drummer, and sousaphonist of Coffee High's seventy-two-piece marching band, perhaps it was only natural that he should think about entering into a career involving music, but he saw himself as possessing no appreciable musical talent and nothing like the personality of his flamboyant older brother Jud. "I was the greenest persimmon on the tree. If you took a bite of me, you didn't like me too much." Jud was the guy "with the overwhelming personality, it was impossible not to like Jud Phillips," but Sam valued himself for his ability to perceive, and bring out, the best in others; he believed in *communication.* And he believed unwaveringly in the communications possibilities that radio had to offer.

His first job was at Muscle Shoals' WLAY, where Jud managed, and occasionally sang in, various gospel quartets and where Jake Hess (later to join the Statesmen) got his start. He moved from there to Decatur, Alabama, then, very briefly, to Nashville's WLAC, finally arriving at WREC in the summer of 1945 with his wife and infant son. He went to work as an announcer and maintenance and broadcast engineer, supervising the big band broadcasts from "high atop the Hotel Peabody Skyway" every night with Marion Keisker. He was inspired equally by the well-bred elegance and "fanaticism for sound" of station owner Hoyt Wooten, who had started the station in his hometown of Coldwater, Mississippi, in 1920, and Phillips himself cut a handsome, almost matinee idol–like figure, though he remained quiet and reserved, a strict teetotaler who continued to be overshadowed by his more gregarious older brother (Jud was now broadcasting on WREC with the Jolly Boys Quartet).

Much as he loved music, though, and, more important, much as he continued to prize radio as an instrument of communication, Phillips was dissatisfied. He found the big band performances drearily predictable — as lofty as the inspiration for the music might be, the musicians, he felt, were mostly just going through the motions. Phillips, a man of fiercely independent spirit, wanted to do something different — "I was shooting for that damn row that hadn't been plowed." He also had a vision that no one else at WREC, evidently, shared: Sam Phillips possessed an almost Whitmanesque belief not just in the nobility of the American dream but in the nobility of that dream as it filtered down to its most downtrodden citizen, the Negro. "I saw — I don't remember when, but I saw as a child — I thought to myself: suppose that I would have been born *black*. Suppose that I would have been born a little bit more down on the economic ladder. I think I felt from the beginning the total inequity of man's inhumanity to his brother. And it didn't take its place with me of getting up in the pulpit and preaching. It took on the aspect with me that *someday I would act on my feelings, I would show them on an individual, one-to-one basis.*"

That was how he came to open his studio in January 1950, with the idea of providing a service, and an opportunity, for "some of [the] great Negro artists" of the mid South that had simply not been available before. "As word got around," wrote the *Press-Scimitar*'s Bob Johnson in 1955, "Sam's studio became host to strange visitors," and Sam insisted on plumbing that strangeness, no matter how sophisticated a veneer they might present to him at first. He recorded cotton-patch blues and slightly more sophisticated rhythm and blues, leasing the sides to the Chess label in Chicago and RPM Records out on the West Coast and doing everything from recording bar mitzvahs and political speeches to getting the concession for the PA system at the Peabody and at Russwood Park, the baseball stadium on Madison. He ordinarily worked no less than an eighteen-hour day, putting in a full schedule at the station, getting to the studio late in the afternoon, returning to the Peabody in the evening for the Skyway broadcasts, then back to the studio, where he might have left the Howlin' Wolf or "Doctor" Isaiah Ross, the discoverer of a cure for the "Boogie Disease," in the middle of a session. It was not uncommon when he came in to work to be greeted with remarks like "Well, you smell okay. I guess you haven't been hanging around those niggers today." The strain of sustaining this kind of schedule eventually led to a nervous breakdown, and he was hospitalized twice at Gartly-Ramsay Hospital, where he received electroshock therapy. It was, he said, the only time in his life that he was ever scared — twenty-eight years old, with a wife and two little boys, no money, no real prospects, nothing but his own faith in himself, and his vision, to sustain him. He quit the radio station unhesitantly, though, when Hoyt Wooten made a sarcastic remark about his absences. "Mr. Wooten," he said, "you are a cruel man," and, in June 1951, left the employ of WREC forever. He had business cards printed that stated: "We record anything — anywhere — anytime. A complete service to fill every recording need." His partner in this venture from the beginning was Marion Keisker, six years older than Sam, well regarded in Memphis even beyond her radio celebrity, a cultured divorcée with a nine-year-old son, who fell hopelessly in love with Sam.

"He was a beautiful young man. Beautiful beyond belief, but still that country touch, that country rawness. He was slim and had those incredible eyes; despite some of the images that have been given of him, he was very, very particular about his appearance with touches of real elegance, beautifully groomed, terrible about his hair. He would talk about this idea that he had, this dream, I suppose, to have a facility where black people could come and play their own music, a place where they would feel free and relaxed to do it. One day we were riding along, and he saw that spot on Union, and he said, 'That's the spot I want.' With many difficulties we got the place, and we raised the money, and between us we did everything. We laid all the tile, we painted the acoustic boards, I put in the bathroom, Sam put in the control room — what little equipment he had always had to be the best. I knew *nothing* about the music, and I didn't care a bit. My association, my contribution, my participation was based totally on my personal relationship with Sam in a way that is totally unbelievable to me now. All I wanted to do was to make it possible for him to fulfill his vision — all I wanted to do was to do what would make him happy."

By the summer of 1953 the fledgling record label had already had one big hit (Rufus Thomas' "Bear Cat") and was well on its way to two others (both "Feelin' Good" by Little Junior Parker and "Just Walkin' in the Rain" by the Prisonaires made the charts in the fall), but the partnership with Jim Bulleit, which had seemed essential to Sam both for Bulleit's financial investment and his expertise when they were starting up the label just six months earlier, was already falling apart. Sam Phillips was never really one for partnerships anyway ("I'm a competitive bastard. My one big mistake was my inability to delegate authority"), and with Jim Bulleit on the road spending money in a manner that Sam considered profligate and responding to Sam's concerns with telegrams that declared "Cold words on paper cannot fully explain this," Sam was in the midst of trying to extricate himself from the arrangement. He had brought in his brother Jud to go on the road with Bulleit, but Jud and Bulleit didn't get along any better than Sam and Jim, so things were at a frustrating impasse in August 1953.

At least that was how Marion always remembered it when she painfully tried to reconstruct the moment when an eighteen-year-old Elvis Presley, shy, a little woebegone, cradling his battered, beat-up child's guitar, first walked into the recording studio. Marion remembered that there had been an argument — she recalled that she was herself in tears because Sam had spoken harshly to her. Sometimes in her memory of that moment Jud was in the back room arguing with Sam over money, sometimes Sam and Jim Bulleit were at Miss Taylor's restaurant next door ("third booth by the window" was the Sun Records office in the absence of any extra space in the crammed storefront headquarters), sometimes the reception area was jammed with people waiting to make a record, sometimes not — but always the young boy with the long, greasy, dirty-blond hair poked his head in the door shyly, tentatively, looking as if he were ready to withdraw at a moment's notice if you just said boo to him, using that look to gain entrance, determined somehow to make himself known.

Elvis had passed 706 Union often, walking, driving — perhaps he had hesitated once or twice outside the door, simply wanting to make sure of the location. When he finally entered, there is little question that he stepped through the doorway with the idea, if not of stardom — because who could imagine stardom? what could it mean? — at the very least of being discovered. In later years he would always say that he wanted to make a personal record "to surprise my mother." Or "I just wanted to hear what I sounded like." But, of course, if he had simply wanted to record his voice, he could have paid twenty-five cents at W. T. Grant's on Main Street, where Lee Denson had made dozens of records, which he kept at home and played for his friends. Instead, Elvis went to a professional facility, where a man who had been written up in the papers would hear him sing.

It was a Saturday. Elvis was working five days a week at M. B. Parker Machinists' Shop, though he would switch soon to Precision Tool, where he and his cousin Gene would work on a shell assembly line. It was hot, and there was no air-conditioning in the waiting room, but the woman behind the desk looked cool in her cotton dress, her blond hair set in a permanent wave, her face a picture of genteel composure and kind respectability. Marion looked up from her typewriter to see the boy approach her almost sideways, figurative hat in hand. Can I help you? she said. She could barely hear his stammered reply — but, of course, she knew what he was there for, what else could he be there for with his guitar and that desperate look of *need* in his eyes? She told him how much it would cost to make a two-sided acetate — $3.98 plus tax, for another dollar you could have a tape copy as well, but he chose the less expensive option. While he sat there waiting, Marion told Jerry Hopkins in a 1970 interview, "we had a conversation, which I had reason to remember for many, many years afterwards, having gone through it with every editor that I tried to talk to during the time that I was promoting him for Sun.

> He said, "If you know anyone that needs a singer. . . ."
>
> And I said, "What kind of a singer are you?"
>
> He said, "I sing all kinds."
>
> I said, "Who do you sound like?"
>
> "I don't sound like nobody."
>
> I thought, Oh yeah, one of those. . . . "What do you sing, hillbilly?"
>
> "I sing hillbilly."
>
> "Well, who do you sound like in hillbilly?"
>
> "I don't sound like nobody."

The truth, Marion discovered, was not that far removed from the boy's improbable self-description. From the first quavering notes of the first song that he sang, it was obvious that there was something different about him, something unique — you could detect his influences, but he *didn't* sound like anyone else. There is a quality of unutterable plaintiveness as Elvis sings "My Happiness," a 1948 pop hit for Jon and Sandra Steele that he had performed over and over in the Courts, a sentimental ballad that couldn't have been further from anyone's imagining of rock 'n' roll, past or present, without a hint of foreshadowing or any black influence other than the clear tenor of Bill Kenny of the Ink Spots — it is just a pure, yearning, almost desperately pleading solo voice reaching for effect, a crying note alternating with a crooning fullness of tone that in turn yields to a sharp nasality betraying its possessor's intentions. The guitar, Elvis said, "sounded like somebody beating on a bucket lid," and the record represents almost exactly what the boys and girls in the Courts must have heard over the last several years, with an added factor of nervousness that Elvis must surely have felt. But even that is not particularly detectable — there is a strange sense of calm, an almost unsettling stillness in the midst of great drama, the kind of poise that comes as both a surprise and a revelation. When he finished the one song, he embarked upon "That's When Your Heartaches Begin," a smooth pop ballad that the Ink Spots had originally cut in 1941, with a deep spoken part for their baritone singer, Hoppy Jones. Here he was not so successful in his rendition, running out of time, or inspiration, and simply declaring "That's the end" at the conclusion of the song. The boy looked up expectantly at the man in the control booth. Mr. Phillips nodded and said politely that he was an "interesting" singer. "We might give you a call sometime." He even had Miss Keisker make a note of the boy's name, which she misspelled and then editorialized beside it: "Good ballad singer. Hold."

When it was all over, he sat in the outer lobby while Miss Keisker typed out the label copy on the blank sides of a Prisonaires label ("Softly and Tenderly," Sun 189). The singer's name was typed underneath the title on each side. Mr. Phillips never came out front, though the boy hung around for a while talking with the woman. He was disappointed that he didn't have a chance to say good-bye. But he walked out of the studio with his acetate and with the conviction that something was going to happen.

Nothing did. Nothing happened for the longest time. All through the fall he would stop by the studio, park the old Lincoln precisely by the curb, turn his collar up, pat down his hair, and manfully stride in the door. Miss Keisker was always very nice, Miss Keisker never failed to recognize him. He would try to make small talk, he would ask if, possibly, she had run into a band that was looking for a singer — he conveyed an impression of longing, of neediness, that always stayed with her. Sometimes Mr. Phillips might be present, but he didn't have time for small talk, he was always busy, he was *making records.* That was what Elvis wanted to do — that was what he wanted to do more than anything else in the world, but he didn't know how to go about it, other than to put himself in the way of it at the only place he knew to do so. Each time he entered the waiting room it was with a somewhat heavier step and somewhat lowered expectations, but he forced himself, he didn't know anything else to do. Gradually he began to doubt that anything would ever happen, and his visits became less frequent. He tried to appear indifferent, but his need showed through. In January 1954 he went in again and cut another little record — Joni James' "I'll Never Stand in Your Way" and an old Jimmy Wakely tune, "It Wouldn't Be the Same Without You," but his lack of confidence betrayed him, and he sounds more abrupt, more insecure, this time than he did the first. He was at an impasse — unlike the hero in comic books and fairy tales, he had not yet been discovered in his true guise, underneath his outer rags. And yet, Marion felt, almost maternally, he was a child who was clearly marked for success of some kind. "He was," she said, "so ingenuous there was no way he could go wrong."

WITH DIXIE LOCKE, SOUTH SIDE JUNIOR PROM, 1955. (MICHAEL OCHS ARCHIVES)

"WITHOUT YOU"

IN JANUARY 1954 he started attending church regularly for the first time since the family had left Tupelo. Vernon and Gladys occasionally went to a service at one of the nearby churches or missions, but for the most part they were content to remain at home, secure in their belief if not in their observance. Vernon was out of work more and more with a bad back; at forty-two — though she admitted to only thirty-eight — Gladys had put on a considerable amount of weight, and Elvis told employers and fellow workers alike that all he wanted to do was to make enough money to buy his mama and daddy a house. For her part, Gladys simply wanted to see her son married, she wanted grandkids, she wanted to know he was happy and settled before she died.

She was pleased, then, when he started going to the Assembly of God Church at 1084 McLemore in South Memphis. The Assembly of God in Memphis had started out in a tent and later moved to a storefront location on South Third and finally into a church on McLemore in 1948. In 1954 Pastor James Hamill, a well-educated, fire-and-brimstone preacher who denounced movies and dancing from the pulpit and encouraged ecstatic demonstrations of faith (such as speaking in tongues) in his church, had been minister for ten years. Over that time membership had grown to close to two thousand, three buses were dispatched each Sunday to pick up congregants without automobiles (one of the stops was at Winchester and Third, just outside the Presleys' door), and since 1950 the famous Blackwood Brothers Quartet and their families had been prominent members of the congregation. When they were in town, the Blackwoods performed frequently at a church service that was renowned for its music (the hundred-voice church choir was well known throughout Memphis), and only recently Cecil Blackwood, a newly married resident of Lauderdale Courts and a nephew of founding member and leader James Blackwood, had started a kind of junior quartet, the Songfellows, with Pastor Hamill's son, Jimmy, a student at Memphis State. They were also members of the Bible study class that met each Sunday at 9:30 A.M. as broader members of a Young Men's Christian group called the Christ Ambassadors.

That was where Dixie Locke first saw Elvis Presley. She had not seen him before, though she and her family were faithful members of the church since its days on South Third, not far from where they lived. Dixie was fifteen and a sophomore at South Side High. Her father worked for Railway Express, and she and her three sisters shared a single bedroom, while her parents slept in the living room. If her father went to bed at 8:00 because he had to go to work early, that was when everyone went to bed.

She had a boyfriend at the time, but it wasn't anything really special. She was bright, attractive, and with two older sisters — one of whom had eloped at fourteen and was now back home — was alert to a world whose existence she could barely have glimpsed. In the half hour before the boys and girls split off into their respective classes, she noticed the new boy, dressed so oddly in pink and black, with his long greasy hair and fidgety manner, as he sought so desperately to become a part of the group. The other kids all laughed at him a little, they made fun of him, but strictly for his appearance — he appeared to be serious about his Bible studies. The other girls thought he was *peculiar:* "He was just so different, all the other guys were like replicas of their dads." And yet to Dixie he was different in another way. "To watch him you would think, even then, he was really shy. What was so strange was that he would do anything to call attention to himself, but I really think he was doing it to prove something to himself more than to the people around him. Inside, even then, I think he knew that he was different. I knew the first time I met him that he was not like other people."

Dixie and her girlfriends went out nearly every weekend to the Rainbow Rollerdrome, east on Lamar (Highway 78 to Tupelo), just beyond the city limits. They rode the bus in their skating skirts; Dixie had one of black corduroy with white satin lining, and she wore white tights underneath. The Rainbow was a big teenage hangout, with a snack bar and a jukebox, an organist who played the "Grand March" for the skaters, and a swimming pool next door. There were dance contests on the floor and generally, on a weekend night, up to six or seven hundred kids, who could gather without any fear of trouble or any concern that they might be getting in with a bad crowd. One Sunday at church, at the end of January, Dixie started talking with some girlfriends about her plans for the upcoming weekend. She spoke loudly enough so that the boys in the groups next to them might overhear, and particularly so that the new boy, who was pretending not to be paying any attention, would know. She wasn't sure that he would come, she thought it almost brazen of herself to be doing this, but she wanted very badly to see him. When she arrived at the rink on Saturday night with her girlfriends, she noticed with a little start that he was there, but she ignored him, pretending to herself that she hadn't seen him until one of her friends said, "Did you know that boy, Elvis Presley, was here?" She said, "Yeah, I saw him," kind of casually, and then watched for a while to see what he was going to do. He was standing by the rail with his skates on, wearing a kind of bolero outfit, short black bullfighter's jacket, ruffled shirt, black pegged pants with a pale pink stripe down the legs. He was leaning up against the rail all by himself, trying to look detached, nonchalantly surveying the floor aswirl with activity, and after a while Dixie realized *he couldn't skate.* She took pity on him at last, went up and introduced herself. He said, "Yeah, I know," and hung his head down, then tossed back his hair. Finally he asked Dixie if she wanted to go get a Coke, "and I said yes, and we went to the snack area, and I don't think we ever went back out to the skating floor the whole night." They talked and talked and talked; it was almost as if he had been waiting to unburden himself all his life. He talked about how he wanted to join the Songfellows, how he had spoken with Cecil and Jimmy Hamill about it and maybe they were going to give him a tryout. It was as if "he had a plan, he knew that he had a talent, there was something for his life that he was supposed to do. It was like from that moment on there was nobody else there."

The first session was over at 10:00 P.M., and Dixie was supposed to go home with her friends, but she told them to leave without her. Elvis asked if she could stay for the second session, and while he was standing there, she pretended to call her mother from the pay phone, but she dialed a number at random (she wouldn't have wanted to admit that she didn't have a phone but had to call her uncle and aunt next door anyway) and gabbled on at length about the nice boy from church that she happened to have run into and how they were going to stay for the second session but she would be home right after midnight. She had never done anything like this before, but she didn't think twice about it. In the end they didn't even stay. After she made the call, he suggested that they go to a drive-in; why didn't they go to K's on Crump Boulevard, where they could get a hamburger and a milk shake? They kept talking as they finally unlaced their skates. He opened the door of the Lincoln for her and was careful to explain that it wasn't his (he wanted to see if she would still go out with him, he explained afterward, if he didn't have a car), and they drove west into town on Lamar until it ran into Crump, talking the whole way.

She sat close to him on the front seat, closer than you ever would on a normal first date, and at K's she kissed him sitting in the parking lot. It was a chaste kiss, a loving kiss — Dixie wasn't planning to keep this a secret for long, even from her mother. She was so swept up in it, he was, too, it was like nothing that had ever happened to either one of them before. When he dropped her off at her door, he whispered that he would call her next week, Wednesday or Thursday probably, about going out on the weekend — there was never any question that they would see each other again, and again. She tiptoed in the door, knowing she was late, even for the late session — she was bound to wake up her parents, her father was going to kill her, but she didn't care, not really, she was truly in love.

HE CALLED THE NEXT DAY. Her aunt called over to her from next door, just as the family was sitting down to a Sunday dinner of fried chicken. When she hadn't seen him at church that morning, her heart sank a little, but she never doubted that she would hear from him. And now he couldn't even wait a day.

They went out that night to the movies, and then again on Wednesday night. She still hadn't let him meet her parents, inventing one excuse or another, for him and for them, but then on Saturday, just a week from the night they had truly met, he came to pick her up at the house and she brought him inside to meet her family, as much because he wanted to as because she knew she had to. She had tried to prepare everyone, but she found when she met him at the door that she was scarcely prepared herself: she had forgotten how *different* he looked, she had forgotten about his hair and his dress, she hadn't thought about the effect it might have on others. At night in bed she had whispered to her sisters about him, and she had confided to her diary that she had at last found her one true love. She had even told her mother what she had done when she called from the skating rink, but she had emphasized that he came from a good family (which she didn't really know — he acted like she was some kind of royalty because she was from South Memphis, though they were as poor as

Job's turkey) and that she had met him in *church.* Now as her father addressed him gravely, and Elvis mumbled his replies, tossing his head back whenever he said, "Yes, sir," and "No, sir," and presenting the gravest, most respectful mien, she wasn't so sure, she knew that she loved him, but she saw him for the first time as her father must see him. There was no way of telling what her father was thinking, he never gave any clue — he gave his full attention without ever saying much of anything. All the boys she and her sisters had ever brought to the house were scared of Mr. Locke, big (six foot two), impassive, but if he ever made up his mind about something he didn't hesitate to let you, or anyone else, know about it, and you just did it, regardless. Her mother was calling her — she didn't want to leave Elvis alone with her father, but she felt she had no choice. In the kitchen, "my mother read me the riot act: 'How can you go out with a boy like that?' — that kind of thing. I was saying, 'Mother, you can't go by the way . . . Just because his hair is long, or he's not dressed like everybody else. . . .' I was really defending him, telling her what a nice boy he was — I had met him at church, after all. And meanwhile I was afraid they would say something that would hurt his feelings and he would just leave."

Eventually they escaped — her sister met him briefly, she was perfectly nice to him to his face, but behind his back she raised her eyebrows so Dixie could see what she really thought. The next day her uncle offered Dixie $2 for the boy if he would just get a haircut. It didn't matter, none of it mattered; that night he gave her his ring, that meant they were going steady, neither of them would see anybody else — ever.

Two weeks later she met his parents. It was a weekday night, cool for February, when he picked her up and drove her back to Alabama Street. She was amazed to discover that even though neither parent was working (Mr. Presley was out of work at the moment with a bad back, and Mrs. Presley's employment at St. Joseph's had evidently stopped) and Elvis' salary at Precision could scarcely have amounted to more than $50 a week, they had a piano, a piano *and* a television set, and he was calling *her* "high class"! She wanted so badly to like his mother, but Mrs. Presley seemed suspicious at first, she seemed nervous and apprehensive, she had a hundred questions for Dixie — where her father worked, how big a family she came from, where she and Elvis had met, how long they had been going out, what school she attended. Mr. Presley was polite, attentive, but he had nothing much to say, "it was almost like he was an outsider, not part of the group." Eventually Mrs. Presley shooed Elvis and his dad to one side to pursue the questioning on her own. Elvis was pacing back and forth, he would come in and out of the room and touch her on the shoulder, as if to say it was all right, then disappear again. He was clearly beside himself, just waiting to get out of there, but it went on and on. And after an hour or two a number of relatives came over — his cousin Gene, whom she had already met, a bunch of other cousins (it seemed like his only friends were his family), and they all sat around and played Monopoly. She was embarrassed and self-conscious, and aware that Elvis would be mad at her if she acted all "prim and proper," if she wasn't just herself. Finally they were able to leave: "He was so relieved, I think he couldn't wait to take me home, so he could come back and say, 'What do you think?' to his mom. You know, they had such a strong love and respect for each other, she was just totally devoted to him, it was like this mutual admiration. A day or two later, I said something like 'I wonder what your mother thinks . . .' or 'I hope . . . ,' something like that, and he said, 'Oh, you don't have to worry about that, she thinks you're neat.' I knew I had her stamp of approval then."

They went out almost every night, even weeknights. If they didn't, they spoke on the phone, long heartfelt conversations, until her uncle and aunt got mad about her monopolizing the line. At one point her dad put a halt to their seeing each other for a few days, but her family soon came "to love him almost as much as I did. They saw that I was serious, and he was always so polite, and they knew it was a very honest relationship, they trusted us together as far as our conduct was concerned. Within a very short time he was just part of the family."

Mrs. Presley, to Dixie, was almost like a second mother, and the Presley house on Alabama became like a second home to her. Some days Mr. Presley would come and pick her up at her house on Lucy after school so she could meet Elvis the moment he got home from work. Sometimes, if Mr. Presley didn't feel like driving, she would ride the bus. "Which was very unusual for those days — that was another one of those things that my mom and dad were not at all in favor of — but I didn't think there was anything wrong with it for me." Not infrequently she visited Mrs. Presley on her own — one time they went to a Stanley Products party together, often they just sat and talked. There was one subject they had in common about which each had an inexhaustible curiosity, but they shared a number of other interests as well. Mrs. Presley showed Dixie her recipes, and occasionally they would go shopping together, maybe even pick out a surprise for Elvis. Dixie found Mrs. Presley to be one of the warmest, most wonderful, and genuine people she had ever met. "In no time we were just great friends. We could call and talk to each other and enjoy each other — whether Elvis was there or not. We could just laugh and have a good time together." But even at fifteen Dixie soon realized that the Presleys were different from her own family in at least two significant respects. One was the role that Vernon played. Perhaps because it was in such sharp contrast to her own father's role and behavior ("I had seen my dad go to work with a brace on his back for years, and he had a very physically demanding job"), his passivity struck her particularly forcefully. "I never saw him be unkind. I never saw him drink or be unruly, I'm sure he was a very loving husband and devoted to his family, and it probably had to do with his self-esteem — but it was like he was an outsider, really, he wasn't really part of Elvis and Mrs. Presley's group. I mean, it sounds weird, but they had such a strong love and respect for each other, and I don't think there was a lot of respect for him during that time. It was almost like Elvis was the father and his dad was just the little boy."

The other striking difference was their view of the outside world. The Lockes regarded the world at large comfortably, as a friendly, for the most part unthreatening sort of place. Coming from a big family herself, having an even larger extended family through the church and all the church activities in which she took part, Dixie was accustomed to a large circle of acquaintances, a constant whirl of social activity, and an open-door policy at home, where friends and family were likely to drop in without notice (they had to — there was no telephone!). The Presleys, by contrast, she felt, regarded the world with suspicion. They had few close friends outside of family; apart from his cousins, Dixie never met any of Elvis' friends. In fact "he just came into our crowd completely, there was nobody he went to school with, nobody from the neighborhood that he palled around with at that point particularly.

"Mrs. Presley was a very humble person, and it was almost like she felt inferior around people where she didn't feel like she quite fit in — maybe she didn't have the right hairdo or the right dress to wear. She had a couple of lady friends from Lauderdale Courts, and one of them had a daughter who really thought Elvis was for her. One night we were all sitting on the porch, and this girl came over — as I remember it she was a very attractive girl — and when she came in, it was as if she belonged there, it was like she was so comfortable with being in the house and being with Elvis that she made me feel uncomfortable. So I just set back and was just kind of reserved and quiet, and Mrs. Presley said, 'Let's have a glass of iced tea' or something. Normally I just would have gotten up and gotten it, but before I could say anything, the other girl said, 'Oh, I'll go fix it.' When she left, I'll never forget, Mrs. Presley got onto me good. She said, 'I could just pinch you. Why did you just set there and let her take over?' She said, 'Don't you ever do that again. You know you're just as at home here as Elvis is. You get up and do something next time, just like you would if you were in your own home.'

"She and I were just so close, sometimes Elvis would talk to me and say things that normally he would reserve for his mother, little pet names and gestures, put his face almost in your face and talk like they talked, how sweet you looked today, that kind of thing, just the way he always talked with his mother. And I would think, 'Oh, don't do that in front of her.' 'Cause that was just for her."

They saw each other all the time. When the weather turned warm, they sat out on the front porch, either at Dixie's house or on the long brick-pillared porch on Alabama — they would sit on the swing and Elvis would sing to her sometimes: "Tomorrow Night," "My Happiness," sweet, tender little ballads. He was slightly inhibited and didn't sing very loud if he thought her family was around. Often they would walk down to the corner and get a purple cow or a milk shake at the Dairy Queen, then go and sit on a bench in Gaston Park, just a few blocks from Dixie's house. A big date was going to the movies at the Suzore No. 2 on North Main, fifty cents' worth of gas, fifty cents for the movies, and a dollar for something to eat at K's or Leonard's afterward. They loved each other, they were committed to remaining "pure" until marriage, they shared everything with each other, there were no secrets. One time there was a crisis at work; Elvis was told if he didn't get a haircut he would be fired. He was so embarrassed by the haircut he got that he didn't want anyone to see him, and it didn't help when Dixie's uncle, who had been telling him to get a haircut all along, kidded him about it. He was so sensitive — Dixie had never met anyone as sensitive as him. One time early in their relationship he got upset with her at a drive-in, about something that she had said in front of his cousin, and he got out of the car and was going to hitchhike home. Another time he got into a fight with his mother and was going to leave — forever. He came over to Dixie's house to say good-bye.

They cried in each other's arms; then she watched him drive off, and promptly drive back again, as she stood on her front porch. They couldn't be separated — ever. They talked about marriage, but they were going to wait. When they got married they wanted their families to share in it.

THEY WENT TO CHURCH together, though not as often as Dixie would have liked. Elvis was good about attending his Bible class, but he didn't always go to the service and sometimes he would just pick her up afterward. Sometimes when they did attend, they would arrive with a group of young people just before the service and sit in the back, making sure that parents and elders knew they were present. Then when the service was well under way and all eyes were on Reverend Hamill, they would sneak out the door and drive down to the colored church at East Trigg, less than a mile away, where the Reverend Brewster delivered his stirring sermons and Queen C. Anderson and the Brewsteraires were the featured soloists. They reveled in the exotic atmosphere, the music was out of this world — but they could only stay a few minutes, they had to get back to First Assembly before they were missed. Sometimes at night they would come back for the WHBQ broadcast of *Camp Meeting of the Air*. Often James Blackwood would be present, and Pastor Hamill's son, Jimmy, and the other Songfellows frequently attended; there was in fact a whole contingent of whites who came to be uplifted by the music and by Dr. Brewster's eloquence and probity of character. Dr. Brewster constantly preached on the theme that a better day was coming, one in which all men could walk as brothers, while across Memphis Sam Phillips listened on his radio every Sunday without fail, and future Sun producer Jack Clement often attended with his father, a Baptist deacon and choir director, "because it was a happening place, it was heartfelt, that's what was happening in Memphis."

They went to the movies — double features — at least twice a week. A couple of times Elvis took Dixie to Humes. Once he sang a song on the talent show in which he told her he had performed the previous year. He paraded proudly in front of his old schoolmates, put his arm around her, talked with some of the guys that he knew from the Courts, while all the while turning her hand over in his — he didn't so much want to introduce her into his world as show her off to it. It was a little bit the same when they visited Tupelo. Once they went with Mr. and Mrs. Presley and visited relatives; another time they went down with Elvis' aunt Clettes and uncle Vester, and once again Elvis showed every respect to his uncles and aunts and cousins down there, but it was definitely a "look at me" kind of thing. He was proud of himself, proud of his clothes, proud of his girl, proud of what he had learned in the city — and why not? In Dixie's view he had every reason to feel that way about himself.

Mostly, though, they stayed close to home, didn't do anything that exotic — it was almost like playing house. Sometimes they would baby-sit for Dixie's cousins and just sit there and watch TV. Sometimes Mr. and Mrs. Presley would go out, leaving them the house to themselves. Much of the time they stayed in the same North Memphis neighborhood where the Presleys had lived for the past five and a half years. The Suzore No. 2 was just around the corner and was cheaper than any of the movie palaces uptown — even if you did run the risk of finding rats underfoot when the lights came up. Charlie's Record Shop moved across the street that spring; the bus stopped right in front of it, and sometimes Dixie met Elvis there. Evidently the proprietor and his wife, Helen, had known Elvis for some time, because after a few visits he introduced her to them, and after that they always greeted her in a friendly way, even if Elvis hadn't arrived yet. There was a jukebox playing all the time and a little soda fountain where you could get a Coke or a NuGrape soda — and then there were the hundreds of 78s, not just the latest hits but r&b hits from years before, too. There were two or three listening booths, and if it wasn't crowded you could hang around for hours sometimes just listening to the music. That was where Elvis first played her the original of one of the songs he sang all the time, Lonnie Johnson's "Tomorrow Night." It was good, but it wasn't as good as Elvis'. That was where she first heard the original versions of a lot of the songs that he sang, and sometimes if he wanted to try a new one he would ask her for the words, because she always had a good memory for music.

He seemed to know quite a few of the kids who hung out there, but he never introduced her. He told her about a record *he* had made a few months before at some little record company out on Union, but he never played it for her, and he never told her that Charlie had put it on the jukebox for a while right in the store, with his name written out in script on the jukebox selection list. Once in a very rare while one or the other of them would actually buy a record — they both had record players at home, and Elvis had a small, treasured collection. Sometimes he would bring some of his favorite records over to her house, and they would just sit there and listen.

More and more she realized how much he loved music. As spring turned to summer, he would sing to her for hours sometimes, free of the self-consciousness that had plagued him initially, particularly around her family. She didn't know whether he was singing to her or just singing for the sake of singing, but his face took on a luminous quality, there was a special expression that he had when he was momentarily at rest. At the Presleys' he was always fooling around on the piano, picking out a tune that they might have heard on the radio — he could play anything after hearing it once or twice, nothing fancy, simply sticking to the melody. Sometimes he would sit at the piano and just sing hymns. Occasionally Gladys might join in, though never Vernon, and Dixie was very self-conscious about her own voice, but they would all gather around the piano in a tight little group, participating if only by their presence and by their approval. "We shared everything, we talked about *everything* — he would talk to me about things that I'm confident he never would have revealed to anyone else. But nothing was ever said about what he wanted to do. Maybe he had deep ambitions that we didn't talk about, because in his mind it was so completely alien, but he wasn't trying to be a musician at night or anything like that. I just thought he was a guy who played the guitar and loved music."

He did talk to her about his ambition to join the Songfellows, but that was just a little amateur quartet out of church. At some point that spring he confessed to her that he had auditioned for the group and been turned down — he was deeply disappointed, and even though he told Dixie that the reason they hadn't taken him was that the guy they thought was going to leave had decided to stay, it seemed obvious that he didn't believe it. "They told me I couldn't sing," he told his father. Jimmy Hamill, the minister's son, said, "Elvis, why don't you give it up?" He was hurt, Dixie said, "but it was like, 'Well, that didn't work out, let's go on to the rest of it.' "

Without fail they attended the monthly All-Night Singings at Ellis that the Blackwood Brothers sponsored. They had each gone on their own before they ever met and happily discovered that this was yet another thing they had in common. They loved the Speer Family and the LeFevres out of Atlanta, Wally Fowler never failed to shake the audience up with "Gospel Boogie," and they thrilled to the Sunshine Boys, featuring the zoom bass of J. D. Sumner, formerly of the Stamps' Sunny South Quartet. The Statesmen and the Blackwoods both had RCA Victor contracts, and in the spring of 1954 the Blackwood Brothers went up to New York and won the *Arthur Godfrey's Talent Scouts* contest, which it seemed everyone in Memphis must have watched. Elvis and Dixie never went backstage at Ellis — they would never have dared, and they had no reason to — but during the intermissions they joined the other fans who clustered around the tables that each group set up to sell their records and songbooks and hung on their every word. They knew James Blackwood, of course; they saw him at church all the time and had great respect for the dignified appearance and professionalism of the group, with their dark suits, precise diction, and carefully worked out harmonies. But it was the Statesmen who remained their favorites — listen to Jake, Elvis would say to Dixie as he hit yet another thrilling high note with that controlled vibrato and the crowd went wild and called for him to do it again. As for Big Chief, he went about as far as you could go, it seemed: the crowd just loved him, they were with him from the moment he first walked out onstage, and when he started in to shaking his leg and dancing around, they just about tore the rafters off. Pastor Hamill wouldn't approve, he didn't think much of quartet singing in any form, despite his son's participation and the celebrity the Blackwood Brothers lent his church. Good Christian people didn't seek out that sort of adulation, good Christian people didn't need to shake their leg and dance the hootchy-koo up onstage, good Christian people were saved by faith, not stardom — but Elvis and Dixie didn't care. "We were just so impressed with them, we practically worshiped Jake Hess, we were like groupies, I guess, the quartets were like part of our family."

They would even go down to WMPS sometimes just to catch the noontime broadcasts that Bob Neal hosted. Dixie had never been to a radio station before, but Elvis was right at home, finding them a seat in the front row, nodding curtly at James Blackwood while looking away from him as if it was accidental — there was never any more contact than that. Elvis couldn't be still, he was fidgeting constantly, drumming his fingers on the side of the chair, his leg going all the time. It drove Dixie's mother crazy, she'd ask her if there was something the matter with him, even bring it to Elvis' attention, and Dixie would defend him without fail, but it embarrassed her, too. She wondered if there *was* something the matter; she supposed he would grow out of it, she just wished he wouldn't do it in public. They enjoyed the broadcasts. Sometimes while Bob was doing the commercials James or one of the other Blackwoods would sneak up behind him and comb his hair down over his eyes and the audience would bust out laughing.

Starting in April they began to go out to Riverside Park every week, two or three times a week, whenever it was warm enough. Sometimes on the weekends they would eat fried chicken on the bluff; McKellar Lake was full of boaters and water-skiers and young couples just having a good time. More often than not, they would double-date with Elvis' cousin Gene, who was going out off and on with Dixie's sister Juanita. Elvis and Gene were goofy together — they acted as if they had some kind of joke going on between them all the time, speaking in a kind of private language that no one else could understand, laughing at things that weren't funny to anyone else. It made Dixie momentarily uncomfortable, as if somehow she were being excluded, as if — despite all the intimacies that they had shared and the ease with which she could have embarrassed *him* (she thought that Elvis must be the most easily embarrassed boy she had ever met) — as if she were somehow the outsider. But then she remembered the innate sweetness of his nature, the dreams and confidences they shared: "He was not a phony, he was not a put-on, he was not a show-off, and once you were around him long enough to see him be himself, not just act the clown, anyone could see his real self, you could see his sweetness, you could see the humility, you could see the desire to please." It was just that he and Gene acted funny together sometimes.

So many nights they ended up at the park, with or without Gene, in a group or by themselves, but whether they came alone or with others it seemed like they always connected with their crowd. They hung out at the pavilion area overlooking the lake, where you could get a Coke or listen to the jukebox and dance at Rocky's Lakeside refreshment stand, a screened-in area especially for teens. Usually there would be at least ten or twelve couples in the parking lot, and, without too much coaxing, Elvis could always be induced to get his guitar out of the backseat and, leaning up against the car, start to play. "He wasn't shy, he just had to be asked — I think he just didn't want to impose. No one else ever did it, no one else had the nerve. He sang songs that were popular and a lot of the old blues-type songs; he did some of the old spirituals, too. You know, it was funny. Right from the start it was as if he had a power over people, it was like they were transformed. It wasn't that he demanded anybody's attention, but they certainly reacted that way — it didn't matter how rough they were or whether they even acted like they were going to be interested or not, they *were,* once he started singing. Like when Pastor Hamill walked up in the pulpit he commanded everyone's attention, it was the same thing with Elvis, it was always that way." Sometimes he would command their attention with a beautiful love song, then change the lyrics to parody the song, but he always kept their attention. "People were just mesmerized, and he loved being the center of attention. I think he could have sung to everybody in the entire city of Memphis and not cared at all."

Sometimes they would just park in the lot overlooking the lake and listen to the radio, looking down at the water. They listened to Dewey Phillips playing the rhythm and blues hits on *Red Hot and Blue,* never country music. They got a big kick out of Dewey's Dizzy Dean impressions, his constant pitch to his audience to go out and buy a "fur-lined mousetrap," and his ads for locally brewed Falstaff beer ("If you can't drink it, freeze it and eat it. If you can't do that, open up a cotton-picking rib and POUR it in"). "Call Sam!" Dewey repeated at frequent intervals, almost as punctuation for his show — but, for his part, Elvis never spoke to Dixie about Sam; she had practically forgotten about the record that he said he had made, and as far as she was concerned they could just keep coming out to Riverside Park forever, Elvis would go on singing to her and their friends, they would get married someday, and life would go on, just as it was meant to be. Every so often a police car would pass by, sweeping the parking lot with the big beam of its spotlight, making sure no boy was taking unwanted advantage, no girl was going to get in trouble. But there was nothing like that to worry about here. You had two level-headed teenagers listening to Dewey Phillips on the radio who knew when it was time to go home.

Toward the end of April, Elvis got a new job. He hadn't been happy with the old one since they made him get a haircut, and the new one on Poplar was just around the corner from the Courts. It involved working for an electrical contractor, Crown Electric, and he was going to be driving a truck, bringing supplies out to the industrial building sites. If he wanted he would have a chance to train as an electrician; it was a long apprenticeship and required going to night school, but the opportunity was there. The owners, Mr. and Mrs. Tipler, seemed very nice — they were warm and considerate and seemed to accept their new employee for who he was.

In fact, Gladys Tipler had been warned by the lady at the employment office that she might find the new applicant's appearance a bit off-putting. But, the woman said, he was a good boy, despite his appearance, and the Tiplers were won over by his polite manner and by his clear devotion to his mother. He just wanted to help her, he told them at his job interview on a Monday, and they hired him on the spot, never regretting the decision, although Mrs. Tipler was bemused that he spent so much time on his hair when he arrived in the morning and every time he came back in from a run. She finally sent him to her hairdresser, Blake Johnson, of Blake's Coiffures at Poplar and Lauderdale, but he would go only after closing time because he was embarrassed. Once in a while at work he might see Paul Burlison, who was well on his way to becoming a master electrician and whom he knew from playing around the Courts and from playing with Dorsey Burnette, yet another employee of Crown. Paul and Dorsey told him about some of the places they played out near the naval base in Millington, and Dorsey told him about one night he had played at Shadow Lawn in Oakland with Johnny Black's brother Bill, and a guitarist named Scotty Moore, from Gadsden, Tennessee, who had only recently gotten out of the navy himself and was now living in Memphis. There had been a big brawl that night, and Dorsey had gotten stabbed in the tailbone. He and his father and his brother, Johnny, had gone out looking for the guys who had done it, but they never found them. Dorsey and Paul invited Elvis to come out and play with them some night if he felt like it, but he told them he didn't think so, he was kind of tied up with other things right now, he might be playing out at the Home for Incurables again, and he had a little thing coming up at the Girls' Club over on Alabama — his voice trailed off in a mumble.

His paycheck came to forty dollars a week, and every Friday he came home and presented it to his father. It was, Dixie noted with some amazement, almost as if it were Elvis' responsibility to take care of his dad. "He just took out enough to last us for the week, fifty cents for gas, a dollar-fifty to get us into the Suzore three times maybe, a little bit extra for food, the rest was for his mom and dad." There was no reluctance about it whatsoever, it was just the way things were; his parents were getting older, he told Dixie, and he wanted to take care of them. And they were just so proud of him, too — Mrs. Presley bragged on him every chance she got, and it seemed like he was equally proud of the strides he had made, for himself and his family. One time he came to pick Dixie up at her house after work, and they must have been doing a dirty job, because he was a mess, wearing greasy overalls with a hole in them. Dixie's mother wanted to take a picture of them both, but he hid behind a clothesline so you couldn't see the clothes he had on.

One Saturday in mid May Elvis floored Dixie. He had run into a mutual friend, Ronnie Smith, at the Cotton Carnival. Dixie knew Ronald from the neighborhood and from South Side High, but Elvis had met him at a birthday party and discovered a mutual passion for music, as well as for cars and girls. With Ronnie he had played a couple of little gigs (the highlight was a Lodge banquet at the Columbia Mutual Towers on Main), but at sixteen Ronald was also a member of a full-fledged professional band led by Eddie Bond, and, he said, Eddie was looking for a singer. Why didn't Elvis stop by? He had a tryout that night, Elvis told Dixie excitedly, at a club called the Hi Hat on South Third, not far from her house. He wondered if she would go with him — he *needed* her to go with him, they would just stay a little while, then they could go to a movie or McKellar Lake or something.

Dixie didn't know what to say; of course she would go, but it was so completely out of the blue. If he had asked her to come see him sing with a professional quartet, now that would have been a shock, but at least it would have been in line with something she might have anticipated, something in keeping with what she and he both saw as a kind of *spiritual* gift. And what if someone saw them, what if one of her parents' friends saw her going into the club or there was a Railway Express co-worker of her father's sitting inside? It didn't stop her, of course. Nor did she ever question Elvis' judgment. "He was just so nervous, I was nervous, too. When we got there, there weren't a lot of people, but there was a dance floor and there were drinks being served, because the man said something to us when we came in about our being too young to even be in there. I had a Coke. We sat at a table and drank Cokes."

The featured performer, Eddie Bond, was a seasoned veteran of twenty-one who had been playing around town since he was fifteen and had just gotten out of the navy. A confident entertainer and self-styled entrepreneur who twenty years later would run for sheriff of Memphis (in 1969 he composed "The Ballad of Buford Pusser," around which the popular movie *Walking Tall* was constructed), Bond came over to the table to say hello. He asked Elvis what he did for a living, and Elvis said he drove a truck for Crown Electric, but Dixie was embarrassed for him because he couldn't stop drumming his fingers on the table. He had gotten a haircut especially for this performance, and he was wearing his bullfighter's outfit with a pink shirt. In no time it was his turn to go onstage. He did two songs by himself, just strumming his guitar and singing; Dixie thought he was wonderful, but before she knew it, it was over. "It was almost like ohh-let's-hurry-and-get-out-of-here, glad-it-was-over type of thing." Before leaving he conferred briefly with Eddie Bond, but Dixie was at a distance and he never told her what was said. In later years Bond would boast jocularly that he was "the only person who ever fired [Elvis Presley] from the bandstand" and explain that it was the club owners who forced him to turn down the fledgling performer. Ronnie Smith was under the impression that Eddie wanted to book him into another, rougher joint across the street so that Eddie could have two bands working at the same time. Elvis for his part took it as a bitter rejection. Bond told him, he confided to his friend George Klein in 1957, that he had better stick with driving a truck " 'because you're never going to make it as a singer.' We were on a train going to Hollywood to make *Jailhouse Rock,* and Elvis said, 'I wonder what Eddie Bond thinks now. Man, that sonofabitch broke my heart.' "

The days went by. More and more, Dixie said, there was talk of marriage. "We came very close one day to getting in the car and driving to Hernando, Mississippi — *anyone* could get married in Hernando. We talked about it several times very seriously, about what we would do after we got married and where we would live. We were seriously talking about it, but I don't know how, one of us always had the good sense to say, 'But what if — ?' I was still in school, and it would have just broken my mom and dad's heart." Dixie was going to start her summer job at Goldsmith's in the cosmetics department soon, but before she did, she and her family were going away on vacation, to visit relatives in Florida for the first two weeks of July. She was worried about that — it would be their first separation, and Elvis got so jealous, he hated for her just to be with other people, let alone other boys. Dixie enjoyed being with people, "but he couldn't stand it if I was doing something that didn't involve him, he was kind of possessive in that respect." Sometimes Dixie thought the whole family was just too wrapped up in themselves, or maybe it was just in their dreams for Elvis; it was so hard to get inside that tight little circle. But then again, she knew that was just the way country people were sometimes.

They picnicked in Overton Park, they went fishing together one time, though Elvis wasn't much of a "nature boy"; he drove her around in the Crown Electric truck and got reprimanded by Mr. Tipler for getting off his route and running late. He always had his guitar in the truck with him, and he would play for his fellow workers at the drop of a hat. Mrs. Tipler told him to "put down that damn guitar, it's going to be the ruination of you," but she said it with an indulgent smile. He was no longer so sure himself that he had the makings of a good electrician, because, as he said in a 1956 interview, he didn't know if he had the requisite attention span. "I was in doubt as to whether I would ever make it, because you had to keep your mind right on what you're doing, you can't be the least bit absentminded or you're liable to blow somebody's house up. I didn't think I was the type for it, but I was going to give it a try."

He was also going to continue to give recording a try. Marion Keisker saw his truck pass by the studio often, and once in a while he would stop in at 706 Union in his work clothes and cast about for a conversational subject, shifting nervously from one foot to the other. He was always asking her if she knew of a band, trying to assume an ease and a familiarity which he obviously did not feel, and her heart went out to him. Dixie, too, sensed that the tryout with Eddie Bond was not simply an isolated incident, though in this one area, evidently, he did not confide his innermost feelings to her. She had no doubt that if he wanted to make a record he would make a record, but she had no idea what making a record really meant — unless it meant getting on the radio. She knew he could never stand to make his living from playing dives and honky-tonks like the Hi Hat, she just wasn't sure what the alternatives were, or how you got to be on Bob Neal's *High Noon Round-Up* with the Blackwood Brothers and Eddie Hill.

On Saturday, June 26, just a week before Dixie was scheduled to leave for Florida, Elvis finally got his chance. Miss Keisker called around noon. "She said, 'Can you be here by three?' " he said in later years, whenever he recounted the story. "I was there by the time she hung up the phone."

What had happened was that, on his last trip to Nashville, in May, to record the Prisonaires, Sam had picked up an acetate from Red Wortham, the song publisher who had originally steered the Prisonaires to Sun. Phillips had listened to the song over and over, a plaintive lament called "Without You," sung in a quavering voice that sounded like a cross between the Ink Spots and a sentimental Irish tenor. It was undeniably amateurish, but there was *something* about it, it had a quality of yearning to it, and Phillips felt with the right voice maybe it could be something. Its purity, its simplicity, above all the very amateurishness of the performance, put him in mind of the kid who had been stopping by — he was not a pest, exactly, but he kept turning up — for the last nine or ten months. What was his name? he asked Marion, who seemed somewhat taken with the boy, a shy, insecure kid ("He was *beyond* shy," Sam thought) who had obviously never sung anywhere in his life. "Elvis Presley," Marion said and made the call.

They worked on the number all afternoon. When it became obvious that for whatever reason the boy was not going to get it right — maybe "Without You" wasn't the right song for him, maybe he was just intimidated by the damn studio — Phillips had him run down just about every song he knew. He wasn't much of a guitar player, but the world didn't need any more damn virtuosos; what the world needed, Sam Phillips was convinced, was *communication,* and that was what he sensed in there somewhere, underlying everything, in this boy's voice. "I guess I must have sat there at least three hours," Elvis told *Memphis Press-Scimitar* reporter Bob Johnson in 1956. "I sang everything I knew — pop stuff, spirituals, just a few words of [anything] I remembered." Sam watched him intently through the glass of the control room window — he was no longer taping him, and in almost every respect this session had to be accounted a dismal failure, but still there was *something.* . . . Every so often the boy looked up at him, as if for approval: was he doing all right? Sam just nodded and spoke in that smooth, reassuring voice. "You're doing just fine. Now just relax. Let me hear something that really means something to you now." Soothing, crooning, his eyes locked into the boy's through the plate glass window that he had built so that his eyes would be level with the performer's when he was sitting at the control room console, he didn't really know if they were getting anywhere or not, it was just so damned hard to tell when you were dealing with a bunch of damn amateurs, but it was only from amateurs, he firmly believed, that you ever got any real freshness of feeling.

When it was over, Elvis was exhausted, he felt limp but strangely elated, too. "I was an overnight sensation," he always told interviewers in later years. "A year after they heard me the first time, they called me back!" Everyone caught the boyish modesty, but they may have overlooked the understandable pride. Mr. Phillips *had* called him back — his perseverance had paid off. And while nothing was said about what would happen next, there was little doubt in Elvis' mind that something would. He had finally gotten his break. He drove over to Dixie's in a strange state of detachment — they went to the movies that night, and he mentioned in passing that he had made a record.

ON THE EVENING of Wednesday, June 30, tragedy struck. Dixie came home the next day to find her mother waiting for her at the door with the gravest expression. She sat Dixie down in the kitchen and told her there had been a terrible accident — the Blackwood Brothers' plane had crashed the night before somewhere in Alabama, it wasn't all of them, it was just R.W. and the bass singer, Bill Lyles, but they had both been killed. Dixie stared at her mother, she couldn't believe it at first, then her eyes filled up with tears. Bill? R.W.? Bill's wife, Ruth, was her Sunday school teacher. She was inconsolable. She called some of her friends. Nobody could believe it. The Blackwood Brothers were their own; the most progressive and businesslike of all gospel groups, they had had their own plane since the fall of 1952. According to the news accounts they had performed at noon with the Statesmen at the Chilton County Peach Festival in Clanton, Alabama. Evidently, the sponsors had asked them to stick around for the afternoon festivities, and when it came time to leave, there was still a big crowd, with automobiles parked all around the field. R.W. wanted to take the plane up before it got dark, to see how much clearance they had for takeoff. When he made his landing approach, everybody thought he was just showing off, but then the plane didn't straighten up, it just bounced and burst into flames, and you could see the charred figures in the plane. James Blackwood, a slight, slender man, screamed that he was going in and started for the plane, but Jake Hess wrapped him in a bear hug and didn't let go until James finally subsided. On the ride back to Memphis that night James said to Jake that he would never sing again, but Jake said he owed it to the people to go on.

Elvis came straight from work to Dixie's house — he didn't even bother to change. It was obvious from his tear-streaked face that he knew what had happened. They didn't say anything, just threw themselves into each other's arms, even with her mother there. They went to Gaston Park that night and sipped on milk shakes and cried and cried. What would happen to the Blackwood Brothers? they wondered. The quartet would just fall apart. Their poor families. It seemed like the world was coming to an end.

The funeral the next day was one of the biggest in Memphis history — it was the first time that a funeral service had ever been conducted at Ellis Auditorium. The Statesmen sang, and so did the Speers and five other quartets. Governor Frank Clement, who had been present at the Blackwoods' last Memphis appearance, on June 18, delivered a sincere and emotional eulogy; Clement, after all, was not only a friend to the quartets, he had presided over the growth of the Nashville recording industry and was one of the key factors in the Prisonaires getting their recording break. There were close to five thousand people present — they opened up the North Hall when the South Hall was filled, and so beloved were the Blackwoods, reported the papers, that "a number of negroes called the Auditorium asking if they could attend the funeral, and the galleries were reserved for negroes, Chauncey Barbour, Auditorium manager, said." The Reverend Hamill preached the sermon, and Dr. Robert G. Lee of Bellevue Baptist Church delivered the prayer. Elvis and Dixie sat with Mr. and Mrs. Presley and held hands. Dixie couldn't believe she was leaving for Florida the next day. She couldn't leave — she didn't want to leave — she wasn't going to leave him, not now. They clung to each other through most of the night, and in the morning Elvis came over as the Lockes packed up for their trip. He left around noon, after an exchange of promises to be true. They would both write, they said, he would try to call — he took down all the numbers and places she would be staying. They could barely let go of each other. Her parents discreetly left them alone. It had been a highly emotional time. When she came back, Dixie reassured him, reassured herself through swollen, tearstained eyes, nothing would have changed, everything would still be the same, they would still have the summer, they would still have their whole lives in front of them.

JULY 28, 1954. (MEMPHIS BROOKS MUSEUM/MICHAEL OCHS ARCHIVES)

"THAT'S ALL RIGHT"

THAT AFTERNOON a young guitarist named Scotty Moore stopped by 706 Union, ostensibly to find out how his record was doing. He had been coming by the studio for several months now, trying to get somewhere with his group, the Starlite Wranglers, trying to get a leg up in the business. The group, which had existed in various configurations since Scotty's discharge from the navy in early 1952, consisted of fellow guitarist Clyde Rush, steel guitarist Millard Yow, and bass player Bill Black, all of whom worked at Firestone, and a variety of interchangeable vocalists. Scotty, who worked as a hatter at his brothers' dry cleaning establishment at 613 North McClean, had recently brought in Doug Poindexter, a baker with a penchant for Hank Williams tunes, as permanent lead singer, and he had had a big star made up with Christmas lights that flashed on and off to advertise the band's name on the bandstand. They had a few regular bookings through the spring — they continued to play the same rough club out toward Somerville where Scotty and Bill had backed up Dorsey Burnette — and they played a couple of clubs around town. They landed a radio spot on West Memphis station KWEM, and Scotty got them a regular booking at the Bon Air, which had previously featured nothing but pop. The next step, clearly, was to make a record.

That was what led the Starlite Wranglers to the Memphis Recording Service. Doug Poindexter asked Bill Fitzgerald at Music Sales, the local independent record distributor, how they "could get on MGM like Hank Williams," and Fitzgerald, who distributed the Sun label among others, suggested that they try Sam Phillips. It was Scotty, as manager of the band and prime instigator of their upward professional mobility, who did this, with some trepidation, one afternoon after he got off work.

He and Sam hit it off almost instantly. Sam saw in Scotty an ambitious young man of twenty-two, not content with the limited vistas that lay before him — he didn't know what he wanted exactly, but he wanted something more than a lifetime of blocking hats or playing clubs and eventually giving it up to go into some little retail business. Scotty was looking for something *different,* Sam sensed, and he was a good listener besides. Soon the two of them got into the habit of meeting several days a week at 2:00 in the afternoon when Scotty got off work — Scotty would just stop by, and they would go next door to Miss Taylor's restaurant for a cup of coffee and talk about the future. To Sam, who at thirty-one had seen more than his share of ups and downs, it was an opportunity to expound upon his ideas to an audience that was not only sympathetic: Scotty clearly *enjoyed* plotting and scheming and dreaming about the changes that were just around the corner. To Scotty, who had grown up on a farm in Gadsden with the feeling that the world had passed him by (his father and his three older brothers had had a band, but by the time Scotty came along, fifteen years after the next-youngest brother, they had given it up) and who had joined the navy at sixteen, this was heaven. He was married for the second time, had two kids living out in Washington with his first wife, and aspired to playing jazz, like Barney Kessel, Tal Farlow, or country virtuosos Merle Travis and Chet Atkins. He was serious but self-taught, he had quit in the middle of his second year of high school, and here was somebody in Memphis telling him, with a conviction that defied gainsaying, that there was a chance that something could happen, that change was on the way. "Sam had an uncanny knack for pulling things out of people that they didn't even know they had. He knew there was a crossover coming. He foresaw it. I think that recording all those black artists had to give him an insight; he just didn't know where that insight would lead. Sam came from pretty much the same background as the rest of us, basically. We were just looking for something, we didn't know quite what it was, we would just sit there over coffee and say to each other, 'What is it? What should we do? How can we do it?' "

Eventually Scotty persuaded Sam to record the Wranglers, and on May 25, 1954, they recorded two sides, which Scotty wrote (he gave half of the credit for one song to Doug Poindexter because he was the vocalist and a third of the other to his brother for writing the lead sheet). The record was released at the beginning of June and never went anywhere — by the end of summer it had sold approximately three hundred copies — but Scotty continued to stop by the studio, knowing that the record wasn't his ticket to the future, the Starlite Wranglers were just a hillbilly band, but feeling somehow that if he stuck close to Sam Phillips he would find out what the future was.

Sometime around the middle of May he started hearing about a young ballad singer with possibilities. There was something different about his voice, Sam said; Sam was interested in trying him out on this new song he had picked up on his latest trip to Nashville to record the Prisonaires. At some point Marion mentioned his name, Elvis Presley — to Scotty it sounded like "a name out of science fiction" — but since Sam kept talking about him, he asked Sam to dig up a telephone number and address, maybe they could get together, maybe this kid really had something. Somehow Sam never seemed to have the information on hand, he always said he'd have Marion look it up the next day, and Scotty was keenly disappointed on this Saturday afternoon to find out that the boy had actually been in the studio just a week before and that they had worked unsuccessfully on the Nashville song. "This particular day," Scotty said, "it was about five in the afternoon — Marion was having coffee with us, and Sam said, 'Get his name and phone number out of the file.' Then he turned to me and said, 'Why don't you give him a call and get him to come over to your house and see what you think of him?' Bill Black lived just three doors down from me on Belz that ran into Firestone — I had actually moved just to be near Bill — and Sam said, 'You and Bill can just give him a listen, kind of feel him out.' "

Scotty called Elvis that evening, right after supper. His mother answered and said that Elvis was at the movies, at the Suzore No. 2. Scotty said that he "represented Sun Records," and Mrs. Presley said that she would get him out of the movies. There was a call back within an hour; Scotty explained who he was and what he wanted to do. The boy seemed to take it all in stride — his voice sounded confident enough, but wary. "I told him I was working with Sam Phillips and possibly would like to audition him if he was interested, and he said he guessed so. So we made an appointment for the next day at my house."

On Sunday, July 4, Elvis showed up at Scotty's house on Belz in his old Lincoln. He was wearing a black shirt, pink pants with a black stripe, white shoes, and a greasy ducktail, and asked "Is this the right place?" when Scotty's wife, Bobbie, answered the door. Bobbie asked him to have a seat and went to get Scotty. "I said, 'That boy is here.' He said, 'What boy?' I said, 'I can't remember his name, it's the one you're supposed to see today.' Scotty asked me to go down to Bill's house and see if Bill would come practice with them — Bill's bass was already in our apartment, because Bill and Evelyn had two kids, and there was more room there."

After a few minutes of awkward small talk, Bill showed up and they got down to business. Elvis hunched over his guitar and mumbled something about not really knowing what to play, then launched into disconnected fragments, seemingly, of every song he knew. Scotty and Bill fell in behind him on numbers like Billy Eckstine's "I Apologize"; the Ink Spots' "If I Didn't Care"; "Tomorrow Night"; Eddy Arnold's latest hit, "I Really Don't Want to Know"; Hank Snow's "I Don't Hurt Anymore"; and a Dean Martin–styled version of Jo Stafford's "You Belong to Me." They were all ballads, all sung in a yearning, quavery tenor that didn't seem ready to settle anywhere soon and accompanied by the most rudimentary strummed guitar. At some point Bill flopped down on the sofa, and there was some talk about how Elvis lived on Alabama, just across from Bill's mother, and how Elvis knew Bill's brother Johnny. Bill, the most affable man in the world and the clown of the Starlite Wranglers ("He never met a stranger," Scotty has said in seeking to describe him), said he had heard from Johnny just the other day, Johnny had been in Corpus Christi since he got laid off from Firestone. They talked a little about the football games down at the Triangle, and Bill said it was funny they had never formally met before, but, of course, he had left home before the Presleys moved into the Courts, he had gone into the army at eighteen, and when he got out in 1946 he was already married. There were a lot of musicians in Memphis, and you couldn't know them all — Elvis didn't happen to know a guitar player named Luther Perkins who lived just around the corner, did he? Elvis met all of Bill's attempts at conversation with perfunctory nods and stammered little asides of agreement that you could barely make out — he was polite enough, but it was almost as if he was filled with a need to say something that couldn't find proper expression, and he couldn't stop fidgeting. "He was as green as a gourd," Scotty would recall, with amusement, as his reaction at the time.

When Bobbie came back with Evelyn and Bill's sister, Mary Ann, they were still playing, but "all of a sudden there was a crowd, we probably scared Elvis," said Bobbie. "It was almost all slow ballads. 'I Love You Because' is the one that I remember." Eventually Elvis left, trailing clouds of oily smoke behind him in the humpbacked old Lincoln. "What'd you think?" Scotty asked, hoping that Bill might have seen something in the boy that he didn't. "Well, he didn't impress me too damn much," said Bill. "Snotty-nosed kid coming in here with those wild clothes and everything." But what about his singing? Scotty asked, almost desperately — he *wanted* the kid to be good for reasons that he didn't even care to examine. "Well, it was all right, nothing out of the ordinary — I mean, the cat can sing. . . ."

That was Scotty's opinion, too. It was all right, nothing special — he couldn't see where the boy had added all that much to the songs that he had sung; Scotty didn't think he was going to make the world forget about Eddy Arnold or Hank Snow. But he called Sam anyway, what else was he going to do after making such a fuss about meeting the kid? What did you think? Sam asked.

"I said, 'He didn't really knock me out.' I said, 'The boy's got a good voice.' I told him a lot of the songs he sang. Sam said, 'Well, I think I'll call him, get him to come down to the studio tomorrow, we'll just set up an audition and see what he sounds like coming back off of tape.' I said, 'Shall we bring in the whole band?' And he said, 'Naw, just you and Bill come over, just something for a little rhythm. No use making a big deal about it.' "

The next night everybody showed up around 7:00. There was some desultory small talk, Bill and Scotty joked nervously among themselves, and Sam tried to make the boy feel at ease, carefully observing the way in which he both withheld himself and tried to thrust himself into the conversation at the same time. He reminded Sam so much of some of the blues singers he had recorded, simultaneously proud and needy. At last, after a few minutes of aimless chatter and letting them all get a little bit used to being in the studio, Sam turned to the boy and said, "Well, what do you want to sing?" This occasioned even more self-conscious confusion as the three musicians tried to come up with something that they all knew and could play — *all the way through* — but after a number of false starts, they finally settled on "Harbor Lights," which had been a big hit for Bing Crosby in 1950, and worked it through to the end, then tried Leon Payne's "I Love You Because," a beautiful country ballad that had been a number-one country hit for its author in 1949 and a number-two hit for Ernest Tubb on the hillbilly charts the same year. They tried up to a dozen takes, running through the song again and again — sometimes the boy led off with several bars of whistling, sometimes he simply launched into the verse. The recitation altered slightly each time that he repeated it, but each time he flung himself into it, seemingly trying to make it new. Sometimes he simply blurted out the words, sometimes his singing voice shifted to a thin, pinched, almost nasal tone before returning to the high, keening tenor in which he sang the rest of the song — it was as if, Sam thought, he wanted to put everything he had ever known or heard into one song. And Scotty's guitar part was too damn complicated, he was trying too damn hard to sound like Chet Atkins, but there was that strange sense of inconsolable desire in the voice, there was *emotion* being communicated.

Sam sat in the control room, tapping his fingers absentmindedly on the console. All his attention was focused on the studio, on the interaction of the musicians, the sound they were getting, the feeling that was behind the sound. Every so often he would come out and change a mike placement slightly, talk with the boy a little, not just to bullshit with him but to make him feel at home, to try to make him feel really at home. It was always a question of how long you could go on like this, you wanted the artist to get familiar with the studio, but being in the studio could take on a kind of mind-numbing quality of its own, it could smooth over the rough edges, you could take refuge in the little space that you had created for yourself and banish the very element of spontaneity you were seeking to achieve.

For Elvis it seemed like it had been going on for hours, and he began to get the feeling that nothing was ever going to happen. When Mr. Phillips had called, he had taken the news calmly to begin with, he had tried to banish all thoughts of results or consequences, but now it seemed as if he could think of nothing else. He was getting more and more frustrated, he flung himself desperately into each new version of "I Love You Because," trying to make it live, trying to make it new, but he saw his chances slipping away as they returned to the beginning of the song over and over again with numbing familiarity. . . .

Finally they decided to take a break — it was late, and everybody had to work the next day. Maybe they ought to just give it up for the night, come back on Tuesday and try it again. Scotty and Bill were sipping Cokes, not saying much of anything, Mr. Phillips was doing something in the control room, and, as Elvis explained it afterward, "this song popped into my mind that I had heard years ago, and I started kidding around with [it]." It was a song that he told Johnny Black he had written when he sang it in the Courts, and Johnny believed him. The song was "That's All Right [Mama]," an old blues number by Arthur "Big Boy" Crudup.

"All of a sudden," said Scotty, "Elvis just started singing this song, jumping around and acting the fool, and then Bill picked up his bass, and he started acting the fool, too, and I started playing with them. Sam, I think, had the door to the control booth open — I don't know, he was either editing some tape, or doing something — and he stuck his head out and said, 'What are you doing?' And we said, 'We don't know.' 'Well, back up,' he said, 'try to find a place to start, and do it again.' "

SAM RECOGNIZED IT right away. He was amazed that the boy even knew Arthur "Big Boy" Crudup — nothing in any of the songs he had tried so far gave any indication that he was drawn to this kind of music at all. But this was the sort of music that Sam had long ago wholeheartedly embraced, this was the sort of music of which he said, "This is where the soul of man never dies." And the way the boy performed it, it came across with a freshness and an exuberance, it came across with the kind of clear-eyed, unabashed *originality* that Sam sought in all the music that he recorded — it was "different," it was itself.

They worked on it. They worked hard on it, but without any of the laboriousness that had gone into the efforts to cut "I Love You Because." Sam tried to get Scotty to cut down on the instrumental flourishes — "Simplify, simplify!" was the watchword. "If we wanted Chet Atkins," said Sam good-humoredly, "we would have brought him up from Nashville and gotten him in the damn studio!" He was delighted with the rhythmic propulsion Bill Black brought to the sound. It was a slap beat and a tonal beat at the same time. He may not have been as good a bass player as his brother Johnny; in fact, Sam said, "Bill was one of the worst bass players in the world, *technically*, but, man, could he slap that thing!" And yet that wasn't it either — it was the *chemistry*. There was Scotty, and there was Bill, and there was Elvis scared to death in the middle, "but sounding so fresh, because it *was* fresh to him."

They worked on it over and over, refining the song, but the center never changed. It always opened with the ringing sound of Elvis' rhythm guitar, up till this moment almost a handicap to be gotten over. Then there was Elvis' vocal, loose and free and full of confidence, holding it together. And Scotty and Bill just fell in with an easy, swinging gait that was the very epitome of what Sam had dreamt of but never fully imagined. The first time Sam played it back for them, "we couldn't believe it was us," said Bill. "It just sounded sort of raw and ragged," said Scotty. "We thought it was exciting, but what was it? It was just so completely different. But it just really flipped Sam — he felt it really had something. We just sort of shook our heads and said, 'Well, that's fine, but good God, they'll run us out of town!' " And Elvis? Elvis flung himself into the recording process. You only have to listen to the tape to hear the confidence grow. By the last take (only two false starts and one complete alternate take remain), there is a different singer in the studio than the one who started out the evening — nothing had been said, nothing had been articulated, but everything had changed.

Sam Phillips sat in the studio after the session was over and everyone had gone home. It was not unusual for him to hang around until two or three in the morning, sometimes recording, sometimes just thinking about what was going to become of his business and his family in these perilous times, sometimes mulling over his vision of the future. He knew that something was in the wind. He knew from his experience recording blues, and from his fascination with black culture, that there was something intrinsic to the music that could translate, that *did* translate. "It got so you could sell a half million copies of a rhythm and blues record," Sam told a Memphis reporter in 1959, reminiscing about his overnight success. "These records appealed to white youngsters just as Uncle Silas [Payne's] songs and stories used to appeal to me. . . . But there was something in many of those youngsters that resisted buying this music. The Southern ones especially felt a resistance that even they probably didn't quite understand. They liked the music, but they weren't sure whether they ought to like it or not. So I got to thinking how many records you could sell if you could find white performers who could play and sing in this same exciting, alive way."

The next night everyone came to the studio, but nothing much happened. They tried a number of different songs — they even gave the Rodgers and Hart standard "Blue Moon" (a 1949 hit for Billy Eckstine) a passing try — but nothing really clicked, and both that evening and the next were spent in more or less getting to know one another musically. Nonetheless, Sam had little doubt of what had transpired in the studio that first night. There was always the question of whether or not it was a fluke; as far as that went, only time would tell. But Sam Phillips was never one to hold back, when he believed in something he just plunged ahead. And so, on Wednesday night, after calling an early halt to the proceedings, he telephoned Dewey Phillips down at the new WHBQ studio in the Hotel Chisca. "Get yourself a wheelbarrow full of goober dust," Dewey was very likely announcing when Sam made the call, "and roll it in the door [of whatever sponsor Dewey happened to be representing], and tell 'em Phillips sent you. *And call Sam!*"

DEWEY PHILLIPS in 1954 was very nearly at the apogee of his renown and glory. From a fifteen-minute unpaid spot that he had talked his way into while managing the record department at W. T. Grant's, he had graduated to a 9:00-to-midnight slot six nights a week. According to the Memphis papers he would get as many as three thousand letters a week and forty to fifty telegrams a night, a measure not just of his audience but of the *fervor* of that audience. When, a year or two later, he asked his listeners to blow their horns at 10:00 in the evening, the whole city, it was said, erupted with a single sound, and when the police chief, who was also listening, called to remind Dewey of Memphis' antinoise ordinance and begged him not to do it again, Dewey announced on the air, "Well, good people, Chief MacDonald just called me, and he said we can't do that anymore. Now I was going to have you do it at eleven o'clock, but the chief told me we couldn't do it, so whatever you do at eleven o'clock, don't blow your horns." The results were predictable.

One night an assistant started a fire in the wastebasket and convinced Dewey that the hotel was on fire, but Dewey, a hero of the Battle of Hurtgen Forest, kept right on broadcasting, directing the fire department down to the station and staying on the air until the hoax was discovered. He broadcast in stereo before stereo was invented, playing the same record on two turntables which never started or ended together, creating a phased effect that pleased Dewey unless it got so far out of line that he took the needle off both records with a scrawk and announced that he was just going to have to start all over and try it again.

WDIA DJ and r&b singer Rufus Thomas referred to Dewey as "a man who just happened to be white," and he never lost his Negro audience, even after the white teenage audience that Sam sensed out there made itself known. He went everywhere in Memphis, paraded proudly down Beale Street, greeted the same people who, the *Commercial Appeal* reported in 1950, had flocked to Grant's "just to see the man 'what gets hisself so messed up.' " He had several chances to go national but passed them up — or allowed them to pass *him* up — by remaining himself. There were two kinds of people in Memphis, the *Press-Scimitar* declared in 1956, "those who are amused and fascinated by Dewey, and those who, when they accidentally tune in, jump as tho stung by a wasp and hurriedly switch to something nice and cultural, like Guy Lombardo." "He was a genius," said Sam Phillips, "and I don't call many people geniuses."

DEWEY STOPPED BY the recording studio after his show. It was well after midnight, but that was as good a time as any for Dewey. "Dewey [was] completely unpredictable," wrote *Press-Scimitar* reporter Bob Johnson, his (and Sam's) friend, in various celebrations of his spirit over the years. "He would call at three or four A.M. and insist I listen to something over the phone. I tried to tell him it was no time to be phoning anyone, but Dewey had no sense of time. Sometimes I wonder if there is a real Dewey, or if he's just something that happens as he goes along." If he was a personality that just unfolded, though, it was because he cared so much about what he was doing. Whatever Dewey did, everyone agreed, was from the heart. Ordinarily, when he stopped by the studio, all he could talk about at first was the show. "Oh God, he loved his show," Sam Phillips said. "He wasn't just playing records and cutting the monitor down. He was enjoying everything he said, every record that he played, every response that he got from his listeners. Dewey could get more excited than anyone you ever saw." And he loved to argue with Sam. To Marion Keisker, Sam and Dewey were so close that she couldn't stand to be in the same room with the two of them — and it wasn't just that she saw Dewey as a bad influence (though she did). She was also, she admitted, jealous; she saw Dewey as a threat. "Dewey loved to argue with Sam, just for the sake of arguing," recalled the singer Dickey Lee. "Talking about how Sam can intimidate people, one night Sam was off on one of his tirades, and right in the middle Dewey had a rubber band and snapped it at Sam and hit him in the head. He thought it was the funniest thing. Sam would get so mad at Dewey, but he loved him. Dewey always referred to Sam as his half brother, even though they weren't related at all."

This particular night, though, there wasn't any arguing. Sam had something he wanted to play for Dewey, he said right off, and he was uncharacteristically nervous about it. Sam Phillips didn't like to ask a favor of anyone — and he didn't really consider that he was asking a favor now — but he was asking Dewey to *listen* to something, he was asking him to consider something that had never previously existed on this earth; this wasn't just a matter of sitting around and bullshitting and letting Dewey absorb whatever happened to come his way. "But, you know it was a funny thing," said Sam. "There was an element of Dewey that was conservative, too. When he picked a damn record, he didn't want to be wrong. 'Cause he had that thing going, 'How much bullshit have you got in you, man, and when are you gonna deliver?' It so happened, by God, that people believed Dewey, and he delivered. 'Cause when he went on the air [he didn't have any scientific method], he just blabbed it right out, 'It's gonna be a hit, it's gonna be a hit, it's the biggest thing you ever heard. I'll tell you what, man, it's gonna knock you out.' And, you know, as much as he respected me and loved me, Dewey had some real hang-ups about what could be done locally — it was like if somebody was five hundred or a thousand miles away there was more intrigue about them. So it was an elongated education process, really, he wanted to make you prove it to him unequivocally. And he was so into the finished product he didn't care how it came about, it was just, what did you deliver for him to make his show great? I think he was just beginning to feel that by God, there was a legitimate record crusader in this town."

Dewey opened a Falstaff and sprinkled some salt in it, then sat back and listened intently as Sam played the tape of the single song over and over. Dewey knew the song, of course; he had played the Arthur "Big Boy" Crudup version many times on his own show. It was the sound that puzzled him. For once there was not much conversation as the two men listened, each wondering what exactly the other thought. "He was reticent, and I was glad that he was," said Sam. "If he hadn't been reticent, it would have scared me to death, if he had said, 'Hey, man, this is a hit, it's a hit,' I would have thought Dewey was just trying to make me feel good. What I was thinking was, where you going to go with this, it's not black, it's not white, it's not pop, it's not country, and I think Dewey was the same way. He was fascinated by it — there was no question about that — I mean, he loved the damn record, but it was a question of where do we go from here?"

They stayed up listening and talking in comparatively muted tones until 2:00 or 3:00 in the morning, when both men finally returned home to their respective families and beds. Then, what to Sam's surprise, the phone rang early the next morning, and it was Dewey. "I didn't sleep well last night, man," Dewey announced. Sam said, "Man, you should have slept pretty good, with all that Jack Daniel's and beer in you." No, Dewey said, he hadn't been able to sleep, because he kept thinking about that record, he wanted it for his show tonight, in fact he wanted two copies, and he said, "We ain't letting anybody know." His reticence, Sam said, was over on that day.

Sam cut the acetates that afternoon and brought them down to the station. He called Elvis after work to tell him that Dewey would most likely be playing the record on his show that night. Elvis' response was not uncharacteristic. "He fixed the radio and told us to leave it on that station," said Gladys, "and then he went to the movies. I guess he was just too nervous to listen." "I thought people would laugh at me," Elvis told C. Robert Jennings of the *Saturday Evening Post* in 1965. "Some did, and some are still laughing, I guess."

Vernon and Gladys did listen. They sat glued to the radio with Vernon's mother, Minnie, and the rest of the relatives listening in their nearby homes, until at last, at 9:30 or 10:00, Dewey announced that he had a new record, it wasn't even a record, actually, it was a dub of a new record that Sam was going to be putting out next week, and it was going to be a *hit*, dee-gaw, ain't that right, Myrtle ("Moo," went the cow), and he slapped the acetate — the acetates — on the turntables.

The response was instantaneous. Forty-seven phone calls, it was said, came in right away, along with fourteen telegrams — or was it 114 phone calls and forty-seven telegrams? — he played the record seven times in a row, eleven times, seven times over the course of the rest of the program. In retrospect it doesn't really matter; it seemed as if all of Memphis was listening as Dewey kept up his nonstop patter, egging his radio audience on, encouraging them to join him in the discovery of a new voice, proclaiming to the world that Daddy-O-Dewey played the hits, that we way uptown, about as far uptown as you can get, did anybody want to buy a fur-lined duck? And if that one didn't flat git it for you, you can go to. . . . And tell 'em Phillips sent you!

For Gladys the biggest shock was "hearing them say his name over the radio just before they put on that record. That shook me so it stayed with me right through the whole song — Elvis Presley — just my son's name. I couldn't rightly hear the record the first time round." She didn't have time to think about it for long anyway, because almost immediately the phone rang. It was Dewey for Elvis. When she told him Elvis was at the movies, he said, "Mrs. Presley, you just get that cotton-picking son of yours down here to the station. I played that record of his, and them bird-brain phones haven't stopped ringing since." Gladys went down one aisle of the Suzore No. 2, and Vernon went down the other — or at least so the story goes — and within minutes Elvis was at the station.

"I was scared to death," Elvis said. "I was shaking all over, I just couldn't believe it, but Dewey kept telling me to cool it, [this] was really happening."

"Sit down, I'm gone interview you" were his first words to the frightened nineteen-year-old, Dewey told writer Stanley Booth in 1967. "He said, 'Mr. Phillips, I don't know nothing about being interviewed.' 'Just don't say nothing dirty,' I told him. He sat down, and I said I'd let him know when we were ready to start. I had a couple of records cued up, and while they played we talked. I asked him where he went to high school, and he said, 'Humes.' I wanted to get that out, because a lot of people listening had thought he was colored. Finally I said, 'All right, Elvis, thank you very much.' 'Aren't you gone interview me?' he asked. 'I already have,' I said. 'The mike's been open the whole time.' He broke out in a cold sweat."

It was Thursday, July 8. Elvis escaped out in the hot night air. He walked back up Main to Third Street and then over to Alabama. Dewey wound up his show and called his wife, Dot. How'd she like it? he asked. "I told him I loved it," Dot told the *Trenton* (Tennessee) *Herald Gazette* in 1978, ten years after Dewey's death. "He went on to say that he believed Elvis had a hit. . . . Dewey cherished that moment with Elvis. He would tell it time and time again."

Sam Phillips was at the studio that night. He didn't see Elvis, and he didn't see Dewey until after the show, but he knew what had happened, he knew that the reaction had come, the phone lines had lit up without anyone thinking about what the singer looked like, "they didn't give a fuck about classifying him, in Memphis, Tennessee, *they liked what they heard*." He knew, too, that now the real work would begin.

* * *

THE NEWS TRAVELED like wildfire. Billie Chiles, a classmate of Elvis' at Humes who had never been exactly entranced by his music, was at a sock hop at the Holy Rosary Catholic Church. "Sometime during the evening a couple went outside to the parking lot," Billie told former *Press-Scimitar* reporter Bill Burk thirty-five years later, "and turned their [car] radio on. . . . They came running downstairs yelling, 'Come up here quick! You ain't going to believe what Dewey Phillips is playing on the radio!' " Another classmate, George Klein, who had been president of the class of 1953, stopped by Dewey's radio show that Saturday night. He had just completed his freshman year at Memphis State, where he was majoring in communications, and had served as a gofer for Dewey, "kind of a baby-sitter," the previous summer, and in fact for much of the past school year. For this summer he had gotten a job working at KOSE, in Osceola, Arkansas, hitchhiking the fifty miles home after his Saturday shift to spend Sunday with his mother and his Memphis friends. This particular Saturday night he stopped by the station, as he generally did, just as Dewey was about to go on the air, and Dewey greeted him, as he generally did, with, " 'Hey mother, when'd you get in?'

"Then he said, 'Guess what? Come here.' And he took a record and put his hand over the label and put it on the turntable. He played the record and said, 'Guess who that is.' I said, 'Shit, Dewey, I don't know. Who is it?' He said, 'You know this guy, you went to school with the boy,' and I knew then it had to be Elvis. 'Sam brought the record by the other night,' he said, 'and I played the sonofabitch fourteen times, and we got about five hundred phone calls. It's gonna be a hit!' "

With all the excitement, Sam Phillips realized, now they were really going to have to come up with something else in a hurry; they *needed* a second side just to be able to put a record out. He felt that nothing they had recorded to date was suitable, so they went back into the studio on Friday night, and sometime in the next couple of days they came up with something equally improbable, equally "different," and equally exciting.

"Blue Moon of Kentucky" had been a hit for Bill Monroe in 1946, well before the term "bluegrass" came into popular usage. In Monroe's version it was a beautiful waltz familiar to anyone who listened to the Grand Ole Opry and revered by every hillbilly musician who had ever picked up a stringed instrument. "We spent three or four nights trying to get a back side," Scotty said, "something that would be in the same kind of vein. We'd gone through this song and that song, just running through them —

I don't think any of them were ever put on tape — and then Bill jumped up and started clowning, beating on his bass and singing 'Blue Moon of Kentucky,' in a high falsetto voice, more or less mimicking Bill Monroe. And Elvis started banging on the guitar, playing rhythm and singing, and I joined in and it just gelled.

"It's funny how they both come about by accident. There was nothing like a direction, there was just a certain . . . feel. You know, Elvis wasn't considered a real good rhythm player on guitar, but you listen to 'That's All Right, Mama,' he starts with the rhythm, just the open rhythm, and then the slap [bass] starts — he had a feel for rhythm on the stuff that we did that's very hard for anybody to do the same way."

"Blue Moon of Kentucky" evolved from a slow, bluesy version in 4/4 time with tentative instrumentation and a rather ornate vocal into a high-spirited declaration of exuberant self-discovery, driven by Elvis' ringing rhythm guitar and a propulsive mix of Scotty's chording riffs and single-string filigree. For the first time Sam made extensive use of what he had come to call slapback, a kind of homemade echo device that was created by running the original recording signal through a second Ampex machine and thereby achieving an almost sibilant phased effect. This undoubtedly added not only to the presence but to the excitement of the recording, and, of course, echo had the capacity of covering up a multitude of sins, but what held it all together most of all was Sam's belief in the uniqueness of what they were doing. What kept the musicians from ever giving up was Sam's lulling faith: "All right, boys, we just about on it now," you can almost hear him saying. "Do it again. Just do it one more time for me." When he felt like he had reached the limit of his creativity, Carl Perkins said of recording for Sam just a year or two later, Sam would coax him to "walk out on a limb, I'd try things I knew I couldn't do, and I'd get in a corner trying to do it and then have to work my way out of it. I'd say, 'Mr. Phillips, that's terrible.' He said, 'That's original.' I said, 'But it's just a big original mistake.' And he said, '*That's what Sun Records is.* That's what we are.' "

"That's fine now" you can actually hear Sam say, at the end of one early take of "Blue Moon of Kentucky." He speaks in a soothing, almost crooning voice, the voice of reason, the voice of confident imperturbability. "Hell, that's different," he says to the three musicians awaiting his verdict. "That's a pop song now, nearly about." And Elvis, Scotty, and Bill all burst out in nervous, self-reassuring laughter.

Almost as soon as the song was cut, Sam got two-sided dubs not just to Dewey, who had had an exclusive now for a couple of days, but to Bob Neal, the early-morning DJ and host of the *High Noon Round-Up* at WMPS, Dick Stuart at the West Memphis station, KWEM, and Sleepy Eyed John, a country jock at WHHM, who also led a big western-style swing band and booked the Eagle's Nest out at the Clearpool complex on Lamar. All three got on the record right away, playing the second side mainly, but Sleepy Eyed John evidently showed some business interest in the young singer, which disturbed Sam. "Sleepy Eyed John hated what we were doing at 706, he made no bones about it. I continued to carry records to him because he played them, but I think he played them because he thought by picking them apart he could make people see that this was not really music." Sleepy Eyed John was a "businessman," not the lowest form of life in Sam's eyes, because Sam considered himself a businessman, but if you were a businessman exclusively, solely interested in making money, you were worth little more than a bucketful of warm spit. To forestall Sleepy Eye, Sam suggested to Scotty that he become the manager of record, just as he was already manager of the Starlite Wranglers. "He was exactly what we needed. Scotty had the demeanor and the manner — he wasn't going to give Elvis any unnecessary problems about 'You do this' and 'You do that,' and you could trust him all the way. We didn't need some hotshot manager — hell, Scotty just wanted to help keep the vehicle together."

On Monday, July 12, just a week after they had first met, Scotty became the official manager. "Whereas, W.S. Moore, III, is a band leader and a booking agent," the agreement read, "and Elvis Presley, a minor, age 19 years, is a singer of reputation and renown, and possesses bright promises of large success. . . ." Scotty got 10 percent off the top, and then at Sam's suggestion the group would divide any income with a 50–25–25 split. The original idea was that Elvis would become part of the Wranglers show, a kind of added attraction, which would make "two acts in one," Scotty said, and in fact that was the way it was set up for the following Saturday at the Bon Air, the Wranglers' regular weekend gig. The record was manufactured that week at Buster Williams' Plastic Products on Chelsea Avenue, in Memphis, and by the time that it was officially released as Sun record number 209 on Monday, July 19, six thousand local orders had already come in. Ed Leek, a Humes classmate who was premed at Memphis State, described going down to the plant and watching the first records come off the press with Elvis, who was "like a little kid at Christmas." Others were hearing the record for the first time. Jack Clement, who was singing with Sleepy Eyed John's band occasionally and studying English and journalism at Memphis State, turned on the radio one morning and heard "Blue Moon of Kentucky" — "it was just what I'd been wanting to hear. It was real. I loved the simplicity of it, and so did everybody I know that heard it. There were some people I know that quarreled with the look, but *everybody* loved the way that it sounded. All it took was one play."

Meanwhile, Dixie was still down in Florida with no idea what was going on. There was only the mysterious telegram that she got at her cousin's house ("We were on the move all the time, so we didn't talk to each other on the phone") — "HURRY HOME. MY RECORD IS DOING GREAT," it read. "I thought, 'What!' And I thought, this can't be for real. But I knew it was."

ON SATURDAY, JULY 17, Sam Phillips carried Elvis out to the Bon Air Club, at Summer and Mendenhall, to execute the first part of the plan that he and Scotty had devised. Dewey mentioned on the air that night that he might stop by after his show, and perhaps that added to the crowd, but it was a normal Saturday-night crowd, "pure redneck," according to Sam, loud, hard-drinking, a little rowdy, in love with their hillbilly music, out for a good time. Elvis and Sam sat at a little table while the band finished its set, and Elvis got more and more nervous. "This was Elvis' first appearance, period, and he was absolutely mortified. Now look, this was a small club, and it was all rednecks — and I don't mean any bad connotation by that — but you had better be careful looking like Elvis did in a redneck joint and not singing hillbilly songs and you want to live. You got a bunch of people drinking, and then you try to come on with some music, untried, unproved, you're unknown. I swear, he just came off real good."

He sang his two songs — they were the only songs the trio really *knew* — and Scotty and Bill hung around for a few minutes, but then it was time for the Wranglers to go back up on the bandstand, and Elvis and Sam left. At that point all of the confidence that he had generated onstage seemed to deflate. "He said, 'Mr. Phillips, I just feel like . . . I failed.' I said, 'Elvis, are you kidding? You were really good.' I didn't say *great,* I said,

'The only thing that could have been better would have been if you had enjoyed it onstage.' You see, I was honest with him, I didn't feed him a line of bullshit, and he couldn't shoot any holes in that."

As for the Wranglers, there was friction, Scotty said, right from the start. To begin with, they hadn't realized they wouldn't all be backing Elvis up, though, of course, that wouldn't have worked, Scotty knew, because they hadn't backed him on the record. Then, too, there seemed to be a resentment based not just on the reception that the kid got, which was nothing out of the ordinary, but on the way he looked, the way he dressed, his whole demeanor — which was. To Sam it was a revelation. He hadn't looked at Elvis Presley as a "physical specimen. I wasn't thinking, 'Is he going to look good onstage, is he going to be a great performer?' I was just looking for something that nobody could categorize." That was what Sam saw at the club that night, and it was what the Wranglers saw, too — but their reactions were entirely different.

Sam called Bob Neal right after the Bon Air appearance. Neal, the WMPS DJ, was putting on a "hillbilly hoedown featur[ing] favorite folk ballads in a sylvan folk setting" and starring, "in person, the sensational radio-recording star" Slim Whitman, of the Louisiana Hayride, who would sing his hits, "Rosemarie," "Secret Love," and, undoubtedly, "Indian Love Call." The show was at the outdoor amphitheater in Overton Park, and Sam asked Neal if he could add this new Memphis act to the bill. Bob, the most affable of entrepreneurs, said sure, as long as Sam got the boy into the musicians' union, which Sam had Marion immediately set about to do. He didn't say anything about it to Elvis at first, because he didn't want to get him too worked up — but he thought he would try to place an ad in the paper with the Poplar Tunes record shop the following week, assuming that it all worked out.

Dixie came home on Sunday, too late to see Elvis that night. The first song that the family heard on the radio when they got back into town was "Blue Moon of Kentucky." On Monday, Dixie called Elvis at Crown Electric first thing in the morning, and he told her to meet him at home after work, he didn't want to have to go home and change and clean up and drive over to her house before seeing her. "I had on a pale blue fitted skirt and a red blouse, and his mom and dad and I were sitting on the porch. They were just so excited they couldn't believe it, they told me about the studio and the record and the people calling and saying, 'Is this your son?' Then I saw him walking down Alabama Street, I could see him a block away, and I couldn't wait for him to get there, and he couldn't wait to get there. And when he came in we had to go over the whole thing all over again. And we had to say, Hi, how you doing? Good vacation? Did you get my telegram? Yeah, I did. And he said something about my outfit, and we were just very polite for a minute, and then he walked in the door like, 'I'm going for a drink or something.' And he said, 'Come here just a minute, Dixie.' So I got up and went in the door so we could get our kiss, because we hadn't seen each other in so long — it had been two weeks! — but we were so polite about it, because we were right there in front of his mother and daddy. It was a sweet day, I can still visualize it, I kept thinking, 'Please don't let him change,' but, you know, after that things were never the same."

They seemed the same for quite some time, though. Dixie rode with him on his route in the Crown Electric truck. They continued to see each other almost every night. They stopped by Dewey's radio show once or twice and sat with Dewey while he screamed and shouted and carried on. One night Elvis put in a plug for Crown Electric, and the switchboard was so jammed with calls the next day that the Tiplers took Elvis off his route and had him answer the phone. The Tiplers were almost as excited about his success as Mr. and Mrs. Presley. They went out to see him the first night he played the club, bringing friends and employees, and were only disappointed that he was not allowed to sing more songs.

Some nights there would be rehearsals over at Scotty's, and Dixie would sit with the wives, Bobbie and Evelyn, older married women in their twenties (Dixie was still not quite sixteen), while they rehearsed. Once they stopped by the Sun studio, but Dixie found Sam a little frightening, not like Dewey, who put you right at your ease, even if he was a little vulgar. Sam was kind of off-putting, though — the force of his gaze, the way it locked in on Elvis, made it seem as if he didn't have much use for, or interest in, Dixie, and as a result she was even quieter than normal in his presence. On the Saturday night after she got home they played again out at the Bon Air, but Dixie, of course, couldn't go because they served alcoholic drinks, so she waited at home for it to be over. When he finally came by to pick her up, he had forgotten his coat, and she rode out to the club with him, but "it was like another world. The people recognized him, and he had to go back onstage and sing again. It was like I was sitting there, thinking, 'I'm not really in this, I'm watching it somewhere.' "

The following week, ads for the July 30 Overton Park show started to appear. One spelled his name "Ellis Presley," one left it out altogether, and the day of the performance there was an ad with Slim Whitman's picture at the top that announced "ELVIS PRESLEY, New Memphis Star Who Sings 'Blue Moon of Kentucky' and 'That's All Right, Mama,' " along with a small Poplar Tunes ad urging patrons to "buy all of Slim Whitman's Imperial Records — Elvis Presley's Sun records" at the record store at 305 Poplar. On Wednesday at lunchtime Marion Keisker took Elvis just down the street to the Press-Scimitar Building at 495 Union. She had hoped to have her old college friend Bob Johnson do the story, but Johnson advised her that they had "a new kid who was handling a lot of that" — Edwin Howard, the editor's son — and maybe it would be more politic to let him write it up. Marion arrived with Elvis in tow, Howard recalled. "I'll never forget. . . . He look[ed] like the wrath of God. Pimples all over his face. Ducktail hair. Had a funny-looking thin bow tie on. . . . He was very hard to interview. About all I could get out of him was yes and no."

The article was headed "In a Spin" and led off with:

> Elvis Presley can be forgiven for going round and round in more ways than one these days. A 19-year-old Humes High graduate, he has just signed a recording contract with Sun Record Co. of Memphis, and already has a disk out that promises to be the biggest hit that Sun has ever pressed. . . . "The odd thing about it," says Marion Keisker of the Sun office, "is that both sides seem to be equally popular on popular, folk, and race record programs. This boy has something that seems to appeal to everybody. We've just gotten the sample records out to the disk jockeys and distributors in other cities, but we got big orders yesterday from Dallas and Atlanta."

True to Howard's recollection, there is not a single direct quote from the subject of the article, and the photograph that accompanies it shows an unsmiling three-quarter view with clip-on bow tie and hair to which grease has been liberally applied in a vain attempt to make it behave — it is standing up a little wildly in front, and two strands have escaped, pointing outward like antennae. He is wearing a western-style shirt-jacket with white-stitched, button-down breast pockets and wide lapels, he appears to be wearing eye shadow, and all in all he looks like a combination of something from outer space and the polite, well-mannered, sober, and sensitive boy that he really was. He looked, Dixie thought, very handsome, and was. He looked, Elvis Presley thought, not quite right, but close to the way he wanted to look.

FRIDAY, JULY 30, was hot and sticky. Dixie and Elvis must have spoken to each other at least half a dozen times during the day. Although he never liked to talk about it, she knew how nervous he must be, and driving up Poplar as they approached the park, she noticed that his fingers drummed an even steadier tattoo than usual on the metal dashboard. Mr. and Mrs. Presley were there — they came with a bunch of other relatives. Some of the boys and girls Dixie knew from church, the ones you would see at the roller rink, and some of their other friends were present, too — but mostly it was an undifferentiated mass who were there to see not "Ellis Presley" but Slim Whitman, the handsome, mustachioed star, or Billy Walker, the Tall Texan, who had just had his first big hit with "Thank You for Calling." These were hillbilly singers, this was a hillbilly crowd — Dixie was scared to death, not for herself but for how Elvis would feel if they just sat there and went, 'Huh?' What if they made fun of him, what if this was the end of his dream?

Sam Phillips was late getting to the show. "I had to park a long ways away, and when I got there he was standing on the steps at the back of the shell looking kind of pitiful — well, maybe *pitiful* is the wrong word, I knew it was the way he was going to look: *unsure*. And he just grabbed me and said, 'Man, I'm so glad to see you, Mr. Phillips. I-I-I-I — ' You know, that was just the way Elvis did. 'I-I-I-I just didn't know what I was going to do.' Well, you know, it's like when somebody's mother is real sick and you tell them everything is going to be all right, and yet you know there's the possibility that his mother might die. I said, 'Look, Elvis, we'll find out whether they like you or not.' And then I said, *'They're gonna love you.'* Now I didn't *know* that, and if you want to call me a liar or a fake for saying something that I didn't know to be the truth — but I believed that once he started to sing and they saw him, I don't mean the stage act, once they heard that voice and the beautiful simplicity of what those three musicians were putting down. . . . You see, Elvis had confidence in me, he saw that when I walked up I always had some kind of assured look, and yet he knew I wasn't going to throw him to the lions either. So I gave him my best clubhouse pitch, not too many curves, 'cause I knew even if he struck out four times and left three people on base each time, after the ball game was over that could be overcome, too."

When Elvis went onstage, Scotty said, his knees were knocking so loud you could almost hear them. Bob Neal made the introduction, and then the three musicians, none of whom had ever appeared in a setting even remotely resembling this one, were on their own. The singer fiddled with the mike, twisting it so hard his knuckles turned white, but when he struck the opening chord of "That's All Right," Scotty and Bill fell in loosely behind him, and he raised up on the balls of his feet, leaning forward into the mike, his lips twisted involuntarily into a kind of sneer, as his legs began to quiver. "I was scared stiff," he explained afterward. "It was my first big appearance in front of an audience, and I came out and I was doing [my first number], and everybody was hollering and I didn't know what they were hollering at."

"We were all scared to death," said Scotty. "Here we come with two little funky instruments and a whole park full of people, and Elvis, instead of just standing flat-footed and tapping his foot, well, he was kind of jiggling. That was just his way of tapping his foot. Plus I think with those old loose britches that we wore — they weren't pegged, they had lots of material and pleated fronts — you shook your leg, and it made it look like all hell was going on under there. During the instrumental parts he would back off from the mike and be playing and shaking, and the crowd would just go wild, but he thought they were actually making fun of him."

He sang his second song, "Blue Moon of Kentucky," which pretty much exhausted the group's repertoire at this point, and the crowd went even wilder. Bill clowned and rode his bass, gave ever more confident whoops in the background, and hit his instrument a double lick. "It was really a wild sound, like a jungle drum or something," Elvis recalled with some wonder. "I came offstage, and my manager told me that they was hollering because I was wiggling my legs. I went back out for an encore, and I did a little more, and the more I did, the wilder they went."

Sam Phillips and Bob Neal stood watching from the wings. This was something beyond either of their wildest expectations. As Elvis sang "Blue Moon of Kentucky" again, for his encore, he showed even greater confidence and more untrammeled movement. "It was a real eye-opener," said Neal, who had had no reason to expect anything whatsoever of this untried, unproven nineteen-year-old. "He just automatically did things right." "They still wanted Slim," said Sam, "but they wanted

Elvis, too. When they got done cheering for Elvis, they were cheering for Slim. And when Slim came out onstage — and this shows you what a great gentleman Slim Whitman was — he said, 'You know, I can understand your reaction, 'cause I was standing backstage and I was enjoying it just as much as you.' How're you going to do better than that?"

Meanwhile, for Dixie there were sharply mixed emotions. She wasn't shocked by his movements, she had seen him do similar things many times just singing for their friends at Riverside Park, "it was his natural way of performing." And it wasn't that different from what Chief did at the All-Night Singings either — even the reaction and the size of the crowd were comparable too. Even so, she said, "I don't think he was prepared for what was about to happen. He knew this was what he wanted to do and that it was breaking for him, but I don't think he [ever] thought everybody would just go crazy. I wanted to tell [some of the girls who were screaming], 'Shut up and leave him alone. What do you think you're doing here?' And I felt like all of a sudden I was not a part of what he was doing. He was doing something so totally *him* that I was not a part of it. . . . And he loved it."

IN THE WEEKS that followed the Overton Park show, Sam Phillips was on the road almost constantly. Ever since starting up Sun Records again the previous year, he had traveled between sixty-five thousand and seventy-five thousand miles, visiting each of his forty-two distributors, meeting jukebox operators, disc jockeys, record-store owners, buyers and sellers. For all the pointedness with which Sam eschewed convention (and conventions), there were very few people in the business that he did not know and who did not in turn recognize and respect the unswerving commitment that drove this slim, elegant, intense young man with the preacher's faith and the piercing gaze. For each of his trips Sam loaded up the trunk of his car with records and set off on a road that ended in a fitful few hours of sleep, more often than not at the local YMCA, before he moved on to meet the next early-morning jock. Meanwhile, Marion kept things going at home, paying bills, fending off creditors, meeting orders, ordering up labels, dealing with the pressing plant, and fulfilling all the other responsibilities that being half of a cash-poor two-person operation entailed. In the six and a half months before "That's All Right" came out, Sun Records had released twelve records, none of them as substantial a hit as Rufus Thomas' "Bear Cat," which had occasioned a bitter lawsuit from Duke Records' Don Robey (he claimed that "Bear Cat" infringed his copyright on Big Mama Thornton's "Hound Dog") and the eventual forfeiture of a considerable amount of money. In the five months following the release of Sun number 209, the company released only three additional records, one of them (the only one to come out before November) the follow-up disc by Elvis Presley. Clearly Sam Phillips' attention was focused on his new artist, and just as clearly it was not simply because of the economic opportunities that he foresaw. For Sam Phillips saw a revolution on the way.

It was not an easy vision to fulfill. When he came around looking for jocks to play Little Junior Parker or Rufus Thomas, trying to sell distributors on their sales potential, the task was easy by comparison: he was dealing with a defined market, and if he happened to believe in the undefined potential of that market, the *crossover* potential, that is, more than his listener, that was merely a matter of degree. Here, though, all the rules were out the window. "I remember talking to T. Tommy Cutrer [the top country jock] at KCIJ in Shreveport, who's one of the greatest guys in the world — and one thing I never did do is try to overpower somebody with my convictions of what I had in my little black bag. 'If you can give me some play on it, I'd appreciate it. If you can't, I understand.' T. Tommy told me, 'Sam, they'll run me out of town.' " Fats Washington, on the other hand, was a paraplegic black man with a rhythm and blues show who had been crippled in the war. "He played my r&b records, all of them. But when I wanted him to play 'That's All Right,' he played it for me, but he said on the air, 'I just want to tell all my listeners I got Sam Phillips in the studio with me here, and he thinks this is gonna be a hit record, and I'm telling him that this man should not be played after the sun comes up in the morning, it's so country.' I'll never forget that statement, but he was honest about it.

"Paul Berlin was the hottest disc jockey in Houston at the time, and I taught him how to run the board. When he was a little chap on Lowenstein's Junior Theater on Saturdays on WREC, I put him on the air and he'd come in after the show and want me to show him the control boards and everything. Then he became the number-one disc jockey in Houston, and he was playing Tennessee Ernie Ford and Patti Page, all the big pop artists of the time, and he told me, 'Sam, your music is just so ragged, I just can't handle it right now. Maybe later on.'

"I never forced myself in any door or left where they felt I didn't at least intend to. I never said, 'Well, you wait and see,' 'cause, hell, I didn't know myself. I worked with the counter people in the distributorships. I talked to unbelievable numbers of jukebox operators and retail [merchants]. On Mondays you would usually see your jukebox operators and give them a whole week to change their program — Wednesday was usually the last day they could come in and get the newest stuff. Retail was usually Wednesday and Thursday, Tuesday if they were out in the country. I'd come in, say, to Atlanta or Dallas, and if there was something the counter person was on the fence about, they would buy in very limited quantity just so they wouldn't get stuck. The thing I would never do was go in and not tell the distributor what reaction I had from other distributors across the country. I told them the truth. Many times I believed so much in what I had that I wanted to tell them things that really wasn't true. But I knew I had to face them again, so I just told them what I felt — and a lot of times I felt real discouraged.

"One night I left Houston going into Dallas on a Sunday night, and I [ran into] a dust storm sixty miles out of there. I'd already checked out of the Sam Houston Hotel, and I'd had bad reports in Houston, they just didn't understand 'That's All Right, Mama.' I turned around and went back [to Houston] to keep from smothering to death. The next morning I got up and drove on into Dallas, and when I got there — Alta Hayes was the counter girl, and she looked at me and said, 'Sam, you look like hell.' I said, 'Well, thank you, you look nice, too, Alta.' She was a good-looking woman and a great person, and she had a great ear, too. She said, 'Well, let's go up to the corner and have a cup of coffee.' We went up there, and I really didn't want a damn thing, and she sat there and told me, 'Sam, look, don't worry about this thing, you look worn out. This guy is going to be a hit, I don't give a damn what they say.' And I said, 'Well, Alta, I hope you're right.' "

It was a lonely path, and one that Sam trod without regard to personal gain or popularity ("I could be a mean motherfucker. Now this may sound like a contradiction, because I needed everybody's help, but I didn't need myself kissing anyone's ass"). He was a man swept up by a belief, in a sound and in an idea. And as discouraged as he might sometimes get, as harsh as the reality of selling this new music might be, he never strayed from his belief, he never allowed himself to be distracted from his main goal. Which was to get them to *listen.*

In Tupelo, Elvis' hometown, Ernest Bowen, who had worked with Vernon Presley for L. P. McCarty and Sons and whose father had employed Vernon briefly after the war, was now sales manager at WELO. Bowen had met Sam Phillips while Sam was still working at WREC and playing the big band music that Bowen loved, and he liked the man — but he didn't like the new music one bit. As a result WELO was not playing this new record by a hometown boy, despite countless requests from local teenagers. "They were just worrying us to death. Sam called and said, 'I understand you're getting requests for Elvis Presley's music.' I said, 'Yeah.' He said, 'You're not going to play it?' I told him it was a bunch of crap." Rather than take offense, Sam patiently explained that he could understand Ernest's feelings but that this was not a question of personal taste: the world had changed, communications had changed, and while Sam himself was still a country boy at heart, it was no longer the days of the horse and buggy and the courthouse square, as great as those days had been. " 'So you might as well start playing it,' he said. So we did, and from there on," Bowen concluded, "the music began to change, and changed rapidly after that. Younger people started listening to radio instead of putting a nickel in the jukebox. I look back on it, and that was where it began to turn."

THERE WAS NO QUESTION that the record was a hit in Memphis. As one of the first national magazine articles announced nearly a year later: "The current greeting among [Memphis] teenagers is still a rhythmical line from the song: 'Ta dee da dee dee da.' " On August 7, 1954, *Billboard,* which under the editorial direction of Paul Ackerman had long championed the cause of Sun ("Paul Ackerman had a great dedication," said Sam Phillips, "to all the talented people who never had a chance"), reviewed the new single in its "Spotlight" section under the heading "Talent." "Presley is a potent new chanter," read the review, "who can sock over a tune for either the country or the r&b markets. . . . A strong new talent." Which was precisely the point Sam was trying to get across. Meanwhile, there was practically no one in town who hadn't heard the record and didn't have an opinion about it. Ronny Trout, who had been Elvis' shop partner at Humes during Elvis' senior year, saw it on a jukebox at the hamburger stand across from the Dairy Delight where he worked and stared in disbelief. "I thought, Surely, no, that's not, it couldn't be. But heck, with a name like that . . . So I invested a nickel and played the first one, 'That's All Right, Mama,' and I said, That's him! Then I had to play the other."

Red West, the star of the Humes football team, who, along with Ronny, still had another year of high school to go, heard Dewey play it on the radio when he was putting in time at bivouac camp at the Memphis Air Force Base. He was flabbergasted to hear someone that he had considered a nonentity, really, on the radio — it was like going into a movie theater and seeing an acquaintance on the screen. "It was bigger than life," he said. "That's the way it was to me. I was happy for him, but it was kind of unbelievable."

Johnny Black was in Texas. "I was in Corpus Christi, and I picked up a Houston station, and they were playing 'That's All Right, Mama.' " He recognized the song and the singer right away, he heard Bill's slapping bass, and he announced to his wife, " 'We're going back to Memphis, 'cause something is happening there, and I want to be a part of it.' "

In the aftermath of the Overton Park show, "That's All Right" was probably the best-selling record in town. Every DJ in Memphis was on it now, and it seemed like everybody was jumping on the bandwagon. Ronnie Smith called up for Eddie Bond to see if Elvis might like to sing with them now, but Elvis said he had been working hard with Scotty and Bill, he couldn't just quit, though he appreciated the invitation. For Elvis and Dixie it was an idyllic time, a momentary lull in the action when everyone knew that it was all bound to explode but they went about their business as if it wasn't. For Dixie, looking back, it was easy to say that this was the point at which it all began to end, this was the point at which she lost him and the world claimed him, but at the time she was just so proud of him; all through that summer she rode around feeling that all eyes were on her, because he was her boyfriend and she was going to be Mrs. Elvis Presley.

They continued to go to Riverside Park, they continued to drink their milk shakes in the little park near Dixie's house and go out to Leonard's for hamburgers and go to the drive-in movies and sit on the front porch and spoon. Elvis asked Charlie Hazelgrove if he would put the record on the jukebox at the Blues Shop, and he brought the record out to the Rainbow skating rink, too, where, the owner, Joe Pieraccini, said, Elvis listened to it on the jukebox over and over again. Some afternoons they would rehearse at Scotty's brothers' dry cleaning plant, and Dixie would sit there, her mind caught up in other things. The Songfellows, Elvis told her, were looking for a new singer now that Cecil had replaced R.W. in the Blackwood Brothers, but he didn't think he would join even if he was asked, he thought he would just see where this new business might lead. Dixie, who had never imagined any calling higher than quartet singer, just nodded. Whatever he wanted to do — things were going along so nicely.

One Sunday evening a week or so after the Overton Park show, she went over to KWEM, in West Memphis, with the band for a brief radio appearance. Several nights they rehearsed in Scotty's living room, with Scotty calling the rehearsal and Bobbie serving sandwiches but Elvis indicating what he wanted to sing. Sometimes he would know no more than two or three lines from a song, and everyone would be ransacking their memory for the lyrics. Sometimes, if it was a song that she and Elvis had listened to at Charlie's, Dixie might help supply the lyrics herself, or Elvis would just ad-lib something and they would move on to the next number. Scotty and Bill took an active role in Elvis' education. "They taught him how to stand," said Bill's wife, Evelyn. "They coached him on how to hold his guitar and to do all this stuff in front of the mike. He had to learn all that." "It was kind of like we adopted him," said Bobbie Moore. "We had to make sure that he got to the dates, we had to make sure that he got home, we had to make sure that he didn't get into trouble. He was just a kid — he was nice, but he could be kind of a brat, too!"

With Elvis everything always had to be funny, Bobbie said, he was always acting up, whereas Scotty, who enjoyed a good joke, too, believed there was a time and a place for everything. One time Scotty and Bill were loading up after their second or third Saturday at the Bon Air while Elvis and Bobbie stood by the car. "Scotty came out, and he put his amplifier in the trunk, and Elvis said, 'I'm trying to get a date with your wife.' Scotty didn't say a word, but I thought, 'Oh-oh, you shouldn't have said that' — because he wasn't, really. Scotty didn't say a word. He went ahead and got in the driver's seat. I said, 'We better get in the car before he leaves.' I knew he didn't take that as a joke."

One night Elvis stayed over after the show. Bobbie wasn't expecting him to, "but then Scotty said, 'You got some linen for the couch?' so I made up a bed. Elvis was never tired, he could stay up all night after a show, and he was always pacing. He wasn't shy! He wouldn't think anything of walking around, poking his head in the bedroom, every time he'd come over he'd look in the refrigerator, walk around, go look out the door. He just couldn't be still. The time he stayed over, the next morning Scotty says, 'Elvis likes his eggs cooked hard as a rock.' So I fried his eggs as hard as I could, 'cause I like mine done, too. He sat there, and he said, 'Can you cook it a little more?' Well, I cooked it until you couldn't get that egg any harder, and he ate a bunch of toast and bacon but only a couple of bites of that egg. That was the first time I ever remember him spending the night away from home. His mother always waited up for him — she said she couldn't go to sleep until Elvis got home — so maybe he called her to tell her he was spending the night."

Scotty took his duties as manager seriously. He and Sam agreed that it made no sense to put Elvis into some of the rough joints that Scotty and Bill had been playing, so he went looking for schoolhouses to book and local Elks Club and Lions Club events within a seventy-five-mile radius of Memphis that might be looking for a singer. He tried his hometown of Gadsden and got turned down by his old principal, who didn't think they'd make enough money to pay the light bill, but he got some dates over in Mississippi and Arkansas starting in September. In the meantime they played out at the Kennedy Veterans Hospital one Saturday afternoon and in the basement rec room of St. Mary's, across from the Courts, where they gained additional exposure if not pay. At Kennedy they played for the paraplegic and quadriplegic ward under the auspices of the B'nai B'rith, and even there they made quite an impact, according to Monte Weiner, a classmate of Elvis' at Humes, whose mother booked the shows. "My mother brought a group out once a month, and she knew of Elvis through me, though I didn't really know him in school. He did it for several months in a row, the first time was right after the record came out, and they'd bring people on stretchers and wheelchairs down to the little room where he was going to perform. I remember they rolled the beds out into the middle of the floor, and I watched their faces while he and his group were performing, doing something completely different from anything I had ever heard before. The patients couldn't move at all, but their facial expressions — it was like they were trying to clap by their facial expressions. It was a really remarkable thing, that's all I can tell you."

JUST ONE WEEK after Overton Park they started playing as the intermission act out at the Eagle's Nest on their own — without the Starlite Wranglers, who had not taken the success of Scotty's new discovery very well at all. In fact the Overton Park appearance seems to have marked the end of the group, although they did not formally break up for another couple of months. Dixie sometimes baby-sat for Evelyn so that she could go out to the show, and the five of them — the Blacks, the Moores, and Elvis — would go out to eat afterward at Earl's Drive-in downtown. Elvis never had any money in his pocket, Bobbie said; since they had joined the union, they no longer got paid on the job but had to go down to the union hall on Monday to collect, so the "girls" generally ended up paying. "Elvis would ask Scotty, 'Can I have another hamburger or a milk shake?' And Scotty would say, 'You'll have to ask her,' " said Bobbie. " 'She's got the money.' " "I found out he didn't like ketchup," said Evelyn. " 'Cause if I put ketchup on my french fries, he wouldn't eat them. It got to where I put ketchup on them every time — otherwise he'd eat every one!"

It wasn't too long before the intermission shows at the Eagle's Nest became a kind of underground sensation. It was Sleepy Eyed John who booked the club, and Sleepy Eyed John whose band continued to play the main dance sets, but from the start Elvis was clearly an attraction. "Elvis Presley Tonight," the little newspaper squib announced. "See and hear Elvis singing 'That's All Right' and 'Blue Moon of Kentucky,' Admission $1.20 (Including Tax)." Sometimes it was "Ladies' Nite, Too (Ladies .50)," and many of the ads cheerfully admonished, "Don't Wear a Tie Unless Your Wife Makes You," but as the momentum built over the course of the month, with perhaps half a dozen different appearances, in addition to one or two at other clubs around town, you didn't need any gimmicks to build attendance. At first Vernon had wanted to take a sock at Sleepy Eyed John because of some of the sarcastic things Sleepy Eye had said about his son's record on the air. He was going to go up to the station, he told Sam Phillips, and take care of him. "I said, 'Now wait a minute, Mr. Presley, that's not the way it works. The worst thing you can do is go over there. All he wants to do is to create some noise. Let's kill the sonofabitch with kindness.' " Vernon was dubious, but he allowed himself to be dissuaded, and when he and Gladys went out to the club, he was glad that he had. Other members of the family came out on occasion: Gladys' sister Lillian and her husband, who remained pessimistic about the boy's prospects; Vernon's brother, Vester, and his wife, Clettes, another of Gladys' sisters, who took a couple of snapshots of a very young, very blond, and somewhat uncomfortable-looking Elvis Presley standing in front of the Eagle's Nest sign.

James and Gladys Tipler came out to the Eagle's Nest, too. They continued to feel great pride in their employee and even brought some of their big construction clients. "He wanted us to come out and see him so he would feel he had some friends in the audience," Mrs. Tipler said. "He had quite a bit of trouble with stage fright." Sometimes he wore his bolero jacket, sometimes he wore a striped sports jacket with a velvet collar that he had recently bought at Lansky's, occasionally he favored western clothes. His favorite colors were pink and black. "I remember the first check he gave me," said Guy Lansky, who had known him from the time he first pressed his face to the Beale Street clothing store window. "It was hard to take. I think it was five hundred dollars from Sam Phillips, and he asked me to cash it for him, and he bought some clothes and some jewelry — I had a little jewelry store on the side. And I was still skeptical of him because of his appearance, I remember running to the bank to see if it was good. Years later, after he got Graceland, I used to take my kids out there, and I remember he showed me that sports coat that he had bought years before — boy, he loved that coat, it was still in his closet."

He seemed to gain more and more of a sense of himself, greater and greater self-assurance onstage and off. "His movement was a natural thing," said Scotty, "but he was also very conscious of what got a reaction. He'd do something one time and then he would expand on it real quick." According to Reggie Young, who was seventeen at the time and would join Eddie Bond's band, the Stompers, the following year, all the teenagers who were out at the swimming pool that gave the Clearpool complex its name (the Eagle's Nest was over the changing room) would rush in as soon as they heard Elvis, Scotty, and Bill start to play. Then all the kids went back outside when Sleepy Eyed John's band took the stage again, fifteen minutes later. "Sleepy Eyed John was all into Ray Price's big western swing band at that time," said his sometime lead vocalist and MC, Jack Clement, who went on to become Sam Phillips' right-hand man at Sun and one of the most brilliantly idiosyncratic producers and confabulators that Nashville ever produced. "Eight or nine pieces, three fiddles, all that kind of stuff — that's where Sleepy Eye thought music was going. Of course nobody agreed with him, and Elvis would come on and do the floor show, just the three of them. He seemed to be handling it all very well, you know, in a young-gentleman fashion, he was kind of reserved but not really shy — that was his demeanor. I was going with my fiancée, Doris, we got married in December, and Doris would come to the dance and sit at a table and when I was up there singing Elvis would be over there trying to get Doris to go out with him. Doris was a very pretty girl — I didn't mind if he flirted with Doris, I liked him. I would get up there and do my set, and then I'd bring him on and he would really cut up."

Marion Keisker saw Elvis frequently all through August. He would stop by the studio from time to time to find out how his record was doing or just to hang around and chat. He remained grateful to Marion, as he would be all his life, for helping him "get his first break," and she in turn saw in him an almost magical quality that both protected him and in turn brought out the best in others. "My total image of Elvis was as a child. His attitude towards people was the equivalent of tipping your hat as you walk down the street — 'Good evening, ma'am, good evening, sir' — but not showing off. He never said a wrong thing from the very first night he appeared on the Dewey Phillips show — he was like a mirror in a way: whatever you were looking for, you were going to find in him. It was not in him to lie or say anything malicious. He had all the intricacy of the very simple."

As for Sam, increasingly he saw in the boy something to mirror his own self-image, the kind of person whose "insecurity drove him, and yet he was an extremely patient person for achieving a kind of success [that his contemporaries could only dream of], he was absolutely, unequivocally going to sing. He was not an eloquent person, but many times without a direct statement he was eloquent in starting something that told you exactly what he was thinking." A person still subject to mood swings ("Sam was a driven man," said Marion) yet one who always maintained the appearance of calm and self-assurance, Sam saw in Elvis the very person that he was but rarely showed. Where Elvis appeared unsure, tongue-tied, incapable of expressing himself, Sam saw in him the same sort of burning ambition, he was only lacking the ability to *verbalize* it.

Sam had always seen it as his mission to "open up an area of freedom within the artist himself, to help him to express what *he* believed his message to be," and here he had found his perfect Trilby. To Sam the person who presented himself had never played anywhere before he entered the Sun studio, "he didn't play with bands, he didn't go to this little club and pick and grin. All he did was set with the guitar on the side of his bed at home. I don't think he even played on the front porch." This was what Elvis conveyed, without words, and in a way it was true. When Elvis was with Scotty, when Elvis was in the Sun studio, it was as if he were reborn.

To Sam, as much as to Marion, he was the personification of an ideal, the embodiment of a vision that Sam had carried with him from the farm in Florence — he represented the *innocence* that had made the country great in combination with "the elements of the soil, the sky, the water, even the wind, the quiet nights, people living on plantations, never out of debt, hoping to eat, lights up the river — that's what they used to call Memphis. That was where it all came together. And Elvis Presley may not have been able to verbalize all that — but he damn sure wasn't dumb, and he damn sure was intuitive, and he damn sure had an appreciation for the total spirituality of the human existence, even if he would never have thought of the term. That was what he cared about."

That was Elvis' mark — he conveyed his spirituality without being able, or needing, to express it. And all these adults with their more complicated lives and dreams and passions and hopes looked for themselves in his simplicity.

On August 28 the record entered the *Billboard* regional charts. It showed up at number three on the C&W Territorial Best Sellers for the week of August 18, behind Hank Snow's "I Don't Hurt Anymore" and a Kitty Wells–Red Foley duet, but it was "Blue Moon of Kentucky" that was the hit. On the strength of these credentials, and on the basis of the record's striking local success, Sam Phillips approached Jim Denny, manager of the Grand Ole Opry, with the idea that the Opry could at least offer the boy a little exposure. After all, Sam adjured Denny, whom he knew from the year he had spent in Nashville, it was no longer the old mule-and-wagon days, wasn't it time to allow something new to breathe? Sam wasn't saying the boy was necessarily going to set the world on fire, but give youth a chance, damnit. Jim Denny listened; he was a hard man, Sam knew — he was not about to win any popularity contests — but he was a fair man, too. He had heard the record, he told Sam, it wasn't really to his taste, but if Sam could give him a little time, well, maybe if the band was in the area at some point he could fit them in. Sam hung up the phone — he was well enough pleased. He could wait as long as he had to. At least Denny hadn't said no.

Others were noticing the waves the new record was making. In Nashville, Bill Monroe, far from being offended at the "sacrilege" which had been committed on his song, approached Carter Stanley, another prominent bluegrass musician, after the Opry one Saturday night. "He said, 'I want you to hear something,' and he had never said anything like that to me before." He played Stanley the "new" version of "Blue Moon of Kentucky." "I laughed a little bit and looked around, and everybody else was laughing except Bill. He said, 'You better do that record [at Stanley's scheduled recording session] tomorrow if you want to sell some records.' . . . He said, 'I'm going to do it [at his own recording session] next Sunday.' " And Monroe helped supervise Stanley's session on Sunday, August 29, then recut "Blue Moon of Kentucky" himself in 4/4 time, as he had said he would, the following week.

The major record labels, too, couldn't help but notice what was going on. Jim Denny, in addition to his duties as general manager of the Opry, was also proprietor of Cedarwood Publishing, which in turn was tied in with Decca Records, and Decca's Paul Cohen pricked up his ears at this new phenomenon. Sam's friend Randy Wood, who operated a big one-stop and mail-order record business in Gallatin, Tennessee, and had enjoyed a good deal of success with his own Dot Record Company, expressed mild interest as well. Meanwhile, RCA Records in New York had come to be aware of this rising new star, and this upstart new label, not simply because of the write-ups in *Billboard* and *Cashbox* but because of the reports they were getting from their own agents in the field. "All of our distributors were aware of Sam Phillips," said Chick Crumpacker, who had become national country and western promotion manager working under a&r (artist and repertoire) director Steve Sholes in April. "There was all this talk about what this insurgent Sun Records was doing, quite a bit of it pejorative. Also, we would get these reports from the field, from Sam Esgro, who was based in Memphis, and Brad McCuen, who had the RCA field from the middle of Tennessee into Virginia and the Carolinas."

McCuen, a thirty-three-year-old transplanted New Yorker, who filed a report to Steve Sholes that summer, vividly recalled his first encounter with Elvis Presley. "My bell-cow area was East Tennessee. If a record made it in the tri-city area of Kingsport, Johnson City, and Bristol on down through to Knoxville, it would go national, so I was just very conscious of that area. One of our best record dealers was Sam Morrison in Knoxville, right on Market Square. He was originally from Massachusetts, I think, and one of the first southern record dealers that I knew to do the New York

City trick of putting a loudspeaker out over his doorsill and playing the music for the market crowd, who had come in to sell their produce. This one particular time Sam grabbed me and said, 'There's something very interesting happening here, it's really weird,' and he went and got Elvis' record, which was just out, and put 'That's All Right' on the player. 'What do you think?' he said. 'I can't get enough of it. I'm selling at least a box a day.' I was amazed, but I said, 'It's just a normal rhythm and blues record, isn't it?' He said, 'No, it isn't, it's selling to a country audience.'

"Well, at just that point an old country man in his fifties came in, I say jokingly he had more hair growing out of his ears and nose than he did on his head, and he said in an easy Tennessee drawl, 'By granny, I want that record.' I couldn't figure it out, because here was an obvious country fan. Then Sam turned the record over, and played 'Blue Moon of Kentucky,' and I figured, 'Well, he probably wants it for that.' But that wasn't it — it was really 'That's All Right.' So I bought two copies of the record and sent one to Steve Sholes, and Steve said, 'You've got to be kidding!' But I told him that Sam Morrison must have gone through about five thousand, and it was selling in Kingsport and the tri-cities area. And Sam Esgro and I kept sending him reports."

On September 8 the *Memphis Press-Scimitar* announced "Fun on a Grand Scale" at the opening of the new Lamar-Airways Shopping Center. The festivities over the next few days would include Indian ceremonies, "Scottish, hillbilly and Indian music groups, radio, television and recording personalities," a twenty-eight-foot "robot" Indian, lavish prizes, and the presence of "a number of celebrities . . . including Mayor Tobey." Also included was the "newest Memphis hit in the recording business . . . Elvis Presley of 'That's All Right, Mama' and 'Blue Moon of Kentucky' fame," who would be appearing along with Sleepy Eyed John's Eagle's Nest band on a flatbed truck in front of Katz Drug Store on opening night, Thursday, between 9:00 and 10:00. "Blue Moon of Kentucky" was number one on the Memphis c&w chart at this point, with "That's All Right" showing up at number seven.

The parking lot was jammed when Elvis arrived with Dixie, and George Klein, who was back at Memphis State for the fall semester, was broadcasting from inside the giant wooden Indian. Scotty and Bill were already present, and Sleepy Eye was all set up onstage, but the crowd seemed restive. It was made up almost exclusively of teenagers — there were lots of them, more than could ever have fit into the Eagle's Nest — and if they didn't equal the size of the Overton Park audience, this time it was obvious who they were there for.

George emerged from the Indian to come up and introduce the band, and Elvis lit up to see his old Humes classmate, the president of the senior class and editor of the yearbook, especially when George said he had been playing the record over the air in Osceola all summer. They caught up with each other very briefly — Elvis hadn't seen George to talk to since graduation, fifteen months before — but it was perfectly evident how their situations had changed. They spoke of friends in common, and then it was time to go onstage. George gave them the big buildup, he mentioned that he had gone to school with this rising young star, he conveyed a sense of significance and respect in his trained announcer's voice that Sleepy Eye would never have suggested, but there was no preparation for the sound that greeted them, for the whoosh of anticipation, the screams, and the mass intake of breath as Elvis Presley bounded to the microphone. Dixie hadn't really seen him perform since Overton Park — and here they were not far from the Rainbow skating rink, where she had first met her "secret love."

Scotty knew that day. "This was the first we could see what was happening. 'Cause it was a whole parking lot full of kids, and they just went crazy." They liked Bill's clowning, and Elvis' gyrations had advanced way beyond Overton even at this point, but it was the beat that really got to them, and it was the kids' response that drove the music to another level. It was so out of control it was almost frightening.

After the show Elvis hung around a little — there were a bunch of people that he knew in the crowd, and they all wanted to talk to him, some of them even wanted his autograph. Looking at him, watching him open up to people in the way she had always known he could, Dixie thought maybe this was as far as he would go, this was success on the highest level that a normal person could ever hope for. George was genuinely excited. He had to go back to making announcements and deejaying inside the Indian, but they really ought to get together sometime, he said. There were some guys in the audience, too, who were muttering under their breath that they didn't see what the big fuss was all about, this guy was weird in his black pants with the pink stripe, his greasy hair and pimply face — it looked almost like he was wearing makeup. In Florida, Lee

Denson heard from his brothers and sisters about the splash that Elvis was making around town, and he couldn't believe it. Here was a kid barely able to form a chord when Lee tried to teach him in the Courts just a couple of years earlier — of all of them he was the *least* likely to succeed. Lee was playing a regular gig while also working as a bellhop in Key West. Ernest Hemingway, the writer, had declared him to be his favorite singer one night at Sloppy Joe's, and here Elvis Presley was stirring up all this fuss. "The difference between me and him," said Lee, "was I went for it. I drove for it. New York, Hollywood — I went everywhere for it. And he fell into the shithole and came up with the gold watch and chain."

TOP: ELVIS, BILL, SCOTTY, AND SAM PHILLIPS, 1954.
(COURTESY OF GARY HARDY, SUN STUDIO)
BOTTOM: WITH BOB NEAL, 1955. (COURTESY OF GER RIJFF)

GOOD ROCKIN' TONIGHT

IT WAS A TWO-HUNDRED-MILE RIDE to Nashville, but the four of them were comfortable enough in Sam Phillips' four-door black 1951 Cadillac, with Bill's bass strapped to the roof. It was Saturday, October 2. Elvis, Scotty, and Bill had played their regular Friday-night gig at the Eagle's Nest; their record "Blue Moon of Kentucky" was near the top of the charts in Memphis and just beginning to break in Nashville and New Orleans; and they had every reason to feel that they had reached the pinnacle of their musical career — because tonight *they were going to play the Opry.*

Jim Denny had finally succumbed to Sam's argument that there was no need to think about putting the boy on as a regular, he didn't have to think of this as a normal "tryout," *just give the boy a chance.* Denny seemed no more convinced than he had been in the first place — perhaps he was just worn down by Sam's persistence — but he agreed to give the young man a one-time spot on Hank Snow's segment of the show. He could perform a single song with his band, the country number "Blue Moon of Kentucky." If it was worth it to Sam and the boys to drive over just for that, well, then, Denny was willing to give them the shot.

In the meantime Sam had also heard from the Louisiana Hayride, the Opry's more innovative rival in Shreveport, which, unlike the Opry, actually *wanted* this new act. The Hayride, which Denny referred to derisively as the Opry's farm club because so many of its big acts eventually defected to Nashville, had discovered Hank Williams in 1948 and broken such stars as Slim Whitman, Webb Pierce, and, most recently, Jim Reeves and Faron Young. But Sam put them off because, he explained to Hayride booking agent Pappy Covington, he wanted to play the Opry first. As soon as the boys had fulfilled this prior commitment, he told Pappy, stretching the truth a little, Elvis could appear on the Hayride. There was no doubt in his mind, he said, that Elvis could make a hit with the Hayride audience, and they could set it up for just a week or two after the

Opry appearance, but he had committed himself to Jim Denny that the boy would appear on the Opry first. He was walking a thin line, he knew. He didn't for a minute want to lose the Hayride, but he wasn't going to give up the opportunity to see a new, untried artist get his national debut on the hallowed Grand Ole Opry.

Ryman Auditorium was like a tattered shrine to the three musicians, none of whom had ever attended, let alone played, a show at the Opry before. They wandered around the dilapidated old building, erected as a tabernacle in 1886 and still retaining the old wooden pews for seats, in something of a daze. They were both overwhelmed at the sense of history contained in the room — the music they had been listening to all their lives emanated from this cramped little stage — and somewhat disillusioned, too, that the Grand Ole Opry was not, well, grander. Backstage the other musicians mingled freely, exchanging small talk and greetings, tuning up, donning makeup and costumes, without any of the formality or protocol that you might have expected from stars but with all of the remoteness, whether real or perceived, of big leaguers sniffing at bushers just up from the minors. Twenty-one-year-old bass player Buddy Killen, who had just started as chief and only song plugger for Tree Music, the publishing house that WSM program director Jack Stapp had set up in 1951, came up to the obviously out-of-place young singer and introduced himself. "[Elvis] said, 'They're going to hate me.' I said, 'They're not going to hate you. You're going to be fine.' He said, 'If they'd just let me leave, I'd go right now.' " Marty Robbins saw evidence of the same insecurity, but when Elvis spotted Chet Atkins backstage, he introduced himself and then, knowing Scotty's admiration for Atkins' playing, pulled Scotty over, too, saying, "My guitar player wants to meet you." Atkins noted with asperity that the kid appeared to be wearing eye makeup.

Probably of all the Opry legends the one they were most leery of running into was Bill Monroe. Many in the country field continued to view the Sun version of "Blue Moon of Kentucky" as a desecration, and even Sam had heard that Monroe was going to take their head off for their untrammeled interpretation of his stately lament ("I'd heard he was going to break my jaw!"). But when they met Monroe, conservatively dressed in dark suit and tie and trademark white hat and at forty-three already an elder statesman possessed of a dignity that permitted neither bullshit nor informality, he came right out and complimented them. As a matter of fact, he told them, he had cut a new version of the song for Decca, due out next week, that followed their pattern.

There were two additional surprises. Marion Keisker, left behind in Memphis to keep the studio doors open, abandoned her post and caught a bus to Nashville, where she thought at first she would just stay out in the audience so as not to spook them but before long found her way backstage and joined the little group. Then Bill peeked out at the audience and, much to his surprise, discovered his wife, Evelyn, and Scotty's wife, Bobbie, in the front row. "I think he was kind of glad to see us," said Bobbie, " 'cause they were wanting to come back to Memphis that night, and Sam was going to stay over in Nashville. You see, they had told Evelyn and me, 'Y'all can't go. We're all going in one car, and there's no room for you.' Well, I accepted that, but then around noon, a couple of hours after they left, Evelyn came over to the house and said, 'Let's go to Nashville.' I said, 'Oh, I don't know about that, we might get in trouble,' but, you know, we really were like Lucy and Ethel, so then I said, 'What the heck!' and we drove over. Bill stuck his head out the stage door and saw us, but when Scotty saw me backstage, it was like he'd seen a ghost!"

At 10:15 Grant Turner announced the Hank Snow segment of the show, sponsored by Royal Crown Cola, and Snow, whose son, Jimmie Rodgers Snow, had just approached Elvis admiringly, got lost in his introduction of a young man from Memphis who has just made a hit record, let's give him a nice round of applause, to the point that he forgot the young singer's name. Elvis bounced out the same way that he always did, as if he had just fallen off a fast-moving train, and did his one number. Scotty and Bill were more nervous than he was — to them, it seemed, there was nowhere to go but down from here, and they could sense from the polite, but somewhat tepid, reception that this was exactly where they were going. Afterward they were like a boxing management team trying to rationalize defeat. Everyone was *nice* to them as they gawked and huddled — they'd gotten a *good* reception, Bobbie and Evelyn insisted, and Bill introduced himself to everyone, laughing and cracking jokes, while Scotty stood off to one side a little stiffly, waiting to be introduced. Before leaving, Sam conferred briefly with Mr. Denny, who confirmed that Elvis Presley just did not fit the Opry mold, but, he told Sam, " 'This boy is not bad.' He didn't give me any great accolades, he just grabbed me by my skinny arm and said, 'This boy is not bad.' Well, people put down Jim

Denny, nobody much liked Jim, he was a damn tough man, but *he did me a favor.*"

They left not long afterward and wandered down the hill to 417 Broadway, the location of the Ernest Tubb Record Shop, where they were scheduled to play the famous Midnight Jamboree (the Jamboree went on the air live from the record store at the conclusion of the Opry broadcast). Their first impression of the shop was how small it was, but maybe that was just because of how crammed it was with record bins and all the people who had already arrived for the start of the broadcast. Someone introduced Elvis to Ernest Tubb, and Tubb, the most gracious and courteous of entertainers, listened patiently as the nineteen-year-old poured out his love for Tubb's music and told him that it was his real ambition to sing country music. "He said, 'They tell me if I'm going to make any money, though, I've got to sing [this other kind of music]. What should I do?' I said, 'Elvis, you ever have any money?' He said, 'No, sir.' I said, 'Well, you just go ahead and do what they tell you to do. Make your money. Then you can do what *you* want to do.' "

Scotty and Bill headed back to Memphis with their errant wives after the broadcast. They felt simultaneously elated and depressed (they had made it to the big time, even if they were now in all likelihood on the road to oblivion), but for Sam Phillips the evening was an unmitigated triumph. To play the Opry — and *then* to get approval, however grudging, from Jim Denny and Bill Monroe! Even the criticism would not hurt. It could be used, Sam was firmly convinced, to further the boy's appeal — if he could just turn around some of this damn rejection he was getting, if he could just straighten out some of the wrongheaded thinking he was encountering, the blind could be made to see, the lame could be made to walk. "I *needed* the attention that I got from the people that hated what I was doing, that acted like: 'Here is somebody trying to thrust junk on us and classify it as our music.' Well, fuck them, *let them do the classifying.* I just had to peak that damn pyramid, or else the damn sonofabitch would have fallen down." And with Elvis Presley, Sam Phillips was sure he had the means to peak the pyramid.

ELVIS PRESLEY'S second Sun single was released on the Monday before his Opry appearance. It was, if anything, an even bolder declaration of intent than the first, especially the strident blues number "Good

Rockin' Tonight," which rocked more confidently than anything they could have imagined in those first, uncertain days in the studio. Maybe Sam still couldn't diagram the path, but, he felt, they were finally beginning to find their way to "that damn row that hadn't been plowed."

They had seized every opportunity they could to get into the studio all through August, but Sam was on the road so much, and the band was working so many weekends (while still holding down full-time jobs), that this was easier said than accomplished. On August 19 they spent hours doing take after take of "Blue Moon," in an eerie, clippity-clop version that resembled a cross between Slim Whitman's "Indian Love Call" and some of the falsetto flights of the r&b "bird" groups (the Orioles, the Ravens, the Larks). After it was all over, Sam wasn't satisfied that they had anything worth releasing, but he never uttered a word of demurral for fear of discouraging the unfettered freshness and enthusiasm of the singer. "The sessions would go on and on," said Marion Keisker, "each record was sweated out. Sam showed patience beyond belief — in a personality that's not really given to patience."

The problem did not appear to have so much to do with time, in any case, as with confidence and direction. They had captured the ring once, seemingly by accident, but now no one appeared to have a clear vision of how to capture it again, and Sam was reluctant to impose his own. "I had a mental picture, as sure as God is on His throne I had a mental picture of what I wanted to hear, certainly not note for note, but I knew the essence of what we were trying to do. But I also knew that the worst thing I could do was to be impatient, to try to force the issue — sometimes you can make a suggestion just [to change] one bar and you kill the whole song. And sometimes you can be too cocky around people who are insecure and just intimidate them. I mean, as far as actually saying, 'Hey, man, don't be scared,' I've never told anybody in my life not to be scared of the microphone — don't go calling attention to the thing you know they are already scared of. I was never a real forward person, because I didn't give a damn about jumping out in front to be seen, but I tried to envelop them in my feelings of security."

Over the course of the next few weeks they made several attempts at "Satisfied," Martha Carson's rousing spiritual hit from 1951, and "Tomorrow Night," the Lonnie Johnson blues ballad which Elvis had crooned so often to Dixie. They made any number of false starts on other tunes, all of them erased because tape was expensive, after all, and they just weren't going anywhere. The slow numbers, Sam said, "would hang you out to dry," but he was determined to give Elvis' creative imagination free play. He was equally determined, said Marion, not to release anything even a jot below the standard they had already set; he wanted to be sure he had done all that he could to make every record as good as it was "humanly possible to make it." From Sam's point of view: "I wanted simplicity, where we could look at what we were hearing mentally and say, 'Man, this guy has just got it.' But I wanted some biting bullshit, too. Everything had to be a stinger. To me every one of those sessions was like I was filming *Gone With the Wind.*"

Finally, starting on September 10, they hit a streak—once again it seemed almost as if they had stumbled onto it by accident, but when they did it was, as Sam Phillips said, as if it had been waiting for them all along. They cut "Just Because," a rollicking, honky-tonk blues which the Shelton Brothers had originally recorded as the Lone Star Cowboys in 1933. The great good humor and burbling effervescence of the new trio version can be traced in equal parts to the singer's confident exploitation of his gospel-learned technique (here for the first time we hear the characteristic Presley drop to a slurred lower register), Bill Black's almost comically thumping bass, and Scotty's increasingly rhythm-driven guitar. "It was almost a total rhythm thing," Scotty said. "With only the three of us we had to make every note count." Although Sam never released this cut or the next one either, a weepy version of Jimmy Wakely's 1941 "I'll Never Let You Go (Little Darlin')" with a tagged-on, double-time ending, both are characterized by the kind of playfulness and adventurousness of spirit that Sam was looking for, the fresh, almost "impudent" attitude that he was seeking to unlock.

With "I Don't Care If the Sun Don't Shine," an even more unlikely transformation took place. Originally written for the Disney animated feature *Cinderella* by Mack David, brother of the celebrated pop composer Hal David (Mack himself wrote such well-known songs as "Bippidi Bobbidi Boo" and "La Vie en Rose"), the song didn't make the film score's final cut, but it was popularized in 1950 by Patti Page and by Dean Martin in conjunction with Paul Weston and His Dixie Eight. The rhythmic approach couldn't have been more different, but it was Martin's version on which Elvis' is clearly based; for all the energy that Elvis, Scotty, and Bill impart to the song, and for all the high spirits of Elvis' vocalizing, it is Martin's lazily insouciant spirit that comes through. It's as if Dennis the Menace met the drawling English character actor George Sanders. "That's what he heard in Dean," said Sam, who was well aware of Martin's influence, "that little bit of mischievousness that he had in his soul when he cut up a little bit — [that's why] he loved Dean Martin's singing."

With the last song of the session, Wynonie Harris' r&b classic "Good Rockin' Tonight," everything finally fell into place. By this time everyone may have been getting a little testy, and no one was really sure whether they had anything or not, but as Scotty said, "Sam had an uncanny knack for pulling stuff out of you. Once you got a direction, he'd work you so hard you'd work your butt off, he'd make you so mad you'd want to kill him, but he wouldn't let go until he got that little something extra sometimes you didn't even know you had." He would insist that they play nothing but rhythm, he would have them change keys just when they finally got used to the one they were in, and he called for tempos so slow sometimes that everyone was ready to scream. "A lot of times it was a tempo that I absolutely knew they weren't going to like, but we were in a situation where we just weren't getting anywhere, and when they came back [to the original tempo], it was like they'd hit a home run."

To Marion Keisker it was like a puzzle to which only Sam had the key. "I still remember the times when everyone would be so tired, and then some little funny thing would set us off — I'd see Elvis literally rolling around on the floor, and Bill Black just stretched out with his old broken-down bass fiddle, just laughing and goofing off. It was a great spirit of — I don't know, everyone was trying very hard, but everyone was trying to hang very loose through the whole thing. [Sometimes] if Elvis would do something absolutely extraordinary and somebody would hit a clinker or something would go wrong before the tape was completed, Sam would say, 'Well, let's go back, and you hold on to what you did there. I want that.' And Elvis would say, 'What did I do? What did I do?' Because it was all so instinctive that he simply didn't know."

Sam's one organizing principle was that it had to be fun. "I could tolerate anything, we could have tensions as long as I knew that we all had confidence in what we were trying to do, and I could get everybody relaxed to the point where they could hear and react to something without that threshold of apprehension where you almost get to a point where you can't do anything right. Every time we did a number I wanted to make sure to the best of my ability that everybody *enjoyed* it."

In the case of this final number, that sense of enjoyment comes through from the very first note, as Elvis' voice takes on a burr of aggression that is missing from the previous recordings, the band for the first time becomes the fused rhythm instrument that Sam had been seeking all along, and there is a sense of driving, high-flying good times almost in defiance of societal norms. "Have you heard the news?" is the opening declaration, drawn out and dramatic. "There's good rocking tonight."

The other dramatic element to declare itself was the quality that Sam thought he had sensed in Elvis from the start, that strange, unexpected impulse that had led the boy to launch himself into "That's All Right, Mama" in the first place — it seemed to come out of nowhere, and yet, Sam felt, he heard something of the same feeling in the sentimental ballads, too. He equated the insecurity that came through so unmistakably in the boy's stance and demeanor with the sense of inferiority — social, psychological, perceptual — that was projected by the great Negro talents he had sought out and recorded. Sam couldn't be sure, he *thought* he sensed in Elvis a kindred spirit, someone who shared with him a secret, almost subversive attraction not just to black music but to black culture, to an inchoate striving, a belief in the equality of man. This was something that Sam felt could never be articulated; each man was doomed to stumble in his own darkness, if only because the stakes were so high.

"I had to keep my nose clean. They could have said, 'This goddam rebel down here is gonna turn his back on us. Why should we give this nigger-loving sonofabitch a break?' It took some subtle thinking on my part — I'm telling you [some] resolute facts here. But I had the ability to be patient. I was able to hold on almost with a religious fervor, but definitely subdued — I wasn't looking for no tall stumps to preach from. And I sensed in him the same kind of empathy. I don't think he was aware of my motivation for doing what I was trying to do — not consciously anyway — but *intuitively* he felt it. I never discussed it — I don't think it would have been very wise to talk about it, for me to say, 'Hey, man, we're going against —.' Or, 'We're trying to put pop music down and bring in black —.' The lack of prejudice on the part of Elvis Presley had to be one of the biggest things that ever could have happened to us, though. It was almost subversive, sneaking around through the music — but we hit things a little bit, don't you think? I went out into this no-man's-land, and I knocked the shit out of the color line."

Sam knew that he had found a kindred spirit in other ways as well. Over the course of the next month, as he worked at trying to set up the

Opry appearance, as he took around an acetate of the new single and encountered the same resistance in Nashville from old friends like WLAC DJ Gene Nobles and one-stop record distributors Randy Wood and Ernie Young, all strictly rhythm and blues men, he nevertheless knew that his instincts had not been wrong. Getting to know the boy a little better, getting him to open up a little more, having the chance to talk to him not just about music but about life and love and women, he sensed a potential that even he had not fully anticipated. "I was amazed. Here I am twelve years older than him, I'm thirty-one and he's nineteen, and I've been exposed to all kinds of music and lived through the damn Depression, and yet he had the most intuitive ability to hear songs without ever having to classify them, or *himself,* of anyone I've ever known outside of Jerry Lee Lewis and myself. It seemed like he had a photographic memory for every damn song he ever heard — and he was one of the most introspective human beings that I've ever met. You see, Elvis Presley knew what it was like to be poor, but that damn sure didn't make him prejudiced. *He didn't draw any lines.* And like [*Billboard* editor] Paul Ackerman said, you have to be an awful smart person or dumb as hell (and you *know* he wasn't dumb) to put out that kind of thinking."

> Elvis Presley, our homegrown hillbilly singer, is continuing his swift, steady stride toward national prominence in the rural rhythm field. Latest honor to come his way is as guest performer with the Louisiana Hayride, to be broadcast Saturday night over KWKH, Shreveport. Louisiana Hayride is about the second or third most popular hillbilly program on the air. The tops is Nashville's Grand Ole Opry, which never takes anyone but long-established stars in the country music field. But Presley has already appeared on the Grand Ole Opry — on October 2 — and neither customers nor fellow performers wanted him to quit. It is unprecedented for Grand Ole Opry to take a performer on the basis of a single record, which is what Presley had until two weeks ago.
>
> — *Memphis Commercial Appeal,* October 14, 1954

SAM CALLED PAPPY COVINGTON, the talent booker for the Hayride, on the Monday after the Opry appearance. They settled on a date less than two weeks away, both because that suited Sam's purposes and because Tillman Franks, who had made the contact for Pappy in the first place, had a chance to book his act, Jimmy and Johnny, into the Eddy County Barn Dance in Carlsbad, New Mexico, if he could find a replacement for them on the Hayride. Jimmy and Johnny had the number three hillbilly hit in the country on Chicago's Chess Records, and Tillman had been offered $500 by Carlsbad promoter Ray Schaffer (as opposed to $24 apiece, Hayride scale). As a result Tillman approached Hayride director Horace Logan about this singer he had heard on T. Tommy Cutrer's program on KCIJ. Tillman had thought the singer was black, and so had Horace, the flamboyant, pistol-toting MC of the Hayride, when Tillman played the record for him. But T. Tommy, who was playing the record only as a favor to Sam Phillips after Sam came through town a couple of months before (the two men knew each other from T.'s brief stint with WREC just after the war), quickly disabused Horace and Tillman of the notion: after all, hadn't Slim Whitman and Billy Walker shared the same stage with the boy in Memphis? And Tillman, a pepper pot of a man possessed of the greatest enthusiasm and love for the music (he had already managed, and lost, Webb Pierce and Bill Carlisle, helped guide Slim Whitman's career, and would go on to manage Johnny Horton while continuing to play bass on the Hayride), got Pappy Covington to take it from there.

The Hayride was a little over six years old at this point. It had been predated by a similar program, the KWKH Saturday Night Roundup, before the war and, as the *Commercial Appeal* stated, was probably the second most popular hillbilly program on the air, with a 50,000-watt clear-channel signal that rivaled the Opry's, reaching up to twenty-eight states, and a CBS hookup that enabled it to reach 198 stations for an hour the third Saturday of every month. The hallmark of the Hayride was innovation, and it was as the Opry's brash younger cousin that the Hayride really made its mark. Hank Williams, Kitty Wells, Webb Pierce, Faron Young, the Carlisles, David Houston, Jim Reeves, all debuted on the Hayride before eventually lighting out for Nashville, and under the leadership of Horace Logan it continued to be a haven for new talent, fast-paced variety, and new directions. The Hayride audiences in the thirty-eight-hundred-seat Municipal Auditorium showed the same kind of enthusiasm as the performers, and Logan placed microphones out among the crowd to register their reaction, whether to something that was going out over the air or to longtime announcer Ray Bartlett (who broadcast during the day as rhythm and blues DJ Groovey Boy) doing unrestrained somersaults and back flips onstage. Shreveport was a lively music town, just on the cusp of oil affluence and with the kind of unassuming racial mix (nothing like desegregation, of course, but with two populations living cheek by jowl, locked in an inescapable cultural alliance) that gave Memphis its own musical flavor. The Hayride had everything, in fact, except an aggressive booking agency to support its acts (Pappy Covington had the job only because he had a lease on the building) and record companies to sign them. This was the principal reason for the one-way migration to Nashville, but in the fall of 1954 it looked as if the supply of new talent might be inexhaustible, and the Hayride had grown accustomed to thumbing its nose at the Opry, which Horace Logan referred to frequently on the air as "the Tennessee branch of the Hayride."

Sam, Elvis, Scotty, and Bill set out for Shreveport, a good seven- or eight-hour ride from Memphis, not long after the boys got off work at their regular Friday-night gig at the Eagle's Nest. They missed the turnoff at Greenville, Mississippi, because Bill had everybody laughing so hard at one of his jokes, and then Scotty almost hit a team of mules as they struggled to make up the time. When they finally got to Shreveport, they checked into the Captain Shreve Hotel downtown — they got a big double room and a smaller adjoining room — and then they had to wait forever while Elvis combed his hair. Sam took the boys around to meet Pappy, who made them feel "like four hundred million dollars, just this kindly, fatherly old man who made you feel like you were the greatest thing that could ever walk into his office. I thought that was the best thing that could happen for these young men and even myself." From there he and Elvis went and paid their respects to T. Tommy, who had until recently been laid up from an automobile accident in which he had lost a leg, though he continued to broadcast from his bed at home. Elvis was wearing a typical black and pink outfit and, according to T. Tommy, "his hair was long and greasy and he didn't look clean. My wife commented afterwards, she said, 'That boy needs to wash his neck.' " T. Tommy, a highly astute, charming, and capable man who kept up a little band of his own at the time and went on to become a Tennessee state senator and a top Teamster official, still had doubts about how far this boy was going to go, and Elvis scarcely opened his mouth the whole time, but Sam was such a believer, and T. Tommy was nothing if not a pragmatist, so he figured, Well, let's just see where it goes.

From there Sam made the rest of his rounds. He stopped by Stan's Record Shop at 728 Texas Street, just around the corner from the auditorium, where they chatted with Stan Lewis, a prematurely white-haired twenty-seven-year-old veteran of the music business who had started out supplying five jukeboxes from the back of his parents' Italian grocery store, then purchased the little record shop that had been his supplier as a full-time business for his wife and himself. Stan's older brother, Ace, was the drummer in T. Tommy's band, alternating with their first cousin, D. J. Fontana, who played with Hoot and Curley on the Hayride as well, and Stan had known Sam Phillips ever since Sam first went into the business. As the principal one-stop and independent distributor in the area, he was without question interested in this new artist — but not *too* interested, because not only was the artist unknown, the genre was untried. Still, Stan had been instrumental in placing Jimmy and Johnny with Chess, previously a blues label almost exclusively, and he was now reaping the benefits of their success. He was *always* open to new talent, he told Sam; what was good for one was good for all.

Elvis meanwhile drifted over to the auditorium. It was bigger than the Opry, with spacious dressing rooms for the stars and a large common dressing room on the second floor. The folding chairs on the floor could be taken up for dances or basketball exhibitions, and the balcony curved around on either side of the stage, giving the room a natural echo. He walked out on the stage with his eyes fixed on the floor, looked up once briefly as if measuring the crowd, and then walked back to the hotel. The Negro shacks in the Bottoms, just a few blocks from the grand auditorium entrance, were not much different than the ramshackle structures of Shake Rag, in Tupelo, or the primitive shotguns of South Memphis; Shreveport's bustling downtown just a couple of blocks away was busy and full of life, and when he ran into Scotty and Bill in the hotel coffee shop, Bill already had his eye on a pretty waitress. . . .

When he arrived back at the auditorium that night, it was completely different, transformed by the presence not just of an audience and musicians in colorful western outfits but by the almost palpable anticipation that something was going to happen. He was wearing a pink jacket, white pants, a black shirt, a brightly colored clip-on bow tie, and the kind of two-tone shoes that were known as corespondent shoes, because they were the kind that a snappy salesman or a corespondent in a divorce case might be expected to wear. Scotty and Bill were wearing matching western shirts with decorative bibs and dark ties. Bill's battered bass looked as if it were held together with baling wire, Elvis cradled his child-size guitar, and only Scotty's handsome Gibson ES 295 lent a touch of professional class to the trio. But everyone was taken with the boy. Tillman Franks, who had dispatched Jimmy and Johnny to Carlsbad but remained behind to play bass in the house band, was almost bouncing with anticipation. Pappy Covington greeted Sam and the boys warmly, as if he hadn't seen them in months. Even Horace Logan, renowned not just for his impresario's instincts but for his frosty air of self-congratulation, seemed to take to the boy — there was something about him that brought out almost a protective quality, even in seasoned professionals.

Sam left to take his seat in the audience. Although he had put up a brave front all day, he really didn't know how it was going to come out, and he felt like he should do his best to at least *try* to cue up a sympathetic response from the crowd. He had to admit that he was worried; the boy looked as if he was scared to death, and even though you could rationalize that they were all experienced veterans by now — all those nights at the Eagle's Nest, the triumph at Overton Park, and of course their Opry appearance — in another way everyone knew that this could be the end of the line.

Horace Logan was out onstage. "Is there anyone from Mississippi? Anyone from Arkansas? Let's hear it from the folks from Oklahoma. Now who here's from Louisiana? Now how many of y'all are from the great state of Texas?" A mighty roar went up as the Western Union clock on the wall registered 8:00 P.M. precisely and the band struck up the familiar Hayride theme, based on the old Negro "minstrel" song, "Raise a Ruckus Tonight." "Come along, everybody come along," the audience all joined in, "while the moon is shining bright / We're going to have a wonderful time / At the Louisiana Hayride tonight."

A tall, skinny singer from Shreveport with a television show in Monroe sidled up to the new sensation — he was barely twenty himself and had been knocked out by Elvis Presley ever since hearing the first record at Jiffy Fowler's Twin City Amusements, a jukebox operation in West Monroe. "I said, 'Hello, Elvis, my name is Merle Kilgore.' He turned around and said, 'Oh, you worked with Hank Williams.' I said, 'Yeah.' He said, 'You wrote "More and More" [a number-one hit for Webb Pierce in the fall of 1954]!' I said, 'Yeah.' He said, 'I want to meet Tibby Edwards.' It was the first thing he said to me. Tibby recorded for Mercury, and he was a star. I said, 'He's my buddy, we room together here in Shreveport.' And I went and got Tibby and introduced him to Elvis. That's how we got to be friends."

JUST A FEW WEEKS AGO," intoned announcer Frank Page's impressively measured radio voice, "a young man from Memphis, Tennessee, recorded a song on the Sun label, and in just a matter of a few weeks that record has skyrocketed right up the charts. It's really doing good all over the country. He's only nineteen years old. He has a new, distinctive style. Elvis Presley. Let's give him a nice hand . . . Elvis, how are you this evening?"

"Just fine, how are you, sir?"

"You all geared up with your band —"

"I'm all geared up!"

"To let us hear your songs?"

"Well, I'd like to say how happy we are to be out here. It's a real honor for us to hav — get a chance to appear on the Louisiana Hayride. And we're going to do a song for you — You got anything else to say, sir?"

"No, I'm ready."

"We're gonna do a song for you we got on the Sun record, it goes something like this . . ." And with that he launched into the first side of his first Sun single.

The cheers that went up from the audience were encouraged by Frank Page and Horace Logan as they stood to the side of the Lucky Strike backdrop. The microphones hanging out over the floor were turned up when Scotty took a somewhat uncertain solo, and the audience politely responded. Elvis was visibly nervous, his knees were practically knocking together, and the jackknife action of his legs was about all, Sam Phillips was convinced, that was preventing him from blowing his brains out. The reaction was not all that different from the one he had gotten on the Opry — he was so ill at ease it was hard for the audience to really like him, even though it was clear to Sam that they might want to do just that,

that they were ready, like Memphis audiences, to respond to the boy's *charm.*

In between shows he went backstage to talk to Elvis. Merle Kilgore noticed them off in a corner huddled together as Sam exhorted Elvis to just relax: the people were there to see him, just let them see what you got, put on your kind of show, if it didn't work, well, the hell with it, at least we can say we tried. Elvis, Merle noted, looked like he was scared stiff, but then Sam Phillips went to take his seat among the audience, after a little while the trio came out to do their two numbers, and this time it was entirely different. Much of the younger audience from the first show had stayed for the second, Tillman Franks observed, and now they were ready for what the new singer had to offer. For Sam it was a moment never to be forgotten.

"There was a college up in Texarkana where Elvis' records had gotten hot, and some of the young people from that college had turned up. Well, when he got through that first number, they were on their feet — and not just them either. Some big fat lady — I mean, it took an effort for her to get up, and she got up and didn't stop talking, right in the middle of the next number, she didn't know who I was, she just said, 'Man, have you ever heard anything that good?' And, honestly, the tonal impact couldn't have competed with the Maddox Brothers and Rose, or the Carlisles, who had been on the week before — I mean, they were *pros.* But Elvis had this factor of communication, I think the audience saw in him the desire to please, he had that little innocence about him, and yet he had something about him that was almost impudent in a way, that was his crutch. He certainly didn't mean to be impudent, but he had enough of that along with what he could convey that was just beautiful and lovely — and I'm not talking about his physical beauty, because he didn't look that pretty then or that good-looking, by conventional standards he should have been thrown off that stage. But I calculated that stuff in my mind: are they going to resent him with his long sideburns — that could be a plus or a minus. But when he came through like he did, it was neither. *He stood on his own.*"

He did the same two numbers that he had for the first show — there were no encores, because Mr. Logan was very strict about encores, you didn't take one unless there was a genuine eruption of the sort that overwhelmed Hank Williams when he sang "Lovesick Blues" seven times in a row and could have kept going all night. For Elvis and Scotty and Bill it wasn't anything like that, but all three grew visibly more confident, and Elvis, for all the terror that had just engulfed him, responded warmly to the crowd's enthusiasm for him. Some of the Hayride veterans, like twenty-seven-year-old Jimmy "C" Newman, who had just had his first big hit on Randy Wood's Dot label with "Cry, Cry Darling," regarded the proceedings with a certain amount of suspicion. "I'd never seen anything like it before. Here comes this guy, I guess you could almost call him an amateur, rings of dirt on his neck, but he had it all right from the start. He didn't work into it, he just knew what he was going to do. We'd just stand in the wings and shake our heads. 'It can't be, it can't last, it's got to be a fad.' "

"I think he scared them a little [in the first show]," said Merle Kilgore. "He was really on the toes of his feet singing. I think they thought he was going to jump off the stage. But when he came back out, he destroyed them — by now they knew he wasn't going to jump off the stage and beat them, and they absolutely exploded."

"What he did," said Jimmy "C" Newman, "was he changed it all around. After that we had to go to Texas to work, there wasn't any work anywhere else, because all they wanted was someone to imitate Elvis, to jump up and down on the stage and make a fool of themselves. It was embarrassing to me to see it — Elvis could do it, but few others could."

IN THE OCTOBER 16 issue of *Billboard,* the same date as the first Hayride appearance, there was a small item in Bill Sachs' "Folk Talent and Tunes" announcing that "Bob Neal of WMPS, Memphis, is planning fall tours with Elvis Presley, the Louvin Brothers, and J.E. and Maxine Brown." Neal, who had not had a great deal of personal contact with Elvis since the Overton Park show, in July, had been out to see the trio several times at the Eagle's Nest and was impressed with their potential. Though he had never been involved in management, he had been booking shows in and around Memphis for the last five years, doing local promotion for Opry and Hayride packages and promoting little shows of his own in Arkansas and Mississippi, anywhere, in fact, within the two-hundred-mile radius of the WMPS broadcast signal. He publicized the shows, of course, on his own popular early-morning program, which was on from 5:00 to 8:00, as well as the *High Noon Round-Up,* featuring the

Blackwood Brothers, Eddie Hill, and other hillbilly entertainment, which Elvis had frequently attended. Neal called Sam Phillips and asked if the group had any representation. Sam said not really — Scotty was handling management for the time being, just taking care of things more or less on an interim basis — and the two men agreed that maybe it would be worth having Bob try some bookings, seeing how it worked out. Bob spoke to Elvis, and the boy seemed agreeable, though he certainly didn't have much to say. And Scotty didn't appear to have any objections; from all that Neal could see, he simply wanted to go back to being a musician. So Bob went ahead and set up some civic club and schoolhouse bookings for November and early December — in towns like Bruce and Iuka, Mississippi; Helena and Leechville, Arkansas — places to which he had brought his shows many times in the past, where folks knew him and enjoyed his ukelele playing and laughed in recognition of his comfortable, carefully honed cornpone humor.

On October 20 the *Press-Scimitar* proudly announced under the headline "Elvis Presley Clicks": "Elvis Presley, Memphis' swift-rising young hillbilly singing star, is now a regular member of the Louisiana Hayride Show. . . . The Hayride specializes in picking promising young rural rhythm talent — and it took just one guest appearance last Saturday for the young Memphian to become a regular." The announcement was somewhat premature (Sam was still working out an arrangement with Pappy Covington and Horace Logan), but Elvis promptly quit his job, and Scotty and Bill quit theirs, too. They did so with the bravest of intentions, but with not a little trepidation, either. "I hated to let him go," said Mr. Tipler, who with his wife continued to go out to the Eagle's Nest, "[but] I could see that he was going places. I just told him, 'I understand that you can't work and stay out all night, too.' I've always been one that if somebody can benefit their self, make more of themselves, I don't never ask them to stay." Vernon, according to Elvis, took a somewhat less sanguine view. "My daddy had seen a lot of people who played guitars and stuff and didn't work, so he said: 'You should make up your mind either about being an electrician or playing a guitar. I never saw a guitar player that was worth a damn.' "

He missed the Hayride for the next two weeks. There had been nothing finalized by the twenty-third, and they were booked at the Eagle's Nest the following weekend, so they hung around Memphis, practiced at Scotty's house, and basked in all the attention that was coming their way.

They felt like great things were about to happen, if they could just get back to Shreveport. Tillman Franks had promised them work, Pappy Covington had assured them that he could get them gigs through the little booking agency that he operated out of the Hayride offices — they were just itching to get on with their new life. But in the meantime the kids would all be out at Clearpool the weekend of October 29–30 — they were playing both Friday and Saturday nights — and it would serve as something of a Memphis send-off.

That Friday night Bob Neal brought a visitor out to the club. Oscar Davis, known as the Baron of the Box Office, was a flamboyant fifty-year-old veteran of the vaudeville, carnival, and country circuits. With his jaunty boutonniere and elegant cigarette holder, his drawling Boston accent and his habit of fixing his listener in his gaze and focusing all of his considerable charm upon him or her, he could boast truthfully that he had spent more money than many millionaires had ever made, which was one reason that he was perennially broke. A true bon vivant, he lived up to the advertising slogan he used for every show that he promoted: DON'T YOU DARE MISS IT!

That was how he happened to be in Memphis at this particular juncture. Oscar had worked promotions on his own for years, he had managed and been associated with stars from Hank Williams to Roy Acuff to Ernest Tubb and Minnie Pearl, and he had established a model for the modern country music promoter, but because of his impecunious ways, he occasionally found himself in the employ of one or another of his protégés. On this trip to Memphis he had been doing advance work for "Colonel" Tom Parker, whom Bob Neal had originally met some years before in connection with an Eddy Arnold show at Russwood Park that Neal had emceed. The Colonel had recently split with Arnold, whom he had guided to unsurpassed heights in the country music field, over "personal differences" and a question of artistic direction. Parker had put Eddy Arnold in pictures; he had hooked him up with Abe Lastfogel, president of the William Morris Agency, and booked him into Las Vegas; he had carefully supervised every last detail of Arnold's career. But Arnold wanted to go into television, and he wanted to spend his own, and the Colonel's, money. The result was that they went their separate ways, a bitter blow to Tom Parker's pride but one that he was well on his way to overcoming with his recent signing of country's new number-one star, Hank Snow, to a limited partnership agreement. Part of the terms of his severance with Arnold were that he would continue to book Arnold on a regional basis, and to that end he had set up a ten-day tour of the mid South in the fall of 1954. Memphis was the fifth date on that tour.

In the course of his Memphis travels, Oscar stopped by the WMPS studio to cut some spots for the show that afternoon and, as was his wont, asked Bob Neal what was going on around town. Neal, who had his finger in a number of pies, gave him a rapid rundown and then happened to mention this young singer, Elvis Presley, with whom he had an upcoming tour. Oscar had heard of Elvis, there was quite a stir about the boy, and he wondered if there might not be a chance to see the kid — maybe he or Tom could do something for him. As a matter of fact, said Neal, the boy happened to be playing out at the Eagle's Nest that night: why didn't they just drive out together and catch the show?

Elvis, Scotty, and Bill were thrilled to meet this larger-than-life character with his stories of the big time, the glamorous world that they could only read about in fan magazines like *Country Song Roundup* and *Country & Western Jamboree.* Davis cut quite a figure in the rough-and-tumble atmosphere of the club, and when he invited Elvis to stop by the show at Ellis Auditorium on Sunday — he would be back in town by then after traveling to Nashville the next day and advancing the upcoming Monday and Tuesday shows there — Elvis jumped at the chance. Maybe, Mr. Davis suggested, he would even be able to introduce Elvis to Eddy Arnold, who was always interested in new talent.

That Sunday at 6:00 P.M. Elvis walked up the familiar steps of the entrance to Ellis Auditorium. The show included Minnie Pearl, guitar virtuoso Hank Garland, local hillbilly star Eddie Hill, and the singing group the Jordanaires, not to mention Robert Powers, the World's Smallest Hillbilly Singer. The man at the box office recognized him immediately and gave him the tickets that had been left in his name, and he attracted a good deal of attention himself sitting up front in his pink shirt and black pants and sharp white shoes. Eddy sang "Don't Rob Another Man's Castle," "I'll Hold You in My Heart," "Any Time," and "I Really Don't Want to Know" (his latest number-one hit), all in that effortlessly flowing voice, with the smooth quartet backing of the Jordanaires.

After the show was over, Bob Neal found Elvis and took him backstage, where he wandered around the unfamiliar setting in a kind of daze. Oscar Davis came over and seemed genuinely pleased to see him; he introduced him to Eddy and to Hoyt Hawkins of the Jordanaires. He had really enjoyed the group's singing, Elvis mumbled with his eyes on the floor. Well, they had enjoyed *his* singing, too, Hoyt said. They had heard his record on the radio when they were out in California with Eddy. He sounded like a quartet singer to them. Elvis blushed and fidgeted with his hands. If he ever got to the point where he had the kind of success that Eddy Arnold had, he said, he would like to get a group like the Jordanaires to sing with him; if he ever achieved that kind of success he would like them to sing behind him on record — did Hoyt think that was possible? Hoyt said he was sure that it was; they did lots of background work in Nashville, it was more and more popular nowadays — they'd love to work with him someday. Oscar seemed anxious for them to go. There was a little coffee shop across the street, maybe he and Elvis and Bob Neal could go over there and have a Coke or a cup of coffee. A heavyset man in a rumpled, ready-made suit with a cigar stuck in his mouth eyed them briefly from across the room, then turned his attention elsewhere. Who was that? Elvis asked Oscar as they exited the backstage area. That, said Oscar, with a respectful but somewhat impatient gesture, was Colonel Parker.

THE FOLLOWING SATURDAY NIGHT he signed a standard union contract with the Hayride for a period of one year. He would receive $18 per appearance as leader; Scotty and Bill would get $12 apiece. And they were permitted to miss five dates a year for outside bookings, though Mr. Logan assured him that informal arrangements could be made if other circumstances arose. Vernon and Gladys accompanied him to Shreveport to sign the contract, and they all stayed at the Captain Shreve Hotel.

That same week, with "Good Rockin' Tonight" number three on the Memphis charts and the first single still showing up on territorial charts throughout the South, *Billboard* ran a review of the new single, once again in the "Spotlight" section. "Elvis Presley," it said, "proves again that he is a sock new singer with his performances on these two oldies. His style is both country and r.&b. and he can appeal to pop." Sam Phillips was delighted. It wasn't simply that this gave him further ammunition in his crusade — it was becoming increasingly clear that there was a groundswell building which distributors and jukebox operators and one-stops could ignore only at their peril. Bill Haley had a couple of records out there that proved the same damn point, and every day Sam was seeing new evidence of it in the country boys who were showing up on his doorstep because they were hearing something in the music that, without being able to put a tag on it, they had recognized all along. And Sam *knew* that a day was coming, he knew as sure as he was born that a day was coming when this music would prevail, he didn't need any damn industry backslapping to convince him of it — but this was *Billboard,* after all, this was Paul Ackerman, a man whom he had yet to meet but for whom he had the deepest respect, and he was hearing the same thing in the music that Sam Phillips was.

Gladys dutifully pasted the review in the scrapbook she was keeping — she couldn't believe how rapidly it was filling up. She and Dixie talked excitedly about his new "career." They chewed over every scrap of information that either of them could come up with, it didn't seem possible somehow that all of this could be happening, and happening so fast — you should have seen the young people in Shreveport, she told Dixie excitedly, they practically went crazy over him, he had to come back and do an encore both shows. And the hotel was so nice, too. . . .

DIXIE WAS WORRIED about Elvis. When he was gone, she worried about him, she prayed for his success and she prayed that the success wouldn't change him. When he was at home, she worried that things were in fact changing, that where just three months ago the main thing on both their minds was marriage and whether they would have the strength to wait, now it seemed his mind was always somewhere else. She wondered if it was on *someone else,* but she didn't think so, she was sure not, it was just that he was always so distracted, and everywhere he went he was recognized, some of the girls were almost shameless the way they called attention to themselves, and he really didn't seem to mind. They stopped by the Chisca to visit with Dewey while he did his radio show, and Elvis went down there sometimes by himself. She didn't know what exactly they did afterward: sometimes they played pool, sometimes they just watched movies in Dewey's garage, and she knew that they went down on Beale, because he told her about meeting B. B. King and about some of the colorful clubs and club owners that he had run into. He seemed really excited about it — he had seen a nattily dressed Lowell Fulson at the Club Handy, and he sang her some of Fulson's brand-new number, "Reconsider Baby," which she might have heard if there was still time to listen to records at Charlie's; he described how Calvin Newborn did the splits while he was playing the guitar at the Flamingo Lounge. The pure enthusiasm, the wide-eyed fascination, the hunger for new experience, were all very much part of the boy she knew, but there was something different about him, too, she knew it and Mrs. Presley did also, but neither one of them wanted to confess it to the other, so they skirted the issue and merely expressed their concern that the boys would drive carefully.

Toward the end of football season Elvis drove by Humes just as the football team was heading out to Bartlett to play a game. One of the star players, Red West, who had been on the team as a freshman when Elvis had tried out junior year, spotted him just as the team was getting on the bus and called out to him. "Congratulations," he said when Elvis got out of his old Lincoln coupe and ambled over. He invited Elvis to come watch the game, so Elvis followed the bus out to Bartlett and, when the game was over, asked Red if he wouldn't like to come out to a show he was doing that weekend, and for the rest of the school year Red accompanied him off and on to shows that were booked on the weekends.

He liked having Red around, it made him feel more comfortable, and Red got along okay with Scotty and Bill, but still he felt strange in Memphis, he felt almost as if people were making more of him than he deserved, as if he were onstage all the time and never quite at ease, never able to be entirely himself. He was becoming a hometown celebrity of sorts and didn't know how to act. On November 8 they played out at Memphis State for a blood drive, and he had his picture taken with Mayor Tobey. "He would look in the papers," said Guy Lansky, "he was worried about what they said about him." Ronnie Smith recalled running into Elvis at WHHM one day, "and he said, 'Come on, Ron, I'll show you my new Cadillac.' We got in the elevator and came back down and went around the parking lot and kept walking until we was in front of the telephone company. That was where his old Lincoln was parked!" Sometimes old friends passed him on the street — he didn't know if they were laughing at him, or if it was because they disapproved, or if they thought he felt somehow that he was above them now.

In Shreveport it was different. It was as if he were a different person; he could create a whole new image for himself and never have anyone bring up the old one. In Shreveport the girls were falling all over themselves to get to him. When he and Scotty and Bill returned to Shreveport the week after Gladys and Vernon came down, they holed up at the Al-Ida Motel in Bossier City, across the river, and the girls started showing up almost as soon as they arrived, as if they sensed his presence. For a kid who had spent scarcely a night away from home in his nineteen years, it was like being away at summer camp: he had always loved flirting with the girls, he loved playing with them and teasing them, but now there was no one around to see that it didn't go too far. And they didn't seem too concerned about it either. In between shows at the auditorium he would peek out from behind the curtain, then, when he spotted someone that he liked, swagger over to the concession stand, place his arm over her shoulder, and drape his other arm around someone else, acting almost like he was drunk, even though everyone knew he didn't drink.

"He was a typical teenager," said Scotty. "Kind of wild, but more like in a mischievous kind of way. He loved pranks and practical jokes. We had to practically beat him with a stick to get him out of bed. His parents were very protective. His mama would corner me and say, 'Take care of my boy. Make sure he eats. Make sure he —' You know, whatever. Typical mother stuff. But it always came down to me. He didn't seem to mind; there was nothing phony about it, he truly loved his mother. He was just a typical coddled son, that's about all you can say, very shy — he was more comfortable just sitting there with a guitar than trying to talk to you. Bill and I would usually be the ones to do most of the talking, and yet he could be very extroverted, too. You know, I'd been all over and he'd never been outside the city limits. He watched and he learned, I never said anything to him because we communicated pretty much without talking anyway — but most of what he didn't know, it was just that nobody had ever told him. When he got to Shreveport, he was just running around, I think, sowing his wild oats."

With Merle Kilgore he would hang out at Murrell's Cafe, on Market Street, opposite the Hayride offices. They would sit for hours sometimes, eating hamburgers and talking about music and eyeing the girls. "He reminded me of Hank Williams," said Merle, who as a fourteen-year-old had met Williams and whose admiration for his idol continued to know no bounds. "Something in his eyes. He'd ask you a question, and his eyes would be asking you another question. It was that look. He'd wait for the answer, but his eyes would be asking the question. I'd only seen that in Hank and Elvis." Sometimes they would go down to the bus station to play pinball with Tibby Edwards or stop by Stan's Record Shop to thumb through the rhythm and blues racks. You ate when you wanted, you slept when you wanted, the girls came running after you — it was a teenager's dream. Every night he called home and spoke to his mother; frequently he called Dixie to express his undying love. But then he was free to do whatever he wanted.

They worked one night at the Lake Cliff Club, where Hoot and Curley played ordinarily. Elvis was attracted to Hoot's pretty daughter, Mary Alice, but he was kind of nervous about asking Hoot, the steel player on Slim Whitman's "Indian Love Call," for permission to take her out. The gig at the Lake Cliff turned into something of a joke. Hoot and Curley had been playing there for six years, and they had their following, but unfortunately their following hadn't been alerted to the fact that they wouldn't be playing at the Lake Cliff that night, and if they didn't throw things, they did practically everything but. By the end of the first set the club had just about emptied out, and it was, in Scotty's assessment, "a complete bust."

On the basis of Tillman Franks' enthusiasm, and his promise of work, they settled in at the Al-Ida for what was intended to be a two-week period in the middle of November, only to discover that Tillman, who had suddenly become persona non grata at the Hayride, couldn't deliver. Just how panicked they must have felt can be deduced from Scotty's vivid memories of being "marooned" in Shreveport, stranded without even the money to pay their hotel bill or buy enough gas to get back to Memphis. In fact they were not stranded for long, and they may simply have spent all their money in expectation of making more. In any case, within days Pappy Covington had work for them in Gladewater, Texas, some sixty miles west of Shreveport.

Pappy called Tom Perryman, a young go-getter who had made his mark in Gladewater at radio station KSIJ, where he had been working since 1949. In addition to deejaying, he had served as engineer, newsman, sports announcer, sales manager, program director, and general manager at various times and also started a local talent show, which he broadcast first from the studio, then, as it grew, from the local community center and the three-hundred-seat movie theater in town. Eventually he put the show on the road, where it played schoolhouses and high school gymnasiums in towns throughout the outlying area. Perryman also booked Hayride shows and occasionally put recording artists with his traveling talent show as a kind of extra draw, which was how he met Jim Reeves, then a DJ in Henderson, Texas, whom he later came to manage and partner in various enterprises. He began to book some of these single artists into clubs and honky-tonks like the Reo Palm Isle in Longview and in general was one of the busiest promoters in Northeast Texas, a territory that appeared to be as music-mad as Memphis or any other region in the country. He had been playing "Blue Moon of Kentucky" since it first came out, "because of the unique arrangement. That sound was just something you never heard." So he was not completely at a loss when Pappy Covington, with whom he had already booked quite a number of shows, called on a Monday morning and wondered "if I had a place where I could put an act right quick.

"He said, 'There are some boys down here that are broke, they don't have the money to get back to Memphis.' Well, I had a friend that had a honky-tonk right out on the Tyler Highway. So I said, 'Yeah, I guess so,' and I called this buddy of mine, and he said, 'Yeah, I'm not doing anything, come on out. Who are they?' I said it was this new act out of Memphis called Elvis Presley. So sure enough, I played that record a lot the next two or three days and come Friday night, here they come. Just Elvis and Scotty and Bill in a Chevrolet with that big old bass on top of the car.

"The way it would work, I would book the show, the club owner would take the bar, and I would take the money off the door. My wife, Billie, would usually work the door. Then we would pay the expenses of the gig, if you had to pay a sponsor or what little advertising there might be. Most of the advertising was done on my [radio] show, and we'd do a live show from the studio, too, promoting that night's performance. Then I would take fifteen percent of the gross, and what was left would go to the act. I never will forget: that first night we took in a total of ninety dollars. That was all we had. Of course I didn't take any of it. I knew those boys needed the money, so I gave them all of it.

"You know, he was really a natural. When Elvis was performing, everyone had the same basic reaction. It was almost spontaneous. It reminded me of the early days, of where I was raised in East Texas and going to these 'Holy Roller' Brush Arbor meetings: seeing these people get religion. I said, 'Man, that's something.' You'd see it in the later years with the big sound systems and the lights, but Elvis could do it if there wasn't but ten people [in the room]. He never realized what he had till later years. He said, 'Man, this sure is a good crowd in this part of the country. Are they always that way?' I said, 'No, man. They never seen anything like you.' Nobody had.

"It won't happen again in this generation or the next, I don't believe. He just came along at the right time with the right thing. Because it was after the war. People my age grew up with the big band music in the forties. But those kids, the generation that were children during the war, they had no music to identify with, they were looking for something they could identify with, and this new sound was a combination of it all."

On Thursday, November 25, Elvis was booked into Houston for the first time, at the Houston Hoedown, where he was listed way down on the bill but made a considerable impression on the MC for the popular live broadcast, KNUZ's Biff Collie, who also happened to have a partnership in the club. Collie, a native of San Antonio and a ten-year broadcast veteran at the age of twenty-eight, was a highly influential figure in radio and in fact the person who had originally gotten T. Tommy Cutrer his job in Shreveport. It was through T. Tommy and Tillman Franks, with whom Biff also went way back, that Biff first heard of Elvis Presley. In fact, he had stopped off in Memphis with Tillman just the week before to see him perform, after first picking up Tillman in Shreveport on the way to the third annual Country Music Disc Jockey convention in Nashville, which Biff had had a considerable hand in organizing. Tillman's act, Jimmy and Johnny, was booked into the Eagle's Nest on Wednesday night with this new Memphis "phenom" that Biff had been hearing so much about, so he and Tillman stopped by the club.

Biff was not that impressed. The boy was "different" enough but not really "sensational"; if anything, Jimmy and Johnny took the show. At the same time he was intrigued by a combination of elements that he saw coming together in one package for the first time — the boy seemed like "a Mississippi gospel singer singing black music, that's about as real as I could figure." On the basis of that observation, not to mention Tillman's unflagging enthusiasm and the recommendation of Bob Neal, whom he saw out at the club that night and with whom he spent time at the convention, he was happy to book him on the Hoedown for $150, and he started playing Elvis Presley records as soon as he got back to Houston.

The reaction to Elvis' Hoedown appearance was good, and he was held over "by popular demand" for two additional nights, but to Biff the nature of his act was about the same as what he had observed in Memphis. The repertoire was extremely limited, and the boy was obviously just learning the ropes, though by now Biff Collie was beginning to see the light, even if he wasn't sure exactly why. "I said, 'Don't you do any slow songs?' He said, 'I don't . . . I don't . . . I like to do these things because they make me feel good, you know.' I said, 'Yeah, they like this stuff that you are doing pretty good, it seems like, but this rhythm and blues stuff is not going to stay forever. You really need to sing some slow songs.' His reaction was, 'I don't like . . . I don't . . . I just like to sing . . . You know, they make me feel good.'

"That night after we were through we went across the street to Stuart's Drive Inn restaurant, and we sat down at a booth and ordered something, and I saw Sonny Stuart come through. His dad was the boss, and he was learning the business at the time. And I winked at him and said, 'Just for fun, get the girl upstairs on the PA to page Elvis Presley.' He said, 'How do you spell that?' And they did it three or four times over a period of fifteen minutes, and, obviously, nothing happened. Nothing at all. And I remember telling Elvis that night, 'One of these days you'll have to have somebody to keep you from getting run over.' And that was — again, it was not because of what he had done there. I just felt like something was going to happen."

The next day Elvis sent a telegram home from Houston. "HI BABIES," it read. "HERE'S THE MONEY TO PAY THE BILLS. DON'T TELL NO ONE HOW MUCH I SENT I WILL SEND MORE NEXT WEEK. THERE IS A CARD IN THE MAIL. LOVE ELVIS."

MEANWHILE, Bob Neal was looking on his new project with increasing enthusiasm; the idea of becoming Elvis Presley's full-fledged manager was beginning to appeal to him more and more. The few dates that they had done together only confirmed his view of the boy's potential. So did the reports that kept coming in from Louisiana and East Texas. And while they had not yet signed any official papers, there was no question in his mind that this was an experiment that could fail only if he chose to walk away from it. Here at last was an opportunity to get in on the ground floor of something instead of just signing on to another Nashville package promotion; it could be a chance of going all the way to the top.

Because that was where Bob Neal quickly judged this kid was heading.

Not much older than Bob's oldest boy, Sonny, and, seemingly, without the ability to articulate what it was he was really looking for, the kid seemed to possess as unerring an instinct for how to connect with an audience — as well as the fierce drive and determination to accomplish it — as Neal had seen in his dozen years in radio and four or five years of serious promotion. In the parts of Mississippi and Arkansas where the Hayride signal came in strongest, he seemed to practically explode, coming out onstage like a sprinter out of the starting blocks, with an energy and a crackling enthusiasm that could barely be contained. In places where he was less well known, on the other hand, "they didn't know exactly how to take him, they just didn't know what to do. Sometimes they were a very quiet audience. A lot of them would come out to the shows because they had been followers of my radio show, and it was a little frustrating to Elvis sometimes. They would gather around to ask me about my family and my kids and so forth, and they would more or less ignore Elvis. [But] the more they sat on their hands, the harder he worked to break them up. His show developed in that sometimes if he was onstage and just through some accidental movement there would be a big scream or reaction, he would automatically remember. On the other hand, if he devised something and got a dead reaction, he would never worry about it, he would drop it and go on to something else. It was just as automatic as breathing to him."

Nearly as important as this natural gift, though, were the two men who made up the remaining two thirds of the trio. They may not have been the best musicians in the world, but Elvis felt perfectly at ease with them, and in those rare instances when his own instincts failed, Bill's always took over. These were *country* audiences they were playing for, and Bill's rough-hewn humor and memory for old Opry routines, in addition to a thoroughly ingratiating personality, always stood him in good stead. Sometimes Bill would come out of the audience dressed like a hobo and yelling, "Wait a minute, I want to play with y'all. I can play just as good as you can!" Other times he might brandish an oversize pair of bloomers that Bobbie and Evelyn had bought for the act or black out his front teeth or tell one of the old jokes about Rotterdam ("Rotterdam socks off!" was the punch line), and the audience always went crazy when he rode that bass, egging Elvis on with both arms uplifted and the bass between his legs like a Brahma bull. He could save Elvis, too, if the boy got too far out on a limb or misjudged the audience for its tolerance of his novelty, vulgarity, or simply his bad jokes. "On some of the early shows," said Scotty, whose unassailable calm and ability to deal with any crisis that came up were just as integral a part of the whole experience, "if it hadn't been for Bill, we would have fallen flat on our face. Because Elvis was such an oddity, if you will, when people first saw him, they were practically in shock. But Bill's antics loosened them up."

Admission, generally, was $1 for adults, 50 cents for children, with 10 percent retained for expenses and 15 percent taken off the top, after the local sponsor or Kiwanis Club had been paid. Sometimes there might be as much as $300 to divide, with $45 going to Bob and the rest split 50–25–25 between Elvis, Scotty, and Bill. Just as often there was less, but one or two commissions of $25 to $45 a week were a nice supplement to a comfortable DJ's salary, and if you added up all the little side benefits that a popular radio personality was heir to, it didn't make for a bad living.

There were any number of other signs that business was likely to pick up in the near future. *Billboard* magazine noted that the records were still ping-ponging around on the charts (the week of November 17, "Blue Moon of Kentucky" was number five in Memphis and "Good Rockin' Tonight" number eight), while in a DJ poll Elvis Presley was named eighth Most Promising C&W Artist behind Tommy Collins, Justin Tubb, Jimmy and Johnny, the Browns, and Jimmy Newman, among others. Meanwhile Bob Neal announced his own third annual listeners' poll, which had Elvis in tenth position behind such country stalwarts as Webb Pierce, Faron Young, Ray Price, Hank Snow, and Kitty Wells. The December 11 issue of *Billboard* reported in its "Folk Talent and Tunes" column that "the hottest piece of merchandise on the . . . Louisiana Hayride at the moment is Elvis Presley, the youngster with the hillbilly blues beat," while Marty Robbins recorded a creditable country version of "That's All Right" for Columbia on December 7.

What struck Neal most of all, though, was the boy's ambition, something he might have missed altogether if it hadn't been for his wife. Sometimes coming back from the shows, on the drive home to Memphis, Elvis would ride with Bob and Helen, so that Bob, who had his 5:00 A.M. show coming up practically as soon as they got into town, could catch some sleep. Elvis would talk to Helen then in a way that he didn't seem able to talk to Bob, or even to Scotty and Bill — he would reveal himself in fragments that Neal would catch in moments between wakefulness and sleep or as Helen would describe it to him afterward. "He would talk about his aspirations and plans," Neal told Elvis biographer Jerry Hopkins. "Helen said he talked not in terms of being a moderate success; his ambition was to be big in movies and so forth. He'd ask her, did she think he could make it, and her response — well, she was a believer, too — she felt that he could go as far as he wanted to. From the very first he had great ambitions to be nothing in the ordinary, but just to go all the way with it."

DIXIE HOPED, with Christmas coming, that Elvis would be able to spend a little more time at home. This would be their first Christmas together, and she really wanted to make it special. When he got back from Texas, he had brought her something in anticipation of Christmas, a pair of shorts and a sleeveless blouse in pale pink. He wanted her to try it on right away, and she was excited, too, because she loved the outfit, but she loved his enthusiasm about it even more. They had never been much for gift giving — they just didn't have the money. But she knew that Christmas this year was going to be different.

Elvis had recently given himself a present, a 1942 Martin guitar that he had bought for $175 from the O. K. Houck Company on Union. He was a little self-conscious about it; it seemed kind of extravagant to pay so much money, but this was the way he now made his living, he told himself, and he never hesitated, except when the man threw his old guitar in the trash. "The man gave me eight dollars on the trade-in," he told anyone who would listen afterward, still a little openmouthed with disbelief. "Shucks, it still played good." He had his first name spelled out in black metallic letters across the blond wood of the D-18, just as he had on his old guitar. It came out smartly on a diagonal below the fret board, and the guitar looked a lot more professional than his other one, but, Elvis joked, he frailed away at it just the same.

They went by Humes for the Christmas show, and all the teachers and kids flocked around, but some of them acted stuck-up, like they thought he was going to act stuck-up first, which didn't seem right at all. They went by Scotty's to rehearse for a session that they managed to get in not long before Christmas. First they did an old blues number that had become a western swing standard in different versions by Bob Wills and his brothers, Billy Jack and Johnnie Lee, over the years. The new version opened up in a beautiful, slow, lilting blues tempo that almost seemed to tease the listener, until Elvis announced, with just a trace of amusement in his voice, "Hold it, fellas, that don't move me. Let's get real, real gone for a change." And plunged into what became known as "Milkcow Blues Boogie." The other side was a new song by a Covington, Tennessee, theater manager named Jack Sallee, whom Sam had met when he came into the Memphis Recording Service to make some promos for his Friday-night hillbilly jamboree. Sam said he was looking for original material for his new artist, and Sallee went home and wrote a song. "You're a Heartbreaker" was the first of Elvis' songs on which Sam Phillips owned the publishing, and it was also the closest that they had come to date to an explicitly country number.

They played the Hayride on the eighteenth, then Bobbie waited for Scotty to come home with her Chevrolet. "Scotty was supposed to be home in time for me to go Christmas shopping. They were using the car, and I was riding the bus. They were supposed to come home Thursday night after a show (Christmas was on a Saturday). I said, 'Well, I'll just wait until you get here and go finish my Christmas shopping.' When they hadn't gotten home by the middle of the afternoon on Friday, I decided that they had stayed over, but I still didn't go out. I said, 'I'm not going to go riding the bus. Scotty just won't get anything for Christmas.' They came in about five-thirty, and I said, 'Why didn't you come home last night?' And they said, 'Elvis wanted to stay in Shreveport and do his Christmas shopping this morning.' I said, 'Okay, Elvis gets what Elvis wants, and you don't get a Christmas present!' But Scotty wasn't too much on that anyway."

Elvis and Dixie spent all day Christmas together, first at Dixie's house, then at the Presleys'. Elvis gave her a suit that he must have bought in Shreveport — she loved it, everything he got her was something she liked, but it wasn't like she thought it was going to be, somehow. Here he had just breezed into town the night before, and now he told her he was going to have to be off again before she even knew it. He was scheduled to play in Houston for Biff Collie at the Cook's Hoedown Yuletide Jamboree on the twenty-eighth, and then at a special New Year's Night broadcast from Eagle's Hall, which Biff had also set up.

She waved good-bye as they drove off and then went over to the Presleys', where she and Gladys alternately shared their pride in the course his life had taken and consoled each other over what they both had lost.

LOUISIANA HAYRIDE. (LANGSTON McEACHERN)

FORBIDDEN FRUIT

ELVIS SIGNED WITH BOB NEAL formally at the start of the year. The official picture, which ran in the trades and in the March issue of *Country & Western Jamboree,* shows him sitting at a desk with a fireplace behind him, pen poised, grin crooked, hair perfectly coiffed. Sam Phillips and Bob Neal stand beside him on either side. Sam has his hand companionably on Elvis' right shoulder, Bob is wearing a broad smile and an elaborately bowed western tie, while all three stare straight into the camera. Because he was still technically a minor, Mr. and Mrs. Vernon Presley signed the contract as parents and legal guardians, with every expectation that this would mark a dramatic upturn in their son's fortunes.

It did, almost from the start. Bob had bookings that would keep Elvis on the road for much of January, with a hometown debut at Ellis Auditorium scheduled for February 6. He was also in the process of making a solid connection with Colonel Tom Parker, who through his new management and booking-agency partnership with Hank Snow was in a position to put Elvis in front of a greatly expanded audience. Though the Colonel at first appeared reluctant to get involved, he was now talking about trying Elvis out on a Hank Snow package tour that started in New Mexico in mid February. For the present Elvis was booked into West Texas the week of January 2 on a Hayride package; then on January 12, 1955, he was scheduled to play the City Auditorium in Clarksdale, Mississippi, for the first time, with the brother-sister duo of Jim Ed and Maxine Brown and "Tater" Bob Neal as MC, and on the thirteenth he played Helena, Arkansas, on the same bill. The following week there was a solid block of bookings in the area around Corinth, Mississippi, with a side excursion to Sikeston, Missouri, then a return to the Gladewater area for a five-day tour the week after that.

He didn't always take the show. Jim Ed and Maxine Brown were a highly polished act. They had had a number-eight national hit the previous summer with "Looking Back to See," were comparative veterans of the Hayride, and had an audience that turned out for them every time. Jim Ed was a big, good-looking guy, just a year older than Elvis and not above preening himself for the girls; his sister, Maxine, was attractive and outgoing, and they never failed to reach a good portion of the crowd. Tom Perryman remembered one show he put on in Gilmer, Texas, near Gladewater, when the Browns actually came out on top. "They did a lot of their harmony gospel songs, and they had their big record, and there was a lot of older family people there. That was the only time I ever saw anybody steal the show from Elvis. Of course it was a big thrill for the Browns." Most of the time, though, they didn't seem to know what had hit them. It wasn't that they were any less popular or that the fans didn't flock around them when they came out after the performance to sign autographs and sell their records; it was just that when that boy was onstage, it was like nothing that had ever been before. Whether people liked it or not, they didn't seem able to think of anything else, and it prevented them from focusing on just about anything that followed.

In Corinth, Mississippi, the show was sponsored by the local Jaycees Club and scheduled to take place at the courthouse, and local DJ/singer Buddy Bain was on the bill. Buddy, who was thirty-one and had had his chance in Nashville, where he had deejayed on WSM after a five-year stint in Knoxville with Chet Atkins, didn't particularly like the new style. He was a traditional country singer himself, who had grown up admiring Gene Autry and Jimmie Rodgers, but he had met Sam Phillips at WLAY in Muscle Shoals, and he knew the Presleys from the Tupelo area, where he had grown up and where his sisters Mary and Marie had worked with Gladys in the sewing room at Reed Manufacturing Company. So when Sam brought not only the first record but the boy himself down to radio station WCMA in Corinth one sweltering day the previous summer, Buddy played it ("Well, I played 'Blue Moon of Kentucky'; 'That's All Right' was a little too much for me") and interviewed Elvis himself for about ten minutes on the air.

By the time he returned to Corinth, in January, Elvis was something of a local phenomenon, and Buddy was featured on the bill, along with his singing partner, fifteen-year-old Kay Crotts from Michie, Tennessee, whom he would marry three years later. Buddy had been plugging the Browns' appearance all week because he had kind of a crush on Maxine ("We had hit it off real good. She wrote to me, and I wrote to her, and I thought something might really come of it until I found out later that she had actually done so many disc jockeys that way, you know, to get them to play her record"), and he was skeptical of the new performer's attraction because he had heard that Bob Neal had paid half a dozen local girls fifty cents apiece to scream, but he was quickly won over.

"You know, they came to make fun of him, but they ended up backstage practically trying to tear him apart. He *was* the show, even then — it wasn't like anything you ever heard. But there was one little thing that happened before the show I'll never forget. They got in in the middle of the afternoon, and we had a little two-story house in Corinth, my mother and I, and we had a girl that would come in and cook for us because my mother was in a wheelchair. Well, I invited Elvis and Maxine and Jim Ed over to the house. And before we had supper, we gave Jim Ed and Maxine my bedroom to lie down in and take a nap. And Elvis said, 'I'd like to lie down, too. The living room sofa's fine for me.' So he lay down on this long red plastic sofa that we had, with his feet over the end, he just went right out. And when I woke him up for supper, the little girl that worked for us, Martha Morris, had filled that table full of food, but all he would eat was some corn bread, and he asked if we didn't have any buttermilk. Well, I chased down to the store for it, and he just crumbled up that corn bread in the buttermilk and ate a whole lot of it and said, 'This is delicious. Just what I want.' After supper was over, my mother was sitting by the window, looking out like she always did, and Elvis went over and said, 'Mrs. Bain, I really enjoyed the meal.' And he kissed her on the cheek, which my mama wasn't used to because *I* didn't even kiss her, I just said, 'Thank you, Mama.' She was a stern woman. When he went out of the room for a minute, she said, 'Who was that slobbering all over me?' I said, 'Mama, that was Elvis Presley.' She said, 'I wondered who that was.'

"Then we all sat down and looked at my scrapbooks. I had lots of pictures from my early career, in Nashville and Raleigh, North Carolina, and the famous Renfro Valley Barn Dance, and he said to me, 'I hope someday I can be as famous as you are. I sure would like to get to Nashville someday.' And you know what I said to him? I remember it as well as if it were yesterday. I said, 'Elvis, if you'll learn you some good country songs, you just might get on the Grand Ole Opry.' Of course he was very polite and thanked me, and then we went to the show."

Backstage at the show Elvis took advantage of his newfound friendship to harmonize with Buddy's singing partner on a Blackwood Brothers song. "We were going to sing a gospel song on our show entitled 'I'm Feeling Mighty Fine.' We all had little practice sessions before going out onstage, and Kay and I were singing over in a corner, and Elvis walked over and said, 'Buddy, scoot on over, you can't sing that song. Let me sing it with Kay.' So he and Kay sang it, and he did his version much different from the way I did mine. 'Cause I did mine just plain, and he did his, 'Well-uh, uh-uh' — you know, like he did. Well, Kay didn't really like it, at least she said she didn't, but I was real jealous of the way they sung it, and he just kept singing it over and over again, there's no telling how many times they sung that chorus, he just didn't know when to stop. But once he got onstage, it was all over." And after the show was done, the mild-mannered boy asked Buddy to point him toward the best-looking girl in the crowd and joked that he would find out if she was wearing falsies or not.

IT WAS ALL LIKE A DREAM from which he was afraid he might one day awaken. It seemed sometimes like it was happening to someone else, and when he spoke of it, it was often with a quality of wonderment likely to strike doubt not so much in his listener's mind as in his own. When he returned home for the show at Ellis, there was a full, four-column spread in the *Memphis Press-Scimitar* by Miss Keisker's friend Mr. Johnson, an affable, easygoing fellow in a battered newspaperman's hat, who spent as much time with Mr. Phillips as he did with the somewhat tongue-tied subject of his story. "Suddenly Singing Elvis Presley Zooms into Recording Stardom," read the headline, with the explanatory introductory phrase, "Thru the Patience of Sam Phillips," running above. The article was accompanied by a photograph of Elvis, Scotty, and Bill in the studio, and underneath the photograph it said, "A white man's voice singing negro rhythms with a rural flavor [has] changed life overnight for Elvis Presley." The body of the text mapped out in plain, accurate, and generally admiring terms the story of his meteoric rise: growing up in Tupelo, moving to Memphis, lugging his guitar every day to Humes. It described how Sam Phillips had discovered his talent, how Dewey Phillips had revealed it to the world, how Elvis had been invited to appear on the Grand Ole Opry, "hillbilly heaven," within a month of the debut of his first record and was today a star of the Louisiana Hayride. The article made note, too, of the phenomenon that had helped give rise to the young man's success and of Sam Phillips' contribution to it. "That's All Right," Johnson noted, was "in the R&B idiom of negro field jazz, 'Blue Moon' more in the country field, but there was a curious blending of the two different musics in both." The last section of the story, headlined "In a Class Alone," stressed the unclassifiability of Elvis' talent and the likelihood of a glowing future for this good-looking young star with the "slumbrous" eyes who, with his new manager, Bob Neal, had recently opened up an office downtown under the title of Elvis Presley Enterprises. "Spin 'em again, boys," wrote Bob Johnson, announcing in bold type everything that Elvis himself had been afraid to even whisper to his friends: the celebrity, the dramatic impact of his success, its scale, the almost unmentionable thrill that went with it.

There were two shows, at 3:00 and 8:00 P.M. The ad in the paper placed him fourth on a "Five Star" bill, with Faron Young and Ferlin Huskey headlining and "Beautiful Gospel Singer" Martha Carson making her Memphis debut, but it was clear from all the attention he was getting that a good deal was expected of him. The first show went fine. He sang his new songs, "Milkcow Blues Boogie" and "You're a Heartbreaker," as well as "That's All Right" and "Good Rockin' Tonight," and he told Ronnie Smith backstage how much fun he was having on the road. He was fascinated, too, with the performance of Martha Carson, a spectacular redhead who looked like a movie star and sang and moved like Sister Rosetta Tharpe when she performed her trademark hit, "Satisfied," and a host of traditional "colored" spirituals. She broke several strings, danced ecstatically at the end of a long guitar cord, and in general created the kind of smoldering intensity and infectious enthusiasm that he sought to achieve in his own performance. He asked Miss Carson afterward if she knew a particular Statesmen number, and he made it clear that "he knew the words to every song that I had ever had out." He told her that he would like to record her song, "Satisfied," someday and that he hoped that they would be billed together again sometime soon. "He was very complimentary and very interested in what I did. I could feel this was sincere, it was from the heart — it wasn't just someone saying this, he just really idolized me, and I could feel it."

In between shows he and Scotty went across the street to a meeting Bob had set up with Colonel Parker. The Colonel had finally added him to Hank Snow's upcoming southwestern tour, which was to start a week from Monday, and Bob said he thought it would be a good idea if they all got together and talked a little bit about the future. In addition to Bob and Colonel Parker, Sam Phillips would also be attending, along with the Colonel's front man, Oscar Davis (whom Elvis had met in connection with the Eddy Arnold show three months before), and Tom Diskin, Parker's associate in Jamboree Attractions, the booking agency in which he and Snow were partners. Ironically, Scotty had contacted Diskin in the fall, at the Chicago office listed in *Billboard,* to see if the agency might be interested in booking Elvis. He had gotten his reply only three weeks earlier, a stock letter of rejection which apparently failed to make any connection between the blind inquiry and the new act in whom the Colonel was now showing interest. The Colonel himself had already seen them perform in Texarkana a couple of months before. Scotty had heard from the booker, Jim LeFan, that the Colonel would be there and even thought he had spotted him standing toward the back of the auditorium. But Parker hadn't come around to see them afterward, and though he spent much of January in touch with Neal about the tour, he had had no direct contact with the musicians until now.

The meeting at Palumbo's did not get off to an auspicious start. The tension in the air was already marked when Elvis and Scotty walked in. Colonel Parker was sitting there with a big cigar, his jaw thrust out, and a pugnacious expression on his face, as Diskin, his young lieutenant, tried to explain to Mr. Phillips that the Colonel didn't really mean anything against the Sun label in particular, that he was just trying to point out the shortcomings that would attach to any small record label, which necessarily lacked the kind of distribution that a major company like RCA, with which the Colonel had been associated for many years through both Eddy Arnold and Hank Snow, could offer. Oscar Davis, sharp as ever with a fresh flower in his buttonhole and his cigarette holder cocked elegantly, just so, was plainly unhappy with his crude associate. And Sam was seething. What did Tom Parker mean — he wasn't going to call that damn mountebank by some phony title — by saying that Elvis was going to get nowhere on Sun? This was a helluva way to start a business conference. His own deep-set eyes bored in on the Colonel, but Parker's gaze never wavered, and both men sat locked in silent combat until finally Bob Neal broke the tension and suggested they discuss some of the specifics of the upcoming tour.

This could be a very fine opportunity for them all, Oscar Davis said with genuine feeling: it would give Sam a chance to get his records into new territories, it would offer young Elvis here an opportunity to expand his audience, and if things worked out it could cement a long-standing relationship — Davis undoubtedly hesitated on the word *partnership* — between Colonel Parker and our good friend Bob Neal and allow it to develop in exciting new directions. The Colonel only glowered, and Oscar was confounded as to just what he could be up to. As for Elvis, Bob had explained to him the Colonel's far-flung connections, not just in the world of country music, but in Hollywood as well. Mr. Phillips had only reinforced what Bob had said. From what he understood, Sam declared before actually meeting him, there wasn't a better *promoter* in the business than Tom Parker, and right now they could certainly use all the help they could get. But what, Elvis might well have been led to wonder at this point, was Colonel Parker's compelling attraction?

THOMAS A. PARKER on first impression was a heavyset, crude, and blustering man with a brilliant mind and a guttural accent, which he claimed to have acquired in West Virginia, where, he said, he had been born forty-five years before. Orphaned as a child (the exact age varied from one telling to the next), he had run away and joined the circus, in this case the Great Parker Pony Circus, which he said was owned by an uncle. From there he had drifted into the carny life, eventually ending up in Tampa, where the Royal American show wintered and where, after half a dozen years "in the life," he had married an older divorcée named Marie Mott in 1935 and settled down. He pursued a number of civilian ventures, eventually becoming field agent (this could be translated as "Chief Dogcatcher," and often was in later years by the Colonel) for the Tampa Humane Society, a privately endowed animal shelter, where he and his family were given a free apartment above the pound. On his own he enterprisingly founded a pet cemetery that offered "Perpetual Care for Deceased Pets" while also promoting and working closely with country singers Gene Austin and Roy Acuff and film star Tom Mix on their Florida tours. Acuff, then known as the King of the Hillbillies, tried to persuade him to move to Nashville, and Parker seemed ready to entertain the idea if Acuff would consider leaving the Opry and giving Parker a free managerial hand. Acuff declined, and perhaps because Tom Parker was not quite ready to give up all his carny ties, this was the point at which they reached a parting of the ways. It wasn't until a few years later, in 1944, when he met twenty-six-year-old Eddy Arnold headlining an Opry tent show tour, that he finally made his move.

Arnold, who had just left Pee Wee King's Golden West Cowboys and signed with RCA Records, was a big, handsome, square-jawed baritone with a full-throated melodic style altogether different from the conventional Nashville approach. Parker must have sensed in him the potential that he was looking for, because he went into show business now with the same creative, full-bore intensity that had always marked him in the carny world. According to Oscar Davis, who first met Parker in Florida while Davis was managing Ernest Tubb, there had never been another manager of this sort before. In his attention to every aspect of his client's career, in his devotion to mapping out a program and to carrying it out in the most meticulous detail, in his use of radio for "exploitation" and his belief that his word was his bond, that a contract, once agreed upon, was a sacred commitment *on both sides*, Tom Parker "as a manager was tops, the greatest in the world. He was an uncanny businessman, very astute, he adjusted the cost so there was never a time when a promoter made more money than he did. If I were to select anyone in the amusement field — and I've been through it from 1912 on up — I would select him; I don't think anyone has beaten him on a deal. He'll read you very quickly. Working with the carnivals taught him that everything wasn't the way that it looks on the surface, that everyone has their weaknesses. Tom was a strong man. He'd lay the law down, and you went that way or you didn't play."

To Biff Collie, the Houston DJ, the difference between the Colonel and Oscar — Davis' chronic impecuniousness aside — was that the Colonel "always thought far beyond where he was," while to Gabe Tucker, who met Parker when Gabe was playing bass for Eddy Arnold and who worked with him on and off for almost thirty years, "his operation was completely different" because of his attention to detail. "Most managers back then would just call up [the local promoter] and say, 'Okay, can you book a tour down there?' And the manager would never leave his office. But he didn't work that way. He'd go out before, check out the place, he'd ask how many seats in the auditorium — not to be smart, but because we knowed percentagewise, if we had a five-thousand-seat auditorium, we knew how many [Eddy Arnold] songbooks to take in and how many we was going to sell. His theory was altogether different than most of them that come to Nashville. He was a carny."

Once he got together with Eddy Arnold he concentrated his focus exclusively on his single client. He moved up to Nashville and virtually moved in with Arnold and his wife, Sally. "When Tom's your manager, he's all you," wrote Arnold in his 1969 autobiography, *It's a Long Way from Chester County*. "He lives and breathes his artist. I once said to him . . . 'Tom, why don't you get yourself a hobby — play golf, go boating, or something?' He looked me straight in the eye and said, 'You're my hobby.' " One of the keys to Parker's success, as Arnold saw it, was his apparent crudity. "Earthy, I guess a lot of people might describe him; uneducated maybe. A lot of times people think they're dealing with a rube. 'Oh, I can take him,' they decide. They don't take him. He's ahead of 'em before they even sit down across a table . . . he fools 'em. They think, because his English might be faulty (he might say a word wrong here and there), 'Oh, I'll handle him.' They walk right into his web!"

Arnold had three number-one hits in 1947 and the following year was persuaded by Parker to reluctantly quit the Opry: there were just too many other opportunities. In October 1948 Parker used his carnival connections to get himself an honorary colonel's commission from Louisiana governor and noted country singer Jimmie Davis, the listed composer of "You Are My Sunshine." From now on, he told Gabe Tucker, who accompanied him to the investiture, "see to it . . . that everyone addresses me as the Colonel." Within a year or two after that he had gotten Arnold into the movies, hooked Eddy up with William Morris, the leading Hollywood talent agency, gotten him on Milton Berle's top-rated television show, and even booked him into Las Vegas. It was a far cry from what any previous country music manager had envisioned for his talent (though a few might have dreamt of it, none achieved it), but eventually the exclusivity of his focus got him into trouble.

In 1953, in an episode that has been widely reported but never fully explained, Eddy Arnold fired him. According to Elvis biographer Jerry Hopkins, who got the story from Oscar Davis, "It was an argument in Las Vegas that made the relationship collapse. Parker had been laying out a two-page newspaper advertisement as a surprise to Eddy . . . and when Eddy walked into the Colonel's room unexpectedly, Parker quickly hid the lay-out, Eddy accused him of doing something behind his back, one thing led to another, and pretty soon Eddy was without a manager, Parker was without a star." It may have had something to do with a weekly television show, too, in which Arnold was persuaded, against the

Colonel's always sober fiscal advice, to invest a great deal of his own money, and it was undoubtedly true, as Gabe noted, that Arnold and Parker "were dissipating much of their energy ironing out the difference in their personalities and private lives." They went on working together in a booking arrangement that was part of an amicable separation agreement, and they never ceased to be personally cordial, but it must have come as a terrible blow to Parker to be abandoned so abruptly by his protégé, in a manner that left him unavoidably exposed in the glare of the show biz spotlight.

Within a year he had rebounded, after initially making his office in the lobby of Nashville radio station WSM, where with Oscar Davis and other independent operators he used the lobby phone to book his acts. "When the phone rang," according to *Billboard* editor Bill Williams, "by agreement whoever was closest answered it by the number . . . and between them they lined up more clients and did more business than the Opry's Service Bureau, which was directly across the hall, while WSM blithely picked up the tab — for years!" By the spring of 1954, though, he was working extensively with Hank Snow, whose "I Don't Hurt Anymore" was the sensation of the first six months of the year. In its November 6 issue *Billboard* announced that Colonel Tom Parker of Jamboree Attractions had "inked a pact with Hank Snow to handle the latter exclusively on personals. After the first of the year . . . he'll take over management of Hank Snow Enterprises, which includes radio, TV, film and recording commitments." He was back in the big time.

And yet, oddly enough, he remained something of an enigma, an unpredictable quantity, certainly, for someone in so visible a position who did not exactly eschew the public eye. Something about his background simply didn't make sense. "No one knows very much about his boyhood," said Oscar Davis, who doubted the story about the Great Parker Pony Circus when he spoke to Jerry Hopkins in 1970. "I never knew if he had brothers or sisters; he's a bit of a mystery." From time to time he would explode in a fit of temper, or perhaps just an outburst of exuberant good humor, in a language that none of his associates recognized or understood. They wondered if he was speaking German, but he always stipulated that it was Dutch, with a twinkle in his eye that left them in little doubt that he was pulling their leg.

He kept nearly everyone, even his closest associates, at arm's length. "You have one fault," he told his brother-in-law, Bitsy Mott. "You make too many friends." His cold eyes belied his occasional warmheartedness; his absolute honesty in business affairs conflicted with the opportunism that always drove him to come out on top not just in formal dealings but in day-to-day affairs as well (he would spend a hundred dollars, it was said, to beat you out of a dollar). "He got a helluva kick," Chet Atkins declared, "out of getting someone to pick up the check. Or out of just beating you in a deal — any kind of a deal." He was capable of real generosity, but more than anything else he loved the game. As Gabe Tucker observed, he lived in a world of mirrors — he never really left the carnival world, in which "they speak a different language. All of them is just like the Colonel; they'll cut your throat just to watch you bleed. But they've got their own laws, it's a game with them, to outsmart you, you're always the pigeon to them." In Gabe's view, and in Oscar Davis', too, everyone else in the Colonel's estimation was a little bit of a fool.

IT WAS LITTLE WONDER, then, that Sam Phillips should take so instant, and visceral, a dislike to the man sitting opposite him in the little restaurant on Poplar. On the other hand, Tom Parker was one of the few people in the business able to provide a match for Sam. These were two very strong, independent men with two very different visions of life. Sam's embraced the sweep of history; it very consciously conjured up the agrarian hero as the focus of the democratic dream. The Colonel's vision, on the other hand, denied history; it centered on the here and now, focusing on survival by wit and instinct in a universe that was indifferent at best. There was room enough for sentiment in the Colonel's view but little for philosophy; Sam was perhaps less inclined to the sentimental gesture but more to the humanitarian impulse. They didn't like each other, clearly, but their needs suited each other, at least for the time being.

And Sam's need for Parker and Jamboree Attractions was, if anything, greater than Parker's need for any untested twenty-year-old. Parker was right in terms of the blunt challenge he had thrown out: Elvis Presley could get only so far with Sun Records. Sun Records could get only so far without a considerable infusion of cash to cover the signing and promotion of new talent, increased pressing costs, expanded distribution, and the wherewithal to provide some kind of breathing space. Bob Neal had been just the thing, Sam was convinced, but in the short time he had been working with Elvis he had taken the boy about as far as he could go on his own — he had brought Elvis to his audience, booked him all through Mississippi and Arkansas, and tied in with other local promoters like Tom Perryman, Biff Collie, and Jim LeFan, so that Elvis Presley was now an authentic regional sensation. The new record had been well reviewed just the previous week in *Billboard* ("Presley continues to impress with each release as one of the slickest talents to come up in the country field in a long, long time"), records were selling like crazy in Memphis, New Orleans, Dallas, Little Rock, Houston, and all over West Texas, and after only three months Elvis Presley was becoming an attraction the likes of which the Louisiana Hayride had never seen. *But he needed a national stage.*

Elvis excused himself to go back to the auditorium with Scotty, and the five men sat around for a little while longer. They talked about details of the tour: money and bookings, the towns and auditoriums (some of them already familiar) that Elvis would be playing during this brief ten-day tour. It was just a start, but if it worked . . . Neal dreamt about television and movies. He didn't say anything, but they were saving out money from their appearances, building up a little fund for a trip to New York to audition for Arthur Godfrey — he hadn't even mentioned it to Sam. They were working almost every night now, he told the Colonel, busting out everywhere they played, creating some kind of sensation or another, just like Colonel Parker had seen in Texarkana. The Colonel grunted. As far as the Colonel was concerned, if this music was going to be made popular it might as well be made popular by Tommy Sands, a young protégé of his in Shreveport — and that was just what he thought he would write to Steve Sholes after his encounter with Phillips today. Wait'll you see the evening show, Bob Neal persisted. Simply on the basis of his own experience, there was little doubt in Neal's mind that Tom Parker was the best in the business. In his heart of hearts he envisioned a kind of partnership of interests. He couldn't wait to begin. Once this tour was over, Neal *knew* there would be more — more tours, more appearances, with or without the Colonel. He couldn't wait to break out of the mid-South territory.

THE TOUR — WITH HANK SNOW HEADLINING, the Carter Sisters and Mother Maybelle, and celebrated comedian Whitey Ford (better known as the Duke of Paducah) — opened in Roswell, New Mexico, eight days later. Elvis was booked into Lubbock, Texas, the night before, where he played the Fair Park auditorium for the second time in little more than a month. Also on the bill was Jimmie Rodgers Snow, Hank's son, who was scheduled to join the tour the next night as well. Just a few months younger than Elvis, Snow was bowled over by his first exposure to this kid in "a chartreuse jacket and black pants with a white stripe down the side, and the kids were just going wild. I'd never seen anyone quite like him — even as a kid he had that something about him, he just *had* it. I had never heard of Elvis Presley when I went out there, I had no idea who he was, the Colonel just called me in — him and Tom Diskin — and said, 'I got you booked with this guy, Elvis Presley, out in Lubbock, Texas.' But we talked that night, we ran around that night, as a matter of fact Buddy Holly was hanging around the show [actually Holly opened the show with his friend Bob Montgomery]. And we just became friends immediately."

They joined up with the others in Roswell and two nights later played Odessa, where Elvis was already something of a local legend from his one previous area appearance, in early January. Typical was the enthusiasm of a nineteen-year-old Odessa musician named Roy Orbison, who had had Elvis on his local TV show the first time he had come to town after seeing him on Dallas' Big "D" Jamboree. Orbison later said of that first encounter: "His energy was incredible, his instinct was just amazing. . . . Actually it affected me exactly the same way as when I first saw that David Lynch film [*Blue Velvet*]. I just didn't know what to make of it. There was just no reference point in the culture to compare it."

Hank Snow might well have agreed, though he would have been looking at the subject from a slightly different point of view. Snow, a proud, aloof Canadian of diminutive stature and iron will, kept his distance from the "young punk," with little evident recollection of the fact that he had introduced him on the Opry just four months earlier and little apparent affinity for the figure he was cutting. Elvis for his part made it clear to Jimmy that he idolized his dad — he knew every one of Hank Snow's songs and persisted in singing snatches of even the most obscure of them ("Brand on My Heart," "Just a Faded Petal from a Beautiful Bouquet," "I'm Gonna Bid My Blues Goodbye"), as if to prove that somehow he belonged.

To Jimmie Rodgers Snow, named for the "Father of Country Music" and with a firsthand view of the cost of success — from sudden uprootings in the middle of the school year to broken promises, bitter disappointment, and the sound of his father's typewriter pecking away as he personally answered every last item of fan correspondence — it was almost as if a vision had entered his world, a vision of peculiar purity and innocence that seemed free of all the frustrating struggle and harsh ugliness of the performer's reality. "He didn't drink, he'd carry a cigarette around in his mouth, one of those filter types, never light it because he didn't smoke, but he'd play with it. I remember how cool he was in my mind. I wanted to sing like him. I wanted to dress like him and do things that I never cared about till I met him. He was the change that was coming to America. With Jimmy Dean and all that. I don't think anybody saw it. Dad had no idea what Elvis Presley would become. Colonel probably saw it more than anybody, but I don't think he saw Elvis Presley for more than an entertainer at that time. I used to ride in the car with him and Scotty and Bill — oh, he was the worst guy in the world to ride with, 'cause he was talking to you the whole time, speeding up and his feet moving all the time, he'd work the stations on the radio dial like crazy, listen to different things, country, spirituals, he loved gospel music. I was just fascinated with him. Watching him comb his hair of a morning using three different hair oils, butch wax for the front like you'd use for a crew cut, one kind of hair oil for the top, another for the back. I asked him why he used that butch wax, and he said that was so when he performed his hair would fall down a certain way. He thought that was cool. I also remember that when he would wear a pair of socks, rather than get them washed he'd roll them up and throw them in the suitcase, and if you opened it up it would knock you down. He'd have that thing full of dirty stuff, and a lot of times he would just throw it away and you'd wonder how this clean-cut-looking kid could be so disorganized, but he always took care of his hair. He would take his socks off sometimes and you could be on the bed next to him, and he'd smell up the whole room, but the women could care less. He was Elvis."

That was the way the crowd reacted, too. Almost immediately the Hank Snow show had a problem. "Dad was in his heyday, he was drawing the crowds, and in many of the places that we performed at the beginning they didn't know Elvis, but it didn't matter if they knew him or not — nobody followed Elvis." It was the oddest thing. This nice, polite, well-mannered boy became transformed onstage in a manner that seemed to contradict everything that you might discern about his private personality. "He was this punk kid," Roy Orbison recalled from his original vantage point in the audience. "Just a real raw cat singing like a bird.

. . . First thing, he came out and spat on the stage. In fact he spat out a piece of gum. . . . Plus he told some real bad, crude jokes — you know, this dumb off-color humor — which weren't funny. And his diction was real coarse, like a truck driver's. . . . I can't overemphasize how shocking he looked and seemed to me that night."

His energy was fierce; his sense of competitive fire seemed to overwhelm the shy, deferential kid within; every minute he was onstage was like an incendiary explosion. "There never was a country act that could follow him," said Bob Neal. "With this type of show he would have a big crowd, and then when he appeared, he just tore them up completely." The trouble was, according to Neal, his competitive spirit got the best of him. He didn't want anyone to dislike him, he especially didn't want any of the other performers to think that he had the *big head,* "but he was up against the tops and he always tried to outdo them."

You have only to listen to the few live recordings from that period that have survived. The repertoire is distinctly limited, and Scotty occasionally gets lost in his solos, but Elvis and the boys just *tear* into each song, whether it's "That's All Right" or "Tweedle Dee" or Ray Charles' brand-new hit, "I Got a Woman." The intensity that you get in each performance bears no relation even to the classic recordings on Sun, and while it may not surpass them, in nearly every case it leaves them sounding dry. If Hank Snow felt angry and humiliated in front of his own audience, though, he knew a commercial trend when he spotted one. Jimmie Rodgers Snow was entranced. Before he left the tour in Bastrop, Louisiana, he invited Elvis to come motorcycle riding with him in Nashville sometime soon. Even the Colonel, who still professed profound disinterest, showed a different side to Elvis than Jimmy had ever seen him show before. "He wouldn't go out of his way for nobody. He was always jumping on my case about being on time, carrying a little bit more, giving me this advice, that advice." He was "a hard-nosed man," said Jimmy, much like his own father, and yet even Parker seemed to have fallen under the spell of this irrepressible youth, he seemed as taken as everyone else by the unfeigned enthusiasm, the undisguised eagerness for experience — only the boyfriends of some of his more uninhibited female fans seemed to take exception. Jimmy had no idea where it was going to end, he was more and more confused about the muddle that his own life was falling into under the growing influence of alcohol and pills, but he *knew* that Elvis Presley had a future in the business.

Elvis himself was increasingly coming to believe it, although he continued to discount the idea to family and friends. Every night he called Dixie as well as his mother from each stop on the tour. He told them how it had gone, he told them with almost wide-eyed wonder how the audience had reacted, he told them who he had met and what they had said. "He was always excited about what happened," said Dixie. "He'd say, 'Guess who I saw.' Or: 'Hank Snow was there.' " It was almost as if he were suspended between two worlds. He studied each performer — he watched carefully from backstage with much the same appreciation as the audience, but with a keen sense of what they were doing, what really knocked the fans out, and how each performer achieved it. Between shows he would seek out opportunities to sing with other members of the troupe, and they were all captivated, much as the audience was, by the young man's ingenuous charm.

He could read every audience; it was, evidently, an innate skill. "I see people all different ages and things," he said years later, trying to explain it. "If I do something good, they let me know it. If I don't, they let me know that, too. It's a give-and-take proposition in that they give me back the inspiration. I work absolutely to them. . . . They bring it out of me: the inspiration. The ham." Even if they didn't respond at first he could always get to them. "He would study a crowd," said Tillman Franks of the Hayride tours. "He would look at them, see that he'd gotten through to them, then give them a little bit more. He had electricity between him and that audience, same as Hank Williams did. Hank just give everything he had — he didn't worry about it, he just did it. But Elvis masterminded the situation. He was a genius at it."

"He knew, of course, that his main thrust was to the women," said Jimmie Rodgers Snow. "I saw grandmas dancing in the aisles. I saw a mother and daughter actually bidding for his attention and jealous of each other. It was uncanny: they would just get totally captivated by this guy." "He was always unhappy about the reaction from the boys," said Bob Neal, "because he very much wanted to be one of the boys and a favorite of theirs, but the boys reacted very violently in many areas because, I suppose, of the way the girls acted. It hurt him. You know, we'd talk about it sometimes for hours at a time, driving; he really couldn't understand it. But there was just no way, apparently, that a lot of these young teenaged fellows would change their minds. They just resented him because of the way the girls reacted to him."

But if that was a cloud on the horizon, it was only the casing for the silver lining. There was no aspect of Elvis' new life with which he was not entranced. When the Carter Sisters and Mother Maybelle joined the tour, he and Scotty both were a little taken with Anita, the youngest sister, and they considered it a great triumph when they could get her to ride with them, away from the watchful eye of Mother Maybelle. On one of the last dates of the tour, near Hope, Arkansas, they got stuck on a back road looking for a shortcut to town, and Scotty tried to make time with Anita in the backseat while the others did what they could to persuade a farmer to help pull them out of the mud. "All of us were in the back of this pickup truck," recalled Jimmy Snow, "just laughing — on our way to Hope to do a show."

Two days later the tour ended in Bastrop. Hank Snow was long since departed (his last show had been in Monroe, Louisiana, the previous Friday), and there was no definite commitment from Jamboree for the future, but there was a sure sense that they had accomplished what they set out to do: they had expanded their audience and had a good time doing it.

THAT SATURDAY, February 26, they made their first trip north, to Cleveland, to play the Circle Theater Jamboree. Bob Neal accompanied the boys in hopes that this might lead to even further exposure, that through the contacts he made at radio stations along the way, or just by being on the scene, *something might happen.* Other than that, he had no firm expectations — they didn't even have a definite place to stay. Tommy Edwards, "the City Slicker Turned Country Boy" and host of the Hillbilly Jamboree, had been playing Elvis' records on WERE since the previous fall and was an unqualified fan; there was a big market for this music in Cleveland, he assured Neal. With all of the southerners who had flocked to town looking for work after the war, in addition to the large black population that occupied the Hough district and a diverse ethnic population, Cleveland was a real music town. Every Friday night there was a rhythm and blues show at the Circle, and the Jamboree had unearthed so many hillbillies that Edwards had invited them to educate him as to what they wanted to hear.

But probably the biggest indicator of the change that was coming in music was the startling success of Alan Freed, who, both on the air and as a concert promoter, had discovered the same young white audience for rhythm and blues that Dewey Phillips had found in Memphis. Freed, as flamboyant as Dewey and as opportunistic in business as Dewey was lacking in business sense, had left Cleveland just months earlier for the even more lucrative New York market, where he continued to crusade for the same kind of music, introduced the all-star rhythm and blues revue (the Drifters, the Clovers, Fats Domino, Big Joe Turner, and half a dozen more premier acts all on the same bill), and claimed to have coined, and even copyrighted, the term "rock & roll." And how about Bill Haley, who was very popular here in town; had Bob Neal ever seen him perform? He had done a rhythm and blues show with his western-style band, the Comets, some eighteen months earlier with Billy Ward and His Dominoes and former heavyweight champion Joe Louis and his orchestra. It seemed like right here in Cleveland all the dividing lines and musical barriers were coming down.

The show that night went fine. Elvis remained largely unheralded in Cleveland (his records were little more than "turntable hits" there, since Sun's distribution did not extend effectively that far), but if Bob Neal had been apprehensive about a northern audience's receptivity to this new music, his fears were quickly put to rest. Elvis went over the same as he had throughout the South: the young people went wild, and the older folks covered their mouths. Bill's souvenir photo sales were brisk, as he mixed easily with the fans and made change from his money belt, and Tommy Edwards sold a fair number of their records (which they had carried up from Memphis in the trunk of Bob's car) in the lobby. After the show Edwards said there was someone he wanted Neal to meet. In fact it was the very person who had put on the Billy Ward–Bill Haley show, just returned from his four-hour Saturday-afternoon shift on WCBS in New York. Maybe Elvis could do another interview, even though they had already done an on-the-air promotion for the Jamboree on Edwards' show that afternoon. They went down to the station, and there they met Bill Randle.

Bill Randle was a legend in radio at that time. Tall, scholarly-looking with black horn-rimmed glasses, he had just been written up in *Time* two weeks before in a story that announced, "For the past year the top U.S. deejay has been Cleveland's Bill Randle, 31, a confident, prepossessing fellow who spins his tunes six afternoons a week (from 2 to 7 P.M. on station WERE)." According to the article, Randle had predicted all but one of the top five best-sellers of 1954, discovered Johnnie Ray, changed the name of the Crew-Cuts (from the Canadaires) as well as finding them their first hit, drove a Jaguar, and made $100,000 a year, with his Saturday-afternoon CBS network show in New York the latest in his series of unprecedented accomplishments. "Randle's explanation of his success: 'I'm constantly getting a mass of records. I weed out those that are obviously bad and play the rest on my program to get listener reaction. Then I feed the results into a machine. I'm the machine. I'm a Univac [computer]. It's so accurate that I can tell my listeners, "This tune will be No. 1 in four weeks."'" When asked if he liked the music that he played, Randle, whose personal taste ran to jazz and classical music and who had been fired from a Detroit radio station several years earlier for refusing to play pop ("It was a tremendous emotional problem switching to popular music. . . . It was almost a physical thing bringing myself to play the records"), Randle declared, cheerfully, in *Time*'s estimation: "I'm a complete schizophrenic about this. I'm in the business of giving the public what it wants. This stuff is simply merchandise, and I understand it."

It was through Tommy Edwards that Randle had first heard Elvis Presley's music, but while Edwards played "Blue Moon of Kentucky" for his country audience, Randle heard something in the blues. It wasn't until he started going to New York in January, though, that he actually started playing Presley, and then he aired "Good Rockin' Tonight" on his CBS show, which according to Randle made him persona non grata at the station for a while.

They did the interview down at the WERE studio that night, as Randle played all three of Presley's Sun records and was altogether won over. "He was extremely shy, talked about Pat Boone and Bill Haley as idols, and called me Mr. Randle. Very gentlemanly, very interesting, he knew a lot about the music and the people and the personalities in Memphis, and it was very exciting." He was almost equally impressed with Bob Neal. "Bob Neal to my mind was a really interesting person. He was very bright. He was a country disc jockey, but he was also a businessman-entrepreneur-hustler — but with a lot of class." Randle invited Neal to stay over at his place, and they stayed up much of the night talking. By the end of the evening Randle was convinced that Neal "had a big artist on his way," and he gave Neal the name of a contact in song publishing who he thought could help get Presley a tryout on *Arthur Godfrey's Talent Scouts*. When they parted in the morning, Randle wished Neal luck with his boy and said he hoped he'd get a chance to see him perform when they returned to Cleveland and the Circle Theater the following month. Then Randle had his Sunday-afternoon radio show to do, and Neal and the boys had a long drive back to Memphis.

Memphis seemed almost tame upon their return. It had been more than three weeks since Elvis had last seen Dixie, their longest separation, and he felt like he had all kinds of things to tell her, but when it came down to it, it seemed like he didn't have all that much to tell. They went to the monthly All-Night Singing at Ellis, where James Blackwood left Elvis' name at the door, then announced that he was in the audience and invited him backstage after the show. They went to the movies — *The Blackboard Jungle* opened that month, with Bill Haley's "Rock Around the Clock" blasting out over the opening credits. For the first time they didn't have to worry about money, they could buy all the new records they wanted at Charlie's and Poplar Tunes and Reuben Cherry's Home of the Blues, where Elvis bought every red and black Atlantic and silver and blue Chess record that he could find. They dropped in to see Dewey Phillips, and Dewey always made a big fuss, announcing in his superexcited pitchman's voice that Elvis was in the studio, firing a few questions at him that Elvis answered with surprising ease on the air. He played football down at the Triangle a few times, but he felt increasingly uncomfortable with the old gang. They stopped by the new office on Union, whose recurrent motif was pink and black: fan club membership cards, stationery, and envelopes all matched Elvis' preferred personal decor, and Bob's wife, Helen, said they had several hundred fan club members enrolled already. On March 15, Elvis signed an amended one-year agreement with Neal, giving Neal a 15 percent commission and subject to renewal in March 1956, when, if necessary, it could be revised again.

Meanwhile, the group had its second recording session in little more than a month. They had gone into the studio at the beginning of February, just before the start of the Jamboree tour, with the idea of recording their next single, but like every other session, this one had come hard. They tried Ray Charles' current hit, "I Got a Woman," already a staple of their live act, as well as "Trying to Get to You," an unusual gospel-based ballad by an obscure rhythm and blues group from Washington, D.C., called the Eagles, but neither one worked out. The one number they did come up with, though, was probably the best they had gotten in the studio to date. Taken from a fairly pallid original by Arthur Gunter that hit the rhythm and blues charts at the end of January, "Baby, Let's Play

House" virtually exploded with energy and high spirits and the sheer bubbling irrepressibility that Sam Phillips had first sensed in Elvis' voice. "Whoa, baby, baby, baby, baby, baby," Elvis opened in an ascending, hiccoughing stutter that knocked everybody out with its utterly unpredictable, uninhibited, and gloriously playful ridiculousness, and when he changed Gunter's original lyric from "You may have religion" to "You may drive a pink Cadillac" ("But don't you be nobody's fool"), he defined something of his own, not to mention his generation's, aspirations. This looked like it could become their biggest record yet, everyone agreed. All they needed was a B side.

While they were out on tour, Stan Kesler wrote it. Kesler, the steel guitarist in Clyde Leoppard's Snearly Ranch Boys, had been hanging around the studio since the fall, when he had been drawn in by the strange new sounds he had heard on the radio ("I never heard anything like it before"). The Snearly Ranch Boys were looking to make a record, which they eventually did, but Sam Phillips picked out Kesler, along with Muscle Shoals–area musicians Quinton Claunch (guitar) and Bill Cantrell (fiddle), to form a kind of rhythm section for a bunch of little country demo sessions he put together in the fall and winter of 1954–55 on artists as diverse as fourteen-year-old Maggie Sue Wimberley, the Miller Sisters, Charlie Feathers, and a new rocking hillbilly artist out of Jackson, Tennessee, a kind of hopped-up Hank Williams named Carl Perkins. He put out limited-release singles on each of these, mostly on a nonunion subsidiary label he formed just for that purpose, called Flip, but with almost all of Sam's energies still focused on Elvis none of the records did anything much.

It was clear, though, that Sam was thinking of the future and seeking ways to expand upon Sun's newfound success. Times were still tough, money remained tight, and Sam was still feeling the pinch from buying out his partner, Jim Bulleit, the year before, but there was no question of his settling for being known as a one-artist producer. Sam Phillips' ambitions were much grander than that: he had great hopes for this new boy Perkins, "one of the great plowhands in the world," as he later described him, and he was "so impressed with the pain and feeling in his country singing" that he felt this might be "someone who could revolutionize the country end of the business." He was equally impressed with yet another young man who had shown up on the Sun doorstep in the wake of Presley's success and continued to hang around until Sam gave him an audition. There was something about the quality of this young appliance salesman's voice — it was in a way akin to Ernest Tubb's in its homespun *honesty* (he kept telling the boy not to try to sound like anyone else, not to worry if his sound and his style were untutored, not even to rehearse too much, "because I was interested in spontaneity, too"). He didn't release a record on Johnny Cash until the following summer, but he was working with him and Perkins and Charlie Feathers and a host of others all through the winter and spring.

That was why Stan Kesler kept hanging around. He sensed that something new was about to happen, and he wanted to be a part of it when it did. When he heard that Sam was looking for material for the next Presley session, he immediately went home and wrote a number called "I'm Left, You're Right, She's Gone" with fellow band member Bill Taylor (trumpet player with the Snearly Ranch Boys) based on the melody of the Campbell's Soup commercial. He borrowed Clyde Leoppard's tape recorder, had Taylor demo the song, and sat around the studio chatting with Marion until Sam came in and listened to it. As it turned out, Sam liked the song, and Elvis must have a little bit, too, because it was the one number that they concentrated on at the session the following week.

What was different about this session was that for the first time they used a drummer. Sam had always said that he wanted to take the trio format as far as he could — and in fact they started out this session as a trio — but Sam felt like there was something missing, and he called up a young musician who had come in with his high school band the previous year to make an acetate of a couple of big band jazz numbers. Jimmie Lott was a junior in high school at the time but unfazed by the action. "I had bronchitis, but I loaded up my drums into my mom's car. Elvis was standing in the doorway of the studio. He had long greasy ducktails, which was not too cool with my [crowd]." They jumped into a Jimmie Rodgers Snow number that Elvis wanted to cut, "How Do You Think I Feel," to which Lott contributed a Latin beat, but they couldn't get it right and soon went back to the Kesler-Taylor composition that Elvis, Scotty, and Bill had been fooling around with all evening. They had run up more than a dozen takes already, trying to transform a simple country tune into a wrenchingly slow blues number patterned on the Delmore Brothers' "Blues Stay Away from Me." Elvis was uncomfortable with the idea of doing a straight-out country tune, and Sam could understand that, but even as they came closer to what they were aiming for, Sam knew they were just getting further apart: hell, they *all* knew it in some part of their souls. The Campbell's Soup melody just wasn't altogether suited to a blues treatment.

Once the drums were added, providing a solid, jangling background, there wasn't so much weight on Elvis' vocals, and he got the pretty, almost delicate tone that Sam had envisioned for the tune all along, breaking his voice in a manner halfway between traditional country style and his newly patented hiccough, with Scotty supplying his smoothest Chet Atkins licks on top of the blues variations that still lingered from earlier versions. It didn't really match some of the other stuff they'd gotten, but it was just the kind of thing Sam felt they needed ("We didn't need that Nashville country, but I wanted the simplicity of the melody line — you know, we had to do a little bit of crawling around just to see where we were before we got into the race"). At the end of the session, as Jimmie Lott was packing up his drums, Sam asked him if he would be interested in working some more with the group, but Jimmie, who would later play in Warren Smith's band and record again in the Sun studio, demurred without much hesitation. "I told him I had another year of school and couldn't."

Just ten days later they went up to New York with Bob Neal. They flew because their booking schedule was so tight that they didn't have time to drive or take the train (*Billboard* of April 2 reported that the group was "set solid through April"). It was the first time that Elvis or Bill had flown, and the first time any of the boys had visited New York. They gawked at the skyscrapers and took a subway ride. Bob, who had been to the city before, pointed out the sights to them while Bill kidded around, crossed his eyes, and acted like a cheerful hick. When they got to the studio, though, the response was decidedly cool, the lady conducting the audition conveyed a "don't call us we'll call you" kind of attitude, and they never even got to see Arthur Godfrey. It was very disappointing to them all, not least to Bob Neal, who had been building this up as an opportunity to break into the big time — television was a *national* market, and Arthur Godfrey was the vehicle by which the Blackwood Brothers had become nationally known. They had been saving up for months for this trip, and now they might just as well have flushed the money down the toilet. Bill Randle's friend Max Kendrick reported back to Randle somewhat indignantly that this new kid just wasn't ready for the big time — he showed up for the audition badly dressed and seemed nervous and ill prepared —

and Randle felt that Kendrick was a little distant as a result for some months thereafter.

Elvis and Scotty and Bill had no time for reflection, however. They hit the road again almost immediately. Scotty and Bobbie's car had finally given out, after more than fifty thousand miles of hard driving in less than six months, and with Bob Neal's help (and in Bob Neal's name) Elvis bought a 1951 Cosmopolitan Lincoln with only ten thousand miles on it. It was the first "new" car he had ever owned. He had a rack put on top for the bass, painted "Elvis Presley — Sun Records" on the side, and was so proud of it that he wouldn't allow anyone even to smoke in it. He didn't keep the car for much more than a month, though, because Bill wrecked it in Arkansas, driving it under a hay truck at a high rate of speed one night.

They were constantly on the go. Sometimes it seemed as if they didn't even have time to sleep. Houston, Dallas, Lubbock and all through West Texas. Hayride shows in Galveston, Waco, and Baton Rouge. Hawkins, Gilmer, and Tyler, Texas, all within calling distance of Tom Perryman's Gladewater radio signal. All the little towns scattered throughout the Mississippi and Arkansas Delta. Back to Cleveland for another date at the Circle Theater. El Dorado. Texarkana. The Hayride. "It was always exciting," in Elvis' view. "We slept in the back of the car, and we'd do a show and get offstage and get in the car and drive to the next town and sometimes just get there in time to wash up [and] do the show." Scotty and Bill were chasing the girls, and the girls were chasing Elvis — and frequently catching up with him. Everywhere he went he created a sensation. "He's the new rage," said a Louisiana radio executive in an interview with the British musical press. "Sings hillbilly in r&b time. Can you figure that out. He wears pink pants and a black coat . . . [and] he's going terrific. If he doesn't suffer too much popularity, he'll be all right."

"This cat came out," said future country singer Bob Luman, still a seventeen-year-old high school student in Kilgore, Texas, "in red pants and a green coat and a pink shirt and socks, and he had this sneer on his face and he stood behind the mike for five minutes, I'll bet, before he made a move. Then he hit his guitar a lick, and he broke two strings. Hell, I'd been playing ten years, and I hadn't broken a *total* of two strings. So there he was, these two strings dangling, and he hadn't done anything except break the strings yet, and these high school girls were screaming and fainting and running up to the stage, and then he started to move his hips real slow like he had a thing for his guitar. . . . For the next nine days he played one-nighters around Kilgore, and after school every day me and my girl would get in the car and go wherever he was playing that night. That's the last time I tried to sing like Webb Pierce or Lefty Frizzell."

Not surprisingly, he was not entirely unaffected by all this adulation. While everyone agreed that he continued to maintain a remarkably polite and deferential manner and never failed to show his elders an uncommon degree of respect, those meeting him for the first time encountered a somewhat different figure than they would have met six months, or even three months, before — more confident perhaps, understandably more suspicious, but overall simply more *himself.* Sometimes this could lead to sudden displays of temper, as at the Hayride, when in a famous local incident he punched the doorkeeper, a teenager named Shorty, in the nose, because Shorty either opened or closed the door on his fans. Everyone was surprised by the incident, no one more so than Elvis himself, who immediately apologized profusely and offered to pay all of the doctor's bills. The Miller Sisters, the performing duo that Sam had been working with, who met Elvis at a show in Saltillo, Mississippi, just down the road from where he was born, found him stuck-up and conceited. "He was really cocky," said one. "I remember Elvis asked me to hold his guitar, and I said, 'Hold it yourself. I'm not your flunky!' " But, of course, that may have just been his way with one woman.

"Elvis Presley continues to gather speed over the South," wrote Cecil Holifield, operator of the Record Shops in Midland and Odessa, Texas, in the June 4 edition of *Billboard.*

> West Texas is his hottest territory to date, and he is the teenagers' favorite wherever he appears. His original appearance in the area was in January with Billy Walker . . . to more than 1600 paid admissions. In February, with Hank Snow at Odessa . . . paid attendance hit over 4000. On April 1 we booked only Elvis and his boys, Bill and Scotty, plus Floyd Cramer on piano and a local boy on drums for a rockin' and rollin' dance for teenagers, and pulled 850 paid admissions. . . . Incidentally, our sales of Presley's four records have beat any individual artist in our eight years in the record business.

With a new Jamboree tour coming up in May, headlined by Hank Snow and covering the entire mid South, Elvis and Scotty and Bill were not about to start looking back. They didn't have the time. Bob Neal was excited and optimistic about all the connections Tom Parker was helping them to make. He felt as if they were finally about to move up to another league.

THE TOUR BEGAN on May 1 in New Orleans, the day after Elvis' fourth Sun single, "Baby, Let's Play House," was released. It was billed as a three-week, twenty-city tour that would employ thirty-one different artists, some of whom would pick up and leave the tour at various points. Headliners were Hank Snow, Slim Whitman, and the Carter Sisters with Mother Maybelle, and Martha Carson and Faron Young would join the show in Florida. In a solution the Colonel devised to prevent the kind of thing that had happened on the last tour, there would be a first half of "younger talent" that included Jimmie Rodgers Snow, the Davis Sisters, and the Wilburn Brothers, with "one of the newest though most exciting personalities in the Hillbilly field . . . [whose] singing style is completely different from any other singer in the field," Elvis Presley, appearing just before the intermission.

There were near-riots almost everywhere they played. Johnny Rivers saw the show in Baton Rouge and decided, "I wanna be like *that* guy," while in Mobile, Jimmie Rodgers Snow remembered Elvis being chased across a football field. There were girls in every city, and after the show Elvis never lacked for company, cruising around town in the pink and white Cadillac he had just acquired to replace the Lincoln (once again he had his name painted in black on the door). Jimmy Snow roomed with him on this tour, "and he would run the women, he'd run two or three of them in one night — whether or not he was actually making love to all three, I don't know, because he was kind of private in that sense and if I thought he was going to run some women in the room with him, I didn't stay. But I just think he wanted them around, it was a sense of insecurity, I guess, because I don't think he was a user. He just loved women, and I think they knew that."

Every night he called his parents at their new home on Lamar just to let them know how he was doing, how the show had gone, to find out how they were. Many nights Dixie was there, and he liked that, both because it saved him a call and because he knew that they were keeping an eye on her. "He didn't want to relinquish that control, regardless of how long he was gone or what he was doing; [he wanted to know] that I was still going to be sitting there. If I wasn't there, he would ask his parents, 'Was Dixie there?' Or: 'Have you heard from her? Has she been over? Did she spend the night?' I think he expected his parents to kind of keep me there while he was gone so I wouldn't do anything else — but it just got to be harder and harder after a while." He wanted to know how they liked the new house — they were still renting, of course, but it was the first time since they had moved to Memphis that they had had a real home of their own. How was Daddy feeling? Was his back any better? No, he reassured Gladys, she didn't have to worry, he was doing just fine — he knew it bothered her the way the audiences did sometimes, but they weren't going to hurt him any. Yes, they were taking good care of the new Caddy, wasn't it the prettiest thing? No, they were being careful. He didn't know if he'd even let Bill drive this one! And how was the pretty little pink and white Crown Victoria he had bought for them? It was the first new car they had ever owned. He tried to reassure her: he was safe, he was happy, he was still hers. But Gladys was not to be reassured. Some part of her feared what was about to happen. Some part of her feared what she saw was happening already. "I know she worshiped him, and he did her," said Dixie, "to the point where she would almost be jealous of anything else that took his time. I think she really had trouble accepting him as his popularity grew. It grew hard for her to let everybody have him. I had the same feelings. He did not belong to [us] anymore."

HE MET MAE BOREN AXTON, publicist for the Florida leg of the tour, at the first Florida date, in Daytona Beach. A forty-year-old English teacher at Paxon High School in Jacksonville, where her husband was the football coach, Axton had gotten into country music through the back door when she was asked by *Life Today*, a magazine for which she did occasional freelance work, to write an article on "hillbilly" music. Though she had been born in Fort Worth, Texas, and grew up in Oklahoma (her brother, David, later became a prominent U.S. senator from Oklahoma), she claimed to have no idea what hillbilly music was. "We listened to the opera, and my teacher taught me classical, and folk songs I knew, but the term 'hillbilly' was foreign to me." Her research took her to Nashville, where she met Minnie Pearl, who introduced her as a country songwriter to powerful song publishing executive Fred Rose. Taking

Mae for what Minnie Pearl said she was, Rose told her he needed a novelty song for a Dub Dickerson recording session that afternoon, and she wrote one, if only to prove her newfound friend correct.

Soon she had gotten a number of her songs cut (Dub Dickerson recorded more of their collaborations, as did Tommy Durdon) while continuing to write stories for fan club magazines. She hooked up with the Colonel in 1953 on a Hank Snow tour and began doing advance press work for him in the Jacksonville-Orlando-Daytona area. As a woman who was both attractive and feisty, Mae claimed to be the only person that she knew ever to get an apology out of the Colonel. Ordinarily, his one response to any form of criticism was "The Colonel is the boss." "You be the boss," she said angrily when he tried this line on her. "Be the big wheel. But don't ever ask me to do another thing for you." Which led to the apology. Despite this incident, or perhaps because of it, she always got along well with the Colonel and for a time even served as Hank Snow's personal publicist. She was energetic and resourceful and proved an excellent local PR woman on a management team that left nothing to chance.

They were scheduled to play Daytona Beach on May 7, and Mae met them at the motel. "I had gotten up real early and gone and done an interview about the show that night and about Elvis, and I came back around eleven, and, you know, the back of the motel was facing the ocean, the little rails were up there, the little iron rails. And I walked out of my door — my room was right near Elvis' — and Elvis was leaning over looking at the ocean. Of course there were a lot of people on the beach, and I said, 'Hi, honey, how are you doing?' And he looked up and said, 'Fine.' He said, 'Miz Axton, look at that ocean.' Of course I had seen it a million times. He said, 'I can't believe that it's so big.' It just overwhelmed him. He said, 'I'd give anything in the world to find enough money to bring my mother and daddy down here to see it.' That just went through my heart. 'Cause I looked down here, and here were all these other kids, different show members for that night, all the guys looking for cute little girls. But his priority was doing something for his mother and daddy."

In the interview he persisted in calling her Miz Axton, and she suggested that he "just make it Mae. That makes it better. . . . Elvis," she said, "you are sort of a bebop artist more than anything else, aren't you? Is that what they call you?"

Elvis: Well, I never have given myself a name, but a lot of the disc jockeys call me — bopping hillbilly and bebop, I don't know what else. . . .

Mae: I think that's very fine. And you've started touring the country, and you've covered a lot of territory in the last two months, I believe.

Elvis: Yes, ma'am, I've covered a lot — mostly in West Texas is where, that's where my records are hottest. Around in San Angelo and Lubbock and Midland and Amarillo —

Mae: They tell me they almost mobbed you there, the teenagers, they like you so much. But I happen to know you have toured all down in the eastern part of the country, too. Down through Florida and around and that the people went for you there about as well as out in West Texas, isn't that right?

Elvis: Well, I wasn't very well known down here — you know, I'm with a small company, and my records don't have the distribution that they should have, but —

Mae: . . . You know, I watched you perform one time down in Florida, and I noticed that the older people got as big a kick out of you as the teenagers, I think that was an amazing thing.

Elvis: Well, I imagine it's just the way we, all three of us move on the stage, you know, we act like we —

Mae: Yes, and we mustn't leave out Scotty and Bill. They really do a terrific job of backing you up.

Elvis: They sure do. I really am lucky to have those two boys, 'cause they really are good. Each one of them have an individual style of their own.

Mae: You know, what I can't understand is how you keep that leg shaking just at the right [general laughter] tempo all the time you're singing.

Elvis: Well, it gets hard sometimes. I have to stop and rest it — but it just automatically wiggles like that.

Mae: Is that it? Just automatically does it? You started back in high school, didn't you?

Elvis: Ah —

Mae: Singing around, public performances with school and things of that sort?

Elvis: Well, no, I never did sing anywhere in public in my life till I made this first record.

Mae: Is that right?

Elvis: Yes, ma'am.

Mae: And then you just went right on into their hearts, and you're doing a wonderful job, and I want to congratulate you on that, and I want to say, too, Elvis, it's been very nice having you in the studio —

Elvis: Well, thank you very much, Mae, and I'd like to personally thank you for really promoting my records down here because you really have done a wonderful job, and I really do appreciate it, because if you don't have people backing you, people pushing you, well, you might as well quit.

Later that night at the show Mae ran into one of her former students, now a student nurse. Elvis was onstage, "and she was just right into it, didn't know who he was, none of them did. But she was just ahhhh — all of them were, even some of the old ones were doing like that. I looked at the faces — they were loving it. And I said, 'Hey, honey, what is it about this kid?' And she said, 'Awww, Miz Axton, he's just a great big beautiful hunk of forbidden fruit.' "

They played Orlando that week, and local reporter Jean Yothers, still evidently in somewhat of a daze several days later, wrote it up in the *Orlando Sentinel* of May 16.

> What hillbilly music does to the hillbilly music fan is absolutely phenomenal. It transports him into a wild, emotional and audible state of ecstasy. He never sits back sedately patting his palms politely and uttering bravos of music appreciation as his long-hair counterpart. He thunders his appreciation for the country-style music and nasal-twanged singing he loves by whistling shrilly through teeth, pounding the palms together with the whirling momentum of a souped-up paddle wheel, stomping the floor and ejecting yip-yip

noises like the barks of a hound dog when it finally runs down a particularly elusive coon.

That's the way it was, friends, at the big Hank Snow show and all-star Grand Ole Opry Jamboree staged last week in municipal auditorium to jam-packed houses both performances. It was as hot as blue blazes within the tired sanctums of the barnish auditorium, but the hillbilly fans turned out in droves and seemed oblivious to the heat. . . . The whole shebang seemed like a cross between the enthusiasm displayed at a wrestling match and old-fashioned camp meeting. . . .

This was my first tangle with a hillbilly jamboree, a poignant contrast to Metropolitan Opera in Atlanta, I must say. I was awed and with all due respect to opera in Atlanta, I got a tremendous boot out of this loud, uninhibited music that's sending the country crazy. . . .

Ferron [Faron] Young was real sharp singing that ditty about living fast, loving hard, dying young and leaving a beautiful memory, but what really stole the show was this 20-year-old sensation, Elvis Presley, a real sex box as far as the teenage girls are concerned. They squealed themselves silly over this fellow in orange coat and sideburns who "sent" them with his unique arrangement of Shake, Rattle and Roll. And following the program, Elvis was surrounded by girlies asking for autographs. He would give each a long, slow look with drooped eyelids and comply. They ate it up. The crowd also ate up a peppy and perspiring Miss Martha Carson calling the parquet-sitting spectators "you folks a-sitten over there on the shelves" and the same Miss Carson breaking two guitar strings and a pick with her strong strumming of This Old House and Count Your Blessings. Fans were forever rushing up near the stage snapping flashbulb pictures during the program, and they all instinctively recognized a tune with recognizable roars before the second plunk of the guitar had been sounded. It was amazing! Hillbilly music is here to stay, yo'all!

On the thirteenth they played Jacksonville. Before the show Mae took Elvis and some of the other musicians out to dinner, and she tried to wheedle him out of the frilly pink shirt he was wearing. "Skeeter Davis was there, and June and Anita [Carter], and some of the boys with Elvis, and I said, 'Elvis, that's vulgar. And it would make me such a pretty blouse.' And Skeeter said, 'I want it,' and June said, 'I want it.' And he just kind of grinned. And I said, 'Elvis, you ought to give it to us, one of us anyway, because they are just going to tear it off you tonight.' Not really thinking about it — knowing the people liked him but not really thinking about it."

That night at the show, in front of fourteen thousand people, he announced at the conclusion of his act: "Girls, I'll see you all backstage." Almost immediately they were after him. The police got him into the Gator Bowl's dugout locker room, where Mae and the Colonel were totaling up the night's receipts. Most of the other acts were backstage, too, Mae recalled, when the fans started pouring in through an overhead window that had been inadvertently left open. "I heard feet like a thundering herd, and the next thing I knew I heard this voice from the shower area. I started running, and three or four policemen started running, too, and by the time we got there several hundred must have crawled in — well, maybe not that many, but a lot — and Elvis was on top of one of the showers looking sheepish and scared, like 'What'd I do?' and his shirt was shredded and his coat was torn to pieces. Somebody had even gotten his belt and his socks and these cute little boots — they were not cowboy boots, he was up there with nothing but his pants on and they were trying to pull at *them* up on the shower. Of course the police started getting them out, and I never will forget Faron Young — this one little girl had kind of a little hump at the back, and he kicked at her, and these little boots fell out."

The Colonel, said Mae, "and I don't mean it derogatorily, got dollar marks in his eyes." It was Jacksonville, said Oscar Davis, that marked the turning point — that was the real eye-opener, the Colonel said to him. By the time the show got to Richmond three days later, it was as if Elvis had never been anything but the Colonel's boy. The whole troupe was staying at the old Jefferson Hotel, and by happenstance RCA c&w promotion manager Chick Crumpacker was in Richmond on one of his three-or-four-times-a-year southern swings to meet DJs, distributors, and field reps. Regional representative Brad McCuen, who had heard Elvis' first record in Knoxville the previous year and, witnessing the reaction to it, sent it on to New York with a glowing report, persuaded Crumpacker to go to the show, and Crumpacker, a sophisticated, serious, and witty Northwestern School of Music graduate who continued to write classical compositions but had a healthy respect for "America's folk music," enthusiastically accepted. Both Crumpacker and McCuen knew the Colonel not only from his present association with Hank Snow and his former management of

Eddy Arnold, RCA's two leading country artists, but because each had briefly accompanied the RCA Country Caravan, which the Colonel had managed the previous year. Both had had interesting experiences with the Colonel. In Jacksonville the previous April, in Chick's presence, Parker had accused publicist Anne Fulchino of "deliberately steering *Life* and *Look* magazine people, whom she had gotten to cover the show, away from him and his wife Marie, who he bragged were responsible for the Caravan's success. When I attempted to explain that this wasn't so, he turned nearly physical and said he would have both our jobs over it." Brad, who had worked extensively with Snow and Eddy Arnold for a number of years, had enjoyed a more congenial relationship overall, but from the opportunity he had had to watch the Colonel in action, he, too, was fully aware of Parker's mania for control, his need to maintain the upper hand, and his predilection for unpredictable acts in order to keep even close friends and associates on their toes. Neither man was entirely certain of the reception they would get, but, true to form, the Colonel surprised them by acting as if he couldn't have been more pleased to see two such old and dear friends.

They were even more surprised by the show they saw that night. Although Chick had been prepared to some extent by McCuen's description of the music, and he might have heard one or two of the records himself in passing, neither one of them had seen the boy perform, and neither was prepared for either the ferocity of his performance or the reaction to it. "We were astounded by the reaction," said Chick, "both among the Richmonders and in ourselves. There were kids in the audience — it was definitely a noisier audience than I remembered from the Caravan the year before. And lo and behold, out comes this guy whose picture we had seen in the trade papers, and he was something else. All the mannerisms were more or less in place. The body language — I don't remember exactly what he sang, but there were frequent belches into the mike, and the clincher came when he took his chewing gum out and tossed it into the audience. This, of course, was shocking, it was wild — but what really got the listeners was his energy and *the way he sang the songs*. The effect was galvanic. It was also somewhat embarrassing, because as friends and promoters of Jimmie Rodgers Snow, we had to watch him be totally eclipsed."

The next morning they had breakfast with the Colonel and Hank Snow. Then to Chick's surprise: "In walks the young star. And the first impression I had is the one that will always stick: that he was so unassuming, he seemed somewhat withdrawn at first, looked nervously around the room, but he had this quality — he was very, very smart behind it all, and he knew how to flatter people. We talked about the show, exchanged views about the crowd, the turnout, the other artists — he was very affable, he would say to Brad and me how much he enjoyed being with us; 'I like you, Chick,' he said. And while this may well have been a ploy, it worked. We liked him, immensely, from the start."

Chick finished up his trip in Louisville, but not before purchasing all four of Elvis' Sun records, two copies of each, one to present to RCA's country and western division head, Steve Sholes. "Throughout that spring and the early part of that summer I did a lot of wishful thinking with Sholes — maybe we could sign this guy. But as far as I know, there were no rumors at this point that his contract was for sale. There was no question that the Colonel had his eye on him, though, the Colonel was *definitely* taking a proprietary attitude, even if nothing was explicitly said or voiced."

TAMPA, JULY 1955. (POPSIE. COURTESY OF GER RIJFF)

MYSTERY TRAIN

BOB NEAL, manager of Elvis Presley," declared the July 9 issue of *Billboard,* "reports that his charge this week begins a fortnight's vacation before embarking on a busy summer and fall schedule being arranged by Col. Tom Parker, Jamboree Attractions, Madison, Tenn."

He had been working steadily, virtually every night, since the show at Ellis Auditorium on February 6, and in that short time he had come further than either he or his manager had ever dared hope. He had opened up new territory, more than held his own with some of the biggest Opry stars, and attracted the favor of a man who had it in his power, Neal insisted, to do even more for him than he had already done.

On balance Bob Neal was well satisfied: he had seen bookings pick up, watched his own and Elvis' material situations dramatically improve, and redrafted their agreement to last until March 1956, with an option to renew. He had also witnessed the kind of growth he would never have taken on faith, an almost exponential progression that had taken place in the boy himself, not just in his stage manner (which would alone have been remarkable enough) but in an appetite for change and self-improvement that seemed to know no experiential bounds. Not that the boy would ever be mistaken for an intellectual — and he was far too jittery to be called introspective. But he soaked up influences like litmus paper; he was open to new people and new ideas and new experiences in a way that defied social stereotype. He was *serious* about his work. Whenever Neal went by the house, he found him with a stack of records — Ray Charles and Big Joe Turner and Big Mama Thornton and Arthur "Big Boy" Crudup — that he studied with all the avidity that other kids focused on their college exams. He listened over and over, seeming to hear something that no one else could hear, while able to carry on a perfectly coherent conversation at the same time on the subject of bookings or the upcoming Florida tour (what were they going to do in Jacksonville for an encore?) or something that Helen needed to know for the fan club, with Dixie all the while sitting by his side.

Vernon was around most of the time — he didn't seem terribly ambitious about going out and looking for a job. Bob was a little worried about that; you could never tell what went on inside a family, and sometimes it seemed to him as if there was "a little rift" between father and son over the father's disinclination to work. "But Gladys kept the family together, she was very down-to-earth, always concerned about his health and well-being, and was always concerned about those of us around him. He was very aware of the fact that she did everything she possibly could to help give him a chance, and he wanted so much to do big things and nice things particularly for his mother. I remember coming back from a show one night, he was commenting to Helen, 'Oh, I just want to be big, because I want to do something for my folks.' He said, 'They're getting old.' I looked at Elvis, and I said, 'Elvis, how old do you think I am?' And he said, 'Well, I don't know.' . . . I was, I think, a year or two older than Vernon."

Elvis was glad to be home while at the same time anxious to be on to the next step. It had all started to get to him a little toward the end of the tour. Just two and a half weeks before, on June 17, on the road between Hope and Texarkana, a wheel bearing caught fire, and he had watched his pretty pink Cadillac burn up. He hadn't had it three months and had played just outside of Tupelo only two days before, where he showed it off and paraded around town in his kelly green suit. For a moment, as Scotty and Bill gave him a hard time and the instruments and clothing sat forlornly by the side of the road, it was like watching all his dreams go up in flames — but then there was business to be taken care of, they had to charter a plane to get to the next show, call Bob, get someone to drive the Crown Victoria down to meet them in Dallas, move *on*. Then on July 4 he found himself playing a picnic with the Blackwood Brothers and the Statesmen Quartet at gospel promoter W. B. Nowlin's All-Day Singing and dinner on the ground in De Leon, Texas. He showed up in his pink suit, according to James Blackwood, but whether or not he knew anything in advance about Nowlin's annual picnic event (it had started seven years earlier with Eddy Arnold and the Stamps Quartet; in 1950 Hank Williams had been booked with the Blackwoods), there was something about the scene that brought him up short: all those families gathered with their kids, eating fried chicken in the afternoon sunlight under the pecan trees in Hodges Park.

"I ain't gonna sing nothing but gospel music today," he told James in the Blackwood Brothers' new bus as they swapped stories and songs, and nothing that James could say would dissuade him. Onstage it was almost as if he were spellbound; he didn't respond when people called out for his songs, "he fell flat on his face," said J. D. Sumner, the bass singer with the group. By evening the spell — if that was what it was — was broken. The whole troupe appeared in Stephenville at a jamboree that also featured Slim Willett ("Don't Let the Stars Get in Your Eyes"), the Faren Twins, and the Stamps Quartet. Elvis did his normal show and got his normal reaction. "It was mighty warm in our rec. hall," reported DJ/promoter Bill Bentley, "but next year it will be cool, as we have decided to air condition it."

Even coming home was not like coming home exactly. For one thing, he was coming home to a new house, the first single-family structure the Presleys had lived in since moving to Memphis, and even though he had slept there before, it was never for more than a night or two, he had been on the road so steadily since they had moved in three months earlier. It was a modest two-bedroom brick bungalow at 2414 Lamar, partway between Katz Drug Store, where Elvis and Scotty and Bill had created such a sensation not ten months previously, and the Rainbow skating rink, where Elvis and Dixie had first met. If you continued east on Lamar, it took you past the Eagle's Nest and, as Highway 78, all the way to Tupelo. It was the road on which the Presleys had first arrived in Memphis, and he didn't know how many times he had traveled it, going in and out of town as a small child and as a young man, but somehow it seemed different now, he felt almost like a stranger. For the first couple of days after he got home he mostly slept.

The next-door neighbors, the Bakers, with three teenagers in the family, two boys and a girl, waited eagerly for their first real glimpse of the young scion of the house. The Presleys didn't have a phone of their own for quite some time — it was difficult to get a new phone installed in those days — so Mr. and Mrs. Presley were frequent visitors to the Bakers' house to make calls, and Mrs. Baker had had a memorable encounter with Mrs. Presley on the night they had moved in. Mr. Presley must still have been moving things from their old house, because he wasn't there when one of her cousins burst in on the Bakers and announced that Mrs. Presley had passed out on the bed. The cousin didn't know if the Presleys had a regular doctor of their own, so Mrs. Baker called her own doctor, who came out and pronounced Mrs. Presley a sick woman — Mrs. Baker understood it was diabetes or a bad heart, something along those lines. Which was a shame in such a young woman. Since then, while they never became exactly friends, Mrs. Baker had felt sorry for Mrs. Presley, the nicest-mannered person but a "nervous creature" who seemed to carry such a burden of sadness that she couldn't stand to even be in the house alone.

The night that Elvis' Cadillac burned up, as the Bakers remembered it, they got the call, but Mrs. Presley seemed to know what was the matter even before she picked up the phone. After that she could scarcely bear to even contemplate the dangers that her son faced out on the road. As much as she wanted success for him, it was almost as if any satisfaction she might take in it was gone. One time she invited Mrs. Baker and her daughter, Sarah, over to the house. "Come here, come here," she said, and showed them his closet, full of clothes in black and pink. She was so proud of all his shoes and the suits hanging up, and she talked about her son in a manner that she talked about nothing else. She convinced Mrs. Baker that he didn't deserve all the criticism that was being directed at him, that he wasn't vulgar in his movements, that he didn't mean anything by it, he just put his whole self into what he did.

Mr. Presley was another story altogether. He was what you might call a very "dry" man, never offering much in the way of amenities or even response. Mr. Baker had even started latching the screen door for a while, because Mr. Presley would walk in without so much as a knock, to use the phone or borrow something, day or night — he didn't mean anything by it, he just didn't know any better, they supposed, but Mr. Baker didn't like it so he put a hook on the door. They watched Vernon in the yard, working with a brother or brother-in-law occasionally, installing air conditioners in new cars whenever, it seemed, he felt like it, and they felt even sorrier for poor Mrs. Presley, but they knew the family was very dedicated to one another — they were even talking about buying the little house someday and adding on a room for Mr. Presley's mother, who stayed with them much of the time.

When he finally got used to being home, Elvis started popping in on the Bakers to make some calls, and to take some, too, showing a graciousness and a natural ease that they could never forget. The first time the two younger kids, Jack and Sarah, saw him, he was on the phone, and he turned to them and introduced himself, as if they would have no idea who he was. It was as if, fourteen-year-old Sarah thought, "he was looking up to you, whoever you were, he certainly didn't want any of us to treat him like he was more important than any of us were."

"We'll have to double-date sometime," he said to eighteen-year-old Don Baker, and though they never did, no one in the family suspected him of hypocrisy; it was all just part of the "mannerliness" that announced in a contradictory way (because it denoted such self-assurance) "I am really someone." When they saw him on the phone, they imagined that he was speaking to Hollywood, to far-off, distant lands, even though he was probably just talking to Scotty, his guitarist, or Colonel Parker in Nashville, who called more and more frequently, it seemed, with details of his upcoming tour. As the days passed they could hear him playing his records, the rhythm and blues music that Dewey Phillips played on the air, through the open windows of the little house on the busy city street on a still, hot summer's day.

THERE WAS SO MUCH TO DO in the little time that he had left. Now that he had a real place of his own, Scotty and Bill came by a few times to rehearse. They played out on the little screened-in porch, and the kids next door and their friends sat out on the grass and listened. "What do you want to hear?" Bill said to them, clowning around, and Elvis favored them with his dazzling smile, asking if they liked the music. With Bob Neal's help once again (the title and financing were still in Bob's name) he purchased another Cadillac, brand-new this time, and at Helen Neal's suggestion had it painted in his customized colors of pink and black. When he drove it down to Lansky's, he showed it off proudly to everyone on Beale and then walked up to Guy Lansky in the store dangling the keys. "He told me to drive it around the block. He said, 'Mr. Lansky, I want you to tell me what you think of it.' He loved it, and this was the biggest mistake I ever made: here I am heavily in debt with all this merchandise, and I think, 'If I drive it around the block, if I wreck this automobile, it's gonna cost me a ton of money.' So I refused him. And he was really disappointed. He felt bad that I wouldn't drive it: he couldn't get over it. He loved that automobile, and here I dropped him. I've felt bad about it ever since."

Dixie came by the house just as often as she ever had. Young Jack Baker and his sister spied on them sometimes holding hands in the backyard, playing with the little white dog that Sarah took care of when the

Presleys were away. Elvis had just taken Dixie to her junior prom, borrowing Bob Neal's brand-new Lincoln for the occasion and double-dating with Dixie's best friend, Bessie Wolverton, and his cousin Gene. He looked handsome in his white tuxedo jacket; she was really proud of him and proud to be able to show him off to all her friends. She tried to make friends with some of his new acquaintances, but she found it harder and harder to fit into his life. She knew Red West, of course — Red had been with him off and on all winter and spring, and since school had gotten out he had started accompanying Elvis regularly on tour. When he went off to college in the fall, she knew, Elvis wanted to get him a car. Red was nice enough, he was always courteous to her, anyway, but some of the new guys who had started hanging around just weren't the kind of people that she and Elvis had ever been drawn to. "They used horrible language, they all smoked, everybody had a drink — it was a group of people I was totally uncomfortable with." More and more, it seemed, he wanted to be with the crowd, they rarely were alone together even in the brief time that they had; "a lot of times he had to go with the guys and party around, that sort of thing." She could understand when he went off to play football with Red at Guthrie Park or down at the Triangle with his old friends, but sometimes it seemed as if he had been swept up in the turmoil himself — he came alive only when other people were around and seemed to crave their attention in a way that neither of them had imagined he ever would.

They had broken up more than once already. Usually the argument was about what *she* was doing while he was away, though really, she suspected, the shoe should have been on the other foot. He couldn't stand for her to have any kind of independent existence, even as he was escaping the very world they had constructed for themselves. What was she doing? Who was she seeing? Where had she been when he called? She wasn't going to lie about it. "Of course I had other friends, the same circle of girlfriends I had always had. I wasn't dating anybody, but we would go out to a canteen called the Busy Betty on Lamar. They had a jukebox, and we'd dance. It got to the point where, Look, you're gone three weeks, and I'm supposed to just sit here every weekend and watch TV? That was the basis of every argument we ever had. He was very possessive and very jealous. I think he knew that what he was asking was unreasonable, but there was nothing he could do about it. It was very dramatic. Several times I gave him back his class ring, or he took it back. And that would last maybe a day, maybe just that night, sometimes before I would get in the house he would drive around the block and come back and say, 'Wait,' and we would sit out on the porch and cry about it. Sometimes my mother would come to the door two or three times and peck on the glass and say, 'Come in,' and I'd say, 'Just a minute.' I thought, you know, 'I can't leave,' because we were both so upset and we were going to break up and we didn't want to break up, because we were still friends. You know, I probably spent more time with his mom and dad than he did with them. When he was out of town, I would go over and stay with them, I spent the night lots of times and slept in his bed while he was gone. Mrs. Presley and I cooked together and ate, and we'd walk. We'd come uptown and just browse around. We'd just kind of console each other."

HIS MIND WAS INCREASINGLY on things that hadn't happened yet — things that Bob Neal and Mr. Phillips had told him would come about, things that Colonel Parker had promised would come to pass before too long in ways that he couldn't altogether imagine. He told Dixie about the Colonel, though she wasn't sure she understood; he talked with Bob about all the ways in which the Colonel would be able to help them out; he talked to his parents all the time about this Colonel Parker, who had done such a great job promoting the last Florida tour. He kept telling them about Colonel Parker, said Vernon, "talking about [what] a great man he had met, how smart he was and all of that. . . . Gladys and I warned him that we really didn't know anything about this man, and anyway, he had an agreement with Bob Neal." Bob would be a part of any arrangement that was made, Elvis assured them. This was something that Bob couldn't really handle on his own. Bob knew that as well as anyone. Bob didn't have the connections that Colonel Parker had. The Colonel had friends in high places. The Colonel had been to Hollywood.

He wanted it as badly as anything he had ever wanted in his life, and he went about getting it in exactly the same single-minded way, even though — it was kind of funny — he could no more name what it was than he could have predicted what was going to happen when he first walked in the door of the Sun studio. Gladys didn't want to hear any more about what the Colonel could do for them; she was simply fearful for her son, while Vernon reacted after a fashion of his own. He was proud of his boy, to the casual acquaintance he showed all the slow-witted pride of a man who'd won the lottery, but to those who knew this handsome, soft-spoken man, withdrawn at times almost to the point of sullenness, he seemed increasingly unsure of himself, increasingly adrift. To Dixie both parents were equally affected. "I think a lot of it had to do with Mr. and Mrs. Presley's resistance to the lifestyle that he was getting into — they had no control over him anymore. It was a very frustrating feeling." And yet the father knew what the boy was saying probably made sense. He liked Bob, he was comfortable with Bob, you could *talk* to Bob — and like he told the boy, he didn't know a thing about this Colonel Parker. But he supposed he was going to have to learn, because the man never stopped calling and sending telegrams; he obviously didn't worry about his long-distance bills. And he was beginning to see that what this Colonel fellow was saying to Elvis was probably true: Memphis wasn't big enough, Sun Records didn't have the kind of national distribution or pay the kind of money that the big companies did, he could see *that*. Marion Keisker detected what she felt was a very noticeable change in manner toward Sam. "I got the feeling that Mr. Presley felt that Sun Records depended on Elvis Presley rather than vice versa. One day he said within my earshot, 'Well, you know, the studio wouldn't be nothing without my boy.' I don't think Sam was even there, but I thought, 'Well, that does it.' The whole picture was changing."

Meanwhile Bob Neal was fielding offers, or at least inquiries, on an almost weekly basis from nearly every major and independent label with whom he had any contact. According to Neal, "Sam had let it be known that he would be interested in talking to them if the money was right," and while Neal made it clear that he did not represent the record company in any way, that he was only an intermediary, most of the offers came through him. Sam always turned them down or upped the ante in such a way that he could be confident that *he* would be turned down. One time Columbia head Mitch Miller, who had been hyped by Bill Randle, the Cleveland DJ (Randle had recently handed Miller "The Yellow Rose of Texas," Columbia's, and Miller's, latest hit), reached Neal on the phone in a West Texas motel. "He said, 'What do you want?' I said, 'I'll find out,' and I called Sam. As I recall, it was around eighteen thousand dollars that Sam was asking that day, so I called Mitch back, and he said, 'Oh, forget it, nobody's worth that much.' " Frank Walker, president of MGM, telegrammed Sam on June 8 after having heard from Sam's brother Jud that Elvis' contract was available, and Sam turned down Decca when they made an offer that met Jud's price. Capitol, Mercury, Chess, Atlantic, Randy Wood's Dot label (currently enjoying great success with Wood's latest discovery, Pat Boone), all exhibited active interest — there were rumblings throughout the entire industry.

And while Sam liked to act as if selling Elvis' contract were the furthest thing from his mind, as though all this was happening solely at the instigation of strangers, or that Bob Neal was going around without authorization just shooting off his mouth, Bob knew that Sam was strapped for cash, that the little record company was stretched to the limit by its very success, and that Jud was pressing Sam for money (he either wanted some return on his investment or cash to buy out the minority interest he had acquired when he helped Sam buy out Jim Bulleit the previous year). As Marion said, Sam was not a "partner-type person in any form or fashion," but Bob knew that if Sam wanted to preserve his vaunted independence, if he wanted to keep his label and move forward in the new directions he was eager to explore, he was going to have to make a hard decision soon.

Bob reported some of the offers to Elvis; others he kept to himself. He didn't want to overwhelm the boy with *possibilities*, and after some years in the business himself he knew that most of them would come to nothing. But it was clear that something was going on — you didn't have so many important people talking about you, looking to jump on the bandwagon, if the bandwagon wasn't getting ready to move out. He thought they were positioned just about perfectly. The July 16 issue of *Billboard* showed "Baby, Let's Play House" at number fifteen on the national country and western charts, and the summer issue of *Country Song Roundup*, with a picture of Hank Snow on the cover, featured the story "Elvis Presley — Folk Music Fireball," following national features in *Cowboy Songs* and *Country & Western Jamboree*. Bob liked the boy — he couldn't say anything bad about him, he was almost like another member of the family. They all went waterskiing on McKellar Lake together and picnicked out at Riverside Park; when Bob's son Sonny ran for student council in the spring, Elvis and Scotty and Bill appeared at the Messick High chapel program in support of his campaign, and Elvis regarded Helen almost like a second mother. Bob couldn't imagine ever losing him, and when he talked to Colonel Parker about all their far-flung plans, it was never with anything less than a sense of partnership in a glowing future. There were certain unpleasant realities to be faced, to be sure: the financial arrangements with Scotty and Bill were going to have to be changed, and they would have to be satisfied with a salaried status rather than the original agreement, which gave 50 percent to Elvis and 25 percent to each of them. But Elvis understood that, and they would have to understand it, too. The kids were coming out to see Elvis now — it wasn't the Blue Moon Boys who were drawing the crowds. With a little luck, and with the Colonel's invaluable assistance, Bob Neal was firmly convinced, from here on in it was going to be nothing but smooth sailing.

On July 11, Elvis went back into the Sun studio. In about a week he would be out on the road again, and it seemed like he had scarcely been home at all. Everywhere he went around town — on Beale Street, at the movies, at a drive-in for a hamburger, just waiting at a stoplight — it seemed as if he was known, it seemed as if something was *expected* of him, and he was always prepared to oblige, with a wink, with a wave, with a knowing but deferential nod of his head. Only in the studio were things still the same: Marion in the outer room, with the venetian blinds slanted to fight the heat, Sam in the control room, waiting, watching, always ready for something to happen, Scotty and Bill reassuringly constant — they would never change. For this session Mr. Phillips had brought in another original number and another drummer. The song was, once again, a country composition by Stan Kesler, the steel guitar player who had written "I'm Left, You're Right, She's Gone," and the drummer was Johnny Bernero, who played regularly with a number of different country bands and worked at the Memphis Light, Gas and Water Company across the street.

The song, Sam knew, was not to Elvis' taste — "he just didn't dig it at first. Maybe it was a little too country, the chord progression, and it was a slow song, too. But I loved the hook line, and I thought it was something we needed at that point to show a little more diversification. So I called Johnny — he was either in there that day, or I called him, 'cause he had played on some other things for me. And we got it going, and he was doing four-four on the beat, and I said, 'That don't help us worth a shit, Johnny.' I told him, 'What I want you to do is do your rim shot snare on the offbeat, but keep it four-four until we go into the chorus. Then you go in and go with the bass beat at two-four.' And by doing that, it sounds like

'I Forgot to Remember to Forget' is twice as fast as it really is. And Elvis really loved it then."

With the next cut there was no need for any such trickery. They were just fooling around without the drummer when they hit on a lick from "Mystery Train," the song Sam had originally cut on Little Junior Parker and the Blue Flames just two years before, and they went from there. It was the driving rhythm-based kind of blues that Sam had been feeding Scotty ever since they started recording, and the three of them fell in with the same natural exuberance that they had first applied to "That's All Right," but with a degree of knowledge — of themselves as much as of any musical technique — that they had not possessed a year earlier. "There was an extra bar of rhythm thrown in at one point," said Scotty, "that if I sat down to play it myself right now, I couldn't, but with him singing it felt natural." "It was the greatest thing I ever did on Elvis," said Sam. "It was a feeling song that so many people had experienced — I mean, it was a big thing, to put a loved one on a train: are they leaving you forever? Maybe they'll never be back. 'Train I ride, sixteen coaches long' — you can take it from the inside of the coach, or you can take it from the outside, standing looking in. Junior was going to make it fifty coaches, but I said, no, sixteen coaches is a helluva lot, that sounds like it's coming out of a small town. It was pure rhythm. And at the end, Elvis was laughing, because he didn't think it was a take, but I'm sorry, it was a fucking masterpiece!"

The last cut they did was a rhythm and blues number, "Trying to Get to You," that they had tried without success earlier in the year. This time it was as free and unfettered as anything they had ever done, even with the addition of Johnny Bernero on drums and Elvis chording on piano, and like "Mystery Train" it aspired to a higher kind of — mystery, for want of a better word. There was a floating sense of inner harmony mixed with a ferocious hunger, a desperate striving linked to a pure outpouring of joy, that seemed to just tumble out of the music. It was the very attainment of art and passion, the natural beauty of the instinctive soul that Sam Phillips had been searching for ever since he first started in music, and there was no question that Elvis knew that he had achieved it.

For the few remaining days of his holiday he cruised around town — with Dixie, with Red and his cousin Gene, he stopped in to see Dewey at the radio station. With Dewey he visited the clubs on Beale, where

Dewey was still hailed as a conquering hero and this white boy who sang the blues was readily accepted as yet another of Dewey's crazy ideas. "Elvis had the feel of Beale Street," said Sam Phillips. "He was probably more at home there than he was on Main. You know, Elvis didn't walk into Lansky Brothers because someone suggested, 'Why don't you buy a chartreuse fucking shirt?' " "We had a lot of fun with him," said WDIA's Professor Nat D. Williams, the unofficial ambassador of Beale. "Elvis Presley on Beale Street when he first started was a favorite man. . . . Always he had that certain humanness about him that Negroes like to put in their songs." That was what he was aiming for, that common human element, and that was what he achieved — there was nowhere he couldn't go that in one sense or another he didn't feel at home, but if that was so, why was it that he felt increasingly like a stranger, as if he alone sensed not only the breadth of possibilities but the dangers lurking in the great world that existed outside of his hometown?

Then he was back on the road, in Texas first, next in a return to Florida that was marked by mounting expectations and increased attention from the press. Few doubted that the Colonel fueled either those expectations or that attention. The show was headlined by philosopher/comic Andy Griffith ("You saw him in U.S. Steel Hour TV production No Time for Sergeants NOW SEE HIM IN PERSON") and also included Ferlin Huskey with His Hush Puppies, Marty Robbins, Jimmie Rodgers Snow, "newcomers" Tommy Collins and Glenn Reeves, and "EXTRA EXTRA By Popular Demand ELVIS PRESLEY with Scotty & Bill." At the bottom of each newspaper ad came Oscar Davis' tag line, *"Don't You Dare Miss It,"* and few Florida country music fans did.

In Jacksonville, the scene of the first riot, in May, there was another near-riot, and "before he could be rescued from his swooning admirers," *Cashbox* reported in an account that could have been written by the Colonel himself, "they had relieved him of his tie, handkerchiefs, belt, and the greater part of his coat and shirt. Col. Tom Parker presented him with a new sports coat to replace the one snatched by souvenir collectors."

The Florida tour ended in Tampa on July 31, and he immediately began another, a five-day package set up by Bob Neal, this time with Webb Pierce, Wanda Jackson, and new Sun recording artist Johnny Cash. They played Sheffield, Alabama, on August 2, then on the third they were booked into Little Rock, where Mr. and Mrs. Presley were scheduled to arrive and sign a contract naming the Colonel "special adviser" to both

Elvis and Bob Neal. Vernon came to the meeting pretty much prepared to sign, but Gladys balked. She was frightened by the riots in Florida, she said, she didn't know why there was such a rush to do anything at this point, she was afraid of what might happen to her boy. Well, that was certainly understandable, said the Colonel — he, too, felt like maybe her boy was being overworked. But if the money was right, why, then, Bob wouldn't have to book him into so many of these little dates, he could even think about taking some time off, maybe going to Florida with Mr. and Mrs. Presley or spending a few days with Colonel and Mrs. Parker over in Madison. The Colonel would never want to see any repetition of what had happened in Jacksonville. Bob Neal pricked up his ears. There was no need to sign anything now, said the Colonel. Once they got things straightened out, though, he could guarantee Mrs. Presley that nothing like the Jacksonville incident would ever happen again.

The Colonel suggested that he and Neal withdraw at this point. He left the senior Presleys in the dressing room with Grand Ole Opry comic Whitey Ford, the Duke of Paducah ("I'm goin' back to the wagon, these shoes are killing me"). Ford, a native of Little Rock, had worked the original Hank Snow tour in February and was a longtime friend and associate of the Colonel's as well as a neighbor. He was also known for his work with church and youth groups, and though he was not on the bill, the Colonel had prevailed upon him to ride over to Little Rock to bolster the Colonel's case. "Mrs. Presley was reluctant," Ford told writer Vince Staten, "very reluctant at first. She didn't want Elvis to make any changes, because he was under all these contracts. But I told her these could all be bought up. . . . I told her I had known the Colonel for years and that he really knew all the angles for producing successful shows." Elvis' friend Jimmie Rodgers Snow had done his best to convey pretty much the same message. "They were country people, and Colonel was very slick — I'm sure they picked up on that. I think they were more concerned with sticking with Bob Neal. The idea was to explain to them that they had to progress and go forward. I probably talked more to Mrs. Presley than to Vernon, because she was really the one who made the decisions."

In the end Gladys' reluctance temporarily prevailed. "He seemed like a smart man," said Vernon, "but we still didn't know too much about him, so we didn't sign." Elvis was bitterly disappointed. He hovered around for what seemed like an eternity, hoping that his parents would change their mind, but when they didn't he had no choice but to accept the Colonel's reassurances. There was nothing to worry about, the Colonel intoned without the slightest hint of doubt, they had made a fine beginning. It would all work out in the end.

He played Camden, Arkansas, the following night and then on August 5 returned to Memphis in a triumphant homecoming concert at the Overton Park Shell, the site of his initial unpremeditated triumph as the misspelled bottom of a bill starring Slim Whitman and Billy Walker. This time he was second headliner (beneath Webb Pierce and the Wondering Boys) of a twenty-two-act bill that marked the finale of "the eighth annual Bob Neal country jamboree series," and the story in the *Press-Scimitar* the next day had images of hometown heroes Elvis Presley and Johnny Cash superimposed on a shirtsleeved crowd of four thousand that jammed the shell while "several hundred had to be turned away." Marion Keisker attended the show, the first time she had seen Elvis perform since the Opry appearance nearly a year before, and described how she "heard someone screaming, and I'm really a very restrained person publicly, but all of a sudden I realized, 'It's me!' This staid mother of a young son — I'd lost my total stupid mind." It didn't altogether surprise her in a way. She adored Elvis, and she was experiencing the most bittersweet feelings of dread, regret, and a measure of anticipation as she watched the drama play itself out.

For the first time since she had known him, Sam simply didn't seem to know what to do. It would clearly be to their advantage for Parker to peddle the contract, and it would probably be to Elvis' advantage at this point, too. Somehow, though, it was as if Sam simply could not commit himself to the bargain he knew he had to make. "Of course I never actually met the Colonel until the [RCA] contract signing, but I felt that Sam had a great deal of contempt for him. I don't know if I ever heard Sam actually say anything pejorative, but I felt that other than Sam's self-interest, he didn't feel it was in Elvis' best interest to go with Colonel Parker even at that point. I think it was the only thing Elvis ever did against Sam's advice, though Sam might deny it. He didn't think it would be a wise thing, but since it seemed inevitable, he didn't fight it. And Elvis was so innately ingenuous. It's when you lie and digress that you get into trouble, but I don't think he ever said a wrong thing into a microphone or camera his whole life."

The day after the concert the new single came out, to be greeted with a *Billboard* "Spotlight" review that declared it "a splendid coupling" and a

"Best Buy" write-up three weeks later that said, "With each release Presley has been coming more and more to the forefront. His current record has wasted no time in establishing itself. Already it appears on the Memphis and Houston territorial charts. It is also reported selling well in Richmond, Atlanta, Durham, Nashville and Dallas."

Meanwhile, the Colonel pulled out all the stops. In the immediate aftermath of their Little Rock meeting, he bombarded the Presleys with phone calls, made sure that his colleague the Duke of Paducah stayed in touch, and consulted with Bob Neal on an almost daily basis so that all parties would fully understand the advantages of the arrangement, not just for the boy but for Neal as well, and for all other parties involved. Noting the Presleys' high regard for Hank Snow, he had Snow, too, make a number of telephone calls. "I think Colonel would have used anybody to influence them," said Jimmie Rodgers Snow, "because they were slow and he was smart enough to realize that he could not directly influence them himself. But I'll tell you what, I think they probably signed not so much because of Parker and what he'd do, but because they liked my dad."

On August 15 they all met once again, in Memphis, and Elvis proudly affixed his signature at the top of a document that named "Col. Thomas A. Parker" as "special adviser to Elvis Presley ['artist'] and Bob Neal ['manager'] for the period of one year and two one-year options for the sum of two thousand, five hundred dollars per year, payable in five payments of five hundred dollars each, to negotiate and assist in any way possible the build-up of Elvis Presley as an artist. Col. Parker will be reimbursed for any out-of-pocket expenses for travelling, promotion, advertising as approved by Elvis Presley and his manager."

The Colonel retained exclusive rights to one hundred appearances over the course of the next year, for which the artist would be paid $200 each, "including his musicians." In addition, in the event that "negotiations come to a complete standstill and Elvis Presley and his manager and associates decide to freelance," the Colonel would be reimbursed for his expenses and, "at the special rate of one hundred seventy five dollars per day for the first appearance and two hundred fifty dollars for the second appearance and three hundred fifty dollars [for the third]," the Colonel retained exclusive territorial rights to "San Antonio, El Paso, Phoenix, Tucson, Albuquerque, Oklahoma City, Denver, Wichita Falls, Wichita, New Orleans, Mobile, Jacksonville, Pensacola, Tampa, Miami, Orlando,

Charleston, Greenville, Spartanburg, Asheville, Knoxville, Roanoke, Richmond, Norfolk, Washington, D.C., Philadelphia, Newark, New York, Pittsburgh, Chicago, Omaha, Milwaukee, Minneapolis, St. Paul, Des Moines, Los Angeles, Amarillo, Houston, Galveston, Corpus Christi, Las Vegas, Reno, Cleveland, Dayton, Akron, and Columbus.

"Colonel Parker," the agreement concluded, "is to negotiate all renewals on existing contracts."

With that Elvis was back on tour, only now as an official member of Hank Snow's Jamboree Attractions. On the surface nothing had really changed, unless it was to embolden the trio to add a permanent fourth member. Going back into Texarkana at the end of the month for the fourth or fifth time in less than a year, Bob and Elvis, Scotty, and Bill made a promotional spot in so casual and disarming a manner that it might have been taking place in someone's living room. "We want to invite everybody out to the show," said Scotty. "And they've all been asking about the drummer who we had up there last time [four months earlier], D. J. Fontana. He's going to be with us. He's a regular member of our band now . . ." "Tell you what," says Bob, "before we call over some other folks here to talk, Elvis Presley, how you doin'?"

"Fine, Bobert," says a relaxed young voice. "How you gettin' along?"

"Oh, doin' grand," says Bob without so much as a blink. "I know all the folks down at Texarkana been raising such a whoop and a holler for you to come down and whoop and holler at 'em that they got this great big double show scheduled for Friday night at the auditorium down there. What do you think about it?" And they engage in an extended colloquy on the subject before Bob introduces "one of the noisiest guys in all this outfit . . . Bill Black, who pumps on the bass and occasionally tells a story or two, and just in general messes things up. Bill, come over and say howdy to your fans in Texarkana."

For a moment we hear the warm molasses drawl of the man that Scotty said "never met a stranger." "Bob, I just wanted to say one thing," he says. "Friday night we'll be down there, and I'll have a brand spanking new pose of Elvis for a picture, and they'll be selling at the same old price of only a quarter. And I'll have about four or five million of them. If anybody would like to have just one, why, I'll have plenty of 'em, before the show, during intermission, after the show — the fact is, I may sell them out there all night long. That's all I got to say."

It is all so relaxed and homespun, it's hard to believe that Elvis Presley is poised on the brink of something — stardom, success, a precipice so steep that it must be at least as fearsome as it is inviting. "I would like to invite everybody out Friday night to see our big show," he declares, at Bob Neal's urging, to promote a crowd. "Because I don't know when we'll be coming back that way. . . . It'll probably be a pretty long while before we can come back to Texarkana," he concludes, with no way of knowing, and not really caring, when that might be.

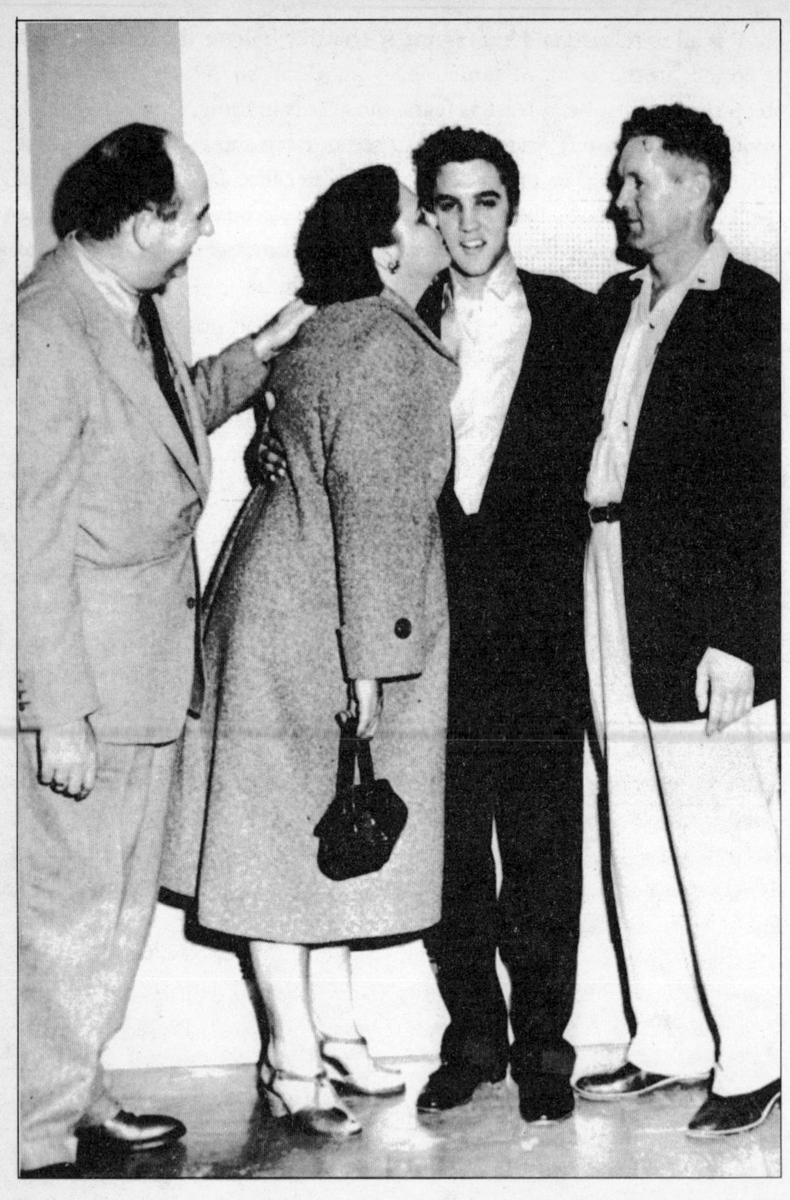

COLONEL PARKER, GLADYS, ELVIS, AND VERNON PRESLEY: RCA SIGNING CEREMONY, SUN STUDIO, NOVEMBER 21, 1955. (COURTESY OF GARY HARDY, SUN STUDIO)

THE PIED PIPERS

THE COLONEL QUICKLY consolidated his position. When Arnold Shaw, the newly named general professional manager of the E. B. Marks publishing company, visited him in Madison in August, the Colonel could talk of nothing but Presley. "What's your interest, Colonel?" Shaw asked him. With something less than full disclosure of the facts but utter candor nonetheless, the Colonel said, "This kid is now managed by Bob Neal of Memphis. But I'll have him when Neal's contract finishes in less than a year." Even Bob seemed to recognize the inevitability of the conclusion and ceded most of his authority to the Colonel while still terming it "a partnership deal." He did renegotiate the Hayride contract with Horace Logan, at the beginning of September, so that when the first year came to an end on November 12, 1955, the Hayride would pick up its option at $200 an appearance, a considerable increase from the $18 union scale that Elvis had been getting up till then. The pretext, according to Logan, was for Elvis to be able to carry a drummer on a regular basis, but the reality was that he was "the hottest thing in show business." The contract stipulated that "artist is given the right to miss 1 Saturday's performance during each 60 [day] period," but Logan added a side agreement penalizing him $400 for every additional show that he missed. Unbeknownst to Neal, evidently, the Colonel urged Vernon not to sign the agreement. He wanted the elder Presleys to withhold their signatures as guardians until he had a better idea of where things stood with a new record deal — but Vernon went ahead and signed anyway.

Neal also had the unpleasant task of telling Scotty and Bill that they were about to go on a fixed salary. What made it even worse was that it was Scotty and Bill who had finally persuaded Elvis to add D.J. on drums by agreeing to share the cost of his $100-a-week salary among them — Elvis wanted a drummer, but he kept saying he couldn't afford it until the other musicians indicated their willingness to pitch in. According to Neal:

"The eventual basic decision [to put the band on salary] went back to Elvis. We talked about it quite a few times, talked about it with his parents, and finally decided that it had to be done. I had to handle that, and I remember that there was quite a bit of unhappiness at that time plus threats that maybe they would quit, but as it worked out they went ahead in that particular situation." Scotty and Bill were inclined to put it down to the Colonel's interference, though Bob was certainly prepared to take the heat. He knew that the worst thing in the world would have been for them to blame Elvis, and he did everything he could to insulate the boy, but it turned out he didn't have to do much. Elvis had a habit of sliding out from under things on his own, and in this case he seemed to do it without any outside help.

For the first time, though, Bob Neal was beginning to wonder about his own role: what exactly was he supposed to *do?* Despite the smoothing over of tempers and the affable addition of D.J., there remained an undercurrent of ill feeling and suspiciousness that had never been present before. There was a sense of uncertainty about what was going to happen next — at one point the Colonel had even suggested that Elvis leave Scotty and Bill and D.J. behind and use Hank Snow's band on an upcoming tour. Bob squelched that before it even got to Elvis, but you could never tell how far that kind of thinking permeated the general atmosphere. Snow's band knew of the rumor, and if they did, how much further did it have to go to get to Scotty and Bill?

It was as if the Colonel were trying to throw everyone into some degree of turmoil — and doing a pretty good job of it, too. Even Sam was edgy about just what was going on. He seemed nervous about business in general: his lawsuit with Duke Records owner Don Robey over Robey's alleged theft of his artist Little Junior Parker was rapidly coming to a boil; he had a radio station that he was about to open up in the brand-new Holiday Inn downtown (the third in a brand-new chain owned by Sam's friend Kemmons Wilson); he had a number of new artists in whom he had faith but whom he had not yet been able to break; and he was obviously feeling the pinch of various unnamed financial pressures. But most of all he seemed thrown into uncharacteristic confusion by the Colonel — he clearly wanted what the Colonel had to offer, which was the promise of some sort of financial security, and he just as clearly feared it, too.

There was a single abortive Sun session that fall to try to get a B side for "Trying to Get to You." Sam once again had Johnny Bernero on drums, and they worked on the Billy Emerson blues "When It Rains, It Really Pours," which had been a favorite of Elvis' since it first came out in January. The mood was edgy, though, the playing tentative, and the session quickly broke up without any of the good feeling or unflagging optimism that had characterized every other recording date. At one point they took a break, Bernero recalled to Sun historian Colin Escott, "when Elvis went up into the control room with Sam. They were up there about thirty minutes. We were just sitting around on the studio floor chewing the fat. Then Elvis came back down and came over to me and said, 'John, we're not going to finish this session, but I really appreciate you coming over.' He gave me fifty dollars. The next thing I knew, Sam had sold his contract."

Meanwhile the Colonel systematically went about his business, which seemed for the most part to consist of playing one potential bidder off against another. There was no question of where the Colonel wanted to end up: he had been doing business with RCA, the label of both Eddy Arnold and Hank Snow, for more than ten years now, and he had been working with the same man for most of that time. Steve Sholes had handled artist and repertoire duties for both Arnold and Snow, and Colonel Parker had extensive connections within the company, all the way up to Singles Division Manager Bill Bullock. At the same time he wasn't going to let RCA take *anything* for granted, nor was he even sure how committed they were to his artist, or to advancing the kind of money that it was going to take to get the boy out of his Sun Records contract. So he continued to actively encourage the other companies in their interest, up to the point where he and Bob Neal were fielding almost daily offers.

Other events were conspiring — or being actively solicited as coconspirators — to move things rapidly along. Hill and Range, one of the most prominent of the BMI family of upstart young song publishers who had taken advantage of the boom in "race" and "hillbilly" recording after the war, was well on its way toward bringing out an Elvis Presley song folio, an event which had its genesis at the Jimmie Rodgers Festival in May. That was where Hill and Range representative Grelun Landon, in company with his friend RCA promo man Chick Crumpacker, had seen Elvis perform for the first time. Knocked out by the show, he had contacted his bosses, Jean and Julian Aberbach. The Aberbachs, Viennese refugees with a long history in European music publishing, had set up Hill and Range in 1945 to celebrate "America's native folk music" (the first part of their title stood for "hillbilly," the second for "the wide-open range") and specialized in "partnership publishing" almost from the start. This was a way of drawing in stars like Ernest Tubb, Bob Wills, Bill Monroe, and Hank Snow, by allowing them for the first time to participate on a 50–50 basis in the publishing end of the business (up till now, almost without exception, the writer had been forced to surrender all of his publishing interests, which represented half of the performance royalties earned by a song, to the music publisher who did him the favor of representing his songs). Landon urged the Aberbachs to contact Sam Phillips right away so that they could get in on the ground floor of this remarkable new phenomenon, and by early summer 1955 they had done so, working out a deal with Phillips and Bob Neal.

Meanwhile, Cleveland DJ Bill Randle, who had had extensive dealings with Hill and Range over the years (everyone stood to gain by this network of informal associations, not excluding the artist, though his songs were likely to come from a source to which his a&r director or an influential DJ like Randle might be tied), approached the Aberbachs on his own. At the same time Freddy Bienstock, the Aberbachs' young chief lieutenant and cousin, who had already heard about Presley from Randle, got a phone call from Hank Snow touting the twenty-year-old performer. The Colonel was not altogether happy about the contract Bob Neal had agreed to on the folio deal, nor was he unaware of Randle's belief, fostered by the Aberbachs' desire to recruit Randle to start a talent management company for Hill and Range, that he would end up as the boy's manager. But Tom Parker had sufficient confidence in his own business acumen, and in his ability to write his own contract somewhere down the line, that he turned a blind eye toward the Aberbachs' maneuverings and Randle's ambitions and simply permitted everyone to think whatever they wanted to think. As he told Arnold Shaw, the first time he had sold an act to a promoter, he had been "taken to the cleaner's. . . . So I went home, found the clause that did me in, cut it out, and pasted it on a piece of paper. The next time . . . I got taken by another clause. . . . One day I put all those smart-assed clauses together — and that's the contract you're holding!"

Randle, in the meantime, was about to shoot a movie short, a self-promotion called *The Pied Piper of Cleveland,* in which he was planning to use the boy, and that might come in handy in the marketing of his contract. Or it might not. It didn't really matter. There was nothing that couldn't be set right so long as you kept your eye on the ball — everyone else, he knew from experience, was likely to take their eye off it. In the Colonel's master plan, if he *had* a master plan, the main thing was to get all the parties working toward the same end without realizing, or even suspecting, that they were not the only ones in the game. In this, in a peculiar way, he and the boy were alike. It did not escape the Colonel's notice that everyone who met the boy, even for an instant, felt that they were the favored one — almost as a result of the boy's innocence and lack of guile. It was a rare gift, something which could not be taught, something which the Colonel particularly appreciated and of which he could wholeheartedly approve. It gave them something in common.

Otherwise it was business as usual: tours, bookings, keeping the publicity machine greased. "[Washington, D.C.–based promoter] Connie B. Gay says that a 19-year-old boy named Elvis Presley will be the next sensation of the country and Western (hillbilly) music field," it was announced in the "TV and Radio People" column of a Tidewater newspaper on September 4. "Presley has crossed bebop with country music and, according to Gay, 'is the hottest thing in the hillbilly field.' " All the DJ polls and fan magazines showed Elvis Presley rising to the top of "the folk music world — not through picking, yodeling, or balladeering — but by belting out his numbers in a rock 'em sock 'em rhythm style." And finally, in an October issue of *Billboard*, under the headline "New Policy Combines Pops-C&W," it was announced, "Col. Tom Parker of Jamboree Attractions, one of the nation's major bookers and promoters of country & western talent, instituted a new policy when he presented a combination of popular and country & western music on a recent one-nighter tour. Parker teamed Bill Haley & His Comets with Hank Snow for an extended tour, which opened in Omaha, Oct. 10. . . . Elvis Presley joined the Snow-Haley tour in Oklahoma City." Even the poster bore out the separate-but-equal angle. "IN PERSON," read the top half. "The Nation's No. 1 Rhythm & Blues Artist Bill Haley and his Comets. Of 'Rock Around the Clock' and 'Shake, Rattle and Roll' fame PLUS Elvis Presley with Scotty and Bill." While at the bottom Hank Snow, the "Singing Ranger," with an "All Star Cast," was showcased with his picture headlining his half of the bill.

The idea was pretty much as the *Billboard* article stated. The Colonel had approached Haley's manager, the almost equally colorful Lord Jim Ferguson, with the pitch that he had this kid: "I can take him over, but I want him to get some experience." To which Ferguson, who was managing one of the hottest acts in the country at a time when it was not clear in what direction the country was likely to go next, had readily assented, given the kid's chart success and the drawing power that Snow could bring to the bill. But for the Colonel the point was something more. RCA was certainly interested — but they weren't *that* interested yet. If they were going to put up the money needed to purchase Presley's contract from Sun, they were going to have to believe not just in the artist but in the movement. This was simply one more way of showing them that there really was something happening out there, that Presley was not just another hillbilly sensation. Once the big-city boys got that point, Colonel Thomas A. Parker was convinced, the rest would be easy.

Elvis himself was thrilled to be on the bill. Bill Haley, out of Chester, Pennsylvania, had had a string of western-flavored records, some more successful than others, since 1946, when he was twenty-one years old. In 1951 he had recorded a cover of "Rocket 88," the Sam Phillips production that has frequently been cited as marking the birth of rock 'n' roll, and since then he had put out a steady stream of releases combining an r&b sensibility with a hillbilly boogie feel and big band, western swing (accordion, steel, and saxophone) instrumentation. It was a mix that defied categorization and made considerable impact on the charts in 1953 and 1954, but it failed to achieve any kind of breakthrough success for Haley until the movie *The Blackboard Jungle* came out in March 1955. Haley's 1954 recording, "Rock Around the Clock," which had sold about seventy-five thousand copies its first time around, was selected to play over the opening credits, and the song went to number one, bestowing upon Haley instant star status (though he would never have another hit that came close to matching it, he continued to work off it profitably until the day he died). His version of Big Joe Turner's "Shake, Rattle and Roll," long a staple of Elvis' show, was a credible act of rhythm and blues homage, and he was poised on the edge of a brief movie career (*Rock Around the Clock*, the lightly fictionalized "Bill Haley Story," with Alan Freed playing a strong supporting role, came out at the beginning of the following year). His music may have lacked the purity and edge that Elvis had achieved in the studio, and certainly his live performances missed out on the smoldering sexuality of Elvis' appearances, but Haley at this point was a *star*, and Elvis was clearly drawn to that stardom, as if it might just rub off on him. Haley for his part was perfectly glad to help a kid who, for all he knew, had never been outside the Memphis city limits before.

"Now this was a long time before he was a big hit, you know," Haley recalled to interviewer Ken Terry. "He was a big tall young kid. He didn't have too much personality at that time. . . . The first time I remember talking to Elvis was in, I think, Oklahoma City. He was standing backstage, and we were getting ready to go on. And he came over and told me he was a fan of mine and we talked — an awful nice kid. . . . He wanted to learn, which was the important thing. I remember one night he went out and did a show and asked me what I thought. I had watched the show, and I told him, 'Elvis, you're leaning too much on ballads and what have you. You've got a natural rhythm feeling, so do your rhythm tunes.' . . . He had the attitude which most young kids do that he was really going to go out there and stop the show and knock Bill Haley off the stage, which at that time was an impossibility because we were number one. And he went out and he was facing Bill Haley fans. . . . When I came back after doing my show he was kind of half crying in the dressing room, very downhearted, and I sat down with him and I told him, 'Look, you got a lot of talent,' and I explained to him a lot of things. He and I buddied together for about a week and a half after that."

In other respects life on the road was just the usual form of insanity: shows increasingly marked by sheer, unrestrained pandemonium; crazy girls who would do anything just about anywhere and, not infrequently, the complications of jealous boyfriends; desperate drives to make the next show after staying up all night in the town where they had played their last one; two or three calls a day home, no matter what else was going on, or who else was around; firecrackers. "Elvis was one of those guys that had a lot of nervous energy," said D. J. Fontana, the newest member of the band. "A superhyper guy — superhyper. Always jumping around or doing something. He never got tired, but when he did, he'd just crash eleven or twelve hours straight in those days. He was always doing something. We'd be driving down the road, we'd never get to a show date on time, because we'd stop every thirty miles to buy firecrackers. He'd make us stop at every other stand, that sucker would. I'd say, 'We've got a bagful.' And he'd say, 'Well, you know, man, we might need some more.' We'd stop and buy some more firecrackers just for something to do."

He was headlining his own show now in many places. In West Texas it was the Elvis Presley Jamboree, with a supporting cast of up to a dozen that included Johnny Cash, Porter Wagoner, and Wanda Jackson. In Lubbock the young singer Buddy Holly, now actively looking for a recording contract of his own, opened the bill for him once again and sought his advice. In Houston he went to see Bob Wills with Tillman Franks on an off night and was amused when Wills told the promoter, Biff Collie, "Bring the young punk back."

He was finally getting used to it, up to a point. He no longer believed it was all just going to go away — even though in interviews he was still inclined, with becoming modesty, to say that he did. Part of him still didn't believe that it was all really happening: the records, the shows, the success, the Colonel, the sex. But part of him — most of him — did. It was all over with Dixie, he realized. He didn't want it to be, but that was the way it had to be. They had talked it over — over and over again. He never really told her that he had been unfaithful, but he knew that she knew. And he knew that she forgave him. It wasn't a life for a decent Christian girl — sometimes when things got quiet or he was alone for a moment and had time to contemplate, he wasn't so sure it was a life for a decent Christian of any sort — but, he thought, he could handle it. And if he couldn't, if it got too much for him, he could always go back, couldn't he? Dixie had told Gladys that it was over, and the two women had cried about it together, but they had agreed they would always be friends because they both loved him so. When she told her own mother, her mother was almost equally upset. "It was hard for my family to accept. They loved him dearly, too. Mother would say, 'Well, what are you going to do if you meet somebody else and get married, and after you get married, Elvis comes back and says, 'Hey, I made a mistake, and I want you to come and be my wife'? And I said, 'Well, I'll just divorce whoever I'm married to and go live with him.' It was so simple in my mind. I thought: 'That's what I'll do.' "

The Presleys, meanwhile, had moved again, just around the corner this time, to 1414 Getwell, which got them off a busy thoroughfare, and they were angry at their former landlord anyway for trying to hold them up, Vernon felt, when they had expressed an interest in purchasing the Lamar Avenue house. Once again they were forced to move in Elvis' absence, and once again Gladys wished that he could simply stop right now, buy a little business with the money he had made, marry Dixie, have three children. But she knew it wasn't to be. And she clung to his telephone calls, they spoke to each other in a language all their own, as she proudly kept track of his growing fame. She kept up her scrapbook religiously. Just as she once saved all of his baby pictures and school reports and memorabilia, now she saved every story she came across that was written about him; she and Vernon looked at them again and again. "When Elvis was a youngster down in Tupelo, Mississippi, folks used to stop him on the street and say, 'Sing for us, Elvis,' " read the latest, in *Country Song Roundup*. "And he would . . . standing on the street corners, in the hot Mississippi sun . . . or in church . . . or at school . . . anywhere someone wanted to hear him, he'd sing." And in the Saturday, October 22, 1955, edition of the *Cleveland Press*, in Bill Randle's column, next to Amy Vanderbilt's and just above a review of a spoken-word recording of T. S. Eliot's *Old Possum's Book of Practical Cats*, was an item called "Turntable Topics," which read: "Turning my life into a frenzy this week was a shooting company from Universal International Pictures. I'm not a Gable at acting, so I'm fortunate to be supported in this film short by Pat Boone, the Four Lads, Bill Haley and his Comets, and the phenomenal Elvis Presley. Called 'Top Jock,' the film will run about 15 minutes when it hits your movie house."

ELVIS PLAYED Cleveland's Circle Theater once again, on Wednesday night, October 19, in an all-star country music jamboree headlined by Roy Acuff and Kitty Wells. The next day Randle's film was scheduled to be shot at 1:00 in the afternoon at the Brooklyn High School auditorium in front of the school's three thousand students, and then at 8:00 that night at St. Michael's Hall, at East 100th and Union. Randle had filmed a number of shorts before — with Peggy Lee and Benny Goodman and Stan Kenton — and in fact the idea was for this one to end up in New York with performances by Patti Page, Tony Bennett, Nat King Cole, and other "legitimate" pop stars. But Cleveland was the jumping-off point and proved hospitable enough until Universal director Arthur Cohen balked at the idea of putting on Presley, after watching his Circle Theater performance and going through initial run-throughs at the high school auditorium the next day. According to Randle: "He thought he was 'pitiful,' completely unacceptable, not worth the time and effort to set up the numbers. I told him about the phenomenal response Presley was getting . . . but Cohen was adamant and proceeded to film the established stars as they went on." Randle then consulted with cameraman Jack Barnett, who agreed to film Presley if Randle would pay for the overtime shooting himself. This proved to be an effective solution, and the show went on.

Pat Boone never forgot the occasion of his first meeting with Elvis Presley. Boone, just twenty-one years old and a student at North Texas State Teachers College (he would transfer to Columbia University the following year), had grown up in Nashville and was married to Red Foley's daughter, Shirley. He had already won Ted Mack's *Original Amateur Hour,* made frequent appearances on the Arthur Godfrey show, and had enjoyed success on two Nashville labels, achieving a national hit on Dot with a cover of the Charms' "Two Hearts" earlier in the year. At the moment his new single, the El Dorados' "At My Front Door (Crazy Little Mama)," was just beginning to climb the pop charts. Randle picked him up at the airport, "and on the way into town he told me about a kid on the show who was going to be a big star, I asked him who it was, and he said, 'Elvis Presley, from Memphis, Tennessee.' I said, 'Oh yeah?' I had lived in Texas, and I had seen his name on some country jukeboxes, and I wondered how in the world a hillbilly could be the next big thing, especially with a name like Elvis Presley. So I was curious, and sure enough, at the high school auditorium where we did this thing, he came backstage, and already he had a little entourage [probably Red and his cousin Gene]. Now, nobody in Cleveland had ever heard of him, so the fact that he had an entourage struck me as funny. I went over dressed in my button-down collar and thin tie and white buck shoes and introduced myself. He mumbled something I couldn't understand, leaned back against the wall with his head down, and never looked me in the eye. So, I said, 'Boy, Bill Randle thinks you're really going to be big,' and he said, "Mmm . . . mrrrbbllee . . . ,' sort of a country twang mumble. I just couldn't tell what he was saying. He had his shirt collar turned up, and his hair was real greasy, and it was, well, he was always looking down, you know, like he couldn't look up. I thought to myself, what's the matter with this guy? I thought his performance would be a catastrophe, that he'd pass out onstage or something."

Elvis was glad to see Bill Haley, whom he had left in Texas just the previous week. DJ Tommy Edwards wanted to take a picture of the two of them together, and while they were backstage in the dressing room, Elvis remarked that he hoped these Yankees liked his music, giving Haley no indication that he had ever played Cleveland before. Randle introduced him to Mike Stewart, a big bear of a man who had been very successful in managing the Four Lads and would one day take over the United Artists label. Stewart was so impressed by both the boy's talent and charm that he called Mitch Miller at Columbia Records the following day, only adding to the chorus of praise that Randle had started and that Miller clearly wished would go away.

The show itself was a great success. Each act did four or five numbers, with Elvis, Scotty, and Bill (D.J. doesn't seem to have made the trip) performing "That's All Right," "Blue Moon of Kentucky," "Good Rockin' Tonight," and his latest coupling, "Mystery Train" and "I Forgot to Remember to Forget," which had entered the national country charts the month before. Pat Boone's fears were not realized. When Elvis hit the stage in his tweedy brown jacket, red socks, white bucks, and white pleated shirt with boldly embroidered front, he looked to Boone "like he had just gotten off a motorcycle. He had his shirt open, and he looked like he was laughing at something, like he had some private joke, you know? He didn't say anything, just went into some rockabilly type song, and the kids loved it. I was really surprised. Then he opened his mouth and said something, and it was so hillbilly that he lost the crowd. Then he sang another song and won them over again. As long as he didn't talk, he was okay. It took me a long time to win that crowd."

It went pretty much the same at St. Michael's, only with greater intensity. Unlike the scene at the high school, where the kids were restrained by the looming presence of their teachers (the athletic director, Mr. Joy, held the doors to keep the students away from Pat Boone), here the girls screamed without restraint and fought to get to Elvis and Boone as they performed. When Presley broke the strings on his guitar, Randle said, and then smashed the guitar on the floor, "it was mass hysteria. We needed police to get him out of the hall, clothes torn, a sleeve ripped from his jacket. Boone also got the same response. He said after the show that he had never believed what had happened could have happened to him. He said for the first time he felt he was going to make it all the way — like Pat Boone."

There was no question that Bill Randle had spotted a winner, and for the entire length of time that he was in negotiations for an executive position with Hill and Range (which ended in November, when he turned down the song publisher's deal and decided to go with a more lucrative stock-option arrangement with the Cleveland radio station WERE), he had no doubt that he was still in the picture. The Aberbach brothers were clearly anxious for him to stay involved with Presley (or was that a ploy to get Randle to sign with them?), the film was just waiting on the New York shoot, and if they could successfully negotiate union problems there, it would emerge as the first movie short devoted to the new music, with the focus on what its subtitle suggested: *A Day in the Life of a Famous Disc Jockey.* Randle maintained good television and Las Vegas connections, which was where he thought the boy's career should be headed. But reality now came jarringly face-to-face with Bill Randle. For Colonel Parker at almost exactly this time took fate into his own hands, went to New York and ensconced himself at the Warwick Hotel, where, armed with an immensely long and improbably detailed telegram from Vernon and Gladys Presley authorizing him to represent their boy, as well as his agreement with Bob Neal, he for the first time formally entertained offers for an artist whose contract he did not, strictly speaking, formally possess.

This was, finally, too much for Sam Phillips. Up till then it had all been something of a dance whose consummation, if preordained, had not yet had to be squarely faced. Now, with a hit record on his hands and new expenses cropping up seemingly every day on every front, Phillips felt as if he was being subverted by the very process that he had himself allowed to be set in motion. "I was pissed off. I got so goddam mad, I called up Bob Neal and I said, 'Bob, you know what the hell you doing to me?' He said, 'Aw, Sam, I ain't doing nothing,' and I said, 'Goddammit, you're associated with Tom Parker and he's putting out this bullshit, after all of what I've been through to get this guy going, he's putting the word out to my distributors that I'm gonna sell Elvis' contract.' I said, 'Man, this is killing me, you're not just messing with an artist contract here, you messing with my life, man. You just don't deal with these people [the distributors] unfairly. They're in this damn thing, too.' I had worked my ass off—driven sixty-five to seventy-five thousand miles a year to gain their confidence, not only on Elvis but going back to the first damn releases on Sun. I said, 'This could cost me the company.' I said, 'This has got to stop.'

"So I called Tom Parker at the Warwick Hotel in New York, and he said, 'Sa-a-am, how you doin'?' And I said, 'Well, I ain't doing worth a damn. Why is it that every distributor I got says that this man is on the block?' I said, 'Look, Tom, this has been going on now basically for three or four months, but I thought nothing of it, 'cause I couldn't get confirmation from Bob Neal that you good friends of mine would be trying to do me in—advertently or inadvertently.' He said, 'Oh, noooo, Sam, no, I don't understand thaaaat.' And then he said, 'But *would* you be interested in selling Elvis' contract?' And I said, 'Well, I just might could be.' 'How much you think you want for him?' He didn't say how much he was thinking—just how much would I take. So I said, 'I hadn't really thought about it, Tom. But I'll let you know.' So he said, 'Well, look, think about it, and let me know.' And I thought about it about thirty seconds and called him back."

The price that he named was $35,000, plus $5,000 he owed Elvis in back royalties, more than anyone had ever paid for a popular recording artist (by comparison, Columbia had paid $25,000 for the contract of Frankie Laine, an established star, in 1951). Thus formally empowered, the Colonel really got down to business with RCA and Hill and Range.

To understand why Sam Phillips would want to sell Elvis' contract in the first place one must understand a complex web of circumstances. To begin with, despite all the success that he had enjoyed in the last year, he was in somewhat desperate financial straits. The demands of manufacturing a hit record (out-of-control manufacturing costs primarily, which had to be paid up front with no guarantee that a great number of the records would not come back as returns from distributors with thirty or sixty days to pay) had stretched his limited resources to the breaking point. In January he had written to his brother Jud: "I have told you repeatedly that Sun liabilities are three times the assets and I have been making every effort possible to keep out of bankruptcy. . . . Anyone less interested in saving face would have given it up long ago, but I intend to pay every dollar the company owes — including you — even while I know there is no possible way to ever get out with a dollar."

In October he finally managed to pay Jud off. He had also completed arrangements to open his first radio station, WHER, with a big band format and an "all-girl" lineup that featured both his assistant, Marion Keisker, and his wife, Becky, among the on-the-air talent. He was working around the clock and beside himself with worry over how he was going to keep his various enterprises afloat. Presley's royalties were already overdue, and he didn't doubt that Tom Parker, as his position became more entrenched, was unlikely to be as forbearing as Bob Neal about contractual niceties. More than anything else Sam Phillips was not about to be beholden to any man. He was *not* going to be known as the proprietor of a one-artist company — he had other artists to develop, he had a number that Carl Perkins had sung to him the other night on the telephone that he believed was going to be a bigger hit than anything he had put out to date, he had no hesitation about selling the damn contract. The only hesitation he had was turning the boy over to that damn barker who called himself Colonel, but, he reasoned, "any time you think you know what the public is going to want, that's when you know you're looking at a damn fool when you're looking in the mirror. I thought, Well, if I can just get some money. . . . But I wanted Elvis to succeed so bad — and this is kind of a selfish thing, but I've got to say it — because I didn't want them to be able to say, '*Well, this was just a fluke.*' "

On Friday, October 28, back home in Madison, Tom Parker got a telegram from W. W. Bullock, RCA's singles division manager, that $25,000 was as high as RCA was willing to go. On Saturday he and his assistant Tom Diskin went over to Memphis to meet with Sam Phillips and Bob Neal at the offices of WHER, which had finally gone on the air that morning after several days of what the newspaper called "ladylike tardiness," equipment delays and problems with the transmitter. Sam had been up three days straight at this point installing the ground system and running all the checks. By apparent coincidence Hill and Range attorney Ben Starr arrived on this very day to work out a deal tied in with the forthcoming Elvis Presley song folio, whereby Hill and Range was licensed to represent the Sun publishing catalogue in Europe as well as to actively promote domestic cover versions of Sun catalogue songs. After listening to Hill and Range's offer, Sam left Starr in the studio and joined the others in the Holiday Inn restaurant next door, squeezing into a booth with Neal opposite Parker and Diskin. Parker brought up the money situation once again, as if to make sure he had heard correctly over what might have been a bad telephone line. Thirty-five thousand? he said. Well, you know that's a lot of money. I don't know if I can raise that kind of money on an unproven talent. He went over great in Jacksonville, but you talking about $35,000. That's right, chimed in Tom Diskin. That's a helluva lot of money. How much money you made on that boy, anyway? According to Sam Phillips: "I said, 'It's none of your goddam business. In addition to that, I didn't invite you down here. I invited Tom Parker.' Tom elbowed Diskin on the outside seat of this booth and said, 'Shut your mouth.' 'Cause, man, I was ready to get up and whip his ass. Or get whipped. Parker said, 'Look, I don't know where we can go.' He said, 'Sam, there's not a lot of people believe in this thing. But how can we work this deal?' I said, 'Well, first thing, you just keep Tom Diskin's mouth shut.' "

They finally worked out an option deal. The option would take effect on Monday, October 31, and allow Parker two weeks to raise $5,000 (until midnight, November 15). The deal was predicated on a $35,000 purchase price — not surprisingly, Sam Phillips did not budge, and undoubtedly part of him was hoping that the price would not be met — and the full amount had to be raised, and the contract executed, within one month, by December 1, 1955. The $5,000 was not refundable, and the deadline would not be extended. It was a gamble on Tom Parker's part. He was committed at this point. If he didn't come through, he was unlikely to get another chance. Mr. and Mrs. Presley believed in him, at least for the time being; Bob Neal had simply caved in; and the boy — the boy, he thought, would follow him to the ends of the earth. The boy simply didn't care. And only the Colonel knew that the money wasn't there.

Sam Phillips, for his part, was also struck by an uncharacteristic moment of doubt. Upon his return to the radio studio, and after having taken care of the Hill and Range business, Sam ran into Kemmons Wilson, the visionary founder of Holiday Inn and the man who was temporarily providing Sam with free office space. If there was anyone whom Sam Phillips looked up to in the realm of business, it was Kemmons Wilson, and suddenly fearful of what he had done, he asked Wilson his opinion. "He said, 'Jesus Christ, thirty-five thousand dollars? Hell, he can't even sing, man. Take the money!' I said, 'Well, I just done it, and I don't know if they will come through or not.' He said, 'You better hope they do.' So I felt better about it — but I was torn."

FOR BOTH TOM PARKER and Sam Phillips the next two weeks were a period of intense, and sometimes frenetic, activity. On Sunday, October 30, Sam set off for Houston with Marion Keisker for a preliminary injunction hearing in federal court on his lawsuit against Duke Records. It was his son Knox's tenth birthday, and he was so worn out by all of his conflicting obligations that he had to pull over in a cow pasture by the side of the road outside of Shreveport to catch some sleep. When he returned to Memphis, he made a conscious point of talking to Elvis about the deal, but after reassuring Elvis that he would speak to Steve Sholes personally, that he would never abandon him, there was not much else to say, and Elvis, never the most verbally expressive of individuals in any case, pretty much conveyed the same attitude that he had already articulated to Bob Neal. "Elvis did ask me once or twice, did I think they

[RCA] could record him as good as they did at Sun," Neal said, "and I said, 'No reason why not.' He didn't really seem too terribly excited, except he was excited by the idea that he was increasing in value all the time. . . . He was not the type that would just get completely broke up over something, it was sort of like, 'I knew this was going to happen. It's great, let's keep it rolling.' "

Tom Parker, on the other hand, spent almost all of his time trying to maneuver RCA into raising their offer, either by indicating the interest of other companies, which by now were in all practical terms out of the picture, or by attempting to tie in the Hill and Range folio deal in some manner beneficial to the purchase price of the contract. By the time of the DJ convention in Nashville, on November 10, the Colonel was sure enough of his deal that everyone knew there was something in the air, but whether RCA was aware that Sam Phillips would not move off his original price or Phillips knew of the RCA shortfall is doubtful. It may well be that the Colonel was simply counting on RCA's increasing commitment to the *idea* of the deal to carry them through the unpleasant financial details.

RCA head of specialty singles Steve Sholes (he oversaw not just the country and western but the gospel and r&b divisions as well) was at the convention as a matter of course, and the Colonel spent as much time as possible with him and publicity director Anne Fulchino, not one of his biggest fans after the scene he had made in Florida the previous year, mapping out variations on his vision of the future. He did not neglect to point out that both *Cashbox* and *Billboard* had selected his boy as most promising new c&w artist in disc jockey polls, and in fact each presented him with a scroll at the convention to go with the plaque he received from *Country & Western Jamboree* for topping their readers' poll with 250,000 votes for "New Star of the Year." Probably the elephant that the Colonel had tethered outside of the Hickory Room of the Andrew Jackson Hotel did not fail to make its implicit point either, while at the same time proclaiming, "Like an elephant Hank Snow never forgets. Thanks Dee Jays."

As for Elvis, he scarcely had time to breeze in and breeze out, flying out of Nashville late Friday night for a few hours at home before taking off again at 10:00 A.M. for Shreveport for an appearance on the Hayride, then flying back to Memphis for an all-star "Western Swing Jamboree" at Ellis Auditorium Sunday afternoon and evening. The convention itself went by like a blur — the Colonel introducing him to many old friends (not to mention Mr. Sholes), Hank Snow taking him under his wing, Bob Neal reining in old friends and colleagues, everyone having fun and doing business. There were girls all over the hotel and parties to introduce you to the girls (if you needed an introduction). Hill and Range representative Grelun Landon brought him proofs of the song folio and showed them to him and Bob Neal: the cover was printed in pink and black, and the back had a studio photograph of Vernon and Gladys Presley, looking youthful and happy (Gladys' mouth was open, her hair had been done by Mr. Tommy at Goldsmith's, she looked as pretty as a doll).

He had never realized before how many friends he had in the business. Biff Collie was here and T. Tommy Cutrer, with his deep booming voice, who had just moved up from Shreveport; all the local DJs and promoters were there, and they were all treating him, he noticed, as if he were somehow . . . *different*. He didn't feel any different, though, he was still just like a kid bouncing on his toes itching to get on with it. When he ran into RCA head of country and western promotion Chick Crumpacker, whom he had met first in Richmond and then in Meridian, Mississippi, the previous spring, he announced proudly, "Hey, I'm with you guys now." And to Buddy Bain, the Corinth DJ who had hosted him at the outset of the year and showed him a scrapbook filled with Opry pictures, he announced proudly, with a big grin, "Buddy, I believe I'm gonna make it. The Colonel just sold my contract to RCA." To which Buddy replied, "I believe you are."

So many people wanted one thing or another from him — he didn't have time to sit still for all that. He didn't mind signing autographs, and he was glad to shoot the breeze about music or any other subject with anyone who came up to him, but he didn't want to talk business with anyone, heck, he didn't know anything *about* business, that's what Bob and Colonel were there for. Mae Boren Axton, the lady from Jacksonville who worked for Colonel in Florida, had been trying to get him to listen to this song ever since he got in — she kept saying it would be his first million-seller, he could have it if he would just make it his first single release on RCA, she was so pleased that he had gotten this wonderful deal. He didn't feel like listening to any songs now, there was so much to do, but Bob finally got him to go up to the room with him and Mae, and he really liked it, he said, "Hot dog, Mae, play it again," and she played it over and over — it was really different, a little like Roy Brown's "Hard Luck Blues," only this was about a hotel, a heartbreak hotel, where the bellhop's tears kept flowing and the desk clerk was dressed in black. He knew the whole song before he left the room. "That's gonna be my next record," he said, nodding at Bob Neal so Mae would know he was serious and maybe leave him alone about it now.

On Sunday he played Ellis in what was billed by the *Press-Scimitar* as a rare local appearance. He was the headliner, with his name above Hank Thompson and Carl Smith, and that new boy from Jackson, Carl Perkins, was at the bottom of the bill. Both his parents were present — Colonel made sure of that, and that they were well treated. Both Colonel and Hank Snow had been calling Mr. and Mrs. Presley regularly to reassure them that everything was all right, that this new RCA deal was really going to come about, and they had even stopped by to visit once or twice at the little house on Getwell. Gladys still didn't like the Colonel, he knew that, but she was finally getting more used to his ways, and while Vernon didn't ever say much, he seemed to know which side his bread was buttered on. At the show that night Elvis wore his oversize red suit and climbed up on top of Bill's bass fiddle with him after popping three or four strings on his guitar. "Scotty's onstage to keep order," said someone in the audience, and after the show was over all the performers signed autographs while still onstage, with Elvis prowling around on the balls of his feet, like a caged tiger, one observer noted, unable to find a release for all that energy.

On November 15, the day the option had to be picked up, the Colonel was still feverishly working out the deal. Bill Bullock continued to balk over the price to the very end, with Parker telegramming him one last time to remind him that time was running out and that if they didn't pick up the option now, he believed the price would simply go up again. Personally, said the Colonel, he believed the price was too high, and, he emphasized, he had nothing to gain from the deal, other than to protect everyone's interests, but he believed that they should go ahead because *the talent was there.* He had managed to stop Sam Phillips from releasing a new Sun single, he said, but the clear implication was that he couldn't stop him for long. He reminded Bullock of the price once again and of the condition that he had inserted, no doubt as one last way of accentuating the difference between himself and Bob Neal, that there would be three national television appearances guaranteed in the contract. Then he pointed out that the banks closed in Madison at 2:00.

Bullock was finally convinced. With his go-ahead, Parker called Phillips to ask if he wanted the money wired to conform strictly to the deadline. No, Sam said, he could just mail it if he wanted, and sent a telegram to that effect. They would have to get together in the next week or so to finalize the deal, and that would, naturally, take place in Memphis. The Colonel went to his bank in Madison and sent the money air mail, special delivery, then wrote to H. Coleman Tily III, RCA's legal representative, and thanked him for all the help he and Bullock had been. The Colonel hoped he had done all right on the deal; he had done the best he could in the absence of their guiding hand. He reminded Tily of the three guest appearances that had to be part of the deal, or else he would lose his credibility with the Presleys, and then he gave instructions as to how his reimbursement check should be made out, with a clear notation that it was a refund, not a commission; as an RCA shareholder he was simply proud to have advanced the money.

In Memphis Sam Phillips felt momentarily bereft. Part of him had never fully believed that the deal would actually go through; part of him knew that it had to. But he plunged back into his recording activity, spent long hours at the new radio studio, started gearing up his new release schedule (he was determined to have "Blue Suede Shoes," the new Carl Perkins record, out by the first of the year), and continued to pursue his claim against Duke Records, which was due for resolution by the end of the month.

Six days later, on November 21, Steve Sholes, Ben Starr, Coleman Tily, the Colonel, Tom Diskin, Hank Snow, local RCA distributor Jim Crudgington, and regional rep Sam Esgro all converged on the little Sun studio for the signing of the papers. Colonel Parker came accompanied by a document dated the same day stipulating that out of the 40 percent in combined commissions due the Colonel and Bob Neal (25 percent to the Colonel, 15 percent to Neal), there would be an even split for the duration of Neal's agreement, until March 15, 1956. The buyout agreement itself was a simple two-page document in which Sun Records agreed to turn over all tapes and cease all distribution and sales of previously released recordings as of December 31, 1955, while the managers "do hereby sell, assign and transfer unto RCA all of their right, title and interest in and to" the previously exercised option agreement. The purchase price was $35,000; RCA undertook responsibility for the payment of all back royalties and held Sun Records harmless from any subsequent claims. Out of all this Elvis Presley would get a royalty of 5 percent as opposed to the 3 percent that he was currently receiving from Sun — this amounted to almost two cents more per record sold, which over the course of a million sales would come to about $18,000.

In addition, as the result of a co-publishing arrangement that the Colonel had entered into with Hill and Range (who probably contributed substantially themselves toward the purchase price), Elvis would now receive half of the two-cent statutory mechanical fee and half of the two-cent broadcast fee on all new Hill and Range compositions that he recorded, which would be registered through his own publishing company. If at this point he were to start writing songs as well, or, perhaps more pertinently, if he were to start claiming songwriting credit for songs he recorded, a practice going back to time immemorial in the recording industry, he could increase his income by up to another two cents per side. Hill and Range, meanwhile, stood to gain an almost incalculable advantage over their competitors in the field by securing not just an inside track, but what amounted to virtually a right of first refusal from the hottest new singing sensation in the country.

After the contract was signed, there was a picture-taking ceremony, with different configurations of the various parties involved. In one Elvis is flanked by the Colonel and Hank Snow, proud partners in Jamboree Attractions, while Bob Neal, to Snow's left, jovially approves; in another Gladys plants a kiss upon her son's cheek and clutches her black handbag as the Colonel pats her on the shoulder and Vernon looks stiffly on. In yet another Sam and Elvis shake hands across RCA attorney Coleman Tily. In all the pictures all the men are beaming — everyone has seemingly gotten exactly what he wanted. After the picture taking a number of the participants dropped by for a brief on-air appearance on Marion Keisker's show in the brand-new WHER studios. "They thought it would be great fun," said Marion, "if they all came over and we announced it. So they all crowded into the little control room, and we did a little four- or five-way interview, well, not really an interview, just a little chat. And in the course of it, I remember, Hank Snow said, 'I'm very proud this boy made his first appearance on the national scene on my section of the Grand Ole Opry.' And he was being such a pompous ass about it, I couldn't help it, but I said, 'Yes, and I remember, you had to ask him what his name was.' That was a rather tactless thing for me to do."

Bob Johnson's story in the *Press-Scimitar* the following day was headlined "Memphis Singer Presley Signed by RCA-Victor for Recording Work."

> Elvis Presley, 20, Memphis recording star and entertainer who zoomed into bigtime and the big money almost overnight, has been released from his contract with Sun Record Co. of Memphis. . . . Phillips and RCA officials did not reveal terms but said the money involved is probably the highest ever paid for a contract release for a country-western recording artist. "I feel Elvis is one of the most talented youngsters today," Phillips said, "and by releasing his contract to RCA-Victor we will give him the opportunity of entering the largest organization of its kind in the world, so his talents can be given the fullest opportunity."

"Double Deals Hurl Presley into Stardom," trumpeted the December 3 issue of *Billboard*.

> Elvis Presley, one of the most sought-after warblers this year, signed two big-time contracts as a recording artist, writer and publisher. RCA Victor beat out the diskery competition and signed the 19-year-old to a three years–plus options contract. Besides which, Hill & Range inked him to a long-time exclusive writing pact and at the same time set up a separate publishing firm, Elvis Presley Music, Inc., which will operate within the H&R fold. . . . Altho Sun has sold Presley primarily as a c.&w. artist, Victor plans to push his platters in all three fields — pop, r.&b., and c.&w. However, RCA Victor's specialty singles chief, Steve Sholes (who will record Presley), plans to cut the warbler with the same backing — electric guitar, bass fiddle, drums and Presley himself on rhythm guitar — featured on his previous Sun waxings.

THE DORSEY SHOW, MARCH 17, 1956. (ALFRED WERTHEIMER)

STAGE SHOW

No matter what people say about you, son, you know who you are and that's all that matters.

— Gladys Presley to her son as quoted by Harold Loyd in *Elvis Presley's Graceland Gates*

The last admonishment I had to Elvis was, "Look, you know how to do it now, you go over there and don't let anybody tell you — they believe enough in you that they've laid some cold cash down, so you let them know what you feel and what you want to do."

— Sam Phillips on his advice to Elvis Presley, late fall 1955

ON TUESDAY, JANUARY 10, 1956, two days after his twenty-first birthday, Elvis Presley entered the RCA studio in Nashville for the first time. Just before Christmas Steve Sholes had sent him a brief note proposing ten titles for his consideration, along with acetate demos and lead sheets for each of the songs. The selection included ballads, novelty numbers, country weepers, blues, and "beat" songs, which Sholes urged him to learn and then let the RCA a&r man know which of them he liked best. About a week before the session, at the Variety Club in Memphis, an after-hours "members only" club for entertainment people and businessmen, Elvis sat down at the beat-up old upright and picked out "Heartbreak Hotel" for Dewey, announcing he was going to cut it in Nashville the following week.

Sholes meanwhile got in touch with Chet Atkins, his Nashville coordinator and one of Scotty's principal inspirations on guitar, about booking the studio and putting together a band for the session. The band was no problem — they would use Elvis' regular group with Chet on rhythm. In addition, Atkins contacted Floyd Cramer, who had just moved to Nashville and had played piano behind Elvis on the Hayride and on tour over the past year, as well as Gordon Stoker of the Jordanaires, the popular quartet who had toured with Eddy Arnold and were singing background on an increasing number of Nashville sessions. He would not be able to employ the full group, Atkins explained to Stoker; RCA had just signed the renowned Speer Family gospel quartet, and he wanted to use Ben and Brock Speer to augment the sound on any ballads they might cut at the session.

Steve Sholes was becoming increasingly nervous. At the DJ convention the previous November, wrote *Billboard* editor Paul Ackerman, the prevailing attitude was, "Anyone who buys [Elvis Presley] will get stuck," and the prevailing attitude at the New York home office was no more comforting. Sholes, ordinarily the most cautious of men, was not unaware that with this signing he had put his neck on the line. He had little doubt that there was enough corporate jealousy to bury him, and it didn't help his state of mind any when Sam Phillips put out his latest release, an upbeat, rambunctious rocker called "Blue Suede Shoes" by twenty-three-year-old Carl Perkins, just before the new year. "Steve was afraid he'd bought the wrong one," Chet Atkins observed, and there is little question that many at RCA would have been exceedingly quick to agree.

In the weeks following the signing, however, RCA as a corporate entity did everything they could to capitalize on their investment. On December 2 they put out their own version of Elvis' last Sun single, "I Forgot to Remember to Forget," still riding high on the country charts after eleven weeks and destined now to reach number one and stay on the charts for another twenty-eight. In addition they rereleased each of the four other Sun singles on December 20, while, in related developments, Hill and Range finally came out with the Elvis Presley songbook and the Colonel announced on December 17 that his boy had been contracted for four appearances on CBS' *Stage Show*, hosted by Jimmy and Tommy Dorsey, which comedian Jackie Gleason produced as a lead-in to his own highly successful Saturday-night show. NBC had also been in the running, the Colonel declared, with fellow RCA artist Perry Como, whose show ran opposite Gleason's, making an unsuccessful bid for Mr. Presley's services. "The most talked-about new personality in the last 10 years of recorded music," declared RCA's full-page ad in *Billboard* on December 3, featuring a dynamic picture of Elvis Presley, legs astraddle, eyes closed, shouting out his blues, and a small italicized notice below: "Bob Neal, manager/under direction of Hank Snow Jamboree Attractions/Col. Tom Parker, general manager."

RCA HAD ITS STUDIO in a building that it shared with the Methodist TV, Radio and Film Commission. The room was big, high-ceilinged, with an arched roof that created a tendency, according to Atkins, for bass notes to "roll around for a long time." The first session was booked for 2:00 in the afternoon, an unlikely hour, but neither Sholes nor Chet was much for night sessions. D. J. Fontana sat attentively behind his drums; it was his first recording date with the group, and he knew that there must be lots of equally good drummers in Nashville. Floyd Cramer, with a young wife to support, was wondering if he had made the right decision leaving Shreveport and whether there would be a living for him in studio work, while Steve Sholes, sitting behind the control room glass with his lead sheets and his song lists and little insight into how the boy was going to react to the new studio and the new situation, couldn't help but feel that this was not a very auspicious beginning from any point of view. To be working with such a ragtag group, especially under such trying circumstances; to feel himself under the jealous scrutiny not just of his own record company but of an entire industry; to be seeking to duplicate the "slapback" sound that was so integral a part of the singer's appeal while his own engineers professed ignorance as to just how Sam Phillips had achieved it — this was not a position he was happy to find himself in. Bill kept chewing gum and cracking jokes, but it was evident that even he felt the tension in the air, and it didn't make Scotty feel any better when, after making small talk with Atkins about the unique qualities of their Echosonic amps, a custom-made item which Scotty had gotten six months earlier after hearing Chet employ it to particular effect on "Mister Sandman," he asked Chet what he wanted them to do. "Just go on doing what you been doing" was his musical idol's characteristically phlegmatic reply. "He was just old Cool Hand Luke himself," said Scotty. "He wasn't there to disturb or anything. [The whole thing] was a drastic change for us at first — at first I think it seemed a little cold. The engineer called take numbers instead of, 'Hey, do it again.' My feeling was not necessarily we're in the big time, just now we had a little more professional atmosphere. . . . We were fresh meat!"

Elvis alone failed to show any sign of strain. He was wearing pink pants with a blue stripe and was clearly excited about the occasion. He flung himself into the first number, Ray Charles' "I Got a Woman," which had been a staple of their stage act for nearly a year, and sang it again and again, zeroing in on the half-time, bluesy finish that had always been a climax of the live performance. There appeared to be no doubt or hesitation. It didn't seem to bother him that for the first time they were hearing the echo effect in the studio (Sam Phillips' slapback was in essence an electronic adjustment after the fact; the only way to get a similar effect in the McGavock Street studio — and then it was only a crude approximation — was by placing a mike and an amp at opposite ends of the long hallway at the front of the building and feeding that back into the main room). He was just biding his time, as he had learned to do from Sam Phillips, until they got it *right*. A couple of times Steve Sholes might have called it a master take, but the boy was insistent, in a nice way, that he could do better, that it wasn't there yet. Atkins, ordinarily unemotional and undemonstrative, was so struck by the performance that he called his wife and told her to come down to the studio right away. "I told her she'd never see anything like this again, it was just so damn exciting."

The next song was "Heartbreak Hotel," the number Mae Axton had brought to the convention, which he had told Dewey he was going to record. It was an odd, almost morbid composition, which Axton had written with Tommy Durden after Tommy showed her a Miami newspaper story about a man who had committed suicide and left a note saying, "I walk a lonely street." "It stunned me," said Mae. "I said to Tommy, 'Everybody in the world has somebody who cares. Let's put a Heartbreak Hotel at the end of this lonely street.' And he said, 'Let's do.' So we wrote it." Mae promised the song to Buddy Killen at Tree Publishing, and she gave a third of the writer's credit to Elvis. "I don't know why," said Buddy, "she said she wanted to buy him a car." Hill and Range tried to get the publishing, but Mae held firm, which must have frustrated Steve Sholes even more.

It was a strange choice by any kind of conventional wisdom: gloomy, world-weary, definitely at odds with the irrepressibly vibrant image that Elvis had projected from the start, both in performance and on all his records to date. In theory it may not have been an altogether comfortable fit, and Sam Phillips pronounced the finished product a "morbid mess," but Elvis clearly believed in it and put everything he had into it, and whatever Sholes' or Chet's personal reservations, the heavy overlay of echo and D.J.'s rim shots created a powerful, emotion-laden atmosphere of upbeat despair.

The entire three-hour evening session was spent putting down "Money Honey," yet another r&b staple of the live act, and the single session that was held the following afternoon was consumed recording the two ballads that Steve Sholes had brought in, with the makeshift three-man vocal group providing only adequate background harmonies. Gordon Stoker in particular was dissatisfied. Stoker, who had met the boy on the Eddy Arnold bill that played Memphis fourteen months before, was upset that his own group had not been used and felt that the sound was unprofessional, with a "quartet" made up of a low bass and two natural tenors. The songs came out all right ("I Was the One" was always Elvis' favorite from the session), but Stoker was not very impressed with Presley's ballad-singing abilities and left the session angry at both Chet and Steve Sholes for showing him so little consideration.

All in all it was a somewhat desultory beginning, and Steve Sholes could not have been happy going back to New York with two r&b covers, a singularly odd original on which Hill and Range didn't even own the publishing, and two ballads unlike anything Elvis Presley had ever recorded before. He couldn't have felt any better when, upon his return, his superiors were so put off by what they heard, Sholes said, that they wanted him to turn around and head straight back to Nashville. "They all told me it didn't sound like anything, it didn't sound like his other record[s], and I'd better not release it, better go back and record it again." Sholes argued that it had taken him two days to get this, if he went back it would just be throwing good money after bad; besides, they had an opportunity for another session in New York at the end of the month and they needed to put something out right away.

Elvis meanwhile remained unfazed by anyone else's doubts. Back in Memphis he appeared on a father's night show at Humes, just as he had appeared the previous month in a Christmas show produced by Miss Scrivener to raise money to help out needy students. He bought himself a new guitar, too, a Martin D-28, at the O. K. Houck Piano Company on Union Avenue, and he stopped by the Chisca to fill in Dewey's radio audience on what he'd been up to lately, talking with Dewey off-air as the records played and Dewey got more and more excited about the world he was entering and the future that stretched out before him.

At the Memphis Recording Service at 706, all attention was focused on the two new Sun releases, Carl Perkins' "Blue Suede Shoes" and Johnny Cash's stark "Folsom Prison Blues." Elvis told Marion and Mr. Phillips all about the Nashville session and the upcoming Dorsey broadcasts; Sam was a big swing band fan and had always pointed to Tommy Dorsey's "Boogie Woogie" as the start of it all. Sam didn't really press him much about the session — he considered Steve Sholes a man of integrity and didn't want to get in the middle of anything. They sat for a few minutes in the little outer office, not really saying much, but secure in the knowledge that things were moving along pretty much according to plan. Elvis felt comfortable with Sam and Marion, he felt at home in the little studio — "there was no place he'd rather be," said Sam, "that's just a fact. If you ever befriended him, he never forgot it. He had difficulty building true friendships, and I had that difficulty, too. I have a lot of friends, but I am just not a person who builds relationships easily. Elvis was the same way. He was just, innately, a loner."

He heard from Steve Sholes again around January 20, just a week before his scheduled departure for New York. Sholes suggested six songs this time, including "Pins and Needles in My Heart," a 1945 Roy Acuff number that Sholes thought he might be able to "get with." A carbon copy of the letter, of course, went to the Colonel, who was busy making plans based on a future that nobody else could see.

The Colonel's vision of the future centered on mass exposure, something he had tried with Eddy Arnold with a good deal of success. With Elvis, though, it was different. "I think there was a big difference in the time. . . . The Eddy Arnold era and the Elvis era were entirely different," said country comedian Minnie Pearl, who worked with the Colonel in both eras. They were different because, according to Pearl, as big a star as Arnold became, Elvis was the Colonel's dream, the perfect vehicle for all the Colonel's elaborately worked out and ingenious promotional schemes. Elvis was the purest of postwar products, the commodity that had been missing from the shelves in an expanding marketplace of leisure time and disposable cash. The Colonel "slept, ate, and breathed Elvis," just as he had Eddy Arnold — but the times had changed, and the personalities of the performers were dissimilar as well: Elvis was fresh-faced and eager to please, pure plasticity in an informational age that required a protean hero.

Television was the key to the deal. The Colonel realized it — hell, Bob Neal had realized it, that was what he had been aiming for when he took Elvis to New York to try out for *Arthur Godfrey's Talent Scouts*. How many people could you reach with one national appearance as opposed to all the one-night stands, the endless promotions and exploitations, that you did before picking up stakes and moving on to the next town? There was no comparison, even for an old carnival hand like Tom Parker. The trick was in controlling the game. You had a boy who could be ruined by any number of variables: sex, scandal, familiarity, loss of self-belief. The idea was to remove him from those variables. The trick was to expose him, but expose him only so much, to define, and control, the level of acceptable danger. The Colonel had a number of powerful allies, a carefully assembled team that included Abe Lastfogel, head of the William Morris Agency, and his second in command, Harry Kalcheim, who had set up the Dorsey contact; Jean and Julian Aberbach of Hill and Range, who along with Lastfogel went back to the days of Eddy Arnold; he had all of his contacts from all of the years with RCA, and he had peripheral players like Bill Randle, with his vast radio audience, working for the Colonel's interests without necessarily even knowing it. All he had to do was to get them working for themselves without working against each other, the key was to put together a team where all the players functioned smoothly but only the team manager knew everyone's function and position. It was a neat trick, but one that he was sure he could pull off — if only the boy came through. And he had little doubt that he would.

THE WEEK BEFORE the first Dorsey appearance Elvis was off on yet another Texas tour. On Saturday night he told the Hayride performers about his upcoming television appearances, and they all wished him luck — he was off for a month now on a Jamboree Attractions tour of the Southeast that was booked around the four consecutive Saturday-night television appearances. According to Maylon Humphries, a Shreveport buddy and occasional performer who was on college break, "He was sitting around in Hoot and Curley's dressing room, and Curley says, 'Elvis, you're going to make a fortune off this,' and he looked down and took a deep breath and says, 'Not really.' And he named what he was getting. 'But, you know, Curley,' he said, 'Mr. Parker says more people will be seeing me on these four shows' — and he didn't say Colonel, he said Mr. Parker — 'than I would be exposed to for the rest of my life on the Hayride.' " Which left everyone with something to think about.

He flew into New York on Wednesday, January 25, with the Colonel and on Thursday met with the powers that be at RCA. Steve Sholes introduced him to Larry Kanaga, the head of the record division, and Sholes almost sank through the floor when Elvis buzzed Kanaga with the electric buzzer concealed in his hand. Then Sholes took him over to the publicity department, where he met Anne Fulchino, the attractive young Bostonian who had modernized pop and c&w publicity practices at RCA but had been pleading with Sholes to bring her the right new artist to work with so that she could really break pop in a big way. "Steve brought Elvis in and introduced him to me. He shook my hand, and he had that electric buzzer. I said, 'Honey, that may be big in Memphis, but it's never going to work in New York.' Fortunately, he had a sense of humor, so we just laughed about it, but he never used that stupid buzzer again.

"He was a very quick study, a cornball kid who was a quick study. We took him to lunch that day, and he didn't know which end of the fork to use, but, you know, he never made the same mistake twice. This was a kid who knew where he wanted to go, and he was very single-minded about it. We had a little discussion that day about what he wanted to do, what the long-range goals were and what the steps would be in the publicity campaign. I explained to him that this should be done very methodically, this should be a long-range plan, I had to know what he wanted to do, and we both had to agree that he was capable of getting there. I was drawing little pyramids in my notebook to show him, and we discussed things like concert tours, I knew there was an acting possibility from the very beginning. He understood all this. He wanted it, and he had the talent. After lunch I asked him to wait in my office, and I went to see Steve. I said to Steve, *'We got him!'* The guy that we'd been looking for."

There was a rehearsal late Saturday morning at the Nola Studios, on Broadway between Fifty-first and Fifty-second, just a couple of blocks from the Warwick Hotel, where the Colonel and Elvis and the band were all staying. The Colonel and a William Morris agent introduced Elvis to the Dorseys and their mother, "and Elvis exhibited a kind of deference and courtesy," observed Arnold Shaw, who had brought Presley to Bill

Randle's attention early on, "that patently puzzled" the Dorseys, not normally known for either their deference or courtesy. Scotty, who was interested in sound engineering, checked out the control booth, while D.J., who had never been to New York before ("We didn't know what to expect. We didn't know what kind of people they were — we figured they'd just gobble us up"), met his boyhood idol, drummer Louie Bellson; Bellson invited him out for coffee and turned out to be a really "nice guy." Elvis hung around at the back of the hall, playing with Hill and Range representative Grelun Landon's five-year-old son and talking to Grelun and Chick Crumpacker, among others, about the time that his car had burned up on the highway. He had seen his whole career "going up in smoke," he said. They had clambered up on a hillside to watch the car burn when all of a sudden the horn went off and died in a crescendo, he told them, like a dying cow. He talked about some of his favorite performers, Bill Kenny and the Ink Spots in particular, and named his favorite movie actor as James Dean, whose "Rebel Without a Pebble," he said, was his favorite film. He was absolutely charming, said Chick Crumpacker, winning in a way that didn't fail to take into account the reaction of his audience.

It was a gloomy day — rain had been pouring down in the aftermath of a storm that had blanketed the East Coast — but when the rehearsal was over Elvis was not averse to doing some sightseeing with Grelun Landon and his son. They bought a ball to toss around in a sporting goods store near Madison Square Garden, stopped off at a coffee shop and ordered milk shakes, and happily soaked up the hustle and bustle of the city. Back at the hotel Scotty and Bill reminisced about some of the early tours, and Bill talked about all the things they had done when they first started out to bolster Elvis and support the act. Scotty was characteristically reserved, while Bill was full of beans in describing some of the scrapes they had gotten themselves into, but with Elvis, said Landon, you simply couldn't tell how relaxed he really was or to what extent he was simply brazening it out. "He knew," said Landon, a sophisticated observer of human nature and, at thirty-three, a music-industry veteran, "what he was doing at all times. I really believe he was like a novelist — he studied and watched what was going on, it was really just second nature with him." There was some talk about "Heartbreak Hotel," which had been released with considerable misgivings by the RCA brass the day before. "I Forgot to Remember to Forget," in its new RCA pressing, was still riding high on the charts, and probably there was no one at RCA, including

Steve Sholes, who wouldn't have picked its clear, crisp, snappy sound over the murky mix and message of the new song. But RCA needed fresh product, they needed to demonstrate their commitment to their new artist, they needed to prove that they had not made a mistake of monumental proportions; they were not about to become the laughingstock of the industry. Just before it was time to go over to the theater Elvis Presley took a nap.

THE SHOW THAT NIGHT, wrote Chick Crumpacker, was not marked by any foreshadowings or harbingers of great success. It was broadcast from CBS' Studio 50, between Fifty-third and Fifty-fourth, and "few had braved the storm. The theater was sparsely filled with shivering servicemen and Saturday nighters, mostly eager for the refuge from the weather. Outside, groups of teenagers rushed past the marquee to a roller-skating rink nearby. Just before showtime, a weary promoter [Crumpacker himself] returned to the box office with dozens of tickets, unable even to give them away on the streets of Times Square."

The series itself was on rather shaky ground; ratings were poor, and in many quarters it was seen simply as the indulgence of one of television's biggest stars, who happened to love the sweet sound of swing. *Stage Show* had started out the previous fall as a half-hour lead-in to Jackie Gleason's *Honeymooners,* which had previously occupied the full hour as *The Jackie Gleason Show.* It proved so weak a lead-in that by March the order would be switched, and the show itself dropped after a single season. Other guests on the night of Elvis Presley's television debut included Sarah Vaughan, whose manager-husband George Treadwell refused to let her follow some untalented "hillbilly" singer, and comic-banjoist Gene Sheldon. In the paper the previous morning it had been announced in Nick Kenny's *New York Daily Mirror* column that "Bill Randle, one of the country's ace disc jockeys, makes a guest appearance on the CBS-TV 'Stage Show' tomorrow night at 8. Bill will present his new pop singing discovery Elvis Presley." It was not Elvis Presley, then, whom Tommy Dorsey introduced but "special guest" Bill Randle, who had been plugging the television appearance on his Saturday-afternoon New York radio network show. "We'd like at this time," said Randle, "to introduce to you a young fellow who, like many performers — Johnnie Ray among them — came out of nowhere to be an overnight big star. This young fellow we saw for the first time while making a movie short. We think tonight that he's going to make television history for you. We'd like you to meet him now — Elvis Presley."

Then Elvis came out looking as if he'd been shot out of a cannon. Wearing a black shirt, white tie, dress pants with a shiny stripe, and a tweed jacket so loud that it almost sparkled, he launched into the first song with no more than a toss of his head to Scotty and Bill, but much to Randle's surprise the song that he launched into was not his new RCA single but Big Joe Turner's "Shake, Rattle and Roll." When it came to the instrumental break, he drew back into the protective shelter of the band, got up on the balls of his feet, spread his legs wide, and let loose.

The reaction of the audience, as Chick Crumpacker recalled it, was something between shock and interest, "a kind of amusement. People tended to laugh as much as applaud at key moments." His hands never stop moving, it looks as if he might be chewing gum, there is a twitchiness to his whole aspect — and yet there is a boundless confidence, too, and his mascaraed visage appears to scan the audience as he seeks . . . connection. In the middle of the song he segues into "Flip, Flop and Fly," another Big Joe Turner number, and you're not sure if it's planned or unplanned, but there is the feeling of something fierce and uncontrolled. Scotty concentrates intently on his guitar playing; Bill — who *is* chewing gum — shouts encouragement: "Go, go, go." And Elvis is gone. At the end of the performance he almost staggers back from the mike, takes a deep bow, and waves, all in one instant. What you take away from it, no matter how many times you watch or how much you are aware of the fluttery movement of the hands, is the sheer enjoyment of the moment. *Elvis Presley is on top of the world.*

"Daddy just sat there," said Jackson Baker, Elvis' fifteen-year-old next-door neighbor of the previous summer, "and he said, 'Elvis is going to be a big star.' We all watched, and it was just so obvious that he was." Bob Johnson wrote in his notes for a future story: "Presley puts intensity into his songs. Over-emotional? Yes. But he projects. He 'sells.' Elvis has arrived. . . . But you can't throw that much into something without it telling. It'll wear him out. It will exhaust him emotionally and physically. He's 20 now [actually he was twenty-one]. If he's wise, he'll slow down a little and live another 20 years."

Probably there were few in Memphis who did not watch — Bob Neal, the mayor, the Lansky brothers, Dixie and her family, Elvis' boyhood friends, all were rooting for him, no doubt. And yet the stars didn't fall from the sky, the ratings didn't even go up appreciably, there was certainly no great press notice of Elvis Presley's television debut, and on Monday morning he was back in the studio recording.

STEVE SHOLES once again had a session in mind that was not going to take place anywhere *but* in his mind. He had lined up a good boogie-woogie piano player named Shorty Long, currently featured on Broadway in the musical *The Most Happy Fella,* to fill out the band, and he had done his best once again to prep Elvis for the session, but he sensed that something was missing. For while he never got any back talk from the boy, and he could sincerely offer nothing but praise to Colonel Parker with respect to the attitude and deportment of his young charge, he suspected that some connection was not being made, that the boy's politeness masked a distance or another point of view that he could not, or would not, articulate.

At Sholes' instigation, in what amounted to standard record company procedure, they started off with "Blue Suede Shoes," the new Sun release that was climbing the charts and provoking such galling afterthoughts at RCA. Recording conditions here in New York were far more satisfactory than in Nashville, the studio on the ground floor of the RCA building on East Twenty-fourth that had once housed the old police academy stables was a comfortable one for Sholes to work in, and the musicians were certainly familiar with the material. After thirteen takes, though, they still hadn't come up with a version to rival the authority of the original, and Sholes could scarcely have been reassured when the boy declared that it was no use doing any more, they couldn't do better than Carl's anyway. Next, at Presley's urging, they launched into a song with which Sholes was surely familiar because it came from an artist with whom he had worked extensively in Victor's "race" series, blues singer Arthur "Big Boy" Crudup. Crudup had written "That's All Right," Presley's first song, and now they did a masterful version of his "My Baby Left Me," in which for the first time the band really started to sound like a unit. D.J.'s drums and Bill's descending bass introed the song. In contrast to the rushed rhythms of the Perkins number or the murky echo of "Heartbreak Hotel," this sounded deliberate, thought out, a vibrant companion piece to the Sun recordings. And yet it can hardly have been of much consolation to Sholes, to whose way of thinking an Arthur Crudup blues was not what they were looking for, no matter how good it might be. *This* was not the potential new pop artist that RCA had signed, this was not the revolutionary new sound that RCA was looking for.

The afternoon session brought more of the same, another wonderful Crudup number, "So Glad You're Mine," plus one of the six songs that Sholes had suggested, a honky-tonker called "One Sided Love Affair" that was particularly suited to Shorty Long's barrelhouse style. If he could get three or four more, Sholes figured, along with the five unissued Sun titles that he had acquired, he would have just enough for an album.

At some point in the process he called Sam Phillips in Memphis and, under the pretext of informing him that they had cut "Blue Suede Shoes" (which he assured Sam he would not put out as a single), sought advice and reassurance concerning the course he was following. He even put out feelers, according to Phillips, for Sam to produce Elvis for RCA on a freelance basis. "I told him he hadn't bought the wrong person. And I told him what I told him when he bought the contract in the first place, just don't try to make Elvis what he's not instinctively. The worst mistake you can make is to try to shape him into some damn country artist, or anything else, if it just doesn't naturally flow that way. I told him to keep it as simple as possible, and I happen to be the greatest admirer of Steve Sholes — he was a person of the utmost integrity and how he could be that way when he was with a major label, quote unquote, I really don't understand — but he was *not* a producer. Steve was just at every session, and he kept his fucking mouth shut."

On the second day of recording a young wire reporter named Fred Danzig showed up for an interview, the first fruits of Anne Fulchino's publicity campaign. "I wrote a thing called 'On the Record' for the radio wire, and I did another version for the newspapers for what was called the United Press Red Letter. I would interview singers and composers and record producers and just give them stuff like that. At some point in 1955 Marion Keisker started writing me from Memphis about this kid, Elvis Presley, who was doing such marvelous things down there, and then he placed ninth in our third annual Disc Jockey Poll. So I knew about him when Annie called me up and told me that he was going to be in New York to do the Dorsey show."

Danzig watched the show on TV and showed up at Fulchino's office at 11:00 A.M. the following Tuesday. She took him down to the recording studio where he found, he later wrote, "a tall, lean young man standing in the hallway waiting for us." He was wearing "a shirt the likes of which I had never seen before. It was a ribbon shirt, light lavender in color. Elvis said it cost $70. I also noted that his blue alligator loafers were scuffed and worn-down at the heels. He had on a gray sports jacket and dark gray slacks. His fingernails were chewed down to where there was no biting room left." His presence was compelling, Danzig said, "just for that face alone. If you saw him on the street, you'd say, 'Wow, look at that guy.' "

They went into the control room to do the interview. In response to a question about his music, the boy started naming blues singers with whom Danzig was somewhat familiar but who "obviously meant a lot to him. I was very surprised to hear him talk about the black performers down there and about how he tried to carry on their music. He talked about how he wanted to buy his parents a house and make life easier for them. I asked him about the shaking and the wiggling, and he told me they hadn't wanted him to jump around so much on TV but that he had told them it was the way he had to perform, it was just the way he did it. He showed me his leather-covered guitar and explained that there was only one other leather guitar case like it. Hank Snow had given him the idea, he said. 'It keeps the guitar from getting splintered when I swing it around and it hits my belt buckle.' " They talked about the movies and how he "wanted to go out to Hollywood and become the next James Dean. And I thought, 'Yeah, well, come on, kid . . .' But that was obviously his goal.

"We talked for about twenty or twenty-five minutes — he wasn't the most articulate kid in the world, but he answered all the questions — when Steve Sholes came in and said they were ready to begin." Elvis invited Danzig to stick around and watch him work, and the first number they tried was "I'm Gonna Sit Right Down and Cry (Over You)," a 1954 r&b number for Roy Hamilton (it was the B side of Hamilton's smash inspirational hit, "You'll Never Walk Alone"). "Gee, those sideburns bother me," Sholes remarked to Danzig wryly. "I wonder if I should get him to the barbershop." But, he added with a mirthful chuckle, "I guess you don't tamper with success. I guess we'll leave them on the kid."

* * *

THE NEXT COUPLE OF DAYS were taken up with sightseeing and a scattering of promotional activities, mostly organized by Anne Fulchino and Chick Crumpacker, with Hill and Range representative Grelun Landon along for the ride. The Colonel by now had gone home to Tennessee, presumably to oversee, in his meticulous fashion, the multiplicity of details surrounding the start-up of the upcoming tour. With his "keepers," Elvis drove out to Trenton to do an interview on perhaps the only station in the New York metropolitan area to air country music. They got lost looking for the station, and Elvis slept all the way out and back. The William Morris people threw a party for him; so did Julian Aberbach, the president of Hill and Range, who had a dinner in Elvis' honor at his home. Julian's wife, Anne Marie, served lamb cooked rare, and Elvis almost gagged on it, explaining that he was not used to "bloody" meat; his taste ran more to hamburgers, well done. "He was extremely polite," said Freddy Bienstock, Julian's cousin, who was also present, "but he was completely lost."

Chick, in what he later came to see as a case of enthusiasm overrunning judgment, scheduled a reception at the Hickory House, on Fifty-second Street above Times Square, but made the mistake of failing to secure a private room. "It might as well have been Grand Central Station the way people were milling in and out, but the savior of the situation was Elvis, who looked around, took stock of things, and then took charge with such aplomb and such charm that he made everybody feel like they were alone with him in the room." He was wearing a hand-painted tie that he had gotten for a dollar in Times Square and the same lavender ribbon shirt that Fred Danzig had remarked upon. What was his reaction to success? he was asked. "It's all happening so fast," he said, "there's so much happening to me . . . that some nights I just can't fall asleep. It scares me, you know . . . it just scares me."

THE SECOND DORSEY SHOW went fine. He sang "Tutti Frutti" and "Baby, Let's Play House," once again failing to plug his new single, which according to *Billboard* was "a strong blues item wrapped up in his usual powerful style and a great beat. . . . Presley is riding high right now with network TV appearances, and this disk should benefit from all the special plugging." Evidently something was bothering Elvis about the show, though, because when Sholes wrote to Parker three days later he said: "I thought Elvis did even better Saturday night than he did on the previous week's show. I understand he was not so pleased but I think he had every right to be happy. You should be very proud of the boy," Sholes went on,

> because as far as I can find out he conducted himself very well after you left. At the press party he mingled with all the guests and made a very good impression there. As a result he is very hot material here in New York and with any luck at all I think we all should do extremely well. . . .
>
> On Friday we didn't have any new material that suited Elvis so we recorded LAWDY MISS CLAWDY and SHAKE RATTLE AND ROLL. Neither one of these would be suitable for single release but I know they will make good selections for the second album.

On Sunday night Elvis was back in Richmond with an Opry troupe assembled by the Colonel that included the Carter Sisters and Mother Maybelle, Ernest Tubb's son, Justin, and Charlie and Ira Louvin, who had already played a good number of dates with Elvis and were Mrs. Presley's favorite country singing group. They were booked every night — in Greensboro, High Point, and Raleigh, North Carolina, then in Spartanburg and Charlotte the first week, with Saturday night off for Elvis to go up to New York to play the third Dorsey brothers show. Oscar Davis acted as the advance man, and the Colonel came in behind him to set up the show, hauling pictures, programs, and all the concessions that he was now personally peddling, taking away a lucrative source of outside income from Bill. Oscar's expansive manner charmed every local newspaperman, promoter, desk clerk, and bellhop in sight, while the Colonel's scrupulous, almost compulsive attention to detail, at such striking odds with the casualness of his appearance, his almost contemptuous dismissal of the niceties of human behavior, virtually guaranteed that everything would be just so. "The Colonel embarrasses me," Oscar frequently complained to his cronies. "Goddam, he embarrasses the hell out of me — runs around like a goddam carny, with his damn shirttail hanging out and no necktie." Parker could become no less infuriated by the way that Oscar threw his money around, but they were the perfect team so long as Oscar didn't quit or the Colonel didn't fire Oscar for giving a stagehand a fifty-dollar tip at any given show.

"We were working near every day," said Scotty. "We'd pull into some town, go to the hotel room and get washed up or go right to the auditorium or movie house, and after we played our shows, we'd get back in the cars and start driving to the next town. We never saw any newspapers. . . . And we didn't hear much radio, because it was drive all night, sleep all day. . . . All we knew was drive, drive, drive." It was, said D.J., like being in a fog.

On Saturday night the whole troupe watched the third *Stage Show* appearance, when Elvis for the first time sang not only "Heartbreak Hotel" but his newly recorded version of "Blue Suede Shoes." The performance of "Heartbreak Hotel" was something of a disaster, with Scotty and Bill hidden away in the shadows, the Dorsey brothers' orchestra contributing an arrhythmic arrangement that Elvis was unable to move or cue, and Charlie Shavers taking a trumpet solo that left the singer with a sickly smile on his lips.

With the exception of the Carter Sisters, the troupe was probably not unhappy to see the young phenom fall on his face. There was a considerable amount of envy already over the attention that Elvis had been getting not just from audiences but from the Colonel himself, who was clearly focusing almost all of his energies and interest on his new acquisition. To Justin Tubb, who had grown up in the business and at twenty had already had three country hits and was a member of the Opry in his own right, everything about the tour was different right from the start. "The audiences were a lot younger, and it was the first time I'd ever seen them start screaming and waving their arms and hollering. You know, country singers and pickers had always been [considered] almost second class, pop musicians looked down on us. The kind of feeling you got was that here was somebody who was kind of using country music to get going, and yet he would go out and do his rockabilly stuff, his real raunchy stuff, and that's what the girls wanted to hear.

"I'm sure there was some real — not jealousy, but envy, because he was happening and you could feel it. Not only in the audiences but in the importance of 'Heartbreak Hotel' just being released and RCA buying his deal and him flying to New York to do the TV show and our all sitting there watching him.

"He was like a diamond in the rough. When he walked offstage, he would be just soaked, just dripping. He worked hard, and he put everything he had into it, and everything he did worked, because the audience just didn't care — we had never seen anything like it before. My feeling was that they didn't capture him on the television show — of course we had already seen him in action, and it could have been envy, but he seemed a little reserved from what we had seen, he seemed a little nervous, they didn't seem to get his magnetism or charisma."

The tour continued. Elvis and Scotty and Bill kept pretty much to themselves, according to Justin. "Elvis always stood in the wings and watched everybody, especially the Louvins, he was a *fan*." Once in a while he would go out to eat with the others, but Red West, who was doing most of the driving, and D.J. were the ones who were more likely to be hanging out. At the end of the second week, Elvis and his three band members flew back to New York from Winston-Salem, North Carolina, to play the TV show with borrowed instruments, while Red loaded up theirs on a little trailer cart that Vernon had had made up and painted pink ("It looked more like a rolling toilet than anything else," said Red in his book, *Elvis: What Happened?*, "[but] the way Elvis' dad went on about that thing, you would have thought it was a goddamned yacht") and took off on the fifteen-hour drive to Tampa. By now the record was finally starting to show some movement. It was just about to debut on the pop charts and had been steadily gaining attention in *Billboard*, particularly in its country and western "Best Buys" column, which declared that sales had "snowballed rapidly in the past two weeks, with pop and r.&b. customers joining Presley's hillbilly fans in demanding the disk." Perhaps as a result of this new flurry of activity, Jackie Gleason Enterprises had picked up the option on Presley's contract and scheduled two more appearances on *Stage Show* for the end of March at the agreed-upon $1,250 each.

Meanwhile on the tour things had already reached something of a boiling point. A few days before that fourth Dorsey appearance, in Wilson, North Carolina, the promoter oversold the show, and the Colonel told the troupe they would have to work a second one at no additional pay that night. Exasperated by Colonel Parker's increasingly peremptory manner (they were beginning to feel as if they were being treated not just as "entertainers," a necessary nuisance in the Colonel's book, but as second-class citizens, little more than stage props on this tour), they banded together and refused to do it. Ira Louvin, who could charitably be described as hot-tempered even under the best of circumstances ("My brother didn't get along with a lot of people," said Charlie Louvin understatedly), went on and on about who did this Presley kid think he was, that no-talent sonofabitch, trying to take over their music — and fuck the Colonel anyway, he was going to go to the Colonel and let him know they weren't going to take this shit anymore.

They had a meeting, with Ira moderating his demands only slightly and Justin Tubb, who had known the Colonel since he was a child (and whose father was as widely respected and loved as anyone in the country music community), making a calmer and more reasoned presentation. But if they thought that Tom Parker was going to be moved by sentiment, or backed into a corner by a unified stand, they had made a serious miscalculation. The Colonel was appalled — *appalled,* he said — that his motives should be questioned in this way. He had heard that Ira was mouthing off and saying, "Fuck the Colonel." "Why did you say that, Iwa?" said Tom Parker in his unmodulated, Elmer Fudd accent. "Why did you say, 'Fuck the Colonel'?" And as for Justin, the Colonel shook his head, the Colonel was surprised at Justin. The Colonel had known Justin's mother, known his father, even given him a little Shetland pony for his birthday when Justin was a small child ("It was old and nearly blind," said Justin, but not to Tom Parker's face), what did Justin mean by coming to him and making these outrageous demands? The Colonel's eyes alternately flashed with fire and filled with tears. As Justin recognized, "he was an old carny, and he grew up the rough, tough way, he was a self-made man — he was brusque, but, I mean, he was the Colonel, I think most of us expected that of him. We didn't bear him any ill will, we just had to make a stand."

In the end the Colonel capitulated — all the performers got paid, and the show went on. But feelings definitely lingered, tempers continued to fester, there was no question in anyone's mind that the Colonel was mad and that Ira Louvin, who sniffed out slights even when there were none, was seething. A couple of days after the incident in Wilson, things came to a head backstage between shows. Elvis was hanging around the dressing room with the Louvins, singing hymns and playing the piano when, in the recollection of Ira's younger brother, Charlie, "Elvis said, 'Boy, this is my favorite music.' Well, Ira walked up and said, 'Why, you white nigger, if that's your favorite music, why don't you do that out yonder? Why do you do that nigger trash out there?' Presley said, 'When I'm out there, I do what they want to hear — when I'm back here, I can do what I want to do.' " Ira flashed and "tried to strangle him," according to Charlie, "and they were very distant from that point on."

In Jacksonville on February 23, Elvis collapsed. He had completed the first night's show at the Gator Bowl and they were loading up the instruments in the parking lot when, in Bill's account, he "fell out cold." They took him to the hospital, where he was kept under observation for a couple of hours and told by a doctor that "I was doing as much work in twenty minutes as the average laborer does in eight hours. He said if I didn't slow up, I'd have to lay off a couple of years." But he checked out of the hospital before morning, because, he told his friends with a wink, the nurses wouldn't give him any rest. And besides, he said to Red, it was all just a stunt to impress Anita Carter. He played the Gator Bowl again that night with undiminished energy and effect. He had no intention of slowing down.

They were back on the Hayride the following week for the first time in a month. A lot had happened in that month, but for Elvis and Scotty and Bill there had been no time to gauge it, and it didn't appear all that different from everything else that had been building and going on for the last year. They did "Heartbreak Hotel" for the first time, said Scotty, "and that damn auditorium down there almost exploded. I mean, it had been wild before that, but it was more like playing down at your local camp, a home folks–type situation. But now they turned into — it was different faces, just a whole other . . . That's the earliest I can remember saying, *What is going on?*"

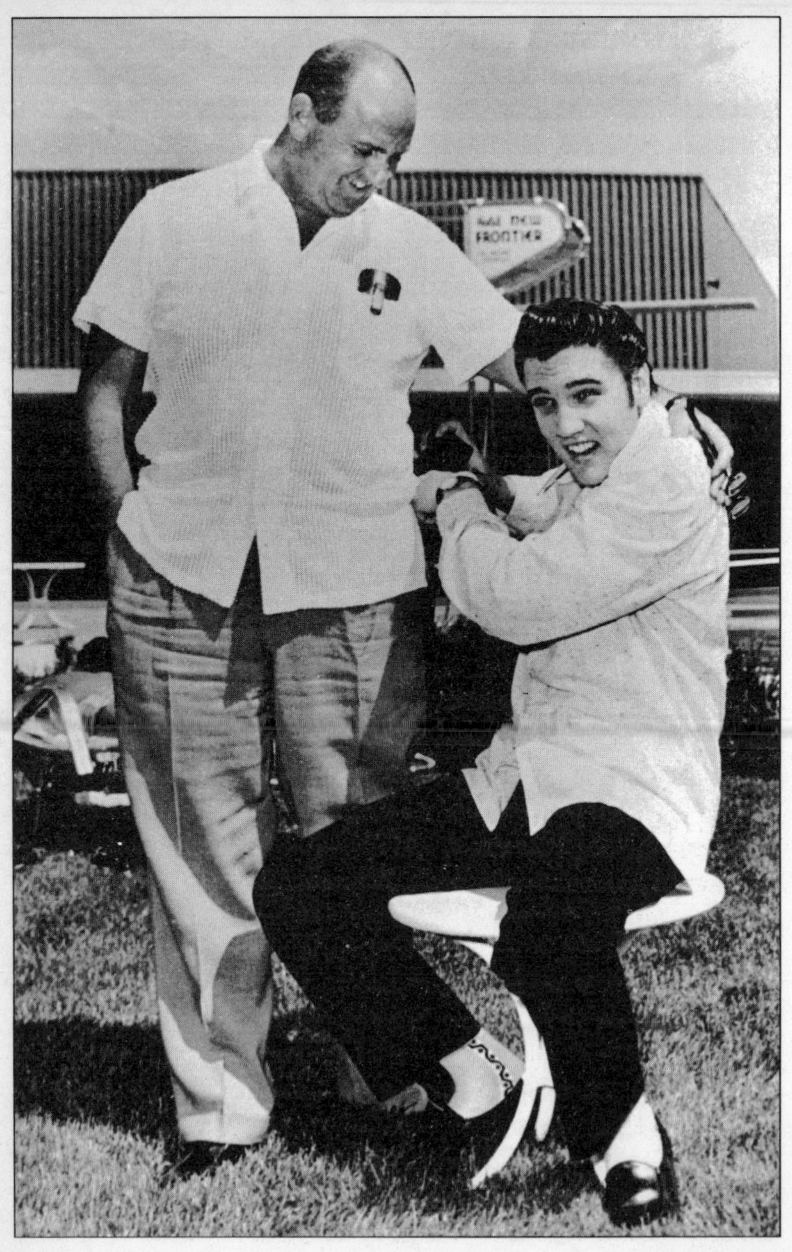

WITH COLONEL PARKER, LAS VEGAS, APRIL 1956. (JAMES REID)

THE WORLD TURNED UPSIDE DOWN

The Elvis Presley who made his sixth and final appearance on the Dorsey brothers' *Stage Show,* on March 24, 1956, was a far cry from the ill-at-ease, fidgety, almost manic gum-chewing figure who had made his television debut just two months before. He strode out purposefully, leaned into "Money Honey," and just poured it on without ever letting up. Even his hair was different, less obviously greasy, more carefully sculpted, and where in earlier appearances his vocal energies appeared to wax and wane and that moment when he pulled back into the shelter of the little group to do his dance seemed as much an attempt to incite a response from the crowd as to invite one, now he regarded the adoring multitudes with a look of amused — not so much contempt as authority. He took their adulation gratefully as his due . . . and then just poured it on some more. When he announced that he would do one side from his latest record, there were screams from the crowd, and "Heartbreak Hotel" took on a sensuous intensity that was dispelled only when he slipped into the small, childish voice he used to break up Scotty and Bill at unpredictable moments. This time it was little more than an allusion, betrayed by the slightest self-amused smile, before he jauntily went on with the show. And then he was gone, coolly, casually striding off the stage and skipping out again for a deep bow. Elvis, as Jimmy Dorsey had announced at the beginning of the show, was off to Hollywood for a screen test.

The band left that night, driving into a snowstorm but stopping off in Dover, Delaware, to visit Carl Perkins in the hospital where he was recuperating from a bad automobile accident in which his two brothers (who played bass and rhythm guitar in his band) were also seriously injured. His song "Blue Suede Shoes" was competing furiously with "Heartbreak Hotel" in the charts, and he had been on his way to New York to appear on *The Perry Como Show,* opposite the Dorsey brothers, when the accident occurred. Elvis meanwhile remained in New York that evening to complete an interview with *Coronet* magazine reporter Robert Carlton Brown in which he mused on his current success. He called his parents every day, he said, because "my mother is always worried about a wreck, or me getting sick. So I have to let her know, because she's not in real good health anyway, and if she worries too much, it might not be good for her." He had just bought his parents a new house, he informed Brown; as a matter of fact "they moved in Tuesday. It's a ranch-type, seven-room house. Three bedrooms, a den, playroom, it's a pretty nice place." As for his father, "he doesn't do any — he takes care of all my business. In other words, he's much more important to me at home than he is on the job. Because I have so much stuff piling up for me when I'm gone, and if he wasn't there to help, when I got home I wouldn't get a bit of rest. He takes care of everything — you know, any business that pops up, any insurance, or just oodles of things that I could mention." And the Colonel? "I read," said the interviewer, "that Colonel Tom Parker has given you a lot of advice and help. What kind?" "Everything," said Elvis without hesitation. "He's the one guy that really gave me the big breaks . . . I don't think I would have ever been very big with another man. Because he — he's a very smart man."

Bob Neal watched bemusedly from the sidelines, now that he was completely, and formally, out of the picture. On March 15, his own contract with Elvis had run out and as per his November 21 agreement with the Colonel, he chose not to exercise the option. On March 26 the Colonel's new status as "sole and exclusive Advisor, Personal Representative, and Manager in any and all fields of public and private entertainment" was formally ratified and his 25 percent commission reaffirmed at the same time. "I suppose," Neal said to Jerry Hopkins in 1971, "really, in many ways, I — felt that I should try to continue in the picture, but at the same time with the things that I had going in Memphis — with my radio show and the promotions, and we owned a record shop . . . had a big family, kids in school and so forth . . . I decided to more or less let things go." While he was undoubtedly gratified by Elvis' own success, it must have galled Neal nonetheless to see the headlines in the trades week after week and to realize that he could, and perhaps should, have been a part of it. "A WINNAH! Presley Hot as $1 Pistol" was the headline in *Billboard* on March 3.

> The hottest artist on the RCA Victor label this week has been none other than the amazing young country warbler, Elvis Presley, who has been on the label for only about two months.
>
> Presley has six hit singles in the company's list of top 25 best sellers, five of which had been previously issued on the Sun label. . . . The coupling of "Heartbreak Hotel" and "I Was the One," cut by Victor, is the label's No. 2 seller, right behind Perry Como's "Juke Box Baby."

By the end of March the single had sold close to a million copies and, in an unprecedented achievement (mirrored only by Carl Perkins' "Blue Suede Shoes" at virtually the same time), was closing in on the top of all three charts: pop, country, and rhythm and blues. Moreover, the new album, released on March 13, stood at nearly three hundred thousand sales, making it a sure bet to be RCA's first million-dollar (at $3.98 retail) album, and the EP containing "Blue Suede Shoes," which RCA had released on the same date as the LP and which was also simply entitled *Elvis Presley* without any additional credit or qualification (as per the Colonel's instructions, neither musicians nor recording supervisors were named), had already started up the charts itself. Steve Sholes, as another *Billboard* headline trumpeted a few weeks later, was definitely having the last laugh.

ON SUNDAY, MARCH 25, after a few hours' sleep, Elvis flew out to the West Coast. He was scheduled to appear on *The Milton Berle Show* the following Tuesday, and his screen test with producer Hal Wallis had been hurriedly set up for the week in between. Wallis, a fifty-six-year-old veteran of the movie business who had made such well-known pictures as *The Maltese Falcon, Casablanca, Yankee Doodle Dandy,* and *The Rose Tattoo* and currently had N. Richard Nash's play *The Rainmaker* in preproduction, had first heard about Presley at the beginning of February from his partner in New York, Joseph Hazen. Hazen's sister-in-law, Harriet Ames, one of the seven wealthy Annenberg sisters, was a "television addict" who happened to be watching the Dorsey show. She called Hazen, who lived across the street from her at 885 Park Avenue, "and I called my partner in California," Hazen remembered. "I said, 'Turn on the television and look at the show. This kid is terrific.' "

Wallis was impressed, he later wrote, with Presley's "originality," but he was probably more impressed with the sales figures and the stir he was creating (not to mention the clear potential to tap into the new youth market, which was crying for a successor to the late Jimmy Dean), factors that were pointed out to him forcefully by Abe Lastfogel of William Morris. The screen test was scheduled to coincide with the Berle appearance, and the Colonel waved off any RCA efforts to set up press or radio promotion for the West Coast trip until all the details with Wallis were nailed down. From Anne Fulchino's point of view, "That's when we really lost control. I remember the Colonel came up to me [just before he went out to Hollywood], and he put his arms around me, and I smelled a rat right away. He said, 'You know, I want to apologize to you for what I did in Jacksonville [this was the incident that took place with Chick Crumpacker on the RCA Country Caravan two years before].' Boy, did I smell a rat then, because he never apologized, even if he was dead wrong, so now I *knew* something was coming. And he said to me, 'You did a tremendous job on Elvis. But,' he said, 'now you can rest.' "

Although Elvis himself had made it plain to the Colonel that he had little interest in just "singing in the movies" — if he was going to do anything in the pictures, he wanted to be a movie *star*, a serious actor like Brando, Dean, Richard Widmark, Rod Steiger — the screen test that he took consisted of two parts. In the first he was given what looked like a toy guitar and told to mime a performance to his recording of "Blue Suede Shoes." The idea, according to screenwriter Allan Weiss, who was present for the test and cued up the record as a then-member of the sound department, was to see if the "indefinable energy" that had showed up on television would translate to film.

There was never any doubt, wrote Weiss, as Presley stepped in front of the camera:

> The transformation was incredible . . . electricity bounced off the walls of the soundstage. One felt it as an awesome thing — like an earthquake in progress, only without the implicit threat. Watching this insecure country boy, who apologized when he asked for a rehearsal as though he had done something wrong, turn into absolute dynamite when he stepped into the bright lights and started lip-synching the words of his familiar hit. He believed in it, and he

made you believe it, no matter how "sophisticated" your musical tastes were. . . .

The number was completed in two takes, and they moved in for close-ups. He protested mildly that he hadn't been "dead-on" in a couple of places. It was explained that the closer shots would be intercut to cover it. I don't think he understood, but with characteristic trust, he did what he was told. No stand-in was provided, and he stood uncomplainingly while the lights were being adjusted—bathed in perspiration.

Then he did two scenes from *The Rainmaker,* a period comedy-drama set in Kansas in 1913 that was scheduled to start shooting in June with Burt Lancaster starring opposite Katharine Hepburn, in which he played the younger brother, a kind of male ingenue role. "I knew my script," Elvis said proudly later that year. "They sent it to me before I came to Hollywood . . . and I got out there and just tried to put myself in the place of the character I was playing, just trying to act as naturally as I could." He had never been in a play before; he had never spoken a single line onstage. He came across, wrote Weiss, "with amateurish conviction — like the lead in a high school play," but if he was wooden from lack of dramatic training, that didn't stop him from telling Mr. Wallis that he didn't think the part was right for him when Wallis sat down with him sometime later to discuss his celluloid future. This character was "lovesick, real shy. I mean, he wasn't real shy. Real jolly. Real happy, real jolly, real lovesick. It wasn't like me. . . . Mr. Wallis asked me what kind of a part I'd like to play, and I told him one more like myself, so I wouldn't have to do any excess acting." But that wasn't what he meant exactly. When the producer laughed, the boy just grinned and let it go, because he couldn't say what he really meant: he couldn't say that he *knew* he could do it, it would be like saying that he knew he could fly. And while he might never have been in a high school play, he had imagined himself up on the screen, he had studied the movies, he studied the actors — the way they presented themselves, the way they cocked their heads, the way they won the audience's sympathy. He had imagined himself a singing star, and it had come true — so why not this, too?

Wallis for his part was struck by the young man's polite, well-mannered demeanor. After dealing with Jerry Lewis for seven years, it would come as a relief to work with such a tractable, essentially malleable young man. And Wallis and the Colonel (whom Wallis found "as fascinating as Elvis" in his own right) were both well aware of the long and profitable tradition by which virtually every popular male singing star, from Rudy Vallee to Bing Crosby to Frank Sinatra, ended up in Hollywood and, if he was lucky, was transformed into a movie star. This rock 'n' roll might not last, but the boy was a real phenomenon, and if he was able — like Crosby and Sinatra before him — to turn that magnetism into the warmth of the all-around entertainer, then they would be able to make a lot of money together.

He and the Colonel quickly came to an understanding that would be formalized by the beginning of the following week in what Wallis characterized — accurately or flatteringly, it would be impossible to say — as "one of the toughest bargaining sessions of my career." It was a three-picture deal which, with options, could be extended for seven years: the price for the first picture was $100,000, for the second and third, $150,000 and $200,000 respectively. For this kind of money Wallis and Hazen had been hoping for an exclusive, but true to his nature the Colonel insisted on keeping his options open, reserving the right to make one outside picture a year for any amount of money that he was able to negotiate.

There was no time to savor the triumph. Elvis was due in San Diego for the Berle show, which was scheduled to be broadcast on April 3 from the deck of the U.S.S. *Hancock,* docked at the San Diego naval station. *The Milton Berle Show* was a definite step up from the Dorseys. Milton Berle, the original "Mr. Television," was still a major star and had booked Presley only as a favor to his agent, Abe Lastfogel. Berle met Elvis and the Colonel for the first time at the airport. "I sat in the middle and Colonel Parker was on the other side and Elvis was on my right. So I said, 'Oh, here's the contract for the show,' and I was about to hand it to Elvis when Colonel Parker grabbed it, says, 'Don't show that boy that contract!' So Elvis didn't know what he was getting. Colonel Parker held a hard hand!"

They went directly to rehearsal, where Scotty and Bill and D.J. met them, having just rolled into town themselves after an arduous cross-country trek. D.J. was thrilled at the presence of the great drummer Buddy Rich, a member of the Harry James Orchestra, but Rich did not return the compliment. The musicians all sniffed when Elvis did not produce any charts, and when he launched into "Blue Suede Shoes," Rich rolled his eyes at Harry James and said, audibly, "This is the worst."

The show itself was one more unmitigated triumph. It was a windy day, and flags were flying in the breeze, with the ocean as backdrop and an audience that was as good-natured as it was enthusiastic. Elvis opened with "Heartbreak Hotel," naturally, after an elaborate introduction by Berle, who came out onstage dressed in an admiral's uniform with plenty of gold braid. The performer that television viewers saw appeared in yet another stage of radical metamorphosis, more self-assured by half, more in command of his look and style than he had been just ten days before — but it is the stark visual imagery that sets off his performance most, as he stands, all in black save for white tie, white belt, and white bucks, legs spread wide apart and at a point of hitherto-unremarked stillness, just inviting the crowd to come to *him*.

They did. The song was greeted by an audience made up predominantly of sailors and their dates with an appropriate mixture of screams and laughter — because it is clear by now that the performer is playing with them. It may not be as clear to the little girls, but there is no aggression in this act, he is teasing them, fooling with them, his laughter is their laughter, for the first time in his life he is one of them. He then introduced "my latest release, 'Blue Schwede Shoes,' " and launched into the song in a loose, carefree manner that far surpassed any of his previous televised efforts. The crowd was with him all the way, and when he went into the repeated, almost mantra-like coda, Bill got on the bass and rode it for all it was worth, hands up in the air, legs sticking out, and whooping as the crowd whooped happily back. It was a moment, a picture, a perfectly lit snapshot, that the Colonel vowed was never going to be repeated: Bill Black was never going to take attention away from his boy again.

Next was a comedy sketch with Berle in which the comedian came out dressed identically to his guest star, only with his pants rolled up and looking like a rube in oversize blue suede shoes. He was, he declared in the broadest Catskills cornpone accent, Elvis' twin brother, Melvin, who had taught Elvis everything he knew. They played with that for a while, with Elvis declaring, "I owe it all to you, Melvin," and then they went into a reprise of "Blue Suede Shoes," which Elvis flung himself into as good-naturedly as he had the earlier rendition, while Berle pranced about the stage and did a limber send-up of his enthusiastic young friend. It would have been hard to detect any sign of resentment, if resentment existed, on the part of "America's newest singing sensation," whether because Berle was spoofing his act or because of the twin-brother routine; it was all just show business, after all — Gladys was probably laughing at home with some of the cousins and Grandma Minnie. They had always enjoyed Uncle Miltie, ever since they got their first television set; he was, of course, a very important and powerful figure in the business, said Colonel Parker, and Elvis should never forget, Mr. Berle was doing them a favor by having him on the show.

There was an appearance the next day at a San Diego record shop and a riot the next night at the conclusion of the first of two appearances at the San Diego Arena. At one point Elvis had to admonish the crowd mildly to "sit down or the show ends," and the girls went back to their seats, but the musicians couldn't get out of the building for a full forty-five minutes after the show was over, and Elvis sat around backstage with some local musicians, talking about the Hayride and his rapid rise to fame. "The crowd was too noisy for most of the numbers to be heard," sniffed the San Diego paper, which noted that his brief appearance followed "a woman vocalist, an acrobatic dance team, a comedian, and a xylophone player," a far cry from the all-star country packages on which he had been appearing. "I changed my whole style," said Glen Glenn, a twenty-one-year-old committed country singer from just outside Los Angeles who had driven down for the show with his guitar player and was introduced backstage by bass player Fred Maddox of the Maddox Brothers and Rose. "We all wanted to be like Elvis after that."

There was no stopping the juggernaut now. Elvis had made his last regular Hayride appearance on Saturday, March 31, flying in from Hollywood in the midst of the Hal Wallis negotiations. The Colonel had extricated Elvis from his contract by paying a penalty of ten thousand dollars and promising that he would do a benefit concert in December for free. The Sunday after the Berle show they played Denver, then flew to Texas for the start of a two-week tour that would be interrupted by a recording session on Saturday, April 14. It had reached the point where no one even knew any longer what day it was; they drove through the night because it was impossible to get to sleep until 9:00 or 10:00 in the morning anyway, Elvis said, he was just too keyed up. There were girls everywhere; more time was spent hiding from them than looking for them. There was, of course, at least one call a day home. He had yet to spend a single night in the new house on Audubon Drive.

Everywhere he went, everyone wanted to know everything about him. They wanted to know how he got started in the business. They wanted to know about his mother and father. They wanted to know about the movies, naturally. He deflected every question with that unique combination of deference and candor. He answered every question with the truth. Yes, he was very excited about his Hollywood contract, it was a dream come true, it just showed that you could never tell what was going to happen to you in your life — but no, he wasn't going to sing in the movies. No, he didn't have any special girl, he had thought he had been in love, he had been in love once, in fact it was only when he started singing that they broke up. He still heard from her, she wrote to him sometimes. Did he still go to church? "I haven't since I been singing, 'cause Saturday night is usually our biggest night, and almost every Sunday we have a matinee or we're on the road . . ." Are you taking good care of yourself? There are rumors that you've been carousing around and don't really know where you're going. "Well, that's about the truth. It really is. I can't deny it, because half the time I — I don't know from one day to the next where I'm going. I have so much on my mind, in other words, I'm trying to keep with everything, trying to keep a level head. . . . You have to be careful out in the world. It's so easy to get turned." And what did he like best about being so successful, aside from the money? "I would say the money in a way, of course that, like you said, is the biggest part, but actually the thing I like about it better is to know that people like — that you've got so many friends."

It was hard work — and it never let up. But no matter how hard he worked, he didn't work any harder than the Colonel. Colonel was up at 5:30 every morning when they were just getting in, and he was there until the last ticket was counted, the last picture sold. He was in everybody's face, it seemed, he didn't let a promoter get away with a single unsold ticket, and he was always on Scotty and Bill about something they had or hadn't done onstage. "He was working for Elvis, period," said D.J., more of a disinterested observer than either of the other two. "He didn't care what you did. That's all he knew, twenty-four hours a day, Elvis. That was his boy." Sometimes, it seemed, Elvis would test the Colonel — he would arrive late for one show after another and then, said D.J., when the Colonel was ready to jump down all their throats, "he'd say, 'Don't you worry about the Colonel. I'll take care of it.' And then the Colonel would jump us and say, 'Hey, you guys have got to get here a little bit earlier.' And we'd say, 'You tell *him*,' and that was the end of it. I think he done it just to make the Colonel mad sometimes."

Scotty and Bill knew the Colonel would just as soon cut their throats as look at them. They'd be gone in a minute, they both agreed, if it was up to the Colonel; he had long ago made that plain. They never really brought it up directly with Elvis, though — they knew Elvis would never consider anything that would change his music, and they doubted that Colonel would ever push him on this point. It was clear what happened if anyone pushed Colonel. Red had had a blowup with the Colonel, and it didn't escape anyone's attention that Red was gone, at least for this tour. In Red's account Elvis had been with a girl, and he wouldn't get out of bed with her.

> When he finally emerged, he looked like he had been mixed up with an eggbeater. . . . Well, we're really late now. It's winter time, and it's sleeting and raining colder than hell. We jump in the car, I drive like a madman through snow and everything to Virginia to this auditorium. . . . We arrive there, I guess we're fifteen minutes late, or something like that. Now it's still snowing like hell, but out in front of the auditorium I see this crazy guy in a T-shirt. I get out of the car, and I notice he is puffing on this cigar, and he has got an expression on his face like he is going to kill me . . . kill *me,* not Elvis. Then I notice that, despite the fact he is wearing a T-shirt in this damn snow, he is so worked up he is sweating. . . . He just looks at me as if he was going to rip a yard from my ass. Right away he starts in, "Where in the hell you been? Do you know what time it is? I got these people waiting, and you're damn well late. You can't keep people waiting. Who do you think you are?"

There was little room for sentiment in the new order of things. The business was changing, the mood was changing, and the show was necessarily changing, too. The crowds were so frenzied by now that you could no longer hear the music. The screams that started up from the moment they took the stage, the tortuous faces and blinding tears — Scotty and Bill watched it all with something like disbelief, playing as loud as they could while all they could hear over the din was the occasional sound of D.J.'s drums. "We were the only band in history," Scotty frequently joked, "that was directed by an ass. It was like being in a sea of sound." It was true, but as intently as they watched him, they could never really tell what he was going to do next. "I'll bet I could burp," said Elvis impishly, "and make them squeal." And then he burped and did.

They chartered a plane out of Amarillo in the middle of the night so that they could get to Nashville in time for the recording session at 9:00 the following morning. Just before dawn they got lost and landed at an airstrip outside of El Dorado, Arkansas, to refuel. It was chilly, and the musicians huddled together in the little coffee shop, yawning and making desultory conversation. It was just light when they took off again. Scotty was sitting beside the pilot, who asked him to hold the wheel for a minute while he studied the map. Just as Scotty took the wheel, the engine coughed and died and the plane started to lose altitude. There was a good deal of confusion, and Bill pulled his coat over his head and cursed the day he had ever let himself be persuaded to go up in this rickety machine, before the pilot discovered that when they refueled they hadn't switched over to the full tank and the airstrip attendant hadn't bothered to refill the empty one. When they finally got to Nashville, Elvis announced half-jokingly, "Man, I don't know if I'll ever fly again."

The session reflected the edginess of everyone's mood. They worked from 9:00 till 12:00, did close to twenty takes of a single song, and ended up with only that one song, a ballad called "I Want You, I Need You, I Love You" that Steve Sholes had come up with for the date. Once again the backup singers were the same mismatched trio that had been assembled for the first Nashville session: Ben and Brock Speer of the Speer Family, and Gordon Stoker of the Jordanaires. Where were the other boys? Elvis asked Stoker during a break. He had played with the Jordanaires in Atlanta just a month before, on the same bill with country comedian Rod Brasfield, Mississippi Slim's cousin, and his brother, Uncle Cyp, and they had made plans to get together in the studio sometime soon. This gave Stoker, who was fuming over the other Jordanaires' exclusion, just the chance he needed. "It was the worst sound on any of Elvis' records. It was a strained sound and a very bad sound. We didn't have a full quartet. Chet didn't even honor Elvis enough to get him a full quartet. Brock was a bass singer, a real low bass singer, and Ben is middle-of-the-road, and here I am first tenor. Elvis was not knocked out by it. He was extremely courteous about it and tactful in everything he said, but he knew exactly what he wanted. So I let him know that I was the only one of the Jordanaires that was asked. Elvis never really had much time for chatting, and that could have been one reason he never had any time to chat after that. But he asked me, 'Can the Jordanaires work with me [from now on]?' And I said, 'We sure can. We'll be there!' "

Steve Sholes was practically beside himself when he heard how the session had gone. He had told the Colonel, how many times had he told the Colonel, he had told Tom over and over again that more preparation time was needed, RCA had a schedule to maintain, he was under increasing pressure to have the second album ready by April 15 for scheduled fall release. "I know you have Elvis on a heavy personal appearance program and I certainly can't blame you," he had written back in February, "but the main purpose of this letter is to point out that we still must get a number of additional recordings from Elvis in the near future." They had gotten not a single one in the intervening months, and now here it was mid April and Tom was still not listening, it was obvious that the boy was not listening (if he was even capable of listening), and Sholes wondered more and more if Nashville was the right place to even try to record him. Chet was his protégé, he had made Chet his Nashville a&r man, but it was obvious that Chet and the boy were not hitting it off at all; he could tell from Chet's noncommittal report, not to mention the fact that they had gotten only the one song, that something was wrong. He waited a couple of weeks, then fired off yet another letter to Tom, complaining once again that attention should be turned to the recordings — but it was like trying to stop a runaway train. At the Nashville session Elvis had been presented with a gold record for "Heartbreak Hotel," and the album had already sold more than 362,000 copies: Sholes was being strangled by his own success.

The session might have continued if there had been a better feeling to it, but Elvis and the boys were anxious to get home for a few hours after being away so long, and Chet just had the one three-hour slot booked anyway. They took their chartered plane back to Memphis that afternoon and on the way ran into some turbulence. This time, Scotty said, "Bill's going berserk. He's scared to death, really he would have jumped out of the plane if he could have. Elvis said, 'Just hang on, Bill, when we get to Memphis we're turning this thing loose.' Then we caught a commercial flight to wherever we had to be the next day."

They continued their Texas tour: San Antonio, Amarillo, Corpus Christi, and Waco, where Elvis gave a brief interview on Tuesday night, shortly before going onstage, to *Waco News-Tribune* reporter Bea

Ramirez. "What do you want to know about me, honey?" he said as he stared out at the four thousand screaming teenagers from backstage, "half scared," wrote Ramirez, "and half unbelieving.

"Elvis, have you any idea just what it was that started the girls going crazy over you?"

"No, I don't. I guess it's just something God gave me. I believe that, you know. Know what I mean, honey? And I'm grateful. Only I'm afraid. I'm afraid I'll go out like a light, just like I came on. Know what I mean, honey?"

Presley has a way with that "honey" business. When he talks, he looks straight ahead, or sort of dreamy like in no direction at all. Then he turns with that "know what I mean, honey?" His face is close, real close. Right in your face — almost. . . .

"Elvis, I hear you walk in your sleep."

"Well, I have nightmares."

"What kind?"

"I dream I'm about to fight somebody or about to be in a car wreck or that I'm breaking things. Know what I mean, honey?" (I don't have any idea what he means.)

"Where are you from?"

"From Memphis, Tennessee."

"Oh yes, that's where all the hillbilly singers come from, isn't it?"

"Maybe so, but I'm no hillbilly singer."

"Well, have you typed yourself, I mean your type of singing?"

"No, I don't dare."

"Why?"

"Cause I'm scared, know what I mean, honey? Real scared."

"What of?"

"I don't know . . . I don't know. Know what I mean, honey?"

At this point I thanked him for his time and started to make a beeline for the door. He grabbed my hand, sat there looking sleepy-eyed into my face and fanned his long lashes while he said:

"Write me up good, will you, honey?"

On Saturday night, April 21, they played two shows at the City Auditorium in Houston. At the end of the first show, when the crowd wouldn't leave, Elvis left the predominantly female audience with the thought that "it's been a wonderful show, folks. Just remember this. Don't go milking the cow on a rainy day. If there's lightning, you may be left holding the bag." As the *Houston Chronicle* reported, "Four thousand females just died." After the show, with the first open date in weeks in front of them, Scotty and Elvis and Bill headed for the Club El Dorado across town, where blues singer Lowell Fulson was headlining. Fulson, who had had a big hit the previous year with "Reconsider Baby," was a regular at the Club Handy and the Hippodrome in Memphis and a big favorite of Dewey Phillips'. During the break Scotty introduced himself and Elvis, and Fulson called them up onstage for a couple of numbers during the next set. For Scotty it was a highly memorable experience. "I remember me and Lowell standing up toe to toe, getting down on some blues." One of those, recalled Lowell, was Big Joe Turner's "Shake, Rattle and Roll." "I don't know what the other one was. Anyway, Elvis sounded good, and the house accepted it, so he [Scotty] said, 'What do you think of him, what do you think of the boy?' I said, 'Well, one thing, he's a pretty boy, and the women will make him. He won't have to work too hard.' He got a big bang out of that. He laughed for a good while."

On the next day, a Sunday, they boarded a flight to Las Vegas.

THE LAS VEGAS BOOKING appears to have come about as something of a last-minute arrangement, since there were no advance notices in the trades. Elvis was booked in for the first two weeks of a four-week Freddy Martin engagement in the thousand-seat Venus Room, at the New Frontier Hotel, at $7,500 or $8,500 a week (both figures have been cited), which the Colonel was said to have demanded in cash because, as he told *Time* magazine, "no check is good. They got an atom-bomb testing place out there in the desert. What if some feller pressed the wrong button?" Bill Randle, the Cleveland DJ who had remained in the picture up to this time (Steve Sholes pointed out to the Colonel in March what a great job Randle was doing for them, to which the Colonel responded somewhat acerbically that he had eyes of his own), occasionally claimed credit for setting up the contract, and he may well have had a hand in it, but the Colonel had his own contacts, and even with so little lead time the Colonel left nothing to chance. When Elvis arrived in Las Vegas, there was a twenty-four-foot-high cutout of Elvis Presley standing out in front of the hotel beside the casino entrance — it was the same action photograph, taken in Florida in the summer of 1955, that graced the cover not only of his first album but of the song folio and any number of additional publicity items. His name was up on the marquee, just below comedian Shecky Greene's, as "Extra Added Attraction Elvis Presley," and in the print ads as "The Atomic Powered Singer."

It was the first sit-down gig of his career. As fellow promoter Gabe Tucker wrote, even the Colonel appeared to be taken in by this newfound elevation in status, which followed statements to his colleagues that he needed to find a whole new kind of venue for his act suitable to Elvis' phenomenal success. Bandleader Freddy Martin, who specialized in pop arrangements of the classics (he started with Tchaikovsky but branched out to Grieg, Rimsky-Korsakov, movie themes, and Khachaturian as well), had been enjoying hits consistently since 1933 and featured a $40,000 floor show, including a seventeen-piece orchestra, twenty-eight singers, twin pianos, dancers, ice skaters, and selections from *Oklahoma!* On opening night, New Frontier vice president T. W. Richardson, who according to Gabe Tucker had first heard Elvis in his hometown of Biloxi and contacted the Colonel about the booking the month before, invited a bunch of friends up from Houston to catch the show. Elvis was the closing act, and as the Freddy Martin Orchestra played their arrangement of "Rock Around the Clock," the curtain rose to reveal a very nervous, very out-of-place hillbilly quartet. Scotty and D.J. and Bill were all wearing light-colored sports jackets, dress pants, bow ties, and white shirts, while Elvis was dressed neatly in loafers, dress pants, and black bow tie, with a light-colored, western-cut checked sports jacket with a dark-cowled collar. From the opening notes of the song that he introduced as "Heartburn Motel" to his stammered attempts to thank Freddy Martin for the nice introduction, you could hear a pin drop. When Elvis started singing, Tucker related, one of Richardson's guests "jumped up from their ringside table and shouted, 'Goddamn it, shit! What is all this yelling and screaming? I can't take this, let's go to the tables and gamble.' "

"For the first time in months we could hear ourselves when we played out of tune," said Bill Black plaintively. "After the show our nerves were pretty frayed, and we would get together in pairs and talk about whoever wasn't around to defend himself." "They weren't my kind of audience," said Elvis. "It was strictly an adult audience. The first night especially I was absolutely scared stiff [but] afterwards I got a little more relaxed and I finally got 'em on my side." "We didn't even know we were failures," said Scotty, but after that night, reported *Billboard,* they no longer closed the show.

Nonetheless he persisted. He played out the full two weeks, and as hometown reporter Bob Johnson wrote, "Elvis, who has played hard audiences before, kept right in there busting guitar strings and shaking his legs and the rafters. . . . And the ice began to break." Bill Randle, who viewed the engagement almost as a social "embarrassment," had arranged to have some of the performances filmed, and Hal Wallis showed up to check out his investment. Judy Spreckels, the attractive twenty-four-year-old divorced sixth wife of sugar king Adolph Spreckels II, whom Elvis had met briefly in California, showed up and served as his "secretary" and aide-de-camp. Curiosity-seeking celebrities like Ray Bolger, Phil Silvers, and Liberace were prominent in the audience, and there is even a film of Elvis and Liberace clowning it up for the cameras. Liberace, one of his mother's favorite performers (Elvis made sure to get the flamboyant showman's autograph), is pretending to play Scotty's guitar, while Elvis flings himself into it, throwing his head back and laughing easily as he sings, perhaps, "Blue Suede Shoes." Not about to be upstaged, Liberace draws a square in the air, pointing at his brother George. It is, in many ways, a picture of perfect innocence.

They played what Elvis calculated to be twenty-eight twelve-minute shows (two shows a night, at 8:00 and midnight, for fourteen nights), and the rest of the time he was free to do as he liked. He and his cousin Gene, whom he described as his "utility man" and who had replaced Red on this tour, rode the Dodgem cars at the local amusement park almost every day, and in two weeks Elvis estimated that he spent more than a hundred dollars on rides for himself and his friends. He lounged around at poolside, flirted with the girls, went to the movies, caught as many acts as he could, stayed up all night long, and if he felt any doubts he kept them to himself. "One thing about Las Vegas pleased Elvis," wrote Johnson, who went out to report on the event, "it never goes to sleep. He had company during those long night hours, and night had become like day to him." It was like being in a city where you played dress-up all the time. Every time he entered a room he created a stir, the showgirls fawned on him, you never knew what was going to happen next. But he didn't drink, he didn't gamble ("It don't appeal to me," he said, explaining why he "never dropped a nickel in a slot machine"); whatever he was doing, whether it was what his mother had raised him to do or not, he wasn't hurting anybody One time he missed an appointment with United Press reporter Aline Mosby because he was at the movies, a Randolph Scott western, but he made it up to her. He saw the Four Lads again and met former teen sensation Johnny Ray for the first time (both were discoveries of Bill Randle's; Elvis had met the Four Lads at the Cleveland show that Randle had filmed). He caught a little bit of Liberace's show at the Riviera, and he went back again and again to catch the lounge act at the Sands, Freddie Bell and the Bellboys.

The Bellboys, a highly visual act who provided both action and comic relief, had had a minor hit the previous year with a song that had been a huge rhythm and blues success for Duke/Peacock artist Big Mama Thornton in 1953. "Hound Dog" had been written by two white teenagers, Jerry Leiber and Mike Stoller, who specialized in rhythm and blues, and was a very odd choice for a male performer, since it was written from a female point of view. Nonetheless, it was the showstopper of Bell's act, even retaining some of the original's rhumba-flavored beat, and it sparked a determination on Elvis' part to incorporate it into his own show. "We stole it straight from them," said Scotty. "He already knew it, knew the song, but when we seen those guys do it, he said, 'There's a natural.' We never did it in Las Vegas, but we were just looking on it as comic relief, if you will, just another number to do onstage."

On the first Saturday of the engagement the New Frontier scheduled a teenage matinee especially for Elvis Presley fans. Proceeds from the show were to go toward lights for a youth baseball park, and finally there was some semblance of Elvis Presley normality. "The carnage was terrific," wrote Bob Johnson in a story that was headlined "The Golden Boy Reaches for a Star While the Music Goes Round and Round and—": "They pushed and shoved to get into the 1000-seat room, and several hundred thwarted youngsters buzzed like angry hornets outside. After the show, bedlam! A laughing, shouting, idolatrous mob swarmed him. . . . They got his shirt, and it was shredded. A triumphant girl seized a button, clutched it as tho it were a diamond."

They played out the rest of the engagement with increasing confidence. Mr. Martin was more respectful, even if he retained a little bit of a tongue-in-cheek attitude toward the whole thing. "We should have five minutes' silence now," he announced after Elvis' act. "Makes me wonder if I've been wasting my time for the last twenty years." One of the casino owners, Mr. Frank Williams of Osceola, Arkansas, gave him an eight-hundred-dollar watch with diamonds for the numbers, and Elvis reciprocated with half a dozen letters of thanks. Even the Colonel, who was initially discomfited by what amounted to the first misstep in a series of otherwise perfectly calculated moves, seemed finally to have come to terms with the value of the experience. In Scotty's view, "I think in one sense it was good, because it was completely different. That's what's funny about Vegas. People that were there, if you'd lifted them out and taken them over to San Antonio, the big coliseum, they'd have been going crazy. It's just a different atmosphere. But we had a ball out there. We really did."

On the last night, which was recorded by a member of the audience and released by RCA twenty-five years later, Elvis still sounds nervous, self-conscious, glad to be done with it all — but aware that he has carried it off. "Thank you very much, ladies and gentlemen," he says as the polite applause dies down. "I would like to tell you, it's really been a pleasure being in Las Vegas. This makes our second week here, and tonight's our last night, and we've had a pretty hard time — stay . . . ah, had a pretty good time while we were here." He introduces "Blue Suede Shoes" by saying, "This song here is called, 'Get out of the stables, Grandma, you're too old to be horsing around,' " and when that doesn't get much of a laugh he turns to the orchestra leader and says, "Do you know that song, Mr. Martin? You do? You know that one about 'Take back my golden garter, my leg is turning green'?" When Martin calls him back graciously for an encore, he says, "Thank you, friends, I was coming back anyway."

"Like a jug of corn liquor at a champagne party," declared *Newsweek*. "Elvis Presley, coming in on a wing of advance hoopla, doesn't hit the mark here," reported *Variety*. *Life* headlined its April 30 story "A Howling Hillbilly Success." Any publicity, said the Colonel, was good publicity. "Heartbreak Hotel" was at number one; "I Want You, I Need You, I Love You" had just been released to advance sales of 300,000; RCA Victor reported that Elvis Presley's records accounted for half of their pop sales; and he was going home to the new house he had been able to purchase with his earnings for himself and his parents. They could write whatever they liked, there was no stopping him now. He really believed that.

He was back in Memphis two days later and stopped by the newspaper office on Tuesday night. "Man, I really like Vegas," he announced. "I'm going back there the first chance I get." He was nettled at a report that a Halifax radio station had given all of its Elvis Presley records away in hopes that it would hear no more. "I didn't know that there were any radio stations in Nova Scotia" was his first reaction, reported the newspaper. "The more they try to ban the stuff, man, the more they'll have to listen to. I mean, man, a lot of people like it, man, it's really hot right now." Then he reminisced about his start in the business just two short years ago. "I was strumming the guitar in Mississippi before I ever came to Memphis," he said. "My father bought one for $12 — it was the best investment he ever made." And then he was off into the night in his "Kelly green frontiersman shirt, black trousers and doeskin loafers," whether on his Harley motorcycle, one of his three Cadillacs, or the three-wheeled German Messerschmidt he had recently purchased, the paper didn't report. He was going to be headlining the big Cotton Carnival bill at Ellis Auditorium one week from tonight, and he had gigs booked in Minnesota and Wisconsin starting on the weekend, but for now he was just going to ride around town.

RUSSWOOD PARK, JULY 4, 1956. (ROBERT WILLIAMS)

"THOSE PEOPLE IN NEW YORK ARE NOT GONNA CHANGE ME NONE"

FOR HIS MAY 15 APPEARANCE on opening night of Memphis' twenty-second annual Cotton Carnival, in which a king and queen were crowned and a midway set up on Front Street, both sides of Ellis Auditorium were opened up for a performance for the first time since Liberace had played the hall. The show was scheduled to begin as close to 7:30 as possible but had to await the landing of the Royal Barge at the foot of Monroe, where the reigning monarchs were to take part in opening ceremonies before traveling to the nearby auditorium to signal the start of the show. Bob Neal was master of ceremonies, and Hank Snow and the Jordanaires were featured, while Eddie Fisher appeared on the Royal Barge and the Carter Sisters, George Morgan, and a host of other country stars were headlining an all-star event at the festival tent on the midway. There was little question, though, that the hometown boy was the focus of this "new and open-to-the-public feature of the Carnival season [that] helps add excitement to its opening night." Country comedian Minnie Pearl flew in for the occasion at the urging of her husband, Henry Cannon, a charter pilot who had recently been flying Elvis all around the country and who had flown him in from La Crosse, Wisconsin, early that morning. "Henry introduced me to him, and he was such a nice man. I always kidded him that he treated me like an old-maid schoolteacher, he was so overly polite — but he always was."

For Elvis, though, this homecoming was a chance to prove himself. " 'More than anything else,' " he had told the *Press-Scimitar*'s Bob Johnson earnestly in Las Vegas just two weeks before, " 'I want the folks back home to think right of me. Just because I managed to do a little something, I don't want anyone back home to think I got the big head.' He wants almost desperately," added Johnson, perhaps not really needing to, "to be thought well of at home."

He arrived accompanied by a police escort to find the usual waiting throng in front of the auditorium. One girl said, "I grabbed his hand, and he grinned and he said, 'Cut me loose,' so I cut him loose. It was heavenly." Vernon and Gladys were already present, seated in a box above the stage on the north side of the hall, eagerly anticipating their first opportunity in some months to see their son perform. In his role as MC Bob Neal whipped up the crowd with sly references to Elvis' upcoming appearance, and one time he even put the spotlight on Elvis' mother and dad, who smiled nervously and took a polite bow. The other acts had a good deal of trouble trying to figure out how to deal with both sides of the auditorium at once, a problem that Hank Snow solved to no one's satisfaction by singing one song to one side, the next to the other. When Elvis came bounding out, however, in black pants, white shirt, and kelly green jacket, he seemed to give the matter no thought at all but, in the words of one thirteen-year-old spectator, simply "staggered all over the stage. Up until he came out I remember thinking, this is a lousy show," recalled Fred Davis, an eighth-grade student at Messick High School where Elvis, Scotty, and Bill had appeared as part of Sonny Neal's student council campaign the previous year. "Then I'd seen him at Ellis with Carl Perkins in November, and he was all over the stage, riding Bill's bass, popping three or four strings, but there was no climax, it didn't seem really practiced, there were just a few screams. This time it was solid noise from start to finish, there were girls in hysterics, I never heard a word he said. No one rushed the stage, no one stood in the aisle, but the flashbulbs were going from start to finish, and I just remember thinking, 'What have I seen?!' "

He opened with "Heartbreak Motel," introduced "Long Tall Sally" as a song by a friend of his whom he had never met (Little Richard), brought the Jordanaires out for "I Was the One," called out to Scotty to "go wild" on "Money Honey," pretended to burp as he introduced "I Got a Woman," on which Bill joined in with a high-pitched call, introduced "Blue Suede Shoes" to wild applause, and then announced that he would be back in just a few weeks in a benefit performance for the *Press-Scimitar*'s Cynthia Milk Fund. And for anyone who wasn't planning to be there, "just remember this one thing, friends, if you're not there, friends, just remember this one thing . . ." At which point he launched into the opening bars of his final song, the still unrecorded "(You Ain't Nothin' But a) Hound Dog." When he got to the end there was even more wild applause, and he looked back at D.J., repeated slyly, "Ladies and gentlemen, remember this one thing," and kicked into a half-time coda, declaring over and over again to the audience the simple one-line message of the song. It was a curious performance, far removed from the loose spontaneity of his Hayride shows of just six months before, but after twenty minutes both he and his fans were exhausted. The last time he had appeared at Ellis he had come out onstage afterward and patiently signed autographs, but with that no longer a possibility, this time he was whisked away into the night before the applause had even died down.

The next day he played Little Rock, then Springfield, Missouri; Des Moines; Lincoln and Omaha, Nebraska. In Kansas City there was a riot: the band was overrun, D.J.'s drums and Bill's bass were smashed, and D.J. was thrown into the orchestra pit, but everyone escaped with their lives and aplomb intact. In Detroit he was billed as "the atomic explosion," but back home in Memphis the review of the Cotton Pickin' Jamboree appearance declared more meaningfully, "Only a few times previously (Billy Sunday, Eddy Arnold, Liberace at his height) have so many persons gathered under one roof in Memphis for one attraction, and the reception had a fire and enthusiasm never in memorable history granted a native son."

Hank Snow meanwhile was just beginning to question what had happened to his money. It had been six months now since they had signed the deal with RCA, and while some tour money might have come his way through the joint Hank Snow Enterprises–Jamboree Attractions booking agency, he had seen not a penny to date from the phenomenal RCA sales, in which the twin management arms of the business should have been equal participants. He had been to his attorney already, who was shocked to discover that there were no formal papers of incorporation and urged Snow to insist on this at least as a first step toward straightening out the partnership's tangled affairs. It was not long after the Memphis show that Snow, who was leery of approaching his partner on any issue of substance for fear of offending him, pressed Parker on this point, and "Parker immediately flew into a rage. Pacing up and down my office floor, he told me he thought we should dissolve our relationship in every aspect of our business. . . . I thought for several minutes and then asked him, 'If we do, what happens to our contract with Elvis Presley?' He twirled his big cigar back and forth in his mouth, pointed his finger at his chest, and said, 'You don't have any contract with Elvis Presley, Elvis is signed exclusively to the colonel.' "

* * *

ELVIS WAS DUE to make his return appearance on *The Milton Berle Show* on June 5. He spent most of the previous week at home for what amounted to the longest extended period of time off he had had (six days) since the beginning of the year. He was too jittery to stay home — after all this time on the road he couldn't really sleep more than three or four hours a night, and Gladys was worried almost constantly that he was just going to burn himself up. "I'm so proud of my boy," she said over and over again, and she would get up early in the morning to run off the fans so Elvis could sleep. Still, there was no escaping them: they lined up politely by the carport from morning till night in the manicured residential neighborhood that the Presleys had moved into at the end of March. All they wanted was a glimpse of Elvis, or any of the family, for that matter. Mrs. Presley answered the doorbell in her housecoat and slippers every time it rang, and sometimes she let them borrow the phone if they said they needed to call their mama and daddy. On a hot day she might even have the new maid, Alberta, bring them a glass of ice water — after all, she said, "they like my boy." Sometimes, she would confide to a friend, she just wished that Elvis would quit right now. He could have a good living, buy himself "a furniture store . . . marry some good girl and have a child — where she would see it and be with it. And she'd be the happiest person in the world," she told Mrs. Faye Harris, an old Tupelo neighbor, "if he would [just] quit and come home and stay with them there in Memphis."

Mr. Presley on the whole was less sanguine about it all. "I wish," he said to a contractor friend named Carl Nichols who was doing some work around the house, "they would all go away." "You wouldn't be here if they did," said his friend. But he still felt like they were all taking advantage of him — of him and his family. He enjoyed playing skill pool in the game room with his son or his brother, Vester, or the various in-laws and cousins, who had virtually moved into the house since they had come up in the world, and he was in the process of having Nichols build him a pool out back because Elvis thought they would all enjoy the chance to cool off in the hot Memphis summertime. But he watched every nickel, and he regarded every newcomer with glowering suspicion, and Elvis had to explain to his friends sometimes that that was just the way his father was.

It wasn't that it didn't feel like home — Gladys had filled the house with what Elvis called "a museum of me," and bought so much furniture that they'd had to pile up a lot of their old things out on the sunporch.

When he surveyed his life, he liked what he saw. He liked the pale green, seven-room ranch house that sat here "out east" in the kind of affluent tract development that he could never have imagined living in back when he was going to Humes High. He was proud of his mama and his daddy — his mama would never change, she never wanted anything for herself, and she was just happy with her kennel and vegetable garden in the backyard. And if the people who lived out here in this nose-up-in-the-air neighborhood didn't think she was as good as any of them, well, they could just kiss his ass. They were all right, though, he supposed. It was just that there was increasingly little differentiation between his public and private lives. Bob Neal had told him it was going to get like this. He hadn't really believed him, but now he didn't know if he cared. It wasn't all that different, as he pointed out to Mr. Johnson at the paper, than the way it had been all along. "It didn't happen all at once," he explained. "Since the beginning, when I first began, it was just the same. The only difference, the crowds are bigger now."

He liked it in a way. The fans were the living representation of his success. Other stars, he read in the movie magazines, resented the demands that were made on them, but he couldn't understand that. The fans, he said over and over again, were his life's blood. Sometimes he stood out in the driveway for hours signing autographs — they were polite for the most part, and besides, he told *Seventeen* magazine reporter Edwin Miller, who was researching a story on him in Memphis that week, "you say no to one person because you had a hundred autographs to sign, they just know you're saying no to them. I never refuse to do anything like that, no matter how tired I am." Sometimes Gladys would have to call him two or three times to get him to come in for supper.

ON THE SECOND DAY that he was home he drove up in the pink Cadillac and found June Juanico, a pretty little girl he had dated one night when he played Keesler Air Force Base, in Biloxi, almost a year before, standing in line with all the others. He recognized her right away and they started in talking, and when he found out that she was in Memphis for the week with some girlfriends, he said he'd call her at her hotel in the morning, maybe they could get together. Later that day, almost on a whim, he stopped by Dixie's house, on Lucy Street. She had just come from rehearsal for her high school graduation that night and was wearing her graduation dress, but when he suggested that they go for a ride she pulled on a pair of jeans, hopped on his motorcycle, and left her parents to explain her absence to her boyfriend when he arrived.

The rest of the week he spent with June — he took her by Humes, stopped by the Memphis Recording Service, went up to the Hotel Chisca, where he introduced her to Dewey, showed her the Courts where he had grown up, and Crown Electric across the street, with the truck he had driven sitting out in the yard. He introduced her to Bernard and Guy Lansky and bought her a motorcycle cap just like his. Then they went out to Mud Island, where he drove his motorcycle so fast that they both got scared, and he made her put her hand on his chest so that she could feel his heart pounding. It was like the first night they had met, the previous June in Biloxi, when they sat out on the White House Hotel pier until 3:00 or 4:00 in the morning, "and I was very nervous — I was afraid of myself. My mother used to tell me, 'Keep a good head on your shoulders. When you get in a compromising situation, think: "What would my mother think of me if she could see me right now?" ' So here's this beautiful boy with his luscious lips kissing me on the back of my neck, and he turns me around gently, and I don't know if he's going to start fondling on me and I felt like it would be all right if he did, so I was trembling, and then when he held me close I could feel him trembling, too. And so we laughed, and he said, 'Which one is more nervous, you or me?' and then we laughed about that."

Mr. and Mrs. Presley couldn't have been nicer. June felt right at home — with Mrs. Presley anyway. She fussed so over June and showed her how Elvis liked his chicken prepared, and when his daddy told him that his new Cadillac was ready for delivery, it didn't surprise her one bit that Elvis asked her if she would go pick it up with him. It did surprise her when it turned out that they had to go to Houston to get it, but June bravely asked her girlfriends to pack a bag and bring it out to the house, and she went on her first plane ride ever, after first swearing to Mrs. Presley that she really was eighteen. In Houston they were booked into separate rooms on separate floors, but she stayed with him after he assured her that he would never hurt her. "Trust me, baby," he said, and she did. They drove the white Cadillac El Dorado back to Memphis the next day, and when they pulled into the driveway, "Mrs. Presley came out and hugged him like he had been gone for weeks." Before they parted on Friday she made him promise that he would come down to visit her in

Biloxi, and he said he had some vacation coming up in July, so he thought maybe he would. They exchanged vows of undying love, and that night he went out to the Overton Park Shell to catch the show that Sam Phillips and Bob Neal were putting on, under the banner of their newly formed partnership, Stars Inc., with Sun artists Carl Perkins, Johnny Cash, Warren Smith, and the recently signed Roy Orbison. Elvis was called upon to take two bows from the audience and signed autographs afterward with Carl, who was by then fully recovered from his automobile accident.

On Saturday, June 2, he flew out to California, where he met Scotty and D.J. and Bill, who had driven out earlier in the week. On the way they had heard a song called "Be Bop A Lula" on the radio for the first time, and they were sure that Elvis had recorded it behind their back. As soon as they saw him, they jumped all over him for going into the studio without them, but he assured them that it wasn't his record, it was by a cat named Gene Vincent. There were shows scheduled in Oakland at 3:00 and 8:00 on Sunday, and then they flew into the Inglewood airport at 4:00 in the morning, leaving little time for sleep before a Berle show rehearsal called for 10:30 A.M.

Elvis felt considerably more at ease with Mr. Berle this time and ran through the material confidently, lounging in the orchestra seats between takes with Irish McCallah, the exotic-looking star of the popular TV series *Sheenah Queen of the Jungle* and meeting the beautiful film star Debra Paget for the first time. There was an opportunity to catch up on business with the Colonel — there was to be a formal presentation of the double Triple Crown Award from *Billboard* for "Heartbreak Hotel" (this meant that the record had topped sales, jukebox, and disc jockey lists in both the pop and c&w categories), he had been signed for Steve Allen's newly announced Sunday-night show, opposite Ed Sullivan, in just a month's time, and an Elvis Presley record was currently number one on each of the three in-store charts, pop ("I Want You, I Need You, I Love You"), r&b ("Heartbreak Hotel"), and country (still "I Forgot to Remember to Forget").

The Colonel's steely gaze bore in on him; it was as if he could read his mind. "If you ever do anything to make me ashamed of you, you're through," the Colonel had said to him more than once already, and he hadn't wanted June to give her real name on the flight to Houston for fear the Colonel might find out. Hearing about the success they were having, though, and feeling the Colonel's reassuring hand on his shoulder, he cast his doubts aside — he knew the difference between a good girl and a bad girl, and the way you treated each. The Colonel was just a cranky old man who worried too much sometimes, things had been going so smoothly lately nothing could seriously go wrong.

He opened with "Hound Dog," the song with which he had been closing his act ever since Las Vegas. He was wearing a light-color checked jacket, dark pants, a two-tone polo shirt, and white socks, and for the first time, surprisingly, he was not even cradling a guitar. Perhaps to make up for its absence he seemed to have carefully worked out new moves, wrists splayed out almost limply in seeming contrast to the ferocity of his vocal attack, fingers fluttering, arms outspread. With Scotty's solo he lurches backward in what might be interpreted as an upbeat adaptation of the shrugging, stuttering, existential hopelessness of a James Dean, there is a jittery fiddling with his mouth and nose, and as the song comes to an end he is dragging the microphone down to the floor, staggering almost to his knees. Scotty and D.J. and Bill keep their eyes glued on him, there is only the slightest flicker of surprise as he points at the audience and declares emphatically, *You* ain't nothin' but a hound dog, then goes into his patented half-time ending, gripping the mike, circling it sensuously, jackknifing his legs out as the audience half-screams, half-laughs, and he laughs, too — it is clearly all in good fun.

"How about my boy?" says Milton Berle with obvious pride and affection as he musses up his hair. "How about him?" Elvis is clearly pleased but does his best not to show it: he yawns, grimaces, rolls his tongue around in his mouth, touches his ear, mugs, and ducks his head as if to say, Who is this guy?, doing everything that he can not to laugh at Berle's nonstop clowning. Before this part of the show is over, Berle, playing the part of the Dutch uncle, seeks to dissuade Elvis from thinking that he could ever get an "ultrasophisticated" movie star like Debra Paget with his sex appeal ("She's not in your league. Stick to Heartbreak Hotel, and stay away from the Waldorf"), then calls Debra out onstage and "introduces" her to Elvis Presley. Whereupon, to Berle's delighted double take, Debra screams, flings her arms around the new teenage idol, and bends him backward in a kiss.

The Milton Berle Show topped Phil Silvers' *Sergeant Bilko* in the ratings for the first time all season, and *Variety* reported that "it was a relaxed and therefore more effective Milton Berle who signed off his program for the season last week with one of his better NBC-TV efforts." But while the immediate response was for the most part favorable and Elvis went on to wildly successful appearances in San Diego, Long Beach, and the Shrine Auditorium in Los Angeles, another reaction was setting in, a reaction that had been building for some time and that culminated now in personal attacks and cries of moral outrage unlike anything that Elvis had encountered to date. "Mr. Presley has no discernible singing ability," declared Jack Gould in the *New York Times*. "The sight of young (21) Mr. Presley caterwauling his unintelligible lyrics in an inadequate voice, during a display of primitive physical movement difficult to describe in terms suitable to a family newspaper, has caused the most heated reaction since the stone-age days of TV when Dagmar and Faysie's necklines were plunging to oblivion," wrote Jack O'Brian in the *New York Journal-American*. "[Popular music] has reached its lowest depths in the 'grunt and groin' antics of one Elvis Presley," fulminated Ben Gross in the *Daily News*. "The TV audience had a noxious sampling of it on the Milton Berle show the other evening. Elvis, who rotates his pelvis, was appalling musically. Also, he gave an exhibition that was suggestive and vulgar, tinged with the kind of animalism that should be confined to dives and bordellos. What amazes me is that Berle and NBC-TV should have permitted this affront." And, under the banner "Beware Elvis Presley," the Catholic weekly *America* suggested that

> if his "entertainment" could be confined to records, it might not be too bad an influence on the young, but unfortunately Presley makes personal appearances.
>
> He recently appeared in two shows in the Municipal Auditorium of La Crosse, Wisconsin. According to the La Crosse paper, his movements and motions during a performance, described as a "strip-tease with clothes on," were not only suggestive but downright obscene. The youngsters at the shows — 4,000 at one, about 1,200 at the second — literally "went wild," some of them actually rolling in the aisles. . . .
>
> Yet the National Broadcasting Company wasn't loath to bring Presley into the living-rooms of the nation on the evening of June 5. Appearing on the Milton Berle show, Presley fortunately didn't go so far as he did in La Crosse, but his routine was "in appalling taste" (said the San Francisco *Chronicle*) and "his one specialty is an accented

movement of the body that hitherto has been primarily identified with the repertoire of the blond bombshells of the burlesque runway" (New York *Times*).

If the agencies (TV and other) would stop handling such nauseating stuff, all the Presleys of our land would soon be swallowed up in the oblivion they deserve.

Juvenile delinquency, a widespread breakdown of morality and cultural values, race mixing, riots, and irreligion all were being blamed on Elvis Presley and rock 'n' roll by a national press that was seemingly just awakening to the threat, the popularity of the new music among the young, and, of course, the circulation gains that could always be anticipated from a great hue and cry. In an age which attached little or no value to vernacular culture in any form and had always focused its fiercest scorn upon the South ("Dogpatch" was about as sophisticated a concept as existed for an appreciation of southern culture), the level of vituperation should perhaps have come as no great surprise — but, after the warm reception that Elvis had gotten almost everywhere that he had appeared throughout the South, and the generally indulgent one that he had received elsewhere, it clearly did. Mrs. Presley was beside herself with anger and shame ("She'd get mad and cuss sometimes, say some low-down things," said Vernon's brother, Vester), and even Elvis seemed taken aback by the onslaught of the debate. "I don't do any vulgar movements," he protested weakly to Aline Mosby, the UP reporter he had stood up in Vegas. "I'm not trying to be sexy," he told Phyllis Battele of the International News Service. "It's just my way of expressing how I feel when I move around. My movements, ma'am, are all leg movements. I don't do nothing with my body."

Only the Colonel kept his cool. Back in Madison the letters were pouring in by the truckload, most of them accompanied by dollar bills for the picture packets that were offered through the fan clubs. After the Berle appearance, Charlie Lamb, the veteran PR man whom Colonel Parker had left in charge back home, hired twenty girls to take care of the overflow: "I hired a doctor's wife to handle the money and keep records of what's coming in with the mail, and I called the bank and told them, 'I got so much money I can't bring it in.' " What did Colonel Parker think about it all? "I'm going to get a wiggle meter to time the wiggles," said the Colonel with imperturbable calm. "When Elvis stops singing, we'll put him on the stage and just let him wiggle!" Only his cigar hid the smirk of the jovial Colonel, "who was the exact opposite," Miss Mosby reflected, "of the serious singer."

NBC TOOK THE THREAT seriously enough, though. Steve Allen, who had already signed Presley to a one-shot appearance at $7,500 (he had received $5,000 apiece for his two Berle appearances), stated on his late-night *Tonight* show that "there has been a demand that I cancel him from our show. As of now he is still booked for July 1, but I have not come to a final decision on his appearance. If he does appear, you can rest assured that I will not allow him to do anything that will offend anyone." An NBC spokesman said, "We think this lad has a great future, but we won't stand for any bad taste under any circumstances." On June 20 a compromise of sorts was reached when NBC announced that Allen would be presenting a new, "revamped, purified and somewhat abridged Presley. He'll wear white tie and tails, glory be," wrote columnist Harriet Van Horne with understandable skepticism. "And he'll stand reasonably still while singing. . . . With so much Bowdlerizing, he may well sing 'Come, Sweet Death' as far as his career is concerned."

It was, said Allen, reflecting back on the experience, "a way of saying something comic." It was also a way, of course, of getting around the Mrs. Grundys of the nation with a big wink. The irony, unfortunately, was lost on Elvis, who seemed bewildered at the force and ferocity of the criticism that continued to be directed at him and his music. It seemed as if all the pent-up forces of puritanism and repression had been unleashed simultaneously to discover in rock 'n' roll the principal source of America's growing moral decadence and the world's ills. What hurt most of all were the denunciations from the pulpit, but even the newspaper articles stung. He said for the record that the critics had a right to their opinions, they were only doing their job, and Elvis was always the first to disparage himself and his talents — but it wasn't fair. He didn't drink, he didn't smoke (except for the little cigarillo Hav-a-tampas that he increasingly enjoyed, though not in public), he did his best to make sure that the boys always conducted themselves like gentlemen. It wasn't supposed to matter how you *looked*.

It was just like in high school — he might have appeared one way, but he was really another. He had always believed that what was important was who you were underneath, but now he was beginning to have his doubts. He treated every girl who deserved to be treated with respect with the respect that was due her, didn't he? And he tried not to swear too much in public and generally set a good example. But when in Charleston he nibbled a reporter's fingers just to get her attention, it made national headlines — "Girl Reporter Bitten by Elvis" — and his mother was upset that now he was being accused of some new form of moral degeneracy until he reassured her that there was nothing to it. In Charlotte on June 26, on the same tour, he uncharacteristically exploded at all the criticism that had been coming at him for the last month and talked seriously about what his music meant to him.

> Elvis Presley is a worried man. Some, that is, for a man with four Cadillacs and a $40,000 weekly pay check. Critics are saying bad things about him. It has been especially rough during the past three weeks. And that is why he bucked his manager's orders to stay away from newsmen in Charlotte Tuesday until showtime. That is why he refused to stay in the seclusion of his hotel room. At 4:10 he couldn't stand it any longer, and with "Cousin Junior" left the room.
>
> He walked quickly to a restaurant a few doors away for a barbecue, flirtation with a few women and a 30-minute round of pool next door.
>
> "Sure I'll talk. Sit down. Most of you guys, though, been writin' bad things about me, man!"
>
> His knees bounced while he sat. His hands drummed a tattoo on the table top.
>
> Eyes, under long lashes, darted from booth to booth, firing rapid winks at the girls who stared at him. "Hi ya, baby," he breathed. And she flopped back in the booth looking like she'd been poleaxed. "This Crosby guy [the critic for the *New York Herald-Tribune*], whoever he is, he says I'm obscene on the Berle show. Nasty. What does he know?
>
> "Did you see the show? This Debra Paget is on the same show. She wore a tight thing with feathers on the behind where they wiggle most. And I never saw anything like it. Sex? Man, she bumped and pooshed out all over the place. I'm like Little Boy Blue. And who do they say is obscene? Me!

"It's because I make more money than Debra. Them critics don't like to see nobody win doing any kind of music they don't know nothin' about."

And he started to eat. The waitress brought his coffee. Elvis reached down and fingered the lace on her slip.

"Aren't you the one?"

"I'm the one, baby!"

Presley says he does what he does because this is what is making money. And it is music that was around before he was born.

"The colored folks been singing it and playing it just like I'm doin' now, man, for more years than I know. They played it like that in the shanties and in their juke joints, and nobody paid it no mind 'til I goosed it up. I got it from them. Down in Tupelo, Mississippi, I used to hear old Arthur Crudup bang his box the way I do now, and I said if I ever got to the place where I could feel all old Arthur felt, I'd be a music man like nobody ever saw."

Yep, some of the music is low-down.

"But, not like Crosby means. There is low-down people and high-up people, but all of them get the kind of feeling this rock 'n' roll music tells about."

Elvis says he doesn't know how long rock and roll will last. "When it's gone, I'll switch to something else. I like to sing ballads the way Eddie Fisher does and the way Perry Como does. But the way I'm singing now is what makes the money. Would you change if you was me? . . .

"When I sang hymns back home with Mom and Pop, I stood still and I looked like you feel when you sing a hymn. When I sing this rock 'n' roll, my eyes won't stay open and my legs won't stand still. I don't care what they say, it ain't nasty."

It was all strangely familiar and yet at the same time surprisingly revealing, the sort of interview he might have given in high school, perhaps, if anyone had thought to interview the strange, silent boy who had attended Humes High, and it was filled with the same odd mixture of crudeness and sensitivity, truculence and hurt. He still seemed to enjoy the anomaly created by the gulf between character and appearance, but it was no longer working in quite the way that he wished. Perhaps this was what he had been thinking of when he confided to Bob Johnson the month before, "Mr. Johnson, you know some things just change when something like this happens. I can't just do like I did."

HE ARRIVED at NBC's midtown rehearsal studio on Friday morning, June 29. He had played Charleston, South Carolina, the night before and was scheduled to play Richmond the following evening, with rehearsal for the Sunday-night show sandwiched in between. Other than the Colonel, only his cousin Junior Smith had accompanied him on the train ride north, and Junior stood staring out at the street while Elvis fooled around at the piano beside him and the Colonel talked business with two William Morris agents and representatives of RCA and Hill and Range. A young photographer named Al Wertheimer, who had taken some publicity shots for RCA at the time of Elvis' fifth Dorsey brothers appearance three months earlier and, in the wake of all the bad press, had been contacted by RCA's Anne Fulchino to take some more, asked if he could shoot some pictures. "Sure, go ahead," said Elvis diffidently. "I couldn't tell if he recognized me," wrote Wertheimer, an admirer of the David Douglas-Duncan school of eloquent, documentary realism, "or if he was just keeping up his side of the conversation." Elvis went on playing as Steve Allen entered, surrounded by his entourage. He was then introduced to the star, who gave him a rather flippant greeting ("Allen eyed him much as an eagle does a piece of meat," recalled Hill and Range rep Grelun Landon, to whom the offbeat, hip-talking comedian had always been "one of my gods") and was handed a script for a "western" skit called "Range Roundup." Playing the part of "Tumbleweed," Elvis rehearsed with Allen, Andy Griffith, and Imogene Coca. "A secretary whispered to Steve as they wrapped up the rehearsal," recorded Wertheimer. "He turned to Elvis, who was studiously flipping back and forth through his script, and said, 'The tailor's here.'

Elvis looked up, confused, and replied, "Yes, sir? What about?"

"Remember, you're wearing tails while you're singing to the hound dog."

"Oh yeah, I remember."

Elvis stepped into a broom closet and reappeared in baggy pants and floppy tails. With the same unlit cigar jammed in a corner of his mouth, Colonel Parker stepped forward to make sure his boy got a custom job. After the tailor made his last chalk mark, Elvis turned to the mirror across the room, snapped the lapels and checked his hair with that half-leer, half-smile that kept me guessing.

The room returned to a chapel-like serenity when the door slammed closed on the last of Allen's group. The Colonel instructed Junior about hotel accommodations and train schedules for a concert in Richmond, Virginia, the following day. Elvis didn't pay any attention. He was back at the piano playing another spiritual.

On a whim, Wertheimer accompanied him to Richmond. Just as in New York, not simply at the Steve Allen rehearsal but on an earlier occasion, when Wertheimer had captured him shaving and sculpting his hair ("Sure, why not?" Elvis had replied when the photographer asked if it was okay to come in the bathroom and shoot some pictures), Elvis was "the perfect subject for a photographer, unafraid and uncaring, oblivious to the invasion of my camera." Perhaps because he was so easily bored, but even more due to his quick inventiveness and tongue-in-cheek humor, "if you just stuck around with him for five minutes there was something happening."

In Richmond there were two shows scheduled, at 5:00 and at 8:00, and after a breakfast of bacon and eggs, milk, home fries, and cantaloupe à la mode, Elvis went up to his room. Wertheimer didn't see him again until about an hour before the start of the first show, when he found him eating a bowl of chili at the Jefferson Hotel coffee shop.

I was hot and sweaty, and he was cool and clean, looking almost dignified in a slate-grey suit, pressed white shirt and white knit tie. It was the white bucks that gave him away.

A woman was with him. She wasn't interested in a quick lettuce and tomato. She was dressed for Saturday night. . . . She was trying to appear casual, not an easy task since a photographer was on the other side of the salt and pepper. Elvis was cool, "Oh, he's the photographer, that's okay, he's with me," as if to say it's only natural to have a photographer on a date. . . . She crossed her legs and in a soft Southern accent asked what he was reading. He was only too happy to oblige, telling her it was the script for the "Steve Allen Show" — "It's gonna be on tomorrow night, are you gonna see the show?" — and talking about learning his lines. . . . Elvis set the script aside and finished his chili, and when he set that aside he turned his full attention to her, talking about how nice her hair was and how pretty her earrings were. He was sweet and natural.

Junior, who had been sitting glowering at the far end of the counter the whole time, tapped his fingers impatiently and said it was time to go. "Go where?" said Elvis. But Junior wasn't in any mood for a joke.

When they got to the theater, Elvis checked out the stage, "feeling its size like a builder inspecting a piece of land." Girls screamed through an open window as Elvis and the Jordanaires tried to rehearse. The Colonel's assistant Tom Diskin was handling the box office while the Colonel was "hunched over [in the lobby] in the middle of the crowd, breaking open bundles of souvenir programs and glossy photos suitable for framing. He gave a handful to a kid.

"'Got enough change on ya, son? Make sure you count your change.'"

The lobby, Wertheimer noted, was papered with glossies. "Nowhere did I see pictures of any other performers. It was wall-to-wall Elvis."

Backstage there was the usual complement of opening acts milling around: Phil Maraquin, the magician; the dancing team of Doris and Lee Strom; a local square-dancing troupe; and the Fliam Brothers, musical comedians. This was the show with which the Colonel had replaced the more traditional country and western caravan of just two months before. A lackluster brass band was rehearsing onstage, and Wertheimer decided it was a safe time to go to the bathroom, but when he heard what he took to be the sound of the show starting, he raced down the staircase to the stage area. There on the landing he discovered Elvis and the blonde from the coffee shop engaged in a ritual dance of courtship, with Elvis "slow, natural, insistent. He slid his arms around her waist. She pressed her arms against his shoulders, pinning the purse between them. He inched forward, she retreated." The photographer snapped picture after picture until at last, in an image destined to become as memorable as Doisneau's classic "The Kiss," "she stuck her tongue out at him and he playfully returned the gesture. The tips of their tongues touched." At this point Wertheimer discreetly withdrew, and not long afterward Elvis faced his loyal fans.

At the end of the second show Elvis left while the band was still playing, and the photographer rode to the train station with the other musicians in a police paddy wagon. There they caught the 10:50 sleeper back to New York; Elvis was already on the train, in an upper berth, "his hand on his forehead, his eyes on the ceiling, watching his own movie."

THEY ARRIVED back in New York early Sunday morning and promptly took a taxi to the Hudson Theater, on Forty-fourth Street, for a full day of rehearsals for the live broadcast that night. They did a quick run-through in which Elvis sang his latest hit, "I Want You, I Need You, I Love You," on a Greek-columned set (it was all part of Allen's comedic concept of presenting low culture in a high-culture setting). "He sang without . . . passion," Wertheimer noted. "He didn't move, he didn't touch the microphone, he stood square, both feet spread and stuck to the ground. After he had finished . . . Steve patted him on the back and told him it was great. Elvis smiled and in a slow, modest voice, he said, 'Thank you, Mr. Allen.' "

Then he met the dog, a female basset hound dressed in collar, bow tie, and top hat. In further keeping with the theme of the show he was going to sing "Hound Dog" to — who else? During the first run-through the dog ignored him. Allen "suggested that they get to know each other." Elvis petted her, sang to her, and in the end prevailed, to the applause of the assembled stagehands and professionals. They then went into the rehearsal of the sketch. At the dress rehearsal, as Elvis stood uncomfortably in his dress shirt and tails waiting to go on, Milton Berle, who was making a cameo appearance on the show, walked by. "Good luck, kid," he said, straightening Elvis' bow tie. "Thank you, Mr. Berle," said Elvis gratefully.

"Well, you know, a couple of weeks ago on *The Milton Berle Show,* our next guest, Elvis Presley, received a great deal of attention, which some people seem to interpret one way and some viewers interpret it another. Naturally, it's our intention to do nothing but a good show." There is a yelping sound from backstage. "Somebody is barking back there. We want to do a show the whole family can watch and enjoy, and we always do, and tonight we're presenting Elvis Presley in his, heh heh, what you might call his first comeback . . ." — Allen laughs again self-consciously, prompting scattered laughter from the audience — ". . . and at this time it gives me extreme pleasure to introduce the new Elvis Presley. Here he is."

If Allen was experiencing extreme pleasure, it was clear that Elvis was experiencing the opposite. He sidled out to the accompaniment of dreamy music, holding the guitar by the neck out from his body, almost as if he were dragging it. He bowed stiffly from the waist, then wiped his nose on his top hat, hiding his face as he handed it to Steve. "Elvis, I must say you look absolutely wonderful," said Allen with a straight face while Elvis tugged at his white gloves, shifted nervously, and looked away. "You really do. And I think your millions of fans are really going to get kind of a kick seeing a different side of your personality tonight."

"Well, uh," said Elvis almost somnambulistically, "thank you, Mr. Allen, uh . . ."

"Can I hold your guitar here?"

"It's not often that I get to wear the, uh, suit and tails . . ."

"Uh-huh," said Allen encouragingly, perhaps wondering if they were ever going to get through this sketch.

". . . and all this stuff. But, uh, I think I have something tonight that's not quite correct for evening wear."

"Not quite formal? What's that, Elvis?"

"Blue suede shoes."

"Ooh yes," said Steve with a double take. The audience laughed and applauded encouragingly.

With his opening number, "I Want You, I Need You, I Love You," for the first time he appeared if not comfortable, at least involved, even in tails. He sang the song with sincerity and feeling, hunching his shoulders, loosening his tie, but for the moment lost in the private reverie which his music provided. The Jordanaires dooh-wahed behind him, out of the picture, as were the musicians, save in silhouette. Even as the last notes were still ringing, Steve Allen bustled out onstage again, this time wheeling the basset, and announced that Elvis was now going to sing "Hound Dog," his next big hit, which he would record the next day. The dog started to look away, Elvis cupped its chin, and there was sympathetic laughter as Elvis glanced balefully, as if sharing a joke with a friend, at the audience. The camera was on the dog as Elvis pointed at her and declared the obvious with a playful snarl. When the dog started to tremble, he held her affectionately and in the course of the song even kissed her once or twice. Apart from nervous titters, there was little response from the audience, but Elvis was a good sport about it all ("He always did the best he could with whatever situation he was given," said Jordanaire Gordon Stoker of the appearance, "and he never, ever insulted anybody"), walking the mike around into the basset's line of vision whenever its attention wandered, sharing his discomfiture openly and amiably. There was a sense of almost palpable relief on the part of all concerned when the song ended and he could finally march offstage after a long, lonely moment in the spotlight.

The embarrassment was only heightened when, after a commercial break, the "Range Roundup" skit (with "Big Steve and the Gang") opened to the strains of "Turkey in the Straw." "Big Steve" was carrying a toy guitar, Andy Griffith had a fiddle and was wearing furry chaps, Imogene Coca was dressed up in a Dale Evans cowgirl skirt, and "Tumbleweed" Presley, looking extremely abashed, was shadowed, like everyone else, by his cowboy hat. At first he literally lurked in the background, throwing in his shouts of agreement in unison with the others with some diffidence and having a good deal of difficulty getting his own lines out (even "You tell 'em, Big Steve" came out in a garbled Memphis accent). But gradually he warmed to the task, and by the time they sang their little western ditty at the end, with each actor taking a verse and all joining in the chorus, he seemed to have entered into the spirit of fun, beating out a rhythm easily on the body of his guitar, throwing a couple of patented, self-referential moves into his cowboy sashay, and singing out his lines with good humor if not abandon. "Well, I got a horse, and I got a gun / And I'm gonna go out and have some fun / I'm a-warning you, galoots / Don't step on my blue suede boots." "Yeah!" said Steve, with the cast ending on a chorus of "Yippy-i-oh, yippy-i-yay, yippy-i-oh-i-yay."

"On his way to the dressing room," reported Wertheimer, "Elvis was intercepted by the William Morris agent with the wire-rimmed glasses whom I had seen Friday morning at the first rehearsal. Shaking Elvis' hand, he said, 'I think the show was terrific. You did a marvelous job. We really ought to get a good reaction to this one.' Tom Diskin, the Colonel's lieutenant, stood by with a wide smile."

Back at his room at the Warwick, Elvis was still not done with his official duties. It had been arranged for him to do an interview on *Herald-Tribune* columnist Hy Gardner's program, "Hy Gardner Calling!," which broadcast locally on WRCA-TV, channel 4. The peculiar conceit of the program was that both parties were filmed "at home," and the show was broadcast "live" at 11:30 P.M. as a split-screen telephone conversation. This particular conversation must have been even more awkward than most. Gardner came across as the ultimate square, while Elvis, perhaps as a result of his experience that evening, suggested more of the James Dean aspect than ever, looking weary and, at times, genuinely lost. Frequently a fluttering hand would drift up to a furrowed brow, his eyes were heavily made up, and overall he presented a perplexing mix of rebellious image and conventional values, resentful truculence and hurt misunderstanding.

Was he getting enough sleep? Gardner wondered. No, not really, "but I'm used to it, and I can't sleep any longer." What would go through his mind to keep him awake? Some of the songs he was going to do, "or some of your plans, or what?" "Well, everything has happened to me so fast during the last year and a half — I'm all mixed up, you know? I can't keep up with everything that's happened." Slightly nonplussed, Gardner asks him about some of the criticism that has been directed at him. Does he feel any animosity toward his critics? "Well, not really, those people have a job to do, and they do it."

But has he learned anything from them?

"No, I haven't."

"You haven't, huh?"

"Because I don't feel like I'm doing anything wrong."

It was not the words so much as the affect — the generational stance not so much that he doesn't understand as that he isn't understood. Over and over again he rejects the rebel label ("I don't see how any type of music would have any bad influence on people when it's only music. . . . I mean, how would rock 'n' roll music make anyone rebel against their parents?") while adopting the stance. Gardner was clearly taken with him and concluded the interview with fatherly advice, suggesting that even the bad publicity may have helped him; it's "made it possible for you to do the kind of things for your folks that you always wanted to. So I sort of think I'd look at it that way, Elvis." "Well, sir, I tell you," said Elvis, repeating words he has said many times but which part of him clearly believes, "you got to accept the bad along with the good. I've been getting some very good publicity, the press has been real wonderful to me, and I've been getting some bad publicity — but you got to expect that. I know that I'm doing the best that I can, and I have never turned a reporter down, and I've never turned a disc jockey down, because they're the people that help make you in this business. . . . As long as I know that I'm doing the best I can." "Well, you can't be expected to do any more," says Gardner reassuringly. "I want to tell you it's been just swell talking to you, and you make a lot of sense." With that the interview concluded, and Elvis was able to set aside the ambivalent feelings and experiences of the last two days and, perhaps, finally, get some sleep.

THE NEXT DAY he seemed hardly the worse for wear. He arrived at the RCA building to find fans carrying picket signs that declared "We Want the Real Elvis" and "We Want the GYRATIN' Elvis"; held yet another press conference, in which he announced that "Barbara Hearn of Memphis and June Juanico of Biloxi, Miss. . . . are the two girls he dates. Miss Hearn has the added distinction of being a good 'motorcycle date' "; and recounted the story of his life once again in painstaking, and painstakingly accurate, detail. Then he entered the studio, shortly before 2:00, and settled down to work.

The studio, according to Al Wertheimer,

> looked like a set from a 1930's science fiction movie. It was a large rectangular space of acoustical tile walls ribbed with monolithic half cylinders. These ran vertically on the long sides of the rectangle and horizontally on the short sides. The high ceiling was rippled with more parallel cylinders and two pipes of fluorescent light. The floor was a series of short strips of wood scaled in a sawtooth pattern of right angles. In the center of the room lay a patch of carpet on which the musicians had placed their instruments.

This was a different kind of session. For one thing, "Hound Dog," the one song they knew they were going into the studio to get, was a number that Elvis and the band had been polishing in live performance for two months now. For another, it was the first session to be attended by Freddy Bienstock, the twenty-eight-year-old Viennese-born "double first cousin" and protégé of the Aberbach brothers, in his capacity as Hill and Range's representative. It was also, of course, the first time that a full complement of Jordanaires was present in the studio. More significant than anything else, though, for the first time the twenty-one-year-old singer was clearly in charge.

They started with "Hound Dog," but perhaps not surprisingly it proved more difficult to capture on record than anyone had anticipated from its easy onstage success. Engineer Ernie Ulrich, as cynical about rock 'n' roll as anyone else in the building, got a good sound mix early on, but then there were seventeen takes without a satisfactory master. The drums, always the driving force in the live show, weren't working right, Scotty was groping toward his guitar solo, the Jordanaires were having some difficulty finding their place, and Shorty Long, the boogie-woogie piano player who had filled in on the last New York session, was just looking for his cues. Steve Sholes was getting visibly discouraged — he was desperate to get material for the second album, and here they were wasting all their time on a single song — but Elvis, who exhibited few points of stillness in any other aspect of his life, maintained absolute concentration. "In his own reserved manner," wrote Wertheimer, "he kept control, he made himself responsible. When somebody else made a mistake, he sang off-key. The offender picked up the cue. He never criticized anyone, never got mad at anybody but himself. He'd just say, 'Okay, fellas, I goofed.' "

On the eighteenth take they finally got something. By now the beat had changed considerably from the way they did it in live performance, and the phrasing of the lyrics had changed even more. It had veered still further from Big Mama Thornton's original Latin-flavored "rhumba-boogie" feel (preserved mainly in the repetition of the final words, *hound dog,* at the end of the opening lines) and become a hard-driving number powered by D.J.'s tommy-gun attack and a solo that Scotty later labeled "ancient psychedelia." With the twenty-sixth take Sholes thought they had it, but Elvis wanted to keep going. After the thirty-first take Sholes announced over the PA, "Okay, Elvis, I think we got it."

> Elvis rubbed his face, swept back his hair and resigned. "I hope so, Mr. Sholes." . . .
>
> The recording had taken over two hours and without the air conditioner turned on (the mikes would have picked up the noise), the air in the room hung low and close. The double doors were opened, admitting cool air, the noise of vending machines and visitors with glowing compliments. Elvis combed his hair, drank the Coke offered by Junior and shrugged in reply to comments about how good the music was. Steve trod lightly. "Elvis, you ready to hear a playback?" As if bad news never had good timing, he said, "Now's as good a time as any."

> Elvis sat cross-legged on the floor in front of the speaker. The engineer announced the take over the PA and let the tape roll. Elvis winced, chewed his fingernails and looked at the floor. At the end of the first playback, he looked like he didn't know whether it was a good take or not. Steve called for take eighteen. Elvis pulled up a folding chair, draped his arms across its back and stared blankly at the floor. . . . The engineer racked take twenty-eight.* Elvis left his chair and crouched on the floor, as if listening in a different position was like looking at a subject from a different angle. Again he went into deep concentration, absorbed and motionless. At the end of the song he slowly rose from his crouch and turned to us with a wide grin, and said, "This is the one."

They ate a late lunch, with Junior taking orders for sandwiches and drinks, and then they began to look for something else to record. Freddy Bienstock had brought in a stack of acetate demos with lead sheets from Hill and Range, and Elvis sorted through them, picking out several by title alone, then listening to them on the studio speaker as Steve broadcast them out from the control room. When he heard the second one, he instantly brightened. "Let me hear that again," he said. "Something I like about that one."

The song was "Don't Be Cruel," a number that Bienstock had acquired through Goldy Goldfarb, a song plugger at booking agent Moe Gale's Shalimar publishing company. It was written by rhythm and blues singer Otis Blackwell, who had enjoyed some success as an artist but was just beginning to enjoy far greater prominence as a writer (his "Fever" had just reached the top of the r&b charts in Little Willie John's classic version). Bienstock, whose principal administrative background had come in running Hill and Range's rhythm and blues division, St. Louis Music, for the past couple of years, was immediately taken with the song. However, he let Goldfarb know in no uncertain terms that if he wanted to get a song recorded by the hottest new act in the business, he would have to give up half the publishing (to Hill and Range) and half the writer's share (to Elvis). As Otis Blackwell later said, "I was told that I would have to make a deal" — but there was little question that it was worth it.

---

*Wertheimer appears to be mistaken in his count, since it was actually the final take that was selected.

Elvis had the song played back for him again and started working it out on the guitar while the others listened for the first time. Then he sketched out a rough arrangement on the piano, which he showed to Shorty Long, who made notes on the lead sheet. By this time he had memorized the lyrics. Scotty tried out a couple of openings, and Elvis suggested that he leave a little more space and told D.J. to "come in behind Scotty and slow it down a little"; then the Jordanaires worked out their arrangement, and after about twenty minutes they were ready for a run-through. After a single rehearsal, Sholes was ready to record, but Elvis wanted to rehearse some more, so they did. The song continued to evolve through twenty-eight takes. It took on a lilting, almost casual, offhand kind of feel, as Scotty virtually sat out except at the beginning and the end, Gordon Stoker of the Jordanaires came to sing a duet with Elvis on the chorus, and D.J. laid Elvis' leather-covered guitar across his lap and played the back of it with a mallet, to get an additional snare effect. It was hardly a formulaic approach, and it was clearly one that left the nominal a&r director baffled. When they finally got the sound that he was looking for, Elvis pronounced, "That felt good," and, though it was late, called for another playback on "Anyway You Want Me," a pleading ballad that he had listened to at the beginning of the session. There was just one rehearsal. "At the fourth take," Wertheimer wrote, "Steve said they had it. Elvis said again, 'That's fine, Mr. Sholes. Let's try it one more time.' "

"I wasn't all that impressed with him, *as a singer,*" said Gordon Stoker. "I mean, I kind of got a kick out of 'Don't Be Cruel,' I was entertained, so to speak, but then with 'Anyway You Want Me,' all of a sudden I took an entirely different attitude, the feeling that he had on that particular sound made the hair on my arm come up. I said to the guys, 'Hey, men, this guy can sing!' "

It was 9:00 by the time the session was over, and the studio was deserted. The guys were talking about going home by train the next morning; they were going to be playing that Milk Fund benefit at the ballpark in town, and then they were going to have the rest of the month off, their first extended break in six months. Everybody was looking forward to it, and Junior was laughing his evil little laugh, his hooded eyes regarding his famous cousin with what seemed like only thinly veiled jealousy. Steve Sholes had some songs he wanted Elvis to hear, but Elvis said he'd have to take them home with him if he was going to get a chance to listen to them at all. Anyway, he'd want acetates of the three songs they'd recorded that day — he wanted to learn the songs exactly the way they'd recorded them so he could do them that way in his shows. Sure, Sholes said, a little reluctantly, he'd get a package over to the hotel in the morning.

There were still some fans waiting outside when they came out of the studio, and Elvis patiently signed autographs while the others waited. By now *The Steve Allen Show* seemed like a million years ago, and the verdict was long since in. Allen had trounced Ed Sullivan in the ratings, the reviews were no more kind toward the stationary Elvis than they had been toward the gyrating one ("A cowed kid," declared the *Journal-American*, "it was plain he couldn't sing or act a lick"), and Sullivan had publicly reiterated that he would not have the singer on his show at any price ("He is not my cup of tea") while privately he had already been in touch with the Colonel. "Hey, Elvis, we gotta get back to the hotel," said Junior. Elvis got into the car. It had been a long day, and now he was hungry again.

HE RAN INTO GENE VINCENT at Penn Station the following morning as they were leaving the city. One of the boys pointed the new rock 'n' roll star out to him, and Elvis walked over and introduced himself, congratulating him sincerely on the success of "Be Bop A Lula." To his surprise Vincent immediately started to apologize. "The first thing he said was, 'I wasn't trying to copy you. I wasn't trying to sound like you.' Just right off the bat, without even being asked. I told him, 'Oh, I know that, it's just your natural style.' " And then the two twenty-one-year-olds compared notes on success.

He spent most of the twenty-eight-hour train ride home relaxing and fooling around. The photographer Al Wertheimer, convinced that this was an historic opportunity that would not pass his way again, took the trip at his own expense and got shots of Elvis catching some sleep, flirting with girls, reading *Archie* comic books, contemplating a giant teddy bear that the Colonel had given him, and listening to the acetates of his songs on a portable record player, over and over again, with obsessive concentration. "How'd it go yesterday at the recording session?" the Colonel asked him in the restaurant car, as Wertheimer recorded the event.

> Elvis replied blandly, "It went pretty well." The Colonel carried on the conversation. "The reaction was terrific on the 'Steve Allen Show.' Better than I thought." Elvis shrugged. He seemed unim-

> pressed. "Glad to hear it." This appeared to be a routine. The Colonel would start a conversation and Elvis would end it. "It's gonna be good to get back home. I'm sure your folks'll be mighty glad to see you," said the Colonel. "Yeah, it'll be good to see 'em."
>
> That was the end of the conversation. The Colonel looked out the window. Tom [Diskin] talked shop. Junior talked to Elvis, and Elvis ate his sandwich. It was two generations sitting at separate tables.

When they finally reached the outskirts of Memphis, Elvis got off at a small signal stop called White Station, made his way across an empty field, inquired for directions to Audubon Drive, and, "still dressed in his suit and white knit tie," Wertheimer noted, "with a wave to us, and a smile that could be seen for a hundred yards, Elvis walked home alone."

He spent the rest of the afternoon at home, signing autographs for the fans, going for a ride on his motorcycle, splashing in the new pool (which Vernon was only filling just now with a garden hose), and playing the RCA acetates for his nineteen-year-old "Memphis girlfriend," Barbara Hearn, an advertising copywriter whom he had known since South Memphis days (she had been going out with Dixie's friend Ron Smith when he first met her) and with whom he had renewed his acquaintance early that spring. Wertheimer got pictures of Vernon shaving, Gladys handing her son a fresh pair of jockey shorts, and the family album, with the only demurral coming from Vernon, who said, " 'But I got shaving cream on.' I told him it was all right. He rinsed off his razor and smiled. . . . 'Well, if that's what you want, okay.' . . . I wondered," wrote Wertheimer, "how a house this open could remain a home."

THE COLONEL ARRIVED sometime after 9:00 with a police escort. He deputized Tom Diskin to take care of the family and Barbara, while he and Elvis rode to the midtown ballpark, home of the Memphis Chicks, in a white squad car. It was a hot night, 97 degrees, and the show had been going on for almost three hours at the old wooden stadium when the police car finally delivered Elvis to the performers' tent at third base. Not a few in the crowd of seven thousand (by comparison, an anti-integration rally led by Mississippi's senior senator James O. Eastland at the Overton Park Shell that afternoon drew thirty-five hundred) had shown up as early as 9:30 that morning, with lunch and supper packed, so as to be sure to get good seats. "The roaring was so loud and long," reported the *Commercial Appeal*, that "extra rations of sleeping pills were passed out to the patients of the four hospitals near the field," with Elvis' name receiving mentions twenty-nine times in advance of his arrival and each mention eliciting uncontrollable screams and squeals.

There was a "bop-dancing" contest, Elvis' signature fourteen-diamond horseshoe ring (worth six hundred dollars) was won in a drawing by seventeen-year-old Roger Fakes, the Colonel sold out the five thousand souvenir programs he had personally donated to the event (when asked by Al Wertheimer why the programs didn't come with a price tag, the Colonel pointed out, "You never want to put a price on anything"), and Dewey Phillips was "cotton-pickin' cute," reported the paper, and "worked like a Trojan" as MC. Among the more than one hundred performers — including four bands, the Dancing Dixie Dolls, the Confederate Barbershop Quartette, the Admiral's Band of Navy Memphis, and a surprise appearance by the Jordanaires, who had flown in from Nashville — was Jesse Lee Denson, who sang Gogi Grant's "Wayward Wind" and with his brother Jimmy told everyone backstage who would listen how he had taught Elvis Presley to play guitar back in the Lauderdale Courts.

Then it was finally time for Elvis to go on, and Dewey did a good imitation of the "old" Elvis and the "new" Elvis, as a squadron of police, firemen, and shore patrol escorted him to the stage. He was dressed all in black save for red socks and the red tie which he and his father had picked out just before the show, and as he sauntered out and greeted Dewey with casual grace, saluting his fans and acknowledging his family in the front row, the place literally exploded. The fans "broke from their seats, swept like a wave up to the stage. . . . Elvis pleaded with them as pleasantly as he could to sit down, but it was like Canute telling the tide to stop. . . . What made [it] all the more remarkable," reflected Bob Johnson in the *Memphis Press-Scimitar*, "was that he had previously played to a packed house in the Auditorium during the Cotton Carnival less than two months ago." To sixteen-year-old Jack Baker, who had been living next door to him just nine months before, "there was this keening sound, this shrill, wailing, keening response, and I remember thinking, That's an amazing sound, and then I realized I was making it, too." When the furor finally died down, and Elvis had graciously accepted a city proclamation designating Wednesday, July 4, as Elvis Presley Day, he turned to the crowd and announced, with that inscrutable mixture of boyish charm and adult calculation, "You know, those people in New York are not gonna change me none, I'm gonna show you what the real Elvis is like tonight."

And he did. After all the personal changes that had taken place, and the dramatic evolution that his career had witnessed in the previous few months, it was perhaps not surprising that the "real Elvis" should be, in Bob Johnson's description, "about halfway between the 'old' Elvis and the 'new' Elvis," but what this really meant was that he was able to control the crowd, to tantalize and manipulate them in a manner that differed significantly even from his appearance a few short weeks before. "He rocked 'em," wrote Johnson, "socked 'em, set them screaming with delight as his sensational individualistic song style throbbed out over the frenzied stadium." He opened with "Heartbreak Hotel," threw in "Mystery Train" and "I Got a Woman," brought out the Jordanaires for "I Want You, I Need You, I Love You" and "I Was the One," roared back with "Blue Suede Shoes" and "Long Tall Sally," and ended, of course, after half an hour, with "Hound Dog."

"When it was time to go," Johnson noted, "he made a quick retreat thru a phalanx of police and Shore Patrolmen to a squad car backed right up to the stage. The excited fans rolled around the car like a wave. Two Shore Patrolmen and a policeman were picked up and carried back as tho they were feathers, but [Police] Capt. Woodward got him in the car all in one piece, and Elvis grinned as the car pushed thru the crowd."

It was a moment of unmitigated triumph, a moment of pure and unsullied splendor that would be forever frozen in time. All Elvis wanted, Bob Johnson had written, was to be "thought well of at home," and now here he was succeeding in front of his family and his hometown in a style, and on a scale, that to anyone else would have been utterly unimaginable.

WITH JUNE JUANICO, 505 FAYARD STREET, BILOXI, SUMMER 1956.
(COURTESY OF JUNE JUANICO)

ELVIS AND JUNE

THE FOLLOWING MONDAY, July 9, he arrived in Biloxi, unannounced and somewhat unexpected. He showed up in his white El Dorado convertible at June Juanico's house on Fayard Street with Red, his cousin Junior, and his friend Arthur Hooton, whose mother had worked with Gladys at Britling's Cafeteria. They waited in the driveway while some neighborhood kids went looking for June. When she got back, she and Elvis made a date for that night, and he left to register at the Sun 'N' Sand Hotel, whose courtyard quickly filled with fans as news of his arrival spread.

That night they went out on the town with June's mother, Mae, and her boyfriend, Eddie Bellman. On their own they revisited many of the sights June had shown him on his visit the previous year. They stayed out late, talking excitedly and making plans. Elvis wasn't sure how long he would be staying this time, he told her; he guessed she would just have to wait and see. All he knew was that he was on vacation for three weeks, footloose and fancy-free. He didn't know what he wanted to do exactly, but he wanted to do *something*. A few days before, he had wheeled into Tupelo on a whim and gone to see both his aunt and his fifth-grade teacher, Mrs. Grimes, who had originally been responsible for his entering the singing contest at the Mississippi-Alabama Fair. Now, it had just been announced, he was going to be returning to headline the fair in September. He was being written up in all the major newspapers and national magazines, and he was going to star in a movie soon. He could buy his mama and his daddy anything they needed, whatever they might want.

The next day he and June spent the whole day together. That afternoon they heard reports on a New Orleans radio station that Elvis Presley had become engaged to a Miss June Juanico of nearby Biloxi, and on the spur of the moment they jumped in the car and drove to New Orleans to dispel the rumors. Elvis got the address of the station at a pay phone, and they just showed up at WNOE, at the St. Charles Hotel, pressing their noses to the plate glass until DJ Hal Murray noticed them, did a double take, and then announced to his amazed listeners that "the man of the hour" had just walked into the studio and hurriedly switched to an interview format.

The only thing he was serious about at this point was his career, Elvis told the radio audience. He didn't have time to even think about getting engaged; right now he was just thinking about his vacation, which he was planning to spend in Florida. "You probably won't have too much of a vacation," interpolated the DJ, "because of the tremendous amount of kids who will be down there and fans —" "Well, I don't mind," he said. "Without them I'd be . . . lost." By the time they left the studio, the hotel lobby was full, and a girl fainted from the excitement and the heat.

From there the party of seven went on to Pontchartrain Beach, where they wandered the midway. Elvis won a host of stuffed animals to join the panda he had won for June at the Memphis Fairgrounds in May which they had christened Pelvis. In the course of the evening, it was reported in the press, Elvis consumed three halves of fried chicken and June three soft-shell crabs. On the way home they stopped off for a snack, and Elvis ordered his eggs over hard with the bacon burnt. When the eggs weren't cooked to his satisfaction, he sent the order back, and when the waitress brought it back again and it still wasn't right, she said, "What do you want, special treatment because you're Elvis Presley?" "No," he said, "I'd just like to be treated like a regular customer," and dumped the plate at the waitress's feet. They got home at 3:45 in the morning, and June responded from her bed to a *New Orleans Item* reporter's queries the next day. "Did I kiss him good night? What do you think? Certainly I kissed him good night. We were standing on the porch. No, not by the garden gate; on the porch. He's wonderful!"

THEY SAW EACH OTHER every night and spent almost all of each day together. Elvis kept telling the press that he was leaving for Florida any day, but he never left. On Thursday they went deep-sea fishing with June's mother and Eddie Bellman, and they had so much fun that he called his parents from the pier and told them to come down. In the meantime, with Eddie Bellman's help, he rented a villa out at the Gulf Hills Dude Ranch, in exclusive Ocean Springs. The crowds at the beachfront hotel had become impossible; there were close to five hundred people waiting for them when they returned from their fishing expedition, and Elvis' Cadillac was constantly covered with addresses, phone numbers, and love notes written in lipstick. When asked by the same reporter who had interviewed him earlier in the week when he was planning to leave for Florida, "keeping a sardonic smile on his lips," Elvis replied, "Well, if this keeps up, probably tonight." By the time that Vernon and Gladys arrived in their pink Cadillac and checked in at the Sun 'N' Sand on Friday, it didn't even matter that Elvis was no longer around; a crowd surrounded the car and grew bigger and bigger as Mrs. Presley stared out silently in curiosity and fear. When they went deep-sea fishing on Saturday, neither of the elder Presleys could have been any happier — Mr. Presley just liked being out on the water, with nobody to bother him or tear at his boy, and Mrs. Presley made Elvis peanut butter and banana sandwiches and fed them to him while he trolled for fish, wiping the crumbs away from his lips when he was done. It was a bright sunny day with a deep blue sky and not a cloud in sight.

On Monday they all drove to New Orleans. They went to the zoo, walked around in a cemetery overhung with Spanish moss, visited June's grandparents, who used to manage the Astor Hotel on Royal Street, and drove by some of the beautiful antebellum mansions in Pass Christian. Mr. and Mrs. Presley held hands, and Gladys asked Vernon if he wouldn't like to live in a big house like that someday. Mrs. Presley obviously liked June. She said, "You know, I've never seen my boy so taken with a girl. You two are planning to get married one of these days, aren't you?" They didn't have to answer, she said. She knew, she just had a feeling. "You just better not let Colonel Parker know how serious you are about June," she told her son. "You know how he feels, especially about marriage." Gladys called June "Satnin'," and June, who had not been able to bring herself to call Mrs. Presley "Gladys" even after she was asked, started calling her "Lovey" for her middle name, Love. "You know, my son's going to make me very proud of him," she confided to June — as if he hadn't made her proud already!

The Presleys returned to Memphis, and Elvis rented a four-bedroom house from the Hack family on Bayview Drive, just on the edge of the Gulf Hills resort, which afforded a greater measure of privacy than the villa could offer. It was a summertime idyll such as neither he nor June had ever experienced before. The next few weeks went by as if they would never end — and as if they would end before they had even begun. Mr. and Mrs. Presley came down again, one or another of the boys would go off from time to time to take care of unspecified business, and occasionally Elvis returned to Memphis, presumably because he had business to take care of, too. Sometimes June suspected that his business had to do with his "Memphis girlfriend," Barbara Hearn — but she didn't care. Not really. For Elvis and June a moment was an eternity, when he was with her he was with her alone, and as she told a reporter mischievously, "It'd be a sin to let something like that go to waste."

At Gulf Hills they rode, they water-skied, they played shuffleboard on a concrete court, they were in and out of the water all day long. At the "Hack House" they had fireworks battles at night behind the high hedge and on the golf course across the street, with everybody running around with little cigars in their mouths to light the fireballs that they threw at one another. Even at the resort they were pretty much left to themselves, so after waterskiing, they might all have dinner in the hotel dining room with June's mother and Mr. Bellman, then walk over to the Pink Pony Lounge and gather around the piano, where Elvis would entertain everyone, and they would all join in on familiar old standards until he ended the evening with a spiritual. He wanted June right there with him all the time and complained when she kept her distance. "He said, 'Other girls I've dated are always right next to me. They act like they're proud to be with me. If I say something, they listen. If I want to say something to you, I have to find you first.' " She knew exactly what he was talking about. Sometimes she would even hang back on purpose, just to see if he would look for her — and he always did. "I said, 'I'm not like your other girlfriends, Elvis, I'm not going to hang on your every word. When we first met, you said, "I like you, June, you're different." Now all of a sudden you want me to be like everybody else.' " No, he protested, but why was she spending so much time talking with the ski instructor when he wanted her to watch *him* ski? "Oh, really," said June. "All you care about is how many guys I've made out with. But, you know, I've gone out with a lot of guys and never really done anything."

"He said, 'Does that mean you're still a cherry?' I said, 'I'm not only a cherry, George. I'm the whole pie.' "

* * *

THEY WERE PERFECTLY MATCHED. June loved to cut up and fool around, and he was surprised to discover that she loved to sing, too. When they went riding, they sang "Side By Side," "Back in the Saddle Again," and "Let the Rest of the World Go By," with June contributing the tenor harmony, and when they were swimming there was always a phonograph sitting beside the pool. Elvis played "My Prayer," a hit by the Platters that summer, over and over again until, just at the point when the lead singer was approaching the climactic high note, "Elvis would always say, 'I'm gonna get that note, I'm gonna get that note, one of these days I'm gonna get that note, here it comes, here it comes . . .' And he'd try to relax and just let it out, and it just wouldn't happen, and he'd scream and go under." He sang all the time — sometimes it seemed he'd rather sing than breathe. June was not particularly a fan of his records, so they stuck mostly to old tunes like "That's My Desire" and "Over the Rainbow" or big-voiced r&b hits like "Ebb Tide" and "Unchained Melody." Not surprisingly, June didn't hesitate to let him know her reservations about his music. "I thought most of his records sounded like he was singing in a tin can. I said, 'Why don't you let some of those guys who do your records hear you sing like this and see if they can find you some of this kind of material? You know, you have a wonderful voice.' "

Most of all, though, they shared a sense of humor. Nearly all the pictures from that time show a smiling, laughing Elvis, relaxed in a way that reveals little self-consciousness, only youth and pride. Healthy, innocent, brimming with energy and a sense that he has arrived, he clowns around in these photographs in a way that the grave-faced youngster of Tupelo days never would, and the rising young star never could, his hat tilted back on his head, his hair mussed up, looking for all the world like the Greek god Pan.

Newsweek ran a column by John Lardner on July 16 excoriating Steve Allen for his attempt to "civilize" Elvis, "to mute and frustrate Presley, for the good of mankind. . . . Allen's ethics," declared Lardner, "were questionable." Ed Sullivan announced on the twelfth that he had changed his mind and was booking Elvis at an unprecedented fifty thousand dollars for three appearances in the fall and winter. Mr. Wallis informed the Colonel that he had just bought a star vehicle for Elvis to make his Paramount debut in six months but in the meantime was loaning him out to Twentieth Century Fox to appear in a western called *The Reno Brothers*, which would start filming at the end of August. And RCA was getting an almost incredible response — even judging by the tumultuous reaction to every other Elvis Presley record they had put out that year — to the coupling of "Hound Dog" and "Don't Be Cruel," which was released on July 13 and within a week was on the verge of going gold.

Meanwhile, Elvis got so sunburnt he was forced to water-ski in long pants and a long-sleeved jersey for a day or two (despite his incongruous dress, "his skill," according to water-ski instructor Dickie Waters, "was almost professional-looking"), and June was in and out of the water so much that she finally just got fed up with fixing her hair and, at Elvis' suggestion, had it all cut off. The world seemed far away, and when it intruded in unwanted fashion there was likely to be a spontaneous response. Elvis for some reason detested Teresa Brewer's "Sweet Old Fashioned Girl," which was popular that summer, and one time after they'd been horseback riding and were sitting around afterward with a giant pitcher of ice water, the song came on the radio. "I told him, 'Here's your favorite song,' " June said, and mischievously turned the radio up. "He took that entire pitcher of ice water and dumped it on his head! That was a typical Elvis thing to do."

The only sobering notes were Elvis' all-too-imminent departure at the beginning of August for yet another Florida tour and the occasional intrusion of others — Red and Junior and sometimes Arthur, whom June called "Arthritis" — on their almost perfect happiness. It wasn't that June didn't like his friends, although she sensed a meanness on Junior's part, not to mention a coarseness on Red's, that flourished when the elder Presleys were away. That she could certainly have lived with — she was confident that she could give as well as she got. What disturbed her far more was their effect on Elvis: he seemed to need their approval so much that he became like them. Her friends didn't have that effect on her, or on him; they were just fun to be around. But Elvis seemed to lose his confidence as well as his temper when he was around his gang. On the one hand, he desperately wanted to be a good influence on them, he shot them a look of sharp rebuke if they ever really got out of line, and he was good to them, too, he was always showing that wonderful generosity of spirit that she loved so much in him. On the other hand, she hated it when he showed off in front of them, when he tried so hard to act like one of the boys that he was no longer even himself. She was a person, too, she told him. She wasn't a possession. She didn't belong to anyone.

"He always wanted me right there, right under his thumb. He'd always be looking for me, and when he found me, it was always, 'Where the hell have you been? Who the hell do you think you are?' This is in front of the guys. He was quick to fly off the handle, and I could be stubborn at times, too! So this one time he's saying, 'You're not going to talk to me like that, you're not going to treat me like that,' and I chewed on his ass in front of them all. Well, he grabbed me — 'Come on!' Just grabbed me by the arm like he was really going to read my beads and pulled me into the bathroom. But when we got in there, I mean he would just take my face in his hands and kiss me and say, 'Baby, I know it. I know you're right . . . and I'm sorry.' But he would not show that to the guys. The guys just did not know that he had a tender heart."

June did, though. She sensed his spiritual side from the first, and she gave him a copy of *The Prophet,* by Kahlil Gibran, a graduation present from a former boyfriend the previous year. "He loved it. I would tell him my favorite chapters — my favorite was on love and friendship, and there was even a little bit on marriage." They read it over and over and talked about it at length, and June thought it calmed him down some — though she doubted that anything would ever really do that. One night they stopped by the hospital to visit a little girl with leukemia whose mother June knew, and then they went to the pier where they had sat out till almost dawn the night they first met. Elvis told June to look up at the moon, to let herself totally relax and not think about anything else, just let herself float in the space between the moon and the stars. If you relaxed enough, he told her, you could get up right there next to them. "How long have you been doing this?" she asked him. "Since I was a little boy," he told her. But he didn't tell just anyone about it. "I learned a long time ago not to talk about it. People think you're crazy when you talk about things they don't understand." His mother, he said, was the only one he had ever really trusted to understand.

She understood. She understood that when she was with him she had something that others couldn't break. And she understood that when he was in public he had something that she was not allowed to threaten. It would be three years, he told her a little apologetically, before he could have a life of his own. Then he could do whatever he wanted to do. Then he would be free to marry, have children, admit in public that he did not simply belong to the public, but until then he had promised the Colonel, this mysterious personage she had never met, that he would never do anything detrimental to his career.

For all of that, though, life in Biloxi was tucked away enough so that they could almost pretend to be leading normal lives, and the town itself was sufficiently accustomed to celebrity that after a while it could simply pretend to ignore them. They went to see *The King and I* at the Saenger Theatre downtown and walked out because, Elvis said, he thought movie musicals were ridiculous, people bursting into song at the drop of a hat just when things were getting serious. They hung around with June's friends, Patty Welsh and Patsy Napier and Buddy Conrad, who drove a sharp new mint green Lincoln Continental, and they went to Gino's Pizza and King William's Cellar in Ocean Springs and, of course, the Pink Pony, typical teenagers, just having fun. All of her friends adored Elvis and wouldn't hear a word against him. One time, as a favor to Eddie Bellman, Elvis made an appearance at Dave Rosenblum's clothing store, where Mr. Bellman owned the ladies' shoe department with Lew Sonnier, and the crowd was so large, the newspaper reported, that it stopped traffic downtown. One night they went to Gus Stevens' famous Supper Club, "the nightclub of the Coast," because Elvis wanted to see the comedian Brother Dave Gardner, and Mr. Gus made a big fuss over them, put them in a private dining room, and had his picture taken with the rising young star.

Toward the end of July Elvis had to go back to Memphis for a week, and when he returned he had a brand-new Lincoln Premiere with a wisteria purple bottom and a white top, which he said would be "less conspicuous." He couldn't get back into the "Hack House," so he rented both sides of a villa which would ordinarily be shared by two families, allowing June and Elvis to maintain their privacy from the guys. With the time of Elvis' departure rapidly approaching, they clung to each other more and more — neither one of them, it seemed, could imagine it ever ending. Finally he said couldn't she just go with him? She asked her mother, and her mother said no, but then Elvis said to just leave everything to him. He had his mother call Mrs. Juanico and assure her that June would be properly chaperoned. Then he went out to Keesler Air Force Base and persuaded the father of June's seventeen-year-old friend Patsy, Sergeant Napier (who June thought would never go for it, not in a million years), to let his daughter accompany them. Then, when Sarge agreed, he enlisted their friend Buddy to drive.

On the last night at the villa, with the older Presleys down for one final visit, June stayed the night, falling asleep in his arms. When she woke up early and started to get dressed, he pulled her back into bed, and they started fooling around, as they frequently did, wrestling and giggling and carrying on. "We had spent night after night falling asleep in one another's arms without anything beyond a lot of kissing and a little touching. Elvis respected women, I think because he respected his mother so much, and he always stopped before I would ever have to say no. But this one time I didn't want to say stop, and I don't think he wanted to stop either, so I got hysterical with giggling — that's what I do when I get nervous — and then my giggling rubbed off on him, and here we were rolling over and over on top of one another without any clothes on just laughing our asses off, because we were both afraid of what we were about to do. And then we stopped, and all of a sudden there was a little tap at the door, and it was Mrs. Presley. She said, 'I heard it was quiet in here, and then I heard giggling, and then I heard quiet again. So I thought I'd better come see. You know, maybe we'd better get June on some pills to keep her from having too many babies.'

"Neither one of us ever said anything about it like 'I'm sorry it went almost that far.' It was more like, 'Boy, we almost did it, June, didn't we?' That was his comment. 'We almost did it, didn't we, baby?' And I said, 'We almost did.' He said, 'That was close, wasn't it?' Like it was fun for him, and it was fun for me, too, and it was close. After that, we really didn't have too many more occasions when we were totally alone. There was only a few times — but it never really got as close as it did that night."

Then he was gone. He would meet them in Miami, he said. Just look for Red or Junior or Gene — any one of those three would take care of them.

THEY ARRIVED in Miami on Friday, August 3, just as Elvis was going on for the first of three daily shows at the Olympia Theatre, a vaudeville redoubt from the 1920s still resplendent with stuffed peacocks and a ceiling twinkling with painted stars in a painted sky. June was immediately ushered backstage, where a *Miami News* reporting team discovered her and recorded that

> she reportedly stroked [Elvis'] brow between stage shows. . . . Furthermore, June Juanico, 18, the Biloxi beauty whom Presley evidently

> prefers to aspirin, admitted that Elvis is as unsteady in love as he is on the stage. "It would be nice if Elvis loved me as much as I love him," June sighed. "But right now he's married to his career and he isn't thinking of marriage." June, whose hair is bobbed Italian-style, said she's going on the Presley tour of six [additional] Florida cities and New Orleans. But when he returns to Memphis, she said, "I don't know just what I'll do."

Interviewed in the tunnel underneath the Olympia stage, June recounted the story of their meeting and subsequent courtship.

> "Well, you know how love is. Eight months went by, and I never heard from him." . . . Overhead, while June was talking and posing for us deep down under the stage, Presley was warming up and she didn't want to miss even one performance. . . . We asked why the girls, especially the younger set, threw such hysterics — and how come she didn't scream. Without missing a knee jerk or bounce June replied: "If you were a member of the opposite sex you'd appreciate him, too. And I do feel like screaming."

They went back to the Robert Clay Hotel after the final performance. Elvis' two-week-old Lincoln was covered with names and messages and phone numbers. There had been reporters underfoot all day, and Elvis was irritated both with himself and with them. At a press conference that afternoon he had stumbled over a question about the Suez Canal crisis, and he felt like he had made a fool of himself. He told June, "Well, I shouldn't have said anything then. I should have waited and thought about it for a second and not come out with anything so dumb." June and Patsy had their own room, of course, and after taking a shower Elvis came back to see them — and to get away from the Colonel and the boys. He lay down on the twin bed with June, touched her as if he couldn't believe she was really there, fooled around with Patsy, a mischievous little sister as no-bullshit and sharp-tongued as June, murmured sweet nothings in June's ear, and then, before she knew it, was fast asleep.

The next day June's interview ran in the newspaper, and the Colonel came storming into the dressing room before the first show. His gaze went first to June, then back to Elvis, and he had the paper in his hand.

"Son, we can't have this kind of publicity," he declared, face red, eyes flaring, rapping the newspaper loudly against his palm. "You've got to do something about this, son," he announced again meaningfully. For the first time since she had known him, Elvis looked really scared. "What is it, Colonel?" he asked, stuttering the way he always did when he was agitated. "Read it yourself, son, and make damn sure you do something about it."

Elvis was still upset after the show — he seemed to blame her for giving the interview, he seemed to feel like if she hadn't talked to "that damn reporter," no one would ever have noticed her presence here in Miami. He was obviously just frustrated and upset, and when he finally calmed down he decided to go car shopping with his manager while June went back to the hotel. On a whim he plunked down $10,800 for a white Lincoln Continental just like Buddy's, with his brand-new lipstick-covered Premiere used as a trade-in. A reporter tracked him down as he lingered in the showroom and asked about June. "Now this is the way it is," Elvis declared nervously. "I got twenty-five girls I date regular. She's just one of the girls." "They show up sometimes eight at a time," chimed in the Colonel, seemingly restored to good humor, "all claiming they're his 'steadies.' One girl even claimed she was my daughter, and I don't have a daughter."

Later, when the Colonel came to Elvis' hotel room, he barely gave June a look. "Here, I thought you might want to see this," he said, handing Gene a copy of the script for the picture they were going to start filming in Hollywood in three weeks. Then he turned on his heel and slammed the door. Elvis grabbed at the script eagerly, and he and June started reading through it, but he got impatient and couldn't resist turning the pages to find out how it ended. He was keenly disappointed when he discovered that the character he played was going to die. "He said, 'June, I don't want to die in my first movie.' I said, 'Why not? I think it's a good idea. I always remember the character who dies. Happy endings you forget. Sad endings stay with you longer.' "

For the final show Elvis told everyone to be sure to be in the cars when he started the last song, not when he finished. He told June to stay away from the Colonel, who would be preoccupied with selling his pictures and souvenirs anyway; after all, he had to feel like he was doing something. In the car as they traveled through the night, they held each other. He put an unlighted cigar in his mouth and made fun of the Colonel, bravely declaring, "You're seeing too much of this girl from Biloxi. She's not good for you, son. You can't be linked to any one girl. For God's sake, don't get her pregnant. You do, and you're through in this business, that's for sure." They laughed till the tears streamed down from their eyes, but June knew his bravery in the dark would never see the light of day. He was trying to look out for them all, Red and Junior and Gene and June and her friends, his family, his fans, they were all counting on him, they were all looking up to him, and some part of him felt like none of this would have been possible, all of it could end in a minute, without the Colonel. So he tried to take care of the problems he could take care of, he did all he could to keep Red and Junior in line, he wanted, thought June, to make everything come out all right.

The next day, in Tampa, the shit really hit the fan. The Miami paper had interviewed June's mother over the telephone and then set her quotes against Elvis' and the Colonel's. Under the headline "Elvis Denies Biloxi Beauty Is His 'Steady,'" Mrs. Mae Juanico was quoted as saying "— in no uncertain terms — that 'The Pelvis' had asked her daughter to be 'his permanently' in three years. . . . 'I don't object to her making the trip,' Mrs. Juanico said. 'He's a nice boy, and June is a good girl. I talked to his parents and they said Elvis would take good care of her. . . . He said he can't get married for at least three years, and he asked her to wait for him.'" The Colonel was rigid with rage, the boys reacted to Elvis' quote that he had twenty-four other girlfriends by saying, "Yeah, that's why he takes us along, we take care of the overflow," and Elvis wanted June to call her mother right away and tell her not to talk to anyone else — he didn't want to hear about her defending her daughter's honor, he just didn't want any more of this shit.

There were two shows that day at the Fort Homer Hesterly Armory, sponsored by the Seratoma Civic Club, with seats at $1.50 and $2.00. There were boxes set up for a stage, no house PA, two microphones, and two amps, with the same incongruous procession of vaudeville acts that Al Dvorin, the Chicago booking agent, had been supplying since the spring, amounting to an hour and a half of mediocre warm-ups preceding the main twenty-minute show. "Fuck you very much," Elvis said over the din, but no one could make out the words, the music, or the remarks. "It was more than obvious," wrote Anne Rowe, a reporter for the *St. Petersburg Times* who was there for an interview, "that he loved every scream and yell . . . and every minute on that stage. He wrestled with the mike, breaking two apart in his frenzy, and finally, with perspiration pouring down his face, he practically tore his jacket off and let go on two more numbers."

He felt like a different person, he told June, when he was onstage: "I don't know, it's hard to explain. It's like your whole body gets goose bumps, but it's not goose bumps. It's not a chill either. It's like a surge of electricity going through you. It's almost like making love, but it's even stronger than that." Did it happen to all entertainers? June asked him. "I don't know. The few I've talked to experience excitement and nerves, but they must not feel the way I do. If they did, they would say more about it, don't you think? They say they get nervous, but after they sing a few lines they calm down. Hell, I don't calm down till two or three hours after I leave the stage. Sometimes I think my heart is going to explode."

He played Lakeland, St. Petersburg, and Orlando, using Tampa as his home base for the first two. When he played Lakeland on Monday, he did an interview backstage with *Tampa Tribune* reporter Paul Wilder, which was scheduled to run the following month in *TV Guide*. Wilder had been with the paper for years and in fact had covered Tom Parker on a regular basis in his column "In Our Town" when the Colonel was merely Tampa's inventive animal-control officer. He had reviewed Elvis' show in Tampa with relative indifference (his daughter, Paula, had covered the teenager's angle with considerably more fervor), but he began his interview, with unimaginable insensitivity, by reading lengthy excerpts from one of the most vicious write-ups Elvis had ever received.

" 'The biggest freak in show business history,' " Wilder read, from Herb Rau's column in the *Miami News*, in a flat, droning voice. " 'Elvis can't sing, can't play the guitar — and can't dance. He has two thousand idiots per show, yet every time he opens his mouth, plucks a guitar string, or shakes his pelvis like any striptease babe in town. . . .' Do you," he asked the startled performer, "shake your pelvis like any striptease babe in town?"

For one of the few times in his career Elvis actually showed anger, not just for himself but for his fans. After first stipulating that Wilder probably knew about striptease babes because that's where he must hang out, he protested the slur on his audience. "Sir, those kids that come here and pay their money to see this show come to have a good time. I mean, I'm not running Mr. Rau down, but I just don't see that he should call those people idiots. Because they're somebody's kids. They're somebody's decent kids, probably, that was raised in a decent home, and he hasn't got any right to call those kids idiots. If they want to pay their money to come out and jump around and scream and yell, it's their business. They'll grow up someday and grow out of that. While they're young, let them have their fun. Don't let some old man that's so old he can't get around sit around and call them a bunch of idiots. Because they're just human beings like he is."

Okay, said Wilder, returning to his readings. But what did he think about Rau suggesting that what his female fans really needed was " 'a solid slap across the mouth?' Have you any comment to that?" "Yeah, but I don't think I should say it." "Okay, okay, this isn't over the air, this is for *TV Guide*," Wilder inexplicably persisted, but Elvis continued to show a remarkable degree of restraint. He still didn't think he should voice his reaction. "Okay —," said Wilder. " 'Cause I'm a singer, not a fighter," said Elvis, to a background of sardonic laughter. What about all this talk about his gyrations? Wilder asked him. "I read a clipping, somewhere you were attributed as saying that Holy Roller —"

"I have *never* used that expression," Elvis exploded angrily. "That's another deal. See, I belong to an Assembly of God church, which is a Holiness church. I was raised up in a little Assembly of God church, and some character called them Holy Rollers —" "Oh, I see. Well, you —" "And that's where that got started. I always attended church where people sang, stood up and sang in the choir and worshiped God, you know. I have never used the expression 'Holy Roller.' " What about the music in his church? Wilder wondered innocently enough. "Do you think you transfer some of that rhythm into your —"

For the first time Elvis seemed to lose his composure altogether. "That's not it. That's not it at all," he practically shouted, obviously stung by an implication far more sweeping than the dismissal of his music. "There was some article came out where I got the jumping around from my religion. Well, my religion has nothing to do with what I do now. Because the type of stuff I do now is not religious music, and my religious background has nothing to do with the way I sing."

After that even Wilder seemed to get it, and he backed off on his questioning, so much so that by the end of the interview he appeared to be totally disarmed. Then, with the show going on in the background, he interviewed his old friend the Colonel, but it was obvious that he never had a chance. Was there a possibility of more frequent television appearances? "I think one of the main reasons that I don't book Mr. Presley on television more often is that to my way of thinking many of the artists today are overexposed on television. . . . My way of thinking may be wrong on this. However, I'll have plenty of time to find out next year. If it doesn't work this way, we'll try something new." The wiggling, and the criticism it provoked? "I have tried to figure out many angles. First of all, for many months we were touring the country, and Elvis had never appeared on television, and the only way people would know about Elvis was by his records. And I have tried repeatedly to play his records and figure out some way where I could see him wiggle while listening to his records. Which is impossible." Elvis' future as an actor? "Well, Mr. Wilder, when we made the screen test for Mr. Hal Wallis at Paramount Studios in Hollywood, they tested Mr. Presley in a singing role, and also, while he was there, they gave him a short story or some play — whatever you call it — and Mr. Wallis decided after seeing the test that Mr. Presley was capable of starring in a dramatic production. When and how I don't know, but Mr. Presley had no training in acting, and I saw the test, and if I was not his manager, I could not be more excited about a new personality than I am now being Elvis Presley's manager, for his acting ability was the greatest. . . . I think Elvis Presley could play any role he makes up his mind to play."

He did three shows in Lakeland, three in St. Petersburg (renamed "St. Presleyburg" for the day), two in Orlando, and two in Daytona Beach. By the time that he arrived in Jacksonville on Friday, August 10, the town had taken on all the trappings of a religious revival. The faithful were gathered as always in a long line in front of the box office from the predawn hours before the first show; a minister was offering up prayers for Presley at the Trinity Baptist Church after declaring that the singer had "achieved a new low in spiritual degeneracy"; reporters from two national magazines, *Life* and *Collier's*, were on hand to cover his every move; a contest winner named Andrea June Stephens was flown in with her mother from Atlanta by *Hit Parader* magazine for a date she had won with an essay entitled "Why I Want to Meet Elvis"; June Juanico was hissed at and gossiped about and cursed as a whore by girls who had read about her or just didn't like the confident way she stood at "his" side; and Judge Marion Gooding, who was determined not to see a repeat of the previous year's performance when "aroused fans ripped nearly all [of Elvis'] clothes off," met with the Optimist Club and prepared warrants charging Presley with impairing the morals of minors, which he said he would serve if the singer acted in a fashion that "put obscenity and vulgarity in front of our children."

Judge Gooding was at the first performance at 3:30 Friday afternoon and subsequently invited the singer to a meeting in chambers. There Elvis expressed his shock at the judge's reaction ("I can't figure out what I'm doing wrong," he said to reporters; "I know my mother approves of what I'm doing"), and the judge repeated his determination to serve the warrants if the show were not toned down. A compromise was reached, and Judge Gooding was satisfied that Presley complied with the agreement, "judging from reports of the later shows." Meanwhile, the *Jacksonville Journal* informed its readers, a representative of the American Guild of Variety Artists told Presley that, because of his suggestive body movements, it would be necessary to post bond and join the guild (which represented exotic dancers, among others), or they would block the show. The Colonel took care of that, and Presley, noted the paper, "kept a nonchalant attitude throughout the day," answering reporters' questions, taking Andrea June Stephens out for a cheeseburger (which Andrea June declined), and, in place of the body movements, wiggling his little finger lasciviously in a move that sent his audience into paroxysms of ecstasy. Back in the hotel room afterward he told June, "Baby, you should have been there. Every time D.J. did his thing on the drums, I wiggled my finger, and the girls went wild. I never heard screams like that in my life. I showed them sons of bitches — calling me vulgar. Baby, you don't think I'm vulgar, do you?" And he put a pair of June's underpants on his head and glided around the room.

WITH THE TOUR'S triumphant conclusion in New Orleans, he returned to Memphis, while June went home to Biloxi. The *Life* magazine team was still with him, and he was never far removed from a reporter's question or a photographer's flashbulb. The *Life* photographer got a picture of the fence that had been installed just a few weeks before, complete with musical staff and notes. It didn't really keep the fans out —

Life also ran a picture of some girls plucking blades of grass from the lawn, and the newspaper reported lines of cars so long that the neighbors called the police. Vernon's brother, Vester, still working full-time at Precision Tool, was now moonlighting as a kind of security guard, but mainly he just chatted with the fans or tried to get them to keep their racket down so Grandma and Gladys could get some rest. There was no question of running them off: Elvis wouldn't hear of it. He knew who he owed his success to.

There were only four days left before his scheduled departure for Hollywood, and he had a lot to pack in. On the first night he went out to the Fairgrounds, and Red got into another fight. The next day Vernon told Red that he didn't want him around anymore, that Red wouldn't be going out to Hollywood with Elvis, because they just didn't need that kind of bad publicity. Red got pissed off and said he was going to join the Marines; he was mad because he didn't hear Elvis speaking up for him, and what else was he going to do, anyway? Elvis saw a lot of Barbara Hearn, and he stopped off to see Dewey down at the radio station almost every night — they laughed and talked about the old days. Dewey was just about to start a TV show, which would go on at 8:00 on Saturday night, just after Lawrence Welk. "You better warn those Welk listeners to grab that dial quick," Dewey told Bob Johnson at the paper, " 'cause if they don't switch quick, I'll be right there at 'em."

Everyone was talking about Hollywood, and no one who knew him doubted that he would make a big success. Sam Phillips told him that he would be another James Dean, and Dewey figured he would just nail all the little starlets he met. He heard from the Colonel out in Hollywood that there were going to be one or two songs in the picture, and that was all right, as long as they didn't take away from the dramatic impact of the role. Was he going to take acting lessons? the reporters all asked. No, he told each and every one, although he had not recited so much as a single line onstage in his life, "I don't think that you learn to become an actor, I think you just, maybe you've got a little bit of acting talent and develop it. If you learn to be an actor, in other words, if you're not a real actor — you're false." On the precipice of something he had never experienced before, he seemed strangely serene — but then why shouldn't he be? Everything he had ever dreamed had come true, so far. "I've made a study of Marlon Brando," he confided to Lloyd Shearer when Shearer had come down to Memphis to do a story for Sunday *Parade* the month before. "I've made a study of poor Jimmy Dean. I've made a study of myself, and I know why girls, at least the young 'uns, go for us. We're sullen, we're broodin', we're something of a menace. I don't understand it exactly, but that's what the girls like in men. I don't know anything about Hollywood, but I know you can't be sexy if you smile. You can't be a rebel if you grin."

STUDYING LINES WITH COSTAR RICHARD EGAN AND DIRECTOR ROBERT WEBB, RIGHT. (MICHAEL OCHS ARCHIVES)

LOVE ME TENDER

HE ARRIVED IN HOLLYWOOD on Friday, August 17. There were signs as he got off the plane at the Los Angeles airport announcing "Elvis for President," but when reporters asked him about it, he indicated no serious interest in the post, declaring, "I'm strictly for Stevenson. I don't dig the intellectual bit, but I'm telling you, man, he knows the most." With that he was off to his hotel, the Hollywood Knickerbocker, on Ivar off Hollywood Boulevard, where the Colonel was already staying and where he and his cousin Gene occupied a spacious suite on the eleventh floor.

He reported to the studio for meetings and costume fittings at the beginning of the following week. Unsure exactly what preparations were required, he had memorized the entire script, not just his own part but everyone else's, too. "I have no trouble memorizing," he told a reporter proudly. "I once memorized General MacArthur's farewell address, and I can still reel off Lincoln's Gettysburg speech from when I memorized it in school." He met his costars, Richard Egan and Debra Paget (to Egan he confided that he had never acted before and that he was "plenty scared"), as well as director Robert Webb, a fifty-three-year-old veteran of the system who was understandably concerned that, with Elvis' late entry, the film, a modest B western, might be turned into a sideshow. To Mildred Dunnock, who was to play his mother in the film, he was a nice boy whose extremely polite and deferential manner indicated an obvious willingness to learn. The person he was most excited about meeting, though, was forty-one-year-old producer David Weisbart, who had produced James Dean's *Rebel Without a Cause* the previous year. Weisbart was talking about filming a documentary-style *James Dean Story*, something, Elvis blurted out to Weisbart, he would like to do "more than anything else." He sat with his legs tucked under him, chewing gum and stroking his chin nervously. "I'd sure like to take a crack at it," he said. "I think I could do it easy."

It was like a magical kingdom, with famous stars constantly strolling by, cowboys and Indians making casual conversation in the commissary, and everyone sneaking a peek out of the corner of their eye to get a look at the latest arrival on the lot. Gene seemed a little bit overwhelmed by it all and took to whittling or retreating to the big dressing room where the Colonel conducted business while Elvis was on the set. For his part Elvis couldn't seem to get enough — it was like the playing out of a childhood fantasy, he just didn't want to reveal by an inadvertent glance or blurted-out words how excited he really was.

On his second day on the set he met twenty-five-year-old Nick Adams, a Hollywood hustler who had originally brazened his way into the cast of *Mister Roberts* two years before by doing impressions of the star, Jimmy Cagney, for director John Ford. Adams, a coal miner's son from Nanticoke, Pennsylvania, had had a supporting role in *Rebel Without a Cause* and was, he announced to all and sundry, currently writing a book about his "best friend," Jimmy Dean. Desperate for success and recognition, he was known to keep meticulous notebooks on Hollywood social life and never failed to send thank-you notes and congratulatory messages to producers, directors, and people of influence in the industry. On this particular day he was roaming the lot, looking to make a connection for the "bad guy" role in *The Reno Brothers* that Cameron Mitchell had just dropped out of. That was when he ran into Elvis. "It's no secret around town that Nick's a go-getter," wrote Army Archerd in *Photoplay,* but "before Nick knew what had hit him, Elvis was saying, 'Gee, I think you're a swell actor.' It didn't take Nick long to tell Elvis how much he'd like to be in his film. He told Elvis how he'd played a 'heavy' in 'The Last Wagon.' 'Gee,' said Elvis, 'I'll tell Mr. Weisbart to look at "The Last Wagon." ' " Though nothing came of it, the point was made, and when Nick offered to introduce Elvis to some more of his, and Jimmy's, friends, their friendship was sealed. Had Elvis met Natalie Wood? He had to meet Natalie. And, of course, this being Hollywood, there were always lots of girls . . .

It was hard to keep track of everything, it was all happening so fast. Every night he called home to tell his mother the latest news. Almost every night he called June. Three songs were now set for the picture, and Colonel was making deals for their delivery to RCA, working out the publishing, and making sure that Elvis got coauthorship. Colonel Parker was staying up nights, Elvis told a reporter, "thinking up ways to promote me." In the midst of it all, Scotty and Bill and D.J. showed up after driving cross-country from Memphis. They had been promised a tryout for the picture, and there was an RCA recording session with Mr. Sholes scheduled for the following weekend.

The tryout was held in the music bungalow on the west end of the lot where Elvis was rehearsing his three songs with Mr. Darby, the musical director. They were asked to play their regular show, but when they got done they were told they were not "hillbilly" enough for the picture. Scotty was furious — if they had known the musical director wanted "hillbilly," he fumed, they would have given him banjos and jugs and Roy Acuff music, that was what they had grown up on, after all. Elvis' mind was somewhere else, though, and the Colonel was certainly not going to stick up for them. As far as the Colonel was concerned, Scotty knew, they might just as well never have showed up.

It was a minor setback — the next picture, Elvis promised them, he would make sure that they were used. He had finally gotten to renew his brief acquaintance with Debra Paget, he told June on the telephone. She was even more beautiful than he had first thought, she was really nice, and . . . Well, who else had he met? June wondered. When Elvis didn't answer, June asked, Well, what did you talk about with Debra? After a long silence he finally said he didn't remember, but he had met Richard Egan. "Oh, I *love* Richard Egan," June simpered. "Oh, really? And just how much do you love Richard Egan?" About as much as he loved Debra Paget, she supposed. Now who else had he met?

On Wednesday the picture started shooting, but Elvis was getting ready for the soundtrack session the following day. On the day of the session Elvis was eager to perform the ballad that would provide a running theme for the movie (and was even then under discussion as a new title for the picture) for Army Archerd, who was on assignment for *Photoplay*. He took Archerd back to the music bungalow, where Ken Darby accompanied him on the grand piano, and Elvis stood "erect, as if he were in a choir," in front of a tall stained-glass window and sang "Love Me Tender." Archerd was astonished both at the stillness of his manner and the straightforwardness of his treatment of the song, which was a rewrite of the Civil War ballad "Aura Lee." "When he finished," wrote Archerd, "it seemed only normal to express our amazement. 'People think all I can do is belt,' he said. 'I used to sing nothing but ballads before I went professional. I love ballads,' " he insisted to the Hollywood columnist with utter sincerity. He was going to start introducing them more into his live act. This was the kind of music he had grown up singing in church.

The session itself went off without a hitch. The film-studio setting may have been a little intimidating at first, with the distinguished conductor-orchestrator Lionel Newman counting off the beat for the little combo and the Ken Darby vocal trio not really up to the kind of support on Brother Claude Ely's "There's a Leak in This Old Building" (retitled, and recopyrighted, as "We're Gonna Move") that the Jordanaires would have provided. Elvis poured himself into "Love Me Tender," though, and when the session was over went off happily with his new pals, Nick Adams and Nick's roommate, Dennis Hopper.

It was a relief once the real work of acting finally began. It was a job like any other — he was up at 5:30 every morning, he told Dewey on the phone, and sometimes he fell asleep talking to June on the phone at night. "This place isn't anything but a workshop," Elvis declared to the Memphis DJ. "I spent one whole day plowing mules. Man, that was rough!"

Richard Egan told him that the trick was to just be yourself, and David Weisbart insisted that acting lessons would probably ruin him, because his greatest asset was his natural ability. The director, Robert Webb, was very patient, taking him aside before the start of each scene and going over it with him so that he could visualize the action and emotion. Webb would break down the lines, too, giving the fledgling actor points of emphasis and breathing points, talking to Elvis in private and showing him the kind of respect that always allowed him to take direction. Everyone liked the kid — they had all thought he would be some kind of hillbilly freak, but he had won them over with the same combination of humility and deferential charm that had worked for him in every other situation in which he had found himself in his twenty-one-year-old life. "I had a nice talk with him one day," Mildred Dunnock recounted to writer Jerry Hopkins, "and he told me a little bit about how he got started. He evidently played the guitar and was very anxious to get on a recording — this was in Memphis. So he kept approaching the man that had the [studio] and just simply couldn't get on it. One night this man took pity on him, or got bored with his asking, and felt finally he'd give him a try. . . . [The night that the disc jockey played the recording] Elvis told me he was so nervous he went to the movie house. He said to his mother, 'I can't listen to this, I just can't listen to it.' So he went down to see the movie, and at about twenty minutes after eleven his mother came rushing down to the movie, to the aisle seat where he was sitting, and said, 'Elvis, come on home, the telephone is ringing like crazy.' And that was the start of his real popularity."

"Before I met him, I figured he must be some sort of moron," said Debra Paget, voicing what she said was a commonly held assumption on the set, but once she got to know him, she, too, came to find him "very sweet, very simple," just not the kind of boy she would care to date. Trude Forsher, a Viennese émigrée, mother of two, and distant relative of the Aberbachs, who had just gone to work for the Colonel as his West Coast secretary, hosted informal meetings in his dressing room in which the Colonel and Abe Lastfogel, the head of William Morris, talked business and Elvis drank milk and fooled around with Gene. Between takes Gene and Elvis would pester her to teach them German and reminisce about their childhood when they played underneath the house in Tupelo with a little toy car. "Gene was just so happy to be with Elvis." The two of them followed her around the lot singing "Trude Frutti."

He was constantly busy with visitors and reporters on the set. He flirted openly with the women reporters and trusted them to see through his bravura facade. "I could make you like me if I tried," he told one reporter. "I'm just teasin' now, but I'd be sweet, and you'd like me because I was sweet, wouldn't you?" With the men he was equally forthright, and he was open about his hopes and fears with one and all. "I'm so nervous," he said in response to a question about biting his fingernails. "I've always been nervous, ever since I was a kid." "From the time I was a kid, well, I knew something was going to happen to me," he told another interviewer. "Didn't know exactly what." To *True Story* staff writer Jules Archer he confessed his genuine disturbance at the reaction to his Jacksonville shows and the preacher who asked his congregation to pray for Elvis' salvation. "I think that hurt me more than anything else at first. This man was supposed to be a religious leader, yet he acted that way without ever knowing who I was or what I was like. I believe in the Bible. I believe that all good things come from God. . . . I don't believe I'd sing the way I do if God hadn't wanted me to. My voice is God's will, not mine."

He signed autographs willingly and met with studio executives' daughters. He and Gene spent $750 on a Saturday night at a Long Beach amusement park. Meanwhile, the Colonel was working without letup to promote his boy, to make sure that the film's title was changed and that the title song, with Elvis' name on the copyright, would run all the way through the picture, to solidify his merchandising deal with marketing king Hank Saperstein, to earn his own newly conferred title (and salary) as "Technical Adviser" to the film. He wore his pink Elvis Presley button everywhere he went on the set and, when asked by a reporter how to obtain one, said, "We'll have to check you over. It's not that easy, you know."

Back at the hotel Elvis was exhausted, frequently by 8:30 or 9:00 at night. Sometimes he and Nick went out together. Mostly he and Gene ordered in room service. He kept June up-to-date on how the movie was going. One night he told her in some wonderment how William Campbell, who played his brother, Brett, had refused the director's orders to wear a hat, because he was so vain about his hair. "He combs his hair even more than I do," he told her — if she could believe that. He was lonely, he missed her, he wanted her to come out. He would arrange for a screen test. What was she up to back home in Biloxi, what was she doing without him?

Everything was going pretty much according to plan. He put himself into the scenes the same way he put himself into the music. He listened intently to the other actors saying their lines, and then he reacted — the character that he played was an innocent, almost a child as he portrayed him, full of hurt and rage and indignation. The only thing that gave him away was his hands. If he didn't have something to do, his hands betrayed him. You could see it in the rushes: his fingers fluttering, just as they did when he was onstage, as he waited for the other actor to get through with his lines, revealing the same lack of training that Mr. Weisbart told reporters was a virtue. "Presley has the same smoldering appeal for teenagers, and the same impulsive nature [as James Dean did]. In his singing style Elvis often expresses the loneliness and yearning of all teenage kids as they break away from childhood and become adults. . . . Elvis is simply a kid who is emotionally honest, and honestly emotional."

On the Friday before Labor Day weekend, Mr. Sholes visited the set, and Colonel got him into a broad-brimmed straw hat while donning a fake goatee and mustache himself for a photograph with other RCA executives to commemorate the occasion. Sholes had flown out the day before with Bill Bullock, manager of RCA's singles division, for the recording session he had been importuning the Colonel for ever since the spring. It was *imperative,* he argued, that they have material for the second album, which was scheduled for November, and Colonel had finally, grudgingly, conceded the point and scheduled a session for Saturday, Sunday, and Monday of the holiday weekend. Also flying out for the session was Freddy Bienstock, and the three men, plus the Colonel's assistant Tom Diskin, met for breakfast each morning in the hotel dining room, with Sholes dressed in his somber suit and tie while the Colonel was suitably decked out for the California sunshine in a colorful western or Hawaiian shirt that barely tucked into his ample waistband.

Sholes had sent out a bunch of songs and arranged with Henri Rene, an arranger-producer at RCA's West Coast office, to make sure that Elvis was supplied with a phonograph player, but every time he made inquiries as to whether or not Elvis had selected material, he was rebuffed with a corny joke or enigmatic double-talk. Freddy Bienstock, the junior member of the trio and the Hill and Range representative who had brought "Don't Be Cruel" to the last session, had arrived with material of his own, and Sholes grew impatient as Bienstock and the Colonel bantered back and forth and spoke with evident good humor of Freddy's cousins the Aberbachs, with whom Steve had been doing business for years. It was a most uncomfortable situation but one he was going to have to get used to: no matter how much bullshit there was to get through, *he* was the one who was responsible in the end for delivery of the product, and he was going to make sure that he delivered.

Since RCA did not have studio facilities of its own in Hollywood, the session was booked into Radio Recorders, an independent studio on Santa Monica. There had been a problem with the Jordanaires' schedule, but that was worked out, and when Elvis walked in the door shortly after 1:00, everyone was there and all set up. The engineer in charge of the session was a twenty-nine-year-old mixer from Dundee, Michigan, named Thorne Nogar who had been assigned the RCA account a year or two before. A quiet man of Scandinavian background and dour mien, he resembled Scotty somewhat in temperament and was neither impressed nor unimpressed by this kid from Memphis, "awful nice kid — he come in there with no pretensions, just a kid off the street." Elvis in turn warmed to the sound recordist's equally unpretentious manner from the start. He liked Nogar's assistant, too, a soft-spoken young jazz drummer named Bones Howe who had just gone to work for the studio and did everything that needed doing, from getting Thorne coffee to cueing up the tape on the reel.

They started off with "Playing for Keeps," a number that Elvis had gotten from Stan Kesler in Memphis (Kesler had written "I Forgot to Remember to Forget" and "I'm Left, You're Right, She's Gone" for him at Sun), and then Bones played the acetate demos, as Freddy handed them to him, over the PA that boomed into the studio. Freddy had a new song "from the pencil of" Otis Blackwell, and, after the great success of "Hound Dog," he had solicited a number from the songwriting team of Leiber and Stoller, too. They had submitted an old tune called "Love Me," which they had originally written as a kind of hillbilly send-up, to their mind "what Homer and Jethro might have done to a legitimate lyric." On this first day Elvis also responded favorably to both "How Do You Think I Feel," which he already knew from Jimmie Rodgers Snow's rhumbaized version (Snow had also recorded a perfectly sincere version of "Love Me"), and a beautiful Eddy Arnold ballad, "How's the World Treating You?" When he liked a song he touched the top of his head so as to hear it again, *from the top.* When he didn't like a number, he simply drew his finger across his throat. By the end of the day they had three songs wrapped and a fourth (Blackwell's "Paralyzed") well in hand. More significantly, there was an overall spirit of optimism and a new order of ascendancy in the studio.

There was no longer any question of who was in charge. Mr. Sholes might still call out the take numbers; he recorded all the session information meticulously in his notebook; he might even request another take or mildly interject a suggestion here and there — but the pace, the momentum, the feel of the session, were all with the boy. Maybe it was his sense of dislocation (Sholes did almost all of his recording at this point in Nashville and New York), and certainly the presence of Freddy Bienstock in the control room, and the central role that Bienstock had assumed, changed things in a fundamental way. It could have been a combination of the Colonel's constant needling and a recognition on his own part, without ever really acknowledging the full truth of it to himself, of the limited, somewhat peripheral and demeaning role of company watchdog into which he had been thrust. Whatever the reason, Steve Sholes seemed at this point to subside into a role of almost avuncular disinterest.

Meanwhile, Elvis ran through the material with the musicians the same way that he always had, he worked out head arrangements for the songs by having Freddy play the dub over and over again, he listened carefully to the final mix with Thorne — whom he called "Stoney," either as a joke or because of a misunderstanding that no one wanted to bother to correct in case it *was* a joke — but he did it all at a pace, and in a manner, different from that of any other RCA session to date. As Bones Howe remarked: "It was always about the music. He would keep working on a song, and he would listen to it played back, and his criterion was always: did it make him feel good? He didn't care if there were little mistakes, he was interested in anything that would make magic out of the record. The sessions were always fun, there was great energy, he was always doing something that was innovative. It was always about whether you had a feeling for music or not, whether you felt what he felt. That's why he liked Thorne so much. Thorne was a very genuine, sincere person, and he wanted Elvis to be completely happy with the records. The trick was that there was no trick. Thorne was there, and the studio was there — it was a level playing field. So he could just come in and do what felt good."

On the second day he recorded two of the songs that Mr. Sholes had brought to the "Hound Dog" session, "Too Much" and "Anyplace Is Paradise," as well as "Old Shep," the Red Foley tale of a boy and his dog with which he had won his first public recognition, at the Mississippi-Alabama Fair, in 1945. At his own insistence he played the piano on this number for the first time on an RCA session, and you can hear in the halting chords and the somewhat stumbling rhythm both the unmistakable emotion and the equally unmistakable valuing of emotion over technique. He nailed down "Old Shep" on the first take, while "Too Much," an oddball piece of pop construction that aimed to emulate "Don't Be Cruel" without either the craft or the charm, took twelve takes and still failed to achieve a satisfactory guitar solo ("It was in an odd key, and I got lost," Scotty confessed, "but it felt good") and "Anyplace Is Paradise," a jaunty, upbeat bluesy number, took twenty-two. He cut three songs by Little Richard (for which Freddy had secured co-publishing), an old tune by Wiley Walker and Gene Sullivan called "When My Blue Moon Turns to Gold Again," which with its lilting country rhythms and easy, unforced fervor would have been equally at home on Sun, and a new song by Aaron Schroeder and Ben Weisman, two of Hill and Range's top young contract writers. He fooled around with some gospel numbers with the Jordanaires and sang "Love Me Tender" to everyone over and over again.

Time meant nothing to him in the studio. If he felt like singing spirituals, he would sing spirituals to his heart's content. It was his way of finding his place; it was all part of the creative process as he had learned it in the Sun studio. If the feeling wasn't there, you waited until it *got* there, you didn't try to define it too precisely before it showed up—and if something else happened to show up while you were waiting, well, then, you took advantage of that. "He ran the session," said Thorne. "He would be right in the center of everything. Like with the Jordanaires, when he sang, we would set it up with a unidirectional mike, so he would be standing right in front of them, facing them, and they would have their own directional microphone, and they would be singing to one another. He could spend two hours on a tune and then just throw it away." If the band wasn't able to do it the way he wanted, said Scotty, he'd just say, "Well, do whatever you can do, then." "He was very loyal," observed Thorne. And he was a movie star.

On Tuesday he was back on the set, working first on the soundtrack, then on the picture, which had now been officially renamed to accommodate the Colonel's marketing plans. He had a number of difficult emotional scenes, but he handled them in stride. When he had to beat up Debra, to prepare the audience for his own obligatory death (the story was a muddled Civil War drama in which Elvis, playing the youngest of four sons and the only one left at home, marries his oldest brother Vance's fiancée, thinking Vance dead. Naturally, when Vance comes back . . .), Webb worked with him extensively on his motivation, and when in another scene Mildred Dunnock as his mother said, "Put that gun down, son," according to Dunnock he was so deep into his character that he dropped the gun right away. "Oh my God, what in the world were you doing?" said the director. "You were supposed to keep on going." "Well, she *told* me to put it down," said Elvis, who may have been fooling—but Dunnock didn't think so. To her: "For the first time in the whole thing he had heard me, and he believed me. Before, he'd just been thinking what he was doing and how he was going to do it. I think it's a funny story. I also think it's a story about a beginner who had one of the essentials of acting, which is to believe."

Meanwhile, he was growing more accustomed to the Hollywood life. He changed hotels, moving to the Beverly Wilshire, along with the Colonel, because his gang of fans had simply overwhelmed the Hollywood Knickerbocker. He was hanging out more and more with Nick and his friends and, through Nick, Natalie Wood, another in the "Rebel" crowd. The gossip columnists reported it as a sizzling romance, and Natalie, who presented him with matching red and blue velvet shirts from her dressmaker, was quoted by the wires as saying, "He's a real pixie and has a wonderful little-boy quality." But while he continued to pester Debra Paget fruitlessly for dates — and had to keep a careful eye (and ear) on his cousin Gene, who was still gawking around like a tourist — with Natalie and Nick, and sometimes Dennis Hopper, he felt more like he was part of a real gang; they all went around together, shared innocent enthusiasms, appreciated one another's work, and disdained pretentiousness and "swank places." One night they descended en masse on the home of Louella Parsons, who had been trying to get an interview with Elvis for some time and who reported with agreeable surprise: "Finally met Elvis Presley, who called on me accompanied by Natalie Wood, Nick Adams and his cousin, Gene Smith, who is a character straight out of a book. Elvis and his gang drink only soft drinks. . . ." In an interview with Albert Goldman years later Natalie described herself, a child of Hollywood, as intrigued by his very conventionality. "He was the first person of my age group I had ever met who said to me: 'How come you're wearing makeup? Why do you want to go to New York? Why do you want to be on your own?' . . . It was like having the date that I never ever had in high school. I thought it was really wild!

"I hadn't been around anyone who was [that] religious. He felt he had been given this gift, this talent, by God. He didn't take it for granted. He thought it was something that he had to protect. He had to be nice to people. Otherwise, God would take it all back."

On September 9 he was scheduled to appear on the premier *Ed Sullivan Show* of the season. Sullivan, however, was recuperating from an August automobile accident and, as a result, was not going to be able to host the program, which Elvis would perform from the CBS studio in Los Angeles. Elvis sent Sullivan a get-well card and a picture autographed to "Mr. Ed Sullivan" and was thrilled to learn that the show would be guest-hosted by Charles Laughton, star of *Mutiny on the Bounty.* Steve Allen, who had presented him in his last television appearance, was not even going to challenge Sullivan on the night in question: NBC was simply going to show a movie.

He opened with "Don't Be Cruel," strolling out alone from the darkened wings onto a stage spotlighted with silhouettes of guitars and a bass fiddle. He was wearing a loud plaid jacket and an open-necked shirt, but his performance was relatively subdued, as every shoulder shrug, every clearing of his throat and probing of his mouth with his tongue, evoked screams and uncontrolled paroxysms of emotion. Then he announced he was going to sing a brand-new song, "it's completely different from anything we've ever done. This is the title of our brand-new Twentieth Century Fox movie and also my newest RCA Victor escape — er, release." There was an apologetic shrug in response to the audience's laughter, and then, after an altogether sincere tribute to the studio, the director, and all the members of the cast, and "with the help of the very wonderful Jordanaires," he sang "Love Me Tender." It is a curious moment. Just after beginning the song he takes the guitar off and hands it to an unseen stagehand, and there are those awkward moments when he doesn't seem to know quite what to do without his prop and shrugs his shoulders or twitchily adjusts his lapels, but the moans which greet the song — of surprise? of shock? of delight? most likely all three — clearly gratify him, and at the end of the song he bows and gestures graciously to the Jordanaires.

When he comes back for the second sequence, the band is shown, with Jordanaire Gordon Stoker at the piano and the other Jordanaires in plaid jackets at least as loud (but nowhere near as cool) as his own. They rock out on Little Richard's "Ready Teddy," but when Elvis goes into his dance the camera pulls away and, as reviews in the following days will note, "censors" his movements. It doesn't matter. The girls scream just when he stands still, and when he does two verses of "Hound Dog" to end the performance, the West Coast studio audience goes crazy, though the *New York Journal-American*'s Jack O'Brian, after first taking note of Presley's "ridiculously tasteless jacket and hairdo (hairdon't)" and granting that "Elvis added to his gamut (A to B) by crossing his eyes," pointed out that the New York audience "laughed and hooted." "Well, what did someone say?" remarked host Charles Laughton, with good humor, at the conclusion of the performance. "Music hath charms to *soothe* the savage breast?"

The show got a 43.7 Trendex rating (it reached 82.6 percent of the television audience), and in the Colonel's view, which he shared gleefully with Steve Sholes, really boosted Presley's stock with an adult audience for the first time. A number of disc jockeys around the country taped the performance and started playing their tape of the new ballad on the air, and that undoubtedly hastened the release of the single, which came out about three weeks later. In the meantime prerelease orders built up to close to a million, and the Colonel pushed RCA to find that millionth customer not only as a confirmation of Elvis' well-established popularity but as a credit to Ed Sullivan, and the power of his show, which could then be proffered to Sullivan as a gratuitous gift.

There were just two more weeks of shooting before Elvis was scheduled to leave for the Tupelo homecoming concert that had been booked in July. Filming was originally supposed to be over by then, but now he was going to have to come back for a few more days after the concert. That was all right. He was enjoying himself now. They had filmed his death scene, which the director said was really going to touch audiences everywhere. Colonel was busy making deals and keeping everyone on the set off balance in a way that irritated some but always tickled Elvis. "We're the perfect combination," Elvis often told friends. "Colonel's an old carny, and me, I'm off the wall." At one point the would-be producers of a rock 'n' roll pastiche called *Do Re Mi* approached Colonel about getting Elvis to sing a couple of songs in the picture for $75,000. Colonel professed to be insulted, then offered to roll the dice for his boy's salary, double or nothing. Other members of the *Love Me Tender* cast claimed to be shocked, and William Campbell was convinced that Elvis' lack of reaction as Colonel told the story indicated an acceptance of his role as chattel or worse, but in Elvis' view, the Colonel was simply a very smart man: "He's a very amusing guy. He plans stuff that nobody else would even think of." And as he made clear to more than one interviewer who tried to cast the Colonel in a Svengali role, "We more or less picked each other." What people didn't understand was that Colonel mostly kept out of his hair. He took care of business, and he left Elvis to take care of his private life. Oh, he could be a pain in the ass sometimes, and he expected Elvis to keep his nose clean in order to maintain his end of the bargain. But for the most part he just left him alone — and he did his best to help Nick out, too. Elvis was glad Colonel liked Nick. Nick didn't have anything better to do, so he was going to come to Tupelo with them. Elvis was looking forward to showing him Memphis for the first time.

They flew into Memphis on Saturday, September 22, and went out to the fair briefly that night. On Monday they visited Humes, where Elvis introduced Nick to his old homeroom teacher, Miss Scrivener, who had sponsored the talent contest in which he had first performed in front of all his classmates senior year. Nick did impressions for Miss Scrivener's class, and Elvis beamed as the kids broke up. He presented the ROTC drill team with $900 for uniforms and gave another teacher a television set "to be used for educational purposes." They visited the Tiplers at Crown Electric, too, and Nick put his feet up on Mr. Tipler's desk while Elvis explained, said his former employer, "how he had his money arranged so he wouldn't get it all at one time." They even went by Dixie's house one afternoon, and she told Elvis she was getting married, and he congratulated her and wished her well.

On Wednesday they left for Tupelo around noon. Mr. and Mrs. Presley, Nick, and Barbara Hearn all drove down with Elvis in the white Lincoln, missing the parade that was being held in his honor but not missing any of the hoopla. Main Street was decked out in bunting and a giant banner that proclaimed "Tupelo Welcomes Elvis Presley Home," while every store window was decorated at the suggestion of fair manager James M. Savery with an "Elvis theme." The fact that it was Children's Day, too, the very day that the children of East Tupelo had been transported to the fair eleven years earlier and Elvis had quaveringly sung "Old Shep," only made the symbolism complete.

Vernon and Gladys were practically overcome. She wore a brocade dress and a locket with a photograph of Elvis around her neck. "It made me feel bad," she told a friend afterward, "to go back there like that and remember how poor we was." Vernon, on the other hand, was practically exuberant. He was wearing a dark suit, white shirt, and tie, with the tie loosened and slightly askew on this very hot day. Outside the big tent in back of the stage he spotted Ernest Bowen, for whom he had had a delivery route when he was working for L. P. McCarty and Sons, the last job he had held before leaving Tupelo. Bowen was now general manager of WELO and trying fruitlessly to gain entry to the tent so he could get an interview for his announcer, Jack Cristil. "All of a sudden this guy hollers at me — I didn't even recognize him, but it was Vernon, all cleaned up and greeting me like a long-lost friend. He wanted to know if he could do anything, and I said, 'Yeah, get me in the tent.' He said, 'Just follow me,' and he just like parted the waves. I asked Vernon, 'How are y'all doing?' He said, 'Oh, we doing just great.' Said, 'The boy is really taking care of us.' And I said, 'Good!' "

Inside the tent, while June Carter was performing, or maybe it was Mississippi Slim's cousin Rod Brasfield, telling jokes for the hometown crowd about his experiences on the Opry or making a Hollywood picture, Elvis told James Savery, with some exaggeration — but probably not much — that this was the first time he had actually been through the main gate; as a kid he had always had to climb the fence. "And just think, you're paying me for it, too!" There was a host of friends, relatives, and acquaintances (and would-be acquaintances) wanting to catch up on old times, with every one of them, seemingly, reminding him of how poor they had all been, of how they, too, had snuck into the fair with him. Elvis graciously received them all, passing off his success, for the most part, as a simple twist of fate, but with the father of one old schoolmate who was attending the University of Mississippi school of pharmacy "so he could amount to something," his answer was a little more revealing. In the account of a New York reporter, "Presley grinned at the older man and replied: 'Shucks, why don't you tell him to just get himself a guitar. That's all he needs.' "

There was an informal press conference before the afternoon show, and Elvis returned to the same theme repeatedly. He couldn't "hardly remember how I looked in overalls," he said. "It's all great," he responded good-humoredly to another question. "I've been looking forward to this homecoming very much. I've been escorted out of these fairgrounds when I was a kid and snuck over the fence. But this is the first time I've been escorted in." How about Natalie? someone called out. "I worry about her when I'm out there where she is," replied Elvis nonchalantly. "I don't think about her when I'm not." The reporters tried in vain to get Colonel Parker to say something, but Mr. and Mrs. Presley, who according to the *Tupelo Daily Journal* seemed "a little bewildered by all the commotion . . . but smiled pleasantly for photographers," expressed their gratitude first to a reporter from the *Journal* and, later, to a radio interviewer. What were their favorite records? the radio interviewer wanted to know. " 'That's All Right,' " said Mr. Presley. " 'Baby, Play House,' " said Gladys. "That's a good one," said Mr. Presley. "And 'Don't Be Cruel,' " added Mrs. Presley. "There's so many of them I can't remember the names," said Vernon. "It was terrific," said the interviewer in summation about the parade he had just determined that they had missed, "and everyone was having such a fine time and I know that you're sorry you missed it and I know that you've heard it was a wonderful parade. . . . Well, I'm sure that you know that the whole town is just wide open to the Presley family."

Mississippi governor J. P. Coleman, whose car had been mobbed by fans who mistook his arrival for their idol's, was backstage, and while they were taking a picture together, Elvis told the governor he thought he might go into politics himself. Oh, what would you run for? asked the governor. "The city limits," said Elvis affably. A highway patrolman asked Elvis to autograph a pile of pictures, and he signed away. Then it was time to go out and do the show, and he manfully made his way into the sea of sound.

He was wearing the heavy blue velvet shirt that Natalie had given him, even in all this heat, and Colonel had arranged for a ceramic model of the RCA dog, Nipper, to be placed onstage. Fox Movietone News was filming the show, and from the first notes of "Heartbreak Hotel" the crowd of five thousand — mostly teenagers, mostly girls — went crazy. There were forty city police and highway patrolmen on hand, but "reporters and photographers had to scramble up on the stage to safety," reported the *Journal,* "when Elvis first opened his mouth and a yelling wave of teenage girls broke for the guitar king." At the conclusion of "Long Tall Sally," Governor Coleman was announced, and after Elvis quieted the crowd ("Excuse me, Governor," he apologized to the startled chief executive), Coleman read off a text that proclaimed the young Tupeloan "America's number-one entertainer in the field of American popular music, [our] own native son." Then Tupelo mayor James Ballard presented him with a key to the city in the shape of a metal-sculpture guitar and declared, "The people of this community and of this city admire you and certainly are proud of you." "Thank you, Mayor, and thank you, ladies and gentlemen, very much, and, uh, and uh —" The crowd's screams drowned out any further comments he might have had in mind.

"I was right at the back of the stage watching him," said Ernest Bowen. "I saw him bring that crowd to hysterics, and he did it by teasing. He knew just how far to walk to the end of that stage, he would lean just far enough so that they could touch the tip of his finger." One time he leaned too far and had a silver button torn from his bright velvet blouse. In the middle of "Don't Be Cruel," fourteen-year-old Judy Hopper, from Alamo, Tennessee, scaled the five-foot-high stage to throw her arms around her idol, who only appeared amused. After that six policemen stayed onstage with Elvis. He ended up with "Hound Dog," naturally, at which point pandemonium really broke loose. "Elvis," shrieked the girls in the front row, among them fourteen-year-old Wynette Pugh, later to become famous as country star Tammy Wynette. " 'Elvis,' they shrieked," reported the *Journal,* "tearing their hair and sobbing hysterically, 'Please, Elvis.' "

After the show photographers got some more shots of Elvis with his mother and father, and a British journalist named Peter Dacre from the London Sunday *Express* ascertained that he would like to go to England, so long as he didn't have to fly ("If something were to go wrong on a plane, there's no land under you. That's a long swim"). Then he was escorted back to his hotel by the four highway patrolmen assigned to him to get some rest for the evening performance.

Fifty National Guardsmen were added for the evening show, which was anticipated to draw half again as many spectators. There must have been close to fifty thousand visitors to town, including sightseers and lookers-on, the biggest crowd that anyone could remember since Roosevelt had visited at the height of the Depression. Elvis was relaxed and chewing gum but disappointed that he wasn't feeling better for the occasion. "I've looked forward to this day for a long time," he said, "and the heck of it is, I'm sick today." He asked for the girl who had crashed the stage that afternoon and was introduced to Judy Hopper, who had her picture taken with him and said, "It was even more thrilling than I dreamed it would be."

The evening performance was, if anything, less inhibited on the part of the audience than the earlier one. At one point Elvis stopped the show to admonish the crowd in a good-natured way that little kids were getting hurt and that he wouldn't go on if they didn't sit back down. They were back up again for "Don't Be Cruel," though, and by the end they were almost out of control. "As howling sirens carried Elvis away, the fairgrounds were wild with crying teenagers," declared the *Journal,* "who fought for a chance for a last look at the boy who put burlesque back in business in a big way."

Elvis and Nick had returned to Hollywood by the weekend, and the film finished shooting within a week, with a Thanksgiving release date planned and more prints expected (575) than for any other film in Twentieth Century Fox's history. Then he was briefly back on tour, with Nick accompanying him and, with the Colonel's blessing, doing impressions to open the show; in Dallas Nick was even served with a summons in a breach-of-contract suit by a Fort Worth process server who didn't know what Elvis Presley looked like.

The Dallas show, which opened the four-day Texas tour on October 11, marked a watershed for the group. There were 26,500 on hand at the Cotton Bowl, which according to the *Dallas Morning News* had not witnessed such hysteria "since a December day in 1949 when a crazy-legged

Mustang named Kyle Rote tied the score against the heavily favored Fighting Irish of Notre Dame." It was the largest paying crowd ever to see an entertainer perform in Dallas (Elvis took home $18,000 out of a $30,000 gross), and from the moment Elvis appeared, waving to the crowd from the back of a Cadillac convertible as he circled the field, a kind of high-pitched, earsplitting, seismic wail went up, there were "screams of anguish" and "shrieks of ecstasy," the papers reported, that never wavered or stopped. The musicians couldn't hear a thing, apart from the crowd, and Elvis, dressed in his kelly green coat and navy blue pants with a black and gold cummerbund, sang by instinct alone, dropping to his knees over and over again, and ending the show by jumping off the stage with the microphone and falling to the ground at the fifty-yard line before being whisked off in a limousine. "It looked like a war out there," said drummer D. J. Fontana. "That's when it really hit me: we went around the park on the back of that Cadillac, and all you could see was just thousands of bulbs going off. I thought, What's this guy done? I just sat on the stage and looked around and thought, This guy draws more than the football players do. One man, and, you know, this park is full of people."

It was the same everywhere he went on this tour. There were riots even when they didn't show up, as teenagers in Temple tore up the Kyle Hotel because they had heard he might be staying there (he was thirty-five miles away, in Waco, at the time). The next night, in Houston, he begged the crowd three times to quiet down and listen, but with little success.

Meanwhile, the single of "Love Me Tender," which had already been certified gold, was about to enter the *Billboard* charts, and Elvis' next movie, a Hal Wallis production called *Lonesome Cowboy,* had been announced to the trades with a projected starting date of December or January. Reporters were pestering him about his draft status (he had gotten his pre-induction questionnaire in Hollywood around the first of the month, but, he said, he didn't know what that meant in terms of being called up, or how soon that might be expected to happen). Everyone wanted to know about his love life, of course. He was getting only four hours of sleep a night, he conceded, but when reporters asked why he didn't take it easier, he suggested that "the Lord can give and . . . the Lord can take away. I might be herding sheep next year." He arrived home exhausted on Monday, October 15, immediately went to see Barbara, and then called June about her upcoming visit at the end of the week. "Well, it won't be long now," he said for what must have been the thousandth time and couldn't resist repeating the joke that Richard Egan pulled on him when he expressed the same sentiment one too many times on the set. "You remind me of that damned monkey," Egan had said. "What monkey is that, Mr. Egan?" Elvis blundered innocently along. "The monkey that was sitting on the railroad track, and the train come along and cut off his tail. That's what he said. 'It won't be long now.' " Elvis laughed and laughed — he loved the joke, and he loved being considered one of the boys enough by Richard Egan that Egan would pull it on him. Then he told June to be packed and ready; he would wire her the money for her flight in a couple of days.

EVERYONE IN BILOXI knew about June's trip, and everyone was excited about it. The owner of Rosie's Dress Shop gave her a new outfit to wear, and the beauty shop trimmed her new pixie hairdo for free. When she went to Western Union on Thursday, she and her friend Patsy announced proudly that they were waiting for a money order from Elvis Presley, but they needn't have bothered — everyone at Western Union already knew she was Elvis Presley's girl from the telegrams they had delivered from Hollywood. She and Patsy waited and waited, going next door to Klein's Bakery, trying to mask their growing discomfiture with cream puffs and coffee. Eventually June went home, utterly humiliated. She was there only a few minutes when the phone rang. It was Elvis, who told her that he had run into a little trouble and would send her the money as soon as he could. She didn't know what to think — she was worried and pissed off — and when her friend Buddy Conrad came by later, the three of them, June, Patsy, and Buddy, proceeded to get drunk.

Only on the next day did she find out what had happened. It was in all the papers. Elvis had been in a fight with a filling-station manager. He had stopped for gas in his Lincoln at the Gulf station at the corner of Second and Gayoso. He asked the attendant to check his tank for a leak — he was getting a gas smell in the air-conditioning vents. When a crowd formed, the manager, Edd Hopper, asked Elvis to move along; he had other customers to take care of, too. By Elvis' account he was unable to move, because of the crowd surrounding the car, and he explained that to Mr. Hopper, but Hopper got mad and reached inside the car and slapped Elvis on the back of the head. With that Elvis leapt out and decked the forty-two-year-old Hopper, who then pulled a knife. By this time there were two policemen on the scene, and one of them restrained Hopper's six-foot-four attendant, Aubrey Brown, who had gone after Elvis and been on the receiving end of a punch himself. "I'll regret this day as long as I live," Elvis was quoted as saying. "It's getting where I can't even leave the house without something happening to me." On his way to the police station, where all three were booked on charges of assault and battery and disorderly conduct, Elvis said, "Maybe you'd better put down Carl Perkins," when asked to state his name.

Western Union called June shortly after she read the account in the paper: the money was finally there. When she went to sign the order, she noticed it had been sent by Vernon, and when she and Patsy arrived at the Memphis airport the following day, it was the elder Presleys who picked her up in the pink Cadillac, not Elvis. Elvis had been acquitted of all charges and advised by Acting Judge Sam Friedman that because of his "avocation" and the fact that "wherever you go you have a large following . . . [you should] try to be considerate and cooperate with businessmen. Avoid crowds where business will be interrupted." The two gas-station employees were fined $26 and $16 apiece, but for Mrs. Presley this was not the end of it. She was frightened of Elvis even going out of the house, she said. She knew her boy, and she knew he could take care of himself, but what if some crazy man came after him with a gun? she said to June, tears streaming down her face. "Now, Mama, he's gone be just fine," said Mr. Presley reassuringly, patting her on the leg. "That was the biggest black eye I ever saw," Patsy declared of the picture of Edd Hopper she had seen in the paper, and that broke the ice a little as Mr. Presley chuckled, but Mrs. Presley was still visibly shaken.

They stayed around the house for most of the first couple of days. They played darts and bumper pool, and Elvis shadowboxed with June in the empty swimming pool, with one hand behind his back. He was clearly feeling restless and trapped, and his mother got mad at him when, in sheer frustration, he flung some darts up at the ceiling, where they stuck until she knocked them down with a broom. "Next time I'm going to use the broom on you," she said with grim affection, but everyone knew she was just worried about him. She fixed his favorite fried chicken and little treats like peanut butter crisscrosses out of her *Better Homes and Gardens New Cookbook.* June and Patsy occasionally went out to the fence, where the fans patiently waited, and they saw Bitsy Mott, the Colonel's brother-in-law, whom they knew from Florida, working security there. They were allowed to talk to the fans from their side of the fence but not to go out on the street and mingle. "You're so lucky," some of the girls said. They all wanted to know what he was really like, they wanted to know what it was like to kiss him. Elvis conscientiously came out two or three times a day to chat and sign autographs, and Gladys sometimes had to call him two or three times to get him to come in.

Finally on Sunday night he couldn't stand it any longer: they were going to go out, he didn't care what his mama thought. One of the local theaters was running the Fox Movietone newsreel of the Tupelo concert, and he wasn't just going to let himself become a *prisoner*. Nothing was going to happen, anyway.

They took the band's black Cadillac limo so as to be less conspicuous, and June paid for the tickets before they dashed inside to watch the picture from a private viewing room. They hadn't been in the theater twenty minutes when two policemen came in to get Elvis' car keys. A crowd had formed outside the theater and was tearing the car apart, scratching names into the paint, breaking windows, ripping out upholstery, and denting the fenders. The policemen moved the car, then came back for Elvis and the two girls, escorting them through an inflamed mob that tore at their clothes and, for the first time, really frightened June. Elvis didn't want his parents to know what had happened, so they left the car at Dewey's and Dewey drove them home. Gladys was surprised to see them back so early, and the next morning Vernon cut the story out of the paper — it had Barbara Hearn as his date and the white Cadillac vandalized — in hopes that Gladys would not learn of the incident.

That afternoon Scotty and Bill and D.J., along with the Jordanaires, came by for a brief rehearsal for the next Ed Sullivan appearance, which was coming up on the weekend. After a brief run-through of the four songs they were going to do on TV, they all sat in a little circle on the floor singing spirituals, with Gladys beaming on the couch. Every so often she would join in and softly sing a line, while June, never shy about her singing, took the alto part on "In the Garden," which had been part of her high school graduation ceremony. Later that night she and Elvis drove out to Mud Island, where they had ridden Elvis' motorcycle at what seemed like 100 miles an hour on her first trip to Memphis.

It was a more contemplative visit this time, sadder somehow; for June there was a sense of almost ominous foreboding. She didn't doubt that he loved her, she knew he was there with her — and yet she didn't know if she could ever get him back. Elvis told her he had just heard from Nick and that Nick was coming to town tomorrow or the next day. He started telling her all about Nick and Nick's friends and Jimmy Dean, but she didn't want to hear. On their way home they passed a milk truck making deliveries. Elvis swung around and waited for the milkman to come back to his truck. He asked the man if he could buy some milk but then found he had no money. The milkman said that was all right, and Elvis just autographed an IOU. They drank the cold milk out of the bottle, and Elvis wiped the milky mustache off his upper lip with the back of his hand, just like James Dean, June thought, in *Rebel Without a Cause*.

It was all right when Nick arrived, but it was somehow, and not all that subtly, different. They drove around town together and talked about many of the same things, but she felt as if, without even bothering to disguise it all that much, she and Nick were competing for his attention. Nick was talking about Natalie all the time — he had even brought a dress of hers as a kind of souvenir and made a big point of how Natalie really filled it out. "I wish you could have invited him some other time," June said to Elvis in a rare moment of privacy, but Elvis insisted that he hadn't invited Nick, Nick had more or less invited himself. "He's just a lonesome little guy struggling to make it in Hollywood," Elvis said, with compassion, of his friend. But Mrs. Presley seemed to sympathize with June. "He sure is a pushy little fellow," she said; she just wished Elvis could be a little more careful in his selection of friends.

One night they went down to the radio station to see Dewey and ran into Cliff Gleaves, a DJ from Jackson, who had met Elvis in passing seven months before. He had just gotten back into town and was hanging around the station on the off chance of seeing Elvis again. Afterward they all went out to Dewey's house, on Perkins, and played pool for a while, but then the men went off into the den, where a movie projector had been set up, while Patsy and June stayed in the living room with Mrs. Phillips. At one point one of the men came out and, with the door momentarily ajar, June saw flickering images of naked bodies. Furiously she marched up to the door, knocked, and then flung it open. She stood in what she called her "Elvis position," her arms folded in front of her, staring blankly ahead. "What the hell are you doing, June?" Elvis said, leaping up in acute embarrassment. "I don't want you watching that shit."

"You can watch that shit as long as you want, Elvis," she said, "but first you can take me and Pat home." And if he thought she was just being a prude, she added, "then y'all can kiss my ass."

The night before she was scheduled to return to Biloxi and Elvis was due to go to New York for the Sullivan show, they all went out to dinner with some wealthy acquaintances of the older Presleys who wanted to provide a special occasion for Vernon and Gladys. It seemed like Gladys was going to fuss with them forever about their manners and their appearance, but then at dinner Elvis gave June his new temporary tooth caps to hold, and she started fooling with them so she looked like a vampire, and soon their hosts were as broken up as they were. "It's about time you kids relaxed and had some fun," said the husband approvingly, as Gladys laughed until the tears ran down from her eyes. Afterward they went to a private screening of a rough cut of *Love Me Tender.* Everyone thought it was wonderful except for Elvis. When June tried to tell him how good he was, he made it clear that he did not want to be just "good." "Quit being so damn hard on yourself, man," Nick muttered, "and give it some time." He had been working for years, he said, to try to get to the point where Elvis was now. "You've proved yourself as an actor, man. Don't worry about it." Elvis took Nick's remarks as highly complimentary, but June put them down more to jealousy.

In the end he wanted her to fly up to New York with him, and if she wouldn't do that, why couldn't she just stay here in Memphis with his parents? He would be back in a few days, and Natalie was going to come visit next week: he wanted her to meet Natalie. Wait a minute, Nick protested, if June was going to stay, he would just call Natalie and tell her to come some other time — there wasn't enough room in the house for everyone. "Don't worry, Nick, I'm not staying," June announced, leaving the room. When Elvis followed her, she told him she wanted to go home, and she wasn't interested in meeting Natalie anyway. "Baby, I didn't invite Natalie," Elvis protested, it was *Nick* who had invited Natalie, and he could just as easily uninvite her.

It was a sour note on which to end the week, and when she got back to Biloxi and went to have her picture taken for the studio portrait that she had promised Elvis, she told the photographer she thought she wanted something really different. They talked about it for a while and finally decided on a picture the photographer had never taken before: the subject in tears. The photograph won second prize in an exhibit sometime later.

WITH NATALIE WOOD OUTSIDE THE HOTEL CHISCA, OCTOBER 31, 1956.
(ROBERT WILLIAMS)

THE TOAST OF THE TOWN

IT WAS A RELAXED, confident, and very much at ease Elvis Presley who made his second appearance on *The Ed Sullivan Show,* still popularly known as the *Toast of the Town,* on the evening of Sunday, October 28. Gone were the explosive nervous energy, the involuntary mannerisms, that had dominated his television appearances of just a few months before; even the self-abashed, somewhat shambling manner of his Sullivan debut had been replaced by a good-natured, almost studied and bemused *playfulness,* a kind of good-humored recognition of common cause both with his audience and that of his host. When he appeared following Sullivan's characteristically stiff, almost wooden introduction, his hair high and a pleased, slightly embarrassed look on his face, it was as if for the first time he really took it all as his due — there appeared to be no rage hiding behind the mask, there was no caged tiger desperate to get out, he acknowledged the response with the deferential distraction of the grand seigneur. He was a recording star, he was a movie star, he was a servant of the Lord and the master of his own destiny; for one brief moment there was not even a hint of imposture in his mind.

He had spent the day primarily fulfilling professional responsibilities and doing good works. After a couple of nights on the town with Nick, Dewey, his cousin Gene, and his new friend, Cliff Gleaves, all of whom he had invited to come up to New York at his expense, he reported for rehearsal at noon, while the Colonel handed out "Elvis for President" buttons at the unveiling of a forty-foot "statue" of the new Hollywood star above the marquee of the Paramount Theatre in Times Square, where *Love Me Tender* would premiere in a little more than two weeks. "The idol of the rock 'n' roll juveniles also surprised an afternoon press interview by demonstrating to adult reporters that he is a polite, personable, quick-witted and charming young man," reported the *New York Times.* "Teenagers are my life and triumph," he declared to the assembled reporters. "I'd be nowhere without them." He wished he could sit down with some of those parents who saw him as a bad influence, "because I think I could change their minds and their viewpoint. Ever since I got to be a sort of name I've examined my conscience and asked myself if I led anybody astray even indirectly, and I'm at peace with my conscience." Somebody asked him if it wasn't teenagers that had recently ripped his car apart. "That means nothing to me, sir. That's a car and I've got other cars, but the idea of doing to others what you'd like them to do to you is what's in my craw. It's in the Bible. . . . I read my Bible, sir, and this is no story just made up for now. My Bible tells me that what he sows he will also reap, and if I'm sowing evil and wickedness it will catch up with me. I'm right sure of that, sir, and I don't think I'm bad for people. If I did think I was bad for people, I would go back to driving a truck, and I really mean this."

At the end of the afternoon, in a public ceremony just as extensively covered by the media, he received an inoculation of the newly developed Salk polio vaccine. He was doing so, he said in a public service announcement he recorded for the March of Dimes, because "so many kids and adults, too, have gotten just about one of the roughest breaks that can happen to a person. . . . We can help these people. And the way to do it is this: join the 1957 March of Dimes." "Halo, Everybody, Halo: Latest Presley Pitch" had been the headline for a recent *Variety* story, which suggested somewhat cynically an "institutional build-up to re-create the rock 'n' roller into an influence for the good" — but that was really missing the point: Elvis didn't need an institutional push, this was what he believed was truly intended for him, this was the real function of fame.

The streets that night were so crowded you could barely get to the studio. There were policemen on horseback, and thousands of fans clamoring to get past the barricades, but Elvis insisted on signing autographs anyway, to the acute discomfiture of his traveling companions. Mr. Sullivan complimented the youngsters in the audience on their comportment; he had asked them not to yell during the songs themselves, he said, and they had kept their promise. A number of the reviews suggested that Elvis had been pressured to tone down his act, that either he or the cameras had been urged to restrain his body movements, but there is no evidence of that: mainly what you see is great good humor, a manner that exudes utter confidence, and a sense of vast amusement both at himself and, lovingly, his audience. Over and over again he stops in the midst of a practiced gesture and shrugs his shoulders, audibly exhales, rolls his eyes, *freezes* — just waiting for the wave that has been momentarily stilled to roll back over him. His eyes twinkle; he smiles and then catches himself and sneers (but affably); he listens to Mr. Sullivan say that Elvis will return for his second appearance on the show in just a couple of minutes and he impishly demurs, then after a brief colloquy agrees that yes, he'll be back. At the conclusion of his third and final segment, he announces the scheduled opening of his new picture and his next appearance on *The Ed Sullivan Show* in January. "And, uh, and uh," he says, momentarily stuck, then recovers with a sincere "Until we meet you again, may God bless you as he has blessed me."

The ratings were not quite as spectacular as they had been for the first show, but Sullivan still beat the principal competition (Mary Martin and Paul Douglas in a special television production of the play *Born Yesterday*) by a margin of two to one and gained an overall 34.6 (57 percent share) Trendex rating.

Elvis shot a new ending for the film the following day at the Junco Studio on East Sixty-ninth Street. Pressure had been building ever since it had been announced he would perish in his first screen role, and there had been pickets all week in front of the Paramount Theatre with suspiciously uniform printed signs that pleaded, "Don't Die! Elvis Presley." Whether prodded by public pressure or perhaps just acceding to the publicity value of the occasion, the studio had acknowledged the protest and flown in director Robert Webb, cameraman Leo Tover, and a crew of technicians. It was going to be a simple shot of the image of Elvis Presley superimposed over the dying Clint Reno and singing the title song of the film as the character expires. There was no need even to change his shoes, and he played the scene in the white bucks he had worn on the television show the night before.

On the next day the new RCA contract which the Colonel had been negotiating for the last couple of months was announced: royalty payments were to be spread out in such a way that Elvis would be guaranteed $1,000 a week for the next twenty years. He had at this point sold well over ten million singles for RCA (this would compute to a record royalty of roughly $450,000), which represented approximately two thirds of RCA's singles business. In fact, *Variety* had declared him a millionaire just the previous week on the basis of their unofficial computations of record royalties, movie income ($250,000, figuring in the new movie that was coming up in a couple of months), song publishing, TV appearances, and personals. It was a situation virtually unprecedented in the record business, rivaling anything that had ever been seen in the larger world of show business, and it didn't even take into account merchandising.

Just three short months before, the Colonel had entered into a deal with a thirty-seven-year-old merchandiser from California named Hank Saperstein for the exclusive right to exploit and commercially promote the Elvis Presley image. Saperstein, who had offices in Beverly Hills, had been in the business for seventeen years and had previously conducted highly successful campaigns for *Super Circus, Ding Dong School,* Lassie, the Lone Ranger, and Wyatt Earp, but, as *Variety* noted, this was the first all-out merchandising campaign in memory aimed at teens, not "moppets." By the time that *The Reno Brothers* started shooting, Saperstein's campaign was fully operational, with something like eighteen licensees and twenty-nine products, many of which (belts, scarves, skirts, jeans, lipstick, charm bracelets, statuettes, publications, and western ties) were laid out on the hood of Saperstein's car in a publicity shot taken on the movie set. By the end of October the program was really getting into gear, with thirty licenses and fifty products to be marketed through Sears, Montgomery Ward, W. T. Grant's, and Woolworth's, among others, and *Variety* was endorsing Saperstein's prediction of $40 million in retail sales over the next fifteen months. This would come to $18 million wholesale, which at the customary 5 percent licenser's royalty would mean $900,000, to be split between Saperstein and Elvis Presley Enterprises equally.

In the offing were hound dogs and houndburgers, and Saperstein, clearly a realistic man, who advertised "promotion in depth," foresaw at least a two-year life to the market. It was just the kind of deal the Colonel loved, and one he knew how to exploit the hell out of both for himself and his boy. In a *Look* magazine article about the Elvis Presley phenomenon, the author, Chester Morrison, quoted the title song of the movie and then remarked:

> There are two grown men who love him true and tender and hope that they will never have to let him go. They are the two who operate the Great Elvis Presley industry, and, Lord, how the money rolls in! . . . Hank Saperstein and Tom Parker are a great pair. They are sardonically gay, as Fred Allen used to be. The Colonel sometimes drops absent-minded ashes from his good cigar onto the folds of his plumpness. Hank is younger, handsomer, taller and he doesn't sag any-

> where. Both of them have a reverence for money and work hard for it. But both of them give the impression that if they didn't get any fun out of making money, the hell with it.

The Colonel was a former carnival man, Morrison noted, who "is happy, but he is certainly not unsophisticated, and he has seen the Tattooed Lady. He genuinely loves those people who come to the carnival, because every last one of them buys a ticket. He is writing an autobiography that should find a place in every home. He calls it *The Benevolent Con Man,* but his alternate and better title is *How Much Does It Cost If It's Free?*"

NATALIE ARRIVED for her Memphis visit on Halloween night. Elvis and Nick picked her up at the airport and showed her the sights, then took her back to the house, where Elvis promised the fans they would come out again in half an hour to talk and sign autographs. After supper they drove around town some more, got ice cream cones, and ended up at the Chisca, where they went up to the "magazine floor" (the mezzanine, in other words) to see Dewey. By the time they came out, hundreds of fans had collected in the street, and they were barely able to recapture the white Lincoln.

The next day Elvis bought himself a new motorcycle, and that night they went for a long ride, with Natalie clinging to Elvis and Nick "chugging along behind," the newspapers reported, on Elvis' old Harley. In the next few days Elvis took Natalie on the standard tour: she met his family, she met his friend George Klein, they drove by Humes, they went out to the Fairgrounds and stopped by Sun, he introduced her to a few of his policemen friends, they even stopped in to see Bob Neal at the new Stars Inc. management firm he had set up in partnership with Mr. Phillips. To Natalie, who was accustomed to celebrity, it was both an eye-opening, and a somewhat numbing, experience. It was, she told a reporter some years later, "like a circus come to town the minute I got off the plane. A mob of people stood outside his house night and day. Someone sold hot dogs and ice cream from a wagon. . . . When we went out on Elvis' motorcycle, we had an instant motorcade behind us. I felt like I was leading the Rose Bowl parade." Elvis was sweet, she told friends and reporters alike, but, she suggested, maybe there was such a thing as being too sweet. According to her sister, Lana, she called home in the middle of her visit and begged her mother to get her out of this. "He can sing," Natalie confided to Lana afterward, as recorded in Lana's memoir, "but he can't do much else." On Saturday Nick and Natalie headed back to Hollywood, after a visit on Natalie's part of only four days.

For Elvis, though, it was good just to have some time to himself. Colonel thought it would be something like two months before they started work on the new picture, and with *Love Me Tender* scheduled to open in ten days, on November 15 in New York, and the day before Thanksgiving in Memphis and everywhere else, he was perfectly happy to be able to concentrate on more mundane matters, like the Beginner Driver Range, "the nation's first police-sponsored behind-the-wheel driving school," whose opening Elvis attended on Monday, November 5, as a past finalist in the annual Road-E-O safe-driving contest for teenagers four years before. " 'If there is anything I can do to set an example, I want to do it,' Presley said to the new class of 31 students, mostly teenagers. No one shrieked or swooned," reported the *Press-Scimitar*. "They did look serious and determined. . . . It was a community project, designed to make Memphis a safer place to live."

Meanwhile, Cliff Gleaves was back in town after his fantasy trip to New York, a tale so improbable that even Cliff, who was accustomed to putting an optimistic spin on the truth, with his DJ's wit, comedian's flair, and philosopher's penchant for positive thinking, was having a difficult time believing it. When he got back, he couldn't seem to run into Elvis again, though, let alone find the opportunity to thank him. He went by the Chisca on a number of occasions, but he never saw him there. He missed him the whole time that Natalie was in town. He started showing up at WMC every afternoon, just as George Klein was finishing his shift as host of *Rock 'N' Roll Ballroom,* and dropped broad hints to George about getting together with Elvis sometime. But while George sprang for dinner almost every night, he never picked up on the hints.

There was another guy, a big fat jolly young fellow named Lamar Fike, who had started hanging around George lately, too, and was interested in getting into radio. He drove a brand-new '56 Chevy, talked like he knew everything about everything, and was desperate to meet Elvis. Cliff was on the verge of telling him to get lost when Lamar happened to flash his billfold, and Cliff, always quick on his feet, said, "Yeah, man, I guess you can come to dinner with us." After that he let Lamar bug them for radio pointers on a regular, paying basis, which didn't get either one of them any closer to Elvis, and Cliff finally came to the conclusion that if this thing was going to happen, it was just going to have to happen on its own. He was nearly at the point of giving up hope, and his room at the YMCA, when he finally ran into Elvis again, and this time turned out to be the charm.

He was on his way to the Chisca on a Monday night, ostensibly to see Dewey, when he saw a pink Cadillac coming toward him on Union. "Hey, Cliff, follow me," Elvis said, leaning out the window and leading him to Madison Cadillac, just a few blocks away.

"At that point my life changed. At that point I made a 180-degree turn with old Elvis. Understand: we pull in. He says, 'I got this car for my mother, and she doesn't have a license, and I don't want to touch it anymore, but I like to keep it tuned. I just bought an El Dorado, but they still got the masking tape on it, and I want to know if you'll do me a favor.' I said, 'Elvis, are you serious?' I had already thanked him for the weekend, and he just said, 'If you can't have fun, what is it? If enjoyment is not in there, what is it worth?'

"He said, 'Cliff, can you take me a couple of places?' Well, no sense in going into the petty details, but about five-thirty he says, 'Cliff, I'd like to invite you home to meet my parents. I'd like you to have dinner with us.' Boom! I said, 'Great!' and we drive out to Audubon Drive, where he lived. After dinner he said, 'Cliff, you know Red West?' I said, 'No, I don't.' He said, 'He was with me, and he joined the Marine Corps.' He said, 'I'm alone now.' He said, 'I like you, my mama and daddy like you' — you see, dinner is over, and we're in the living room now. 'I'm alone now, and I'd really like for you to be with me. When I invited you to New York, I really wasn't thinking that way.' I said, 'Elvis, I'll tell you what. I have obligations here and there.' I said, 'To do that, you know — the obligation factor, I really can't take that offer. I have to be a free agent, free spirit, I can't be obligated. But as a *friend* — that's a different ball game.'

"He said, 'You mean the only thing stopping you from joining me is that?' I said, 'That's about it.' He said, 'Cliff, let's go get your clothes.' That night I moved into my bedroom on Audubon Drive. Elvis' bedroom is down at the end, down the hallway is what they call Natalie's room, because that's where Natalie Wood stayed when she was there, and Elvis' mother and father are at the other end of the house. Three bedrooms, two baths — no problem. I moved in bag and baggage. His mother said,

'That was Natalie's room, now it's yours.' From that point on, he always wanted me there."

Cliff found life with the Presleys utterly beguiling. Elvis, as he saw it, was "an innocent. He didn't know about the tricks, the 'worldly ways'; he operated on sheer instinct. Never was there any arrogance — he was simply not going to let people trying to get to him be denied. He did not have the 'informal schooling' of being out in the world too long. He wasn't out there just a little bit when he walked into Sun Records: only thing he knew was his parents' home to Sun to making money to fame. He had no introduction to the world." His parents? "Vernon was not an innocent, 'cause he'd been burned. Vernon was finely tuned to the world, a dollar was a dollar to Vernon, a quarter is a quarter. One night at dinner Elvis said, 'Daddy's a hard man, but you can't blame him. You got to know what happened to him.' Then they explained it all. Vernon said, 'Hey, Cliff, I offered to work as long as the man would let me work it off — but he refused.' He said, 'Cliff, that was hard.' "

Gladys, on the other hand, was simply proud of her boy — no more, and no less, than when he had won the singing prize at the fair. "It wasn't that [she knew that] he was going to come along and tear the world up, it was just something that was in him. Vester came along and taught him a couple of chords, nobody paid much attention, it was just an isolated event, but she was very proud of him. She said, 'I just hope to hell we all live.' 'Cause it upset her, she was not thrilled with his big-time success, she was not carried away by the fame, the only thing that counted was Elvis."

At night they would frequently sit around listening to gospel music: the Blackwood Brothers, Sister Rosetta Tharpe, the Clara Ward Singers, the Statesmen Quartet — Elvis would always point to the singing of Jake Hess as they listened. Often he would sit at the organ and sing the songs himself, as Mr. and Mrs. Presley nodded appreciatively. For Cliff it was something of an education, because though he considered himself a "spiritual" person, he had never heard this kind of music before. For Cliff it was something of a trial, too. There was no smoking or drinking allowed in the house, and Cliff was not by nature an abstemious person, but he abided by house rules. "Elvis did not want to be around people when they were drinking. He had tremendous willpower, and he just felt like people who were out of control — how many times did he say,

'Cliff, I just can't afford being around people who are not in control of themselves.' "

One night they were invited over for "cocktails" by a wealthy young couple with "old Memphis" roots who lived up the street. Frank Pidgeon, whose family owned the Pidgeon-Thomas Iron Company, had written the insurance on the house, and Betty Pidgeon was the granddaughter of E. H. "Boss" Crump, who had virtually ruled Memphis from his election as mayor in 1910 until his death in 1954. Elvis was reluctant to go at first — the neighbors had been unremitting in their rejection, he felt, not just of him and his family but of his fans. He could understand their being upset at the disruption which his presence had caused the once-quiet little street, and he had done everything he could to accommodate their concerns, but there had even been public discussion of buying the Presleys out, which Elvis had countered by offering to buy the neighbors out in turn. As one Memphian wrote to Elvis biographer Elaine Dundy, "From the point of view of the world I was born and raised in, the world of the country club etc., he was referred to . . . as an embarrassment."

Cliff recalled the social occasion vividly. "Elvis said, 'Mama, I don't want to go, these people got a lot of money, and I don't fit in, I don't feel comfortable, I just don't want to do it.' She said, 'Son, these people don't want anything from you. They've already made their mark in the world, and they are prominent people from two prominent families here — you know that she's a Crump. What they are doing is welcoming you to the neighborhood, that's all. You can't give them anything, they are just proud of you, another Memphian who is making his own mark in the world.' "

They drove the short distance up the street, arrived a little late, and declined the bourbon and sodas they were offered, taking Cokes instead to wash down their Cheez Whiz crackers. Elvis seemed "a little nervous at first" to Pallas Pidgeon, who was eight at the time, "but he was very nice, very friendly and accommodating. Daddy asked if he would mind calling my father's first cousin, who lived in Plainfield, New Jersey, and she was a great fan of his. So we put the long-distance call through to her. Then we called my aunt, the youngest daughter of my grandparents, who were also there — she was at St. Catherine's School in Richmond, and her whole dorm went crazy. Then I asked him if he would mind calling my best friend, Louise, and he did the same thing. 'Louise, this is Elvis.' It was just incredible. Then we went on a tour of the house, and we went in the bedroom, he and Cliff and my mother and I, and I had a lot of stuffed animals on the bed, and he asked me when my birthday was, and he said he would send me a teddy bear, which he never did, but at least I could dream about it for a few months."

He was hurt that people judged him without knowing him, he told Marion Keisker one day when he stopped off at Sun. Mr. Phillips was busy a lot of the time — Johnny Cash was really hot now, and he was trying to get Carl back on track, and he had some new boys he was excited about — but Elvis always felt comfortable just stopping by and talking to Marion with the sun beating down on the blinds and the sights and sounds of a recording session coming through the window cut into the partition wall. He was still upset by that Jacksonville preacher who had been written up in *Life* magazine, he told her. "The only thing I can say is they don't know me."

As the date of the movie opening approached, he became more and more nervous, he felt increasingly on display, even in his own hometown. He finally took the Colonel's advice and got out of town for a little while, taking a vacation in Las Vegas, which saved him from having to make excuses when the reporters inevitably asked for his reaction to the reviews. It was all in keeping with the new management strategy of removing him from the public eye (the Colonel indicated that he might have to start charging reporters for interviews with Elvis soon), but at the same time it suited the very impulse that had led him to duck into the Suzore No. 2 the night that Dewey played his record for the first time.

In Vegas he was a celebrity among celebrities, and while his comings and goings were duly noted, it was from a distance, and with a casual disinterest, that left him pretty much on his own. He stayed at the New Frontier with his cousin Gene and attended all the shows. At the outset of his visit he dated Marilyn Evans, a dancer at the New Frontier, and invited her to come see him in Memphis in December. Then he met Dottie Harmony, a blond eighteen-year-old dancer from Brooklyn who had come to town to do a show at the Thunderbird and who had a girlfriend at the Frontier who was getting married. He kept sending emissaries over to her table to see if she would join him, but she told them to get lost "until all of a sudden I looked over, and there was Elvis on his knee, saying, 'Ma'am, you're the most beautiful woman I've ever seen in my life.

Would you have a drink with me?' " They started seeing each other almost exclusively, he came to see her show, "we spent almost every single day and evening together, except for when I worked." On November 14, the night before the *Love Me Tender* premiere in New York, he attended Liberace's opening at the Riviera and was introduced from the front row by the flamboyant entertainer, who was dressed in gold-sequined cutaway and matching pants. Afterward they exchanged jackets and instruments, cutting up for the cameras and singing and playing songs like "Girl of My Dreams" and "Deep in the Heart of Texas." "Elvis and I may be characters," commented Liberace, "but we can afford to be."

He and Dottie were totally caught up in each other. "He was just the nicest guy. He used to call his mother every night, and he made me call mine. He would tell me stories about how his family had all lived together in this one room and how his father used to pray every night that things would get better and how happy he was now that he could make it better for his parents. It's a little hard to believe, but we mainly just hung around. We would go out to the airport and watch the planes take off. One night we stopped and helped an old man change a tire. You know, we were just kids." They would fight on occasion, usually about the attention Dottie got from other men ("I knew everybody in town, and I think that bothered Elvis, but I said, 'What's good for the goose is good for the gander' "). Sometimes when they fought, Elvis would rip the phone out of the wall, "but next thing I knew it was always fixed again." One night they went to see Billy Ward and His Dominoes, one of Elvis' favorite r&b groups, whose young lead singer, an unbilled Jackie Wilson, in addition to reprising the various Dominoes hits ("The Bells," "Rags to Riches," "Have Mercy Baby"), also did an Elvis Presley medley in his act. He did "Hound Dog" and one or two other numbers that didn't impress their originator all that much, but then he did "Don't Be Cruel," slower and with more dramatic impact than the record, and Elvis went back to see him four nights running. Nick came into town to visit, and a couple of other Hollywood pals, too, but mostly it was just the two of them double-dating with Gene, and before Elvis left he made Dottie promise that she would spend Christmas with him in Memphis.

June had read about Natalie and him in the Memphis papers. He had telephoned her the day that Natalie left, but by the time she called back, Gladys said he was in Las Vegas and she wasn't sure when he'd be home.

The two of them had a nice long chat anyway, but Elvis didn't call when the movie opened, he missed her birthday on November 19, and she was less and less inclined to blame it on the Colonel.

The movie premiered with great hoopla on the fifteenth. There were fifteen hundred teenagers lined up when the doors opened at the New York Paramount at 8:00 A.M. for the first show, and there would have been more in attendance if truant officers hadn't combed the lines. When the film opened on November 21 at Memphis' Loew's State and 550 other theaters across the country, it did record-breaking business and by the end of the month was reported by *Variety* to be enjoying "sock grosses," which "underscored the need for the industry to develop players and subject matter to bring out the juvenile audience sector." It outperformed Marilyn Monroe's earlier *Bus Stop* and *The Seven Year Itch* in the same or similar locations, was running neck and neck with *Giant* and *The Ten Commandments,* which opened around the same time, and, it was reported, the concession business was "astounding."

The reviews were for the most part extremely condescending, if occasionally granting Elvis a certain measure of grudging respect. *Time* was particularly derisive, asking, "Is it a sausage?" of the new, sleekly packaged Hollywood image, while the *New York Times* gave Elvis backhanded credit for failing to recognize the film's limitations and providing an animated performance in the midst of a lusterless vehicle. "Richard Egan is virtually lethargic as the brother who comes home from war," Bosley Crowther wrote, "and Debra Paget is bathed in melancholia," while "Mr. Presley . . . goes at it as though it were 'Gone With the Wind.' " Perhaps the most interesting review appeared in *The Reporter,* which led an all-out assault on popular culture with a vilification of Elvis Presley ("Presley resembles an obscene child") and his so-called "music" (a "vacillation between a shout and a whine") but posed the pertinent question: "Who is the new hero? How does he look, move, talk and dress?" And went on to answer it by comparing Elvis with Brando and James Dean, and characterizing the new hero as possessing

> mannerisms by Brando out of the Actor's Studio. . . . First of all he does not walk: he slouches, ambles, almost minces. His hand gestures are all tentative, incomplete, with arms out in front as though he were feeling his way along a wet-walled underground passageway, or folded back against the body as though he were warding off a blow.

> . . . The new hero is an adolescent. Whether he is twenty or thirty or forty, he is fifteen and excessively sorry for himself. He is essentially a lone wolf who wants to belong.

The Colonel's only public comment was his advice to theater operators to be sure to empty the house after every matinee showing. Otherwise, the Colonel said, Elvis' fans would stock up on food and camp out in the theater all day, thereby depriving theater owners of a valuable source of revenue.

Elvis himself was embarrassed, according to Cliff, both by the inadequacy of his own performance and by the reaction of his fans. " 'I'll never make it,' he said, 'it will never happen, because they're never going to hear me 'cause they're screaming all the time.' He really meant that." At the same time he was what he had always wanted to be: a movie star. Critics might tear him apart, he told reporters at the Ed Sullivan news conference just two and a half weeks before the movie's opening, and if they did he might have to rethink his approach, but he could see a lifetime career in the movies, long after he had stopped singing. "I'm not going to quit," he said, "and I'm not going to take lessons because I want to be me."

WITH B. B. KING AT THE WDIA GOODWILL REVUE, DECEMBER 7, 1956.
(ERNEST WITHERS. MIMOSA RECORDS PRODUCTIONS INC. / MICHAEL OCHS ARCHIVES)

THE END OF SOMETHING

IT WAS A TUESDAY AFTERNOON in early December. Cliff and Elvis were cruising down Union Avenue with Marilyn Evans, the dark-eyed dancer from Las Vegas whom he had dated before meeting Dottie Harmony. As they drove by 706, it looked, in the words of Marion Keisker, like a "chicken coop nested in Cadillacs." There was obviously a session going on, and on an impulse Elvis wheeled the car around and parked out in front of the studio. Once inside, he found Carl Perkins and his brothers Jay and Clayton, with "Fluke" Holland on drums and a new blond-haired boy on piano, working on a couple of Carl's new tunes. The session quickly broke up — they were just listening to playbacks at this point anyway — and, after general greetings all around, Mr. Phillips introduced him to the piano player. His name was Jerry Lee Lewis, he was from Ferriday, Louisiana, and he had a new single just out, his first on the Sun label — but, it turned out, he didn't really need much of an introduction, he wasn't shy in the least. As a matter of fact, he would have talked Elvis' ear off if Elvis hadn't already been talking with Carl and Mr. Phillips about Hollywood and Las Vegas and the new RCA single that was coming out in January: the B side would definitely be Stan's song "Playing for Keeps," on which Mr. Phillips had the publishing. Sam was pleased to hear that, and Elvis and Carl were enjoying catching up on old times, but the piano player was getting impatient with all this small talk — he just wanted to get back to the piano.

Eventually a jam session did develop. They fooled around with "Blueberry Hill" and "My Isle of Golden Dreams," and then someone provided an acoustic guitar out of the trunk of his car, and Elvis began to warble "You Belong to My Heart," a 1945 Bing Crosby hit from the Disney animated feature *The Three Caballeros*, rolling his *r*s in the Latin manner with exaggerated, eye-rolling passion. Next they launched into a bunch of spiritual numbers with Carl and the band pitching in and the new boy echoing Elvis high-spiritedly on every number and taking the lead on some. "This is fun!" says Jerry Lee. "You ought to get up a quartet," someone suggests, and a woman — maybe Marilyn — requests "Farther Along" from this "Rover Boys trio." Elvis does imitations of Bill Monroe, and of Hank Snow singing an Ernest Tubb song. Has he heard the new Chuck Berry single? someone asks him. Yes, he likes "Brown Eyed Handsome Man" better than "Too Much Monkey Business," and without further ado they are off and running on that. Carl has just gotten back from being out on tour with Berry, he says. Man, he just set out behind the stage and — he shrugs helplessly at Berry's prolific genius and creativity. Which just sets them off again on another pass at "Brown Eyed Handsome Man."

Almost from the start Sam had the tape recorder turned on. He was all set up for a session anyway, and he realized immediately that this could be an historic occasion. "I told Jack Clement [who was in the control room, too], 'Man, let's just record this. This is the type of feel, and probably an occasion, that — who knows? — we may never have these people together again.' " He didn't fail to recognize the potential for publicity either, and he called Johnny Cash, currently Sun's biggest star, who showed up briefly with his wife, and Bob Johnson at the *Press-Scimitar,* who came by with a UP reporter and a photographer in tow. "I never had a better time than yesterday afternoon," wrote Johnson, a little disingenuously, in the paper the next day, as he added: "If Sam Phillips had been on his toes, he'd have turned the recorder on when that very unrehearsed but talented bunch got to cutting up. That quartet could sell a million." Phillips himself sent the write-up out to DJs with a note headlined "Our Only Regret!," the regret being that "each and every one of you wonderful D.J.'s who are responsible for these boys being among the best known and liked in show business could not be here *too!*"

If they had, they would have been amazed. "I heard this guy in Las Vegas," Elvis reports to his captivated audience, "there was a guy out there [with Billy Ward and His Dominoes] that was doing a takeoff on me — 'Don't Be Cruel.' He tried so hard till he got much better, boy, much better than that record of mine." There are polite murmurs of demurral. "No, wait now, I mean, he was real slender, he was a colored guy, he got up there and he'd say —" And here Elvis begins to perform the song in imitation of the singer imitating him. "He had it a little slower than me. . . . He got the backing, the whole quartet, they got the feeling on it, he was hitting it, boy. Grabbed that microphone, and on the last note he went all the way down to the floor, man, looking straight up at the ceiling. Man, he was cutting out. I was under the table when he got through singing. . . . And all the time he was singing, them feet was going in and out, both ways, sliding like this. . . . He's a Yankee, you know," said Elvis, remarking with bemusement upon the singer's strange pronunciation of "tellyphone" and coming back to the song yet again, even trying "Paralyzed," the Otis Blackwell song he had recorded in September, in similar fashion. "All he needed was a building or something to jump off of," says someone, won over by the sheer enthusiasm of Elvis' description. "That's all he needed," agrees the unknown singer's foremost admirer, "that would have made a big ending."

They sang "No Place Like Home" and "When the Saints Go Marching In" with the blond-haired boy on piano ("The wrong man's been sitting here at this piano," said Elvis when Jerry Lee took his place. "Well, I been wanting to tell you that all along," responded Jerry Lee without missing a beat. "Scoot over!") and "Is It So Strange?," the number Faron Young had given him some months ago which he and June had taken as a twisted symbol of their love. He didn't know if he was going to record it, though, he said; Faron didn't want to give him any of the publishing. When he sang "That's When Your Heartaches Begin," the song he had cut in this very studio the summer after his senior year, he told everyone, "I recorded the sonofabitch and lost the dub on it." He thought it could still be a hit, he said. With the right arrangement and the same kind of deep baritone voice that had been featured in the background of the Ink Spots' original, he thought it could still sell.

Throughout the session people drift in and out, the guitar is passed around, while Snearly Ranch Boys piano player and sometime session musician Smokey Joe Baugh contributes his gravelly comments and harmonies. You can hear comments by unidentified women and children, doors slamming, and musicians departing (the Perkins brothers exit fairly early in the proceedings), which leaves a clear field for singers and piano pickers almost exclusively. At the end of the day Jerry Lee Lewis finally gets a chance to really show off his wares as he storms through both sides of his new single as well as "You're the Only Star in My Blue Heaven" and "Black Bottom Stomp." "That's why I hate to get started in these jam sessions," says Elvis affably, "I'm always the last one to leave. . . .

"Jerry, it was good to have met you," he says to the brash newcomer, inviting him to come out to the house sometime, while good-byes are being exchanged all around. "It was totally extemporaneous," said Sam Phillips, the proud progenitor, "everything was off mike, if it was on mike it was by accident — I think this little chance meeting meant an awful lot to all those people, not because one was bigger than another, *it was kind of like coming from the same womb.*" "I never saw the boy more likeable," wrote Bob Johnson, "than he was just fooling around with those other fellows who have the same interests he does."

Three nights later Elvis was among other fellows with much the same interests, but under entirely different, if no less newsworthy, circumstances. WDIA, which had been broadcasting since 1949 with programming aimed exclusively at Memphis' black population, but with white management, news announcers, and engineers, had established a Goodwill Fund almost from its inception with the goal of helping "needy Negro children." Each year the station put on a revue on the first Friday of December, which for the last several years had taken place at Ellis Auditorium. In 1956 the headliners were Ray Charles, former WDIA disc jockey B. B. King, the Magnificents, and the Moonglows, along with a gospel segment that featured the Spirit of Memphis Quartet and the Happyland Blind Boys. Each year's show featured a theme acted out by the current DJ staff, and this year's had to do with a contingent of "hep Choctaws," led by Chief Rockin' Horse (Rufus Thomas) and his bride, Princess Premium Stuff (Martha Jean the Queen), who are determined to introduce rock 'n' roll to a recalcitrant, and hopelessly square, rival tribe.

One of the engineers at the station, Louis Cantor, who doubled as a part-time gospel and r&b announcer under the names of Deacon and Cannonball Cantor, had graduated from Humes a year ahead of Elvis and George Klein and was a fellow student with Klein at Memphis State, as well as a fellow congregant at Temple Beth El Emeth. Wouldn't it be something, the powers that be at WDIA speculated, if they could get Elvis Presley to make a guest appearance on the show? Cantor approached Klein, who spoke to Elvis about it. He would be thrilled, he said, to put in an appearance, but he couldn't, of course, perform — that was something the Colonel had drilled into him since the very beginning of their association.

He and George showed up on the night of the show and stood quietly in the wings as some of his biggest heroes appeared onstage. Ray Charles sang "I Got a Woman" to Princess Premium Stuff; Phineas Newborn, Sr., led an all-star pit band dressed in Indian costumes of its own; and the ubiquitous Professor Nat D. Williams, master of ceremonies both here and at the amateur talent shows at the Palace Theatre as well as a popular columnist in the Negro press, crowned the station's "Miss 1070," as he did every year. "I was fourteen," said Carla Thomas, Rufus' daughter, a member of the highly disciplined Teen Town Singers, who sang backup for many of the singers on the show and had a performing spot of their own, "and I told my girlfriend, 'That's Elvis Presley back there in the wings.' We were on the completely other side, but I could see it was Elvis. She said, 'That's not Elvis Presley, he's not on the show.' I said, 'I know.' He was just watching from the wings. They didn't announce him until the very end, because they didn't want everybody to get carried away, and when they did and he came out and did his little 'How you doing?' everybody said, 'More! Do a little something for us.' So he did a little shake, and he tore everybody up."

"I told them, If you put Elvis into the front of the show, the show is over," said Carla's father, Chief Rockin' Horse for this evening, "so they took me at my word and put Elvis on near the end. I took Elvis onstage by the hand, I had this great big headdress with all the feathers, and when I took Elvis out there and he did that little wiggle that they wouldn't let him do on television, the crowd just went crazy. They stormed all backstage, beating on the doors and everything!"

After the show was over he stood backstage talking quietly and having his picture taken with B.B. and Miss Claudia Marie Ivy, the newly crowned WDIA queen. "To all who were in earshot," reported the *Tri-State Defender* to its black constituency proudly, "Presley was heard telling King, 'Thanks, man, for the early lessons you gave me.' Arthur Godfrey would surely call that 'humility.' "

"He stayed around a long time after the show," said Carla. "My sister Vaneese and I had our pictures taken with him, and there was an old piano backstage and he played some little runs on it. The audience was gone, and there were just the people getting dressed, and finally the stage manager said, 'All right now, y'all got to go.' He stayed that long, and we were just having a lot of fun. I remember *that* Elvis."

The accounts in the Negro press in succeeding weeks and months were just as positive, with one exception. Various reports pointed out that Elvis freely acknowledged not only his debt to B.B. but, implicitly, to black music in general, and the *Memphis World* cited an account of six months earlier that had Elvis "crack[ing] Memphis segregation laws [on June 19] by attending the Fairgrounds Memphis amusement park on East Parkway, during what is designated as 'colored night.' " For the most part there was little question that he was a hero in the black community. Nat D. Williams alone demurred. In his column in the December 22 issue of the *Pittsburgh Courier*, he wrote:

> Maybe it's the Indigo Avenue's blase blues sophistication, native ignorance of the important, or just pur-dee meanness, but ordinarily nobody generally excites Beale Streeters enough to cause them to cue up to buy tickets or crash lines for autographs. . . . But Elvis Presley has 'em talking. And they ain't talking about his "art." You see, something happened the other night that the average Beale Streeter doesn't altogether dig or appreciate.

What the average Beale Streeter didn't dig or appreciate, Nat D. went on, appeared to be a variation on the same thing that so disturbed the white middle-class (and middle-aged) mainstream.

> A thousand black, brown and beige teen-age girls in the audience blended their alto and soprano voices in one wild crescendo of sound that rent the rafters . . . and took off like scalded cats in the direction of Elvis. It took some time and several white cops to quell the melee and protect Elvis. The teen-age charge left Beale Streeters wondering: "How come cullud girls would take on so over a Memphis white boy . . . when they hardly let out a squeak over B. B. King, a Memphis cullud boy?" . . . But further, Beale Streeters are wondering if these teen-age girls' demonstration over Presley doesn't reflect a basic integration in attitude and aspiration which has been festering in the minds of most of your folks' women folk all along. Huhhh?

Just six days later, on December 13, Hal Kanter, the screenwriter and director for *Lonesome Cowboy*, Elvis' first Hal Wallis production, which was scheduled to start shooting in mid January, flew into town. Kanter, a thirty-seven-year-old native of Savannah, had started out writing comedy skits in the pioneer days of TV, worked on a couple of Bob Hope movies, directed television's top-rated *George Gobel Show*, and most recently written screenplays for Tennessee Williams' *Rose Tattoo* and Dean Martin and

Jerry Lewis' *Artists and Models* for Hal Wallis — but this would mark his celluloid directorial debut. Elvis was slated to make his final appearance on the Louisiana Hayride two days later, the charity performance at Hirsch Coliseum that the Colonel had worked out back in April (along with the ten-thousand-dollar buyout) so as to free him of all contractual obligations, and Wallis thought it would be a good idea for Kanter to get a sense of the flavor of his star performer's life, since *Lonesome Cowboy* was intended to be something of a rock 'n' roll biopic.

Elvis met Kanter at the airport with Cliff and Gene and Freddy Bienstock, too, the dapper twenty-eight-year-old Hill and Range representative with the pronounced Viennese accent. Bienstock wasn't quite sure what he was doing there, except that he sensed that Elvis was a little nervous about Kanter coming to visit his home and he wanted to make an impression on the "Hollywood director." The first thing he did once they got to the house was to put Kanter in the same vibrating chair in which he had installed Bienstock upon *his* arrival, flipping the switch that set the chair in motion without any warning, which gave Kanter something of a surprise. Then he proudly showed off the house before his mother announced it was time for dinner. They had fried chicken and okra and greens, but Alberta, the maid, had forgotten to put any water on the table, and Kanter was parched, so he asked if he could please have some water. Elvis, being, naturally, a little embarrassed, "started screaming for the maid," Freddy recalled, "and he yells 'Alberta, some water please!' So she comes in with a pitcher of water and puts it in the middle of the table, but she didn't bring any glasses. So Kanter was looking at the water, and Elvis screams, 'Alberta, you forgot the glasses!' And Kanter says, 'It's all right, a straw will do.' Which I thought was very funny — but Elvis resented it. He didn't take to strangers easily, and later on in the evening, when I was getting ready to go back to New York, he came to me and said, 'Listen, man, you got to come with me [to Shreveport]. This director, I don't really know how to approach him — he's supposed to be directing my next movie, and he turns out to be a fucking comedian!' "

Things weren't beyond salvaging, though — Elvis was simply embarrassed, and Kanter was understandably feeling his way. After dinner they sat around in the recreation room, shot some pool, and talked about the movie. Hal Wallis had specifically enjoined the director from bringing a script, but after Elvis had expounded on his theory of screen acting (the ones who lasted were the ones who didn't smile much), Kanter hastened to reassure him that this wasn't just another "jolly" film where Elvis would sit around grinning all the time; in fact he wouldn't have to smile at all if he didn't really want to. You know, Elvis is a really good actor, Gene volunteered to Kanter. I'm sure he is, said Kanter agreeably. He had seen the screen test and he thought it was very good. " 'Man, that screen test ain't nothin'. You oughta hear him do his piece. Elvis, do that piece of yours for him.' Elvis said, 'Naw, I don't want to, I don't —' He said, 'Go ahead, do the piece.' I said, 'What piece are you talking about?' He said, 'Oh, it's a little something I learned.' And I said, 'What is it?' He said it was General MacArthur's speech to Congress, his farewell address. I said, 'Why did you learn that?' He said, 'I don't know. I just wanted to see if I could memorize it, and I did.' "

The next day Elvis gave Kanter a tour of Memphis, and that night they left for Shreveport in the Lincoln, with Scotty and Bill driving the instruments in the big yellow Cadillac limo. Kanter rode with Elvis in the front seat, while cousins Gene and Junior and the Colonel's brother-in-law, Bitsy Mott, rode in the back. At one point everybody was asleep except Elvis and the director, "and we passed a dog, an old dog howling in the night, and he said how much he envied that dog. That dog had a life of his own. He said, 'He goes out at night, and he's doing this, and he's doing that, and nobody knows what he's up to, but he's having more fun — and when the sun comes up he's back under the front porch, just thinking, and nobody knows the life he's been living during the night.' "

They pulled in to Shreveport at 5:00 A.M. and registered at the Captain Shreve, where the fans were already gathered in force and making enough noise that Elvis had to stick his head out of his room window to ask them to please let him get some sleep. "He awoke in late afternoon and breakfasted with two travelling companions," wrote Kanter in an article entitled "Inside Paradise," which was published in *Variety* some three weeks later. The story bore no specific reference to Elvis Presley, but it could have been about no one else, starting with its striking lead about "the young man with the ancient eyes and the child's mouth . . . [who] awoke from the nightmare of poverty to find the brilliant sun of Fame suddenly burst in his eyes. . . .

> The lobby of the hotel had been swarming with camera-equipped hordes waiting for his brief flight to the auditorium; police had been detailed to keep order; one was posted at his door in the hallway. . . .

Now, the hours drag by for the young man. He reads a magazine, plays some records, chats with his travelling companions, looks over the newspapers, signs a few autographs for the hotel manager. Now it is time to dress. He takes his time, stretching out every movement to consume more minutes, to eat away the hour remaining.

On schedule the assistant manager arrives with the two burly police who escort him to the waiting patrol car. Down the service elevator, through the kitchen, into the alley where the patrol car hums, poised for immediate flight. . . .

Another squad of police wait at the stage entrance of the auditorium, leaning heavily against the throng of fans straining for a glimpse of their hero. A shout goes up as the car wheels into view. It turns into screams, high-pierced, splitting the night air, beseeching, fanatic, as he leaps from the car and hurdles himself past clutching hands into the comparative safety of the auditorium.

Backstage there are milling scores who want to slap his back, shake his hand, "remember me" him. Then the reporters, the photographers, the disk jockeys with their tape-recorders, city officials, civic dignitaries, fan club presidents, business associates. Talk. Laugh. Shake. Smile. Pose. Answer. Listen. Stand. Sit. Walk. See. Sign. Hear. Acknowledge. Deny.

A nerve-shattering hour and then the moment to appear onstage. The introduction is drowned by the shout that goes up at the merest hint he is next on the bill. The shrill, deafening, roof-lifting screams continue.

"That's the night my car got stomped in," said Horace Logan, the head of the Hayride, who introduced Elvis wearing his trademark Stetson hat and pearl-handled six-guns. "I parked it right behind the dressing room behind the Coliseum, and the little old girls stomped the roof in standing on top of it trying to see Elvis. That was the night they had roped off the front of the stage, about twenty-five feet. Nobody was supposed to get down there, and when we got there, they were jammed up against the stage. And the fire chief said, 'Get them to move back or there is no show.' Well, you're talking about eight thousand people on the lower floor, they had to move their chairs back, all eight thousand of them would have had to move. Now how am I going to do that? I told the fire chief, I said, 'I'll tell them there is not going to be any show, but I'm going to tell them who canceled it — and they'll kill you!' Then I got an inspiration. We had some kids out there in iron lungs, and I told them, 'Folks, I'm sorry to have to do this, but these young people over here in the iron lungs are the only ones I'm going to allow down here. Every one of you has got to back up and move over, so we can put those kids in the front.' And they did it."

The show itself lasted for about half an hour, and there was screaming from start to finish. Hal Kanter, who had admittedly come to scoff, came away a true believer. When he had driven out to the Coliseum earlier in the day with Bill, the fans had converged on the car, thinking it was Elvis', and he thought he was going to be torn apart. Then, after they realized their mistake, he saw something he could scarcely believe. "I saw a young girl open her purse and take out a Kleenex, and she wiped her hand on the car, took some dust, put it in the Kleenex and folded it and put it back in the purse. I thought, 'My God, I've never seen any kind of devotion like this anywhere, about anything.' "

At the show that night he saw further evidence of this same strange sense of almost trancelike absorption. He saw a young girl who looked as if she were about to strangle herself by swallowing her hand. "She appeared to have her hand in her mouth all the way down to her wrist, and I was wondering, how can a little girl like this get her whole hand down her throat? And then at one point she pulled her hand out of her mouth, and I found out she didn't have a hand at all. She was just sucking on the stump. And I thought, 'God, I've got to get that in the picture!' " He saw twins clapping to the music, one twin using her left hand, the other using her right. Most of all, he saw a kind of mass hysteria, and a mass adulation, that he had never seen before or since. "I'm a man who saw Al Jolson on the stage, and I never saw anything like the reception that Al Jolson got until Elvis Presley — and he made Al Jolson seem like a passing fancy."

Nobody had seen anything like it before. If there had been any doubt that Elvis Presley had outgrown the Hayride, that doubt was now erased. It was, in a way, the end of the Hayride itself. Though it would limp along for another few years, how could it follow an act like this? Webb Pierce had succeeded Hank Williams, Slim Whitman and Faron Young had succeeded Webb Pierce, and Elvis Presley had succeeded them all — but who was going to succeed Elvis Presley?

Backstage there was an uproar of activity. Paul Kallinger from 150,000-watt station XERF in Mexico, which broadcast unimpeded, and essentially unregulated, just across the border from Del Rio, Texas, got Tillman Franks to introduce him, but Elvis spent at least an equal amount of time with Tillman's daughter, Darlene. Even Sandi Phillips, a reporter for the Broadmoor Junior High School student newspaper, got an interview. She was there with a group of girls from Broadmoor, and they all went backstage after the show. "I said I was a reporter for the *Bulldog Bark*, and there were all these guards, and they weren't going to let me in, and then all of a sudden this man says, 'Let her in,' *and it was him* — I'm getting goose bumps just telling this — and he said, 'Hey, little lady, you want an interview or something?' Something like that. And his hair was flopping around, and he was sweating, and he had a towel around his neck, and I had a little pad and pencil and I was wearing jeans and a Levi shirt and I had a ponytail, and I asked him a few questions (who knows what in hell I asked him?), and he answered whatever I asked, and he kissed me on the cheek, and I remember going out into the hall and all my girlfriends were just screaming at the top of their lungs and I just fell into their arms and, of course, I wouldn't let anyone touch me or wash that spot for weeks."

DOTTIE HARMONY FLEW IN from Hollywood the following week to celebrate Christmas with the Presley family. There had been a snowstorm, and her plane was delayed, so when she got to Memphis there was nobody at the airport to meet her, and she fell asleep disconsolately next to a heater. "The next thing I knew, I heard a whole bunch of kids shouting, and I open up my eyes, and there are a bunch of girls with banners that say, 'Go home, Dottie Harmony.' Then I heard screams, and in comes Elvis, who proceeds to pick me up and carry me out to the Lincoln, and we went home, where he introduced me to his mom and dad."

Dottie found Mrs. Presley a totally sympathetic figure — Gladys hugged her and made a big fuss over her — and while Vernon didn't show anywhere near as much personality, "they were very affectionate with each other, and he was very much so with Elvis, too." Within an hour of her arrival Gladys had bundled her up and given her a Christmas list. "Mind you, I'd never met any of the people on this list, and I don't know what I'm supposed to get them. I got the female list, and Elvis took the males, and we went to this big department store downtown, walked in, and he tells me, 'We'll meet here when we're done.' So I went about my business, bought gifts left and right, and I had a whole bunch of presents stacked up and waiting when all of a sudden I saw him running right past me, out the door to the car—'cause he had a whole bunch of fans running after him. About twenty minutes later, Cliff came back and got me, and we went home and had dinner."

Dottie spent a little over two weeks at the house, sleeping in Elvis' room while he stayed down the hall. He spoke to her parents in Brooklyn several times on the phone to reassure them that she was all right; they rode around town in matching motorcycle outfits, and he introduced her to his friends and showed her where he had grown up and gone to school. The Colonel came by on a number of occasions, but he barely acknowledged her presence. "He acted like I wasn't even there. I remember one time, he wanted to talk to them about some kind of money deal and he asked me to leave, and Elvis' mother said, 'Doroty'—she always called me Doroty—'stays right here. Doroty is part of the family.' He didn't like that one bit."

Mrs. Presley talked about her garden ("Doroty, we've got tomatoes as big as your two fists") and cooked black-eyed peas and greens and a coconut cake for Elvis almost every night. The fan magazines had a field day, but it wasn't, said Dottie, "anything like you might think. We used to read the Bible every night, if you can believe that—he used to read aloud to me and then talk about it. He was very religious—there was nothing phony about that at all. At six o'clock at night he made me go out and sign autographs with him, which I thought was so ridiculous. I said, 'I mean, what do people want my autograph for, Elvis?' He said, 'Just sign it.' He said he wouldn't be where he was if it wasn't for his fans. He really felt that way."

Elvis tried to get Dottie to give up smoking ("I knew I didn't have to worry about that, because he promised to stop chewing his nails if I did"), and he lectured her frequently on the "many lives he had seen ruined by drink." One time she and Gladys managed to get him out of the house, "and we cracked a beer. One beer!" On Christmas Day they all exchanged gifts under a white nylon Christmas tree. Gladys wore her brocade dress and a red Santa hat, and there were pictures in the newspapers of Elvis and Dottie, of Elvis surveying his presents (including any number of stuffed animals and teddy bears), of Dottie opening *her* presents, even of a touch football game at the Dave Wells Community Center two days later, with Red home on leave and Elvis wearing tennis shoes and rolled-up dungarees, hair flopping across his forehead and a determined expression on his face.

June saw the pictures in the paper and fumed. "Here I am, I'm being good, I'm being faithful, I'm not doing anything — and I've had lots of offers to go out. And then Christmas Day we were home till about noon, but then we were invited to some friend's house. I even made myself a brand-new blue velvet dress to wear for Christmas Day, and I felt really pretty. I'm thinking, This is Christmas, and he's got to call. When I woke up on Christmas Day, I was thinking about Elvis Presley — but he wasn't thinking about me. Because Dottie Harmony was there. Well, that really clinched it for me, it really broke my heart, I had no idea it was all just this game. He called me afterwards and said that he had called and we didn't answer, and that's probably true, but right after that I met someone and started going out with him, and he just swept me off my feet, eased my heartache, and asked me to marry him, and I said yes."

Scotty and Bill saw the pictures, too, and it only reinforced their growing feeling that they were on the outside looking in. Christmas was a bleak season for them that year. Although they had worked a lot of dates the first half of the year, since August there had been no more than two weeks' worth of work, and this didn't add up to much on a $100-a-week retainer (even when they were working, they were earning $200 a week tops and were enjoined from making any product endorsements or taking any free goods). "We were broke, flat broke," said Scotty's wife, Bobbie. After living in Elvis' old house on Getwell for a few months, they had moved in with her three sisters and a brother-in-law in a big house on Tutwiler, near Sears, and Bobbie was having to hide money from Scotty in a jewelry box just to be sure to have enough to pay the bills. Scotty and Bill (and D.J., too, in a good-humored subsidiary role) gave an interview to the *Press-Scimitar* in mid December in which they spoke in only slightly veiled terms of their straitened financial and social circumstances. They didn't see as much of Elvis as they once had, they conceded — "just can't be that way." He was still fun to be around, though; "[he's] always got some jazz going, likes to keep up chatter and joking," said Bill. "I don't think anyone should criticize him until they try to put themselves in his shoes and figure out what they would do." They used to split the money three ways before D.J. came into the group, reported the newspaper, but "when [Elvis] hit the real big time, they realized that different financial arrangements would have [to be] made, and were happy that they came out of it as well as they did." The real purpose of their "press conference" was to announce that they had just been given permission by management (which explicitly did not permit them to work with anyone else or "appear as a unit without Elvis in between tours") to make a record of their own, an instrumental that RCA would put out sometime after the first of the year. They were very excited about this new opportunity. "We don't even know how they will title us yet," said Bill. "Maybe as 'Elvis' Boys.' "

ON JANUARY 4, 1957, Elvis' new single was released, and he reported for his pre-induction physical. He asked Dottie if she could stick around and go in with him, and she and Cliff accompanied him to the examination center at Kennedy Veterans Hospital, on Getwell, where he had performed in the rec room not long after his first record came out. Ordinarily there would have been forty or fifty men processed on any given day, but the army had decided that Elvis should be put through on an "off day," all by himself. No one was supposed to know about it (the notice had been telephoned, not mailed), but there was a legion of photographers and reporters waiting when they pulled up in the rain. Dottie waited in the car at first, then joined Cliff inside, and Elvis announced to them both with a broad smile that he thought he had passed the intelligence test. Then she flew back to California, and Elvis left for New York on the train later that evening to play *The Ed Sullivan Show* for the third and final time.

The Ed Sullivan appearance could best be described as the triumph of inclusion over exclusion, the boldfaced embrace and declaration of respectability that civilization inevitably has to offer. With the gold lamé vest that Barbara had given him for a Christmas present worn over the blue velvet blouse that he had worn for his appearance in Tupelo, Elvis looked something like a Middle Eastern pasha, while the Jordanaires, dressed in checked salesmen's sports jackets, gave their booster's all behind him. For his first segment he delivered an easygoing medley of his biggest records (it was not that they were any bigger in *size*, he hastened to kid his totally rapt audience, as per custom), concluding with a rendition of "Don't Be Cruel" that owed everything, from finger rolls to his pronunciation of "tellyphone" to the big pumped-up ending, to the performance by Jackie Wilson he had witnessed in Las Vegas. Then he did "Too Much" and "When My Blue Moon Turns to Gold Again," the lilting 1941 hit that he had included on his second album, and thanked his thoroughly mesmerized audience for the best Christmas he had ever had — and for the 282 teddy bears that they had sent him. After another break he came out again, this time dressed in one of his loudly tweedy sports jackets and, with eyes closed, straining up on his toes, he sang a song that Ed Sullivan introduced as "sort of in the mood that he'd like to create," the spiritual "Peace in the Valley."

"Elvis, ladies and gentlemen," said Ed, "inasmuch as he goes to the Coast now for his new picture, this will be the last time that we'll run into each other for a while, but I —" Screams from the audience. Elvis laughs. "Now wait a minute." Ed holds up his hand. "I wanted to say to Elvis Presley and the country that this is a real decent, fine boy, and wherever you go, Elvis, all of you . . . we want to say that we've never had a pleasanter experience on our show with a big name than we've had with you. So now let's have a tremendous hand for a very nice person." Elvis is clearly gratified and, with a generous gesture, includes both the band and the Jordanaires in his circle of acclaim, as Ed shakes the hand of each backup singer. There will be no more appearances on the show, the Colonel has made that clear by setting what amount to prohibitive terms for all three networks: if they want Elvis in the future, they will have to pay a $300,000 fee, which will cover two guest appearances and an hour-long special. But Ed's gesture does not seem to be motivated by the normal show business considerations; he appears genuinely taken with the young man. And Elvis for his part is just as genuinely thrilled — he says as much to friends and fellow musicians — to receive recognition and validation from someone so widely respected, so experienced in the business. "This is a nice boy, and I want you to know it," Ed repeated that same night in a television interview with Hy Gardner, on *Hy Gardner Calling!* "He could so easily have his head turned by all that's happened. But it hasn't. . . ."

By then, though, Elvis was already on the long train ride back home. He wanted to spend his twenty-second birthday with his mother and father before leaving for the Coast in a couple of days. On Tuesday he celebrated quietly at the house and made plans with his parents to join him in California several weeks later. The draft board announced that same day that he was an "A profile," which meant that he would be classified 1-A, or draftable, as soon as his local board received the report, though he would probably not be called up for six or eight months. It didn't matter, Elvis told reporters who telephoned, he was happy to serve, he would simply go whenever he was called. He knocked around Memphis for the next couple of days, got a haircut at Jim's Barber Shop, on the corner of Beale and Main, stopped by the police station just to shoot the bull (in December it had been reported that he told his "home town police friends" that he thought Debra Paget was the prettiest of the Hollywood stars, but Kim Novak was a good-looking girl with a good figure, and Rita Moreno really knocked him out), saw Dewey and George at their respective radio stations, and briefly dropped by the place that Dixie worked. She was married now, she told him. She had gotten married not long after the last time she had seen him with Nick. "Well, I'll see you around," he said, and then he was on the train to California with Cliff and Gene, stocked up with Reese's peanut butter cups and comic books and movie magazines, and looking forward to making what he felt would amount to his real movie debut, his first chance at a genuine starring role.

WITH YVONNE LIME, IN FRONT OF GRACELAND, EASTER WEEKEND, 1957.
(ROBERT WILLIAMS)

LOVING YOU

THE MOVIE HAD BEEN RETITLED *Loving You* (after a new Leiber and Stoller ballad of that name, expressly written for the picture) by the time that Elvis arrived in Los Angeles by train on January 11. It had been planned with all the characteristic care and attention to detail of a typical Hal Wallis production, with the casting of seasoned stars (Wendell Corey and Lizabeth Scott) who were unlikely to overwhelm the new "singing sensation," the secondary interest of another Hal Wallis discovery (eighteen-year-old Dolores Hart, née Hicks, whom Wallis was said to have found in a campus production of *Joan of Lorraine* just weeks before), colorful contract players like James Gleason in significant minor roles, a carefully prepared script, and an experienced studio crew. It was, in short, the kind of lighthearted, fresh-faced picture with which a major studio might have introduced an exciting new star twenty, or even five, years before, but it was worlds away from the flurry of rock 'n' roll exploitation features that had sprung up in the previous year to fill the void that *Variety* had pointed to in its review of *Love Me Tender*.

With a customary two-month studio shooting time and its newly commissioned score alone, *Loving You* would have differed substantially from *Rock Around the Clock* or *Don't Knock the Rock*, for example, the two 1956 quickie productions by exploitation master Sam Katzman which set a rock 'n' roll movie trend for even more rudimentary filmic exercises like *Rock, Rock, Rock* (filmed in less than two weeks) to follow. Each of these movies presented stars like Bill Haley and DJ Alan Freed who, in the face of adult opposition, conspire to put on a show that inevitably includes a panoply of rock 'n' rollers — from Little Richard, the Platters, and Fats Domino to such Las Vegas staples as the Treniers and Freddie Bell and the Bellboys — trotted out on a soundstage to lip-synch their latest hits.

What the Colonel and Hal Wallis had in mind was something quite different. Their idea, linked by a partnership of convenience and a shared canniness which had approached similar challenges and similar partnerships in the past, was to build a career that would last, a career that could survive musical trends, which inevitably come and go, while permitting an incandescent talent to continue to shine. In keeping with that goal, the Colonel knew, it was necessary to *distance* his boy from the hurly-burly; he was becoming increasingly concerned that the very controversy that had originally fueled Elvis' fame was now serving to limit it. He had worked hard to get his boy on Ed Sullivan and pointed with pride not only to the ratings, which clearly reflected a substantial, and substantially growing, adult audience, but to Sullivan's public endorsement and embrace — and he was now determined to work just as hard to achieve success in the movies.

The Colonel had always paid close attention to newspaper accounts and never failed to note criticism. In Elvis' case he had exploited it for a time, assuring RCA that he knew what he was doing and that, if they didn't like it, they could just step off the merry-go-round. Now it was time for them *all* to step off the merry-go-round. The criticism had simply become too intense, and it was becoming all too clear that rock 'n' roll now served as a lightning rod for a more and more sharply divided society. Denounced from the pulpit, derided in the press, increasingly linked to the race issue, and even subject to congressional hearings, the music was being used to stigmatize a generation. New York congressman Emanuel Celler, chairman of the Antitrust Subcommittee of the House Judiciary Committee, which was looking into the issue of "payola," declared that while "rock 'n' roll has its place [and has given] great impetus to talent, particularly among the colored people," the music of Elvis Presley and his "animal gyrations . . . are violative of all that I know to be in good taste."

To the Colonel it was all business. The attacks, the whipped-up emotion, the moral outrage — these were simply the actions of concerned businessmen, secular and ecclesiastic, determined to protect their investment in society. But the Colonel was determined to protect his investment, too, and to that end, without ever announcing his policy or spelling it out in specific detail, he was prepared to remove Elvis from the fray, he was committed to the idea of getting him off the road and out of the glare of needless, negative publicity. Elvis' business was communication, after all, and what better way to communicate with his audience all around the world than from the silver screen, where the image always flickered, the candle burned but never flamed — and fame, carefully nurtured, need never go away?

Meanwhile, Wallis, a veteran of seven of the first eight Martin and Lewis pictures and one of the most careful polishers of image and fame, however unlikely the source, was not about to overlook his own investment. He recognized in the Colonel a kindred spirit. "He was a genius," he said of Parker in a quote that might well have been applied to himself, "at getting every possible inch of financial mileage out of his astonishing protégé," and he was somewhat taken aback by Hal Kanter's rather cavalier take on the whole phenomenon. When Kanter, in recounting his experiences on the road, mentioned the girl he thought had swallowed her hand and suggested that perhaps they could find an attractive amputee from central casting, Wallis, who had thoroughly enjoyed the recitation up to that point, reacted with horror. "Oh God, you can't put *that* in the picture," he said. Leave the satire to Frank Tashlin, whose *The Girl Can't Help It* at Twentieth Century Fox was a clever takeoff on rock 'n' roll, with Edmond O'Brien, as a love-struck gangster, warbling songs like "Rock Around the Rock Pile" and Jayne Mansfield competing for attention with Gene Vincent and Little Richard. Hal Wallis was not simply in the business of exploiting fads, and he was as determined as Tom Parker to see to it that Elvis Presley's career was a long, and mutually profitable, one. As far as he was concerned, *Loving You* was going to be good entertainment, a typical name-above-the-title Hollywood production, with the best of the "new music," a clever (but not too clever) script, and a wholesome Hollywood patina to spread over any recognizable real-life details. It would be a picture you could take the whole family to.

NOT DUE AT THE PARAMOUNT STUDIO until the beginning of the week, Elvis reported to Radio Recorders at noon on Saturday, January 12, the day after his Hollywood arrival, for his first RCA session since September. He might more easily have recorded in Nashville during his time off in November and December, but he was adamantly opposed to working anymore under such uninspired conditions, unless he absolutely had to. With the second album out and nothing of any substance left in the can, Steve Sholes had been begging the Colonel for more studio time, and Parker had at last grudgingly conceded it to him on the two weekends that framed the start of the picture — *unless* Paramount should happen to change its plans. The principal purpose of the session was to record an extended-play "inspirational" album of four or five titles, something Elvis had publicly stated to be his ambition since his start in show business, along with a follow-up single to "Too Much," which was currently number two on the charts. In addition, it appeared that he would cut studio versions of several of the songs intended for the motion picture, so as to avoid the problem they had run into with *Love Me Tender* and be able to offer recording-quality sound on at least some of his RCA movie soundtrack releases.

Steve Sholes would be present, of course, but with Freddy Bienstock serving as de facto a&r man, he had been virtually relegated to a timekeeper's role, and he was fed up with being the constant butt of the Colonel's jokes. On principle he refused to address Parker by any other title than his Christian name. Still, he was a good company man, and that was the limit of his personal rebellion, until, on the second or third day of his visit, he told the Colonel that he wouldn't be able to join him and Bienstock and Tom Diskin for their daily breakfast meeting, due to an unavoidable early meeting at RCA. "That sonofabitch just doesn't want to have breakfast with us," declared the Colonel indignantly to Freddy Bienstock. The next morning Colonel had everyone there an hour and a half early, and they caught Sholes sneaking into the dining room. "Must have been a short meeting, Steve," remarked the Colonel caustically. "And, of course, Steve had to sit down at the table," recalled Bienstock, "and he hated all of it. He felt perhaps that he was too important an executive to play along with Colonel Parker. You know, the Colonel knew a lot of practical jokes and so forth, and he was a difficult man and had, always, all kinds of demands and requests, and Steve was just too impatient a man to put up with all of this."

The sessions themselves went smoothly enough. In addition to the religious and movie titles, Elvis recorded "That's When Your Heartaches Begin," the Ink Spots number which he had spoken of at the "Million-Dollar Quartet" session in December, as well as Otis Blackwell's latest, "All Shook Up," which Elvis thought was a good phrase for a refrain. For this he received a co-writing credit, his last (after the one third Mae Axton had given him for "Heartbreak Hotel" and the songwriter's share Hill and Range had insisted on for "Don't Be Cruel" and the *Love Me Tender* soundtrack) for a long while.

Hill and Range had its own deal in place by now, which got around the question of credit by simply getting a one-third cut-in from every songwriter who wanted to have his song recorded by Elvis Presley. What this meant was that the songwriter signed a document surrendering one third of his songwriter's royalties, which were paid by the record company to the song publisher. Once the publisher received them, they were split, under ordinary circumstances, 50–50 with the writer(s), but in this case one third was to be reserved out, to be "paid to Elvis Presley personally." As a result the writer, or writers, ended up getting 33⅓ percent, instead of 50 percent, of these "mechanical royalties." The performance royalties, on the other hand (which were calculated on the basis of live performance and jukebox and air play) were not affected. They were collected by the performing-rights societies ASCAP and BMI and paid directly to songwriter and publisher alike. The understanding was that this agreement would apply only to songs first recorded by Elvis Presley and only in their original version. This got around Elvis' embarrassment at taking credit for something he didn't do ("I've never written a song in my life," Elvis insisted vociferously on a number of public occasions, going on to declare in one interview, "It's all a big hoax . . . I get one third of the credit for recording it. It makes me look smarter than I am") while at the same time neatly sidestepping his contractual agreement with RCA to give the record company a reduced publishing rate on all songs authored, or coauthored, by him.

It would be virtually impossible at this point for a non–Hill and Range song to find its way to a session — unless, of course, Elvis introduced it, and then Hill and Range was bound to secure a substantial piece of the publishing before RCA might see fit to clear it for release. Still, the publishing house liked to cover all bets, and on the second day of the session, after Elvis had recorded "Peace in the Valley" and "Precious Lord, Take My Hand" — two staples of the Hill and Range religious catalogue by Thomas A. Dorsey, the father of modern black gospel music — there was a suggestion from Jean Aberbach, the younger of the two brothers who had founded the firm. Since Elvis was recording religious music anyway, offered the debonair forty-five-year-old Aberbach, why not try a holiday release like "Here Comes Peter Cottontail," with which the firm had had great success? Freddy, somewhat more attuned to the likes and dislikes of their successful young partner-client, was horrified, but Jean, for the first and only time in what would turn out to be a very long association, persisted. "I mean, you had to be mad to think Elvis is going to record 'Peter

Cottontail,' " recalled Freddy, "and I told him that, but Jean had no sense for songs and he insisted. So he brought a lead sheet down to Radio Recorders, and he put it on Elvis' stand while Elvis was having something to eat, and Elvis comes back and looks at it and said, 'Who brought that Bre'r Rabbit shit in here?' " Whereupon Jean conceded defeat ("Jean could laugh at himself, and when he saw Elvis' reaction, he died laughing — he just disappeared"), but he got the last laugh anyway when he snuck an instrumental version of the song onto the motion picture soundtrack.

On Monday Elvis reported to the studio for makeup and wardrobe tests. This would be his first Technicolor film, and he'd always thought that actors with dark hair, like Tony Curtis, lasted the longest and looked the best. The makeup man said that with his eyes he should photograph well with black hair, so they dyed it and Mr. Wallis liked the way it looked, and they went with the darker coloring. From the start he felt more comfortable on the Paramount lot than he had ever felt at Fox. Mr. Wallis treated him with affectionate respect, and it was clear he was not being seen as just the latest freak, to be trotted out and eyed suspiciously by the rest of the cast and crew until he had proved himself. Hal Kanter greeted him with the fond familiarity that only shared experience can bring, and he immediately took to the music director, an easygoing guy with a pencil-thin mustache named Charlie O'Curran, who was married to Patti Page (he had previously been married to Betty Hutton) and who rolled up his sleeves and went to work with Scotty, D.J., and Bill.

They spent the week first rehearsing, and then recording, the film soundtrack on the Paramount soundstage. It quickly became evident that Elvis was uncomfortable in the big open space, with people wandering in and out, but whether because Radio Recorders was all booked up or because Hal Wallis truly believed that he had the best facilities for motion picture recording, with a two-track 35-millimeter sound system that allowed you easily to bring up the vocal, tone down the instrumentation, and introduce ambient sound, they persisted at Paramount throughout the week. There were moments of exasperation when, for example, sultry Lizabeth Scott, the thirty-four-year-old smoky-voiced heroine of countless films noirs, strolled in during a take, perhaps to get a closer look at her costar. Songwriter Ben Weisman, too, showed up unannounced at a session. Weisman, a protégé of Jean Aberbach's who had gotten his first Elvis cut a few months earlier with "First in Line" and had then written

"Got a Lot O' Livin' to Do" for the film, was tipped off to the recording session by Aberbach and flew in from New York with his songwriting partner, Aaron Schroeder — at their own expense — to make sure that the song got cut. On the afternoon that Weisman and Schroeder arrived, Elvis was struggling with the movie's title cut, and it didn't seem like he would ever get to their song. He had already recorded a version of it at Radio Recorders, but Weisman was getting increasingly worried that the number wouldn't make it into the movie.

"So I do things sometimes that are very unorthodox, I've learned sometimes you've got to do things that are a little off-the-wall. Aaron and I were sitting in the control booth waiting for our song to be recorded, and I told Aaron during an intermission that I was going out there to meet him. Aaron says, 'Don't go. You don't belong out there.' But I went anyway, and it happened that Elvis was sitting in the corner of this big studio with nobody around him, playing guitar, and there was a piano right next to him. So I sat down at the piano — he was playing the blues — and I jammed with him. He didn't look up. After a chorus or two, he looks up and says, 'Who are you?' I said, 'My name is Ben Weisman.' He said, 'Ben Weisman. Didn't you write . . .' He said, 'Wow.' He was so impressed. He liked the way I was jamming with him. He got up, and he yelled out, 'Guys, get out here,' and on the spot they all got together again, and I was there watching, and I went back in the control room, and they did the tune."

Because Wallis had so little faith in Elvis' musicians ("I need them like I need a hole in the head," Wallis told Elvis, who insisted that he needed his boys behind him), he made sure to have a couple of experienced studio musicians for the session. Hilmer J. "Tiny" Timbrell, an affable native of British Columbia in his mid thirties, played rhythm guitar, while Dudley Brooks, forty-three-year-old assistant music director at Paramount and an alumnus of the Lionel Hampton band, played piano and served as de facto arranger of the sessions. "Dudley was a little, short, heavyset guy, black as the ace of spades," said Radio Recorders engineer Thorne Nogar, who met him at the recording studio just a few days later. "For some reason Elvis took a liking to him, and he would sit there at the piano, and Dudley would say, 'Well, El, you play it this way — no, use that finger.' He kind of taught Elvis."

The band gelled, but the sessions didn't, and even Wallis was forced to admit that the studio soundstage was not the ideal setting for an Elvis

Presley recording. They went back to Radio Recorders the following week to fix up the soundtrack (in the end they wound up using a judicious mix of studio and soundstage recordings), but Wallis was hooked by now and even attended some of the sessions. "I was fascinated by the way Elvis recorded," he wrote in his autobiography. "Never bothering with arrangements, he and his boys noodled around, improvised, ad-libbed, and worked out numbers for hours. Finally, he would rehearse a number straight through. Night after long night I watched and listened, fascinated. . . . I never said a word, just observed."

SOME OF THAT SAME easygoing faith and fascination carried over when production started up the following week. Hal Kanter had adapted what might have been a conventional Hollywood musical ("Hey, kids, let's put on a show") into a witty treatment of fame and disaffection. Here the wily manager was transformed from a cigar-chewing carny into a beautiful, if inaccessible, woman (Lizabeth Scott); the faithful musicians, who might have been left behind but in the end were warmly reembraced, became, in this version, Wendell Corey alone; and Elvis' character was rendered with faithful perplexity as a pained innocent in a Technicolor world. The music was incorporated into the script in a way that celebrated its wholesome joyousness, the very "spirituality" that Sam Phillips had spoken of from the start, without confronting any of its troublesome social, or generational, implications. Ben Weisman and Aaron Schroeder's "Got a Lot O' Livin' to Do" ran like a trouble-free theme throughout the film, and there was lots of snappy repartee playing off its audience's, or its author's, knowledge of the real-life drama. The Trouble in Jacksonville, for example, is put up on the screen in the form of a campaign to ban Deke Rivers' music, while The Gas-Station Fight in Memphis — or perhaps it is The Hotel Fight in Toledo — here is transformed into a café fight in which Elvis is goaded into performing a wonderful version of "Mean Woman Blues," then knocks his tormentor into the jukebox which has, miraculously, provided his musical accompaniment.

Elvis was seemingly attuned throughout, in character in a way that he had been able only fitfully to achieve in his debut film, and his musical performances were marvelous representations of his stage act, not the real thing exactly but close enough to leave no one in the audience in any doubt as to what the fuss was all about. What was most striking, however, was not his energy, which was considerable, nor his very convincing representation of emotion (mostly inner turmoil and wounded pride, in the manner of James Dean) but the occasional indication of a stillness at the center, those rare moments of true ease which gave promise of the kind of long-term career that a Spencer Tracy, or even a Bing Crosby, could enjoy and that Hal Wallis could well envision for his latest discovery.

He felt at ease with his fellow actors as well. He liked Wendell Corey, whose acting tips he appreciated (and for whom he later named a cat), and he felt perfectly comfortable with Dolores Hart, who was younger and did not have even *his* experience in the movies. His romance with Dottie seemed to be cooling, helped along by the Colonel's obvious skepticism of her motives ("The Colonel never wanted anyone to get close," Dottie felt, though she continued to remain in touch with Elvis' mother), and the Colonel stepped in on one or two other occasions, too, when he felt that one of Elvis' Hollywood acquaintances might be "unsuitable." But for all that, there was no question he felt more at home in Hollywood, dating starlets like Rita Moreno, with whom he went to see Dean Martin at a Hollywood nightclub, and Yvonne Lime, a Paramount player who had a small part in the picture and who was more like a hometown date, "a lot of fun to be with," Elvis told *Press-Scimitar* reporter Bob Johnson. "Mostly we'd go to movies or just ride around looking at things. Sometimes we would play records."

Less idyllic was the situation that seemed to be developing with Scotty and Bill, and with D.J. to a lesser extent. They didn't like Hollywood, they were bored just sitting around waiting to be called, and they couldn't help but feel the slights, real or imagined, that they saw continually coming their way. To relieve the boredom on the set they would jam with Elvis between takes. An electrician would plug them in, and they always drew a crowd, up to the point that Kanter had to beg, "Will you please stop? We're trying to do some work here!" Off the set they hung around with Charlie O'Curran, a man who enjoyed his liquor and could ask them out to his house in Santa Monica without even calling his wife, Patti. For the most part, though, they were on their own, seeing little of Elvis even though they were only two or three floors below him at the Hollywood Knickerbocker and, in Scotty and Bill's case in particular, hurt and resentful at the separation. Aspiring rockabilly singer Glen Glenn (né Troutman), who had first met Elvis in San Diego in April 1956 and had subsequently become good friends with the band, came by often to see Scotty and Bill, and Bill would frequently bring him up to see Elvis, who was his main inspiration.

"Lots of times Bill would go up with us, knock on the door, and then he would go back down. It wasn't that easy to get in, but he always made sure. There were always a lot of girls sitting around on the couch and stuff, talking. One night I remember Elvis had all the acetates for the soundtrack from *Loving You*, and he had that old Smiley Lewis song, 'One Night,' too — that wasn't in the movie, but he cut it at Radio Recorders at the same time — and he was bragging on it 'cause he played guitar on that. We sat there listening to every one of those songs, and the girls were setting around and Black had already left — he kept playing 'One Night' over and over. 'That's a good fuckin' record,' he said.

"Bill got real mad one time, 'cause they wouldn't let us in upstairs — I think it was mainly the Colonel didn't want Elvis to see anybody that night, but Bill said, 'I ought to go up there and just hit him right in the nose.' He knew I loved Elvis, and it meant a lot to Bill that he could actually take me up there to meet him. He was very bitter, because he thought that Elvis could have put his foot down and done more. Scotty never would say much, but Bill felt like him and Scotty was the band, they should be with Elvis, these other guys were just along for the ride."

That was the only real cloud on the horizon, though. Cliff and Gene ("Cuz") were getting to feel more at home in Hollywood, too, so much so that Elvis was embarrassed at times and felt compelled to restrain their more unencumbered speech and behavior, his cousin's in particular. His father had shipped out his new white Cadillac so that he could cruise around town in style. All in all, despite "a little homesick[ness]," he felt like he was fitting in just fine.

About three weeks into filming, Vernon and Gladys Presley came out with their friends the Nicholses for an extended stay. They had been scheduled to arrive sometime earlier, but Gladys had not been feeling well and checked into Memphis' Baptist Hospital for a series of tests. It was an undefined ailment, a kind of general malaise, brought on perhaps by worry. "I was suffering some nausea and pain in my left shoulder," she told the newspaper, but after the tests had been carried out, she announced with some relief, "There is no surgery in sight." On their first morning at the lot, reported a somewhat disingenuous press release, "the officer of duty at the main studio gate was approached by a . . . man [who] said, with a Southern accent, 'Howdy, officer, can you tell me how to get into this place? We've got a boy working here?' " Vernon was wearing a light-colored suit, round-brimmed, pushed-back hat, and a too-short tie bunched up by an ornamental tie clip, while Gladys wore a simple pinned-back hat and an elegant new jacket over a dark dress. After it was ascertained what exactly their boy did on the lot, they were ceremoniously ushered in. Elvis showed them all around, and within days of their arrival both they and their friends bought poodles, whom they named Pierre and Duke (Gladys led Duke, named for John Wayne, around by a fake diamond necklace collar), and Vernon introduced Carl Nichols to one and all as his "decorator," which puzzled Hal Kanter until it dawned on him that Nichols was by profession a housepainter.

Gladys was entranced. She had worried before coming out that her boy might be made fun of, but she delightedly told friends and relatives afterward, "There's somebody to comb his hair for him and even a man to help him get dressed and another man to ask him if he's ready to work." On weekends they went sightseeing, touring neighborhoods dotted with imposing mansions, as Elvis pointed out Debra Paget's house, Red Skelton's showplace, the homes of the stars. One time they went to the movies, and he took eighteen-year-old Paramount contract player Joan Blackman to see *The Ten Commandments,* but Gladys had to keep shushing him as he enthusiastically explained every scene from a biblical or "technical," cinematic point of view. Scotty Moore's wife, Bobbie, came out for a week, and she and Scotty took the elder Presleys to Burbank for the filming of Tennessee Ernie Ford's popular weekly show, where Vernon and Gladys were introduced from the audience and later met Tennessee Ernie and his wife backstage.

One day when they visited the set, on a whim Hal Kanter shot some film of them and then invited them to come back to see themselves in the daily rushes the next day. Gladys was concerned that she looked fat, but Vernon reassured her that she looked fine, and overall they were so delighted with the results that Kanter got the idea of including them in the audience in the climactic show scene. When he broached the idea to Elvis, Elvis said he was sure that they would love it. So in the final Coast-to-Coast broadcast that caps the picture and refutes all the mean-spirited critics of rock 'n' roll, there is Elvis rocking away onstage, and there is Gladys seated on the aisle — with Vernon beside her, and the Nicholses beside *him* — clapping away in time to the music, intent on nothing but her boy. It is perhaps the musical high point of Elvis' career in films, yet another reprise of "Got a Lot O' Livin' to Do" which combines illusion and reality in such a way as to heighten the attraction of each. Elvis swivels his leg sharply, then good-naturedly drags it behind him. He stands at the lip of the stage and, along with the Jordanaires, who are dressed in matching cowboy outfits, leads the audience in hand clapping, then jumps down and comes dancing up the aisle. Gladys' gaze never wavers. For a moment he is standing to her left, and as she claps along she never takes her eyes off her son. Then he backs away, climbs back up on the stage, and the number is over, the studio audience is still applauding, Gladys along with all the rest — but for her it is different, different even than for the man beside her. For her it is the pinnacle of everything she has ever dreamed or imagined. Her gaze is transformed by love.

They returned home in mid March with the Nicholses after a month-long stay in Hollywood. Elvis would be coming home in about a week — but then he would be off again in May, to make the new picture that the Colonel and MGM had jointly announced would make Elvis Presley, by one manner of accounting anyway, the highest-paid star in motion picture history. For his new movie, tentatively entitled *The Rock*, Elvis would get $250,000 up front plus a range of additional benefits (office, travel, staff, not to mention the Colonel's fee for technical assistance), with 50 percent of the film's net profits assigned to Elvis on the back end. It was, remarked *Time* magazine in its May account, "unheard of."

Elvis handled it all with the utmost good grace and aplomb; everyone on the set agreed that he remained the same simple, thoughtful, almost unnaturally controlled and polite young man you might ever hope to meet — but there were at the same time unmistakable signs of pressure. He blew up at Gordon Stoker of the Jordanaires, who had come to Hollywood to record with him and be in his picture, for making a record with Tab Hunter (whose "Young Love" had just beaten out "Too Much" for the number-one pop position) — even though he had always said the Jordanaires were free to record with whomever they pleased. The next day he apologized, and apologized profusely. You don't have to do that, said Stoker, taken a little bit aback. " 'You don't have to apologize to me or to anybody,' I told him. 'Yes, I do,' he said. I never will forget it as long as I live. He said, 'See that man sweeping the floor right there?' We were on the movie set. 'If I hurt his feelings, it would bug me till I went and apologized to him. I guess I'm a weird guy.' " He supposed he was just getting antsy; he was really beginning to miss his road trips, and he was just looking forward to getting back out there and working off some of this excess energy.

At the wrap party Hal Kanter put a good deal of effort, and not a little of his own money, into thanking a cast and crew who he felt had given their all on this, his first picture. Due to some last-minute business involving a two-shot with Elvis and Lizabeth Scott, he was late getting to the party, and when he arrived he found the Colonel operating out of a booth decorated with RCA promotional material and a banner declaring "Elvis and the Colonel Thank You." Colonel Parker was handing out Elvis Presley albums which had been provided by the record company and publicity pictures of Elvis with his autograph printed on them, and he was raffling off an RCA Victrola, giving everyone a number. "It cost me several thousand dollars, but it turned out to be *his* party!" remarked Kanter. The Colonel greeted him warmly, welcoming him to the festivities, and Kanter was reminded once again of the book that Parker had asked him to help write. "All I have is the title," the Colonel had told him, recapitulating a familiar theme, "but I guarantee that it's gonna be a best-seller." What was the title? Kanter asked, going for the bait. "It's called *How Much Does It Cost If It's Free?*" The reason he knew it would be a best-seller, the Colonel hastened to assure the movie director, was that RCA had guaranteed to buy ten thousand copies of the book the moment it was published.

ELVIS SPOKE TO HIS PARENTS on the telephone on Saturday just before boarding the train for home. They were both excited. They had just seen a house, an estate, really, and they thought he would be excited about it, too. They had made an appointment to go back to see it again on Tuesday after he got home. He sent a telegram to June to meet him when the train stopped in New Orleans. She went with some ambivalence but with more of an intention to pay him back for all the hurt that he had caused her, and when he told her that he wanted her to accompany him to Memphis — he had a surprise that she would really love — she told him that she was engaged. He didn't believe her at first, but then he never told her his surprise, just looked at her blankly as the train pulled away.

Graceland turned out to be beyond his wildest expectations. Built in 1939 in Whitehaven, about eight miles south of downtown Memphis, it was written up by Ida Clemens in the *Memphis Commercial Appeal* in the fall of 1940 as the new country home of Dr. and Mrs. Thomas D. Moore. "Located well back from Highway 51 in a grove of towering oaks, it stands proudly on land that has been in the family nearly a century. . . . As you roll up the drive you sense its fine heritage from the past in its general feeling of aristocratic kindliness and tranquillity." The facade of Tishomingo limestone and the Corinthian columns of the entrance portico were remarked upon. "Polished with the quiet manners characteristic of today's beauty, the palatial home is a noteworthy example of the Georgian colonial style" with an "air of subtle luxury that pervades the exterior [and] seeps through the walls and penetrates every room in the house. . . .

" 'Our entire home is centered around music,' " Mrs. Moore told the *Commercial Appeal* reporter, alluding to her fourteen-year-old daughter, who went on to a distinguished career as harpist for the Memphis Symphony, and proudly showing Miss Clemens around the eighteen-room house, with its parlor that opened up for entertainment to a full seventy-five-foot length and its beautifully planted 18¼ acres. This was what remained of Mrs. Moore's family's almost 500-acre Hereford cattle farm after her great-aunt Grace (for whom the house was named) sold off much of the rest of the land for a subdivision and shopping center and Mrs. Moore herself subsequently gave away another 4½ acres to the Graceland Christian Church just before putting her home on the market.

Elvis got in after midnight Monday night and went out to see the estate first thing on Tuesday with his parents and a reporter in tow. Accompanying the family was Mrs. Virginia Grant, a young real estate agent whom Gladys had met early in February in the parking lot of Lowenstein's East department store. Mrs. Grant had had a number of properties to show them, but they were leaving for California the next day and didn't contact her again until their return. They didn't like the first house, a sprawling ranch on seven acres, and Mrs. Grant was feeling a little bit discouraged when Gladys said, "Don't you have anything to show us with a Colonial home?" All of a sudden the image of Graceland, which had only recently come on the market and which she had never been inside, popped into her head, and though Vernon at this point thought that he might like to move to California, Gladys prevailed upon him to look at the property.

"This is going to be a lot nicer than Red Skelton's house when I get it like I want it," Elvis told the *Press-Scimitar* reporter enthusiastically after going through the house for the first time, and before the deal was done or a firm offer even made, everyone in Memphis knew that Elvis Presley was going to pay $100,000 for Mrs. Moore's beautiful old southern mansion. "We've found a house that we like very much, and we will buy it if we can come to terms," said Vernon, ever cautious and aware that the price was not going to come down if they did not indicate some reluctance. Elvis was simply not one to negotiate, though. He knew how happy the house would make his mother ("I think I am going to like this new home," Gladys announced publicly. "We will have a lot more privacy and a lot more room to put some of the things we have accumulated over the last few years"), and within a week the deal was done. The price was $102,500. Hugh Bosworth, the listing agent, took their old house at an assigned value of $55,000 in trade, and the Presleys put down $10,000 cash and took out a mortgage of $37,500. In fact, the only barrier to really cashing in on the deal was the Colonel's decision that they would have to turn down a bubble gum manufacturer's bid at a "fabulous" price to strip the newly installed wood paneling from the house on Audubon, chop it up, and distribute it as prizes with his bubble gum. The Colonel said this would conflict with merchandising deals they already had in place.

Within a couple of days renovations had begun. Sam Phillips had just moved into *his* new house, out east in the higher-priced Memphis suburbs, earlier in the year, and on Sam's recommendation Elvis contacted Sam's decorator, George Golden, a forty-three-year-old former Lipton tea salesman with a taste for the eclectic and a flair for self-promotion. To advertise his business, Golden had several flatbed trucks cruising around Memphis, day and night, decked out with illuminated "three-foot-wide miniature rooms, built to scale, complete with carpet, wallpaper and a two-foot sofa, upholstered in chartreuse satin. That sofa with the shiny satin really caught everyone's eye." It evidently caught Elvis' eye, or at least the futuristic touches and bold "lush life" style that marked Sam's house did, and he wanted something on an even grander scale for himself. For his bedroom, he told the newspapers, he was going to have "the darkest blue there is . . . with a mirror that will cover one side of the room. I probably will have a black bedroom suite, trimmed in white leather, with a white [llama] rug [like Sam's]." The entrance hall, he said, would be decorated with a sky effect, with tiny lights for stars and clouds painted on the ceiling, and he intended to build "a swimming pool on the south side of the house with a large sunken patio leading up to the pool," a six-foot pink stone wall, purple walls with gold trim for the living and dining rooms, and a number of other resplendent touches.

When it actually came down to it, he gave up the purple for pavilion blue at his mother's request (her son, like most young people, she said understandingly, liked "dark, cozy colors"), and according to Golden, there were two priorities that asserted themselves most strongly. "One was that he had the most beautiful bedroom in Memphis for his mother. Number two, he wanted a soda fountain — a real soda fountain with Cokes and an ice cream thing — so his young friends could sit and have a soda." He had an eight-foot-square bed built for himself and a fifteen-foot sofa custom-built for the living room, and with all the other touches that were planned — the swimming pool, the gates with the musical motif which Golden would have custom-made, the chicken house that Gladys wanted, the painting that Mr. Nichols was going to have to do throughout the house, and the structural repairs that were needed — he seemed ready to pay as much again for the renovations as he had paid already for the house. He just wanted it all to be ready by the summer, when he got home from making his next movie.

For now he scarcely had time to think. He had another disturbing run-in downtown when he was accused of pulling a gun on a nineteen-year-old Marine who claimed that he had insulted his wife. The gun turned out to be a prop Elvis had brought back from Hollywood, Elvis had never even met Private First Class Hershel Nixon's wife, and the whole thing was settled in Judge Boushe's chambers the day before he went back out on the road, but it was beginning to seem like he couldn't go anywhere in Memphis anymore without something happening.

On the same day as the incident with the Marine, there was an announcement in the paper that Elvis would be returning to Tupelo for an appearance at the Mississippi-Alabama Fair in the fall. "The fair wanted Elvis back," the *Press-Scimitar* reported, "[and] offered his manager, Col. Tom Parker, a guarantee of $10,000 for an appearance. Parker turned [them] down. 'Elvis has been thinking about returning to Tupelo ever since last year,' Parker said. 'He has spoken about it a number of times. We'll come to Tupelo, but all money over actual expenses will go to build a youth recreation center for boys in the East Tupelo section, where Elvis grew up.' " He was excited about that, and he was excited about the upcoming tour, too. Cliff had remained in California to try to promote his "career," and Elvis was increasingly disinclined to take along his cousin Junior, whose behavior was becoming more erratic—but Gene, of course, would be with him, as always, and Arthur Hooton would be going out again for the first time in a while, and his friend George Klein was going to be accompanying him for the first time ever.

"I had gotten fired from WMC because they quit playing rock 'n' roll. One night I was up at HBQ visiting Dewey, and Elvis dropped by and said, 'What are you doing, GK?' And I said, 'Well, I got fired, Elvis.' He said, 'You want to come work for me?' I said, 'What do I do?' He said, 'Nothing.' I said, 'Really, what do I—' He said, 'You're just my traveling companion.' I said, 'Elvis, you know I'll just go along for the ride.' He just wanted some hometown guys with him so he wouldn't get lonesome.

"Mrs. Presley always liked me, I don't really know why—she liked my mother, too. She told me, 'George, when you go out on the road with Elvis, he has some bad habits, so please watch him because he's my baby.' She said, 'Make sure you go through his pockets before you send his clothes to the wash because he'll leave money in his pants. And he has a bad habit of walking in his sleep.' She told me how to handle it. She said, 'He's a very nervous young man, and when he gets up to walk in his sleep, you talk to him real soft. And when he talks back to you, you talk back to him real soft: "That's right, Elvis, now why don't you come back to bed?" ' So then I knew how to handle it."

The first date on the tour was in Chicago on March 28. Elvis had a press conference at the Saddle and Sirloin Club at the Stockyards Inn in the afternoon, and that night he unveiled the $2,500 gold-leaf suit that the Colonel had had made up for him. The idea had come from the gold cutaway that Liberace wore in Las Vegas, and the Colonel had Nudie Cohen, Hollywood tailor to the stars (or perhaps a certain kind of star, including all the bespangled country and western luminaries), come out to the movie set in his steer-horn-decorated Cadillac to measure him for it. There were twelve thousand in attendance at the International Amphitheatre, with a $32,000 gross, and thirteen girls passed out during the performance, but what stood out most for the Colonel was the first time Elvis fell to his knees like Al Jolson and left fifty dollars' worth of gold spangles on the floor. He went up to Elvis after the show and asked him please not to do it again. Elvis wore the suit the following night at the Kiel Opera House, in St. Louis, which sold out for only the second time in its history (the first was for Liberace), but after that for the most part he stopped wearing the suit pants, substituting dark slacks to set off the jacket, sometimes wearing the gold slippers and bow tie, sometimes not. After a while he came to be embarrassed by it — it was as if he were advertising the suit rather than the other way around.

For his part, George was having a ball. The shows themselves were outrageous, there were bomb threats and riots, the atmosphere was charged, and after the show there were always girls to "promote." George served as a kind of scout and advance man ("Elvis knew I could talk"). But after a while he was forced to carry identification with him — a picture of Elvis and him together — just to prove he was who he said he was. The Colonel didn't much like it, George knew; what was he going to do about it, though? Colonel was always worrying about potential trouble, and George tried to be careful in his selection process. He told the girls they had nothing to worry about, it was a good bunch of guys, no drunken orgies or wild sex scenes, but in the end who was he going to please, Elvis or the Colonel? There was only so much the Colonel could expect from Elvis, and the Colonel understood that, too.

"Hysterical Shrieks Greet Elvis in His Gold Jacket and Shoes" read the headline in the Detroit paper, which complained that "the trouble with going to see Elvis Presley is that you're liable to get killed." "Convent Suspends Eight Elvis Fans," declared the *Ottawa Citizen* with reference to the expulsion of eight girls from the Notre Dame Convent school for attending the Ottawa show. In Philadelphia, in his first major appearance in the Northeast, he was pelted with eggs by Villanova University students, and in a headline that could have summed up the general journalistic reaction, under the sarcastic banner of "Music (?) Review," the *Toronto Daily Star* trumpeted, "All Too Plainly Visible Elvis Is Barely Audible."

In Canada, Oscar Davis finally made his move. Playing on the split that had clearly grown up between Elvis and his musicians, Davis, who was still doing all the advance work for his onetime protégé but dreamt of a day when he could once again operate on his own, approached first Scotty and Bill, then D.J., and then the Jordanaires, about having him represent them. *They* were not tied to the Colonel, he argued, but they were clearly being exploited — and he could just about guarantee them that the boy would not risk losing his entire musical troupe over a matter of a few dollars. His importunings did not fall on deaf ears. Scotty and Bill were more than ready to make the leap, and in the end D.J. was, too: Presley was making millions, and they were still on $200-a-week pay when they were working, $100-a-week retainer when they were not. In the end the Jordanaires were the lone holdouts, but without them there was simply not enough leverage. "He offered us a better deal than what the Colonel had offered us," said Gordon Stoker, "but I think we more or less didn't trust him. He was beautifully dressed, and he didn't have the bull that the Colonel had, but he was a con artist, too. A beautiful con artist, immaculately dressed, always sharp as a tack — but that's the reason we didn't fall for it."

They played ten cities in ten days — big cities, far removed from their former regional base — and the tour grossed more than $300,000 with a commensurate sale of programs and souvenirs. It generated coverage, controversy, and cash, and from nearly every point of view could not fail to be accounted a success, but if anything was needed to confirm the Colonel's growing conviction that this was a phenomenon that had orbited out of control ("All those sweet little girls out there, they're fucking animals," he had told Hal Kanter), this tour served to do it. It wasn't just the riots, egg throwing, and ridicule, nor even the concerted effort by the Catholic Church to paint Presley as some kind of a moral pariah (in St. Louis, Catholic schoolgirls had burned him in effigy and recited prayers "as public reparation for excesses committed by teenagers"). It was just too damn out of control — and it was becoming increasingly impossible even to do the show. "Girls screamed and hundreds of flash bulbs were discharged," reported the *St. Louis Post-Dispatch* of a typical scene, "making the hall look as if it were under an artillery barrage. Presley clung to the microphone standard and staggered about in a distinctive, distraught manner, waiting for the noise to subside a bit. . . ." *He couldn't even hear himself.* Perhaps thinking of this, Gordon Stoker came to feel that he sought protection in the group; "on some numbers he worked almost just up in our face because he would feel more secure this way."

In Philadelphia, speaking to a group of high school newspaper reporters, Elvis expressed suitable humility in the face of a flurry of not particularly respectful questions ("Is it true you can't get married before you're twenty-three — that it's in your contract?"). What were his most memorable high school experiences? he was asked. When he didn't answer, the reporter persisted: "Well? Didn't you have any?" What did he think of his first movie? "It was pretty horrible. Acting's not something you learn overnight. I knew that picture was bad when it was completed. I'm my own worst critic. But my next picture is different. I know I done a better job in it." And what of the future? "I just take every day as it comes," Elvis told the teenage reporter, who identified herself as Rochelle. "I don't plan too far ahead. There'll be record albums, of course, and movies, too. Don't know anymore; maybe I'll go back to driving a truck."

And then he was home. The work on Graceland was proceeding, but the house wasn't close to ready and the Presleys were still living on Audubon when Yvonne Lime came to visit the Friday of Easter weekend. The first thing that Elvis did was to take her out to see his new home, and he proudly showed both it and her off on Saturday as a newspaper photographer snapped pictures. In one photograph, which went on the UP wire, they are standing in front of the mansion holding hands, the pillars and the portico in the background. Yvonne is wearing a striped, pajamalike outfit and looking up adoringly at an Elvis who appears studiedly sincere. In another shot they are clowning around, holding up a window frame in front of them, Yvonne more animated but still wholesomely perky. Yvonne was surprised to discover how small and cramped the house on Audubon Drive was, she reported in *Modern Screen* magazine, made even more cramped by all the furniture Elvis had bought and all the fan mail that was boxed up on the porch. They ate meat loaf and mashed potatoes and after dinner sat out on lawn chairs in the back. Elvis held Yvonne's hand and Gladys' and declared that they were his "two best girls."

On Saturday night they went over to Sam's new house for a party, and Elvis checked out the decor. Sam's wife, Becky, a DJ and big band authority on WHER, was the perfect hostess; Dot and Dewey Phillips were there; and, of course, Sam's eleven- and nine-year-old sons, Knox and Jerry, immaculate in their Lansky's-bought clothing and carefully sculpted DAs, hung on Elvis' every word and gesture. Elvis introduced Yvonne to many of his old friends and acquaintances, and as the evening wore on and it started to rain, the party gravitated to the living room, where he began to sing spirituals and hymns. "It was a thrilling experience," Yvonne wrote. He sang "on and on, until day began to break and it was Easter morning." For Dot Phillips, who had known Elvis informally ever since her husband had played the first record, it was one of the most moving moments of a long acquaintance. They ended up out by the pool as the sun came up on Easter morning, with Elvis singing and Becky serving scrambled eggs just as hard as Elvis liked them.

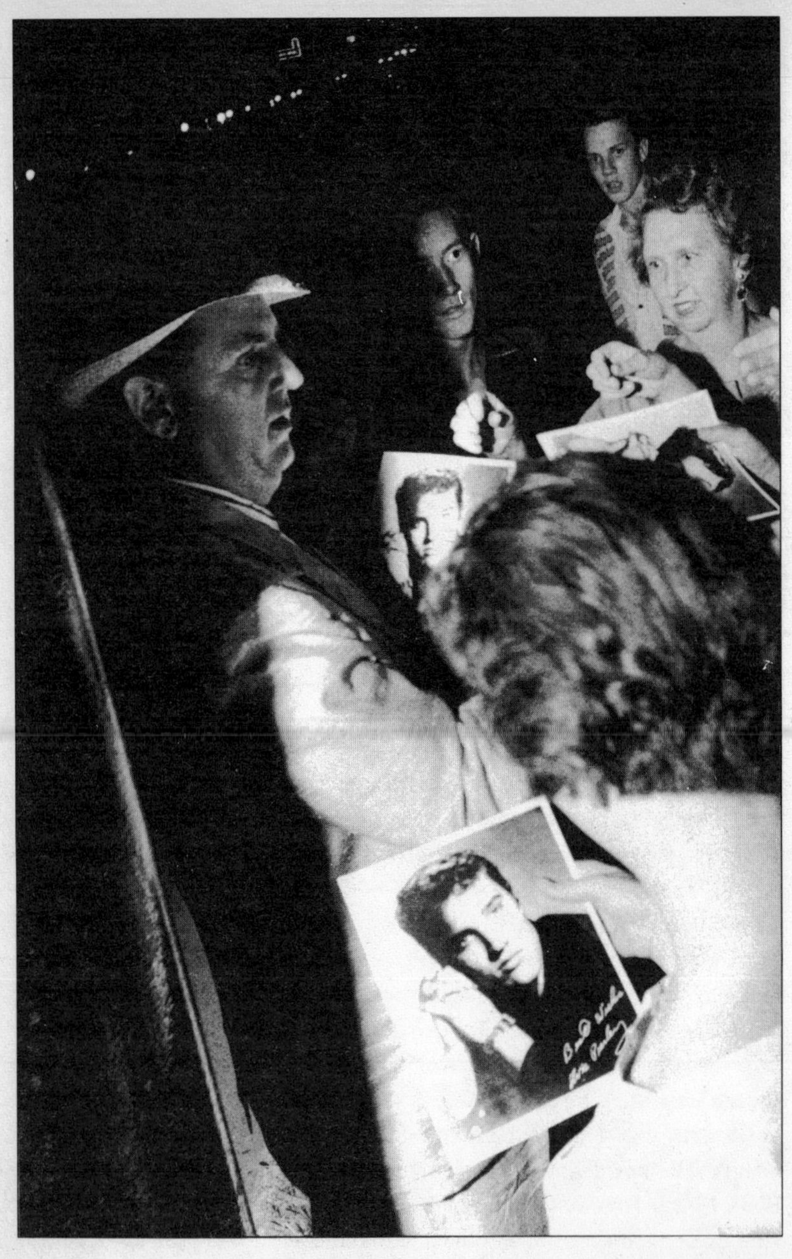

COLONEL PARKER, WITH FANS. (ALFRED WERTHEIMER)

JAILHOUSE ROCK

HE WAS STAYING at the plush Beverly Wilshire, occupying the penthouse apartment plus the Presidential Suite. Scotty and D.J. and Bill tried it, but they didn't like it — it was too far removed from the hustle and bustle — so they moved back to the Knickerbocker, in the heart of downtown Hollywood. Elvis had plenty of friends to keep him company in any case. George and Gene and Arthur Hooton ("Arthritis") had ridden out with him on the train, and Cliff, of course, was there to meet them when they arrived. Junior had wanted to come, too, and Elvis had told him that he could join them in a little while — if he didn't fuck up. The Colonel's brother-in-law, Bitsy Mott, had a single just down the hall, and Colonel and Mrs. Parker were staying on another floor. There were always girls at the soda fountain downstairs looking for dates — pretty little starlets, beautiful girls looking to break into the business, it was known for that reason as "the Mink Farm" to some. It was nice.

It had been the usual long, boring train ride out. Gene and Arthur slept most of the time, but George was excited just to be going to Hollywood. He read lines with Elvis until he knew most of the script himself, and they talked about a lot of things. What was success, Elvis wondered aloud, if you couldn't share it with your friends? Part of him still couldn't believe it was real. "One time he turned to me, and he said, 'I wonder how the people feel, George.' I said, 'What do you mean?' He said, 'When I went to audition for Arthur Godfrey, they told me to watch the mailbox. Well, man, every day for two weeks I met that mailman — I couldn't wait. And I never got a response. I wonder how they —' I said, 'Well, Elvis, I guess they're kicking themselves in the seat of the pants.' . . . He kind of laughed about it, and then he told me about a couple more gaffes, but the thing about it was, he had so much drive, so much determination and energy, he just knew he was going to make it and nothing was going to stop him."

He reported to the recording studio on Tuesday, April 30, with Freddy, Steve Sholes, a number of other RCA officials and MGM executives, plus the band (augmented once again by Dudley Brooks on piano) and Thorne Nogar all in attendance. It was a good, productive session, going from 10:00 in the morning till 6:00 at night. The only thing that made it different from previous sessions — aside from the fact that there was no battle over using the movie studio soundstage, once the Colonel had made it clear that there was not going to *be* any battle — was the presence, and the contributions, of the film's two principal songwriters.

Jerry Leiber and Mike Stoller had been commissioned, more or less, to write the score. Just two years older than Elvis, but with a string of r&b hits (including "Hound Dog") going back into their teens, they had not exactly leapt at the opportunity. In fact, Jean Aberbach had practically had to lock them in their New York hotel room the month before just to get them to settle down long enough to write four songs (the other two had then been farmed out). As hipsters of long standing and deep-seated belief, their attitude, simply stated, was: who was this lame ofay moving in on their territory? They had hated the job he had done on "Hound Dog"; "Love Me," the second song they gave him, was their idea of a joke; and they hadn't been particularly impressed by the two songs of theirs that he had recorded for *Loving You* either. They were scarcely prepared, then, for the person they actually met at Radio Recorders, where Big Mama Thornton's original version of "Hound Dog" had been cut four years earlier, with the same songwriters present and the same recordist, Thorne Nogar, engineering.

"We thought we were the only two white kids who knew anything about the blues," said Mike Stoller, "but he knew all kinds of stuff." "We thought he was like an idiot savant," echoed Jerry Leiber, "but he listened a lot. He knew all of our records. He knew Eddie 'Cleanhead' Vinson. He loved Ray Charles' early records. And he was a workhorse in the studio — he didn't pull any diva numbers." They fenced warily for a while, trading enthusiasms, and Elvis and Mike sat down at the piano to play some four-hand blues. Afterward, Jerry and Mike ran through the title song they had written for the new picture, and Elvis smiled approvingly at Leiber's hoarse, knowing vocal and said, "Okay, let's make it."

They got three songs on the first day, but then, on the following day, their luck ran out. The movie studio was concerned, evidently, at the amount of time that had been spent recording three titles, and someone spoke to the executive in charge of production about it. As Elvis warmed up at the piano singing spirituals with the Jordanaires ("The thing that really surprised us was that there was no clock," said Mike Stoller. "It was amazing — Jerry and I just weren't used to that"), the studio man prodded Thorne and asked him if he couldn't do something. Then at lunchtime, in Gordon Stoker's recollection, he approached the Jordanaires and told them, " 'Get him off this stuff. In fact, if he starts singing [gospel], don't sing with him.'

"So Elvis came back from lunch and started at the piano and we didn't sing. And he said, 'Hey, what's wrong with you guys?' And it fell to my duty to say, 'Elvis, they told us we couldn't sing with you.' He got up and said, 'If I want to bring you guys out here and sing the entire week of spirituals, this is what we'll do.' And he left, just walked out and left."

Elvis didn't come back into the studio at all on the following day, but when he returned on Friday it was as if nothing had happened, except that, seemingly by the tacit consent of all concerned, Leiber and Stoller were now in charge. To Freddy Bienstock it was a logical enough progression: "They came in because we pushed them in, and they were certainly more talented as record producers than Steve Sholes was." And whatever reservations Elvis might have felt, he was now completely caught up in the enthusiasm of the moment, in Leiber's manic flood of ideas ("Elvis thought Jerry was completely crazy," said Bienstock, "with those two different-color eyes, one brown, one blue"), in Stoller's patient musical coaching of Scotty and the other musicians, in the inspired lunacy that for the moment seemed to have come back into the recording studio. "He was completely open," said Mike Stoller. "I played piano to demonstrate — in fact I played piano on some of the sides — and Jerry would sing. And then we would stay on the floor while he was recording, with Jerry sort of conducting with body English. Frequently we'd have what we thought was a take, and he would say, 'No, let me do it again,' and he would just keep doing it. As long as he *felt* like doing it. Sometimes it got better, but other times we knew we had it, and he would just enjoy himself, and then he would say 'Let's hear it,' and then, 'Yeah, that one had it.' In many ways he was a perfectionist, and in other ways he was very relaxed in the studio — a strange combination."

However relaxed he may have been feeling at this point, though, there was an incident toward the end of the session that betrayed some of the longtime tensions in the group. Bill Black was feeling increasingly frustrated not just at the indifference with which he saw himself and Scotty being treated but by his own difficulties in trying to learn how to play the electric bass (the electric bass had just come into common use, achieving almost instant adoption in all fields but bluegrass, because it was compact, amplified, and for the precise fretting it allowed). Bill had only recently gotten a Fender bass of his own, and he couldn't get the ominous, rhythmic intro to Leiber and Stoller's "(You're So Square) Baby, I Don't Care," one of the highlights of the film score. He tried it again and again, got more and more pissed off and embarrassed by his failure, and finally just slammed the bass down, slid it across the floor, and stormed out of the studio, while everyone watched in disbelief. "Most artists," said Gordon Stoker, "would have said, 'You pick that bass up and play it, buster, that's your job,' but not Elvis. You know what Elvis did? Elvis thought it was funny. He picked it up and played it himself. He just picked up that bass, put his foot up on my chair, and played that song all the way through."

They were in the studio for more than seven hours altogether, and when they were done they had virtually completed the entire soundtrack. There were still overdubs to do (like the vocal for "Baby, I Don't Care"), but they had recorded a typically witty, specially commissioned, more than slightly cynical set of songs "mostly by Jerry Leiber and Mike Stoller," as the film credits would declare, a set of self-contained "playlets" of the tongue-in-cheek variety (listen to "Jailhouse Rock" sometime if you doubt the satiric intent) that Leiber and Stoller had pioneered in their work with the Coasters. They had done different versions for different stages of the character's musical evolution (Vince Everett, whom Elvis played, was, needless to say, a singer), some intentionally flat in their affect, some with the undeniable Presley touch. It was, all in all, an exciting enterprise and the kind of thing that could at least make the musical interludes endurable — so long as it was necessary to make musicals at all.

On Monday he reported to the studio for costume fitting and met some of the cast and crew. It was a different kind of studio, and a different kind of set, than the *Loving You* shoot at Paramount — MGM seemed a little more imposing, and the set, without the presence of Hal Wallis constantly hovering over the proceedings, a little more impersonal — but in the end people everywhere were pretty much the same, and the similarities were bound to outweigh the differences. Elvis was assigned the Clark

Gable dressing room, and when they drove in through the Thalberg Gates for the first time, secretaries and executive secretaries and office workers poured out of their offices in such numbers that security had a real problem on the lot. Richard Thorpe, the sixty-one-year-old director, a veteran of scores of low-budget pictures delivered on a tight schedule from 1923 on, showed no great personal enthusiasm (he was known as a man who refused to discuss anything to do with the film in progress over lunch) but was cordial enough, and Elvis had little doubt that he could win him over, whether by charm or by persistence. He was getting to know the game. His mother had taught him these people weren't any different than anyone else, and Colonel had certainly reinforced the lesson.

He met his leading lady, Judy Tyler, who had played Princess Summerfall Winterspring on the children's show *Howdy Doody* and had more recently appeared as a regular on *Caesar Presents,* Sid Caesar's comedy-variety hour, and in the Rodgers and Hammerstein musical *Pipe Dream,* on the Broadway stage. Judy had just gotten married to a young actor named Gregory Lafayette, so that eliminated any chance of anything going on there, but he liked Judy, and he liked Mickey Shaughnessy, his costar, who had played strong secondary roles in a number of pictures (including *From Here to Eternity*) and did an imitation of Elvis in his nightclub act. He met the choreographer, too, Alex Romero, who was already planning the big dance sequence that was scheduled to be shot at the beginning of the following week. Romero had a dub of the song for the sequence, "Jailhouse Rock," and showed Elvis some of the steps that he had devised for it along the lines of a typical Gene Kelly or Fred Astaire number.

"Elvis looked at me, and I looked at Elvis and Cliff," said George Klein, who had gone to the rehearsal room with the others, "and — Alex Romero was a really nice guy, and he said, 'Elvis, will you please try it?' And Elvis got up to copy his steps, and, just from the first instant, you could tell it wasn't going to work. And Elvis said, 'Man, it's not me.' So Alex, being such a sharp guy, said, 'Have you got any of your records in your dressing room?' And we put the records on — 'Don't Be Cruel' and 'Hound Dog' and 'All Shook Up.' And Alex said, 'Would you just show me what you do onstage?' Well, Elvis would go along if he thought you knew what you were doing, so he went through about three songs, and Alex Romero said, 'I got it. See you later, Elvis.' And Elvis said, 'What do you mean you got it?' He said, 'Elvis, what I'm going to do is I'm going to go home tonight and I'm going to take what you do and work it into the routine, and it's going to be you, what you normally feel comfortable doing onstage, but I'm going to choreograph it.' The next day we came back to that same little rehearsal hall, and Alex Romero's choreographed the scene so it looks like you're watching Elvis. He put 'Jailhouse Rock' on and put little markings on the floor, and said, 'Elvis, just do what you feel comfortable doing.' So Elvis whipped through it, and, man, he had it. And then he couldn't wait to do the dance sequence!"

He liked show people. He enjoyed being back in Hollywood. It was good running around with Nick again — there was always something happening, and the hotel suite was like a private clubhouse where you needed to know the secret password to get in and he got to change the password every day.

On the weekend Nick called up his friend Russ Tamblyn, who had a small, one-bedroom beach house on the Pacific Coast Highway just south of Topanga Canyon, and asked if he could bring his friend Elvis over. Tamblyn, who at twenty-two had been in the business from early childhood on, both as an actor and as a dancer, and who saw Nick as something of a hustler, said sure, come on out.

"I'll never forget it. I mean, no one could forget it. First, because Elvis was so big at the time. And, second, when he came, they drove up in three limousines, and there were Elvis and all of his cousins and hangers-on and girls — it was like fifteen or twenty people pouring out of these limos, and then they came in. It was nuts — I thought Nick was just going to bring Elvis over, and it ended up like twenty people came pouring into the room. They brought in soft drinks, and I had a record on, it was a Josh White record, that Elvis just flipped over. I can't remember the title, but it was a weird song, it was a good one with a real low, gutty guitar sound — I could never quite figure what it was about — and we played it about ten times in a row until Elvis finally asked if he could borrow it. Everybody else was sort of partying out on the porch, which was right out on the beach, and Elvis and I were over in front of the record player, and as he listened to the music, he started doing his dance with his knees like he does, and I said, 'Great.' I said, 'Throw those knees.' I guess just being a dancer, I could see where a couple of suggestions might help, so I said, 'Throw those knees out more.' So I showed him, and he said, 'What did you do? Show me again.' So the music was on, and we were standing there dancing in front of the record player, and I remember a girlfriend I had at that time was coming over that night and she told me later she came in and she couldn't believe it, 'There you were dancing with Elvis!' But he was really interested. It wasn't that I technically knew that much, but I was a street dancer, and I understood what he was doing, and I could see right away where with little exaggerated movements it would look better — it would just put it on another level and make it a little stronger, and he got some of that in *Jailhouse Rock.*"

Principal shooting started the following Monday, May 13, and began with the dance sequence that Alex Romero had worked on with Elvis the previous week. The set was a skeletal scaffolding with barred doors suggesting cells on two levels. There was a fireman's pole for the inmates on the upper level to slide down, and a cast of professional dancers was outlined in silhouette behind bars at the start of the number. The dancers then swing out on the cell doors in their striped prison shirts and white-stitched denims and jackets. Miming the song's story line, they escape, only to return in the end to their cells, because the party that the warden has thrown — the "Jailhouse Rock" of the title — is so much fun that who would ever want to leave? Elvis flung himself into the number with utter abandon ("He couldn't wait to do it," said George Klein), so much abandon, in fact, that on Tuesday he swallowed one of the temporary caps for his teeth as he was sliding down a pole. He told the assistant director, Bob Relyea, that he thought he could feel something rattling around in his chest, and Relyea called a doctor to the set, but after examining him the doctor reassured Elvis and Relyea that it was just Elvis' imagination, no more than a scratch. "So now we get the entire crew and all the dancers down on their hands and knees looking for the [cap], 'cause it's very very small and it must be on the floor someplace, and we decide it's all in his mind. About an hour later he comes up after a take and says to me, 'You know that scratch that I think I feel? It's moved. It's over to the left now.' And I said, 'No, no, it's all in your mind.' So about an hour later, after a take he came up and said, 'Ah, it's in my mind? Listen to this.' And then, when he was breathing, you could hear a whistling sound!"

Elvis called George Klein from the Cedars of Lebanon Hospital. It turned out that he had aspirated the cap, which had lodged in his lung, so the next day a surgeon went in and got it out. Oddly enough, there was a scene just like this in the movie, where Vince Everett, the character Elvis played, is punched in the throat by his former cellmate, Hunk Hogan, and everyone is gathered around him toward the end of the picture anxiously waiting to see if he will ever sing again. In this case, according to Relyea, the scene in the recovery room was not much different, with Colonel Parker present and the doctor coming in to announce that everything was fine. " 'We got it,' he said, 'we just had to, we had to part the vocal cords and put the tool through and get in the lung.' And he said, 'Then the darn thing broke in two, and we had to get one piece out and then — it's like arthroscopic surgery — get the other piece out.' When he got to the part about separating the vocal cords to put the instrument through, it got Colonel Parker's attention!"

Elvis was a little hoarse for a couple of days, and when he got back on the set he ran into Russ Tamblyn, who was getting ready to go out on location for *Peyton Place*. "I remember they were rehearsing, and I watched a little bit. When he got done with what he was doing, he came over and got me and said, 'I want to show you something.' And he took me back to his dressing room, and we went inside and he shut the door and said, 'I've been working on this,' and he started going into this dance, and sure enough he had really gotten his knees out further and gotten his elbows back and was doing more with his arms. He wanted to show me how he had been practicing, *but he didn't want anybody else to see.*"

Meanwhile the retinue had grown by the addition of one. Lamar Fike, who had been hanging around with George and Cliff in Memphis the previous fall in hopes of an introduction, was down in Texas visiting his mother when he read in the newspaper that Elvis was in the hospital. He had been calling George regularly for the past couple of weeks suggesting that he might like to come out, and George had been telling him things were kind of tight, everybody was busy, "in other words I didn't want to be responsible for him." At this point Lamar took matters into his own hands, jumped into his '56 Chevy, and drove straight to the Beverly Wilshire, without asking permission of anybody. When he showed up, all three hundred pounds of him in chartreuse shorts and yellow cowboy boots, George wasn't there, but according to his understanding, Cliff met Lamar at the door. "He went into his con, and Cliff went into his con, and Lamar said, 'Man, can I come in?' And Cliff said, 'Man, it's kind of tight. I mean, Elvis is real particular here in Hollywood.' So, finally, Cliff goes and tells Elvis, he says, 'Elvis, there's a guy here from Memphis. He's hung out with me and George, and he's kind of jolly and he's kind of funny and he drove all the way from Texas. Can he come in tonight and party with us?' So Elvis said yeah, and Lamar made an impression like he always does and that's how he worked his way into the group."

ONCE THE DANCE SEQUENCE was finished, the picture moved along at a brisk pace. There were none of the relatively complicated setups of *Loving You,* and Richard Thorpe worked fast anyway. For George, just being on the lot was like a fantasy come true. "Cliff, Arthur, and I were on the payroll now — of course Gene was already on the payroll. I'll never forget, he said, 'I'll pay all you guys' expenses, if you need any money you know you can always come to me. But Colonel says we're making a movie so I've got to put you on salary for tax purposes.' So he put us on salary at fifty dollars a week. Gene and Cliff and Arthur, they'd get bored on the set and would just lay down and go to sleep in the dressing room, but I was all over that lot like crazy, I didn't want to miss a thing. The first day we got there Glenn Ford was there, he'd just finished a picture for MGM. And he was talking to Elvis, he was telling Elvis something — he was a real nice guy — and he was going through these motions just like he did in movies, and I said, 'God, he acts just like he does in the movies, Elvis!' And Elvis says, 'Shut up, shut up.' He didn't want me to sound like I was starstruck, but me and Cliff were, you know.

"Whenever there was a break in the action, I'd jump off this soundstage and run over to another soundstage and watch Yul Brynner work or John Ford or Kim Novak — she was unloading some stuff from her car, and I told Cliff, I said, 'Shit, I'm going to go over and talk to her. She might not say a word to me, but I got to talk to Kim Novak!' I remember, they were making *Saddle the Wind* with Robert Taylor and Julie London, and one day I go over to the set 'cause Anne Francis was on the set and I wanted to see what she looked like. So I'm on the set standing in the background watching — it was an open set — and Vince Edwards walks over to me and starts talking. He said, 'Hey, man, ain't you with Presley?' 'Cause I guess everybody on the lot noticed who was with Elvis. And I said, 'Yeah,' and he introduced himself, and we start talking and he said, 'Man, I'm a big fan.' Now he was just starting out in Hollywood, but he'd been a big swimming champion at Ohio State, and he said, 'You want to meet Anne Francis?' And I said, 'Sure.' So when they took a break, he said, 'This is Elvis' buddy.' And he said, 'I'd like to meet Elvis,' so I said, 'Come over to the set.' Well, Vince came over, and immediately Cliff liked him and Elvis liked him and I liked him, so Elvis invited him up to the Beverly Wilshire and he started coming every now and then."

Edwards became a regular member of the group, and he introduced them to an actor named Billy Murphy, who had been in *Sands of Iwo Jima* with John Wayne, and to Sammy Davis, Jr., too, who came up one night and scared the hell out of Elvis with his impression of Dr. Jekyll and Mr. Hyde. Murphy was a Hollywood character, a few years older than the others, who walked up and down Hollywood Boulevard dressed in black — black pants, black shirt, black hat, black gloves — and carrying an unproduced screenplay that he had written about Billy the Kid in a bold, illegible script. "Elvis was just infatuated with him," according to George, "we all were, because he was just so colorful and interesting. Some directors were scared of him, I think, because he was very physical, even threatened one or two of them. He was friends with Robert Mitchum and Rory Calhoun on a first-name basis, he had a certain way of walking, kind of like Mitchum, and he had a pet phrase that we all picked up: 'You bet your life, mister, and you may have to.' It came out of an old Clark Gable movie, really, but we picked it up from Murphy. Nick Adams would tell us wild stories about him. I think he just became a little too erratic for Hollywood."

Mitchum himself stopped by one afternoon, because he wanted Elvis to play the part of his brother in the upcoming production of *Thunder Road,* a moonshiner's tale which he was producing and for which he had written the story. Elvis was thrilled at the visit, and at the offer — Mitchum had gotten him "all shook up," he told Russ Tamblyn, who arrived just after Mitchum's departure — and listened enthralled to Mitchum's real-life tales of growing up hard in the South and doing time on a Georgia chain gang.

In the evenings they would go to the movies sometimes, the whole gang of them; it was, according to Vince Edwards, like "The Clan of Elvis Presley," with the limos pulling out of the Beverly Wilshire full of cousins and kin. "When we got to the theater," said Russ Tamblyn, "we all got out and bought our tickets and formed a line. Now by this time a crowd has formed, you know, they'd see all these strange-looking characters get out of the cars and wonder, who the hell is this, so if there wasn't a problem before, there is now. Anyway, there would be two lines right up to the ticket taker, and Elvis would be the last one, or if he had a girlfriend, the girlfriend would come out with him, and Elvis would go right between the two lines, and everybody would be so blown away they'd just move back. I always thought Elvis loved the entourage, and he loved playing the part — he seemed to have an instinct for entrances."

They went out to Russ' beach house one or two more times, and with Russ on the verge of leaving to shoot his new movie in Maine, Elvis asked if he could rent it for the next couple of months. He was still seeing Yvonne Lime occasionally, but he was dating Anne Neyland, a former Miss Texas whom he had met on the MGM lot, and Venetia Stevenson, too, when a rumor that he was about to marry Yvonne in Acapulco broke at the end of May. "When I get married," he told the press, after the Colonel's official denials, "it'll be no secret. I'll get married in my hometown of Memphis, and the whole town'll be there."

He wasn't really serious about anyone for the time being, though. He was enjoying the single life, and when he got bored he just had to tell the guys to hunt up some girls in the lobby of the hotel. He would have them brought up to the suite, offered one observer, "and Elvis would go in the other room, he'd go in the bedroom or somewhere, and then when they came back with the girls, the girls would sit there for maybe ten or fifteen minutes, and finally one of the cousins would go in the bedroom and come out himself and another ten minutes would go by — and then in would come Elvis. And there would be like a silence, and then the cousins would say, 'Oh, Mary Jane, this is Elvis,' and the girls would be totally gone." For the more experienced girls it wasn't like with other Hollywood stars or even with other more sophisticated boys they knew. They offered to do things for him, but he wasn't really interested. What he liked to do was to lie in bed and watch television and eat and talk all night — the companionship seemed as important for him as the sex — and then in the early-morning hours they would make love. "He had an innocence at that time," said one of them. "I'm sure it didn't last. But what he really wanted was to have a relationship, to have company. He was very clean-cut about it. There were a lot of things that he didn't like. And another thing that you could not do around him was mention drugs, he was dead set against it. There was a lot of grass around in Hollywood at that time, and what the cousins said was, 'If you got any dope, don't bring it out around Elvis.' If anyone wanted to turn on, they had to go away and not do it around Elvis."

In a wholly unlikely turn of events, one of the newcomers to the scene was songwriter Mike Stoller. Stoller had gotten a part in the movie when

Jerry Leiber, who, in the eyes of the film's casting director, *looked* more like a piano player than his piano-playing partner, begged off film work for a dentist's appointment. Stoller shaved off his goatee to play the part, looking exceedingly uncomfortable on-screen without it. He found film work boring but, to his surprise, enjoyed the opportunity it gave him to get to know Presley a little better. "He was very comfortable in the recording studio, but not so much on the set. I remember one time a couple of extras were sitting around, and I witnessed this whole thing — these two guys were playing cards and talking about their families, you know, the baby, the car payments, that kind of stuff. And one of them said something to the other, and they started laughing. Elvis came through at that moment, and he turned around and zap, right on them, and he said, 'Boy, you think you're so hot, huh?' They didn't know what he was talking about, and he was already in a sense omnipotent — but he thought they were laughing at him.

"I know he was very insecure, and I think that he used the Colonel in this as protection in a different way than the Colonel was using him. My own feeling was that he felt comfortable surrounded by his friends, and I think that also worked to the Colonel's idea of keeping him exclusive, keeping him isolated and insulated so that no one could get to him and he could never become too commonplace. I felt a little sorry for him because he didn't have a shot at becoming a whole person: in twenty minutes he would go from being arrogant and high-handed to frightened. He would order people about, and the next minute he would be saying, 'Can I get you a sandwich? Do you want some pie?'

"I used to hang out in the dressing room with the entourage, and one day we were horsing around, and Elvis said, 'You know, Mike, I'd really like you to write a ballad, a real pretty ballad, for me,' and that week Jerry and I wrote a song called 'Don't,' and we made a demo of it up at Hollywood Recorders with [rhythm and blues singer] Young Jessie singing, and I came back to the set and gave him the record and he loved it and eventually recorded it. But we caught hell for not going through the proper channels. I was supposed to tell Jean and Julian [Aberbach] and to play it for Freddy — and then *Freddy* was supposed to play it for Elvis. The Colonel was very upset — it was supposed to work the way it always worked, they didn't want any loose cannons around.

"One day after the shooting he invited me up to the hotel — I think we had a Coke downstairs, and then we went up to his suite on the top floor. And we went in and shot some pool and ate some peanuts, and we're kidding around and talking about songs and music, and then the Colonel came in and it was like a scattering of birds: they all flew away. I was in the middle of a pool shot and looked up and nobody was there. When Elvis came back, he looked terrible. He said, 'Mike, the Colonel's all upset because you're here, and I guess you gotta go.' I said it was all right and took off. They just didn't want anybody around, especially a songwriter — it was okay to work with him in a controlled area, but to be able to get to him and perhaps influence him, present him with a song. . . . That was the kind of control the Colonel had."

"I don't feel like I'm property," Elvis told columnist Joe Hyams, while lunching alone in his dressing room on a bowl of gravy, a bowl of mashed potatoes, nine slices of well-done bacon, two pints of milk, a large glass of tomato juice, lettuce salad, six slices of bread, and four pats of butter. "I can't get it into my head that I'm property. People tell me you can't do this or that," he went on, "but I don't listen to them. I do what I want. I can't change, and I won't change." He was a hard worker, he said, he had worked hard all his life, and even though he got lonely as hell sometimes ("A lot of times I feel miserable, don't know whichaway to turn"), he still loved every minute of it. "If I had to drop it all I could do it, but I wouldn't like it." And what about the Colonel? Hyams asked. "I've got an idea of how to handle me better than anyone else has as far as keeping me in line," said Elvis. "Colonel Parker is more or less like a daddy when I'm away from my own folks. He doesn't meddle in my affairs. Ain't nobody can tell me 'you do this or that.' Colonel Parker knows the business and I don't. He never butts into record sessions, I don't butt into business. Nobody can tell you how to run your life."

He studied the daily rushes religiously every night. He was still dead set against acting lessons — it was like the difference between an opera singer and a singer who sang from the heart, he explained to George Klein; formal study might rob him of his spontaneity. But, as a great believer in self-improvement and self-education, he never left the studio at night without carefully scrutinizing his performance. "I always criticize myself in films," he told an interviewer a few months later. "I'm always striving to be natural in front of a camera. That takes studying, of a sort."

He was serious about it, and he felt like he was getting somewhere. Mr. Thorpe wasn't very approachable, but he sought tips wherever he could get them, asking assistant director Bob Relyea for suggestions, thanking character actor Glenn Strange for his patience in a difficult scene. "He interacted with everybody," said Relyea. "One of the first days we were shooting a scene, and we were held up — and one of the crew just said, 'Well, we should have a song.' So he got his guitar out and played a song. It wasn't any, 'No, no, I don't do that, uh, don't embarrass me.' He just said, 'Give me my guitar!' He had all these qualities that you knew that he could succeed at whatever he wanted to do. He probably would have been good as a schoolteacher, he would have been a good mechanic. He was so dedicated and focused, he knew what it was about: he knew what tomorrow's work was going to be."

It was into this volatile mix of work and play, of desperate deal making and disingenuous denial, that Dewey stepped when he arrived for a Hollywood vacation several weeks into filming. He was all excited about the trip, which Elvis had even offered to pay for because, Bob Johnson wrote in the *Press-Scimitar,* "he wanted Dewey to spend a lot of time with him, and to watch him at work at MGM. . . . He didn't put him in with the other fellows, but put Dewey up in a room in his own personal suite. . . . Elvis took Dewey to his dentist and spent about $400 getting Dewey some of those fancy porcelain caps just like Elvis' for his teeth. He took him around to the various studios and stars' homes, proud of his strange friend from Memphis."

Unfortunately, "strange" appeared to be the operative word. Dewey, as Scotty said, "acted just the way he did around Memphis. Of course everyone in Memphis knew him, but out there he was just out of his league." He showed up on the set on the first day, got bored, and left after fifteen minutes. He got thrown off another set for taking pictures. Elvis took him over to the soundstage where they were making *The Brothers Karamazov* and introduced him to Yul Brynner, whereupon Dewey spontaneously observed, "You're a short little mother, aren't you?" and Elvis, mortified, apologized for his friend. "It was a star-crossed situation," observed George Klein. "Elvis loved Dewey for what he'd done for him, but by the same token he was embarrassed by what Dewey was doing in Hollywood. We went to see Sammy Davis, Jr., at the Moulin Rouge, and they introduced Elvis, and Dewey jumped up between Elvis and the spotlight and said, 'Dewey Phillips, Memphis, Tennessee,' and there's Elvis standing up to take a bow. We didn't get mad. We just said, 'That's crazy Dewey.' I mean, Elvis knew how Dewey was."

Before he left, Elvis played him a dub of his new single, "Teddy Bear," from *Loving You,* and Dewey flipped over it, it was a damn hit, he said and asked to hear it again. When he got on the plane, according to Dewey's report to Bob Johnson, "we even shed a few tears. I told him I'd never be able to repay him for all the nice things he'd done for me. His last words to me were, 'Phillips, be sure and say a prayer before you get on that plane.' "

Unfortunately Dewey had taken some stowaway luggage on board: against Elvis' explicit instructions, he had appropriated a copy of the new single, which was not due for release until June 11 and which, against all protocol and advice, he played on the air immediately upon his return. The Victor people were furious, the Colonel was furious — it only vindicated what he had been saying about Elvis' Memphis friends all along — and Elvis was furious, too. The headline in the *Press-Scimitar* was "These Reports True — Elvis and Dewey Had a Falling Out."

In the meantime shooting on the movie was rapidly coming to an end. When it was finished, it offered a neat little parable in black and white on the debilitating effects of fame (Vince Everett turned bigheaded before fate intervened) and the discrepancy that could exist between a truculent and much-criticized exterior and the essential sweetness that might lie underneath. It was a point Elvis had been arguing by deed, if not by word, for years, and one to which he clearly took, in a performance that marked an even further advance over the significant progress shown in *Loving You.* You couldn't really say that he had achieved an acting style, because in each scene he was a little different: there were traces, of course, of Dean and Brando — Brando particularly in the penitentiary scene where Elvis was flogged and registered silent suffering while naked to the waist — but, not surprisingly, the most striking resemblance was to a young Robert Mitchum, or perhaps it was Billy Murphy he was thinking of. In any case, it was a most creditable performance, and one of which Elvis could be proud as he departed for home at the end of June.

The train ride home was relatively uneventful, though it might have been less boring for Elvis if he had been aware of the behavior of his increasingly erratic cousin Junior Smith. Junior bunked with George, because at this point no one else could stand him. "He was drinking a lot, and when he'd get drunk he'd get mean. And he smoked in bed at night, and everyone was afraid he'd set the cabin on fire. So Elvis said, 'George, do you mind if Junior stays with you?' And I said no, because for some reason Junior and I hit it off, we'd kid around and tell old stories and it was fine. Well, this particular night he'd had a few drinks and he gets up and starts packing his bag, and it's about three-thirty in the morning, and I said, 'Junior, where in the shit are you going?' And he said, 'I'm getting off this fucking train.' I said, 'Junior, what are you going to do?' He packed his bag, and I said, 'Man, don't wake up Elvis, Junior.' He said, 'I ain't gonna wake up Cuz.' So he pulls that fucking cord that stops the train, and the conductor comes running down to our little booth, and Junior says, 'Stop this motherfucker, I want to get off.' And I started talking to him, and the conductor started talking to him, and we finally calmed him down and got him back to bed."

Elvis couldn't wait to get home to see the renovations and stay overnight at Graceland with his parents, who had already moved in. So impatient was he that, after trying to get June to meet him in New Orleans, only to find out that she had been married on June 1, he got off the train in Lafayette, Louisiana, rented a car with Cliff, and drove the rest of the way home. "When we got there, the wall, the limestone wall, was not finished, and the gate was not up, and these little sticks guided you up the driveway with these orange markers because the asphalt was not fixed yet. Well, we made the little curve, got out, and went up to the door, and he stopped — it was about eleven-thirty at night, and he says, 'Well, Cliff, here goes.' He opened the door, and there was a little foyer there, and he went in, and, standing under the chandelier in the extended part of the foyer, were his mother and father. And she said, 'Welcome home, son.' And we talked for most of the night. It was not the excitement you might expect. Not, you know, 'Hey, we made it. We're on top of the world.' That never came out of that family — it was against their nature. They just talked. 'It's nice.' 'They've done a good job.' Elvis' father explained to him, 'We've still got to do this or that . . . I think this man here charged a little too much. I think we ought to change this guy, get another contractor . . .' That kind of talk." Had they completed the hog pens and chicken coop out back? Elvis wondered. Elvis' mother told him she had put in the garden.

THERE WAS NOTHING PLANNED, there was nothing that he had to do, there was nowhere that he needed to be. "Teddy Bear" and "Whole Lotta Shakin' Going On," the new song that Sam had put out on

Jerry Lee Lewis, were vying for number one, "Love Letters in the Sand" was still going good for Pat Boone, seventeen-year-old Ricky Nelson was doing all right with his first record, and he liked Tommy Sands, too — "There's plenty of room for all of us," he reassured his friends when they started running down one artist or another, though he didn't ever want to be taken for granted, either. The world premiere of *Loving You* was scheduled to be held in Memphis on July 9 at the Strand Theatre on South Main, and he was planning to attend. In the meantime he wanted to make sure that everything at Graceland was just right. He had heard that geese were good for keeping down a lawn, so he took one of the Cadillacs, drove it down to Mississippi, and filled up the backseat with sixteen geese, which, not surprisingly, left a substantial deposit. Another time he took over from Vernon on the driving mower, heading straight for his mother's tulip bed. He was just fooling around, but then his mother started to yell, "Elvis, Elvis, don't!" and a look of panic came over her face, which only added to the temptation. Tulips flew everywhere, and his mother eventually started laughing, too, but Mr. Presley was worried that he was going to be blamed.

Then on the night of July 3 he heard that Judy Tyler had been killed with her husband in an automobile crash out west. She had played the record company girl who became his manager and love interest in *Jailhouse Rock,* and he was devastated. He showed up at George's house with Arthur at 10:00 the following morning, an unheard-of hour. "I was still living across from Humes with my mother, and she came into the bedroom and said, 'Elvis is at the door.' I said, 'No, Mom, Elvis is not at the door.' He was real serious, so I said, 'What's wrong, man?' but he just wanted to take a ride. So we got in the car and he said, 'Hey, man, Judy got killed.' So we drove around for a while and he explained it to me, he just felt so bad."

He was determined to go to the funeral, he told the newspapers later in the day, even if it meant missing the premiere. "She was at the peak of success," he said, fighting back tears. "Nothing has hurt me as bad in my life. . . . I remember the last night I saw them. They were leaving on a trip. Even remember what she was wearing." He didn't know if he could stand to look at the movie now, he said. "I just don't believe I can." In the end he didn't attend the funeral. It was his mother, not the Colonel, who told the papers a couple of days later that he would just send flowers, he didn't want to disrupt the service.

That Sunday he met a girl he had been seeing on TV ever since getting home. Anita Wood was nineteen, a beauty-contest winner, blond, pert, and talented, who had been appearing with Wink Martindale on the *Top Ten Dance Party* on WHBQ for the past few months. She was from Jackson, Tennessee, originally, like Wink, and Cliff knew her from there, while George knew her through Wink. Elvis had George check the situation out, and when George came back and said she'd like to meet him, he had George call her up. The first time she was busy, and when she had to decline a second time, she thought he would never call again, but the third time George called she was free. They drove by the Strand to see the cutout of Elvis that the theater had put out in anticipation of the movie opening in two days. George and Cliff were in the backseat, and Lamar, too, and they went out for hamburgers at Chenault's afterward. Then he gave her a tour of his new home and its grounds: the swimming pool, the six cars, his collection of teddy bears, from which he lightheartedly selected one as a gift. He showed her his bedroom, but she told him she didn't feel comfortable there, so they went back downstairs and spent the rest of the evening talking and playing records and singing at the piano. At the end of the night he took her home to the room she rented in Mrs. J. R. Patty's house, and they chastely kissed good-night.

After that they kept almost constant company. Elvis didn't attend the *Loving You* premiere, which set box office records in Memphis and, a few weeks later, across the country, but he took Anita and his parents to a special midnight showing, which they all enjoyed. During the day they frequently drove around in an old panel truck that guaranteed anonymity, as Elvis showed her all the places that meant something to him in his life. He was painstaking, almost compulsive, about pointing out to her the route he had walked to the store, where he had played as a child, where his friends and cousins lived, the places where he had worked and played. He dreaded going into the army, he told her, and started calling her "Little" because of the size of her feet. Sometimes he would talk baby talk to her the same as he would talk to his mother. It was all very down-to-earth and flattering, too, if only for the way he simply adored her. He didn't play the big star, he was just like a boy that you would meet and fall in love with and then expect to marry — and his family was so welcoming, too. "I just can't wait," Gladys told her, not long after Anita had become a regular fixture, "to see that little ol' baby walking up and down the driveway." She had been sick a lot lately and stayed up in her room. "She had a heart problem, I think, and she was overweight with fluid — her ankles and her legs would swell a lot. . . . She never ceased to worry about Elvis."

They drove all around on his motorcycle and went horseback riding and played badminton out on the lawn. There was a special dining room reserved for them in the back room at Chenault's Drive-in; they went out to McKellar Lake on occasion or to the Fairgrounds to ride the Dodgems and the Pippin, the oldest operating wooden roller-coaster ride in the country. The guys were with them almost constantly, George or Cliff, Lamar, Arthur, the cousins. Once in a while Elvis would run into one of his old friends and invite him up to the house. Buzzy Forbess from the Courts came by one evening, and Elvis surprised him by fooling around with a classical harp he had just bought, but to Buzzy there were just too many people sitting around holding out their hands, and the atmosphere was kind of forced, so he didn't go back for a while. George Klein brought around a friend named Alan Fortas, who had been an All-City tackle at Central High, then went on to Vanderbilt University and Southwestern before dropping out and going to work at his father's junkyard. George, who knew him through the temple and a number of other Jewish organizations, needed a ride out to Graceland one night.

"George didn't drive, he was one of the few people who didn't, so he asked me if I'd like to go out to meet Elvis. Of course I was an Elvis fan, I had seen him in a couple of shows at the Overton Park Shell and Russwood Park, and I had been out to the Eagle's Nest. So I said, 'Man, I'd love to,' and I picked George up, and we went out there and, of course, Elvis was a big football fan and he remembered me from high school and showed me all around the house. Well, I left after a couple of hours, I didn't want to overstay my welcome, and when I left, he said, 'Well, I'll see you again, Alan.' So a couple of nights later George called and said, 'Elvis asked about you and wanted to know why you hadn't been back.' 'Well,' I said, 'I didn't want to press my luck.' He said, 'Oh, he liked talking to you. Come back out.' So I went out, and when I left that night, he said, 'I'll see you tomorrow night.' One thing led to another, and every night I left he said, 'I'll see you tomorrow night, Alan.' "

Elvis seemed to really take to him. Before long he started calling him "Hog Ears," just as he called Lamar "Mr. Bull" and George "GK." It was cool going out to Graceland — you never knew what was going to happen. Where else were you going to find donkeys in the swimming pool (courtesy of Colonel Parker) and peacocks on the lawn? As the summer wore on, Elvis started renting out the Fairgrounds through a friend of George's named Wimpy Adams, and they would have it to themselves from midnight till sunrise. They rented out the Rainbow Rollerdrome, too, from Joe and Doris Pieraccini, and had skating parties where the guys put on knee and elbow pads and divided up into teams, playing rough games of tag and roller derby, with one of the cousins acting as referee. One night, Alan recalled in his memoir of that time, Elvis was "more keyed up than usual" when they piled in the car to go home.

> Lamar and I climbed in the front seat, and Elvis and Anita sat in the back. We were just tooling along, when all of a sudden Anita announced in a loud voice, "My cunt hurts!" What? My mouth dropped down to my ankles. Maybe I misunderstood. I cleared my throat, Lamar did the same, and we drove on a little farther. Then Anita burst out again. "Did y'all hear me? I said, 'My cunt really hurts!' " . . . It wasn't until we got back to Graceland that I found out that Elvis had told Anita the whopping lie that "my cunt hurts" is a Hollywood expression for "my rear's sore." And every time she yelled it out, it was only because Elvis nudged her. . . . She had no idea what it meant.

Alan didn't think much of the cousins and the uncles and the aunts — they were, he wrote, "an odd lot. . . . Sometimes I'd talk to Gene and it was almost like talking to a retarded person. I didn't know if he was acting or whether he was really that dumb." Mostly they just had a helluva time, though. They went everywhere and they did everything on the slightest whim. The only place they didn't go was to the Hotel Chisca. Ever since getting back, Elvis had studiously avoided the radio station, and now he wouldn't even come to the phone when Dewey called. Dewey had apologized right after he got back — almost under duress, it seemed — and there had even been a brief period of rapprochement, but then Dewey began to feel aggrieved that Elvis wasn't coming by with a sack of Krystalburgers anymore, and he started telling anyone who would listen that he thought Elvis had the big head.

One night he came by the house at 3:00 in the morning, ranting that Elvis had forgotten his old friends, and when he was turned away at the gate, he "climbed the fence," the paper reported, "and went in and roused the household shouting: 'I'm through with you, Elvis.' Elvis is said to have doubled him in spades. One person close to Elvis said, 'What made it especially bad is that Mrs. Presley is so nervous, especially since Liberace's mother got hurt.' " The story was quite different, according to an obviously remorseful Dewey. It was only about 1:00 A.M., he thought, and he'd gone out there to retrieve a Polaroid camera that Sam Phillips had given him for Christmas. He needed it back, because he was about to take the rest of his vacation and he wanted to take some pictures. "It wasn't really late for Elvis," he said. "They wouldn't let me in and I still haven't got my camera. I said some things I shouldn't have said. . . . I still love that boy like a brother. Or maybe it would be better to say like a son."

There were lots, of course, of other nights at Graceland. One night the great rhythm and blues singer Ivory Joe Hunter, whose anthemic 1950 hit, "I Almost Lost My Mind" (remade with even greater success as "Since I Met You, Baby" in 1956), was one of Elvis' favorites and whose "I Need You So" Elvis had recorded in February, came out to the house. Brother Dave Gardner, the comedian whom Elvis had first met in Biloxi the previous summer, was in town recording a follow-up to his unexpected pop hit, "White Silver Sands." Somehow or other he had hooked up with Ivory Joe, and he called up Elvis and asked if he could bring him over. Elvis was thrilled, and they were all sitting on the white couch in the living room swapping stories when, according to George Klein, "Elvis said, 'Ivory Joe, I sure do like your songs. You ain't got any more of them for me, do you?'

"Now Ivory Joe was a real friendly guy. Great big 'Hey, baby, how you doing, baby?' kind of guy. You just immediately liked him. And he said, 'Well, baby, I just have — I got one just for you.' So we went in the piano room, and he sang 'My Wish Came True,' and Elvis said, 'Shit, I'm cutting that at my next session!' Which he did, even though it didn't come out for a couple of years. And they sat there for hours, mostly singing Ivory Joe's songs, a few of Elvis' — man, I just wish I'd had a tape machine."

"He is very spiritually minded," said Hunter, who had felt some trepidation to start off with because, "frankly, I'd heard he was color prejudiced." The rumor had been circulating throughout the Negro community that spring and summer, in fact, that Elvis Presley had said, "The only thing Negroes can do for me is buy my records and shine my shoes." After determining that "tracing the rumored racial slur to its source was like running a gopher to earth" (the remark was said to have been made either in Boston, which Elvis had never visited, or on Edward R. Murrow's national television show, on which he had never appeared), *Jet* magazine sent a reporter to the set of *Jailhouse Rock* to confront the singer himself. "When asked if he ever made the remark, Mississippi-born Elvis declared: 'I never said anything like that, and people who know me know I wouldn't have said it.' " The reporter, Louie Robinson, then spoke to some people who *were* in a position to know and heard from Dr. W. A. Zuber, a Negro physician in Tupelo, that Elvis used to "go around with quartets and to Negro 'sanctified' meetings," from pianist Dudley Brooks that "he faces everybody as a man," and from Elvis himself that he had gone "to colored churches when I was a kid, like Reverend Brewster's," and that he could honestly never hope to equal the musical achievements of Fats Domino or the Ink Spots' Bill Kenny. "To Elvis," *Jet* concluded in its August 1 issue, "people are people, regardless of race, color or creed." And to Ivory Joe Hunter, who verified the matter for himself, "he showed me every courtesy, and I think he's one of the greatest."

All in all it was a peculiarly lazy, idyllic kind of existence, an adolescent daydream that seemed like it could go on forever. In the basement the jukebox was playing all the time, and the soda fountain was fully stocked. If he felt like it, he might fix a visitor a milk shake, and with no fans around to observe him, he could smoke the little Hav-a-tampas that he and the guys all enjoyed without compunction — but without inhaling either. According to Bettye Maddox, a DJ at WHER whom Elvis met after seeing her do a commercial for Honeysuckle Cornmeal on Dewey's *Pop Shop* TV show, "It was like a magic spell — it was like each night you knew something magic was going to happen, but you didn't know what it was." Some nights Anita would call and Bettye would be out there, and he would just tell the guys to say that he was busy. Venetia Stevenson flew in from Hollywood to stay with him, and there was a trio of fourteen-year-old girls that he had known since the previous fall (one of their fathers operated a garage that Vernon patronized); they came around from time to time, and he roughhoused with them and had pillow fights and kissed and cuddled some ("We'd tickle, fight, laugh, mess around," said one, "but all you'd have to say is 'Stop!' and he'd roll over and quit"), until Lamar had to drive them home. But mostly it was Anita. She saw him almost every night, though she told a reporter a couple of months was much too early to tell whether there was anything really "serious" to it.

From Alan Fortas' perspective there was a quality of wholesomeness, whether internally or externally determined, that was almost unreal, and largely attributable to Mrs. Presley's presence. "It never got wild at Graceland," he wrote. "People respected Graceland as the Presleys' home. And the language never got [too] rough around there, either. . . . If anybody said 'goddamn,' he erupted in a rage . . . 'You can use any other word you want to, but don't use the Lord's name in vain!' " He had his high school class picture up on the wall, and he would point it out to everyone, in George's presence, saying, "Look who's up there at the top." And they would always say, "Who is that, Elvis? It's hard to see." He would say, "That's George Klein. He was one of the few guys that was nice to me in school," to George's acute discomfiture and radiating pride.

Vernon couldn't have been happier — everybody came to him for decisions, he had plenty to do, Elvis deferred to him on money matters, he was as proud as one of the peacocks on the lawn. For Gladys, on the other hand, there was a clear sense of resignation, a pervasive air of sadness; she didn't seem able to ever really settle in to her new home. "She never did go nowhere after they moved out there," said her sister Lillian. "She used to go to the grocery store, but she quit going to the grocery store. She never was satisfied after she moved out there — I think the house was too big, and she didn't like it. Of course she never told Elvis that." When her cousin Frank Richards visited with his wife, Leona, that summer, Gladys confessed to her, "I'm the most miserable woman in the world," and Alan always recalled her "sitting by the window in the kitchen, daydreaming, or looking out in the backyard at her chickens." Every so often she'd have a beer or two with Cliff. "We never did that at Audubon, but up at Graceland we'd be sitting and chatting in the kitchen, maybe two or three times a week in the afternoon — that was it — and Elvis would come in and shake his head like, 'My God, you people are going to hell, drinking beer like this.' I'm serious! She just said, 'Son, Cliff and I are going to have a beer, whether you like it or not.' And he'd turn around and shake his head and just walk out without saying another word." It was all right, she told Lamar, if Elvis blew up at him, or at any of them, once in a while. " 'When Elvis gets mad at you,' she said, 'always remember, it's from the mouth out.' That was one of her expressions. She knew him better than anybody. She could tell what he was going to do before he did it. She was scared to death something was gonna happen to him. She used to say, 'I hope I'm in the grave before he is. Because I could never stand to see him dead before me.' "

Toward the end of the summer Freddy Bienstock came down to go over material for the upcoming session in Hollywood in September. "It was the second time that I went to Memphis, ostensibly to play songs for him. I was told that he wasn't going to get up till about three o'clock, and it was a hot day, so I went into the swimming pool and a couple of ducks jumped in and one of them clipped me on the ear, and I jumped out of that pool so fast. . . . He had all kinds of animals around, and he had built columns around the pool — he told me afterwards that he had the idea of building these columns from seeing the movie *The Philadelphia Story*. Anyway, he showed me around — he was very proud of Graceland without putting on any airs about it — and in the evening we all went out to dinner. I hadn't eaten very much, so I was really looking forward to a terrific dinner. We were driving in two limousines, and he said to Lamar, who was an endomorph for sure, to call the restaurant on the car phone — they were very rare in those days — he wanted a private dining room reserved for him. So I thought this is really going to be a lovely dinner. He said, 'We may as well order now, so when we get there the food will be ready and we don't have to wait.' The first order was a hamburger and an orange pop, and, you know, then a ham and cheese sandwich and a Pepsi-Cola, a bacon sandwich and a glass of milk, and so forth, and when it came to me I didn't want to be different, so I ordered another cheese sandwich and an orange pop. And then, when it came to paying the bill, the whole thing came to, I think, fourteen or fifteen dollars, and Elvis pulled out a twenty and grandly says, 'Keep the change.' "

THE SCENE AT THE TRAIN STATION as he left for the Coast at 11:00 on the night of August 27 threatened to get out of hand. The Colonel had set up a whirlwind tour of the Pacific Northwest (five cities in four days) to precede the September 5–7 recording session that Steve Sholes had finally gotten him to allow Elvis to do. George, Lamar, and Cliff, who would once again be his traveling companions, had all driven to the station with his parents and him, while his uncle Travis and aunt Lorraine had come in their own car, but Anita was without question the center of attention. "Anita is number one with me — strictly tops," Elvis told the small crowd of fans and reporters who had gathered to see him off. He then embraced his mother several times, reported the paper faithfully, "and she reminded him to 'Be good, son,' as he boarded the train. 'Take care of yourself, boy,' said Mr. Presley. . . . Elvis kissed Anita twice for photographers (and about five times for himself) before hopping aboard. As the train moved away, Anita burst into tears and Mrs. Presley put her arm around her. The Presleys and Anita walked arm in arm out of the station to the Cadillac again, with Uncle Travis, himself moist-eyed, following."

And then they were gone. Anita had just won the Mid-South Hollywood Star Hunt the previous Thursday and was traveling to New Orleans to take part in the finalists' competition, which promised a small movie role to the winner. He was keeping his fingers crossed, he told her, but for himself Elvis was just looking forward to getting back to work. The promoter for the tour was Lee Gordon, the same flamboyant Australian entrepreneur who had booked them in the Northeast the previous spring and was imprecating Colonel Parker — so far without any success — to agree to an Australian tour. Jerry Leiber and Mike Stoller, the songwriters, were all set for the Hollywood session. And Elvis was going to have Millie Kirkham, the soprano who had done a good deal of Nashville session work with the Jordanaires and whose backup vocals he had admired recently on a Jimmy "C" Newman release, flown in specially for the session. He hadn't heard anything from the draft board lately, though there were rumors in the papers every day, and maybe that would work out, maybe the Colonel could fix it — why would the government want to give up all those millions of dollars in taxes?

The tour went pretty much according to plan. There were riots in virtually every city, but security was generally good, and he enjoyed teasing the crowd, dancing suggestively and lying down and writhing on the stage, sometimes with a model of RCA's trademark dog, Nipper. "A chunky, effeminate-looking man with long hair, later identified as a member of Presley's entourage, seemed almost in a trance as he snapped his fingers, wiggled his body and shouted over and over: 'Yeah man, yeah man, yeah, yeah, yeah,' " reported the *Tacoma News Tribune*. "I lose myself in my singing," Elvis told one press gathering. "Maybe it's my early training singing gospel hymns. I'm limp as a rag, worn out when a show's over." His first love was "the old colored spirituals," he told a press conference in Vancouver. "I know practically every religious song that's ever been written," he boasted proudly.

He ended every show with "Hound Dog," which he had taken to introducing as the "Elvis Presley national anthem." Meanwhile, the Colonel, never one to miss a trick, was selling nearly as many "I Hate Elvis" buttons as "I Love Elvis" ones. In Vancouver a small contingent of Canadian Mounties was not up to the task of holding back a crowd of almost twenty-five thousand at Empire Stadium, and for the first time the Colonel, who had protested bitterly over the size of the force, Mounties or no Mounties, was impelled to actively intervene.

"The Colonel came out and pulled Elvis offstage," said George Klein, "and the MC said, 'You are going to have to get back in your seats, or we can't go on with the show.' Meanwhile, the Colonel told Elvis, 'Elvis, don't tease this crowd. These people are crazy.' Well, if you tell Elvis not to do something, that's the surest way you're going to get him to do it, so he goes back onstage and the first thing he does is, 'Wellllll . . .' And here come fifty thousand more people! So the Colonel runs out again — this is the first time I ever saw Colonel Parker go out onstage — he got mad, and he went onstage because he was protecting his property. And he said, 'Okay, you can stay on the field if you act right and you don't tear the stage up. Otherwise Mr. Presley's not going to be performing.' And he says to Elvis, 'Elvis, please don't do an hour. Do thirty minutes tonight.' So Elvis did about forty-five or fifty minutes, and when we left that stage the last thing we saw was the stage being turned over — sheet music flying up in the air, they grabbed music stands, instruments, drumsticks, everything they could get. That was a pretty scary night."

"A gang moved into our town," declared the *Vancouver Province*. It was nothing more than "subsidized sex," sniffed the paper's music critic, Dr. Ida Halpern. The performance "had not even the quality of a true obscenity: merely an artificial and unhealthy exploitation of the enthusiasm of youth's body and mind." Meanwhile, Elvis heard from Anita that she had won the talent contest in New Orleans. She told him excitedly that she would join him in Hollywood the following week, and he sounded really happy and told her not to be nervous and said that he was really looking forward to showing her around.

The session went smoothly enough. Mr. Sholes had just been promoted to head of pop a&r — it hadn't been announced yet, but he and Mr. Bullock were celebrating. That still didn't stop Colonel from getting in his little zingers every chance he got. The principal aim of the session was to record a Christmas album, and Elvis wanted to get in the right mood, so Mr. Sholes arranged to have a tree in the studio and made sure that there were wrapped presents under it. Elvis had never been satisfied with the version of "Treat Me Nice" he had recorded for the movie, so he did it again, and he cut "Don't," the ballad that Jerry and Mike had written for him in June, as well as a beautiful version of Ivory Joe Hunter's "My Wish Came True," on which he coached the Jordanaires to mimic the harmonies of the Statesmen and in particular Jake Hess' habit of crisply enunciating his syllables. Freddy tried to sneak in a song that he had pitched without success back in January — he figured Elvis would never remember it — but he didn't get more than eight bars into it when Elvis said, "I've heard that song before, and I don't like it any better now than I did then."

They recorded a number of Christmas standards, including a re-creation of the Drifters' arrangement of "White Christmas" from a couple of years before and the Ernest Tubb country standard, "Blue Christmas." With "Blue Christmas" Elvis wanted the sound that Millie Kirkham had created on Ferlin Husky's "Gone," and he had her singing a soprano obbligato all the way through. "It was horrible," said Kirkham, who was six months pregnant at the time. "It was sort of comical. It wasn't supposed to be, but the longer it goes the funnier it gets — but he liked it. He was a star, but he was so much fun to be around. He was very polite to everybody, amazingly so to me. When I walked in, he said, 'Get this woman a chair!' I was the only female, of course, but if one of the guys happened to say something off-color he would just say, 'Wait a minute, guys, we got a lady in the room,' and they were never offended. We always used to say they laughed on cue." Toward the end of the session they ran out of material, and Jerry and Mike went back into the mix room, where they concocted "Santa Claus Is Back in Town," a wonderful double-entendre blues that Elvis delivered with great panache.

Scotty, D.J., and Bill were watching the clock with increasing apprehension as the three-day session came to a close. They had been promised the opportunity to record some instrumentals on Elvis' time when the session was over. Actually, the idea had been kicking around for close to a year now, but this time they had a firm commitment for studio time, and they had worked up some tunes, and Elvis was even talking about playing piano on one or two. When it came down to it, though, Elvis felt tired, or was simply not in the mood, and Tom Diskin came into the studio and said, "That's it." Scotty and Bill protested that they had a deal, but Diskin told them Colonel said they could do it another time and told everyone to pack up, unmoved by either their anger or protestations. Bill hit the roof, muttering to himself and slamming his electric bass into its case, while they waited for Elvis to stand up for them — but he never did. He didn't say a word, in fact, and, as had so often been the case, seemed to slide out of the situation without even acknowledging that he knew what was going on.

Scotty and Bill went back to the hotel, but the gnawing feeling of resentment wouldn't go away; it just grew stronger and stronger until, finally, later in the evening, they wrote up a letter of resignation which each of them would personally sign and send. They had expected more from Elvis, they had expected to *share* in his success, and here they were still only making two hundred dollars a week on the road and responsible for their own expenses. They were in debt, they needed financial help, they just wanted some fucking respect. Within the formal constraints of a letter they were barely able to touch on their long-standing feelings: the fact that they had had only one raise in two years; the cutback in personals to the point that they had played only fourteen dates so far this year; the way in which the Colonel had prevented them from making any endorsements and, as they saw it, simply "squeezed us for a matter of dollars"; the way in which they had been cut off from all access to Elvis — it was almost as if, Bill felt, they were no longer even permitted to talk to him.

When they approached D.J. with the letter, he declined to sign it. He felt that he had been treated fairly, he explained; he had come in as a salaried employee, he had always gotten paid, he had no real complaints. "Bill was pretty pissed, but I explained my reasons, and they said, 'Okay, don't worry about it.' " Then they had the letter delivered to Elvis at the Beverly Wilshire Hotel.

Elvis read the letter, shook his head, said "Aw, shit," and passed it around. He obviously couldn't believe that Scotty and Bill would do something like this to him, that they would humiliate him, in front of the world, in this fashion. It flashed through his mind that maybe this was the beginning of the end: first Dewey, then them. *Where was their fucking loyalty?* Then he was pissed off. If they had just come to him, he told the guys and anyone who would listen, they could have worked something out. Now he would *never* take them back. They had probably been hired by someone else — Ricky Nelson or Gene Vincent or one of them. He was wild with grief. Anita, who had arrived from Memphis only that evening, tried to console him. Colonel and Diskin stayed out of his way — the boy would work it out for himself, Colonel said, while Steve Sholes expressed the hope, several times, that the separation would be permanent. In Sholes' view Elvis could do better, he could get better musicians, brighter musicians, quicker learners, any day of the week.

The last couple of days in Hollywood were bittersweet. Elvis showed his girl the sights and, before he left, gave her a ring to signify his feelings. He bought it in the Beverly Wilshire jewelry shop, and it was described as eighteen sapphires surrounding a diamond and "very expensive" by "bug-eyed" hotel employees. It was just a "friendship ring," Anita said, showing it off proudly to reporters, but, secretly, she felt differently.

The news of the split with Scotty and Bill had reached Memphis by the time Elvis got home on September 11. He called Scotty the following day and offered a raise of $50 across the board, but Scotty said that he would need $10,000 in addition to the raise, if only "out of the kindness of [Elvis'] heart," just to get out of debt. Elvis said he would think about it, but in the meantime Bob Johnson sniffed out the story and interviewed Scotty and Bill for a feature that ran the next day in which both musicians expressed their disappointment, and described the disagreement, in sorrowful but explicit terms. The crux of the matter, said Scotty, was that "[Elvis] promised us that the more he made the more we would make. But it hasn't worked that way."

Elvis' reaction was not surprising: he felt even further betrayed and released a statement to the newspaper to accompany an interview in which he told *his* side of the story.

"Scotty, Bill, I hope you fellows have good luck," Elvis' statement read. "I will give you fellows good recommendations. If you had come to me, we would have worked things out. I would have always taken care of you. But you went to the papers and tried to make me look bad, instead of coming to me so we could work things out. All I can say to you is 'good luck.' " So far as promises were concerned, Elvis said, "I have a good memory and I don't remember ever telling them [anything like] that." To *Press-Scimitar* reporter Bill Burk, Elvis spoke of "certain people close to him who have tried to persuade him to drop his musical group during the last two years. He would not name these people, but said he told them he would not because they were good musicians and because of sentimental reasons. 'We started out together,' he said, 'and I didn't want to cut anyone out of anything. . . . These boys could have had a job with me as long as I was making a dime.' "

Their resignations, he told Burk, came at a particularly crucial time. "He plays the Tupelo Fair (which he called 'my homecoming') Sept. 27. He said he just received the dates of his next tour, which will be in October. . . . Elvis said he would immediately begin auditioning for a new guitar player and bass player during the two weeks before the Tupelo Fair. 'It might take a while,' he said, 'but it's not impossible to find replacements.' "

"We're both pretty stubborn," Scotty conceded to the press. "I guess he can be stubborn longer because he's got more money."

HE ARRIVED IN TUPELO with Anita and his parents, along with Cliff, George, Lamar, Alan, and another friend, named Louis Harris. There was as much excitement in town about his upcoming appearance as there had been the previous year, but it was of a different sort, and mindful of his generous donation toward a youth center, the lead editorial in the paper offered an admonitory note to the community to "Let Our Welcome for Elvis Be Truly Warm." Elvis had been "the best ambassador any town could have," declared the *Tupelo Daily Journal,* and "he needs to feel appreciated in at least one community in America for just being himself." The paper was full of stories about the riots in Little Rock over school integration, and there was even a story with a Memphis dateline about white students from still segregated Humes High School jeering at Negro students on their way to nearby Manassas, but in Tupelo, the paper noted on the front page, while the annual 4-H Club style show would be held in front of the grandstand, "the Negro junior Jersey show will start at 10 A.M. in the Negro section of the fairgrounds."

Mr. Savery, the fair manager, had them all over to dinner, and Jack Cristil from WELO spent as much time interviewing Anita as he did Elvis.

Did they have marriage plans? the reporters all shouted at him at the press conference in the tent before the performance. "I haven't found the girl yet," he said, staring straight at Anita with a look meant just for her. After a slow advance sale, the grandstand was filled to capacity; the band — with Nashville's Hank "Sugarfoot" Garland on guitar and Chuck Wiginton, a friend of D.J.'s from Dallas, on bass — sounded tight; Colonel made sure that they put up a big banner announcing that *Jailhouse Rock* was coming soon; and he worked the crowd, and himself, up into the usual frenzy. But somehow it wasn't the same. It didn't feel right, he told D.J. afterward. Garland was a helluva guitarist, but you could tell the difference on "Don't Be Cruel"; Garland could really *play*, but he didn't hit that intro the way that Scotty did.

A feeling of melancholy had stolen over him, as if, somehow, it was all coming to an end. He felt badly let down by Scotty and Bill — he didn't understand why they had done this to him. And even though things were back to normal with Dewey as of last week, he wasn't sure they could ever really be the same again. He had stopped by Sun, but things were different there, too, with Marion gone. She and Sam had had a big fight, and she had gone off and enlisted in the air force. The draft was hanging like a dark cloud over his head. Every day there were stories in the paper about it, and reporters wanted to know what he was going to do.

The week after the Tupelo homecoming, he decided to take them back. Scotty and Bill played a miserable two-week engagement at the Dallas State Fair and then formalized the arrangement, with everyone swallowing his pride a little and the Blue Moon Boys returning on a per diem basis. There were no hard feelings, Scotty said. It was a matter of money all along. For Elvis, though, it would have been hard to say what it was exactly. One day he heard "Jailhouse Rock" on the radio and declared, "Elvis Presley and his one-man band," with a rueful shake of his head. It seemed like everything was plunging headlong forward, and he didn't know how to hold it back.

PORTRAIT. (ALFRED WERTHEIMER)

WALKING IN A DREAM

"HERE. READ THIS!" said a reporter, shoving a magazine article into Elvis' hands. "Rock 'n' roll smells phony and false," declared Frank Sinatra in the story's text. "It is sung, played, and written for the most part by cretinous goons and by means of its almost imbecilic reiteration, and sly, lewd, in plain fact, dirty lyrics . . . it manages to be the martial music of every sideburned delinquent on the face of the earth. . . . [It] is the most brutal, ugly, desperate, vicious form of expression it has been my misfortune to hear."

And what was Elvis Presley's response to that? he was asked, standing in front of a roomful of reporters. It was an hour before his October 28 performance at the Pan Pacific Auditorium, which would mark his Hollywood debut. "I admire the man," said Elvis. "He has a right to say what he wants to say. He is a great success and a fine actor, but I think he shouldn't have said it. He's mistaken about this. This is a trend, just the same as he faced when he started years ago. I consider it the greatest in music," Elvis added mischievously, throwing the reporters a little off balance. "It is very noteworthy — and namely because it is the only thing I can do. . . ."

"Is that all you have to say?"

"You can't knock success," declared Elvis and went on to answer questions about his income, his sideburns, his draft status, and any plans he might have for marriage, before taking the stage in gold jacket and dress pants at 8:15.

He was determined to impress his celebrity-studded audience, and he did. In front of a sold-out, paid attendance of more than nine thousand (at the Colonel's insistence, even Hal Wallis was required to buy his own ticket), he flung himself about, "wiggled, bumped, twisted," and at the conclusion of the fifty-minute performance rolled around on the floor with Nipper in a manner longtime critic Jack O'Brian of the *New York*

Journal-American declared "far too indecent to mention in every detail."

The audience went wild, but the newspapers took a somewhat dimmer view. "Elvis Presley Will Have to Clean Up His Show — Or Go to Jail," declared one headline, while O'Brian characterized the music as "a terrible popular twist on darkest Africa's fertility tom-tom displays" and *Los Angeles Mirror-News* entertainment editor Dick Williams noted: "If any further proof were needed that what Elvis offers is not basically music but a sex show, it was proved last night." His performance, wrote Williams, resembled "one of those screeching, uninhibited party rallies which the Nazis used to hold for Hitler," and many parents who had attended with their children, including actors Alan Ladd and Walter Slezak, expressed equal outrage to authorities and the newspapers. The result was that the Los Angeles Vice Squad contacted the Colonel, who told Elvis that he would have to cut out some of the dancing and in general tone down his act. What was Elvis' reaction? the Colonel was asked. "This isn't the first time," said the Colonel. "You know, they done it a couple of times before." Did Elvis complain about not being able to dance? "Naw, he didn't complain. . . . He just said, 'Well, if I don't dance tonight, maybe I don't have to take a shower tonight.' " "Colonel Parker said that?" declared Elvis incredulously. "He couldn't have! You see," Elvis explained, genuinely upset, "I take a shower every night, whether I dance or just sing."

When the police showed up with movie cameras on the second night, the show *was* considerably toned down, and the only person to object was Yul Brynner, "whose bleeding heart," wrote Jack O'Brian, "led him to protest [the censorship] as if it were an invasion of someone's privacy." Brynner, declared O'Brian olympianly, was "ridiculous." Elvis, for his part, kept his own counsel.

Still, he felt good about it. He had done what he did best in front of a town in which he was only beginning to feel comfortable — and it had caused just as much of a stir as it would have in Memphis or Saskatchewan. The single of "Jailhouse Rock" was currently at number one, the film had just had its world premiere in Memphis at the same theater where Elvis had ushered as a teenager and was scheduled to open in theaters throughout the country the following week, and the Colonel had estimated that, with the deal they had with MGM, Elvis was likely to make more than two million dollars when it did. As he said to one reporter who raised the question of what he would do if his popularity were to decline,

"You can't stay on top forever. Even if I stopped singing tomorrow, I'd have no regrets. I had a ball while I was there."

There was a party that night at his suite, and everyone was there: Sammy, Nick, Vince Edwards, Venetia, Carol Channing, Tommy Sands, a whole bunch of pretty girls, even seventeen-year-old Ricky Nelson showed up, riding the crest of his first big Imperial hit. Elvis knew that Ricky was friendly with Scotty and Bill, but he and Ricky had never really talked, and Ricky was just hanging around on the edge of the party when Elvis pushed his way through the crowd, picked him up in the air, and said, "Man, I just love your new record." He loved *The Adventures of Ozzie and Harriet,* too, he watched it all the time, he told Ricky, and he wondered whether Ricky's brother, David, was here tonight. When *Photoplay* editor Marcia Borie told Elvis that Ricky was about to go out on tour for the first time and could use some advice, Elvis took Ricky aside and filled him in. "You'll never know how much tonight has meant to me," Nelson told Borie later in the evening. "Imagine Elvis Presley watching our show. He repeated episodes I'd even forgotten about. He remembered them word for word. And he gave me some great tips about things to do on my tour. I still can't believe it." Cliff, Nick, and Sammy Davis, Jr., entertained the guests with impressions, and Elvis' date for the evening was Anne Neyland.

One week later he sailed for Hawaii. The three shows scheduled there were the last of a broken six-day tour (San Francisco, Oakland, Hollywood, and Hawaii) that seemed to have been arranged at the last minute and was elongated even further by the four-day boat ride. The Colonel and the Jordanaires and the band, of course, all flew over, but Elvis stuck to his promise to his mother not to fly unless it was absolutely necessary. There was one small surprise at the dock: Billy Murphy showed up with his bags packed just as the ship was about to sail. Elvis had invited him sometime earlier, but there had been no further discussion of the subject, and now a mild flurry of confusion arose before someone finally purchased a ticket for him. Other than that, the cruise was a dull one, made up of typical tourists and retirees and a notable absence of eligible girls. Cliff, who continued to aspire to Hollywood hipness, followed Billy around to the point that Murphy finally told him, "Cliff, you're colorful and you're interesting, but you're ninety percent exaggeration and ten percent lies." Which kind of took the wind out of Cliff's sails and gave the others something to chew on. When they finally arrived, Elvis enjoyed his first view of Hawaii; the Australian promoter, Lee Gordon, did his usual good job of promoting the shows; and Elvis even went down to the beach in shorts on the last night to sign autographs.

They were back in Hollywood by November 17, with nothing, really, to do. The Colonel didn't want him making any recordings — RCA had more than enough in the can — and the new movie deal with Twentieth Century Fox had fallen through when Hal Wallis refused to release Elvis from his contractual obligation to make another picture with Paramount first. There was no further touring planned, and he had no particular reason to be home, so he returned to Las Vegas, where he had spent a couple of weeks in October going out with showgirls and catching every act in town. On this visit he met a fresh-faced, twenty-one-year-old singer named Kitty Dolan, whom he formally "dated," as he had dated Dottie and June before, as well as the stripper Tempest Storm, to whom he announced, at an appropriate moment, "I'm as horny as a billy goat in a pepper patch. I'll race you to the bed."

It was a strangely unsettled time. The draft wasn't going to go away, his career seemed to be in a temporary state of limbo, even the tour — with the exception of his appearance at the Pan Pacific — had been without any real luster. There had been the usual riots, there had been the usual challenge of provoking the crowd into a frenzy, of teasing them until they were aroused past the point of turning back — *but there was nothing new.* It was all something he had done before, all just the playing out of a masquerade. For the first time in a long time he was no longer sure what was supposed to happen next. Perhaps the one real surprise had come in San Francisco when security guards came backstage to tell him that there was a rabbi outside insisting that he had to see Elvis. George scrutinized the scribbled note and realized to his astonishment that it was Rabbi Fruchter, his old rabbi from Temple Beth El Emeth, but he couldn't for the life of him figure out how Rabbi Fruchter would know George was there or what the connection with Elvis might be. "Elvis said, 'Oh, we used to live underneath him on Alabama Street, he was really nice to me, he'd loan me money, and sometimes he'd ask me to turn on the lights for him on Saturday.' So I went and got him, and Elvis hugs him and shakes hands with him, and at the press conference he introduces Rabbi Fruchter, and the reporters all look at this rabbi, and they just couldn't relate!"

Some guys from Tupelo showed up at the same performance, and Elvis recalled them, too, riding on a train with George sometime later. "We'd be going through some little country town, and he'd say, 'Shit, this reminds me of Tupelo.' He said, 'You remember when we were in San Francisco, George, and those guys came up to us, and all they wanted to talk about was Tupelo? They kept saying, "Elvis, remember back in Tupelo?" And all I was thinking was, "Fuck Tupelo. I want to forget about Tupelo." ' He wasn't putting down Tupelo. He just meant he was glad to get out. Tupelo was a little small town where there really wasn't much to do. Memphis was where everything had happened for him."

BACK HOME IN MEMPHIS the same overhanging miasma continued to prevail. In the midst of public celebration an unsettling sense of spiritual malaise would overtake him, which he might share, occasionally, with friends or reveal, almost despite himself, in public statements. After the Easter service at First Assembly, for example, which he had proudly attended with Yvonne Lime, he had sought out the Reverend Hamill. "He said, 'Pastor, I am the most miserable young man you have ever seen. I have got more money than I can ever spend. I have thousands of fans out there, and I have a lot of people who call themselves my friends, but I am miserable. I am not doing a lot of things that you taught me, and I am doing some things that you taught me not to do.' " To *Photoplay* magazine he announced, in what the magazine described as a state of dejection and what might more accurately be seen as a moment of near-desperation: "I never expected to be anybody important. Maybe I'm not now, but whatever I am, whatever I will become will be what God has chosen for me. Some people I know can't figure out how Elvis Presley happened. I don't blame them for wondering that. Sometimes I wonder myself. . . . But no matter what I do, I don't forget about God. I feel he's watching every move I make. And in a way it's good for me. I'll never feel comfortable taking a strong drink, and I'll never feel easy smoking a cigarette. I just don't think those things are right for me. . . . I just want to let a few people know that the way I live is by doing what I think God wants me to. I want someone to understand."

He visited Lansky's one night at 9:00 or 10:00, "and we had a big feast for him," said Guy Lansky. "I went down to the deli to pick up corn beef and salami, we had a beautiful spread for him, and all he wanted was potato salad. He reached over and got that quart of potato salad and said, 'That's all I'm going to eat.' And I said, 'How about a corn beef sandwich, Elvis?' And he said, 'No, Mr. Lansky, this is all I want. Give the rest to Lamar. He's my garbage disposal.' He got a big laugh out of that, but Lamar didn't take it so pleasantly. There were still some customers in the store, and Elvis said, 'Give them anything they want' — I mean, up to a certain limit. I said, 'You're on, Elvis. Whatever they want.' Man, they couldn't get over it, the customers — and of course it was mostly black customers in Lansky's at that time — but for his entourage he didn't buy them anything, he never bought them anything. I couldn't figure that one out."

On December 6 he attended the WDIA Goodwill Revue once again. His appearance didn't cause the commotion that it had the year before, but he had his picture taken with Little Junior Parker (the originator of "Mystery Train") and Bobby "Blue" Bland, and he was quoted in the paper as saying that this music was "the real thing. . . . Right from the heart." You couldn't beat it, he said, watching from the wings and smiling and swaying to the music. "The audience shouted in time to the solid rhythm," reported the paper. " 'Man,' grinned Elvis, 'what about that!' "

It was a strangely desultory Christmas. The tree was taken down out of storage, Elvis distributed a considerable amount of money to local charities as well as the United Fund and the March of Dimes, the Christmas album reached the number-one chart position even as it encountered vicious criticism (from Irving Berlin, among others) for what was seen as a desecration of the traditional Christmas spirit. The Colonel told him he had two more movies definitely lined up upon the completion of the new Hal Wallis production, a specially tailored adaptation of the Harold Robbins novel *A Stone for Danny Fisher.* The first of the outside projects was an unnamed picture for Twentieth Century Fox, the other a Hank Williams biopic for MGM — both, if he bothered to read the trades, at enormous sums of money — but he doubted somehow that either was ever going to get made.

About ten days before Christmas he started getting serious pitches from the army, the navy, and the air force about what they could do for *him.* They had suggestions for various kinds of deals — the navy proposed an "Elvis Presley company" that could be specially trained, and the air force offered a deal where he would merely tour recruiting centers around the country—but when he and the Colonel talked it over, he could see that the Colonel was right once again, it would merely serve to inflame public opinion and create a vicious backlash if he did not go in and receive the same treatment as every other citizen.

Then, on December 19, he got word informally from Milton Bowers, chairman of the draft board since 1943 and former president of the Memphis School Board, that his induction notice was ready and that he could simply stop by the draft board to pick it up. Bowers didn't want to put it in the mail, he said, for fear that the news would be leaked by someone who saw the letter addressed in an official Selective Service envelope.

Elvis dropped in at the Sun studio the next day, just after picking up his notice, and announced cheerfully, "Hey, I'm going in," but with George and Cliff and the other guys he was somewhat more revealing. "We were at Graceland," said George, "and I walked in. First thing he did was hand me the note. I said, 'What's this?' He said, 'Read it.' And I opened it up, and it said: 'GREETINGS.' I said, 'Oh no, Elvis.' He said, 'Yeah, I've been drafted.' He was devastated—just down, depressed. I said, 'Damn, what are we going to do?' He said, 'Man, I don't know.' He said, 'The Colonel says we might could get a deferment to make *King Creole*, but he says I probably got to go.' I said, 'Well, man, there's no war going on'—we were trying to make him feel better, me and Cliff and Arthur, and Gene. Cliff said, 'Wait a minute, Elvis, they'll never take you. You're too big! You're the biggest thing in show biz. They won't let them take you, the kids won't let them. Elvis, just think'—and Cliff's a real quick thinker, and he said, he immediately zeroed in, 'Elvis, you're paying the government ten million dollars a year in taxes, you know there's no war going on. It's all—' And so he kind of got Elvis' mind off it, but the last thing Elvis said when he got on the damn bus to go in the army was, 'Fuck Cliff Gleaves!' "

James Page, a *Press-Scimitar* reporter, caught up with him well after midnight as he was coming in from a night on the town. There were dozens of fans still at the gate maintaining a mournful vigil when Elvis roared up in his Continental. He professed himself relieved to have the situation finally resolved and expressed sincere feelings of gratitude for "what this country has given me. And now I'm ready to return a little. It's the only adult way to look at it."

"Would you like to go into Special Services?"

"I want to go where I can do the best job."

"What about your movie contracts?"

"Don't know — just don't know."

"How about a look at your draft notice?"

Elvis grinned sheepishly: "Man, I don't know what I did with it."

The search was on.

"Maybe in the kitchen," someone suggested. It wasn't.

"Last time I saw it, it was right there," said Elvis and pointed to a place in the front hall. No notice.

Finally: "Here's the envelope — the notice must be in my parents' bedroom."

One thing sure: There is a notice for Elvis and "I'll do what I have to — like any American boy."

He left for Nashville that same night to deliver his Christmas present to the Colonel. It was a little red Isetta sports car, and he loaded it onto a rented truck, which he drove, with Lamar and Cliff following in the Lincoln. They arrived at the Colonel's home in Madison early the next morning, but there was already a gang of reporters and photographers waiting. He and the Colonel posed for pictures in the car. "It is snug," observed Parker. "It is only a small, small way of showing my feelings for you," replied Elvis on the record. "Now isn't he a sweet kid?" Colonel said to the newspapermen, his eyes "dewing up." "He could have just sent something in the mail." In addition, Elvis answered questions about the draft (who knew, he said, he just might reenlist when his hitch was up) and even tried on an army surplus set of fatigues, which a photographer thoughtfully provided and in which he looked exceedingly uncomfortable. " 'I guess I'll be wearing this stuff for real, soon,' he said, looking ruefully down at the green twill." Whatever private feelings he had he kept to himself or reserved for the private conference that he and the Colonel had, as per custom, behind closed doors.

Gordon Stoker came out at the Colonel's direction to pick up the Jordanaires' four thousand dollars in Christmas bonuses, and Elvis asked if he'd be going to the Opry that night. "He told me, 'If I had some kind of clothes, I'd go with you guys. Well, I called Mallernee's down on Sixth — I happened to know the man who owned the store — and I told them, 'I'm going to bring Elvis Presley in there to get something to wear down to the Grand Ole Opry tonight, but if any of the salesmen or anyone makes anything over him, he'll walk right out in the middle of a fitting, so don't tell anyone he's coming.' Anyway, surprisingly, he picked out a tuxedo with a tux shirt, tux tie, even tux shoes. I was shocked. I thought he'd just buy a suit or a sports coat. But that's what he wore down to the Opry that night."

His draft situation was really bugging him, Stoker felt; he still couldn't understand why the Colonel hadn't fixed things better, but he didn't say much about it. At the Opry that night he just walked out onstage and waved and visited with old friends backstage. How were things going? asked T. Tommy Cutrer, who had promoted him in Shreveport and was announcing the Opry now. "He said, 'It's lonesome, T.' I said, 'How can you talk about that, with thousands of people . . .' He said, 'Well, I can't go get a hamburger, I can't go in some little greasy joint, I can't go waterskiing or shopping' — and he loved to go shopping. By this time he'd dyed his hair and had on makeup, which was strange to me. The only one of the Opry stars that would make up back then was Ferlin Husky, and that was to go onstage. So I said, 'Cat, why you got that shit on you?' He said, 'Well, that's what the movies want.' But he never changed a bit, he was always the same."

He had his picture taken with old friends and current Opry stars: he and the Colonel posed with the Duke of Paducah and Faron Young and booking agent Hubert Long, and he was pictured with his arm around an absolutely thrilled-looking Brenda Lee (who at thirteen looked no older than ten), with Johnny Cash, Ray Price, Hawkshaw Hawkins, the Wilburn Brothers, even Hank Snow, who seemed to hold no grudge against his onetime protégé even if his feelings toward his former partner were less than mixed. Jimmie Rodgers Snow, too, came by with his fifteen-year-old fiancée to say hello, "and he asked me what I was doing. I said, 'Nothing special, why?' And he said, 'Why don't you come over to Memphis around the first, we'll have some fun.' And I said, 'Fine.' " Then he changed back into the clothes he had worn on the trip over and, according to Gordon Stoker, threw his new tux into a barrel full of stage ropes before setting off on the 230-mile drive back to Memphis.

By Monday morning the draft board had received a letter from Paramount studio head Y. Frank Freeman requesting a sixty-day deferment for Elvis on the basis of financial hardship: the studio had already spent between $300,000 and $350,000 in preproduction costs for *King Creole* (formerly *Sing, You Sinners*) and stood to lose that amount or more if Elvis Presley were not permitted to film it. That was all very well, declared draft board chairman Milton Bowers, the board might very well look favorably upon such a request, but the request had to come from the inductee. On Tuesday, December 24, Elvis wrote to the draft board, explaining that as far as he was concerned he was ready to enter the army immediately, but he was requesting the deferment for Paramount "so these folks will not lose so much money, with all they have done so far." He concluded by wishing the three board members a merry Christmas. Three days later the request was granted, which the Colonel called "very kind," adding, "I know of nothing that would prevent his induction when his deferment is up. And I don't think Elvis would consider making another request, because I know how he feels personally about it." "I'm glad for the studio's sake," Elvis said. "I'm glad they were nice enough to let me make this picture because I think it will be the best one I've made."

Jimmie Rodgers Snow arrived on the afternoon of New Year's Day, and Lamar picked him up at the airport. Snow had been undergoing something of a spiritual crisis of late, brought on by his recognition of an increasing dependence on pills and alcohol, but he and Elvis just picked up where they had left off a year and a half before. "When I first arrived there was somebody at the door getting his signature on a special delivery. He just tossed it on the couch, didn't even open it until much later when he said, 'Oh yeah, my gold record.'

"He introduced me to all his friends, and we ran around all night and slept all day. When we would come downstairs probably at two or three in the afternoon, his mother would always be there, sitting in the kitchen drinking a beer. He'd go up and kiss her, and we'd go down and shoot pool or sing at the piano, talk about what we were going to do that night, which was either go see his movie, *Jailhouse Rock*, at the theater with a bunch of girls or go roller-skating, things like that. When we went to the movies, he rented the whole theater, and he'd sit beside me and say, 'What did you think of me in that scene? How'd I do? Was I flat on that note? Did I hold it too long?' He was just the same. He used to love for me to imitate Winston Churchill, put a cigar in my mouth and sound just like Churchill — he'd want me to do that for everybody, and he loved it every time. It was nothing for him to be driving down the street at night and all of a sudden put his brakes on, open the car door up, jump out, make a face back at the cars behind him, and get back in and drive off and laugh.

"Sometimes he'd get serious and sit down at that white piano, and we'd sing gospel songs. And, of course, I'd been a Christian in 1950, '51, I didn't stay with it very long but I was being tugged on at that time by God to go into the ministry, get married and give up my career. So we'd get serious, which I didn't really want to because I was fighting it then, but we'd talk about the Lord and he would voice his feelings, and then we would get off of it and go into fun things."

Cliff and Lamar got into a fight that week over a badminton game, and Lamar finally egged Cliff to the point that Cliff hit him over the head with his racket. Mr. Presley was pissed off, and Mrs. Presley got so upset that Elvis had to fire the two of them. He apologized as they were packing, trying to sort out what was theirs and what was his ("Oh, just keep it," he said of every item), and he told them he was sure that once things had cooled down he could hire them back. It was just that his mama was so nervous with everything that was going on that she couldn't have that kind of uproar around the house. "She just couldn't cope with [the idea of] him being gone," her sister Lillian said. Vernon was tight-lipped about it, but Gladys' mood was increasingly somber, and her eyes were limpid pools of sadness.

He asked George to accompany him once again to California, but George had just started a new job deejaying at WHUY out in Millington, so he couldn't go. He gave Jimmy Snow the script for *King Creole,* "because he wanted to know if I'd be interested in going out to California with him and maybe do a part in the film. And it was in the bedroom upstairs as I was reading the script that I made my decision, which I told him about the next day. I told him I really appreciated the opportunity. It was something I had wanted to do all my life. 'But,' I said, 'strange as it may seem, I think I'm going to go back and quit the business and go into the ministry.' Which he thought was wonderful, he was very complimentary and wished me a lot of luck and anything he could do, just let him know. So that's what I did."

He celebrated his twenty-third birthday on January 8 with a party at home and asked Alan Fortas if he would accompany Gene and him to California. "I was working for my father in the junk business, and Elvis asked me if I thought I could get off for a little while. I said, 'You know how that is, Elvis. You work for your father, you can do what you want to.' He said, 'Good, we leave for California in two days.' " At the last minute he took Cliff back, but Lamar remained in the doghouse for the time being, so when they embarked on January 10 it was just Gene, Cliff, and Alan, plus the Colonel, "security chief" Bitsy Mott, Freddy Bienstock, and Tom Diskin. There were huge crowds at every stop, alerted, Alan felt sure, by an intentional leak from the Colonel's organization. "That was the first time I'd been around the Colonel, and I thought, 'Man, this guy is tough.' He was just — he didn't trust anybody. Didn't like anybody. At least that was the impression he gave. You didn't know if he was serious or kidding — of course he was just looking out for one person: Elvis. He just didn't want people taking advantage."

They arrived in California on January 13 and reported immediately to the studio, with soundtrack recording scheduled to begin at Radio Recorders two days later. This time there was no question of where they were going to record. Hal Wallis was finally convinced that Elvis knew what he was doing, and Jerry Leiber and Mike Stoller, at Elvis' request, were in charge. Leiber and Stoller had been hired by RCA the previous fall as perhaps the first independent a&r men in the business (while they were on salary with RCA, they also continued to maintain a profitable relationship with Atlantic, producing the Coasters, along with numerous other side ventures). Elvis was clearly their primary responsibility at the label, and it had been suggested that they would have a relatively free hand, but so far it hadn't worked out the way they had hoped.

Jerry was living in New York at this point and going out with former MGM board chairman Nick Schenck's daughter, Marty Page, whose best friend was divorced from the well-known agent Charlie Feldman. "Charlie was very much connected to people like Moss Hart and Cole Porter, and he took a shine to me and was going to try to groom us as Broadway writers. He liked what we did, but he thought it was kind of kid stuff and now we were ready for the big time, which was Broadway and film. He said to me, 'You know what would be marvelous? I have a property that would make an incredible musical motion picture. It's called *A Walk on the Wild Side* [the celebrated novel by Nelson Algren], and it would be great for Elvis Presley.' He said, 'I'm sure I can get Elia Kazan to direct, and I think we might get Budd Schulberg to write the screenplay, and you two guys would write the book.' He said, 'It's perfect. He's handsome, he's innocent, and he's a victim.'

"I took the idea to the Aberbachs, who were the closest to Colonel Parker. They watched me in complete silence as I spun this story for about twenty minutes and made the pitch, and finally Jean said in his

Viennese accent, 'If you ever try to interfere with the business or artistic workings of the process known as Elvis Presley, if you ever start thinking in this direction again, you will never work for us again.'

"It wasn't long after that, to be very frank, that we both got bored, because we knew there were no possibilities left. It was just going to be another one like the last one, every movie the same. I mean, you had three ballads, one medium-tempo, one up-tempo, and one break blues boogie, usually for a production number. It was too fucking boring. I told Stoller, 'If I have to write another song like "King Creole," I'll cut my fucking throat — maybe theirs first.' We talked about — you know, maybe we're burning up a license to print money. I said, 'You know what? Burn it up.' 'Cause we could have made fucking history, and those assholes only wanted to make another nickel the same way."

The sessions proceeded without incident. Leiber and Stoller contributed three songs, plus a fourth that wasn't used, and for the first time experienced session players were employed to create a semiauthentic Dixieland sound. Perhaps the two most interesting songs were "Crawfish," a duet with rhythm and blues singer Kitty White, which was written by songwriters Ben Weisman and Fred Wise as a street vendor's cry, and Leiber and Stoller's "Trouble," a Muddy Waters–styled blues intended somewhat tongue in cheek but delivered by Elvis with untempered ferocity. In Jerry Leiber's view, " 'Trouble' was the same kind of song as 'Black Denim Trousers.' They're both send-ups, and the only people who are going to take them seriously are Hell's Angels and Elvis Presley. I suppose there was a bit of contempt on our part. You know, when the guy sang, Ba boom ba ba boom, 'If you're looking for trouble,' you know, 'just come looking for me' — there's something laughable there. I mean, if you get Memphis Slim or John Lee Hooker singing it, it sounds right, but Elvis did not sound right to us. But I would be tolerant. Just like [rhythm and blues bandleader-arranger] Maxwell Davis was tolerant of me when I first walked in, this little white kid with a twelve-bar blues, and he said, 'That's nice.' He said, 'I think that's nice.' He didn't say, 'That's full of shit, you don't know what you're doing.' He said, 'That's nice.' It's a sort of tolerant attitude with a little bit of tongue in cheek. So in the early days that's where we were coming from. It sounded sort of comical to us, but strangely enough to the mass market it wasn't. It was somewhat generational and somewhat cultural, but they bought it."

They wound up the session in two days. In reality, the score was independent of the picture; the character that Elvis played was a singer, it was true, but the story was up-from-poverty, and the protagonist might better have remained the boxer that he was in the novel in terms of the dramatic impact of the story.

Elvis had read the book in preparation for making the film. He was determined to do his very best, because, he told Alan Fortas, this could be it for him. He got together with his new friend Kitty Dolan to run lines with him and spoke with concern of what his absence from the scene for two years might mean. The director, Michael Curtiz, was a sixty-nine-year-old Hungarian émigré who had been directing films since 1919 and had made such notable pictures as *Casablanca, Mildred Pierce,* and *Young Man with a Horn.* Elvis was a little taken aback at first when Curtiz told him he would have to cut his sideburns and lose fifteen pounds for the role, and he had a great deal of trouble initially understanding Curtiz's accent. "You just didn't have a lot of fooling around with Curtiz — I mean, he would embarrass the hell out of you," said Jan Shepard, who played Elvis' sister in the movie. "But no matter what Curtiz would ask of Elvis, he would say, 'Okay, you're the boss.' Curtiz said he thought Elvis was going to be a very conceited boy, but when he started working with him, he said, 'No, this is a lovely boy, and he's going to be a wonderful actor.'

"The first time I met Elvis was when we went to the doctor's office for the insurance. I was sitting there, and he walked in with his little group from Memphis, and then we worked together alone for about a week, because we did the opening of the show. He was just really young, carefree — it was like letting a kid loose in a candy store, he was just a lot of fun and buoyant, not guarded at all. There was a five-and-dime store on our set, and in the morning I would find earrings and little bracelets, little five-and-dime stuff on my dressing room table. I used to call him the last of the big-time spenders!

"He was very concentrated, very focused on playing Danny. For a kid coming in and just beginning his career he had a great sense of timing; there was great honesty in his acting. He was a very good listener, and he just became that young boy, he became Danny in the show. Just like in his music, he really got involved in his acting, you'd look in his eyes and, boy, they were really going."

With Walter Matthau as the heavy, Dolores Hart once again as the fresh-faced ingenue, Carolyn Jones as the offbeat vamp, and Dean Jagger as the weak, ineffectual father (a stock-in-trade for every teen picture since *Rebel Without a Cause*), the cast that Wallis had assembled was a uniformly good one, and there was a uniformly positive spirit on the set. "I almost hesitate, I creep up to the sentence," Walter Matthau told a BBC interviewer, "he was an instinctive actor. Because that almost is a derogation of his talents. That's saying, 'Well, you know, he's just a dumb animal who does it well by instinct.' No, he was quite bright, too. He was very intelligent. Also, he was intelligent enough to understand what a character was and how to play the character simply by being himself *through* the means of the story. Michael Curtiz used to call him Elvy, and he'd call me Valty. He'd say, 'Now Elvy and Valty, come here, now, Valty, this is not Academy Award scene. Don't act so much. You are high-price actor. Make believe you are low-price actor. Let Elvy act.' But Elvy didn't *over*act. He was not a punk. He was very elegant, sedate . . . refined and sophisticated."

In Carolyn Jones' observation "he was always asking a lot of questions. God, he was young! I didn't think anybody could be *that* young! He was always talking about his folks and about the house he'd just bought them." Jones suggested that in order to really learn his craft he should consider taking acting lessons, and the guys took up one of her lines in the film, "Take a day out of your life and love me," as a kind of sardonic commentary, to be trotted out on any number of occasions, in a wide variety of social settings.

One Sunday when he was feeling blue, he told Jan, he spent most of the day just talking to his mother on the phone, and he was both disturbed and amused by George's telephone account of how Dewey had been fired from his midnight television show. The show had commanded a number-one rating in its afternoon slot, until it had been forced off the air to make room for Dick Clark's network-syndicated *American Bandstand*. It was in the fourth night of its present incarnation when Harry Fritzius, a noted young abstract painter who appeared in an ape suit on the air, explicitly fondled a life-size cutout of Jayne Mansfield in an altogether human way. "He embarrassed the station, and he embarrassed me personally," said station manager Bill Grumbles. Dewey would continue on the air with a Saturday-evening show and his nightly radio spot, but his sidekick Harry Fritzius was finished, "probably the best thing that ever happened to me," declared Fritzius. "I'm twenty-five, and it's time I found something to do with my life."

Crazy old Dewey, the guys all said, and Elvis was tempted to join them. He thought about giving Dewey a call, but he knew the complications that could cause, and he wasn't sure that he wanted to deal with them now, when everything seemed to be spinning out of control. And yet, for all of his worries, he had probably never felt more relaxed or at home on a set. He saw Pat Boone on the Paramount lot one day and greeted him smilingly with an impromptu rendition of "April Love"; on the soundstage he serenaded cast and crew alike; and he even got to meet Marlon Brando, after a fashion. He and Jan Shepard were in the commissary. "Sophia Loren and Carlo Ponti were sitting at a table next to us, and I remember Cornel Wilde came over and asked for an autograph for his daughter. Elvis said, 'Can you believe that Cornel Wilde wanted my autograph?' He was stunned by it. Then I said, 'Elvis, did you know Marlon Brando is sitting right behind you?' He had his back to him, and he almost started shaking, and I said, 'You know, he keeps looking over.' He was just like, you know, 'I couldn't, oh I couldn't, you know, it's Marlon Brando' — like that. So I said, 'Well, when we get up, all you have to do is push your chair back and you're going to go right into him.' So as we got up to go, he bumped into Brando, and Brando got up, of course, and then they shook hands, and when we went out he said, 'Oh my God, I shook hands with Marlon Brando!' "

February 1 was the only day open for RCA recording, and with his induction date rapidly approaching, Steve Sholes was desperate to get a final studio session in. Elvis had rehearsed two numbers for the upcoming date at a January 23 soundtrack session, but he was insistent that Leiber and Stoller, who had returned to New York after the initial session the previous week, be there. Dutifully, the Colonel had Tom Diskin inform Sholes that their presence was required — Elvis by now considered them a kind of "good-luck charm." Sholes wrote, telegrammed, and attempted to call, but all to no avail, because Stoller was unable to locate his partner, who was lying incommunicado in the emergency ward of a Harlem hospital with pneumonia. "Nobody knew where I was, *I* didn't know where I was for a couple of days. When I came to my senses, I started calling around. I called Mike, and I got out of the hospital, and when I got home there was a stack of telegrams jammed under my door, and they were all about the same thing: 'You must come to L.A. immediately.'

"I called the Aberbachs, and I got Julian on the phone. He said, 'You must come to California immediately. Presley is ready to record, and he will not go in the studio without you.' I said, 'I don't think I can come immediately, but I'll see.' So I called my doctor, and he told me absolutely not to go anywhere for two weeks, and I called them back and they started to get real nasty. Finally, Parker got on the phone and said, 'Boy, you better get your ass out here or else.' He said, 'By the way, did you get my contract for the new projects?' I said, 'No, it might have slipped by. I opened up about eight telegrams, and they were all the same, so I figured the rest weren't any different.' He said, 'You better open up the rest.'

"So I opened them up, and there was in fact another piece of mail from Colonel Parker's office, and it said, 'Enclosed you'll find the contract. Please execute and return.' And I looked at the piece of paper, and it had nothing on either side, but it had a line at the bottom with a space for my signature. And on the right-hand side was a line for Tom Parker that was signed by him. So I got on the phone and said, 'There must be some kind of mistake, Tom. There's just a blank piece of paper here with a place for my name.' He said, 'There's no mistake, boy, just sign it and return it.' I said, 'There's nothing on the paper.' He said, 'Don't worry, we'll fill it in later.'

"We never worked with him again. That was it. We never talked to each other again."

The session was a disaster. They spent eight hours in the studio and got two barely usable tracks. Elvis was a wreck — it was as if the magic had worn off, and for the first time the Colonel was embarrassed both for his boy and for the waste of RCA's (and Elvis' and his own) time and money. Two weeks later Elvis wanted to go back into the studio to repair the damage, and there was some talk among all the parties about arranging another session, but that would have meant Colonel acknowledging some degree of failure to Steve Sholes, and he was not prepared to do that. So in the end Sholes had to make do with what he had. For the Colonel the whole experience underlined one fundamental point: never let *anyone*, let alone a songwriter, get in the middle of your business. In future, he stressed emphatically to his brother-in-law, Bitsy Mott, keep those people away from Elvis, watch very carefully *anyone* who got anywhere near him, and, for God's sake, keep them away from the suite.

Toward the end of February, just before most of the cast and crew were scheduled to depart for New Orleans for a week of location shoots, Dolores Hart staged a surprise birthday party for Jan Shepard at her home. Although Elvis was invited, no one expected him to show up, and Jan was surprised enough just to discover most of her fellow cast members, along with young Paramount contract players like Ty Hardin and Edith Head's assistant, Pat Richards. "But I was really shocked when Elvis walked in, and he had this big stuffed tiger cat on his shoulders. We named it 'Danny Boy,' because he always used to sing that song on the set. The other thing was, I had all these little kids in the neighborhood who wanted pictures of him, and we had this running gag, where I kept saying, 'Elvis, bring some pictures in for my birthday.' So his *second* gift to me was a movie camera with a light bar and, I think, three rolls of film, and he said, 'Go ahead, take your pictures now.' Which I did, even though I'd never used a movie camera before!

"It was wonderful. Everyone was cooking and helping out in the kitchen, and we all had dinner, and Ty Hardin, who had studied to be an engineer, made a cake that looked like a theater, with a marquee and everything. Then after dinner we sat in the living room, and Elvis sat down at the piano and Ty had brought his guitar and started playing, and then Elvis took the guitar and Dolores had her clarinet, and Dolores' mother was dressed up like Topsy and was doing a number from Topsy. It was kind of a free-for-all, just, you know, just a very relaxing time, and he stayed till the end, which was really amazing, but there was nobody there that was going to interfere with him. It was really nice."

Red West showed up the next week on a two-week leave from the Marines. He had stopped by Graceland to pay his respects, and Mrs. Presley called Elvis on the phone, and Elvis invited him to fly out the next day. "When I got up to say goodbye," Red wrote in *Elvis: What Happened?*, "she just sort of called me back, and I heard her say what she had said a hundred times: 'Bob, look after my boy.' " Red arrived in Hollywood, "a crew-cut hick sonofabitch in a Marine uniform on a Paramount movie set," they had their first extended reunion in more than a year, and Elvis asked him if he wanted to go to New Orleans with the troupe two days later.

While most of the film company flew, Elvis and his friends rode the train. Red, Cliff, Gene, and Alan all accompanied him, along with Carolyn, her husband, Aaron Spelling, and Nick Adams, whom Red met for the first time and who amused everyone with his impressions on the long trip. In New Orleans, the Colonel, who had argued bitterly against a location shoot for security reasons, was, not surprisingly, proved right. "Hal Wallis loved locations," said Alan Fortas, whose opinion of the Colonel was considerably higher than it had been at the start. "He said, 'I had

Dean Martin and Jerry Lewis in their prime. I had this star and that star . . .' Colonel said, 'I don't care who you had, Wallis, you never had Elvis Presley.' "

Cliff was given a line in the picture ("See you next week, baby," he said to a prostitute while dressed up in a sailor's uniform), and the guys got a big kick out of kidding Alan that he would soon be making his movie debut as well. They had him walking around in makeup all day with Kleenex stuck into the collar of his shirt, convinced that his scene would be coming up any minute. Meanwhile, Cliff met a kid whose father owned a clothing store and conned him out of blazers for the whole gang. According to George, who joined the group in New Orleans, "Cliff said we worked for Elvis, and it would be real sharp if all of Elvis' guys wore blazers, uniform-style. The guy said, 'Yeah?' Cliff said, 'Man, I'll tell you what, what do those blazers sell for?' The guy says, 'About fifty dollars apiece.' Cliff said, 'There are five guys that work for Elvis, there's Elvis and Colonel Parker. We need seven blazers, but we ain't gonna pay for them. Here's what we are going to do for you. You give us the jackets, and you can advertise that Elvis' traveling companions and Elvis Presley are wearing clothes from your clothing store.'

"We said, 'Cliff, Colonel Parker is going to have a fit, Elvis has never endorsed anything.' Cliff said, 'Don't worry about it,' and next day, man, everyone has a brand-new blazer, and the guy even has one for Colonel Parker. So Cliff tells him, 'There's Colonel Parker, you just go over there and say, "Colonel Parker, I'm so-and-so, and I'd like to present you with this blazer as a gift." ' Well, he goes over and presents the blazer, and Colonel immediately picks up something is wrong, and he comes over and says, 'Cliff, what the hell are you doing? You know Elvis doesn't endorse anything. He never has, and we don't intend to start now.' And Cliff says, 'Wait a minute, Colonel, look, Elvis wanted us to have these blue blazers, and Elvis wanted one, so if Elvis went down and bought one, Colonel, and he bought one for all of the guys, the guy is going to say the same thing anyway, so we might as well just get them for free.' The Colonel said, 'That makes sense,' and he just kind of shook his head and walked away. But we all got blue blazers."

They took the train back to Hollywood, and Hal Wallis threw a breakup party at the studio commissary. He wasn't worried about the army, Elvis told columnist Vernon Scott, who was present. It couldn't be any worse than the merry-go-round he'd been on for the past two years, and he certainly knew what hard work was — he'd been working since he was fourteen. "Had to. Got a job at Loew's State Theatre in Memphis as an usher. They fired me for fighting in the lobby. . . . I've worked in factories, drove a truck, cut grass for a living, and did a hitch in a defense plant. I'll do whatever they tell me, and I won't be asking no special favors." It was going to be harder on his folks, he said, than it would be on him.

Just to get everyone in the spirit of his usual "pull-out-all-stops" promotion campaign, the Colonel had a big bunch of balloons made up with "King Creole" written on them, and he led Trude Forsher, the William Morris agents, and everyone else he could commandeer around the lot carrying the balloons before marching into the commissary and releasing them to the ceiling. Elvis posed politely for pictures, showed off the prop Civil War blunderbuss that he had been given as a gift, and ate a little bit of cake decorated with the figure of an army private peeling potatoes.

Then he was off to Memphis, with less than two weeks until his formal induction. He was so impatient to get home that, once again, he got off the train, this time renting a fleet of Cadillacs in Dallas. He was met by a *Commercial Appeal* reporter when he arrived at Graceland at 6:30 on Friday night, March 14. The questions were all about his new movie and the army. How did his parents feel about his going in? "Well, my mother hates to see her son go in service," he said candidly, but added: "My mother is no different from millions of other mothers who hated to see their sons go, though." As far as the movie went, he had reason to be proud. "It was quite a challenge for me because it was written for a more experienced actor," he said. It was, he felt without false modesty, his best performance to date, one in which he had acquitted himself well in truly distinguished company. But what about his popularity? asked the reporter. Did he think it would slip while he was in the army? "That's the sixty-four-dollar question," replied Elvis plaintively. "I wish I knew."

ON THE STEPS OF GRACELAND, AUGUST 14, 1958. (JAMES REID)

"PRECIOUS MEMORIES"

THE TEN DAYS that he had left before going in were a blur of activity. On Monday he met Dewey down at Poplar Tunes, and a lot of misunderstandings, reported Bob Johnson, seemed to just fall away. Elvis bought Dean Martin's "Return to Me," Nat King Cole's "Looking Back," Pat Boone's "Too Soon to Know," Jo Stafford's "Sweet Little Darling," Don Gibson's "I Can't Stop Loving You," and "Maybe" by the Chantels. He got a haircut at Jim's Barber Shop, his second in less than a month, and declared that he liked the new crew cut style so much he intended to get it cut even shorter before induction.

On Wednesday he looked at cars with Anita, who was now customarily described in the national press as both a "Hollywood starlet" and a "frequent companion," but it was also reported in the papers that he was entertaining a parade of women, "no fewer than twelve beautiful girls," by one count. "I screwed everything in sight," he told a friend years later in an uncharacteristic, and perhaps inaccurate, display of sexual bravura, while to reporters he simply commented, "I'd be crazy to get married now. I like to play the field."

Whoever his companion for the evening, every night he would go in a group to the movies, to the skating rink after it was closed, back to Graceland after all other sources for fun were exhausted, in what seemed like an almost desperate attempt to pack in every last element of civilian experience, a vain effort to stave off the inevitable moment by hiding himself in the crowd.

Over the course of the week he let the last of the boys go, wrote Bob Johnson, about to be without their company for the first time in more than two years. He had "fed them, clothed them, paid them in return for simple duties, but mostly their job was just to keep him company in a rather extraordinary world where new friends could have no understanding of a world he knew." He said good-bye to Scotty and Bill: "It was just

'So long, see you when I get out,' " said Scotty, who detected little nervousness. "We were just like two mules turned out to pasture." Over the weekend he gave Anita a 1956 Ford. She felt he was dreading the army, "because it was something unknown to him, he didn't know what to expect, but it was something that he had to do — he could have gotten out of it, but he wanted no part of that." He told her that he had to do what was expected of him and reassured his mother that he was going to be all right. "I can make it," he said. "I can do this." To Barbara Pittman, who had known him from childhood, he was somewhat more unbuttoned. "He was very upset about it. He kept saying, 'Why me, when I can stay here and make so much more money? My taxes would be more important than sticking me in the service.' He was crying. He was hurt. He couldn't understand why he had to go." Judy Spreckels, who described herself as "like a sister" ("Girls come and go," she said, "but sisters stay forever"), flew in from the Coast to provide support.

On his last night of freedom he was up all night with his friends. He and Anita and some of the boys went to the drive-in to see Tommy Sands in *Sing, Boy, Sing,* the story of the rise and fall of a rock 'n' roll star told in somewhat harder-hitting terms than any of Elvis' movies. Sands, just twenty but a recording artist from the age of fourteen, and a longtime protégé of Colonel Parker's, had gotten the role, originally written for Elvis, only through the intercession of the Colonel. "We pulled in to the drive-in in the Cadillac limousine," said George Klein, "and Nick Adams was playing a combination of all of Elvis' sidekicks in the movie — he played me and Gene and Cliff and Arthur, all rolled into one. It was kind of cold, and we all wanted to stay up with him until the last minute, you know, and keep his mind occupied so he wouldn't have to think about leaving the next day. And I think he appreciated that, but we got quite a kick not so much out of Tommy Sands as out of Nick Adams playing all the other guys." Afterward they went to the skating rink for the eighth night in a row, and when it finally came time to leave, "he got in and out of the panel truck three times," the owners told writer Vince Staten. "He didn't want to go."

He hadn't eaten or slept when dawn came up. "Overnight," he said, "it was all gone. It was like a dream."

* * *

He showed up at the draft board in the M&M Building at 198 South Main at 6:35 the next morning and parked just south of the Malco Theatre. He was accompanied by several cars full of friends and relatives and was greeted by a couple of dozen photographers and reporters, including representatives of the British press. It was raining lightly, and he was half an hour early. He was wearing dark blue trousers, his loud gray-and-white-checked sports jacket, a striped shirt, and pink and black socks, and he was carrying a pigskin shaving kit. Gladys looked as if she were about to cry, while Vernon gripped her hand tightly. Lamar gave everybody a laugh by pretending that he wanted to enlist, too, but at 270 pounds there was little likelihood that he would be taken. Anita looked prettily composed while Judy remained in the background and the Colonel hovered on the edge of the proceedings, making sure that everything went off without a hitch. Among the recruits was an old friend from Lauderdale Courts, Farley Guy, who told reporters it was "the same old Elvis." "If I seem nervous," said Elvis, "it's because I am," adding that he was looking forward to the army "as a great experience. The army can do anything it wants with me. Millions of other guys have been drafted, and I don't want to be different from anyone else." At 7:14 the thirteen inductees left the draft board in an olive drab army bus. They were bound for the Kennedy Veterans Hospital several miles away, where they would be examined and processed. The army of newsmen, friends, fans, and relatives all followed, but not before Anita got special permission from Recruiting Sergeant Walter Alden to visit Elvis at the induction station that afternoon in order to say a special good-bye.

At Kennedy he was examined, weighed, and pronounced fit, all under the scrutiny of reporters' pencils and pads, microphones, and cameras. The picture of him in *Life* magazine the following week revealed a well-nourished white male, still showing some evidence of baby fat, standing on the scale in his underpants with his eyes on either side of the height-measuring extender. His gaze is distracted, his mouth is downcast, and you could imagine either that he was momentarily lost in thought or frozen in fear. To the *Life* reporter he simply said, "Heaven knows I want to live up to what people expect of me." In conversations with other photographers and newsmen "Elvis recalled that in the days before he became famous, he pawned his old guitar for $3 'five or six times.' Also, he remember[ed] that in 1952 he sold a pint of his blood to Baptist Hospital for $10. Elvis said his has always been a happy family and is happy today, but that money brings a lot of headaches. . . ."

The army provided a box lunch of a ham sandwich, a roast beef sandwich, a piece of apple pie, an apple, and a container of milk, which Elvis wolfed down, explaining that he hadn't eaten since the previous night. "Man, I was hungry," he said. Then he lay down on a rec room couch and took a nap for half an hour. More friends and relatives continued to show up, and a telegram from Governor Frank Clement arrived, declaring that "you have shown that you are an American citizen first, a Tennessee Volunteer, and a young man willing to serve his country when called upon to do so."

Outside, the Colonel was marching around handing out more balloons that advertised *King Creole,* while the crowd grew larger and larger and the Presleys looked increasingly stricken. The army brass were growing nervous that they would not fulfill the quota of twenty (including volunteers as well as draftees) necessary to requisition a bus and get out of Memphis *today*. Finally a draftee named Donald Rex Mansfield, who had just arrived on the bus from Dresden, Tennessee, and was not slated to go in until the following day, was rushed through processing, and Private Elvis Presley, serial number 53 310 761, was put in charge of the 150-mile bus trip to Fort Chaffee. He rapidly embraced his mother, who was virtually inconsolable by now, and his father, who was openly weeping. "Good-bye, baby," he said to Anita as the bus was about to pull out. "Good-bye, you long black sonofabitch," he said, referring to his black Cadillac limousine standing at the curb. The other recruits laughed nervously. That, reported Rex Mansfield, broke the ice. After that he was, at least nominally, "one of the boys."

A CARAVAN OF CARS containing newsmen and fans followed the army bus out of Memphis, and when it made its regular scheduled stop just across the Mississippi at the Coffee Cup restaurant in West Memphis, there was a crowd of close to two hundred already assembled, and the bus driver had to bring sandwiches and drinks back to the bus. At Fort Chaffee, the information officer, Captain Arlie Metheny, a native Arkansan and twenty-year vet, had been anticipating the arrival since January, but nothing in his previous experience (not even his stint as information officer during the Little Rock integration crisis) could have fully prepared him for the mob scene that erupted when the bus finally pulled in at 11:15 that night. More than a hundred civilian fans, forty or fifty newsmen, and another two hundred dependents of military personnel descended on the hapless new recruit, with the Colonel leading the greeting committee. The newsmen followed Elvis into a reception room for roll call and photographed him making his bed over and over again for the cameras, though when a photographer hid in the barracks to get a shot of a sleeping Private Presley, that was too much for even the army's tolerance, and Captain Metheny had the photographer thrown out. Throughout it all Elvis bore up with extraordinary patience, presenting a bright, cheerful exterior, offering up quips and self-deprecating statements, entertaining all requests without demurral, refusing only to sign autographs while he was "in ranks."

He estimated that he slept no more than three hours and was up well before 5:30 reveille the next morning, dressing and shaving while the others were just waking up. The Colonel and twenty photographers joined him for breakfast at 6:00 ("It was good, but I was so hungry I'd eat anything this morning," he was reported as saying), and then he was scheduled for five hours of aptitude tests, a two-hour postlunch lecture on a private's rights and privileges, a brief classification interview, the issuance of seven dollars in partial pay (What are you going to do with all that money? reporters shouted. "Start a loan company," Elvis replied good-humoredly), and, finally, the bestowal of the standard-issue GI haircut. There were fifty-five reporters and photographers standing around waiting to record this historic moment. "Hair today, gone tomorrow," said Elvis, holding some of the hair in his hand and blowing it away for photographers, but he was flustered enough that he forgot to pay the barber the sixty-five-cent fee and, to his embarrassment, had to be called back. He spotted a phone booth and went off to telephone his mother. When reporters sprinted after him, Colonel Parker blocked their way. "I think a boy's entitled to talk to his mother alone," said the Colonel.

On Wednesday he was issued his uniform, and the Colonel, clowning for the cameras, tried to get him to try on a western string tie with it. "No, sir. If I wore a string tie in here, I'd have to take the punishment, not you," Elvis replied, as the Colonel declared to the photographers, "I wish you boys would stop taking pictures of yourselves." That afternoon there was an announcement (surprising only because it came sooner than expected) that Elvis Presley would be assigned to the Second Armored Division — General George Patton's famous "Hell on Wheels" outfit — at Fort Hood, just outside Killeen, Texas, for basic training and advanced tank instruction. He had been a good soldier so far, announced post commander General Ralph R. Mace; "at least in my opinion, he has conducted himself in a marvelous manner." And Hy Gardner wrote a column in the form of a letter to Elvis' fellow soldiers, proclaiming Elvis a credit to his country:

> Where else could a nobody become a somebody so quickly, and in what other nation in the world would such a rich and famous man serve alongside you other draftees without trying to use influence to buy his way out? In my book this is American democracy at its best — the blessed way of life for whose protection you and Elvis have been called upon to contribute eighteen to twenty-four months of your young lives. . . . I hope you go along with my sentiments.

SIX OF THE THIRTEEN original Memphis draftees were assigned to Fort Hood, including Rex Mansfield and William Norvell, whom Elvis immediately dubbed "Nervous" Norvell. After being chased for more than two hundred miles by a convoy of devoted fans ("I'd hate to see anyone get hurt," said Elvis worriedly. "Maybe if I wave . . ."), the chartered Greyhound bypassed the usual stops in Dallas and Waxahachie, where hundreds of people had already gathered, finally stopping for lunch in Hillsboro, Texas, at 1:30. Captain J. F. Dowling assigned two of his largest men to sit on either side of Elvis: "I think we must have set some kind of record. We went twenty-five minutes before anyone recognized him." When they finally did, there was a small riot, and it took at least another twenty-five minutes before they could make their way out of the restaurant. "Elvis was very nice about the whole thing," said Captain Dowling. "Some of the men ordered meals that exceeded the allowance on the meal ticket, but Elvis said he'd pick up the check for the difference. And before we got him on the bus, he managed to buy cigarettes and candy, which he passed out to the boys. As we left Hillsboro, the girls were fighting over who would keep the chair that Elvis had sat in."

At Fort Hood things were under substantially more control from the start. The information officer, Lieutenant Colonel Marjorie Schulten, had already made the determination, before the bus arrived, that she was going to take a different approach than the one that had been tried at Fort Chaffee. "He was due in on [March] twenty-eighth about four P.M.," she told writer Alan Levy. "Beginning at eleven A.M. the media people started to come in here. I've never seen so many people. . . . When I saw a Fort Worth editor with a reputation for never leaving his swivel chair, I knew this was an event." Colonel Parker stopped by not long afterward to offer, Levy observed, "his services, advice, and moral support. Lieutenant Colonel Schulten turned to 'Colonel' Parker and, couching her words in the respect accorded a higher-ranking person — particularly one who made all his rank 'on the outside' — she told him: 'Colonel Parker, the Second Armored Division will not be able to train this boy at the rate these requests are coming in. You have an enormous investment, so you may not like what I'm about to do here and now.' Parker, whose most detailed pre-induction plans had never anticipated a woman officer, . . . surrendered to the inevitable with a meek, 'Well, Colonel, you're the boss.' "

What she was about to do was declare Elvis Presley off-limits to newsmen and photographers after his first day at Fort Hood. "You will have carte blanche as promised," she said, "but just this one day. After today, nothing!" And that was the policy she stuck to.

The first few days were extremely difficult for a very homesick, very isolated Elvis Presley. The others just watched, some of them ragged on him a little ("Boy, you ain't wiggling right," someone was likely to call out as he ran past, and "Miss your teddy bears, Elvis?" was a common put-down), but mostly it was Elvis' own private battle, Rex Mansfield observed, as he struggled desperately to find his equilibrium and be accepted as one of the guys. Gradually he was, and gradually he relaxed a little, too, but recruit instructor Sergeant Bill Norwood, who befriended him and allowed him to make private calls from Norwood's home, witnessed his homesickness and tears at first hand and worried what would happen if the others saw him like this. "When you come in my house," he told Elvis, "you can let it all out. Do whatever you want to, and don't worry about anything. But when you walk out of my front door, you are now Elvis Presley. You're an actor. You're a soldier. So, by God, I want you to act! Don't let nobody know how you feel on the inside."

He got his marksman medal with a carbine, sharpshooter with a pistol, and he was named acting assistant squad leader for his squad along with Rex for his squad and "Nervous" Norvell for his. Gradually, he said, he came to be accepted. "I didn't ask for anything, and they didn't give me anything. I just did the same thing everybody else did. I made it very well." He just didn't know who to trust.

The Colonel came to see him once or twice to get his signature on some pieces of paper and report to him on sales and strategy. It was reassuring to hear news of his career, even if he cared little about the facts and figures, but when a Waco businessman named Eddie Fadal, whom he had first met during a five-day Texas tour in January 1956, came to see him two weeks into basic, it was as though he had found a long-lost friend. Fadal, in his thirties, married with two daughters, was one of those not so rare individuals who had responded more than instantly to Elvis' appeal. He had in fact quit his job as a Dallas DJ after Elvis' spur-of-the-moment invitation to go out "as a general flunky," in Fadal's words, on that brief 1956 tour, and he had rejoined him for another few days when Elvis returned with Nick Adams for a performance at Waco's Heart O' Texas Coliseum later that year. "I thought, he probably won't remember me, but I'm going over to the base and see. I went through a lot of red tape at the gate, and I went to see the sergeant of the day room, and he gave me a lot of flak, too, but finally he went to get Elvis for me. And sure enough, he did remember me. I invited him to come to our house when he could get away, told him that we'd give him a home away from home, provide him with privacy and home-cooked food and all of those things, and he said, 'Sure, I'll be there.' He said, 'I can't come for another two weeks, but I'll be there.' I thought to myself, 'Yeah, I'll bet you will,' but, true to his word, in two weeks my telephone rang. . . ."

In the meantime Anita had come down at the invitation of Sergeant Norwood and his wife, who made their home on the post available to her. When she first arrived, Elvis was assigned to guard duty for twenty-four hours, but Sergeant Norwood suggested that, according to army regulations, he could get out of the assignment if he could find a substitute of equal rank. Elvis approached Rex Mansfield and offered him twenty dollars to take his place. "I told him straightaway that I would be glad to pull his guard duty, but in no way would I take his money," wrote Rex, who had observed with distaste the competition for Elvis' attention. "I said to him that I would do this for any other GI whose girl was waiting to see him. . . . This was the real beginning of our friendship."

Elvis brought Anita with him to Waco to visit Eddie Fadal. "He called me from the circle at the confluence of all the highways that come into Waco, and I had a hard time finding him because he didn't stay right where I thought he would be. But he followed my car and he followed me out to my house, and from then on it was every weekend." Nervous Norvell accompanied him once or twice with his wife, who had come to Texas to keep Anita company. But mostly it was just Elvis and Anita and the Fadals. They sang and played records, and Elvis called home at least once a day. "He'd say, 'Mama,' and I imagine she would say, 'Son.' And then it would just go on from there — it was weeping and sobbing, and crying. He thought his career was over. He told me many times, 'It's all over, Eddie.' He told me, 'They aren't going to know me when I get back.' I said, 'Elvis, it's not over. It's just beginning. You're never going to be forgotten.' He said, 'Naw, it's all over. That's it.' He firmly believed that."

Toward the end of basic, Anita got word that she would be recording in New York during the first week of June, and one night as they sat around the piano, Elvis prompted her to sing Hank Williams' "I Can't Help It (If I'm Still in Love with You)" and Connie Francis' brand-new hit, "Who's Sorry Now?," while he mostly sang gospel. Someone turned on a tape recorder, and you can hear Eddie saying to Anita, "I can't wait till your first record comes out." "It better be a good one," Elvis jumps in. "I wish they'd let me pick it." If they did, he says, it would be a song like "Happy, Happy Birthday, Baby," which the whole gang has just been singing. Or it might be something like "Cold Cold Heart," something with some heartbreak in it. "What I'm afraid of is they're going to put her on something a little too modern, a little too popular, you know what I mean?" "It will just die out quick?" "No . . ." "It'll catch on and then fade?" "No, what I'm talking about — they're gonna give her some music I'm afraid is more of a Julie London type. They got to give her something like Connie Francis sings. Something with some guts to it." Anita demurely assents to any and all suggestions, and they go back again and again to "Happy, Happy Birthday" as Elvis sings along with the Tune Weavers' record and ends the impromptu recital with a beautiful, self-accompanied version of "Just a Closer Walk with Thee" while one of the Fadals' daughters cries in the background. Eddie had little doubt that Elvis was going to marry Anita someday. They were so comfortable with each other, and he was so obviously at home in her company and in the Fadals' house. "His mother said to me later that he told her the Fadals had provided him with a home away from home."

Furlough was scheduled to begin at 11:00 A.M. on Saturday, May 31, but at the last minute it was moved up to 6:00 A.M., and Anita and the Colonel were waiting at the post gate. Elvis dropped them in Dallas, where they caught planes to Memphis and Nashville respectively, and then continued on his way with Rex Mansfield and "Nervous" Norvell. He dropped Nervous off on Lamar Avenue and then took Rex to Graceland, where hundreds of fans were waiting at the gate when they arrived. Elvis didn't stop the car, wrote Rex, because he was tired and impatient to see his folks, but he promised to come out later to sign autographs. "The treatment which I received from Elvis upon our arrival . . . was really amazing to me. After the usual hugs and kisses to his mother and dad and the warm welcome to his old friends, he turned all of his attention to me." He showed Rex around the mansion, which Rex in his memoir sought to describe, "but mere words have limitations and seeing is better for believing. . . . I had never before seen the inside of any house, even in the movies, that was as beautiful and luxurious as Graceland Mansion. . . .

"Elvis then amazed me further by, personally, going to the trouble to take me to my parents [when they arrived at his brother-in-law's house in Memphis]. We went out the back gate of his home through a big field in one of his many other limousines (a black Cadillac). Two of his best friends . . . went with us, Lamar Fike and Red West [who] was in the Marines at that time but had taken a leave to be with Elvis during his leave. . . . In parting . . . Elvis asked me to spend [the last] few of my fourteen days' leave with him at Graceland and I could travel back to Fort Hood with him. I eagerly accepted his offer."

HE FELT AS IF he had been transported back into the world to which he truly belonged — but it was no more than a tantalizing vision, he knew it was all destined to disappear. Everything seemed just the same, it was like old times, with everyone gathered at Graceland, friends, family, the fans at the gates. So what's it like in the service, *Cuz?* Junior asked with that slightly malevolent sneer. Now you boys be careful, his mother said, as they all went off to go roller-skating or to the Fairgrounds, now that the weather was warm again. There were business meetings with the Colonel, the Colonel was talking to him all the time about boring business matters, decisions that had to be made.

And what about Anita spending so much time with him in Texas?

hometown reporters asked. "Well, I know the papers had us engaged, married, and everything else, but it just looked that way." How did he like army food? "I've eaten things in the army that I never ate before, and I've eaten things that I didn't know what it was, but after a hard day of basic training, you could eat a rattlesnake." Army hours? "I'm used to them. I don't sleep more or less than I used to, just do it at different hours. Here on leave, I'm having trouble staying awake after midnight, where I used to stay up all night." Had he written many letters home? "I've never written a letter in my life." Why was he wearing his uniform the whole time he was on leave? "Simple. I'm kinda proud of it." And his overall impression of the army? "It's human nature to gripe, but I'm going ahead and doing the best job I can. One thing: the army teaches boys to think like men."

He went with his parents to a specially arranged screening of *King Creole,* got a haircut at Jim's, and bought a new red Lincoln Continental convertible. He had a recording session scheduled in Nashville for the following week, which the Colonel had finally granted in the face of Steve Sholes' near-hysterical pleas. Sholes saw them going into the wilderness for two years with no more than four releasable songs in the can and only himself to be blamed if the whole thing should suddenly fall apart. The Colonel practically made him crawl — it is evident from their correspondence that Sholes had to virtually tie himself down to keep from expressing his true feelings — but, ironically, as frustrating as the last session had been, this time everything gelled and in ten hours, over the course of a single night, they got five nearly perfect sides. For the first time Scotty and Bill were not in the studio with him, and D.J. was relegated to a supporting role, but they were scarcely missed, as top Nashville session players took their place and the session exploded with a kind of live-wire energy and musical humor that hadn't been present for a while. There was Hank Garland on guitar, bassist Bob Moore, Floyd Cramer playing piano, and Buddy Harman on drums, while Chet Atkins came out of the booth to contribute rhythm guitar. In addition, the Jordanaires had a new member, Ray Walker, singing bass, and every time his part came up, "[Elvis] tried to throw me every way he could. He'd move his lips and not say anything, and then he'd say his line. He was giving me a rough way to go!" Tom Diskin, speaking for the Colonel, expressed his concern that the instruments were coming through too loud and might override Elvis' voice, but Sholes reassured him that it would all be balanced out in the mix.

By the time that Rex returned to Graceland, the whole gang was assembled, including Nick Adams, who had flown in from Hollywood, and Rex felt a distinct chill in the air. "I could feel their mistrust and resentment," he wrote. "Later on I caught myself having those same resentments. . . . It was a jealous feeling like maybe Elvis would not pay as much attention to me and more attention to the new guy. Anyway, I made up my mind these guys had better accept me because I was planning to be around for a while." Anita, too, had returned by now ("Naturally we both just felt awful when I had to go to New York for my recording session just when he came home on furlough, but we both knew it had to be"), and it was reported that she spent the last hours alone with him "without friends or parents around."

When he left to go back to the base in the new red Lincoln early Saturday morning, he felt both exhilarated and depressed: exhilarated because it had been so easy to slip back into the old life, depressed for much the same reason, because he couldn't stand to let it go just like that. The Colonel had been making a study of army regulations, and back at Fort Hood, Elvis conferred with Sergeant Norwood, who advised him that once basic training was completed, permission would customarily be granted for a soldier to live off-post — *if* he had dependents living nearby. Within days Vernon and Gladys, who were indeed Elvis' legal dependents, had packed up and were en route in the white Fleetwood with Vernon's mother, Minnie, while Lamar led the way in the Lincoln Mark II. By June 21 they were ensconced just outside the Fort Hood gates in a rented three-bedroom trailer, and when, almost immediately, that proved a little cramped for five adults, they rented a house in the middle of Killeen from Judge Chester Crawford, who was planning on taking a two-month vacation, starting July 1.

Elvis brought his parents over to meet the Fadals the first weekend they were in town and then, again, for a Fourth of July cookout the following week. His mother took immediately to Eddie's wife, LaNelle. "She and my wife would go to the grocery store and purchase the things that Elvis liked. And then she would put on her little apron and go in the kitchen and start fixing it. She was jolly, just home folks, and we had a merry time." Eddie had by now added on a wing to his house with its own customized hi-fi, decorating it in pink and black so that Elvis would feel more comfortable on the weekends when he came to stay. During the week, Eddie visited with the Presleys while Elvis was on duty.

"Gladys would be sitting there in a rocking chair wearing a housecoat and barefoot, just as homey as anybody could be. Elvis loved banana cream pies, and there was a restaurant here that made them called the Toddle House. I'd take him a couple of those pies on a Tuesday or a Wednesday along with the latest magazines and a batch of 45s. A good friend of mine, Leonard Nixon, owned a record store, and every new 45 that came out he would call me and say, 'Elvis would like to hear this one, I know.' He'd just give them to me, the newest things by Connie Francis and Fats Domino and Sam Cooke, artists that Elvis really liked. We'd visit for an hour or so before Elvis got there, and then everything started jumping. They had to start fixing dinner, and the fans would gather at the door, and, you know, it was just a lot of hectic times, because they knew when he'd be home."

It was good times again for the Presley household, even though Gladys was not particularly looking forward to going to Germany when Elvis' company was shipped overseas ("I just can't see myself over there in a foreign country," she told Lamar. "I've left nothing over there, and I'm not trying to find anything"), and Vernon was primarily concerned with the impact that all of this might have on his son's career. For himself, during the week Elvis remained totally taken up with advanced basic, which consisted of training to become a tanker — Elvis placed third in tank gunnery, and occasionally he took over the company drum for marching — but he lived for the weekends. Anita came down some, but mostly he and Lamar and Rex ("Rexadus," as he dubbed him) and a bunch of other guys headed out for Dallas or Fort Worth, where there was an airline stewardess school, or just hung out at the Fadals' in Waco, where they would eat and fool around and play touch football. "There was always a parade of cars," said Eddie proudly. "Every time my wife would see him driving up, she'd say, 'Oh oh, I've got to feed twelve or fifteen people.' But only Elvis would stay over."

Gladys was unfailingly gracious to the stream of visitors who arrived in Killeen on official business, social business, or no business at all. The Colonel came several times and closeted himself with Elvis and Vernon. "He would come into the living room," said Eddie, "and talk with whoever was there, me and Gladys and Lamar mostly, but they talked their business behind closed doors. We never knew what went on in there, but sometimes Elvis would come out mad, and after the Colonel would leave he would cuss and fume, but other times it was amicable and he came in with a good feeling and a smile on his face. There were times that they disagreed, but [it] had nothing to do with Elvis' artistic endeavors. The Colonel had nothing to do with that, but he had everything to do with the business side, which I think was the way it should be."

A DJ named Rocky Frisco showed up one time after bicycling five hundred miles from Tulsa on a publicity stunt. When he arrived in Killeen, it was only to discover that Elvis was out on bivouac, but Gladys invited him to visit with them every day, and "I was made to feel every bit as welcome there as if I were family." Vic Morrow, who had played the gang leader in *King Creole,* stopped by one time, and Vince Edwards and Billy Murphy detoured through Killeen on their way to Dallas, knowing only that Elvis was stationed there but not where he lived. They had just pulled into a service station to ask directions when Lamar ("We called him 'Old Elephant Ass' ") spotted the Hollywood plates and took them out to the house. Elvis was still on duty, Gladys told them. She insisted that they stay for dinner, though, and Vernon set them up in a little tin trailer out back. Elvis finally arrived home, and they had a happy reunion, but then Vince and Billy got increasingly spooked in the trailer after everyone else had gone to bed. Around one in the morning, said Vince, "we didn't care what he would think, the goddam animals started making so much noise we just had to get our ass out of there and get to a motel." So they left without even saying good-bye.

Fans showed up at their doorstep, neighbors complained about the traffic, some girls set up a booth by the side of the road on Elvis' route home with a sign declaring "Please Stop Here, Elvis," and one day Elvis did. Eddie Fadal ferried fan club presidents back and forth to the bus stop in Temple, and Mrs. Presley was never less than courteous, but as the summer wore on she started to feel more and more poorly, her color was bad, and she wasn't able to keep anything down. She called her doctor in Memphis, Dr. Charles Clarke. "She said to me, 'Dr. Clarke, tomorrow's Wednesday.' I said, 'Yes, ma'am.' She said, 'Ain't you off on Wednesday? Well, I want you to fly out here to see me, 'cause I'm sick.' I said, 'Mrs. Presley . . .' I jumped around for some excuse. I said, 'I'm not licensed to practice in Texas.' She said, 'You ain't?' She said, 'Well, I'll just have to get somebody to drive me up there. I need to get Elvis a mess of greens out of the garden anyway.' That was just the way she talked. She was a very sweet person. I remember sometime back she was having a lot of stomach trouble, and I had put her on what we called a 'soft diet.' She came back sometime later and said, 'Doc, I done just what you told me. I ain't put nothing in my stomach. I've been very careful — I ain't put nothing but Pepsi-Cola and watermelon.' That was her soft diet!"

Elvis put his parents on the train for Memphis in Temple on August 8, a Friday. On Saturday Gladys was admitted to the hospital. Dr. Clarke was not sure just what was the matter with her: "It was a liver problem, but she was not jaundiced, as I recall. It wasn't a typical hepatitis. I called every consultant we could latch on to, and we tried our best to diagnose it. Apparently she had some sort of clotting phenomenon that involved her liver and internal organs."

By Monday he was still unsure of the diagnosis, but he knew that it was serious. He telephoned Elvis, who had just begun his six weeks of basic unit training and was unable initially to get leave. Elvis called practically every hour for news of his mother, and "finally he said, 'If my leave doesn't come through by tomorrow morning, I'll be there tomorrow afternoon anyway.' I said, 'Now, Elvis, don't go AWOL. All the young men in the world are watching you. You're a model. Don't do that.' I said, 'Give me the name of your colonel, and I'll get you out if it's come to this.' I said, 'I know the chairman of the Military Affairs Committee. I'll call him.' So he gave me the name of his colonel, and I called the colonel. The colonel said, 'Well, Doctor, if it was anyone but Elvis Presley, we'd let him go, but let Elvis go and they'll say we're giving him special privileges.' I simply said to the colonel — these are my very words — I said, 'Look, Colonel, I'm having to sit down with the press of the whole world here and talk to them every day. Now if they say you gave him special privileges, I will back you to the hilt if you let him go.' But I said, 'Furthermore, Colonel, if you *don't* let him go, I'm going to sit down with them, and I'm going to burn your ass.' I told him that in so many words. I spent five and a half years in the army myself. I was chief of cardiac surgery at Walter Reed during World War II, and I knew how to handle colonels. Elvis was here in a matter of hours. The colonel saw the handwriting on the wall."

Elvis and Lamar flew from Dallas on Tuesday evening, August 12, and Elvis went straight to the hospital. "Oh my son, oh my son," exclaimed Gladys, who had already expressed concern about his flying to come see her. He spent an hour or so in the hospital room and found her a little better than expected. Her condition was still grave, said Dr. Clarke, but his visit had done her a world of good. He left his father at the hospital, where Vernon was camped out on a folding cot beside Gladys' bed. The pink Cadillac was parked so she could see it from her window. "I walked in one morning," said Dr. Clarke, "and she said, 'Look at that pink Cad out there in the parking lot.' She said, 'I like that special, 'cause Elvis give it to me.' The thing she was proudest of in her whole life was working as a nurse's aide at St. Joseph's Hospital."

Elvis came back early the next morning and spent several hours with her, then returned in the late afternoon with a bunch of friends, who hung out in the waiting room while he visited with his mother. She was in better spirits than the day before and spoke volubly about a wide range of subjects. He stayed till nearly midnight and promised her he'd be back early the next morning to take some of the flowers home.

At 3:30 A.M. the phone rang at Graceland. "I knew what it was before I answered the telephone," Elvis said. Vernon had been awakened by what he described as his wife "suffering for breath." He propped up her head and called for a doctor, but before the doctor was able to get there she was gone. Elvis arrived within minutes and sank to his knees, with his father, beside the bed. When Lamar brought Vernon's mother, Minnie, to the hospital just minutes later, "we got off the elevator, and I could hear Elvis and Vernon wailing. I had never heard anything like it before in my life — it was like a scream. I came down the hall, and Elvis saw me and he grabbed hold of me and said, 'Satnin' is gone.' "

They waited at the hospital for the hearse to come and take her away. Elvis was inconsolable, touching the body over and over, until hospital attendants had to ask him to stop. From the hospital Elvis called Sergeant Norwood at the base, and Anita Wood, who was in New York to do *The Andy Williams Show*. It was 5:30 in the morning, and her mother answered the phone. Elvis could barely speak, said Anita. She promised she would come right after the show that night.

When reporters came to the house at mid morning, they found Elvis and his father sitting on the front steps of Graceland, utterly bereft. They had their arms around each other and were sobbing uncontrollably, oblivious to the presence of anyone else. Elvis was wearing a white ruffled dress shirt with the sleeves rolled up, khaki continental pants, and unbuckled white buck shoes. His mother's death, he told reporters without embarrassment or shame, had broken his heart. "Tears streamed down his cheeks," wrote the *Press-Scimitar* reporter. "He cried throughout the interview. 'She's all we lived for,' he sobbed. 'She was always my best girl.' " Looking down the curved driveway, he said, "When Mama was feeling bad we used to walk with her up and down the driveway to help her feel better. Now it's over."

Hundreds of fans had assembled outside the gates and were keeping vigil when they moved the body to the house in the early afternoon. Elvis had announced that he wanted the funeral at home, in the traditional manner, because his mother had always loved his fans, and he wanted them to have a chance to see her. The Colonel overruled him, however, citing security, and the viewing at Graceland was limited to friends and family. The body was placed in a silver casket and lay in state in the music room. Gladys was clothed in a baby blue dress which her sister Lillian had never seen her wear, and Elvis struggled with tears once again as he recalled his mother's simplicity, her imperviousness to the blandishments of wealth and fame. "My mama loved beautiful things, but she wouldn't wear them," he declared with bitter emotion.

Nick Adams was flying in from the Coast, Cliff Gleaves was coming from Florida, and Vernon's father, Jessie, was riding the bus from Louisville. When Dr. Clarke arrived at the house ("I mean, they insisted that I come out and be with them at the home"), he found a chilling scene. "The expression of grief was just profound. He and his dad would just be pacing around, walk up to the front door with their arms locked around each other, and I remember the father saying, 'Elvis, look at them chickens. Mama ain't never gonna feed them chickens no more.' 'No, Daddy, Mama won't never feed them chickens anymore.' Just that sort of abject grief."

All day there was a mounting crescendo of tears and emotion. Some of Elvis' relatives, according to one source, were dead drunk in the kitchen. As Dr. Clarke saw it, the Colonel was doing his best "to make an extravaganza out of it." When Alan Fortas came in, "Elvis was in a daze. His voice was small and strained. 'My baby's gone, Alan, she's gone!' 'I know, Elvis,' I said. 'I'm sorry. She was a nice lady.' Then he took me over to view the body. . . . Except when he got up to greet visitors, he just sat there with her, almost as if they were the host and hostess of their own little party. It was a pitiful thing to watch." Junior picked up Eddie Fadal at the airport, and Elvis led him to the casket. "Just look at Mama," he said. "Look at them hands, oh God, those hands toiled to raise me." He couldn't stop touching her, Gladys' sister Lillian said. He would hug and kiss her and rock back and forth, whispering endearments, pleading with her to come back. "They couldn't get him to stop, until they were afraid for him, you know, and finally they had to cover over the coffin with glass." Telegrams arrived from Dean Martin, Marlon Brando, Ricky Nelson, Sammy Davis, Jr., Tennessee Ernie Ford, and present and soon-to-be Tennessee governors Frank Clement and Buford Ellington.

In the evening Sam and Dewey Phillips both came out to the house. Dewey was a mess. He had been fired from WHBQ the month before, and his behavior, under the influence of drink, pills, and congenital eccentricity, was becoming more and more erratic, but he and Sam stayed the whole night and did their best to comfort Elvis, who would not leave his mother's side. "After a time," said Sam, "I persuaded him to come to the kitchen, and we sat down, and I just listened to him. He knew I wasn't going to give him any damn bullshit or try to make him artificially feel good about it. . . . Elvis kept talking about the body and how he didn't want to give it up to anyone else. I eventually got Elvis away from the casket and we sat down by the pool. I'll never forget the dead leaves by the pool. I was able to convince him that he should let his mother go. I knew just enough to know which part of him to touch and in what way."

Anita finally arrived at 2:30 Friday morning. Everybody was camped out in the kitchen and living room. Nick, who had arrived with a cut over his eye from a fight scene with Frank Lovejoy, set up a makeshift bed next to Elvis' so he could keep him company through the night. George, Alan, Lamar, and a bunch of the other guys, too, were all set for the duration. Anita found Elvis and Vernon sitting on the steps in front of Graceland. He hugged her when he saw her, and they both cried, and he said, "Come in, Little. I want you to see Mama." She didn't really want to, because she'd never seen a dead body before, but he said, "Come on in, Little, Mama loved you. I want you to come and see her, she looks so pretty." He took her to the music room, "and there was a glass over her covering her up, but the top was up all the way so that the entire length of her body was exposed, and he took me over there and started talking about how pretty she looked, and then he patted on the top of the table where her feet were, and he said, 'Look at her little sooties, Little, look at her little sooties, she's so precious.' "

The Colonel cleared out most of the stragglers at that point, and Dr. Clarke administered a sedative to Elvis. The Memphis Funeral Home came for the body at 9:00 that morning while Elvis was still asleep.

The funeral was scheduled for 3:30 that afternoon, with the Reverend

Hamill presiding. By the time the service started, close to three thousand people had filed by the body, and there were sixty-five police outside to control the crowds. The chapel was filled to overflowing with nearly four hundred mourners jamming the three-hundred-seat hall. Chet Atkins attended, but Bill and Scotty did not. Elvis was wearing a dark brown suit and tie and had to be helped from the limo. Before the service started, Dixie, married and a mother by now, arrived with her aunt and entered the little alcove where the family sat, to pay her respects. "When I went in the room, Elvis and his dad were sitting there, and he just burst up out of his chair and grabbed me before I was in the door: it was like, 'Look, Dad, here's Dixie.' Like I was going to save the world. And we just hugged and comforted each other for a minute — there were twenty or thirty people sitting there, and it was almost time for the service to start — but it was a very emotional thing for both of us, and for his dad, and he said, 'Will you come out to Graceland tonight? I just need to talk to you.' And I said, 'Well, I'll try.' He was just so shaken over it. It just broke my heart to see him like that." When the Blackwood Brothers, who were stationed behind the altar room, sang "Precious Memories," Vernon could be heard to exclaim, "All we have now are memories," with Elvis sobbing out, "Oh Dad, Dad, no, no, no. . . ." The Blackwood Brothers had been Gladys Presley's favorite quartet, and Elvis had arranged for them to fly in from South Carolina. Every time they finished a song, said J. D. Sumner, who was singing bass, "he would send a note back for us to sing another one. We were supposed to sing three or four songs, and we wound up singing something like twelve. I never seen a man suffer as much or grieve as much as he did at the loss of his mother."

The Reverend Hamill preached on a theme suitable to the occasion. "Women can succeed in most any field these days," he said, "but the most important job of all is being a good wife and a good mother. Mrs. Presley was such a woman. I would be foolish to tell this father and this son, 'Don't worry, don't grieve, don't be sorrowful.' Of course you will miss her. But I can say, with Paul, 'Sorrow not as those who have no hope.' "

Several times during the service he almost collapsed. "I sat right behind him during the ceremony," said Anita, "and he would just cry out." When the service was over and the mourners had filed out, he and Vernon and James Blackwood and his friend Captain Woodward, of the Memphis Police Department, stood by the coffin alone. "He went over to the casket," said James, "and kissed his mother and said, 'Mama, I'd give up every dime I own and go back to digging ditches, just to have you back.' He was sobbing and crying hysterically. He came over and put his arms around me and just laid over on my shoulder and said, 'James, I know you know something of what we're going through.' He said, 'You don't know it, but I was in the audience at R.W. and Bill's funeral at Ellis Auditorium after the crash. So you know what I've been experiencing.' And I said, 'Yes, I do,' but I hadn't known that he was there until that day."

The scene was no less emotional or chaotic at the cemetery. The streets were lined with onlookers as the funeral procession left town on Bellevue, becoming Highway 51 as it reached Forest Hill Cemetery two or three miles short of Graceland. The grave site was crowded with an additional five hundred onlookers. "Some spectators," wrote Charles Portis in the *Commercial Appeal* the next day, "seemed to be honestly bereaved, but the majority craned their necks and chattered." Mr. Presley tried to comfort Elvis, but every time he did, he would himself dissolve in a paroxysm of grief. "She's gone, she's not coming back," he declared hopelessly over and over again. Elvis himself maintained his composure a little better until, toward the end, he burst into uncontrollable tears and, with the service completed, leaned over the casket, crying out, "Good-bye, darling, good-bye. I love you so much. You know how much I lived my whole life just for you." Four friends half-dragged him into the limousine. "Oh God," he declared, "everything I have is gone."

It was a mob scene back at Graceland, with friends and relatives milling around in helpless confusion, Elvis inconsolable, and the Colonel at his command post in the kitchen, when Dixie came out early that evening. She had no intention of intruding on his grief. "I didn't mean to see him that night, because he was already surrounded by people. I was wearing shorts, and I had my hair in rollers, and I was just going to tell him I'd see him the next night. I stopped at the gate, and none of the Presleys were down there — it was like Grand Central Station, and all these little girls were trying to get in, and I sat there for a minute and watched all the commotion. And I went up to the guard — it was somebody I didn't know — and said, 'Will you just call up to the house and tell Elvis that I'm down here, and that I'll come out tomorrow night to visit with him, if that's good.' So the guy says, 'Okay, I'll tell him,' but I was sure he wasn't going to give him the message.

"Then I went back to get in the car, and my car wouldn't start, and while I was sitting there one of Elvis' cousins came up and said, 'Aren't you Dixie?' And I said, 'Yes.' He said, 'Elvis is waiting on you at the house.' I said, 'No, I don't want to see him tonight. I've got my hair rolled up, and I'm not dressed. I was planning to see him tomorrow night.' He said, 'No. You'd better come up. He's already called down to see if you're here at the gate.' He took my keys to the car, and he took me up to the house, and Elvis came out the front door and just enveloped me. We went in the house, and the only person we saw was his grandmother. I said, 'Where is everybody? I thought you had all these people.' Because, I don't think this is an exaggeration, I think there were at least twenty or thirty cars out front. He said, 'There were — but I told them to get lost.' And I did not see or hear a soul the whole time we were there, except the maid was in the kitchen and he went in and asked her to bring us some lemonade, and we went in the wing where the piano was and we talked and he sang 'I'm Walking Behind You on Your Wedding Day,' and we sat there and cried.

"We talked about his mother and rehashed from the time that I'd met her and all the things that we'd done that were funny and silly. And he expressed how special it was just to be with somebody you knew from those many days back that loved you and accepted you for just what you were back then. He said, 'I wonder how many of my friends that are here now would be here if it were five years ago.' He said, 'Not very many, because they are all looking for something from me.' And he told me about one of the guys who was singing backup for him at the time who had just given his heart to the Lord. He had been in the world for a long time and was just really messed up, and he told Elvis that he was having to walk away from the life that he was leading, and Elvis said, 'I wish I could do that.' It was just so sad. I said, 'Why don't you? You've already done what you wanted to do. You've been there, so let's just stop at the top and go back.' He said, 'It's too late for that. There are too many people. There are too many people that depend on me. I'm too obligated. I'm in too far to get out.'

"That was the last time I saw him. Well, not the last time, because I went back the next night, all dressed up, but, you know, the next night the house was all full of people. You know, it was like, this is the way it will always be. That was his lifestyle. That was his life. It just reinforced to me that what I was seeing that night was really it. We both realized that.

He was in it, and there was no way out. He couldn't come back to my lifestyle any more than I could have gone on to his."

He was grieving almost constantly, the papers wrote. "He'd cry all day," said George, "and we'd get him calmed down, and the next day it would start all over again." On Saturday he returned once again to the Memphis Funeral Home, this time for the funeral of Red West's father. Red, who was still in the Marine Corps and stationed in Norfolk, Virginia, had requested emergency leave as soon as he heard of Gladys' death. It was denied, but then he heard of his father's illness that same morning. He was on his way home when he got word of his father's death. He was forced to miss Gladys' funeral because he had to attend to the details of his father's the next day, and he was flabbergasted when Elvis showed up at the funeral home. "Man, he had gone through a trial the day before. . . . He was out of it. But just before the service started Elvis appeared at the doorway. He was with Alan Fortas and Gene Smith and Lamar Fike. They were all very respectfully dressed. Elvis almost had to be carried over to me. . . . He came over to me and sort of half fell into my arms. 'My mama was here yesterday just where your daddy is, Red,' Elvis told me. He couldn't say too much more."

That afternoon they went out to the cemetery to visit Elvis' mother's grave, which couldn't have seemed like much of an idea to any of his friends but which none of them could talk him out of. "After a near emotional breakdown," reported the *Press-Scimitar,* "Elvis had a fever of 'near 102,' his doctor reported. 'I went down and checked him over and gave him some cold drugs,' the doctor said. 'I called again Sunday and he was feeling better and eating a little, so I didn't go down.' "

His leave was extended by five days, and his friends tried to cheer him up. He bought a new van, and the whole gang traveled with him around the countryside — they went to the movies and the Rainbow Rollerdrome — but it wasn't the same. Even the Tennessee Highway Patrol got into the act, as they took him on morning helicopter rides over Memphis and taught him how to operate the controls. All of Memphis, the whole world, in fact, grieved with him, as more than a hundred thousand cards, letters, and telegrams came into the Colonel's headquarters in Madison. None of it made any difference. One day he ran into an old schoolmate and neighbor from the Courts, George Blancet, driving down Bellevue. "He rolled his window down, and his eyes were teary and he called me by name. I told him I was sorry his mother had died. He just said, 'I don't know how I'm gonna make it.' Something like that. It was a statement of desperation."

Toward the end of the week his dentist, Lester Hofman, came by with his wife, Sterling, to pay their respects. "This was the first time we had been there. I was racking my brain about what to do — should I send flowers? I really didn't know — when I got a call saying, 'Dr. Hofman, can you come out to the house? Elvis would like to see you.' When we got there, the room was full of all his buddies. We looked around and we didn't see a face we knew. I sat next to this young fellow, and he said, 'Who are you here to see?' I said, 'We're here to see Elvis.' He said, 'Well, you're not going to see him. He hasn't been out of his room.' I said, 'Well, that's his privilege. It's up to him whether he wants to see us.' Then we were talking with Vernon, and Vernon said, 'Just a minute, I'll get Elvis.' Five minutes later Elvis walked in, and he went like this and the room cleared. We told him how sorry we were, and he said to Sterling, 'Mrs. Hofman, I don't know if this is the right time, but the newspapers have made my house so laughable' — that was the word. He said, 'They have made it sound so laughable, I would love to have your opinion of my home.' She said, 'Elvis, I really didn't come here to go through your home. We came here to be with you.' He said, 'But I want your opinion.' He took us all through the house, my taste is not so marvelous, but it was very attractive, it all fit — there was a modern sculpture on the chimney over the fireplace, and I had the same sculpture in my office, it was called 'Rhythm.' Anyway, when we got back to the living room, he said, 'What do you think?' and Sterling said, 'If you give me the key, I'll swap you. And I won't even move a dish!' Then Sterling said to him, 'Did you ever think one day, you might have all of this, it's just so beautiful.' He said, 'Mrs. Hofman, I never thought I'd get out of Humes High.' "

On Sunday he returned to Fort Hood. He left instructions that nothing was to be changed, nothing was to be the least bit disturbed in his mother's room, all was to be kept exactly as it had been. The simple inscription on his mother's gravestone read: "She was the sunshine of our home."

THE LAST FEW WEEKS at Fort Hood went by in a haze. Vernon, Elvis' grandmother Minnie, Lamar, Junior, and Gene were all living at the house in Killeen, and Red joined them when he got out of the Marines in the first week of September. It was, as Red described it, a kind of "open house" atmosphere in which everyone tried almost desperately to cheer up Elvis. They'd stay up all night occasionally; "sometimes a whole team of us would sit around with a guitar and sing ourselves hoarse." Things were never again the same, wrote Rex Mansfield in his memoir of army days. "We all suffered (his whole outfit) with and for Elvis' great loss . . . and there remained a certain sadness with all of us throughout the rest of our training."

The Colonel came down a couple of times to huddle with Elvis over embarkation plans and future RCA releases. Anita, who was constantly fending off rumors of impending marriage ("Heavenly days, I just can't imagine it"), visited frequently in between performance dates and television appearances. Elvis' grandmother, she noted, was doing her best to take Gladys' place. She fixed all his favorite foods: sauerkraut and crowder peas, sliced tomatoes and brown gravy, and bacon cooked till it was burnt. Whatever he liked she would fix for him, and there was still an extraordinary sense of closeness among Elvis, his father, and his grandmother, but now it was a closeness tied to grief. Sometimes he and Anita talked about her coming to see him when he was in Germany, but the thought existed more in the realm of fantasy than reality.

Once in a while they would go to the drive-in in Waco with Eddie Fadal, and Elvis and Eddie attended an r&b revue in Fort Worth ("I don't remember who they all were, but we parked by the stage door, and they all came out to the car and greeted him") and almost caused a riot at a Johnny Horton show in Temple. "It was at the auditorium in downtown Temple," said Shreveport native Jerry Kennedy, still in his teens but playing guitar for Horton at the time. "I was sitting on those big doors that used to come up at the back of auditoriums, where you can back a truck into, and this car pulled up, and all these guys bailed out of it with Elvis in uniform, and they said, 'Hey, can you let us in the back door?' I said, 'I guess. Since it's you.' So I went down and opened the back door, and he came in, and then we went onstage. Johnny did four or five songs, and then he said, 'I want to extend a warm welcome to somebody who is visiting me backstage.' He said something about his mother, and so forth, and I remember, I was standing there thinking, 'Don't do this. Oh God, he's not going to do that.' And he did, and then he said, 'I'd like for him to step out and take a bow. Elvis . . .' And the people got up and just rushed the stage, and I grabbed my guitar and got away!"

The last weekend that he was at Fort Hood, Kitty Dolan, the young singer whom he had met in Las Vegas the previous fall, came for a visit. When she arrived, she found the living room full of girls. "I Was One Girl Among Many" read the headline over her article in *TV and Movie Screen.* She fully appreciated the sincerity of the others, though, and their genuine desire to try to alleviate his grief. One fan told of visiting Graceland and how Gladys had proudly shown her the home and the pink Cadillac that her son had given her. "What other boy would love his parents so much?" Gladys had said to her, the girl reported, as tears came to Elvis' eyes. After dinner they sat around singing songs, ending with a gospel session with a bunch of the guys. "At two A.M. we said good night," Kitty told columnist May Mann. "When he kissed me, I said with a little laugh, 'What is this with you and Anita Wood? I've been reading all the stories.' Elvis smiled and said, 'She has a good press agent.' And then he kissed me again."

There is a group picture from Elvis' last night in Killeen taken with Vernon, Lamar, Eddie, Junior, and Red, along with two or three of the fan club presidents. Elvis has his arms around Eddie's and his father's shoulders. He is wearing his marksman and sharpshooter medals, and he is surrounded by friends, but he looks alone and lost, his eyes blank, his mouth downturned, as if he were about to cry. After the picture was taken, he asked Eddie if he would lead the group in prayer, and then they left to take him to the troop train in the drizzling rain. "He shipped out that very night," said Eddie. "I rode with Elvis and Anita in his new Lincoln Continental, with Elvis driving. Then Anita and I drove home and we sat there with Vernon for a while. We were really in mourning, he'd never been out like that before, and we were [worrying]: how are they going to treat him, are they going to resent or embrace him, you know, how is he going to take it?"

THE TRAIN RIDE to New York was uneventful for the most part. One of four special troop trains moving approximately 1,360 soldiers to the Brooklyn Army Terminal to ship out for Germany as replacements for Third Armored Division troops, it was, ironically, routed through Memphis, and word got out. When the train pulled in, there was a crowd of fans already waiting, along with George Klein, Alan Fortas, and several other of Elvis' friends. The train took about an hour to refuel, "and this gorgeous brunette came up to me," said Klein, "I don't know if she went to Ole Miss at the time, but she was a typical Ole Miss beautiful girl, and she said her name was Janie Willbanks, and she asked if I would introduce her. I did, and about two weeks later I get this call from Germany saying, 'Who in the hell was that girl? Man, she was good-looking! Tell her to send me some pictures and write to me.' That was when I first got the indication that it might not be all that serious with Anita."

One of his fellow soldiers gave Elvis a book called *Poems That Touch the Heart,* compiled by A. L. Alexander ("Creator of Radio's GOOD WILL COURT"), and he leafed through it, reading several of the poems, including "Mother" ("Again your kindly, smiling face I see"), "Friendship," and "One of Us Two" ("The day will dawn, when one of us shall harken / In vain to hear a voice that has grown dumb"), but one in particular really hit home. It was called "Should You Go First," and he stared at it for some time, until he practically knew it by heart: "I'll hear your voice, I'll see your smile / Though blindly I may grope / The memory of your helping hand / Will buoy me on with hope. . . ."

Mostly, though, he didn't like to be alone with his thoughts, and the other boys wanted to hear about Hollywood and Hollywood starlets and the movies. The train was delayed several times as it ran into commuter traffic, and somewhere in Delaware or New Jersey a brash, pint-size young soldier named Charlie Hodge, who had done everything he could to get together with Elvis at Fort Hood but had never really gotten the chance, showed up in the train car that Elvis and Rex and Nervous Norvell were riding in. Charlie had sung with the Foggy River Boys on Red Foley's Ozark Jubilee and had even met Elvis once backstage at Ellis Auditorium in 1955. He was not at all shy about drawing on mutual show biz connections, and before long they were talking about Wanda Jackson and country comedian Uncle Cyp and the passion that they shared for quartet music. Charlie was "bound and determined to meet Elvis," observed Rex, but he "really was one of the funniest guys you could meet; the type you could not help but like and Elvis liked him instantly." They spent the rest of the train ride trading stories and separated only when the train finally got into the Brooklyn Army Terminal at Fifty-eighth and First Avenue, a little after 9:00 A.M. There Elvis Presley, the public figure, became the center of attention once again.

It was a scene worthy of P. T. Barnum, Cecil B. DeMille, or the Colonel at his most extravagant. There were 125 newsmen waiting impatiently, all of RCA's top brass, Elvis' father, his grandmother, Anita, Red and Lamar, the Aberbachs and Freddy Bienstock, plus the Colonel with his full entourage. Elvis would be out shortly, army spokesman Irving Moss explained, but in the meantime he wanted to go over protocol: for the first ten or fifteen minutes still photographers would be permitted to take pictures; then there would be a press conference proper; following that, the newsreel and TV cameras would have their chance; then Pfc. Presley would board the ship's gangplank for photographers, with eight buddies selected at random from off the train; finally, there would be a small group of newsmen permitted on board. Would he be carrying a duffel bag? someone asked. No, said Moss, his duffel bag had already been loaded on board, but when that answer didn't satisfy the press, the army spokesman proposed that a duffel bag could be *borrowed*. "I want to say one more thing, ladies and gentlemen. Since this terminal has been established, [during] World War I and through World War II and to date, there have been millions of troops going through here and among them have been thousands of celebrities in the various fields of the arts, sciences, sports, and the entertainment field. It has not been, nor is it, the policy of the army to single out any of these people for press conferences. However, in this particular instance . . ." "What are we waiting for?" called out one reporter as it became evident that Elvis Presley had arrived. "All right, bring him out." "Let's go, for heaven's sake," came the "angered squawks from photographers, desperately shoving each other to get a clear shot at Presley."

Then, at last, Elvis emerged from behind the blue backing where he had been chatting with the Colonel, stood for a moment for photographers, smiled graciously for the cameras, signed autographs, kissed a WAC named Mary Davies whom the army had produced for the occasion, did his best to oblige every shouted request, and finally sat down at the table with Information Officer Moss in front of a cluster of microphones. He was carrying a shiny calfskin attaché case and clutching the book of poems he had had on the train. What was the train ride like? he was asked. What were his medals for? What did the *a* in his name stand for? "A-ron," he explained, pronouncing the *a* long. Yes, his father and his grandmother and Lamar were going to accompany him to Germany. Would he ever sell Graceland? "No, sir, because that was my mother's home." The guys in his outfit had been great. "If it had been like everybody thought, I mean everybody thought I wouldn't have to work, and I would be given special treatment and this and that, but when they looked around and saw I was on KP and I was pulling guard and everything, just like they were, well, they figured, he's just like us, so . . ."

He'd come in for a lot of criticism in his career. What did he think of the charges that his music had contributed to juvenile delinquency? "I don't see that. Because if there is anything I have tried to do, I've tried to live a straight, clean life, not set any kind of a bad example." "Elvis —" "I will say this, excuse me, sir, I will say there are people who are going to like you and people who don't like you, regardless of what business you are in or what you do. You cannot please everyone." What about his great success? Did he feel that he'd been lucky, or that he had talent? "Well, sir, I've been very lucky. I happened to come along at a time in the music business when there was no trend. The people were looking for something different, and I was lucky. I came along just in time." And did he miss show business? "I miss my singing career very much. And at the same time — the army is a pretty good deal, too." But surely he didn't miss the fans grabbing at his clothes, invading his private life, threatening his safety? He did, he said, he missed even that, "because that is my greatest love — like I said, entertaining people. I really miss it."

And marriage? Did he think there was an ideal age to get married? "Well, as you're growing up, a lot of times you think you're in love with someone, and then later on in your life you find out that you're wrong. Actually you didn't love them, you only thought you did. And I was no different. Several times as I was growing up I would have probably married, and my mother and dad talked to me and told me, 'You better wait and find out that this is just what you want,' and I'm glad that I did." When was the last time he thought he was in love? "Oh, many times, ma'am, I don't know, I suppose the closest that I ever came to getting married was just before I started singing. In fact, my first record saved my neck." There is general laughter, and then someone asks him if he'd like to say something about his mother.

"Yes, sir, I certainly would. Ahhh, my mother . . . I suppose since I was an only child we might have been a little closer than — I mean, everyone loves their mother, but I was an only child, and Mother was always right with me all my life. And it wasn't only like losing a mother, it was like losing a friend, a companion, someone to talk to, I could wake her up any hour of the night if I was worried or troubled about something, well, she'd get up and try to help me. And I used to get very angry at her when I was growing up. It's a natural thing — a young person wants to go somewhere or do something, and your mother won't let you, and you think, 'Why, what's wrong with you?' But then, later on in the years you find out, you know, that she was right. That she was only doing it to protect you and keep you from getting into trouble or getting hurt. And I'm very happy that she was kind of strict on me, very happy that it worked out the way it did."

The press conference went on for nearly an hour, and when it was over, he posed for more pictures and signed more autographs as Information Officer Moss tried to extricate him from the crowd. The people would get mad if they were turned down, Elvis said in an aside to the army information officer. "Come on," said the Colonel, urging the RCA executives forward. "We all eat off him, let's get in the picture. The boy is mighty sad." Then there were more photographs to be taken outside on the dock and activities to be staged for the newsreel cameras. "I think I'm talking for all the guys," said one of the eight army "buddies" picked at random for the task, "when I say that we learned a lot about people in general when we were lucky enough to have Elvis with us. . . . He gives so much of himself to all the people around him that you just can't help but improve a little through the association. He's a lonely guy in many ways, and a little afraid of what tomorrow will bring for him and his loved ones."

He marched up the gangplank with a borrowed duffel bag slung over his shoulder as the army band, under the direction of Chief Warrant Officer John R. Charlesworth, struck up "Tutti Frutti." He did it not once but eight times for news crews and photographers, with the two thousand relatives who were there for their own leave-takings waving and screaming on cue. Once on board, he was closeted in the ship's library with the Colonel, Steve Sholes, Bill Bullock, and various other members of the industry entourage. He recorded a brief Christmas message for the fans, which, together with an edited version of the press conference, to be entitled "Elvis Sails!," would help keep him in touch with his public. He conferred anxiously with the Colonel, Freddy, and the Aberbachs and promised them that he would do his very best. "He was resigned," said Anne Fulchino, the RCA publicity chief, who had scarcely seen him since launching that first national publicity campaign for a bright-eyed youth in early 1956. "He was concerned about interrupting his career, he was worried that his records would stop selling. I said there was no reason they should, but I know he was thinking about that." He took out one of the postcards with which the Colonel had supplied him to present to fans and fellow soldiers alike. "May God bless you," he wrote on it as he handed it to her. He seemed trapped, cornered, she thought, his eyes frantically searched the room. Why don't you come along, too? he said, suddenly, to Red, who was just standing there with Lamar. Red could fly over with Vernon and Grandma and Lamar. "Daddy will fix up the tickets," he said. They would have themselves a ball.

Then there was a brief interview in the library. For the first time that day, in public he sounds tired, even a bit downcast. He hasn't eaten since early morning, he says, but he doesn't feel like he could eat anything right now. What are his thoughts? he is asked, as the time for departure approaches. "Well, I'm going to be very honest about it," he says haltingly. "I'm looking forward to Germany, I'm looking forward to seeing the country and meeting a lot of the people, but at the same time I'm looking forward to coming back here, because here is where I started. Here's where all my friends, my business and so forth . . ." Would he like to send any special message to his fans? "Yes, I would. I'd like to say that in spite of the fact that I'm going away and will be out of their eyes for some time, I hope I'm not out of their minds. And I'll be looking forward to the time when I can come back and entertain again like I did." "Well, thank you, Elvis," the interviewer concludes, with fifteen minutes left before departure. "I know you want to talk to Colonel Parker, your close friend and your manager. All we can do is wish you a wonderful trip and all the best luck in the world and come home soon."

The band played "All Shook Up," "Hound Dog," and "Don't Be Cruel" as the ship got under way. Elvis stood out on deck handing out pictures and postcards to his fellow servicemen and throwing kisses back to the pier but stopped for a moment "to rotate his shoulder, snap his fingers and buckle his knees. His admirers shrieked," reported the *New York Herald-Tribune*. "Colonel Parker beamed. The Department of Defense man from Washington who had overseen the operation wiped his brow and sighed." And Elvis waved. And waved again for the cameras. And again, and again.

ON THE TRAIN TO MEMPHIS, JULY 3–4, 1956. (ALFRED WERTHEIMER)

Notes

THE MAJORITY OF THE INTERVIEW MATERIAL is my own, but Jerry Hopkins' interviews of various figures for his 1971 biography, *Elvis*, have been a unique, and invaluable, resource. They were made available by the Mississippi Valley Collection at Memphis State University (MVC/MSU) through the kind efforts of Dr. John Bakke. In addition, Stuart Goldman and Adam Taylor were good enough to share information and interview material assembled for their 1993 film, *Elvis in Hollywood*. Many other people contributed their time and resources, and I have tried to indicate my thanks and indebtedness both in these notes and in the acknowledgments that follow.

PROLOGUE: MEMPHIS, 1950

3 the Mississippi Delta begins: David Cohn, *Where I Was Born and Raised*, p. 12.

4 The newcomer, Dewey Phillips, is twenty-four years old: Much of the account of Dewey Phillips' early background comes from " 'Phillips Sent Me' Has Become Vital Part of City's Lexicon" by Ida Clemens, *Memphis Commercial Appeal*, June 9, 1950.

4–5 That is why Sam Phillips: Sam Phillips' early background, as well as his account of his first meeting with Dewey Phillips, comes from interviews with Sam Phillips, 1979–93. All subsequent quotes are from these interviews, unless otherwise specified.

5 "Negro artists in the South who wanted to make a record": "Man Behind the Sun Sound," *Melody Maker*, c. 1957, as cited by Mike Leadbitter in "Memphis," *Blues Unlimited* Collectors Classics 13.

5–6 "genuine, untutored negro" music; "Negroes with field mud on their boots": Robert Johnson, "Suddenly Singing Elvis Presley Zooms into Recording Stardom," *Memphis Press-Scimitar*, February 5, 1955.

6 The ostensible reason: Interview with Sam Phillips, 1988; letter from Sam Phillips to "Mr. J. Edward Connolly, June-bug, 8 — 50," published in *Kicks* 7, 1992. The letter to Connolly seems to belie Phillips' contention that he was not trying to sell Dewey to Connolly, but this was at the very beginning of their acquaintance, and by August, Dewey and Sam had their first (and last) release out on the aptly named "The Phillips" label.

8 "so nervous he was bug-eyed": Vernon quoted in *Elvis Presley*, prepared by the editors of *TV Radio Mirror*, 1956, p. 10.

8 the Presleys gave the impression: "Elvis by His Father Vernon Presley" as told to Nancy Anderson, *Good Housekeeping*, January 1978.

8 In February 1949: All information on the Presleys' housing from the time of their arrival in Memphis comes from Memphis Housing Authority records, kindly made available by Rick Hawks, whose "adoptive aunt" was Housing Authority adviser Jane Richardson.

TUPELO: ABOVE THE HIGHWAY

11 "industry rising in the midst of agriculture": *Mississippi: The WPA Guide to the Magnolia State*.

11 "Over the years": Dale Dobbs, "A Brief History of East Tupelo, Mississippi," *Elvis Presley Heights, Mississippi, Lee County, 1921–1984*, compiled by members of the Elvis Presley Heights Garden Club.

12 Gladys Presley, everyone agreed: The principal, and best, source for background information on Gladys and Vernon Presley, and the Smith and Presley family backgrounds, is Elaine Dundy's *Elvis and Gladys*.

13 Aron (pronounced with a long *a*): This is how Elvis pronounces it at his army press conference on September 22, 1958.

13 "when one twin died": "Elvis Presley Part 2: The Folks He Left Behind Him," *TV Guide*, September 22–28, 1956.

13 Gladys was never able to have another baby: In *Elvis Presley Speaks!*, the book-length bio by Memphis reporter Robert Johnson that came out in 1956, Vernon says, "That was just one of those things that couldn't be. . . . We spent a lot on doctors trying to change it, but there wasn't anything we could do."

13 The physician's fifteen-dollar fee: William Thomas, "Delivering Elvis Paid $15 — From Welfare," *Memphis Commercial Appeal*, January 6, 1980.

13 "she worshiped him": Jerry Hopkins interview with Faye Harris (MVC/MSU).

13 "Elvis was so sure": *Elvis Presley*, prepared by the editors of *TV Radio Mirror*, 1956, p. 6.

13 "My mama never let me": C. Robert Jennings, "There'll Always Be an Elvis," *Saturday Evening Post*, September 11, 1965, p. 78.

14 "common laborer": This was Elvis' own phrase in a number of interviews.

14 In 1937 Gladys' uncle Gains: Dundy, *Elvis and Gladys*, p. 72.

14 "when Elvis was just a little fellow": *TV Radio Mirror*, p. 8.

14 "My daddy may seem hard": Both Cliff Gleaves and Charlie Hodge cited this phrase in separate interviews, and George Klein alluded to similar conversations.

14 "It was no big disgrace": Interview with Frank and Corene Randle Smith, 1990.

14–15 "afraid that he would get run over": Interview with Corinne Richards Tate, 1990.

15 "crying his eyes out": Dundy, *Elvis and Gladys*, p. 84.

15 "In 1940 they moved": Ibid., p. 87; friendship with Sales and Annie Presley documented in *Elvis Presley Heights*, p. 47.

15 "Though we had friends": "Elvis by His Father Vernon Presley" as told to Nancy Anderson, *Good Housekeeping*, January 1978, p. 156.

15–16 "Mrs. Presley would say": Interview with James Ausborn, 1990.

16 "[one time] I asked him": *Good Housekeeping*, p. 157.

16 " 'When I grow up' ": Recollected by both Gladys (in Martha Lopert, "The Boy with the Big Beat," *Celebrity*, winter 1958) and Vernon (in Edwin Miller, "Elvis the Innocent," *Memories*, May 1989, from a May 1956 interview). This story combines the two accounts.

16 "an average student," "sweet and average": Dundy, *Elvis and Gladys*, p. 107; Pat Chism, "Teacher Recalls Elvis' Favorite Tune While at Lawhon Was 'Old Shep,' " *Tupelo Daily Journal*, July 28–29, 1956; Kathy Jarman, "Milam Report Card Reveals Elvis as an 'Average' Student," *Tupelo Daily Journal*, October 6, 1977.

16 "and we couldn't": Larry Geller and Joel Spector, *"If I Can Dream,"* p. 288.

16 The picture that you see of him: This picture was in the Tupelo Museum in 1989.

16–17 "I'd tramp all over town": *TV Radio Mirror*, p. 8.

17 On August 18, 1945: Dundy, *Elvis and Gladys*, p. 108.

17 became a deacon in the church: Ibid., p. 109; *Good Housekeeping*, p. 157.

17 the Presleys, like every other member: Interview with Frank and Corene Randle Smith.

17 "I sang some": *Saturday Evening Post*, p. 78.

17 he "trioed" with his mother and father: Army Archerd, "Presley Takes Hollywood," *Photoplay*, December 1956, p. 94.

18 two doors down from the Presleys: *Elvis Presley Heights*, p. 156.

18 the two couples would share: Ibid., p. 48.

18 The newspaper did not cover: In 1994 Bill Burk discovered a photograph of a ten-year-old Elvis Presley standing onstage after the contest, wearing glasses and flanked by the first-, second-, and third-place winners. Elvis, as he always said, had come in an unofficial fifth. The photograph and accompanying interviews will appear in Burk's *Early Elvis: The Tupelo Years*.

18 "I'll never forget": *TV Radio Mirror*, p. 26.

19 (the tornado of 1936): *Mississippi*.

19 "Son, wouldn't you rather": *TV Radio Mirror*, p. 26.

19 "I always played the guitar": Interview with Frank and Corene Randle Smith.

20–21 the hillbilly star of the station: Background on the Brasfield family of comedians, Rod, "Boob," and Cyp, from Linnell Gentry's *A History and Encyclopedia of Country, Western, and Gospel Music; The Country Music Story* by Robert Shelton; *Nashville's Grand Ole Opry* by Jack Hurst; and 1989 and 1990 interviews with Charlie Hodge and James Ausborn respectively.

21 "He was a good entertainer": Interview with Bill Mitchell, 1990.

21 Archie Mackey's memory: Interview with Archie Mackey, 1990.

21 "He was crazy about music": Interview with James Ausborn.

22 "He always knew": *Elvis Presley Speaks!*, p. 16.

22–23 Tex Ritter was making a personal appearance: The Tex Ritter story is from a 1990 interview with James Ausborn.

23 "I took the guitar": 1972 interview.

24 To Ernest Bowen: Interview with Ernest Bowen, 1990.

24 "All of us were country kids": Interview with Willie Wileman, 1990.

25 "It was unbelievable": Interview with Roland Tindall, 1990.

25–26 "Elvis would bring": Ibid.

26 "He brought his guitar": Interview with James Ausborn.

26 A classmate, Shirley Lumpkin: Dundy, *Elvis and Gladys*, pp. 120–121.

26 "All the socializing": Interview with Roland Tindall.

27 You walked by the Elks Club: My tour guide for the North Green Street area of Tupelo was Jimmy Young, a lifelong resident, who was good enough to drive me around and point out all the sights.

27 Several times a year: The basis for this description of a revival on North Green Street comes from Ernest Bowen, although I have taken the liberty of adapting it and introducing an eyewitness. In the August 1, 1957, edition of *Jet* magazine, Dr. W. A. Zuber, a black Tupelo physician, spoke of Elvis going "to Negro 'sanctified' meetings."

28 On his last day of school: Vince Staten, *The Real Elvis: Good Old Boy*, p. 42; Dundy, *Elvis and Gladys*, pp. 124, 132. The date is based on the fact that Elvis' first day in the Memphis school system, as recorded on his high school record, was November 8, 1948. Also, see below.

28 They moved on a Saturday: *TV Radio Mirror*, p. 9.

28 "We were broke, man, broke": James Kingsley, "At Home with Elvis Presley," *Memphis Commercial Appeal, Mid-South Magazine*, March 7, 1965.

28 According to Gladys: *TV Radio Mirror*, p. 9.

28–29 "I told Elvis": Ibid., p. 8.

29 "There were times": *Good Housekeeping*, p. 157.

MEMPHIS: THE COURTS

33 The Presleys lived: This, and all subsequent information on the Presleys' living situation, is from Housing Authority records, as supplied by Rick Hawks, and Jerry Hopkins' interview with Housing Authority adviser Jane Richardson.

33 ("We always found"): Jerry Hopkins interview with Jane Richardson (MVC/MSU).

34 "like we'd come into the money": Interview with George Blancet, 1989.

34 you just did it: Interview with Buzzy Forbess, 1991.

34 Stanley Products (Tupperware-like) parties: Interviews with Barbara Pittman and Jimmy Denson, 1989.

34 "They treated him": Jerry Hopkins, *Elvis*, p. 38.

35 "He was particular": Interview with Lillian Fortenberry, 1988.

35 "He never spent": "Elvis by His Father Vernon Presley" as told to Nancy Anderson, *Good Housekeeping*, January 1978, p. 157.

35 "If one has no scruples": *Humes Herald*, 1953.

35 At first Gladys: Joseph Lewis, "Elvis Presley Lives," *Cosmopolitan*, November 1968, p. 94.

35 "He was a gentle, obedient boy": Robert Johnson, *Elvis Presley Speaks!*, p. 18. (Miss Susie Johnson was *Press-Scimitar* reporter Bob Johnson's aunt.)

35 "He was during his first years": Ibid., p. 18.

36 According to a classmate: Elston Leonard, "Elvis Presley: The New Singing Rage," *Tiger*, c. 1956. George Klein, another student in the class, also tells this story to date the beginning of his friendship with Elvis.

36 "My older brother": Interview with Barbara Pittman.

36 Gladys was working: *Elvis Presley Speaks!*, p. 17.

36–37 "Paul lived on the third floor": Interview with Buzzy Forbess.

37–38 "The first evening he came in": *Elvis Presley Speaks!*, p. 17.

38 "With the three of us": Interview with Buzzy Forbess.

38 One time Farley's mother: Vince Staten, *The Real Elvis: Good Old Boy*, p. 44. The quote from Jane Richardson comes from Jerry Hopkins' interview.

38 "He even practiced two or three songs": Interview with Buzzy Forbess.

38 In one typical 1951 segment: Air check, *Red Hot and Blue*, December 2, 1951.

38 "If you have a song": Lydel Sims, "Rocket Becomes Flying Disc, Spins Toward Record Glory," *Memphis Commercial Appeal*, March 28, 1951.

38 "Do like me": This is an adaptation of one of Dewey Phillips expert Charles Raiteri's fine evocations of Dewey's patter and style.

40 He had run away from home: Various interviews with Jimmy Denson, 1989–92.

40 made the papers for performing: Rhea Talley, "Early A.M. Audition Needed by Lee Denson, Guitarist," *Memphis Commercial Appeal*, August 5, 1956.

40 He didn't want to teach Elvis: Interview with Lee Denson, 1989.

41 Lee's friends Dorsey Burnette and his younger brother, Johnny: Background information on the Burnettes comes from interviews with Jimmy and Lee Denson, 1989; Johnny Black, 1990, 1991; Evelyn Black, 1993; also Ian Wallis interview with Paul Burlison, 1989.

41 In the summertime there were informal dances: Interview with Jimmy and Lee Denson. This is supported by interviews with various other Courts residents, including Johnny Black, 1990, and Evelyn Black, 1993.

41 "We would play under the trees": Interview with Johnny Black, 1990.

41 When he missed a note: Interview with Jimmy and Lee Denson.

42 "She used to come out": Michael Donahue, "Elvis: The Project Years," *Memphis Commercial Appeal, Mid-South Magazine*, August 11, 1985.

42–43 "Elvis was a great kisser": Bill E. Burk, *Early Elvis: The Humes Years*, pp. 110–111.

43 "He tried not to show it": Robert Palmer, "Sam Phillips: The Sun King," *Memphis*, December 1978.

43 He sings Eddy Arnold's: The repertoire was specified in an interview with Buzzy Forbess. Buzzy also mentioned Bing and Gary Crosby's catchy (and up-tempo) "Play a Simple Melody."

44 ("Wild-looking guys"): 1972 interview.

44 ("It was just something"): Ibid.

44 she was very proud of the job: Interviews with Gladys' physician, Dr Charles Clarke, 1989, and Ronny Trout, 1991.

44 a 1941 Lincoln coupe: This has been described on some occasions as a 1942 model (and, more specifically, as a Lincoln Zephyr), but it is specified as a '41 Chrysler in the Housing Authority report.

44–45 "My daddy was something wonderful": Edwin Miller, "Elvis the Innocent," *Memories*, May 1989, p. 13.

45 One time, Vernon recalled: *Elvis Presley*, prepared by the editors of *TV Radio Mirror*, 1956, p. 17.

45 "Elvis saw the street": *Elvis Presley Speaks!*, p. 26.

45 the firemen, who welcomed any diversion: Ibid.

45 "One time we were hanging around": Interview with Johnny Black, 1990.

46 "we don't have any Negro conductors": David Tucker, *Lieutenant Lee of Beale Street*, p. 146.

46 "He came down": Interview with Guy Lansky, 1990.

46 "I suppose that was where I saw him": Jerry Hopkins interview with Bob Neal (MVC/MSU).

46–47 "I mean, we didn't know Elvis Presley": Interview with Jake Hess, 1991.

47–48 Once a month Ellis was filled: A great deal of the background on the All-Night Singings, and quartet singing in general, comes from extensive interviews with Jake Hess and James Blackwood; early videos of the Blackwood Brothers and the Statesmen supplied by Mary Jarvis, James Blackwood, and Jake Hess; various writings by Charles Wolfe (including "Presley and the Gospel Tradition" in *Elvis: Images and Fancies*) and *The Music Men* by Bob Terrell.

47 "the big heavy rhythm beats": C. Robert Jennings, "There'll Always Be an Elvis," *Saturday Evening Post*, September 11, 1965, p. 78.

48 "He went about as far as you could go": Interview with Jake Hess.

48 "Oh, no, not again": Interview with Johnny Black, 1990.

48 "I moved everything": Interview with Lillian Fortenberry, 1988.

48 He sang quite a few: Elvis' musical repertoire is supplied from interviews with Buzzy Forbess, Lee Denson, Johnny Black, and Ronald Smith, as well as various published interviews with Paul Burlison.

48 Some evenings Vernon and Gladys: "Elvis by His Father Vernon Presley" as told to Nancy Anderson, *Good Housekeeping*, January 1978, p. 157.

48 "He grabbed it out of my purse": Billie Wardlaw quoted in Bill E. Burk, *The Young Elvis*, pp. 111–112.

48 Occasionally Buzzy and the other boys: Interview with Buzzy Forbess.

49 According to a teacher, Mildred Scrivener: Mildred Scrivener, "My Boy Elvis," *TV Radio Mirror*, March 1957.

49 "It got so hard on him": *Elvis Presley*, prepared by the editors of *TV Radio Mirror*, 1956, p. 10. Actually Gladys went back to work at St. Joseph's in August, but the same principle applied.

50 "I really felt sorry for him": Red West et al., *Elvis: What Happened?*, p. 17.

50 "He would wear dress pants": Interview with Ronny Trout.

51 One time he got a home permanent: The "permanent" was described in various manifestations in interviews with Ronny Trout, Jimmy Denson, Barbara Pittman, and "Mary Ann," a neighbor in the Courts, who is quoted in Jane and Michael Stern's *Elvis World*, p. 151.

51 he stopped by St. Joseph's: Interview with Ronny Trout.

51 Perhaps he attended the Midnight Rambles: Interviews with Ronny Trout, George Blancet, George Klein, et al.

51–52 "the same place," he later recalled: 1972 interview.

52 "We just thought he was pretty": Interview with Evelyn Black.

52 Rabbi Alfred Fruchter and his wife, Jeanette: Staten, *The Real Elvis*, p. 61.

52–53 On April 9, 1953: Interviews with George Blancet, George Klein, Buzzy Forbess, Ronny Trout, and Red West, as well as the program of the event.

53 "I wasn't popular in school": 1972 interview.

53 "While other students were dashing around": Scrivener, "My Boy Elvis," *TV Radio Mirror*, March 1957.

53 Toward the end of the school year he took: "Elvis's Prom Date Remembers a Shy Guy in Blue Suede Shoes," *People*, 1989; also *The Young Elvis* by Bill E. Burk and "Elvis: Wallflower at Own Prom," *Fort Lauderdale News and Sun Sentinel*, May 23, 1989.

54 "we are reminded at this time": *Humes Herald*, 1953, p. 33.

"MY HAPPINESS"

All quotes from Sam Phillips and Marion Keisker are from the author's interviews, 1979–93 (Phillips) and 1981–89 (Keisker), unless otherwise noted.

57 On July 15, 1953: Clark Porteous, "Prison Singers May Find Fame with Record They Made in Memphis," *Memphis Press-Scimitar*, July 15, 1953. Further information on the Prisonaires from interviews with Sam Phillips; "The Prisonaires," *Ebony*, November 1953; and Colin Escott's liner notes, and research for, *Just Walkin' in the Rain*, the Prisonaires' album on Bear Family, and his own history of Sun (written with Martin Hawkins), *Good Rockin' Tonight: Sun Records and the Birth of Rock 'n' Roll.*

58ff Sun Records, and the Memphis Recording Service, were a two-person operation: Background on the Memphis Recording Service and Sun Records stems, primarily, from numerous interviews with Sam Phillips and Marion Keisker over the years and Escott and Hawkins' *Good Rockin' Tonight*.

58 renting for $75 or $80 a month: Interview with Sam Phillips, 1990. Vince Staten sets it at $150 a month in *The Real Elvis: Good Old Boy*, and various other figures have been suggested.

59ff Marion Keisker would have been: Background on Marion Keisker from interviews and conversations, 1981–89; obituary by Colin Escott, *Goldmine*, February 9, 1990.

59 and where Jake Hess (later to join the Statesmen) got his start: Interviews with Jake Hess, 1991, 1994. Jake continued to cross paths with the Phillipses and in Memphis sang on WREC with the Daniel Brothers Quartet, which Jud managed. Hess was so impressed with the warmth and kindness of Sam's future wife, Becky, who was working at WLAY when he first met her, that years later he named his daughter for her.

60 He was inspired equally: Interview with Marion Keisker, 1981.

60 Hoyt Wooten, who had started the station: Robert Johnson, "Wooten Sells T-V, Radio Stations," *Memphis Press-Scimitar*, November 3, 1958.

60 he remained quiet and reserved: This surprising self-description of a young Sam Phillips was borne out in interviews with Marion Keisker, Biff Collie, Jake Hess, and T. Tommy Cutrer, among others.

60 "some of [the] great Negro artists": "Man Behind the Sun Sound," *Melody Maker*, c. 1957, as cited by Mike Leadbitter in "Memphis," *Blues Unlimited* Collectors Classics 13.

60 "As word got around": Robert Johnson, "Suddenly Singing Elvis Presley Zooms into Recording Stardom," *Memphis Press-Scimitar*, February 5, 1955.

62 the partnership with Jim Bulleit: Interviews with Sam Phillips and Marion Keisker; Escott and Hawkins, *Good Rockin' Tonight*.

63 "to surprise my mother": March 24, 1956, interview.

63 "I just wanted to hear": Robert Johnson, *Elvis Presley Speaks!*, p. 8.

63 "we had a conversation": Jerry Hopkins interview with Marion Keisker (MVC/MSU).

64 "sounded like somebody beating on a bucket lid": *Time*, May 14, 1956, and *passim*.

64 "We might give you a call sometime": C. Robert Jennings, "There'll Always Be an Elvis," *Saturday Evening Post*, September 11, 1965, p. 78.

64 He even had Miss Keisker: This is a combination of Marion's story as related in Jerry Hopkins' biography (here Sam comes in after the recording is done) and Robert Johnson's account in *TV Star Parade* (September 1956), where it is Sam who takes the boy's name.

It must be noted that this is one scenario, and one scenario only. Over the last twenty years there has sprung up a raging controversy. The nub of the controversy consists of a dispute between Sam Phillips and Marion Keisker over who actually recorded Elvis Presley that first time, which in essence boils down to who turned on the tape recorder when he walked in off the street to make a "personal" record for his mother. The first detailed published version that I am aware of, Bob Johnson's 1956 *Elvis Presley Speaks!*, based on extensive reporting by Johnson since early 1955, was clearly Marion's version. In it she had Sam Phillips coming in "before the record session was completed. It took about fifteen minutes." Subsequent stories by Johnson (and other newspaper and magazine stories) fudged the issue with language that *could* have indicated the presence of both parties. Marion's account remained the same, however, until her death, with minor variations, which occasionally offered explanations for Sam's absence and, in her well-known interview with Jerry Hopkins, had her making a tape copy of the young singer partway into his performance so that she could play it for Sam afterward. As she said to me in 1981, disclaiming credit for anything other than thinking of Sam: "I knew nothing about r&b, I knew nothing about country, and I didn't care whether I did. I was totally enamored of Sam. All I wanted was for Sam to do whatever would make him happy." And it clearly hurt her, as she said, to be branded a liar.

I knew Marion for the last ten years of her life. In our friendship I knew her to be a truthful person, always, but Marion would have been the first to tell you that memory is a creative function, and many aspects of her story contradicted others: for example, if the waiting room was full of people and she got acquainted with Elvis while others were taking their turn, who was recording the others? These internal contradictions in no way disprove her story; they only indicate the difficulties of ascertaining "the truth."

Sam didn't weigh in with his version until 1979, when he broke what amounted to two decades of silence and spoke first to Robert Palmer, then to me and, subsequently, to many others. Sam's version, essentially, claimed credit for the recording (he didn't need to claim credit for the discovery, since that was not the issue here) and registered first disbelief, then indignation, that Marion's story should indicate an ability on her part to operate the delicate disc-cutting machinery, let alone Sam's permission to do so. Marion, who referred to herself as a "mechanical idiot," described to me just how she operated the lathe when I first met her — before I ever spoke about it with Sam or was fully aware of the controversy, though not before Marion and Sam had discussed the matter thoroughly between themselves. Marion said, "Who do you think recorded Buck Turner [Sam's first partner, who had a daily radio show that was frequently transcribed in the studio] when Sam wasn't there? You know, everything didn't just stop during his absence. It couldn't."

I've spoken to numerous people familiar with the Sun operation over the years. All agree, from what they know of Marion and the technical operation of the lathe, that not only could Marion have operated it, she probably did. But none could recall ever seeing her do so. I tried to contact her son, who she said was frequently in the studio with her, but was unable to get a response from him. I've spoken to a number of people — though not a great number — who made "personal" records in those years, and all of them recall Marion out front and Sam doing the recording.

None of which proves anything.

Toward the end of Marion's life there was some talk of a compromise between the two versions, and I've often felt that Marion was offering an olive branch by bringing Sam more frequently into the studio at the conclusion of the session (upon his return from Miss Taylor's restaurant). Sam has remained steadfast that he alone operated the lathe. Whatever version one would like to choose, I don't think any proof is possible in the absence of a credible, impartial witness, and I honestly don't think it makes any difference. I would like to think that this is simply a dispute on a specific point of fact between two honorable people who simply have remembered a scene, which could scarcely have had much significance to either one until long after the event, in different ways. The reason that I have chosen the version that I have presented is that it best fits Marion's "crowded room" scenario, while allowing both Sam and Marion to fulfill the roles that were clearly theirs: Marion, as Elvis portrayed her, was the one who listened, the one who responded to his need, and he was always grateful to her for this. Sam, as Marion conceded in every word, gesture, and deed, and as Elvis himself consistently indicated over the years, was solely responsible for the music. Sam possessed the vision. That is the nub of both Sam's and Marion's version. Who flicked the switch simply should not represent an issue of earthshaking importance.

65 Miss Keisker was always very nice: The picture here of Elvis tentatively putting himself in the way of discovery is based on Marion's impressionistic portrait, not a chronological sequence that recalled him coming into the studio on specific occasions. It makes sense to me in terms of the person that both she and Sam portrayed as well as the aspirations he possessed and the skeletal chronology of events.

"WITHOUT YOU"

All quotes from Dixie Locke are from the author's interviews, unless otherwise noted.

67ff the Assembly of God Church at 1084 McLemore: Background information on the First Assembly of God Church comes from James Blackwood; Dixie Locke; Vince Staten's *The Real Elvis: Good Old Boy*; Bill E. Burk's *Early Elvis: The Humes Years*; Ronald Smith; and Bill E. Burk.

74 One time there was a crisis at work: Interviews with Lillian Fortenberry, 1988, and Dixie Locke, 1990.

75 the colored church at East Trigg: Background information on the East Trigg Baptist Church and the remarkable Dr. William Herbert Brewster comes from "William Herbert Brewster, Sr.," *We'll Understand It Better By and By*, edited by Bernice Reagon; *The Gospel Sound: Good News and Bad Times* by Tony Heilbut; also Horace Boyer's 1979 interview with Dr. Brewster; Bill E. Burk's interview with the Reverend James Hamill in *Early Elvis*, p. 117; and my own interviews with Sam Phillips, James Blackwood, Jack Clement, George Klein, Lamar Fike, et al.

76 Charlie had put it on the jukebox: There are a number of different versions of this story. Johnny Black remembered clearly hearing the record in Charlie's; Ronald Smith recalled just as clearly Elvis bringing him to see it on the jukebox at the Pantaze Drug Store, opposite Ellis Auditorium; and Elvis' aunt Lillian Fortenberry placed it in a drugstore near Sun.

77 "They told me I couldn't sing": Elaine Dundy, *Elvis and Gladys*, pp. 175–176.

77 "Elvis, why don't you give it up?": Jimmy Hamill quoted by his father in Burk, *Early Elvis*, p. 118.

78 Pastor Hamill wouldn't approve: Ibid.

79 Sometimes while Bob was doing the commercials: Interview with James Blackwood, 1988.

80 ("If you can't drink it, freeze it"): Dewey's pitch adapted from Randy Haspel's version in "Tell 'Em Phillips Sencha," *Memphis*, June 1978.

80–81 Toward the end of April, Elvis got a new job: Background information on Crown Electric and James and Gladys Tipler comes from Elston Leonard's "Elvis Presley: The New Singing Rage," *Tiger*, c. 1956; *Elvis* by Jerry Hopkins; Jerry Hopkins' interviews with the Tiplers (MVC/MSU); the 1987 BBC television documentary *Presley: "I Don't Sing Like Nobody"*; and "Elvis Presley Part 2: The Folks He Left Behind Him," *TV Guide*, September 22–28, 1956.

81 Dorsey told him about one night: Interviews with Scotty Moore, 1990, and Bobbie Moore, 1992; Ian Wallis interview with Paul Burlison, 1989.

81 Dorsey and Paul invited Elvis: This is an imagined conversation, but it is based on interview material — with Ronald Smith, Paul Burlison, Jimmy Denson, and Barbara Pittman, as well as a 1963 *New Musical Express* interview with Johnny Burnette — that makes it clear that he played places like the Home and the Girls' Club, the basement rec room of St. Mary's across the street from the Courts, on an increasingly regular basis. In addition, both Dixie Locke and Ronald Smith felt certain that he did not, and *would* not, play "joints" at this time. He even made this distaste clear to Sam Phillips and Bob Neal when he was embarking upon his professional career.

81 his parents were getting older: Jerry Hopkins interview with Bob Neal (MVC/MSU), in addition to interview with Dixie Locke.

82 (a Lodge banquet at the Columbia Mutual Towers): Interview with Ronald Smith, 1993; Buzzy Forbess, too, spoke in a 1991 interview of Elvis playing guitar at a number of dances put on at the Columbia Mutual Towers building by the Junior Order of the Oddfellows Lodge, to which Buzzy belonged.

82–83 The featured performer, Eddie Bond: The experience with Eddie Bond was described by Dixie Locke and Ronald Smith in separate interviews, while Elvis' recollection of the event in later years comes from an interview with George Klein. Eddie Bond's take on the incident is described somewhat differently in "Eddie Bond: A Reluctant Rockabilly Rocker Remembers" by Charles Raiteri, *Goldmine*, August 1, 1986.

As a final footnote, the Hi Hat was, evidently, a "higher class of joint," and the reason for the tryout in the first place, according to Ronald Smith, was that the owners, Tom and Mary, an older couple who had formerly been Arthur Murray dance instructors, wanted to institute a classier policy of entertainment, featuring waltzes and popular music. Since Eddie Bond by his own admission was strictly a country singer, and Elvis at this stage was strictly a pop singer, it seemed to be a perfect fit. Ron put the dismissal down to jealousy to some degree, but Eddie told Charles Raiteri in the *Goldmine* interview, "The big shots that run this place . . . sat at the front table like they was runnin' the Peabody and just stared at us. . . . I called 'em the 'Board of Directors.' [That] night . . . [the] old lady says, 'I'll tell you what you gone do. You gone get rid of that snaky-lookin' fella. If you don't, I'm gone fire all of you.' " Bond thought it was something of a matter of personal hygiene as well. "Elvis wasn't the cleanest guy you'd find, I'll guarantee you," he told Raiteri, further explaining the owners' distaste.

83 "We came very close": Elvis, too, spoke of how close the couple came to marriage. "I got out of school, and I was driving a truck. I was dating a girl and waiting for her to get out of school so we could get married," he said in a 1972 interview, only one of many times he referred to Dixie in similar fashion in subsequent years.

84 "I was in doubt": March 26, 1956, interview.

84 "She said, 'Can you be here?' ": 1972 interview.

84–85 Sam had picked up an acetate: This account is based primarily on interviews with Sam Phillips in 1979 and 1990. In the 1990 interview Sam told me that Wortham had an uncle who was a guard at the prison, and the uncle steered Wortham toward another prisoner, a short-termer, perhaps white, who recorded the acetate.

The role that this one-sided acetate has been assigned in history is quite different than the actual song will bear. Marion, I'm sure putting together two different stories, and knowing Sam's evolving thinking nearly as well as Sam himself, always said that this was the moment at which Sam realized his vision: "If I could find a white man who had the Negro sound and the Negro feel, I could make a billion dollars," she quoted Sam correctly, though, as she always said, the quote was missing Sam's underlying vision and irony ("Sam could not have cared less about the money") when it subsequently appeared in print. Far more misleading, however, is the context in which the quotation has generally been placed. All it takes is one listen to the acetate (which is in the possession of Dr. John Bakke at Memphis State and which was heard in part in the BBC documentary *Presley: "I Don't Sing Like Nobody"*) to realize that there could have been nothing less overtly African-American-sounding than this particular acetate or this particular song. Moreover, Elvis had given no one, least of all Sam Phillips, reason to think that he was drawn to black music in particular at this point.

Unquestionably, Sam Phillips heard something different in his voice, and there is equally little question that Phillips was coming to recognize at this time both the limitations of the "race" market and the unlimited possibilities, and untapped potential, in the popular appetite for African-American culture. One other side note of contention: Marion always said that Sam wanted to put out the demo as it was but couldn't find the singer. Sam has consistently denied that. You couldn't put out a record in that form, he has said, and the singer was secondary to the song in this case anyway. Listening to the demo tends to confirm Sam's view, though who knows — Sam Phillips prized originality above all else, and he may have heard something sufficiently different here to tempt him to put it on the market.

85 "I guess I must have sat there": Robert Johnson, *Elvis Presley Speaks!*, p. 10.

86–87 On the evening of Wednesday, June 30: In addition to interviews with Dixie Locke, James Blackwood, and Jake Hess on the crash and their own (and Elvis') reaction to it, I have relied on the accounts in the *Memphis Press-Scimitar* and *Commercial Appeal*, July 1–3, 1954.

"THAT'S ALL RIGHT"

All quotes from Sam Phillips, Marion Keisker, Scotty Moore, and Dixie Locke are from the author's interviews, unless otherwise noted.

89 The group, which had existed in various configurations: Background on the Starlite Wranglers from interviews with Scotty Moore, Bobbie Moore, and Evelyn Black, as well as Colin Escott and Martin Hawkins' *Good Rockin' Tonight: Sun Records and the Birth of Rock 'n' Roll.*

89 how they "could get on MGM": The quotation is from "Scotty Moore: The Guitar That Changed the World," interview by Robert Santelli, *Goldmine*, August 23, 1991.

91 Sometime around the middle of May: The dating, and the circumstances, are primarily from interviews with Scotty Moore.

91 "I told him I was working": Jerry Hopkins interview with Scotty Moore (MVC/MSU).

92 After a few minutes: The repertoire is based on various interviews with Scotty Moore over the years, the conversation on Scotty's description of Elvis' manner, with likely topics supplied in interviews with Scotty, Bobbie Moore, Evelyn Black, and Johnny Black. The whole question of whether Elvis knew Bill (he was certainly meeting Scotty for the first time) before they got together on this occasion is a somewhat vexed one. By all logical standards he *should* have known Bill, having lived across the street from Bill's mother for the past year or so and having known Bill's brother Johnny for quite some time. There is no question that Bill's wife, Evelyn, recognized Elvis, but neither Scotty nor Bobbie was aware of Bill's knowing Elvis, and Elvis always denied any prior acquaintance in his early interviews. It certainly seems possible that theirs was a nodding, but not a speaking, acquaintance. "[He] intended to use my brother on the fiddle," Bill told Bob Johnson in 1956 (*Elvis Presley Speaks!*, p. 10), but whether this was the literal truth or simply family politics is impossible to say.

93 The next night everybody: This description of the first night in the studio is based primarily on extensive interviews with Scotty Moore and Sam Phillips. The actual order of recording is impossible to determine, but Lee Cotten makes a good case for "Harbor Lights" coming first in his *All Shook Up: Elvis Day-by-Day, 1954–1977*, and there is little question that "I Love You Because" was recorded at the first session, prior to "That's All Right." Interestingly, Elvis' friend from the Courts, Buzzy Forbess, was under the impression that Elvis recorded "Blue Moon of Kentucky" first, a piece of misinformation fostered by Elvis when the record came out in what must have been a moment of embarrassment. "I never sang like [that] in my life," Elvis told *Jet* magazine in 1957, "until I made that first record. . . . I remembered that song because I heard Arthur (Big Boy Crudup) sing it and I thought I would like to try it. That was it."

95 "This is where the soul of man never dies": Robert Palmer, *Deep Blues*, p. 233.

95 It was a slap beat: Colin Escott, liner notes to Bill Black Combo album.

96 "we couldn't believe it was us": *Elvis Presley Speaks!*, p. 10.

96 "It just sounded sort of raw": Trevor Cajiao interview with Scotty Moore for "We Were the Only Band Directed by an Ass," *Elvis: The Man and His Music* 10, March 1991, p. 19.

96 "We thought it was exciting": Jerry Hopkins interview with Scotty Moore (MVC/MSU).

96 "It got so you could sell a half million copies": Edwin Howard, "He's Made $2 Million on Disks — Without a Desk," *Memphis Press-Scimitar*, April 29, 1959.

96–97 The next night everyone came to the studio: The exact chronology of these two nights is guesswork to a certain extent. There are no written records. I have Elvis singing "Blue Moon" (though he probably did not record an acceptable take of it until mid August), because he was singing the song when he first met Scotty and Bill, and at this point they were casting about, somewhat desperately, for a second side. We know that Dewey broke the record on the air at least by the Friday after it was first recorded, but which night exactly is somewhat open to conjecture. I have tried to follow what seemed to me the most logical progression, based primarily on the most persuasive of Sam Phillips' accounts of how, and why, he contacted Dewey.

98 "Dewey [was] completely unpredictable": Johnson's comments are constructed from columns in the *Press-Scimitar* on August 22, 1956; October 1, 1968; and June 20, 1972, all of which cover much the same ground.

98 "Dewey loved to argue": Interview with Dickey Lee, 1988.

99–100 Dewey opened a Falstaff: This account of Dewey and Sam's meeting is based primarily on interviews with Sam Phillips in 1988, 1989, and 1991.

100 "He fixed the radio": *Elvis Presley*, prepared by the editors of *TV Radio Mirror*, 1956, p. 21.

100 The response was instantaneous: Carlton Brown, "A Craze Called Elvis," *Coronet*, September 1956. This seems the most considered account of the overwhelming reaction.

100–101 "hearing them say his name": Elaine Dundy, *Elvis and Gladys*, pp. 180–181.

101 "Mrs. Presley, you just get": Elston Leonard, "Elvis Presley: The New Singing Rage," *Tiger*, c. 1956, p. 13.

101 "I was scared to death": Elvis interviewed on Dewey's death in the *Memphis Commercial Appeal*, September 29, 1968.

101 "Sit down, I'm gone interview": Stanley Booth, "A Hound Dog to the Manor Born," *Esquire*, February 1968.

101 It was Thursday, July 8: The story has been told many times, but this seems to me the most logical date by the sequence of events described. Recording would appear to have definitely taken place on Monday, July 5. Leaving some time for it all to settle in, one would imagine that Sam's meeting with Dewey would logically wait until Wednesday, which would leave Thursday for the actual making of an acetate before the Thursday-evening show. But obviously, this is only informed conjecture, and likely to remain so.

101 "I told him I loved it": Larry Johnson, "Memories of Elvis Shared by Close Friend," *Trenton Herald Gazette*, August 17, 1978.

102 "Sometime during the evening": Bill E. Burk, *Early Elvis: The Humes Years*, p. 131.

102 Another classmate, George Klein: Interview with George Klein, 1989.

102–103 "We spent three or four nights": Jerry Hopkins interview with Scotty Moore (MVC/MSU).

103 "All right, boys": Interview with Carl Perkins, 1979.

103 "That's fine now": This can be heard in conversation between takes on the album, *The Complete Sun Sessions*.

105 "like a little kid at Christmas": Telephone interview with Ed Leek, 1988.

105 Jack Clement, who was singing: Interviews with Jack Clement, 1978, 1989.

105 On Saturday, July 17: This can be dated because it was Dewey and Dot Phillips' sixth anniversary.

107 Dixie rode with him on his route: Various interviews with James and Gladys Tipler, including *Elvis* by Jerry Hopkins; Jerry Hopkins' interviews with the Tiplers (MVC/MSU); the 1987 BBC television documentary *Presley: "I Don't Sing Like Nobody"*; and "Elvis Presley: The New Singing Rage" by Elston Leonard in *Tiger*, c. 1956.

108 She had hoped: Interview with Marion Keisker, 1981.

108 "I'll never forget": Burk, *Elvis: A 30-Year Chronicle*, p. 7.

110 "I was scared stiff": Paul Wilder interview, August 6, 1956.

110 "It was really a wild sound": 1972 interview.

110 "I came offstage": Paul Wilder interview.

When Elvis referred to "my manager," the interviewer asked him who his manager was at the time. Momentarily flustered, Elvis stammered, "Bob . . . Bob Neal," who became his manager several months later. It's hard to say for sure whether it was in fact Neal or Sam Phillips, who clearly was there to provide reassurance and inspiration, who explained the crowd reaction to him, but given the context, and the fact that Neal was the "manager" of the show, it seems likely that it was Neal who, essentially, pushed him back out onstage.

110 Elvis sang "Blue Moon of Kentucky" again: What he sang for his encore is purely supposition at this point. Scotty said they *could* have sung "I Love You Because," because they had rehearsed it — but he doubted that they did. In his recollection "That's All Right" and "Blue Moon of Kentucky" were not simply the only songs that they knew well enough to perform in this kind of setting, they were the only songs that the audience would have wanted to hear. No one else that I have interviewed to date, or whose interview I have read, has offered persuasive testimony to the contrary, but there may well be someone out there who actually knows!

110–111 "It was a real eye-opener": Jerry Hopkins interview with Bob Neal (MVC/MSU).

111–112 he had traveled between sixty-five thousand and seventy-five thousand miles: Trevor Cajiao, "The Most Important Man in the World: Sam Phillips Talks to *Now Dig This*," pt. 2, *Now Dig This* 84, March 1990, p. 17.

112 "I remember talking": Escott and Hawkins, *Good Rockin' Tonight*, p. 67.

112 "He played my r&b records": Escott interview of Sam Phillips as quoted in ibid. and Charles Raiteri liner notes to the Dewey Phillips air checks album, *Red Hot & Blue*, on the Zu Zazz label.

112 "Paul Berlin was the hottest": *Now Dig This*, p. 20.

113 "One night I left Houston": Ibid., edited down from a more discursive account, with permission.

114 "The current greeting": *Cowboy Songs*, June 1955.

114–115 "I thought, Surely, no": Interview with Ronny Trout, 1991.

115 Johnny Black was in Texas: Interview with Johnny Black, 1990.

115 Ronnie Smith called up for Eddie Bond: Interview with Ronald Smith, 1993.

115 he brought the record out to the Rainbow skating rink: Vince Staten, *The Real Elvis: Good Old Boy*, p. 92.

116 The Songfellows, Elvis told her: There are persistent rumors that Elvis tried out again for the Songfellows at around this time. Neither Sam nor Scotty nor Dixie nor James Blackwood recalled a specific tryout, but it would not be unlike Elvis to compartmentalize his activities in such a way that they would not be aware of it.

Vernon Presley offered the most specific recollection. "Later, after he made a couple of records professionally," Vernon declared in his January 1978 *Good Housekeeping* article with Nancy Anderson, "Elvis came to me and said, 'Daddy, you know the Song Fellows? They want me to join them now.' My answer to that was, 'To hell with the Song Fellows! You're doing good with what you've got going, and I don't believe I would change.' "

116 "They taught him how to stand": Interview with Bobbie Moore and Evelyn Black, 1993.

116–117 "It was kind of like we adopted him": Interview with Bobbie Moore, 1992.

117 they played out at the Kennedy Veterans: Ibid.

117 "My mother brought a group out once a month": Interview with Monte Weiner, 1993.

119 "He wanted us to come out": *Tiger*.

119 According to Reggie Young: Interview with Reggie Young, 1989.

119–120 "Sleepy Eyed John was all into Ray Price's": Interview with Jack Clement, 1989.

120 "he didn't play with bands": Elizabeth Kaye, "Sam Phillips: The *Rolling Stone* Interview," *Rolling Stone* 467, February 13, 1986, p. 56.

121 On the strength of these credentials: Jim Denny's role was detailed in interviews with Sam Phillips in 1979, 1988, and 1990.

121–122 Others were noticing: Mike Seeger interview with Carter Stanley, spring 1966, as quoted in *Bluegrass: A History* by Neil V. Rosenberg, with additional material from Rosenberg; also, "Joe Meadows: Mountain State Fiddler" by Ivan M. Tribe, *Bluegrass Unlimited*, October 1978.

122 "All of our distributors": Interview with Chick Crumpacker, 1989.

122–123 "My bell-cow area": Interview with Brad McCuen, 1988.

124 "This was the first we could see": Jerry Hopkins interview with Scotty Moore (MVC/MSU). In addition I interviewed Scotty, Dixie Locke, George Klein, and a number of bystanders about the performance.

124–125 In Florida, Lee Denson: Interview with Jimmy and Lee Denson, 1989.

GOOD ROCKIN' TONIGHT

All quotes from Sam Phillips, Marion Keisker, Scotty Moore, and Dixie Locke are from the author's interviews, unless otherwise noted.

127 Jim Denny had finally succumbed: Sam first met Jim Denny in 1944 when he applied for a job as an announcer at WSM, the Opry's mother station. When he didn't get the job, and his future partner, Jim Bulleit, did, Bulleit sent him down the street to WLAC, where Bulleit had already won a job that he was now going to pass up.

127–128 In the meantime Sam had also heard: Interviews with Sam Phillips, 1979, 1990, 1991.

128 Twenty-one-year-old bass player Buddy Killen: Interview with Buddy Killen, 1989.

128 Marty Robbins saw evidence: Alanna Nash interview with Marty Robbins in her book *Behind Closed Doors: Talking with the Legends of Country Music*, p. 443.

128 when Elvis spotted Chet Atkins: Interview with Chet Atkins, 1988.

128 Probably of all the Opry legends: Interview with Sam Phillips, 1988.

128–129 But when they met Monroe: Interviews with Sam Phillips and Bill Monroe, 1980. Also Neil Rosenberg's *Bluegrass: A History* describes the meeting, as does *Bluegrass 1950–1958: Bill Monroe*, the Charles Wolfe and Neil Rosenberg booklet that accompanies the Bear Family boxed set of Monroe's music of the same name.

129 There were two additional surprises: Interviews with Marion Keisker, 1981, and with Bobbie Moore and Evelyn Black, 1993.

129–130 Before leaving, Sam conferred briefly: Interview with Sam Phillips, 1988.

This contradicts the well-known version that has Denny telling Elvis to go back to driving a truck — but then so does the account of every eyewitness that I have interviewed. The almost universal acceptance of the story by members of the music community who were not present appears to be based on two factors: Denny's personal chilliness and somewhat autocratic manner, and Elvis' genuine dislike of the man for that reason. But Denny, if anything, was giving Elvis a break, not denying him one, and if it would not have been out of character for him, in another well-known part of the story, to have referred slightingly to Elvis' music as "nigger music," such attitudes were common, as Chet Atkins has frequently pointed out, in many segments of the country music community at that time. The story that Elvis cried all the way back to Memphis is based on thirdhand testimony; as Marion Keisker said, "There was only Sam and Elvis and me in the car. We were in good spirits. I'd like to see where that other person was sitting."

130 They left not long afterward: Interview with Ernest Tubb, 1976; also interviews with Justin Tubb, 1989, and Bobbie Moore, as well as the *Ernest Tubb*

Discography (1936–1969) by Norma Barthel. According to Tubb and his son, Justin, Elvis wrote a note to Ernest afterward, thanking Tubb for his kindness and advice. It should perhaps be borne in mind that what Elvis said to Ernest Tubb, a childhood idol, might have been more in the nature of politeness, an unerring instinct for deference, or, as Marion said, never putting a foot wrong. It is not necessarily a statement to be taken literally, though Ernest obviously did.

132 as good as it was "humanly possible": Jerry Hopkins interview with Marion Keisker (MVC/MSU).

132 the Shelton Brothers had originally recorded: The Shelton Brothers were originally the Attlesey brothers. The song is credited to the Attleseys and guitarist Leon Chapplear, but it clearly goes back to an earlier blues and "minstrel" tradition. The Attlesey lineage is spelled out in Billy Altman's liner notes to *Are You from Dixie? Great Country Brother Teams of the 1930's*, on RCA.

133 With the last song of the session: This more or less follows the order suggested by Lee Cotten in *All Shook Up: Elvis Day-by-Day, 1954–1977* (Cotten appears to have been working from RCA executive Steve Sholes' notes), and Ernst Jorgensen's definitive discography. It must be emphasized, however, that there can be no certainty as to order in the absence of a true recording log.

133 To Marion Keisker it was like: Jerry Hopkins interview with Marion Keisker (MVC/MSU).

135ff Sam called Pappy Covington: This account is based on interviews with a myriad of sources, including Sam Phillips, Scotty Moore, Tillman Franks, Billy Walker, Frank Page, and Horace Logan. Unfortunately, there is nearly as much dispute over Elvis' arrival at the Hayride as there is over his arrival at the Memphis Recording Service, or at the Opry, for that matter. According to Horace Logan, it was he who first contacted Sam Phillips (though Tillman Franks, with whom he fell out just around this time, played an unspecified part), and it was he who first introduced Elvis onstage. Both Slim Whitman and Billy Walker, who appeared on the bill at Overton Park, have suggested credibly in published interviews that they brought the news of the young Memphis phenomenon back to the Hayride, while Tillman's story seeks credit for nothing but the need to find a substitute for Jimmy and Johnny on the Hayride bill. From talking with most of the principal players, I think the scenario I have presented is as logical a version as one might come up with, but that doesn't mean it happened that way.

136–137ff The Hayride was a little over six years old: Background information on the Hayride comes from interviews with Horace Logan, Tillman Franks, Frank Page, T. Tommy Cutrer, Merle Kilgore, and Alton and Margaret Warwick, among others. Also the 1984 PBS documentary *Cradle of the Stars* and "Saturday Night Live" by Joe Rhodes in *Westward* (the *Dallas Times-Herald* magazine), October 10, 1982.

138 He stopped by Stan's Record Shop: Interview with Stan Lewis, 1990; also Robert Trudeau, "Stan the Record Man," *Upstate*, December 8, 1983.

138 He walked out on the stage: Interview with Horace Logan, 1991.

138–139 He was wearing: This is a composite picture put together from descriptions of Elvis' appearance that evening and contemporaneous photographs. I don't know of a photograph from that first performance itself.

139 Horace Logan was out onstage: Interview with Horace Logan. Logan fully described his working methods.

140 "Elvis, how are you this evening?": This dialogue, which prefaces performances of "That's All Right" and "Blue Moon of Kentucky," appears on *Elvis. . . . The Beginning Years*, on the Louisiana Hayride/RCA label. Despite Horace Logan's claim, the interlocutor appears to be Frank Page (though it's always possible that Logan preceded Page). The tape seems to be authentic, and I don't know any reason to question its dating (the dialogue is certainly awkward enough to signal a first appearance). In any case, it's well worth a listen.

140–141 The cheers that went up: Interviews with Sam Phillips, Merle Kilgore, Tillman Franks, Jimmy "C" Newman, Curley Herndon, et al., 1989–92.

142 "I'd never seen anything like it before": Interview with Jimmy "C" Newman, 1990.

142 "I think he scared them": Interview with Merle Kilgore, 1989.

143 "My daddy had seen": 1972 interview.

143 He missed the Hayride for the next two weeks: There has been some debate over this issue. There is no question that Elvis returned to the Hayride and signed a contract on November 6, 1954, or that he missed the October 30 broadcast. I had believed from oral testimony, and from a story in "*The Cashbox* Country Roundup" of November 6, 1954 (which quoted Marion Keisker on the success of his second week's appearance), that he played the Hayride on October 23. But he does not appear to have been listed in the lineup, and Scotty's recollection is that there was at least a two-week gap while Sam was "negotiating the contract — not that there was all that much to negotiate, at twenty-four dollars a week or whatever it was." Sam, meanwhile, recalls clearly that they did *not* return until at least three weeks later, after the contract had been arranged.

144ff That Friday night Bob Neal brought a visitor: This account of Oscar Davis' discovery of a fresh young talent is based on several interlinked sources: Jerry Hopkins interviews with Oscar Davis and Bob Neal (MVC/MSU); a joint interview with both Colonel Parker and Oscar Davis carried out briefly in the aftermath of Elvis' well-known interview in August 1956; Gordon Stoker's recollections to me (and others) of meeting Elvis backstage at the Eddy Arnold show, long before Elvis had made his mark; my interview with Hoyt Hawkins' widow, Dot Hawkins; ads and a review in the *Memphis Press-Scimitar* of Eddy Arnold's October 31 show; and the documented fact that by early January the Colonel was well aware of exactly who Elvis Presley was.

At the time of that first meeting, Oscar Davis told Hopkins, "Scotty Moore was acting as [Elvis'] manager. . . . They were somewhat excited about getting me in the picture with them, and we agreed to meet the following Sunday when Eddy Arnold would be in town and I would be in town." In the 1956 interview Parker credited Davis with "introducing" him to the boy (he refused to acknowledge that Davis actually discovered him), though it is unclear whether he actually met Presley at the time, and Davis made a point to Hopkins that he tried to keep his find secret from the Colonel. Both Parker and Davis stipulated that an Eddy Arnold concert in Memphis was the occasion, and Davis declared that "I called him to the Colonel's attention on the Sunday which we played [there]." The working out of this scenario has involved some guesswork, obviously, but the only discrepancy that I am aware of is that Davis remembered going to see Elvis perform at a little "airport inn." The fact that Elvis was advertised at the Eagle's Nest the weekend of the Eddy Arnold show seems to resolve the discrepancy.

Background on Oscar Davis and Tom Parker stems from numerous interviews, including invaluable ones with Grelun Landon, Gabe Tucker, and Sam Phillips, as well as extensive documentation in Marge Crumbaker and Gabe Tucker's *Up and Down with Elvis Presley*; *Elvis* by Jerry Hopkins; *It's a Long Way from Chester County* by Eddy Arnold; *Elvis and Gladys* by Elaine Dundy; *Elvis and the Colonel* by Dirk Vellenga; and *Elvis* by Albert Goldman.

145–146 he introduced him to Eddy and to Hoyt Hawkins: Interview with Gordon Stoker, 1989.

146 they had enjoyed *his* singing, too: Jerry Hopkins interview with Neal Matthews (MVC/MSU).

146 The following Saturday night: Interview with Horace Logan. The actual contract is available and has been widely reproduced.

147 They stopped by the Chisca to visit: Elvis' relationship with Dewey was documented in interviews with Sam Phillips, Dixie Locke, June Juanico, and Dickey Lee, among others, as well as by Jonnie Barnett's extensive interviews with Harry Fritzius and Charles Raiteri's exhaustive research for his fine screenplay on Dewey.

So far as the issue of Elvis on Beale, this is an old, and much-debated, question. I have spoken with innumerable Beale Streeters, and read the testimony in *Beale Black & Blue* by Margaret McKee and Fred Chisenhall. Although Rufus Thomas has adamantly insisted he never saw Elvis on Beale until the December 1956 WDIA Goodwill Revue, I don't have any problem placing Elvis on Beale; it is just a question of when. From speaking with Elvis' childhood friends, and considering the nature of the young man, I find it far more likely that he would start going down to the clubs once he had achieved a certain measure of confidence and respect, and if WDIA's Professor Nat D. Williams was Beale Street's uncrowned mayor, Dewey Phillips was something like a roving ambassador from another galaxy. There is nothing in the interviews with Beale Street habitués that I have conducted or read that would indicate a distinction in the mind of the speaker between a young Elvis Presley who had not recorded at all and a young Elvis Presley who had simply recorded locally but was not widely known, at least not in the black community. That, as I see it, is the cause of the confusion. Robert Henry, for example, who is quoted in *Beale Black & Blue* as having "taken him to the Hotel Improvement Club with me," was cited in much the same role in the *Press-Scimitar* on Elvis' death with one telling exception: "I met him through Dewey Phillips," Henry said. You can read the interviews with Billy "The Kid" Emerson (*Living Blues* 45/46, spring 1980),

Sunbeam Mitchell (by David Less, unpublished), and Calvin Newborn with this chronology in mind, and I don't believe there is anything in any of them that would sharply contradict it. And when an even younger, even less well known white boy is recalled hanging out in the clubs at a presumed earlier date, the question naturally arises: How did you know it was Elvis? In the absence of an introduction, the presumption must be that the name was attached retrospectively. This is all, in other words, inductive (but not, I hope, circular) reasoning, and persuasive only to the point that it is actually proved, or disproved, by documented events. Putting the description in the form of a dialogue with Dixie is a narrative device, however: the conversation may have happened, but it is not a memory that I have gotten from Dixie, and it is simply a means of threading together a chronological story in a manner that seems to me reasonably plausible.

148 Toward the end of football season: Jerry Hopkins interview with Red West (MVC/MSU); Red West et al., *Elvis: What Happened?*; Trevor Cajiao interview with Red West for *Elvis: The Man and His Music* 22, March 1994; interview with Buzzy Forbess, 1991.

148 "He would look in the papers": Interview with Guy Lansky, 1990.

148 Ronnie Smith recalled running into Elvis: Interview with Ronald Smith, 1993.

148 Sometimes old friends passed him: He speaks of this happening, at a later date, to Bob Neal in Robert Johnson, *Elvis Presley Speaks!*, p. 30.

148 he didn't know if they were laughing: He cites this fear in his Warwick Hotel interview in March 1956.

149 In between shows at the auditorium: Interview with Maylon Humphries, 1991.

149 With Merle Kilgore: Interview with Merle Kilgore.

149–150 Sometimes they would go: Interview with Maylon Humphries.

150 They worked one night: Interviews with Curly Herndon, 1991; Scotty Moore; D. J. Fontana, 1988, 1991; and Tillman Franks, 1991–93.

150–152 Pappy called Tom Perryman: Interview with Tom Perryman, 1989.

Scotty Moore confirmed how the connection came about and the nature of the relationship. "A lot of times," Perryman recalled, "the boys would come by after the show. Elvis would look after our three kids when we took the baby-sitter home. Hamburgers and banana pudding."

152–153 On Thursday, November 25: Interview with Biff Collie, 1990.

In addition to the quotes, much of the background material on Biff Collie comes from this same interview. Additional information on Collie from interviews with Tillman Franks and T. Tommy Cutrer, while the Eagle's Nest incident was illuminated by Franks as well as by the story "The Notorious 'Country' Johnny Mathis" by Bill Carpenter, which appeared in *Goldmine*, May 28, 1993. The telegram was on display for a time at the Elvis — Up Close Museum, across from Graceland, and was published in *Goldmine*, August 10, 1990, in a story by Joe Haertel, "Retracing Elvis's Memphis and Tupelo Footsteps."

153–156 Meanwhile, Bob Neal was looking on his new project: Jerry Hopkins interviews with Bob Neal (MVC/MSU).

154 "they didn't know exactly how to take him": This description of Elvis' development as a stage performer is assembled from various points in Jerry Hopkins' interviews with Bob Neal (MVC/MSU).

154–155 Sometimes Bill would come out of the audience: Interviews with Bobbie Moore, 1992, and Bobbie Moore and Evelyn Black, 1993.

156 Elvis had recently given himself: *Elvis Presley Speaks!*, p. 16; Robert Johnson, "Suddenly Singing Elvis Presley Zooms into Recording Stardom," *Memphis Press-Scimitar*, February 5, 1955; *Country & Western Jamboree*, April 1955.

157 a new song by a Covington, Tennessee, theater manager: Colin Escott and Martin Hawkins, *Good Rockin' Tonight: Sun Records and the Birth of Rock 'n' Roll*, p. 72.

FORBIDDEN FRUIT

All quotes from Sam Phillips, Marion Keisker, Scotty Moore, and Dixie Locke are from the author's interviews, unless otherwise noted.

160 "They did a lot of their harmony gospel songs": Interview with Tom Perryman, 1989.

160–162 In Corinth, Mississippi: Interviews with Buddy and Kay Bain, 1989, 1990, 1994.

162 It was all like a dream: Elvis referred to this fear again and again, that somehow his success would turn out to be all an illusion, from his earliest recorded interviews on. "I think about things that have happened," he told Edwin Miller in May 1956 ("Elvis Presley," *Seventeen*, fall 1956), "and it's kind of like a dream. A year and a half ago, I was nothing." To Bob Johnson he insisted that, despite this dreamlike atmosphere, he would never forget "who I am and where I came from and my friends and how this all happened."

162–163 there was a full, four-column spread: *Memphis Press-Scimitar*, February 5, 1955.

163 He was fascinated, too: Interview with Martha Carson, 1989; Dave Byers, "Martha Carson: 'The Rockin' Queen of Happy Spirituals,' " 1983.

163–164 In between shows he and Scotty went across the street: Scotty recalled the experience in 1988, 1989, and 1992 interviews; Sam Phillips spoke of it in 1989 and 1990 interviews; and the Texarkana date has been frequently cited in print, at least as early as a November 20, 1957, AP story on the Colonel, though New Boston, Texas, has also been mentioned. In a 1991 interview Tillman Franks recalled booking Elvis into Texarkana and El Dorado, Arkansas, with T. Tommy Cutrer at this time and said of Jim LeFan, "He always told of how he got Elvis with the Colonel. In fact he made a life story of it!" So far, however, I am not aware that anyone has been able to discover an exact date.

164–165, 169–170 The meeting at Palumbo's: This account has been put together primarily from interviews with Sam Phillips and Scotty Moore, along with

Oscar Davis' colorful, if somewhat confused, description to Jerry Hopkins (MVC/MSU). Davis gives the most vivid account by far of the Colonel's frontal assault, but both Scotty's and Sam's impressions of Tom Parker in the aftermath of the meeting, and the Colonel's subsequent attempt to sell Tommy Sands, not Elvis Presley, to RCA as a harbinger of the new music, bear out the somewhat unfortunate contretemps that resulted, at least initially, from this meeting.

165 Thomas A. Parker on first impression: Much of the specific background on the Colonel here comes from Marge Crumbaker and Gabe Tucker's *Up and Down with Elvis Presley*; Dirk Vellenga's *Elvis and the Colonel*; and Albert Goldman's *Elvis*.

165–166 Acuff, then known as: Elizabeth Schlappi, *Roy Acuff*.

166 According to Oscar Davis: This description of Colonel Parker has been put together from various points in Jerry Hopkins' interview with Oscar Davis (MVC/MSU).

166 To Biff Collie, the Houston DJ: Interview with Biff Collie, 1990.

166 Gabe Tucker, who met Parker: Interview with Gabe Tucker, 1990.

167 "When Tom's your manager": Eddy Arnold, *It's a Long Way from Chester County*, pp. 46–47.

167 From now on, he told Gabe Tucker: Crumbaker and Tucker, *Up and Down*, p. 74.

167–168 In 1953, in an episode: Jerry Hopkins, *Elvis*, p. 101.

168 Arnold and Parker "were dissipating": Crumbaker and Tucker, *Up and Down*, p. 71.

168 making his office in the lobby: Jerry Hopkins interview with Bill Williams (MVC/MSU); the story is told in Hopkins' *Elvis*, p. 102.

168 By the spring of 1954: *Billboard* passim.

168 "No one knows very much": Jerry Hopkins interview with Oscar Davis (MVC/MSU).

168–169 "You have one fault": Vellenga, *Elvis and the Colonel*, p. 126.

169 As Gabe Tucker observed: Interview with Gabe Tucker.

169 everyone else in the Colonel's estimation: "Everyone has weaknesses," Oscar Davis told Jerry Hopkins (MVC/MSU). "He'll read you very quickly. Helluva guy."

171–175 Snow was bowled over by his first exposure to this kid: Interviews with Jimmie Rodgers Snow, 1990, 1993, 1994.

A note on the spelling of Jimmie Rodgers Snow's name. Snow was named, obviously, for his father's musical idol. He came to identify himself, however, as "Jimmy," both as an artist and, in later years, as a minister. Hence the discrepancy in spelling.

One final note. Jimmy Snow believes that he played Lubbock with Elvis a month earlier than this booking, operating as a kind of scout for his father and Colonel Parker. After extensive interviews with Billy Walker, who headlined Elvis' first, brief West Texas tour; Tillman Franks, who booked it; and "Pappy" Dave Stone, who booked the Lubbock gigs in both January and February (not to mention Bill Griggs' article "Elvis Presley in Lubbock" in *Rockin' '50s*, August 1992), I have come to the conclusion that this is just a matter of the normal telescoping and expansion of memory — but I remain open to correction.

171 "His energy was incredible": Nick Kent, "Roy Orbison: *The Face* Interview," *The Face*, 1989.

172–173 "He was this punk kid": Ibid.

173 "There never was a country act": Jerry Hopkins interview with Bob Neal (MVC/MSU).

173 The trouble was: Robert Johnson, *TV Star Parade*, September 1956, p. 65.

174 "I see people all different ages": 1972 interview.

174 "He would study a crowd": Interview with Tillman Franks.

174 "He was always unhappy": Jerry Hopkins interview with Bob Neal (MVC/MSU).

175–176 the startling success of Alan Freed: My primary source for background on Alan Freed was John Jackson's biography *Big Beat Heat: Alan Freed and the Early Years of Rock & Roll.*

176–177 "For the past year the top U.S. deejay": *Time*, February 14, 1955, © 1955. Reprinted by permission.

177 ("It was a tremendous emotional problem"): *Cleveland Plain Dealer*, September 15, 1956.

177–178 "He was extremely shy": This and subsequent quotes by Randle are from Ger Rijff and Jan van Gestel, *Memphis Lonesome*.

178 On March 15: Jerry Hopkins interview with Bob Neal (MVC/MSU); also Report of Guardian Ad Litem re the Estate of Elvis A. Presley, Deceased, in the Probate Court of Shelby County, Tennessee (this reproduces the Colonel's agreement with Neal on November 21, 1955).

179 While they were out: Interview with Stan Kesler, 1987.

179 this new boy Perkins: Colin Escott and Martin Hawkins, *Good Rockin' Tonight: Sun Records and the Birth of Rock 'n' Roll*, p. 130.

180 Jimmie Lott was a junior: Ibid., p. 73.

181 Just ten days later: With respect to dating, the session that produced "I'm Left, You're Right, She's Gone" has been dated with some definitiveness as March 5, though this, too, may be subject to revision. I have placed the Godfrey tryout during the week of March 15, because, by Bill Randle's account, it had to follow the group's meeting with Randle on February 26 (Randle says that he gave Bob Neal the name of the Godfrey contact at this time). Since they were booked solid the weeks of March 6 and March 21, I placed the Godfrey tryout here. From all that Bob Neal said to Jerry Hopkins, and from my own interviews with Scotty Moore, March seems to make sense, but, as should be clear by now, the date is no more than an educated guess. The information on the trip itself is from those same interviews, while Bill Randle's perspective is described in Rijff and van Gestel, *Memphis Lonesome.*

182 after more than fifty thousand miles: Jerry Hopkins interview with Scotty Moore (MVC/MSU).

182 a 1951 Cosmopolitan Lincoln: Interview with Merle Kilgore, 1989.

182 "It was always exciting": 1972 interview.

182 "He's the new rage": Jules J. Paglin, "Louisiana Disc Jockeys," *Melody Maker*, December 31, 1955 (as reprinted in *Blues World* 31, June 1970).

182–183 "This cat came out": Paul Hemphill, *The Nashville Sound: Bright Lights and Country Music*, pp. 272–273.

183 The Miller Sisters, the performing duo: Hank Davis, "The Miller Sisters," *DISCoveries*, June 1989.

184 "one of the newest": Souvenir program accompanying the "Hank Snow All Star Jamboree" tour.

184 Johnny Rivers saw the show: Steve Roeser, "Johnny Rivers: The Man Who Made the Whisky," *Goldmine*, September 6, 1991.

184 Jimmy Snow roomed: Interview with Jimmie Rodgers Snow, 1990.

185–186 He met Mae Boren Axton: Interview with Mae Boren Axton, 1988.

186–188 In the interview he persisted: Mae told me about this interview before I heard it, and we spoke about it afterward. Actually putting a date on it has proved to be a persistent problem. In the course of the interview Mae refers to Elvis having previously played Florida, which would lead one to wonder about its actual date. It certainly *sounds* like a first meeting, and my best guess about the somewhat tentative references to earlier touring is that this was a way to indicate a wider celebrity than the singer actually possessed. The evident intention of the interview was to publicize his appearances throughout Florida over the next week; at least that is the most logical explanation I can come up with. The fact that the Jacksonville riot of May 13 is not referred to indicates to me that the interview predates the actual tour.

188 "and she was just right into it": Interview with Mae Boren Axton.

189–190 "Skeeter Davis was there": Ibid.

191–192 Parker had accused publicist Anne Fulchino: This account and the subsequent quotes by Crumpacker are from interviews and letters, 1989–94.

192 Chick finished up his trip: The next time Chick saw Elvis was at the third annual Jimmie Rodgers Festival in Meridian, Mississippi, on May 25. Founded to honor the "Singing Brakeman," who was widely hailed as the Father of Country Music, the festival also served as a kind of trade convention about midway between one annual DJ convention in Nashville and the next. Elvis and Scotty and Bill made a big impression on the '55 festival, practically causing a riot in their appearance at the football stadium and coming to the inescapable attention of Steve Sholes, Chick's boss at RCA. Hill and Range was also represented in the person of Grelun Landon, and there were innumerable other performers and industry figures getting a look at this new phenomenon for the first time.

The reason I mention all this is that in recent years a story has sprung up that this was not Elvis' first trip to Meridian. In 1953, so the story goes, Elvis hitchhiked to Meridian two days short of high school graduation, performed in an amateur contest to some acclaim, and then borrowed ten dollars from a festival official to get back home. I first heard this story in 1980 when I was in Meridian for the festival and have tried to track it down ever since. I have never found any evidence to support the story, and, while it is always possible that hard evidence will turn up, it seems more likely that this is yet another case of two stories merging: the first that of an unknown young singer who appears hungry and talented (and anonymous) in 1953, the second the appearance two years later of a rapidly gathering sensation still largely unknown to an older generation. It would not be at all inconceivable that these two stories could become legitimately confused. In any case, Elvis enjoyed a real triumph at Meridian in 1955 among both his peers and his elders.

MYSTERY TRAIN

All quotes from Sam Phillips, Marion Keisker, Scotty Moore, and Dixie Locke are from the author's interviews, unless otherwise noted.

195 a man who had it in his power: Neal and Parker conferred in Memphis all day on June 17, just one month after the Jacksonville "riot." According to the July 2 *Cashbox*: "Bob Neal . . . flew into Nashville last weekend for a meeting with Col. Tom Parker . . . [and] signed an exclusive contract with Hank Snow Enterprises, allowing the company to represent Presley in all phases of the entertainment field. Neal, however, will continue as exclusive manager of Presley."

195–204 On balance Bob Neal was well satisfied: Not only the quoted material but the appraisal of Elvis' career, his listening habits and avidity for knowledge, all stem from Jerry Hopkins' interviews with Bob Neal (MVC/MSU).

196 "I was, I think, a year or two": Neal was in fact about a year younger than Vernon.

196 paraded around town in his kelly green suit: Elaine Dundy, *Elvis and Gladys*, p. 223.

196–197 Then on July 4 he found himself: Information on the De Leon date from interviews with James Blackwood and J. D. Sumner in 1988, 1990, and 1991; also *Country & Western Jamboree*, October 1955, as supplied by Wayne Russell, and Bob Terrell's *The Music Men*. Colin Escott's biography, *Hank Williams*, points out that Hank Williams was booked in 1950 but showed up drunk and didn't perform.

197–199 The next-door neighbors, the Bakers: Interviews with Jackson Baker in 1989, 1990, and 1992, as well as a joint telephone interview with Jack, his sister, Sarah, and their mother, Eve, in 1990. Just when the Presleys got their phone became a matter of some debate among the Bakers, but even if the Presleys had their own line by July, as might well be expected, both Jackson and Sarah's memories of him on their hall phone are so vivid that it seems clear that he must have continued to make some calls from their home even afterward.

199 "He told me to drive it": Interview with Guy Lansky, 1990.

201 He kept telling them about Colonel Parker: "Elvis by His Father Vernon Presley" as told to Nancy Anderson, *Good Housekeeping*, January 1978, p. 157.

202–203 Meanwhile Bob Neal was fielding offers: Jerry Hopkins interviews with Bob Neal (MVC/MSU).

Additional information on the other labels' interest in Elvis comes from interviews with Jerry Wexler, Jerry Leiber and Mike Stoller, Grelun Landon, and Sam Phillips, as well as Colin Escott and Martin Hawkins' *Good Rockin' Tonight: Sun*

Records and the Birth of Rock 'n' Roll (the MGM telegram); Arnold Shaw's *The Rockin' '50s*; Bill Randle in *Memphis Lonesome* by Ger Rijff and Jan van Gestel; Vince Staten's *The Real Elvis: Good Old Boy* (on Randy Wood's offer); and Albert Cunniff, "Muscle Behind the Music: The Life and Times of Jim Denny," pt. 3, *Journal of Country Music*, vol. 11, no. 3 (on the involvement of Jim Denny, Jud Phillips, and Decca Records).

206 "Elvis Presley on Beale Street": Margaret McKee and Fred Chisenhall, *Beale Black & Blue*, p. 95.

206 "before he could be rescued": *Cashbox*, August 13, 1955.

206–208 Mr. and Mrs. Presley were scheduled to arrive: The account of this Little Rock meeting is based primarily on Vince Staten's interview with Whitey Ford in *The Real Elvis*, Vernon Presley's testimony in his *Good Housekeeping* story, and — for the specific context in which the Colonel's wooing of the Presleys was taking place — my own interviews with Sam Phillips, Marion Keisker, Jimmie Rodgers Snow, Hank Snow, Gabe Tucker, Mae Boren Axton, Lillian Fortenberry, and Scotty Moore, as well as Jerry Hopkins' interviews with Marion Keisker and Bob Neal (MVC/MSU).

207 maybe her boy was being overworked: Jerry Hopkins interview with Marion Keisker (MVC/MSU).

207 spending a few days with Colonel and Mrs. Parker: Jerry Hopkins, *Elvis*, p. 117.

207 "He seemed like a smart man": *Good Housekeeping*, p. 157.

208 she "heard someone screaming": Jerry Hopkins interview with Marion Keisker (MVC/MSU).

208 "Of course I never actually met the Colonel": Interview with Marion Keisker, 1988.

209–210 a document that named "Col. Thomas A. Parker": Report of Guardian Ad Litem re the Estate of Elvis A. Presley, Deceased, in the Probate Court of Shelby County, Tennessee.

THE PIED PIPERS

All quotes from Sam Phillips, Marion Keisker, Scotty Moore, and Dixie Locke are from the author's interviews, unless otherwise noted.

213 When Arnold Shaw, the newly named general professional manager: Arnold Shaw, *The Rockin' 50s*, pp. 4–7. Shaw had accompanied Chick Crumpacker to Meridian in May.

213 The contract stipulated: The contract that I have seen does not stipulate the four-hundred-dollar penalty, but Horace Logan has referred to it frequently in interviews and in his interview with Rob Finnis said of Elvis, "He probably thought I pocketed it!" In any case, it clearly came into effect in the spring of 1956, when Elvis in effect left the Hayride, and it clearly stymied the Colonel. The Colonel's role, and his frustration with Vernon, were clearly delineated by the Colonel to me, within the context of a story about Vernon signing the renewal while the Colonel was in New York trying to sell Elvis' contract. Since the Hayride contract is dated

September 8, and the Colonel was in New York a month and a half later, I can only think that this is another case of memory telescoping events — unless, of course, the renewal was backdated. But Bob Neal's pride in negotiating that renewal ("We negotiated a deal that was quite a thing then," he told Jerry Hopkins [MVC/MSU]) would suggest otherwise.

213 share the cost of [D.J.'s] $100-a-week salary: Max Weinberg, *The Big Beat: Conversations with Rock's Great Drummers*, p. 115.

213 he kept saying he couldn't afford it: Jerry Hopkins interview with Scotty Moore (MVC/MSU).

214 "The eventual basic decision": Jerry Hopkins interview with Bob Neal (MVC/MSU).

214 Scotty and Bill were inclined: Scotty has always spoken of a royalty understanding that would have gone into effect at some undefined (but clearly indicated) point in the future, but I don't think that is what came into play here.

Scotty's expectation was based on conversations at the very outset of Elvis' career. "It was never on paper. Bill and I would split half of one percent, one quarter percent each. Strictly on record royalties. This came about from several conversations sitting on the steps in front of the house on Alabama just pipe-dreaming, a few weeks, I'm guessing, after the first record came out. [We were thinking]: 'With all the commotion going on in Memphis, we better tighten up our business stuff here. We're liable to have to go across to West Memphis!' We had already agreed to a three-way split, with expenses equal. He said, 'Okay, we'll do this on everything [including record royalties].' I told him, from what little I knew about the music business, 'No, that won't work. 'Cause if we do anything, you'll be the headliner, you'll be the main guy. There will be problems down the road if we go into anything like this on record royalties.' I said, 'If you want to give us a *token* —' And that's what it would have amounted to. But it never did start."

In later years, understandably, this became a source of considerable bitterness, but at the time I would guess it was as much a case of legitimately hurt feelings as of financial claims.

215 "when Elvis went up into the control room": Colin Escott and Martin Hawkins, *Good Rockin' Tonight: Sun Records and the Birth of Rock 'n' Roll*, p. 83.

215–216 Hill and Range, one of the most prominent: Information on the folio deal comes specifically from interviews with Sam Phillips, Grelun Landon, and Freddy Bienstock. Information on the Aberbach family and Hill and Range from Russell Sanjek, *American Popular Music and Its Business*, vol. 3; *Billboard Music Week*, January 30, 1961, as cited in *Country Music, U.S.A.* by Bill Malone; and research generously provided by Tony Scherman. Bill Randle's views are articulated in *Memphis Lonesome* by Ger Rijff and Jan van Gestel.

216 Randle's belief, fostered by the Aberbachs' desire: The political intricacies of all this are somewhat unclear. Randle spoke of the specifics of the Hill and Range connection in an interview with the *Cleveland Plain Dealer*, December 6, 1984, and is quoted to this effect in Rijff and van Gestel, *Memphis Lonesome*, as well. There seems little question that he fully believed that, had he taken the Aberbachs' offer, he would have become Elvis Presley's manager — though perhaps this is another instance of memory cropping and enlarging to some degree (possibly the Aberbachs offered him the position of Elvis' *song* manager, which Freddy Bienstock later became). In any case, when I tried a blunter version of this scenario on the Colonel, he professed utter ignorance of any part that Bill Randle may have played and deemed it the most ridiculous thing (my scenario) he had ever heard — at least from me. I hope I have improved on it since then.

217 "the folk music world": "Rockin' to Stardom," *Country Song Roundup*, winter 1955–56.

217–218 The Colonel had approached Haley's manager: John Swenson, *Bill Haley*, p. 66.

219 "Now this was a long time": Ken Terry interview with Bill Haley, as cited in ibid.

219 "Elvis was one of those guys": Peter Mikelbank, "D.J. Fontana: Elvis' Drummer Capsulizes the King's Career," *Goldmine*, August 14, 1987.

220 they were angry at their former landlord: Interview with Eve and Sarah Baker, 1990.

221 "Called 'Top Jock' ": The title was subsequently changed to, alternatively, *The Pied Piper of Cleveland* or *A Day in the Life of a Famous Disc Jockey*, with the latter also used as a subtitle to the former.

221 the idea was for this one: "Randle Short Scuttled by IBEW Ruling," *Billboard*, December 3, 1955.

221–224 According to Randle: Rijff and van Gestel, *Memphis Lonesome*, pp. 19–20.

222–223 Pat Boone never forgot: The information on Pat Boone's meeting with Elvis Presley comes from "Pat Boone" by Jeffrey Ressner, *Rolling Stone*, April 19, 1990; Dave Booth's interview with Boone; and an unsourced clipping included in Ger Rijff and Poul Madsen's *Elvis Presley: Echoes of the Past*. In each interview Boone discusses exactly the same moment in virtually the same language, but each offers a slightly different emphasis with more, or less, detail at certain points. The two quotations that I have included here are edited versions combining elements of all three interviews.

222 he hoped these Yankees liked his music: John Haley and John von Hoelle, *Sound and Glory*, p. 109.

224 if they could successfully negotiate union problems: They didn't. Filming was shut down in New York by an International Brotherhood of Electrical Workers dispute on November 26. What was shot in Cleveland had yet to be seen as of spring 1994.

225 "I have told you repeatedly": Escott and Hawkins, *Good Rockin' Tonight*, pp. 80–81.

226 "ladylike tardiness": *Memphis Press-Scimitar*, October 28, 1955.

227–228 "Elvis did ask me once or twice": Jerry Hopkins interview with Bob Neal (MVC/MSU).

228–229 The convention itself: Interviews with Chick Crumpacker, Grelun Landon, Buddy Bain, Buddy Killen, Mae Boren Axton, Galen Christy, et al.

230 On Sunday he played Ellis: The description of the concert comes primarily from Fred Davis, who was there.

231–232 The purchase price was $35,000: This is my understanding of the deal. RCA paid Sam Phillips $35,000 as specified, beyond the initial $5,000 deposit which Tom Parker had made (and for which he was reimbursed). Presumably, the $5,000 represented the back royalties that Phillips owed Elvis, who was specifically exempted from any future royalty payments. Beyond that, RCA and Hill and Range kicked in an additional $6,000 total as a signing bonus for the artist. This was paid to Parker, who deducted a 25 percent commission, which he split, after expenses, with Bob Neal. It has been speculated for years that Hill and Range put up a substantial amount of the purchase price itself, up to $15,000, but I have found nothing either in the contract or in the negotiations that led up to it to confirm that arrangement, nor has anyone I have spoken to confirmed it from a position of knowledge. At the same time it remains a logical possibility.

STAGE SHOW

All quotes from Sam Phillips and Scotty Moore are from the author's interviews, unless otherwise noted.

235 *The last admonishment I had:* Interview with Sam Phillips, 1992.

235 About a week before the session: Interview with George Klein, 1988.

236 At the DJ convention: "What Has Happened to Popular Music?," *High Fidelity Magazine*, June 1958; "Sholes Has Last Laugh," *Billboard*, April 21, 1956, covers much the same ground.

237 The room was big, high-ceilinged: Chet Atkins, *Country Gentleman*.

238 Tommy showed her a Miami newspaper story: The story appeared in the *Miami Herald* of October 1, 1955, as documented in Arena Television's *Tales of Rock 'N' Roll: Heartbreak Hotel*, broadcast in 1993.

238 Mae promised the song to Buddy: This account is based primarily on interviews with Buddy Killen, 1989, and Mae Boren Axton, 1988. Buddy's account is at odds with Mae's mainly in terms of the availability of the song prior to Elvis' recording of it. In Buddy's recollection he got the song from Mae in July, at the same time that she introduced him to Elvis, but the date of the *Miami Herald* headline would seem to disprove that scenario.

239 a "morbid mess": *New York Post*, October 3, 1956.

239 Stoker, who had met the boy: Interview with Gordon Stoker, 1989.

239 "They all told me": Tandy Rice interview with Steve Sholes, Country Music Foundation collection, used by permission.

239 a father's night show at Humes: Robert Johnson, *Elvis Presley Speaks!*, p. 44.

239 a Christmas show produced by Miss Scrivener: "Elvis Presley," prepared by the editors of *TV Radio Mirror*, 1956, p. 31.

240 "I think there was a big difference": Shelley Ritter interview with Minnie Pearl, 1990.

241–242 According to Maylon Humphries: Interview with Maylon Humphries, 1991.

242 Steve Sholes introduced: Interview with Chick Crumpacker, 1992; additional interviews with Arlene Blum and Lorene Lortie, 1993.

242 "Steve brought Elvis in": Interview with Anne Fulchino, 1992.

242ff introduced Elvis to the Dorseys: Interviews and correspondence with Grelun Landon, 1988–94; also, unpublished manuscript by Landon.

242–243 "and Elvis exhibited a kind of deference and courtesy": Arnold Shaw, *The Rockin' '50s*, p. 11.

243 ("We didn't know what to expect"): Jerry Hopkins interview with D. J. Fontana (MVC/MSU).

243 talking to Grelun and Chick Crumpacker: Interview with Chick Crumpacker, 1989.

244 The show that night: Chick Crumpacker liner notes to *Elvis* (RCA LPM 1382) and interviews and correspondence, 1989–94.

245 "Daddy just sat there": Interview with Jackson, Sarah, and Eve Baker, 1990.

245 Bob Johnson wrote in his notes: *Elvis Presley Speaks!*, p. 45.

246 it was no use doing any more: Grelun Landon, "Elvis Presley: The Tape Keeps Rolling." RCA publicity package, 1984.

247 On the second day of recording: Interview with Fred Danzig, 1993.

248 "a tall, lean young man": Manuscript copy of "The Day No One Wanted Elvis — But Me" by Fred Danzig.

248 They went into the control room: Interview with Fred Danzig.

249 The William Morris people threw a party: Interviews with Freddy Bienstock and Grelun Landon; also Martha Lopert, "The Boy with the Big Beat," *Celebrity*, winter 1958, p. 62.

249 a reception at the Hickory House: Interviews and correspondence with Chick Crumpacker; also interviews with Arlene Blum and Fred Danzig.

250 "I thought Elvis did even better": Booklet for *Elvis: The Complete 50's Masters*.

250 "The Colonel embarrasses me": Interview with Gabe Tucker, 1990.

251 "We were working near every day": Jerry Hopkins, *Elvis*, p. 125.

251ff To Justin Tubb: Interview with Justin Tubb, 1989, and subsequent correspondence.

252–253 ("My brother didn't get along"): Jimmy Guterman interview with Charlie Louvin, 1987.

253 "Fuck the Colonel": Interview with Chet Atkins, 1988.

253 "Elvis said, 'Boy' ": Howard Miller, *The Louvin Brothers*, p. 47.

253 Ira flashed: Jimmy Guterman interview with Charlie Louvin.

254 In Jacksonville on February 23: Robert Johnson, "Elvis Himself," *TV Star Parade*, September 1956, p. 65; also *Elvis Presley Speaks!*, p. 45. Other sources include the *Jacksonville Journal* (as cited in Morrie and Virginia Kricun, *Elvis: 1956 Reflections*); my interview with Justin Tubb and Jimmy Guterman's with Charlie Louvin; also James Poling, "Elvis Presley: Go, Cat, Go," *Pageant*, July 1956, p. 12, and Red West et al., *Elvis: What Happened?*, p. 109.

THE WORLD TURNED UPSIDE DOWN

All quotes from Scotty Moore are from the author's interviews, unless otherwise noted.

258 "I suppose," Neal said: Jerry Hopkins interview with Bob Neal (MVC/MSU).

259 Hazen's sister-in-law: Interview with Joseph Hazen, 1993.

260 Wallis was impressed: Hal Wallis and Charles Higham, *Starmaker*.

260 From Anne Fulchino's point of view: Interview with Anne Fulchino, 1993.

260–261 "The transformation was incredible": Allan Weiss, "Elvis Presley: Rock Music Phenomenon," in Danny Peary, ed., *Close Ups: The Movie Star Book*. Used by permission.

261 "I knew my script": August 6, 1956, interview.

261 This character was "lovesick": Will Jones, "Squeals Drown Presley's Songs," *Minneapolis Tribune*, May 13, 1956.

Just when Elvis delivered this opinion is a matter of conjecture. As of April 13, he evidently still believed he would be making *The Rainmaker* starting in June (this is borne out by an interview with Jay Thompson in Wichita Falls, Texas, on April 9 and his interview in the *Press-Scimitar* four days later), but whenever he spoke to Wallis, and whatever words he actually used, I believe that the feelings represented here — not to mention the combination of verbal confusion and emotional assurance — ring true.

261–262 Wallis for his part: All Wallis quotes from Wallis and Higham, *Starmaker*; information gleaned from *Starmaker*, correspondence with Nick Tosches, interview with Joseph Hazen, and other accounts.

262 Berle met Elvis and the Colonel: Andrew Solt interview with Milton Berle.

264 At one point Elvis: *Variety*, April 11, 1956.

264 "The crowd was too noisy": San Diego newspaper story, as quoted in Ger Rijff, *Long Lonely Highway*, p. 78.

264 "I changed my whole style": Interview with Glen Glenn, 1990.

264 The Colonel had extricated Elvis: Interview with Horace Logan, 1991. In Elvis' interview with Jay Thompson on Monday, April 9, he speaks of his final night on the Hayride as being "last Saturday night," but March 31 was advertised as his final appearance. The figure of ten thousand dollars is stipulated in the revision of his Hayride contract.

264 a recording session on Saturday, April 14: This session has always been listed as taking place on April 11, but Ernst Jorgensen called my attention to a number of discrepancies in scheduling, and a story in the *Press-Scimitar* on April 13 makes it clear that Elvis recorded on the fourteenth.

265 everyone wanted to know everything: All quotes are from Elvis' interview at the Warwick Hotel on March 24 but reflect fairly both the kind of questions he continued to be asked and the answers that he gave.

265–266 "He was working for Elvis, period": Interview with D. J. Fontana, 1991.

266 Scotty and Bill knew the Colonel: One of the Colonel's early schemes, according to both Scotty and D.J., was to replace them with Hank Snow's band for the ostensible purpose of saving money. The difference in musical styles was of little or no concern to him, they felt.

266 In Red's account Elvis: Red West et al., *Elvis: What Happened?*, pp. 120–121.

267 "I'll bet I could burp": Interview with Gordon Stoker, 1989.

267 They chartered a plane: Interviews with Scotty Moore, 1988, 1989; also *Memphis Press-Scimitar* account, May 4, 1956.

267 "Man, I don't know if": Interview with Chet Atkins, 1988.

267–268 "It was the worst sound": Interview with Gordon Stoker.

268–269 Elvis gave a brief interview: "Elvis Gives Out with Crazy Cool Interview," *Waco News-Tribune*, April 18, 1956.

270 Scotty and Elvis and Bill headed for the Club El Dorado: Interviews with Scotty Moore and Lowell Fulson, 1989.

270 "no check is good": *Time*, May 16, 1960.

271ff It was the first sit-down gig: Principal sources for this account of the Las Vegas booking are interviews with Scotty Moore and D. J. Fontana; stories in the *Memphis Press-Scimitar* and *Commercial Appeal*; Robert Johnson, *Elvis Presley Speaks!*; *Billboard* and *Variety* coverage; Marge Crumbaker and Gabe Tucker's *Up and Down with Elvis Presley*; Bill Randle's comments as detailed in Ger Rijff and Jan van Gestel, *Memphis Lonesome*; RCA's recording of the final show as presented on *Elvis: The Complete 50's Masters*; various contemporary interviews with Elvis Presley; Bill Dahl's story on Freddie Bell ("Remembering Rock," *Chicago Tribune*, December 5, 1990); and Jonny Whiteside's interview/memorial to Johnnie Ray, "Who's Crying Now," *LA Weekly*, March 9–15, 1990.

It should be noted that it has frequently been assumed that Elvis was fired from this engagement because he left after two weeks and Freddy Martin stayed on. In fact it would appear from all indications that Elvis was hired for the first two weeks of Martin's engagement only. He went on to regular scheduled gigs starting in St. Paul on May 12 and going through the entire next week, which included a headlining appearance at the Cotton Carnival in the middle of what would have been his fourth week in Vegas. I think the confusion initially arose from trade accounts that had him "replaced on the bill by Roberta Sherwood" (*Variety*, May 9, 1956). This came in the midst of a negative article, and indeed in the midst of a negative sentence ("The more sophisticated gambling clientele didn't dig his frenzied antics, and Presley was replaced . . ."), but I believe from interviews and all other indications that it was booked as a two-week engagement from the start and that the announced replacement was a planned one, the conjunction ("and") merely sequential. This, too, however, is subject to revision.

271 one of Richardson's guests: Crumbaker and Tucker, *Up and Down*, p. 38.

271 "For the first time in months": *Elvis Presley Speaks!*, p. 53.

271 "After the show our nerves": Elston Leonard, "Elvis Presley: The New Singing Rage," *Tiger*, c. 1956, p. 14.

271 "They weren't my kind of audience": *Elvis Presley*, prepared by the editors of *TV Radio Mirror*, 1956, p. 43.

271 "It was strictly an adult audience": May 14, 1956, interview, La Crosse, Wisconsin. See the *Memphis Commercial Appeal* of May 9 for a similar interview, in which he declares, "Man, I really liked Vegas. I'm going back there the first chance I get."

272 "Elvis, who has played hard audiences": Robert Johnson, "The Golden Boy Reaches for a Star While the Music Goes Round and Round and —," *Memphis Press-Scimitar*, May 4, 1956.

272 They played what Elvis calculated: Richard Lyons, "Presley Irked by Overtime — Even at $4000 an Hour," *Memphis Commercial Appeal*, May 9, 1956.

272 "One thing about Las Vegas": *Elvis Presley Speaks!*, p. 55.

273 "The carnage was terrific": *Memphis Press-Scimitar*, May 4, 1956.

274 eight-hundred-dollar watch with diamonds: The gift is shown in a photograph accompanying the *Press-Scimitar* story. The thank-you notes are specified by Marge Crumbaker and Gabe Tucker in *Up and Down with Elvis Presley*.

274 "Like a jug of corn liquor": "Hillbilly on a Pedestal," *Newsweek*, May 14, 1956.

274–275 He was back in Memphis: *Memphis Commercial Appeal*, May 9, 1956.

"THOSE PEOPLE IN NEW YORK ARE NOT GONNA CHANGE ME NONE"

277 this "new and open-to-the-public feature": *Memphis Commercial Appeal*, May 13, 1956.

277 "Henry introduced me to him": Shelley Ritter interview with Minnie Pearl, 1990.

277–278 "I grabbed his hand": *Memphis Commercial Appeal*, May 13, 1956.

278–279 Vernon and Gladys were already present: This account is based primarily on Fred Davis' firsthand testimony, as well as the *Press-Scimitar* story of May 16 and a fortuitous recording of the Little Rock concert the following day, which followed virtually the same format.

279 Hank Snow meanwhile was just beginning: Hank Snow with Jack Ownbey and Bob Burris, *The Hank Snow Story*, Champaign, University of Illinois Press, forthcoming, p. 390. Used by permission.

There has been all kinds of speculation on the subject of Snow's break with Parker over the years, and in the absence of an alternative version from the Colonel, this seems as plausible an explanation as any. In his book, *Up and Down with Elvis Presley*, coauthored with Marge Crumbaker, Gabe Tucker posits that the Colonel said to Snow, "Hank, you put in everything you make, and I'll put in everything I make, and we'll buy this boy's contract . . ." When Snow demurred, as Parker knew that he would, Parker cut him out of the deal. Tucker and Crumbaker portray the denouement in much the same way. "Have we signed that damn kid or not?" Snow says of the RCA deal. "No, we haven't," the Colonel replies. "I have signed him."

One essential factor not to be discounted is that Snow was a proud man and would never have been able to brook the idea of being "taken." In the words of his son: "I don't think that my dad realized at that time what had happened," and this would help explain his reluctance to pursue, or even to fully explain, the matter.

280 "I'm so proud of my boy": Interview with Cliff Gleaves, 1990.

280 Mrs. Presley answered the doorbell: Interview with Pallas Pidgeon, 1990; Robert Johnson, *Elvis Presley Speaks!*, p. 64; Jerry Hopkins interview with Faye Harris (MVC/MSU).

280 "I wish," he said to a contractor friend: Interview with Guy Lansky, 1990.

280–281 Gladys had filled the house: Edwin Miller, "Elvis the Innocent," *Memories*, May 1989. Miller's account of his visit at precisely this time was written up first in a 1956 issue of *Seventeen* and, later, in this more reflective article.

281 "It didn't happen all at once": *Memphis Press-Scimitar*, May 4, 1956.

282–283 The rest of the week he spent with June: Interview with June Juanico, 1991.

283 On the way they had heard a song: Peter Cronin interview with Scotty Moore, 1992.

283 "If you ever do anything to make": Albert Goldman, *Elvis*, p. 505.

284–285 "it was a relaxed and therefore more effective": *Variety*, June 13, 1956.

285 "Mr. Presley has no discernible": *New York Times*, June 6, 1956.

285 "The sight of young (21) Mr. Presley": *New York Journal-American*, June 9, 1956.

285–286 under the banner "Beware Elvis Presley": *America*, June 23, 1956.

286 ("She'd get mad and cuss"): Shelley Ritter interview with Vester Presley, 1991.

286 "I don't do any vulgar movements": Aline Mosby, "Presley Sexy? He Denies It," *New York World Telegram*, June 15, 1956.

286 "I'm not trying to be sexy": Phyllis Battele, *New York Journal-American*, June 18, 1956.

286 "I hired a doctor's wife": Interview with Charlie Lamb, 1990.

286–287 "I'm going to get a wiggle meter": *New York World Telegram*, June 15, 1956.

287 a one-shot appearance at $7,500: Allen indicated this figure in his interview with Andrew Solt, though the amount has also been cited as $5,000. The higher figure would seem to explain Ed Sullivan's unprecented bid ($50,000 for three appearances) after the Allen broadcast.

287 "there has been a demand that": *New York Journal-American*, June 13, 1956.

287 On June 20 a compromise of sorts was reached: Ibid., June 21, 1956.

287 It was, said Allen: Andrew Solt interview with Steve Allen.

288–289 Elvis Presley is a worried man: Kays Gary, "Elvis Defends Low-Down Style," *Charlotte Observer*, June 27, 1956.

290 "Mr. Johnson, you know some things": *Memphis Press-Scimitar*, May 4, 1956.

290–295 He arrived at NBC's midtown rehearsal studio: This particular detail, along with extended and attributed quotations, comes from Alfred Wertheimer's book, *Elvis '56: In the Beginning*, © 1979, and is used by permission. All observations are from Wertheimer's point of view, unless otherwise specified, and are used with grateful acknowledgment. This credit carries through to the end of the chapter, wherever noted.

291 "if you just stuck around with him": Anita Houk, "Lensman's Early Look at Elvis Was Rare, Personal," *Memphis Commercial Appeal*, August 11, 1991.

294 ("He always did the best he could"): Peter Cronin interview with Gordon Stoker, 1992.

297–302 The next day he seemed: Once again Alfred Wertheimer's firsthand observation (in words and pictures) was an invaluable source of visualization, information, and insight. In addition, interviews with Freddy Bienstock and Chick Crumpacker were of great help, along with Grelun Landon's, Scotty Moore's, and D. J. Fontana's recollections. Finally, Chick Crumpacker took Ernst Jorgensen and me on a guided tour of the old RCA neighborhood and building, which is now a division of Baruch College, in which Studio B has been astonishingly preserved as a television teaching studio.

297 "Barbara Hearn of Memphis": Rhea Talley, "Memphis, Biloxi Girls Share Top Spot in Elvis' Date Book," *Memphis Commercial Appeal*, July 8, 1956.

299 As Otis Blackwell later said: "Otis Blackwell: The Power Behind Elvis," *Essence*, May 1978. For additional information on Otis Blackwell, see Gary Giddins, "Just How Much Did Elvis Learn from Otis Blackwell?," *Village Voice*, October 25, 1976.

300 "I wasn't all that impressed": Peter Cronin interview with Gordon Stoker.

301 He ran into Gene Vincent: New Orleans radio interview, July 1956.

302–304 It was a hot night, 97 degrees: Most of the detail on the Russwood Park show comes from *Press-Scimitar* and *Commercial Appeal* coverage the next day. Early editions of the *Press-Scimitar* had attendance at fourteen thousand, but the figure was corrected by the end of the day. Robert Johnson's account in the *Press-Scimitar* was particularly vivid, as was Alfred Wertheimer's in *Elvis '56*.

303 The fans "broke from their seats": Robert Johnson, "Elvis Sings and Thousands Scream," *Memphis Press-Scimitar*, July 5, 1956.

303 "there was this keening sound": Interview with Jackson Baker, 1990.

304 "He rocked 'em"; "When it was time to go": *Memphis Press-Scimitar*, July 5, 1956.

304 All Elvis wanted: Ibid., May 4, 1956.

A note on the title of this chapter: The quotation comes from Jackson Baker's recollection of the event in a 1989 interview. Stanley Booth uses a variant of the same quote in his classic February 1968 story for *Esquire*, "A Hound Dog to the Manor Born." The only reference in newspaper accounts is in Bob Johnson's July 5 story in the *Press-Scimitar*, which states: "Elvis joked about his recent appearance on the Steve Allen show, when he had to restrain some of his wriggling," but no direct quotation is made.

ELVIS AND JUNE

All quotes from June Juanico are from the author's interviews, telephone conversation, and correspondence, 1991–94, unless otherwise noted. June's own unpublished manuscript gives a wonderful picture of the period and should not remain unpublished for long.

307–308 they just showed up: Thomas Sancton, "Elvis Dates Biloxi Girl," *New Orleans Item*, July 11, 1956; also interviews with June Juanico.

308 In the course of the evening: Ruth Sullivan, "Slim Elvis Presley Is Heavy on the Diet," "The Grapevine" (column in a New Orleans newspaper), July 1956.

308 "Did I kiss him good night?": *New Orleans Item*, July 11, 1956.

308–309 The crowds at the beachfront hotel: Kay Freeman, "Elvis Presley Catches Spanish Mackerel; Dodges Crowd of 500 Coast Rock, Roll Fans Thursday," *Biloxi Daily Herald*, July 15, 1956.

310 "It'd be a sin to let something like that go to waste": *Miami News*, August 4, 1956.

312 Meanwhile, Elvis got so sunburnt: Harry Reeks, "During Vacation on Gulf His 'Mob' Proves Active," publicity handout, July 1956.

314 Toward the end of July: *Memphis Press-Scimitar*, July 23, 1956.

315 a vaudeville redoubt from the 1920s: Philip Chapman, "The Girl Who Got Presley," *TV Radio Mirror*.

315–316 she reportedly stroked [Elvis'] brow: Sandy Schnier and Damon Runyon, Jr., "Hey, Gals! Elvis Has 2 Steadies," *Miami News*, August 4, 1956.

317 "Now this is the way it is": Bella Kelly, "Elvis Denies Biloxi Beauty Is His 'Steady,' " *Miami News*, August 5, 1956.

318 Mrs. Mae Juanico was quoted: Ibid.

319 "The biggest freak in show business history": *Miami News*, August 4, 1956.

322 "aroused fans ripped": "Elvis — a Different Kind of Idol," *Life*, August 27, 1956.

322 a fashion that "put obscenity and vulgarity": *Jacksonville Journal*, August 10, 1956 (as quoted in Morrie and Virginia Kricun, *Elvis: 1956 Reflections*).

322 ("I can't figure out what I'm doing"): Ibid., August 11, 1956.

323 Dewey was just about to start: *Memphis Press-Scimitar*, August 22, 1956.

323 "I don't think that you learn to become an actor": August 6, 1956, interview.

LOVE ME TENDER

All quotes from June Juanico and Scotty Moore are from the author's interviews, unless otherwise noted.

327 "I'm strictly for Stevenson": *New York Herald-Tribune*, August 18, 1956.

327 "I have no trouble memorizing": Harold Stone, "Meet Mr. Rock 'N' Roll," *Top Secret*, November 1956, p. 54.

327 he was "plenty scared": Army Archerd, "Presley Takes Hollywood," *Photoplay*, December 1956.

327 Elvis blurted out to Weisbart: Ibid.

328 On his second day on the set: Ibid. There is also a charming account of his friendship with Elvis by Nick Adams in the May 1957 issue of *16* (vol. 1, no. 1), begun under the editorship of Memphis' Robert Johnson.

328–329 Colonel Parker was staying up nights: Martha Lopert, "The Boy with the Big Beat," *Celebrity*, winter 1958.

329–330 Elvis was eager to perform: *Photoplay*.

330 It was a job like any other: *Memphis Press-Scimitar*, September 1, 1956.

330 The director, Robert Webb: *New York Post*, October 3, 1956.

330–331 Webb would break down the lines: Jerry Hopkins interview with Mildred Dunnock (MVC/MSU).

331 "Before I met him": Albert Goldman, *Elvis*, p. 218.

331 Trude Forsher, a Viennese émigrée: Interview with Trude Forsher, 1993.

331 "I could make you like me if I tried": Joe Hyams, "All Alone with Elvis Presley," *New York Herald-Tribune*, September 23, 1956.

331 "From the time I was a kid": Atra Baer, "The Real Presley," *New York Journal-American*, September 23, 1956.

331 To *True Story* staff writer Jules Archer he confessed: Jules Archer, "Is This Unassuming Rocker America's Newest Rebel?," *True Story*, December 1956, as reprinted in *DISCoveries*, January-February 1988.

331 He and Gene spent $750: *New York Journal-American*, September 23, 1956.

332 "We'll have to check you over": *Photoplay*.

332 "Presley has the same smoldering appeal": *True Story*.

332–336 On the Friday before Labor Day weekend: Interviews with Freddy Bienstock, Scotty Moore, Thorne Nogar, Bones Howe, Gordon Stoker, D. J. Fontana, and Trude Forsher.

336 "Well, do whatever you can": Peter Cronin interview with Scotty Moore, 1992.

336 the picture, which had now been officially renamed: Bob Thomas, "Vulgah? Not Me," *New York Post*, September 4, 1956.

336 Mildred Dunnock as his mother: Jerry Hopkins interview with Mildred Dunnock (MVC/MSU).

337 "He's a real pixie": *Tupelo Daily Journal*, September 13, 1956, as quoted in Morrie and Virginia Kricun, *Elvis: 1956 Reflections*.

337 "Finally met Elvis Presley": *New York Journal-American*, September 20, 1956.

337 "He was the first person": Goldman, *Elvis*, pp. 219–220.

337 Elvis sent Sullivan a get-well card: *Photoplay*.

339 "We're the perfect combination": Interview with Cliff Gleaves, 1991.

339 sing a couple of songs in the picture: This was cited as a hundred-thousand-dollar offer on occasion.

339 William Campbell was convinced: Goldman, *Elvis*, p. 201.

339 the Colonel was simply a very smart man: March 24, 1956, interview.

339 "He's a very amusing guy": August 6, 1956, interview.

339 "We more or less picked each other": Ibid.

339 Colonel liked Nick: Sidney Skolsky, "Tintyped: Elvis Presley," *New York Post*, November 21, 1956. Skolsky had Colonel and Nick writing a book together called *Elvis Presley: Actor, Singer and Man*.

339 On Monday they visited Humes: Mildred Scrivener, "My Boy Elvis," *TV Radio Mirror*, March 1957. On December 1 the *Memphis Press-Scimitar* ran a picture of the drill team modeling the new equipment and carrying a banner which stated the band's new name, the EP Rebels.

340 Nick put his feet up: Jerry Hopkins interview with James and Gladys Tipler (MVC/MSU).

340 "It made me feel bad": Elaine Dundy, *Elvis and Gladys*, p. 260.

340 Bowen was now general manager: Interview with Ernest Bowen, 1990.

340–341 "And just think, you're paying me": *New York Post*, October 2, 1956.

341 He couldn't "hardly remember": *Tupelo Daily Journal*, September 27, 1956.

342 "The city limits": Peter Dacre, "Eyewitness to Presleymania."

342 There were forty city police: *Tupelo Daily Journal*, September 27, 1956.

342 "I was right at the back of the stage": Interview with Ernest Bowen.

343 in Dallas Nick was even served: *Dallas Morning News*, October 12, 1956.

344 "It looked like a war out there": Interview with D. J. Fontana, 1988.

344 teenagers in Temple: *Memphis Press-Scimitar*, October 13, 1956.

344 Reporters were pestering: *Dallas Morning News*, October 12, 1956.

345–346 Elvis had been in a fight: *Memphis Press-Scimitar*, October 19, 1956.

346 "I'll regret this day as long as I live": *New York Post*, October 19, 1956.

346 advised by Acting Judge Sam Friedman: *Memphis Commercial Appeal*, October 20, 1956.

THE TOAST OF THE TOWN

351 "The idol of the rock 'n' roll juveniles": *New York Times*, October 29, 1956.

351–352 "Teenagers are my life and triumph": Gordon Sinclair, "Sinclair Says Elvis 'Fine Lad,' Hopes to Last for 40 Years," *Toronto Star*, October 29, 1956.

353 The ratings were not quite as spectacular: *Variety*, October 31, 1956.

353 he played the scene: There are pictures of Elvis shooting the scene in his white bucks in Ger Rijff's *Faces and Stages*.

354–355 In the offing were hound dogs and houndburgers: Chester Morrison, "The Great Elvis Presley Industry," *Look*, November 13, 1956; additional background on merchandising in Mike Kaplan, "Elvis a Millionaire in 1 Year," *Variety*, October 24, 1956, and Louis M. Kohlmeier, "Heartbreak, Hound Dogs Put Sales Zip into Presley Products," *Wall Street Journal*, December 31, 1956.

355 "like a circus come to town": Joseph Lewis, "Elvis Presley Lives," *Cosmopolitan*, November 1968.

355–356 According to her sister, Lana: Lana Wood, *Natalie*, p. 45.

356 "the nation's first police-sponsored behind-the-wheel driving school": *Memphis Press-Scimitar*, November 6, 1956.

356–357 Meanwhile, Cliff Gleaves was back in town: Interviews with Cliff Gleaves, Lamar Fike, and George Klein. Needless to say, Cliff, Lamar, and George do not agree on every detail.

357–359 "At that point my life changed": Interview with Cliff Gleaves, 1990.

359–360 Elvis seemed "a little nervous at first": Interview with Pallas Pidgeon, 1990.

360 "The only thing I can say is they don't know me": Jerry Hopkins interview with Marion Keisker (MVC/MSU).

360 (the Colonel indicated): Dick Kleiner, "20 Questions with Elvis Presley," *Memphis Press-Scimitar*, December 1, 1956.

360–361 Then he met Dottie Harmony: Interview with Dottie Harmony, 1993.

361 he attended Liberace's opening: *Memphis Press-Scimitar*, November 15, 1956.

362 Perhaps the most interesting review: Gerald Weales, "Movies: The Crazy, Mixed-up Kids Take Over," *The Reporter*, December 13, 1956.

363 The Colonel's only public comment: *New York Journal-American*, October 8, 1956.

363 Elvis himself was embarrassed: Interview with Cliff Gleaves.

363 "I'm not going to quit": *Toronto Star*, October 29, 1956.

THE END OF SOMETHING

365 a "chicken coop nested in Cadillacs": Jerry Hopkins, *Elvis*, p. 107.

366 Sam had the tape recorder turned on: Interviews with Sam Phillips, Jack Clement, Carl Perkins, and Johnny Cash, 1979.

366–368 "I heard this guy in Las Vegas": *The Million Dollar Quartet* (RCA 2023-2-R).

368 One of the engineers at the station: Interviews with George Klein and Louis Cantor, 1993. Cantor's *Wheelin' on Beale* is an invaluable source of information on the radio station and the era.

369 "I was fourteen," said Carla Thomas: Interview with Carla Thomas, 1980. Sam Cooke's brother L.C., then a member of the Magnificents, also remembers the show, and Elvis' enthusiasm for his brother's gospel singing, vividly.

369 "I told them, If you put Elvis": Interview with Rufus Thomas, 1988.

369 "To all who were in earshot": *Tri-State Defender*, February 2, 1957.

369–370 the *Memphis World* cited an account: *Memphis World*, June 23, 1956, and July 6, 1957, as supplied by Louis Cantor.

370 Maybe it's the Indigo Avenue's blase blues: *Pittsburgh Courier*, December 22, 1956, as cited in *Beale Black & Blue*, by Margaret McKee and Fred Chisenhall, and *Wheelin' on Beale*, by Louis Cantor.

371–372 Elvis met Kanter at the airport: Interviews with Hal Kanter, 1993, and Freddy Bienstock, 1992.

372 " 'Man, that screen test ain't nothin' ": Interview with Hal Kanter for *Elvis in Hollywood*, 1993.

372–373 "He awoke in late afternoon": Hal Kanter, "Inside Paradise," *Variety*, January 9, 1957.

373–374 "That's the night my car got stomped in": Interview with Horace Logan, 1991.

374 "I saw a young girl open her purse": Interview with Hal Kanter for *Elvis in Hollywood*, 1993.

375 Even Sandi Phillips: Interview with Sandi Phillips Kallenberg, 1992.

375–376 Dottie Harmony flew in: Interview with Dottie Harmony, 1993.

377 June saw the pictures in the paper: Interview with June Juanico, 1991.

377 "We were broke, flat broke": Interview with Bobbie Moore, 1992.

377–378 an interview to the *Press-Scimitar*: Robert Johnson, "These Are the Cats Who Make Music for Elvis," *Memphis Press-Scimitar*, December 15, 1956.

378 his pre-induction physical: Interviews with Dottie Harmony and Cliff Gleaves, 1990.

378 the gold lamé vest that Barbara had given him: "Elvis Likes Barbara," *16*, May 1957.

379 they will have to pay a $300,000 fee: *Newsweek*, October 8, 1956; see *Time*, November 4, 1957, for a slight variation.

379 Elvis for his part is just as genuinely thrilled: Interview with Gordon Stoker, 1989.

379 "This is a nice boy": *TV Star Parade*, April 1957.

380 he was happy to serve: *Memphis Press-Scimitar*, January 8, 1957.

LOVING YOU

384 while "rock 'n' roll has its place": John Jackson, *Big Beat Heat: Alan Freed and the Early Years of Rock & Roll*, p. 146.

385 "He was a genius": Hal Wallis and Charles Higham, *Starmaker*, p. 148.

386–388 on the second or third day of his visit: Interview with Freddy Bienstock, 1992.

386 Elvis thought was a good phrase: October 28, 1957, interview.

388 On Monday Elvis reported to the studio: There has always been a good deal of controversy about when exactly Elvis started to dye his hair. Given his experimentation with hairstyles from high school on, this confusion is certainly understandable, and not of any great critical importance, but according to George Klein, he had never seen Elvis with black hair before he came back from the filming of *Loving You*, and this was the story that Elvis told George of how it came about.

388–389 Songwriter Ben Weisman, too, showed up: Interview with Ben Weisman, 1989.

389 ("I need them like I need a hole in the head"): *Memphis Press-Scimitar*, September 14, 1957.

390 "I was fascinated by the way Elvis recorded": Wallis and Higham, *Starmaker*, p. 151.

391 He liked Wendell Corey: Interviews with Glen Glenn, 1990, and Hal Kanter, 1993.

391 "a lot of fun to be with": Robert Johnson, "Elvis' Hollywood Diary," *16*, July 1957.

391–392 the situation that seemed to be developing: Interview with Glen Glenn; also interviews with Scotty Moore.

392 "a little homesick[ness]": *Memphis Press-Scimitar*, March 7, 1957.

392 "I was suffering some nausea": *Memphis Press-Scimitar*, January 29, 1957.

392–393 On their first morning at the lot: Dick Williams, "Behind the Scenes with *Loving You*," as cited in Bill DeNight et al., eds., *Elvis Album*, p. 90.

393 "There's somebody to comb his hair": C. Robert Jennings, "There'll Always Be an Elvis," *Saturday Evening Post*, September 11, 1965, p. 79.

393 One time they went to the movies: Albert Goldman, *Elvis*, pp. 231–232.

393 Scotty Moore's wife, Bobbie, came out: Interview with Bobbie Moore, 1992.

393 One day when they visited the set: Interview with Hal Kanter.

394 It was, remarked *Time* magazine: *Time*, May 27, 1957.

394 He blew up at Gordon Stoker: Interview with Gordon Stoker, 1989.

395 he was really beginning to miss his road trips: *Memphis Press-Scimitar*, March 19, 1957.

395 At the wrap party Hal Kanter: Interview with Hal Kanter.

395 He sent a telegram to June: Interview with June Juanico, 1991.

395–396 Built in 1939: Ida Clemens in the *Memphis Commercial Appeal*, October 27, 1940, as cited in Jane Brown Gillette, "Elvis Lives," *Historic Preservation*, May/June 1992.

396 Accompanying the family was Mrs. Virginia Grant: *Graceland*, pp. 30–31.

396–397 "This is going to be a lot nicer": "Singer Is Interested in Purchasing Graceland," *Memphis Press-Scimitar*, March 23, 1957.

397 ("I think I am going to like this new home"): William Leaptrott and Tom Johnson, "Presley Is Eager to Redecorate," *Memphis Press-Scimitar*, March 26, 1957.

397 The price was $102,500: Goldman, *Elvis*, p. 234. Contemporary accounts have the purchase price at "around $100,000," but Goldman seems to have good specific figures (although I have adjusted the mortgage upward by $500, in order to make the addition come out right).

397 Sam Phillips had just moved into: Interview with Knox Phillips, 1989.

397–398 "the darkest blue there is": *Memphis Press-Scimitar*, March 26, 1957.

398 there were two priorities: Shelley Ritter interview with George Golden, 1993; additional information on Golden from Dewey Webb, "Goodness Graceland! Elvis' Interior Decorator Tells All!" *Phoenix New Times*, July 28–August 3, 1993.

398 He had another disturbing run-in: *Memphis Press-Scimitar*, March 22–26, 1957.

398 Elvis would be returning to Tupelo: *Memphis Press-Scimitar*, March 22, 1957.

399 "I had gotten fired": Interview with George Klein, 1991.

400 "Hysterical Shrieks Greet Elvis": Press coverage from this tour is extensively documented in Ger Rijff, *Faces and Stages*.

400–401 In Canada, Oscar Davis finally made his move: Interviews with Scotty Moore, Gordon Stoker, and D. J. Fontana.

401 ("All those sweet little girls out there"): Interview with Hal Kanter.

401 ("as public reparation for excesses"): *New York Journal-American*, March 31, 1957.

401–402 In Philadelphia, speaking to a group: Carol Gelber, "Press Conference: High School Reporters Keep Their Poise Interviewing Elvis," *Philadelphia Evening Bulletin*, April 6, 1957.

402 Yvonne Lime came to visit: Yvonne Lime, "My Weekend with Elvis," *Modern Screen*, 1957.

402 On Saturday night they went over to Sam's new house: Ibid.; interviews with Sam and Knox Phillips; Dot Phillips' recollections in "Memories of Elvis Shared by Close Friend" by Larry Johnson, *Trenton Herald Gazette*, August 17, 1978.

JAILHOUSE ROCK

All quotes from Scotty Moore, George Klein, Russ Tamblyn, Cliff Gleaves, and Jerry Leiber and Mike Stoller are from the author's interviews, unless otherwise noted.

405 He was staying at the plush Beverly Wilshire: Interview with George Klein, 1993.

407 " 'Get him off this stuff' ": Jerry Hopkins interview with Gordon Stoker (MVC/MSU).

407 "They came in because we pushed them in": Interview with Freddy Bienstock, 1992.

408 "Most artists," said Gordon Stoker: Interview with Gordon Stoker, 1989.

409–410 "Elvis looked at me": Interview with George Klein for *Elvis* in Hollywood, 1993.

411–412 He told the assistant director: Interview with Bob Relyea for *Elvis* in Hollywood, 1993.

412–413 Cliff met Lamar at the door: Cliff's account essentially bears out George's.

413 "Cliff, Arthur, and I": Interview with George Klein for *Elvis* in Hollywood, 1993.

413–414 "Whenever there was a break": Interview with George Klein, 1993.

414 scared the hell out of Elvis: Sammy Davis, Jr., et al., *Why Me? The Sammy Davis, Jr., Story,* pp. 77–81. This is supported by interviews with George Klein et al., as well as newspaper accounts.

414 Mitchum himself stopped by: Interviews with George Klein, Russ Tamblyn, and D. J. Fontana.

414 "The Clan of Elvis Presley": Interview with Vince Edwards, 1990.

415 "When I get married": AP report, June 6, 1957.

417 "I don't feel like I'm property": Joe Hyams, "The Highest Paid Movie Star Ever," *New York Herald-Tribune*, May 16, 1957.

417 "I always criticize myself": October 28, 1957, interview.

417–418 he sought tips: Interview with Bob Relyea for *Elvis in Hollywood*, 1993.

419 Before he left, Elvis played: Robert Johnson, "These Reports True — Elvis and Dewey Had a Falling Out," *Memphis Press-Scimitar*, summer 1957.

421 "There's plenty of room for all of us": *Tacoma News Tribune*, September 2, 1957.

421 He had heard that geese: Shelley Ritter interview with George Golden, 1993.

421 "I was still living across from Humes": Interview with George Klein for *Elvis in Hollywood*, 1993.

421 "She was at the peak of success": *Memphis Press-Scimitar*, July 5, 1957.

422 At the end of the night: *Memphis Press-Scimitar*, September 14, 1957.

422–423 After that they kept almost constant: 1987 BBC television documentary *Presley — "Cut Me and I Bleed."*

423 They drove all around on his motorcycle: *Memphis Press-Scimitar*, September 14, 1957.

423 Buzzy Forbess from the Courts came by: Interviews with Buzzy Forbess, 1991, 1994.

423–424 "George didn't drive": Interview with Alan Fortas, 1990.

424 One night, Alan recalled in his memoir: Alan Fortas, *Elvis: From Memphis to Hollywood*, p. 61.

424 Alan didn't think much of the cousins: Ibid., p. 56.

425 One night he came by the house at three: Robert Johnson, "These Reports True," *Memphis Press-Scimitar*, summer 1957.

425–426 One night the great rhythm and blues singer: Interviews with George Klein, Barbara Pittman, Quinton Claunch, and Bettye Berger.

425–426 "He is very spiritually minded": Mike Hellicar, "Elvis Sings Spirituals Like a Negro, Says Ivory Joe Hunter," *New Musical Express*, c. May 1961.

426 The rumor had been circulating: Louie Robinson, " 'The Pelvis' Gives His Views on Vicious Anti-Negro Slur," *Jet*, August 1, 1957.

426 "It was like a magic spell": Interview with Bettye Berger, 1989.

426–427 a trio of fourteen year old girls: Albert Goldman, *Elvis*, pp. 252–254.

427 a couple of months was much too early: *New York Journal-American*, September 11, 1957.

427 "It never got wild at Graceland": Fortas, *Elvis*, p. 58.

427 "She never did go nowhere": Interview with Lillian Fortenberry, 1988.

427 "I'm the most miserable woman in the world": Elaine Dundy, *Elvis and Gladys*, p. 292. In Dundy's book the visit is dated earlier, but Corinne Tate, the Richardses' daughter, told me that it took place just after Judy Tyler's death.

427 "sitting by the window": Fortas, *Elvis*, p. 79.

427–428 Every so often she'd have a beer: Interview with Cliff Gleaves, 1990.

428 It was all right, she told Lamar: Interview with Lamar Fike, 1988.

428 Toward the end of the summer: Interview with Freddy Bienstock.

428–429 The scene at the train station: *Memphis Press-Scimitar*, August 28, 1957.

429–430 "A chunky, effeminate-looking man": *Tacoma News Tribune*, September 2, 1957.

430 "A gang moved into our town": *Vancouver Province*, September 3, 1957, as cited in AP report, September 3, 1957.

431 the harmonies of the Statesmen: Jerry Hopkins interview (MVC/MSU) and 1992 Peter Cronin interview with Gordon Stoker.

431 Freddy tried to sneak in a song: Interview with Freddy Bienstock.

431 "It was horrible": Interview with Millie Kirkham, 1989.

431–434 Scotty, D. J., and Bill were watching the clock: This articulation of Scotty and Bill's feelings, and their subsequent playing out, is based on stories that ran in the *Memphis Press-Scimitar* on September 13 and 14, 1957, as well as numerous interviews with Scotty Moore, Bobbie Moore, Evelyn Black, Reggie Young, Glen Glenn, D. J. Fontana, Alan Fortas, and George Klein.

432 "squeezed us for a matter of dollars": Interview with Scotty Moore, 1989.

432–433 Elvis read the letter, shook his head: Interview with George Klein, 1990.

433 a ring to signify his feelings: *Memphis Press-Scimitar*, September 11, 1957.

433 He called Scotty the following day: *Memphis Press-Scimitar*, September 14, 1957.

433 "[Elvis] promised us": *Memphis Press-Scimitar*, September 13, 1957.

434 the lead editorial in the paper: *Tupelo Daily Journal*, September 27, 1957.

435 It didn't feel right: Interviews with D. J. Fontana, 1991, and George Klein, 1990.

435 "Elvis Presley and his one-man band": Interview with George Klein, 1990.

WALKING IN A DREAM

All quotes from George Klein, Cliff Gleaves, and Jerry Leiber and Mike Stoller are from the author's interviews, unless otherwise noted.

437 "Rock 'n' roll smells phony and false": Frank Sinatra, as quoted in Linda Martin and Kerry Segrave, *Anti-Rock*, pp. 46–47.

437 And what was Elvis Presley's response?: Press conference, as reported in the *Los Angeles Times, New York Post, New York Journal-American, New York Herald-Tribune*, October 29–30, 1957.

437–438 "wiggled, bumped, twisted": Jack O'Brian, "L.A. Outraged at Presley," *New York Journal-American*, November 8, 1957.

438 including actors Alan Ladd and Walter Slezak: Carla Phillips, "My Story of Elvis," fan club publication.

438 What was Elvis' reaction?: *New York Post*, October 30, 1957.

439 even seventeen-year-old Ricky Nelson showed up: Joel Selvin, *Ricky Nelson*; Philip Bashe, *Teenage Idol, Travelin' Man*; Albert Goldman, *Elvis*.

439–440 One week later he sailed for Hawaii: Interviews with George Klein, Cliff Gleaves, and Vince Edwards, in addition to press coverage in the *Honolulu Star Bulletin*.

440 "I'm as horny as a billy goat": Tempest Storm, *The Lady Is a Vamp*, p. 168.

441 After the Easter service: Bill E. Burk, *Early Elvis: The Humes Years*, p. 118; also Alanna Nash interview with the Reverend James Hamill; Steve Turner's *Hungry for Heaven*, pp. 33–34; and Yvonne Lime, "My Weekend with Elvis," *Modern Screen*, 1957.

441 "I never expected to be anybody important": Louis Larkin, "God Is My Refuge," *Photoplay*, July 1957.

441–442 He visited Lansky's: Interview with Guy Lansky, 1990.

442 this music was "the real thing": *Memphis Press-Scimitar*, December 7, 1957.

442–443 About ten days before Christmas: Robert Johnson and Thomas N. Pappas, "Army, Navy Recruiters Make Offers to Elvis," *Memphis Press-Scimitar*, December 1957; additional *Memphis Press-Scimitar* articles, December 1957; interview with George Klein, 1993.

443 Elvis dropped in at the Sun studio: Interview with Jack Clement, 1989.

443 "We were at Graceland": Interview with George Klein for *Elvis in Hollywood*, 1993.

443–444 James Page, a *Press-Scimitar* reporter: *Memphis Press-Scimitar*, December 21, 1957.

444 He left for Nashville that same night: *Nashville Tennessean*, December 22, 1957; also *Nashville Banner*, December 21, 1957.

444–445 Gordon Stoker came out: Interview with Gordon Stoker, 1993.

445 How were things going?: Interview with T. Tommy Cutrer, 1990.

445 Jimmie Rodgers Snow, too, came by: Interview with Jimmie Rodgers Snow, 1993.

446 On Tuesday, December 24, Elvis wrote: *Memphis Commercial Appeal*, December 28, 1957.

446 He concluded by wishing: Alan Levy, *Operation Elvis*, p. 14.

446–447 Jimmie Rodgers Snow arrived: Interviews with Jimmie Rodgers Snow, 1990, 1993.

446–447 an increasing dependence on pills and alcohol: Interview with Jimmie Rodgers Snow, 1990; Jimmy Snow, *I Cannot Go Back*, pp. 57–58ff.

447 "She just couldn't cope": Interview with Lillian Fortenberry, 1988.

447–448 "I was working for my father": Interview with Alan Fortas, 1990.

450 Elvis had read the book: Both Alan Fortas and George Klein spoke in separate interviews of Elvis' unusual preparations for the role.

450 He got together with his new friend Kitty Dolan to run lines: May Mann, *Elvis and the Colonel*, pp. 47ff.

450 "You just didn't have a lot of fooling": Interview with Jan Shepard, 1992.

451 "I almost hesitate, I creep up to the sentence": BBC interview with Walter Matthau, as quoted in Gerry McLafferty, *Elvis Presley in Hollywood*.

451 In Carolyn Jones' observation "he was always": Joseph Lewis, "Elvis Presley Lives," *Cosmopolitan*, November 1968.

451 Jones suggested: Interview with Cliff Gleaves, 1991.

451 One Sunday when he was feeling blue: Interview with Jan Shepard.

451 It was in the fourth night: *Memphis Press-Scimitar*, January 14, 1958.

452 He saw Pat Boone: Interview with Jan Shepard.

453–454 Toward the end of February: Ibid.

454–455 "Hal Wallis loved locations": Interview with Alan Fortas.

455–456 He wasn't worried about the army: Vernon Scott, "Elvis at Home, Awaits Clippers," *New York World-Telegram*, March 15, 1958.

456 the Colonel had a big bunch of balloons: Interview with Trude Forsher, 1993.

456 Elvis posed politely for pictures: Levy, *Operation Elvis*, p. 21.

456 He was met by a *Commercial Appeal* reporter: James H. White, "Elvis Back in Town, with Sideburns Clipped and the Army on His Mind," *Memphis Commercial Appeal*, March 15, 1958.

"PRECIOUS MEMORIES"

459 On Monday he met Dewey: *Memphis Press-Scimitar*, March 18, 1958.

459 "no fewer than twelve beautiful girls": Alan Levy, *Operation Elvis*, p. 22.

459 "I screwed everything in sight": Larry Geller and Joel Spector, *"If I Can Dream,"* p. 236.

459 He had "fed them": *Memphis Press-Scimitar*, March 18, 1958.

459–460 "It was just 'So long' ": Interview with Scotty Moore, 1989.

460 he was dreading the army: BBC interview with Anita Wood.

460 To Barbara Pittman, who had known him: Interview with Barbara Pittman, 1989.

460 ("Girls come and go"): *Memphis Press-Scimitar*, March 24, 1958.

460 "We pulled in to the drive-in": Interview with George Klein for *Elvis in Hollywood*, 1993.

460 "he got in and out": Vince Staten, *The Real Elvis: Good Old Boy*, p. 139.

460 "Overnight," he said, "it was all gone": 1972 interview.

461–462 He showed up at the draft board: *Memphis Press-Scimitar*, March 24, 1958; additional sources are Alan Fortas' *Elvis: From Memphis to Hollywood*; Levy's *Operation Elvis*; and *Elvis the Soldier* by Rex and Elisabeth Mansfield.

461 not before Anita got special permission: *New York Post*, March 24, 1958.

461 The picture of him in *Life*: *Life*, April 7, 1958.

461–462 "Elvis recalled that in the days": *Memphis Press-Scimitar*, March 24, 1958.

462 The army provided a box lunch: *New York Post*, March 24, 1958.

463 refusing only to sign autographs: *New York Journal-American*, March 25, 1958.

463 "Start a loan company": Levy, *Operation Elvis*, p. 51.

463 He spotted a phone booth: Ibid., p. 52.

463 "No, sir. If I wore a string tie": Ibid., p. 54.

464 Hy Gardner wrote a column: *New York Herald-Tribune*, March 28, 1958.

464 After being chased for more than two hundred miles: Levy, *Operation Elvis*, pp. 61–63.

464–465 At Fort Hood things were under substantially: Ibid., pp. 59ff.

465 recruit instructor Sergeant Bill Norwood, who befriended him: Albert Goldman, *Elvis*, pp. 278–279.

465–466 "I didn't ask for anything": 1972 interview.

466–467 a Waco businessman named Eddie Fadal: Interview with Eddie Fadal, 1993.

466 Elvis approached Rex Mansfield: Mansfield, *Elvis the Soldier*, pp. 16–18.

467 Someone turned on a tape recorder: This has been available on a number of bootlegs over the years, starting off with *An Evening with Elvis* (Memphis Flash 92447).

468 "The treatment which I received": Mansfield, *Elvis the Soldier*, pp. 20–21.

469 "Well, I know the papers had us engaged, married": *Memphis Press-Scimitar*, June 3, 1958; UPI reports, June 3; Levy, *Operation Elvis*, p. 69.

469 He went with his parents: UPI report, June 14, 1958.

469 "[Elvis] tried to throw me every way": Jerry Hopkins interview with Ray Walker (MVC/MSU).

470 By the time that Rex returned: Mansfield, *Elvis the Soldier*, pp. 22–23.

470 Anita, too, had returned by now: Levy, *Operation Elvis*, p. 71; "Anita Wood Reveals — Why Elvis and I Couldn't Marry," fan magazine article excerpted in Bill DeNight et al., eds., *Elvis Album*; and UPI report, June 14, 1958.

470–472 Elvis brought his parents over: Interview with Eddie Fadal.

471 ("I just can't see myself over there"): Goldman, *Elvis*, p. 280.

472 A DJ named Rocky Frisco: Bill E. Burk, "Rocky Road Led to Meeting Elvis," *Elvis World* 20, June 1991.

472 Vince Edwards and Billy Murphy detoured: Interview with Vince Edwards, 1990.

472–473 She called her doctor in Memphis: Interview with Dr. Charles Clarke, 1989. Dr. Clarke's account of his forcefulness with army authorities is supported by news clippings of the time.

474 She was in better spirits: UPI report, August 14, 1958.

474 "we got off the elevator": Interview with Lamar Fike, 1988.

474 When reporters came to the house at mid morning: UPI report, August 14, 1958.

474–475 "Tears streamed down his cheeks": *Memphis Press-Scimitar*, August 14, 1958.

475 "When Mama was feeling bad": UPI report, August 14, 1958.

475–476 Hundreds of fans had assembled: This account of Gladys' "waking" draws on news accounts, Goldman's *Elvis*, and Elaine Dundy's *Elvis and Gladys*, as well as interviews cited.

475 When Dr. Clarke arrived at the house: Interview with Dr. Charles Clarke.

475 "Elvis was in a daze": Fortas, *Elvis*, pp. 91–92.

475 Junior picked up Eddie Fadal: Interview with Eddie Fadal.

476 "They couldn't get him to stop": Dundy, *Elvis and Gladys*, p. 325.

476 In the evening Sam and Dewey Phillips: Colin Escott and Martin Hawkins, *Good Rockin' Tonight: Sun Records and the Birth of Rock 'n' Roll*, p. 90.

476 "Come on in, Little": BBC interview with Anita Wood.

477 "When I went in the room": Interview with Dixie Locke, 1990.

477 "All we have now are memories": *Memphis Press-Scimitar*, August 16, 1958.

477 Every time they finished a song: Interview with J. D. Sumner, 1990; also interviews with James Blackwood, 1988, 1991.

477 The Reverend Hamill preached: *Memphis Commercial Appeal*, August 15, 1958.

477–478 "He went over to the casket": Interview with James Blackwood, 1991.

478–480 "I didn't mean to see him that night": Interview with Dixie Locke.

480 "He'd cry all day": Shelley Ritter interview with George Klein, 1993.

480 On Saturday he returned once again: Red West et al., *Elvis: What Happened?*, pp. 153–154.

480 "After a near emotional breakdown": *Memphis Press-Scimitar*, August 18, 1958.

480 his friends tried to cheer him up: Interview with Eddie Fadal; Fortas, *Elvis*, p. 93.

480–481 "He rolled his window down": Interview with George Blancet, 1989.

481 Toward the end of the week his dentist: Interview with Lester and Sterling Hofman, 1989.

482 It was, as Red described it: West et al., *Elvis*, p. 155.

482 Things were never again the same: Mansfield, *Elvis the Soldier*, p. 29.

482 ("Heavenly days, I just can't imagine it"): *New York Journal-American*, August 28, 1958.

482 Elvis and Eddie attended an r&b revue: Interview with Eddie Fadal.

482 a Johnny Horton show in Temple: Interviews with Jerry Kennedy, 1990, and Eddie Fadal; also 1993 interviews with Galen "Corncob" Christy, who promoted the show and played on it, and Tillman Franks, who managed Johnny Horton and played bass in Horton's band.

Christy did not remember the exact date of the concert but thought it was just before he went into the army himself, in mid September. His recollection was of asking Elvis how things were going. " 'It's like prison,' " said Elvis, who had met Christy at the 1955 DJ convention in Nashville. "He said, 'I tried to go to church the other day, and I disrupted the church service.' He thought that was not right: that a human being would disrupt the worship of the Lord."

483 The last weekend that he was at Fort Hood: Kitty Dolan, "I Shared Elvis' Love," *TV and Movie Screen*, March 1959.

483 "At two A.M. we said good night": May Mann, *Elvis and the Colonel*, p. 68.

483 he asked Eddie: Interview with Eddie Fadal.

483–484 The train took about an hour: Interview with George Klein, 1990.

484 One of his fellow soldiers gave Elvis a book: Elvis named the book, and the poem "Should You Go First," at his pre-embarkation press conference. He said that he had read several other poems, and I have taken the liberty of guessing which ones. He said that he preferred poetry to short stories.

484 Charlie was "bound and determined": Mansfield, *Elvis the Soldier*, p. 33; also interview with Charlie Hodge, 1989.

484–487 It was a scene worthy of P. T. Barnum: The scene is fully audible in recordings of the press conference — and visible to a degree as well in film clips. It is particularly well described in Ren Grevatt's "On the Beat," *Billboard*, September 29, 1958.

487 "Come on," said the Colonel: *New York Journal-American*, September 28, 1958.

487 "I think I'm talking for all the guys": Ibid.

487–488 "He was resigned": Interview with Anne Fulchino, 1993.

488 Why don't you come along, too?: In West et al., *Elvis*, Red has Elvis asking both him *and* Lamar at this point, but since he had already announced in the press conference that Lamar would be accompanying him, this is my best guess at the actual scenario.

Bibliography

REFERENCE

Cotten, Lee. *All Shook Up: Elvis Day-by-Day, 1954–1977*. Ann Arbor, Mich.: Pierian Press, 1985.

———. *Shake, Rattle & Roll: The Golden Age of American Rock 'n' Roll*. Vol. 1, *1952–1955*. Ann Arbor, Mich.: Pierian Press, 1989.

Dellar, Fred, Roy Thompson, and Douglas B. Green. *The Illustrated Encyclopedia of Country Music*. New York: Harmony Books, 1977.

Elvis: Like Any Other Soldier. Reprint of the 1958 2nd Army Division Yearbook. Port Townsend, Wash.: Osborne Productions, 1988.

F.B.I. Files for Elvis A. Presley. Released under the Freedom of Information Act.

Federal Writers' Project of the Works Progress Administration. *Mississippi: The WPA Guide to the Magnolia State*. Golden anniversary ed. Jackson: University Press of Mississippi, 1988.

———. *The WPA Guide to Tennessee*. Knoxville: University of Tennessee Press, 1986.

Gart, Galen, comp. and ed. *First Pressings: Rock History as Chronicled in Billboard Magazine*. Vol. 1, *1948–1950*. Milford, N.H.: Big Nickel Publications, 1986.

———. *First Pressings: Rock History as Chronicled in Billboard Magazine*. Vol. 2, *1951–1952*. Milford, N.H.: Big Nickel Publications, 1986.

———. *The History of Rhythm & Blues*. Vols. 1–7 (1951–1957). Milford, N.H.: Big Nickel Publications, 1991–1993.

———. *The History of Rhythm & Blues, Special 1950 Volume*. Milford, N.H.: Big Nickel Publications, 1993.

Gentry, Linnell. *A History and Encyclopedia of Country, Western, and Gospel Music*. Nashville: Linnell Gentry, 1961.

Hardy, Phil, and Dave Laing. *Encyclopedia of Rock, 1955–1975*. London: Aquarius Books, 1977.

The 1953 Senior Herald. Humes High School Yearbook. Reprint, Port Townsend, Wash.: Osborne Enterprises, 1988.

Report of Guardian Ad Litem in re the Estate of Elvis A. Presley, Deceased, in the Probate Court of Shelby County, Tennessee. Number A655.

Stambler, Irwin. *Encyclopedia of Pop, Rock and Soul*. New York: St. Martin's Press, 1977.

Stambler, Irwin, and Grelun Landon. *Encyclopedia of Folk, Country and Western Music*. New York: St. Martin's Press, 1969.

Whisler, John A. *Elvis Presley: Reference Guide and Discography*. Metuchen, N.J.: Scarecrow Press, 1981.

Worth, Fred L., and Steve D. Tamerius. *All About Elvis*. New York: Bantam Books, 1981.

———. *Elvis: His Life from A to Z*. Chicago: Contemporary Books, 1988.

DISCOGRAPHIES, SONG AND RECORD GUIDES

Blackburn, Richard. *Rockabilly: A Comprehensive Discography of Reissues*. N.p.: Richard Blackburn, 1975.

Cotten, Lee, and Howard A. DeWitt. *Jailhouse Rock: The Bootleg Records of Elvis Presley, 1970–1983*. Ann Arbor, Mich.: Pierian Press, 1983.

The Elvis Presley Album of Juke Box Favorites, No. 1. New York: Hill and Range Songs, 1956.

Escott, Colin, and Martin Hawkins. *Sun Records: The Discography*. Vollersode, West Germany: Bear Family, 1987.

Hawkins, Martin, and Colin Escott. *Elvis Presley: The Illustrated Discography*. London: Omnibus Press, 1981.

Jancik, Wayne. *Billboard Book of One-Hit Wonders*. New York: Watson-Guptill, 1990.

Jorgensen, Ernst, Erik Rasmussen, and Johnny Mikkelsen. *Elvis Recording Sessions*. Stenlose, Denmark: JEE Productions, 1984.

Jorgensen, Ernst, Erik Rasmussen, and Roger Semon. Sessionography and Discography for *Elvis: The King of Rock 'N' Roll: The Complete 50's Masters* (RCA 07863-66050-2), 1992.

Kingsbury, Paul, ed. *Country on Compact Disc: The Essential Guide to the Music*. New York: Grove Press, 1993.

Pavlow, Big Al. *The R & B Book: A Disc-History of Rhythm & Blues*. Providence: Music House Publishing, 1983.

Tunzi, Joseph A. *Elvis Sessions: The Recorded Music of Elvis Aron Presley, 1953–1977*. Chicago: JAT Productions, 1993.

Weisman, Ben. *Elvis Presley: "The Hollywood Years."* Secaucus, N.J.: Warner Brothers Publications, 1992.

Whitburn, Joel. *Pop Memories, 1890–1954: The History of American Popular Music*. Menomonee Falls, Wis.: Record Research, 1986.

———. *Top Country Singles, 1944–1988*. Menomonee Falls, Wis.: Record Research, 1989.

———. *Top Pop Records, 1955–1972*. Menomonee Falls, Wis.: Record Research, 1973.

———. *Top R & B Singles, 1942–1988*. Menomonee Falls, Wis.: Record Research, 1988.

BOOKS OF MORE GENERAL INTEREST

Alexander, A. L., ed. *Poems That Touch the Heart*. Garden City, N.Y.: Doubleday, 1941.

Amburn, Ellis. *Dark Star: The Roy Orbison Story*. New York: Lyle Stuart, 1990.

Arnold, Eddy. *It's a Long Way from Chester County*. Old Tappan, N.J.: Hewitt House, 1969.

Atkins, Chet, with Bill Neely. *Country Gentleman*. Chicago: Henry Regnery, 1974.

Atkins, John, ed. *The Carter Family*. London: Old Time Music, 1973.

Bane, Michael. *White Boy Singin' the Blues: The Black Roots of White Rock*. New York: Penguin Books, 1982.

Bane, Michael, and Mary Ellen Moore. *Tampa, Yesterday, Today and Tomorrow*. Tampa: Misher and King Publishing, 1981.

Banks, Ann, ed. *First-Person America*. New York: Vintage Books, 1981.

Barthel, Norma. *Ernest Tubb Discography (1936–1969)*. Roland, Okla.: Ernest Tubb Fan Club Enterprises, 1969.

Bashe, Philip. *Teenage Idol, Travelin' Man: The Complete Biography of Rick Nelson*. New York: Hyperion, 1992.

Benson, Bernard. *The Minstrel*. New York: G. P. Putnam's Sons, 1977.

Berry, Chuck. *Chuck Berry: The Autobiography*. New York: Harmony Books, 1987.

Biles, Roger. *Memphis in the Great Depression*. Knoxville: University of Tennessee Press, 1986.

Black, Jim. *Elvis on the Road to Stardom*. London: W. H. Allen, 1988.

Blaine, Hal, with David Goggin. *Hal Blaine and the Wrecking Crew*. Emeryville, Calif.: Mix Books, 1990.

Blumhofer, Edith L. *Restoring the Faith: The Assemblies of God, Pentecostalism, and American Culture*. Urbana: University of Illinois Press, 1993.

Booth, Stanley. *Rythm Oil: A Journey Through the Music of the American South*. London: Jonathan Cape, 1991.

Bowles, Jerry. *A Thousand Sundays: The Story of the Ed Sullivan Show*. New York: G. P. Putnam's Sons, 1980.

Branch, Taylor. *Parting the Waters: America in the King Years*. New York: Simon and Schuster, 1988.

Braudy, Leo. *The Frenzy of Renown: Fame and Its History*. New York: Oxford University Press, 1986.

Buckle, Phillip. *All Elvis: An Unofficial Biography of the "King of Discs."* London: Daily Mirror, 1962.

Burk, Bill E. *Early Elvis: The Humes Years*. Memphis: Red Oak Press, 1990.

———. *Early Elvis: The Tupelo Years*. Memphis: Propwash Publishing. Forthcoming.

———. *Elvis: A 30-Year Chronicle*. Tempe, Ariz.: Osborne Enterprises, 1985.

———. *Elvis Memories: Press Between the Pages*. Memphis: Propwash Publishing, 1993.

———. *Elvis Through My Eyes*. Memphis: Burk Enterprises, 1987.

Cain, Robert. *Whole Lotta Shakin' Goin' On: Jerry Lee Lewis*. New York: Dial Press, 1981.

Cantor, Louis. *Wheelin' on Beale*. New York: Pharos Books, 1992.

Capers, Gerald M., Jr. *The Biography of a River Town: Memphis, Its Heroic Age*. 1966. Reprint, Memphis: Burke's Book Store.

Carr, Roy, and Mick Farren. *Elvis Presley: The Illustrated Record*. New York: Harmony Books, 1982.

Cash, Johnny. *The Man in Black*. New York: Warner Books, 1975.

Cash, June Carter. *From the Heart*. New York: Prentice Hall Press, 1987.

Cash, W. J. *The Mind of the South*. 1941. Reprint, New York: Vintage Books.

Chapple, Steve, and Reebee Garofalo. *Rock 'n' Roll Is Here to Pay*. Chicago: Nelson-Hall, 1977.

Choron, Sandra, and Bob Oskam. *Elvis! The Last Word*. New York: Citadel Press, 1991.

Cocke, Marian J. *I Called Him Babe: Elvis Presley's Nurse Remembers*. Memphis: Memphis State University Press, 1979.

Cohn, David. *Where I Was Born and Raised*. Notre Dame, Ind.: University of Notre Dame Press, 1967.

Cohn, Nik. *Rock from the Beginning*. New York: Pocket Books, 1970.

Conaway, James. *Memphis Afternoons*. Boston: Houghton Mifflin, 1993.

Country Music Foundation. *Country: The Music and the Musicians*. New York: Abbeville Press, 1988.

Country Music Magazine, editors of. *The Illustrated History of Country Music*. Garden City, N.Y.: Doubleday, 1979.

Crumbaker, Marge, and Gabe Tucker. *Up and Down with Elvis Presley*. New York: G. P. Putnam's Sons, 1981.

Dalton, David. *James Dean: The Mutant King*. New York: Dell, 1974.

Dalton, David, and Lenny Kaye. *Rock 100*. New York: Grosset and Dunlap, 1977.

Daniel, Pete. *Standing at the Crossroads*. New York: Hill and Wang, 1986.

Davis, Jr., Sammy, Jane Boyar, and Burt Boyar. *Hollywood in a Suitcase*. New York: William Morrow, 1980.

———. *Why Me? The Sammy Davis, Jr., Story*. New York: Farrar, Straus and Giroux, 1989.

DeCosta-Willis, Miriam, and Fannie Mitchell Delk. *Homespun Images: An Anthology of Black Memphis Writers and Artists*. Memphis: LeMoyne Owen College, 1989.

Delmore, Alton. *Truth Is Stranger than Publicity*. Edited by Charles K. Wolfe. Nashville: Country Music Foundation Press, 1977.

DeWitt, Howard A. *Elvis — The Sun Years: The Story of Elvis Presley in the Fifties*. Ann Arbor, Mich.: Popular Culture, Ink., 1993.

Dollard, John. *Caste and Class in a Southern Town*. 3d ed. New York: Doubleday Anchor, 1957.

Dundy, Elaine. *Elvis and Gladys*. New York: Macmillan, 1985.

———. *Ferriday, Louisiana*. New York: Donald Fine, 1991.

Dunne, Philip. *Take Two: A Life in Music and Politics*. New York: McGraw-Hill, 1980.

Elvis Presley. Prepared by the Editors of *TV Radio Mirror Magazine*. New York: Bartholomew House, 1956.

Elvis Presley Heights, Mississippi: Lee County, 1921–1984. Compiled by Members of the Elvis Presley Heights Garden Club. Tupelo, Miss., 1984.

Elvis Presley Speaks! Text by Robert Johnson. New York: Rave Publishing, 1956.

Escott, Colin, and Martin Hawkins. *Good Rockin' Tonight: Sun Records and the Birth of Rock 'n' Roll*. New York: St. Martin's Press, 1991.

Escott, Colin, Martin Hawkins, and Hank Davis. *The Sun Country Years: Country Music in Memphis, 1950–1959*. Vollersode, West Germany: Bear Family Records, 1987.

Escott, Colin, with George Merritt and William MacEwen. *Hank Williams: The Biography*. Boston: Little, Brown, 1994.

Falkenburg, Claudia, and Andrew Solt, eds. *A Really Big Show: A Visual History of the Ed Sullivan Show.* Text by John Leonard. New York: Viking Studio Books, 1992.

Farren, Mick, ed. *Elvis in His Own Words*. London: Omnibus Press, 1977.

Finnis, Rob, and Bob Dunham. *Gene Vincent and the Blue Caps*. London: Rob Finnis and Bob Dunham, n.d.

Fortas, Alan. *Elvis: From Memphis to Hollywood*. Ann Arbor, Mich.: Popular Culture, Ink., 1992.

Fowler, Gene, and Bill Crawford. *Border Radio*. Austin: Texas Monthly Press, 1987.

Fowles, Jib. *Star Struck: Celebrity Performers and the American Public*. Washington, D.C.: Smithsonian Institution Press, 1992.

Frady, Marshall. *Southerners: A Journalist's Odyssey*. New York: New American Library, 1980.

Gabree, John. *The World of Rock*. Greenwich, Conn.: Fawcett, 1968.

Gaillard, Frye. *Watermelon Wine: The Spirit of Country Music*. New York: St. Martin's Press, 1978.

Garbutt, Bob. *Rockabilly Queens: The Careers and Recordings of Wanda Jackson, Janis Martin, Brenda Lee*. Toronto: Robert Garbutt Productions, 1979.

Gart, Galen, and Roy C. Ames. *Duke/Peacock Records: An Illustrated History with Discography*. Milford, N.H.: Big Nickel Publications, 1990.

Gelatt, Roland. *The Fabulous Phonograph, 1877–1977*. New York: Collier Books, 1977.

Geller, Larry, and Joel Spector with Patricia Romanowski. *"If I Can Dream": Elvis' Own Story*. New York: Simon and Schuster, 1989.

Gibson, Robert, with Sid Shaw. *Elvis: A King Forever*. London: Elvisly Yours, 1987.

Gillett, Charlie. *The Sound of the City: The Rise of Rock and Roll*. Rev. ed. London: Souvenir Press, 1983.

Goldman, Albert. *Elvis*. New York: McGraw-Hill, 1981.

———. *Elvis: The Last 24 Hours*. New York: St. Martin's Paperbacks, 1991.

Goldrosen, John, and John Beecher. *Remembering Buddy: The Definitive Biography of Buddy Holly*. New York: Penguin Books, 1986.

Graceland: The Living Legacy of Elvis Presley. San Francisco: Collins Publishers San Francisco, 1993.

Green, Douglas B. *Country Roots: The Origins of Country Music*. New York: Hawthorne Books, 1976.

Greenwood, Earl, and Kathleen Tracy. *The Boy Who Would Be King*. New York: Dutton, 1990.

Gregory, James, editor. *The Elvis Presley Story*. New York: Hillman Periodicals, 1960.

Gregory, Neal, and Janice Gregory. *When Elvis Died*. Washington, D.C.: Communications Press, 1980.

Grissim, John. *Country Music: White Man's Blues*. New York: Paperback Library, 1970.

Gruber, J. Richard, organizer. *Memphis: 1948–1958*. Memphis: Memphis Brooks Museum of Art, 1986.

Guterman, Jimmy. *Rockin' My Life Away: Listening to Jerry Lee Lewis*. Nashville: Rutledge Hill Press, 1991.

Hagarty, Britt. *The Day the World Turned Blue: A Biography of Gene Vincent*. Vancouver: Talonbooks, 1983.

Haining, Peter, ed. *Elvis in Private*. New York: St. Martin's Press, 1987.

Halberstam, David. *The Fifties*. New York: Villard Books, 1993.

Haley, John W., and John von Hoelle. *Sound and Glory*. Wilmington, Del.: Dyne-American Publishing, 1990.

Hammontree, Patsy Guy. *Elvis Presley: A Bio-Bibliography*. Westport, Conn.: Greenwood Press, 1985.

Hand, Albert. *Meet Elvis*. An Elvis Monthly Special: Manchester, 1962.

Harbinson, W. A. *The Illustrated Elvis*. New York: Grosset and Dunlap, 1976.

Harbinson, W. A., and Kay Wheeler. *Growing Up with the Memphis Flash*. Amsterdam: Tutti Frutti Productions, 1994.

Hawkins, Martin, and Colin Escott, comps. *The Sun Records Rocking Years*. London: Charly Records, 1986.

Hemphill, Paul. *The Nashville Sound: Bright Lights and Country Music*. New York: Simon and Schuster, 1970.

Hill, Wanda June. *We Remember, Elvis*. Palos Verdes, Calif.: Morgin Press, 1978.

Historic Black Memphians. Memphis: Memphis Pink Palace Museum Foundation, n.d.

Hodge, Charlie, with Charles Goodman. *Me 'n Elvis*. Memphis: Castle Books, 1988.

Holmes, Richard. *Footsteps: Adventures of a Romantic Biographer*. New York: Viking, 1985.

Hopkins, Jerry. *Elvis*. New York: Simon and Schuster, 1971.

———. *Elvis: The Final Years*. New York: St. Martin's Press, 1980.

———. *The Rock Story*. New York: Signet Books, 1970.

Horstman, Dorothy. *Sing Your Heart Out, Country Boy*. Rev. Ed. Nashville: Country Music Foundation Press, 1986.

Hurst, Jack. *Nashville's Grand Ole Opry*. New York: Abrams, 1975.

The Impersonal Life. Marina del Rey, Calif.: DeVorss, 1988.

Jenkins, Mary. *Elvis: The Way I Knew Him*. Memphis: Riverpark Publishers, 1984.

Jenkinson, Philip, and Alan Warner. *Celluloid Rock*. New York: Warner Books, 1976.

Jones, Ira, as told to Bill E. Burk. *Soldier Boy Elvis*. Memphis: Propwash Publishing, 1992.

Juanico, June. *Elvis — In the Twilight of Memory*. Unpublished manuscript.

Kienzle, Rich. *Great Guitarists: The Most Influential Players in Blues, Country Music, Jazz and Rock*. New York: Facts on File, 1985.

Killen, Buddy, with Tom Carter. *By the Seat of My Pants*. New York: Simon and Schuster, 1993.

Kirby, Edward "Prince Gabe." *From Africa to Beale Street*. Memphis: Music Management, 1983.

Lacker, Marty, Patsy Lacker, and Leslie S. Smith. *Elvis: Portrait of a Friend*. New York: Bantam, 1980.

Laing, Dave. *Buddy Holly*. London: Studio Vista, 1971.

Langbroek, Hans. *The Hillbilly Cat*. Self-published, n.d.

Latham, Caroline, and Jeannie Sakol. *"E" Is for Elvis: An A to Z Illustrated Guide to the King of Rock and Roll*. New York: New American Library, 1990.

Lemann, Nicholas. *Out of the Forties*. New York: Simon and Schuster, 1983.

———. *The Promised Land*. New York: Alfred A. Knopf, 1991.

Levine, Lawrence W. *Black Culture and Black Consciousness: Afro-American Folk Thought from Slavery to Freedom*. New York: Oxford University Press, 1977.

Levy, Alan. *Operation Elvis*. New York: Henry Holt, 1960.

Lewis, Myra, with Murray Silver. *Great Balls of Fire: The Uncensored Story of Jerry Lee Lewis*. New York: Quill, 1982.

Lichter, Paul. *The Boy Who Dared to Rock: The Definitive Elvis*. New York: Doubleday Dolphin, 1978.

Lornell, Kip. *"Happy in the Service of the Lord": Afro-American Gospel Quartets in Memphis*. Urbana: University of Illinois Press, 1988.

Loyd, Harold. *Elvis Presley's Graceland Gates*. Franklin, Tenn.: Jimmy Velvet Publications, 1987.

Lydon, Michael. *Rock Folk: Portraits from the Rock 'n' Roll Pantheon*. New York: Dial, 1971.

Lytle, Clyde Francis, ed. *Leaves of Gold: An Anthology of Prayers, Memorable Phrases, Inspirational Verse and Prose*. N.p., n.d.

Malone, Bill C. *Country Music, U.S.A.: A Fifty-Year History*. Austin: American Folklore Society, University of Texas Press, 1968.

———. *Southern Music: American Music*. Lexington: University Press of Kentucky, 1979.

Malone, Bill C., and Judith McCulloh. *Stars of Country Music: Uncle Dave Macon to Johnny Rodriguez*. Urbana: University of Illinois Press, 1975.

Mann, May. *Elvis and the Colonel*. New York: Drake Publishers, 1975.

Mansfield, Rex, and Elizabeth Mansfield. *Elvis the Soldier*. Bamberg, West Germany: Collectors Service GmbH, 1983.

Marcus, Greil. *Dead Elvis*. New York: Doubleday, 1991.

———. *Mystery Train*. 3d rev. ed. New York: Dutton, 1990.

Marsh, Dave. *Elvis*. New York: Times Books, 1982.

Martin, Linda, and Kerry Segrave. *Anti-Rock: The Opposition to Rock 'n' Roll*. Hamden, Conn.: Shoe String Press, Archon Books, 1988.

Matthew-Walker, Robert. *Elvis Presley: A Study in Music*. London: Omnibus Press, 1983.

McIlwaine, Shields. *Memphis Down in Dixie*. New York: E. P. Dutton, 1948.

McKee, Margaret, and Fred Chisenhall. *Beale Black & Blue: Life and Music on Black America's Main Street*. Baton Rouge: Louisiana State University Press, 1981.

McLafferty, Gerry. *Elvis Presley in Hollywood: Celluloid Sell-Out*. London: Robert Hale, 1989.

McNutt, Randy. *We Wanna Boogie*. Hamilton, Ohio: HHP Books, 1988.

Michael Ochs Archives. *Elvis in Hollywood*. Text by Steve Pond. New York: New American Library, 1990.

Miller, Jim, ed. *The Rolling Stone Illustrated History of Rock & Roll.* New York: Random House, Rolling Stone Press, 1976.

Miller, William D. *Memphis During the Progressive Era: 1900–1917.* Memphis: Memphis State University Press, 1957.

———. *Mr. Crump of Memphis.* Baton Rouge: Louisiana State University Press, 1964.

Morris, Willie. *North Toward Home.* Boston: Houghton Mifflin, 1967.

Morthland, John. *The Best of Country Music.* Garden City, N.Y.: Doubleday Dolphin, 1984.

Muir, Eddie, ed. *'Wild Cat': A Tribute to Gene Vincent.* Brighton, U.K.: Self-published, 1977.

Murray, Albert. *South to a Very Old Place.* New York: McGraw-Hill, 1971.

Nash, Alanna. *Behind Closed Doors: Talking with the Legends of Country Music.* New York: Alfred A. Knopf, 1988.

Palmer, Robert. *Baby, That Was Rock & Roll: The Legendary Leiber & Stoller.* New York: Harcourt Brace Jovanovich, 1978.

———. *Deep Blues.* New York: Viking, 1981.

———. *Jerry Lee Lewis Rocks!* New York: G. P. Putnam's Sons, 1981.

———. *A Tale of Two Cities: Memphis Rock and New Orleans Roll.* I.S.A.M. Monographs: Number 12. Brooklyn: Institute for Studies in American Music, 1979.

Palmer, Tony. *All You Need Is Love: The Story of Popular Music.* New York: Viking Press, Grossman Publishers, 1976.

Parker, Ed. *Inside Elvis.* Orange, Calif.: Rampart House, 1978.

Parker, John. *Five for Hollywood.* New York: Lyle Stuart, 1991.

Passman, Arnold. *The Deejays.* New York: Macmillan, 1971.

Pearl, Minnie, with Joan Dew. *Minnie Pearl: An Autobiography.* New York: Simon and Schuster, 1980.

Peary, Danny, ed. *Close Ups: The Movie Star Book.* New York: Workman, 1978.

Percy, William Alexander. *Lanterns on the Levee: Recollections of a Planter's Son.* Baton Rouge: Louisiana State University Press, 1973.

Perkins, Carl, with Ron Rendleman. *Disciple in Blue Suede Shoes.* Grand Rapids, Mich.: Zondervan Publishing House, 1978.

Pleasants, Henry. *The Great American Popular Singers.* New York: Simon and Schuster, 1974.

Poe, Randy. *Music Publishing: A Songwriter's Guide.* Cincinnati: Writer's Digest Books, 1990.

Porterfield, Nolan. *The Life and Times of America's Blue Yodeler: Jimmie Rodgers.* Urbana: University of Illinois Press, 1979.

Presley, Dee, Billy Stanley, Rick Stanley, and David Stanley, as told to Martin Torgoff. *Elvis, We Love You Tender.* New York: Delacorte Press, 1980.

Presley, Priscilla Beaulieu, with Sandra Harmon. *Elvis and Me.* New York: G. P. Putnam's Sons, 1985.

Presley, Vester. *A Presley Speaks.* Memphis: Wimmer Brothers Books, 1978.

Presley, Vester, and Nancy Rooks. *The Presley Family Cookbook*. Memphis: Wimmer Brothers Books, 1980.

Quain, Kevin, ed. *The Elvis Reader: Texts and Sources on the King of Rock 'n' Roll*. New York: St. Martin's Press, 1992.

Raines, Howell. *My Soul Is Rested*. New York: G. P. Putnam's Sons, 1977.

Reagon, Bernice Johnson, ed. *We'll Understand It Better By and By*. Washington, D.C.: Smithsonian Institution Press, 1992.

Rheingold, Todd. *Dispelling the Myth: An Analysis of American Attitudes and Prejudices*. New York: Believe in a Dream Publications, 1993.

Rijff, Ger. *Faces and Stages: An Elvis Presley Time-Frame*. Amsterdam: Tutti Frutti Productions, 1986.

———. *Long Lonely Highway*. Amsterdam: Tutti Frutti Productions, 1985.

———. *Memphis Lonesome*. Amsterdam: Tutti Frutti Productions, 1988.

———. *The Voice of Rock 'n' Roll: Elvis in the Times of Ultimate Cool*. Rotterdam: It's Elvis Time, 1993.

Rijff, Ger J., and Jan van Gestel. *Elvis: The Cool King*. Amsterdam: Tutti Frutti Productions, 1989.

———. *Fire in the Sun*. Amsterdam: Tutti Frutti Productions, 1991.

———. *Florida Close-Up*. Amsterdam: Tutti Frutti Productions, 1987.

Roark, Eldon. *Memphis Bragabouts*. New York: McGraw-Hill, Whittlesey House, 1945.

Rodriguez, Elena. *Dennis Hopper: A Madness to His Method*. New York: St. Martin's Press, 1988.

Rosenberg, Neil V. *Bluegrass: A History*. Urbana: University of Illinois Press, 1985.

Rovin, Jeff. *The World According to Elvis: Quotes from the King*. New York: HarperCollins, Harper Paperbacks, 1992.

Russell, Tony. *Blacks Whites and Blues*. London: Studio Vista, 1970.

Russell, Wayne. *Foot Soldiers and Kings*. Brandon, Manitoba: Wayne Russell, n.d.

———. *Foot Soldiers and Kings*. Vol 2. Brandon, Manitoba: Wayne Russell, n.d.

Sanjek, Russell. *American Popular Music and Its Business: The First Four Hundred Years*. Vol. 3, *From 1900 to 1984*. New York: Oxford University Press, 1988.

———. *From Print to Plastic: Publishing and Promoting America's Popular Music (1900–1980)*. I.S.A.M. Monographs: Number 20. Brooklyn: Institute for Studies in American Music, 1983.

Sawyer, Charles. *The Arrival of B. B. King*. Garden City, N.Y.: Doubleday, 1980.

Schlappi, Elizabeth. *Roy Acuff: The Smoky Mountain Boy*. Gretna, La.: Pelican Publishing, 1978.

Schroer, Andreas. *Private Presley: The Missing Years — Elvis in Germany*. New York: William Morrow, 1993.

Selvin, Joel. *Ricky Nelson: Idol for a Generation*. Chicago: Contemporary Books, 1990.

Shaw, Arnold. *The Rockin' '50s*. New York: Hawthorne Books, 1974.

Shelton, Robert, and Burt Goldblatt. *The Country Music Story: A Picture History of Country and Western Music*. New York: Bobbs-Merrill, 1966.

Siegel, Don. *A Siegel Film: An Autobiography*. London: Faber and Faber, 1993.

Sigafoos, Robert A. *Cotton Row to Beale Street*. Memphis: Memphis State University Press, 1979.

Smith, Wes. *The Pied Pipers of Rock 'n' Roll: Radio Deejays of the 50s and 60s*. Marietta, Ga.: Longstreet Press, 1989.

Snow, Hank, with Jack Ownbey and Bob Burris. *The Hank Snow Story*. Champaign: University of Illinois Press. Forthcoming.

Snow, Jimmy, with Jim Hefley and Marti Hefley. *I Cannot Go Back*. Plainfield, N.J.: Logos International, 1977.

Stanley, Billy, with George Erikson. *Elvis, My Brother*. New York: St. Martin's Press, 1989.

Stanley, David. *Life with Elvis*. Old Tappan, N.J.: Fleming H. Revell, 1986.

Stanley, Rick, with Michael K. Haynes. *The Touch of Two Kings: Growing Up at Graceland*. N.p.: T2K Publishers, 1986.

Staten, Vince. *The Real Elvis: Good Old Boy*. Dayton: Media Ventures, 1978.

Stearn, Jess, with Larry Geller. *The Truth About Elvis*. New York: Jove Publications, 1980.

Stern, Jane, and Michael Stern. *Elvis World*. New York: Alfred A. Knopf, 1987.

Storm, Tempest, with Bill Boyd. *The Lady Is a Vamp*. Atlanta: Peachtree Publishers, 1987.

Sumner, J. D., with Bob Terrell. *Elvis: His Love for Gospel Music and J. D. Sumner*. N.p.: The Gospel Quartet Music Company and Bob Terrell, 1991.

Swaggart, Jimmy. *The Campmeeting Hour: The Radio Miracle of the 20th Century*. Baton Rouge: Jimmy Swaggart Evangelistic Association, 1976.

Swaggart, Jimmy, with Robert Paul Lamb. *To Cross a River*. Plainfield, N.J.: Logos International, 1977.

Swenson, John. *Bill Haley: The Daddy of Rock and Roll*. New York: Stein and Day, 1982.

Terrell, Bob. *The Music Men: The Story of Professional Gospel Quartet Singing*. Asheville, N.C.: Bob Terrell Publisher, 1990.

Tharpe, Jac L., ed. *Elvis: Images and Fancies*. Jackson: University Press of Mississippi, 1979.

Thompson, Charles C. II, and James P. Cole. *The Death of Elvis: What Really Happened*. New York: Delacorte Press, 1991.

Thompson, Sam. *Elvis on Tour: The Last Year*. Memphis: Still Brook Publishing, 1992.

Tobler, John, and Stuart Grundy. *The Record Producers*. New York: St. Martin's Press, 1982.

Toll, Robert. *Blacking Up: The Minstrel Show in Nineteenth-Century America*. New York: Oxford University Press, 1974.

Torgoff, Martin, ed. *The Complete Elvis*. New York: G. P. Putnam's Sons, 1982.

Tosches, Nick. *Country: The Biggest Music in America*. New York: Stein and Day, 1977.

———. *Dino*. New York: Doubleday, 1992.

———. *Hellfire: The Jerry Lee Lewis Story*. New York: Dell, 1982.

———. *Unsung Heroes of Rock 'n' Roll*. Rev. ed. New York: Harmony Books, 1991.

Townsend, Charles R. *San Antonio Rose: The Life and Music of Bob Wills*. Urbana: University of Illinois Press, 1976.

Tribute: The Life of Dr. William Herbert Brewster. 2d ed. Memphis: Brewster House of Sermon Songs, n.d.

Tucker, David. *Lieutenant Lee of Beale Street*. Nashville: Vanderbilt University Press, 1971.

———. *Memphis Since Crump: Bossism, Blacks, and Civic Reformers, 1948–1968*. Knoxville: University of Tennessee Press, 1980.

Turner, Steve. *Hungry for Heaven: Rock and Roll and the Search for Redemption*. London: W. H. Allen, 1988.

Van Doren, Mamie, with Art Aveilhe. *Playing the Field: My Story*. New York: G. P. Putnam's Sons, 1987.

Vellenga, Dirk, with Mick Farren. *Elvis and the Colonel*. New York: Delacorte Press, 1988.

Vernon, Paul. *The Sun Legend*. London: Paul Vernon, 1969.

Vince, Alan. *I Remember Gene Vincent*. Liverpool: Vintage Rock'n'Roll Appreciation Society, 1977.

Wade-Gayles, Gloria. *Pushed Back to Strength*. Boston: Beacon Press, 1993.

Wallis, Hal, and Charles Higham. *Starmaker: The Autobiography of Hal Wallis*. New York: Macmillan, 1980.

Ward, Ed, Geoffrey Stokes, and Ken Tucker. *Rock of Ages: The Rolling Stone History of Rock & Roll*. New York: Summit Books, 1986.

Weinberg, Max, with Robert Santelli. *The Big Beat: Conversations with Rock's Great Drummers*. New York: Billboard Books, 1991.

Wertheimer, Alfred, with Gregory Martinelli. *Elvis '56: In the Beginning*. New York: Collier Books, 1979.

West, Red, Sonny West, and Dave Hebler, as told to Steve Dunleavy. *Elvis: What Happened?* New York: Ballantine Books, 1977.

Westmoreland, Kathy, with William G. Quinn. *Elvis and Kathy*. Glendale, Calif.: Glendale House Publishing, 1987.

White, Charles. *The Life and Times of Little Richard: The Quasar of Rock*. New York: Harmony Books, 1984.

Wiegert, Sue. *Elvis: For the Good Times*. Los Angeles: The Blue Hawaiians for Elvis, 1978.

Wiegert, Sue, with contributions by Elvis friends and Elvis fans. *"Elvis: Precious Memories."* Los Angeles: Century City Printing, 1987.

———. *"Elvis: Precious Memories."* Vol. 2. Los Angeles: Century City Printing, 1989.

Williams, William Carlos. *In the American Grain*. New York: New Directions Press, 1956.

Winters, Shelley. *Shelley II*. New York: Simon and Schuster, 1989.

Wood, Lana. *Natalie: A Memoir by Her Sister*. New York: G. P. Putnam's Sons, 1984.

Woodward, C. Vann. *The Burden of Southern History*. Rev. ed. Baton Rouge: Louisiana State University Press, 1968.

———. *Thinking Back: The Perils of Writing History*. Baton Rouge: Louisiana State University Press, 1986.

Wren, Christopher S. *Winners Got Scars Too: The Life of Johnny Cash*. New York: A Country Music/Ballantine Book, 1971.

Wynette, Tammy, with Joan Dew. *Stand By Your Man: An Autobiography*. New York: Simon and Schuster, 1979.

Yancy, Becky, and Cliff Linedecker. *My Life with Elvis*. New York: St. Martin's Press, 1977.

Yogananda, Paramahansa. *Autobiography of a Yogi*. Los Angeles: Self-Realization Fellowship, 1974.

Zmijewsky, Steven, and Boris Zmijewsky. *Elvis: The Films and Career of Elvis Presley*. New York: Citadel Press, 1991.

CLIPPINGS, COLLECTIONS, PICTURE BOOKS, AND MEMORABILIA

Burk, Bill E. *Elvis: Rare Images of a Legend*. Memphis: Propwash Publishing, 1990.

Clark, Alan. *Buddy Holly and the Crickets*. West Covina, Calif.: Alan Clark Productions, 1979.

———. *Elvis Presley Memories*. West Covina, Calif.: Leap Frog Productions, 1982.

———. *The Elvis Presley Photo Album*. West Covina, Calif.: Alan Clark Productions, 1981.

———. *Gene Vincent: The Screaming End*. West Covina, Calif.: Alan Clark Productions, 1980.

———. *Legends of Sun Records*. West Covina, Calif.: Alan Clark Productions. Various volumes, 1986 to present.

———. *Rock-a-billy and Country Legends*. West Covina, Calif.: Alan Clark Productions.

———. *Rock and Roll in the Movies*. West Covina, Calif.: Alan Clark Productions. Various volumes.

———. *Rock and Roll Legends*. West Covina, Calif.: Alan Clark Productions. Various volumes.

———. *Rock and Roll Memories*. West Covina, Calif.: Alan Clark Productions. Various volumes.

Cortez, Diego, ed. *Private Elvis*. Stuttgart: FEY Verlags GmbH, 1978.

Curtin, Jim. *Unseen Elvis: Candids of the King*. Boston: Little, Brown, 1992.

DeNight, Bill, Sharon Fox, and Ger Rijff. *Elvis Album*. Lincolnwood, Ill.: Beekman House, 1991.

Esposito, Joe. *Elvis: A Legendary Performance*. Buena Park, Calif.: West Coast Publishing, 1990.

Fox, Sharon R., ed. *Elvis, His Real Life in the 60s: My Personal Scrapbook*. Chicago: Sharon Fox, 1989.

Hannaford, Jim. *Elvis: Golden Ride on the Mystery Train*. Vols. 1 and 2. Alva, Okla.: Jim Hannaford, 1986.

Kricun, Morrie E., and Virginia M. Kricun. *Elvis: 1956 Reflections*. Wayne, Pa.: Morgin Press, 1991 and 1992.

Lamb, Charles. *The Country Music World of Charlie Lamb*. Nashville: Infac Publications, 1986.

Life: 1946–1955. New York: Little, Brown, New York Graphic Society, 1984.

Loper, Karen. *The Elvis Clippings*. Houston: "The Elvis Clippings," n.d.

Michael Ochs Rock Archives. Garden City, N.Y.: Doubleday, 1984.

Now Dig This. *The King Forever.* Wallsend, Tyne and Wear, U.K.: Now Dig This, 1992.

O'Neal, Hank (text). *A Vision Shared: A Classic Portrait of America and Its People*. New York: St. Martin's Press, 1976.

Parish, James Robert. *Solid Gold Memories: The Elvis Presley Scrapbook*. New York: Ballantine Books, 1975.

Rijff, Ger, and Poul Madsen. *Elvis Presley: Echoes of the Past*. Voorschoten, Holland: "Blue Suede Shoes" Productions, 1976.

Tucker, Gabe, and Elmer Williams. *Pictures of Elvis Presley*. Houston: Williams and Tucker Photographs, 1981.

Tunzi, Joseph A. *Elvis '69: The Return*. Chicago: JAT Productions, 1991.

———. *Elvis '73: Hawaiian Spirit*. Chicago: JAT Productions, 1992.

PERIODICALS

I couldn't begin to list all the periodicals, past and present, that I have consulted. Just for the briefest of references, I have found *Now Dig This*, *Goldmine*, *DISCoveries*, *New Kommotion*, *Kicks*, *Country Music*, and *Picking Up the Tempo* particularly useful (and frequently invaluable) over the years. In addition, I have consulted the following Elvis publications extensively: *Elvis: The Man and His Music*; *Elvis: The Record*; *Elvis World*; *Because of Elvis*; *Elvis International Forum*; and *Graceland Express*. *Musician's* special 1992 report, "Elvis Presley: An Oral Biography," with interviews conducted by Peter Cronin, Scott Isler, and Mark Rowland, offered an insightful portrait. Finally, Orbis' *History of Rock*, vols. 3 and 5, published in 1981 and 1982, has good pictures and interesting background on the early career, and life and times, of Elvis Presley.

For detailed reference to specific articles and periodical sources, however, please see the Source Notes (page 491).

A Brief Discographical Note

MUCH OF THE WORK THAT would once have gone into pointing people toward the best of Elvis Presley on record has finally been done (or is in the process of completion) by RCA/BMG. Thanks to the efforts of Ernst Jorgensen and Roger Semon, the vast majority of Elvis' essential performances are now available on two five-CD sets. *Elvis: The King of Rock 'N' Roll: The Complete 50's Masters* (RCA 07863-66050-2) and *Elvis from Nashville to Memphis: The Essential 60's Masters* (RCA 07863-66160-2) contain just about everything in the way of studio masters over this two-decade period, with a '70s set as well as a two-CD gospel compilation in the offing.

The Complete 50's Masters alone could, really, serve as the soundtrack to this book, including everything from the first acetate to the last in-uniform '58 session, with such bonuses as Elvis' embarkation press conference, his 1956 Las Vegas show, a number of 1955 Hayride performances, and a 1955 radio-station acetate of Elvis, Scotty, and Bill doing a charming, unselfconscious version of the Clovers' "Fool, Fool, Fool." The only other essential purchases that I can think of would be *The Sun Sessions* (RCA 6414-2), which offers a fascinating glimpse of the creative process by way of alternate takes, outtakes, and studio chatter; *The Million Dollar Quartet* (RCA 2023-2), which offers an equally fascinating and even more unbuttoned view, with wonderfully ragged harmonies from Elvis, Jerry Lee Lewis, and Carl Perkins and the incomparable audio spectacle of hearing Elvis imitate Jackie Wilson imitating him; the nine scattered Hayride performances, which are included on *Elvis . . . The Beginning Years* (Louisiana Hayride 3061); and *The Essential Elvis*, volumes 1–3, a series of outtakes compiled by Jorgensen and Semon, of which volume 2, *Elvis Presley Stereo '57* (RCA 9589-2-R), provides a particularly fresh slant on familiar tunes.

With that said, the Elvis archaeologist has only just begun his journey. There is a whole paleontological dig out there comprising all the music that Elvis listened to and the music that influenced him most (the Statesmen, the Blackwood Brothers, Arthur Crudup, Martha Carson, Eddy Arnold, the Ink Spots, the Golden Gate Quartet, Sister Rosetta Tharpe), but I think I'll postpone that for a later time. So consider this just a start.

I should point out in any case that the best compilation highlighting the origins of Elvis' music is one that doesn't yet exist. Andy Franklin has assembled a wonderful anthology called *Fit for a King*, which gives us the whole panoply of Elvis' music by bringing together the first thirty songs that he recorded in their original versions, by artists as diverse as Roy Hamilton and Dean Martin, Bing Crosby and Ray Charles. It is a frequently startling, and always gratifying, documentation, beautifully annotated, scrupulously researched, and pointing out better than anything else could the catholicity and breadth of Elvis' musical taste. Let's hope that licensing problems can be overcome and that *Fit for a King* will see the light of day sometime soon.

Acknowledgments

IN WRITING A BOOK over so long a period (and one that stretches back well beyond its formal start), one incurs debts that one can never repay. Literally hundreds of people have helped me with my research and my interviews, and I thank them all. The following are just some of the people who gave me a hand over the weeks, months, and years:

Mrs. Lee Roy Abernathy, Curtis Lee Alderson, J. W. Alexander, Hoss Allen, Terry Allen, Chet Atkins, James Ausborn, Mae Axton, Buddy and Kay Bain, Eva Mills Baker and Sarah Baker Bailey, Jimmy Bank, Jonnie Barnett, Dick Baxter, Bob Beckham, Fred and Harriette Beeson, Bill Bentley, Bettye Berger, Freddy Bienstock, Steve Binder, Evelyn Black, Johnny Black, James Blackwood, George Blancet, Arthur Bloom, Arlene Piper Blum, Barbara Bobo, Barbara Boldt, Dave Booth, Stanley Booth, Joella Bostick, Ernest Bowen, Horace Boyer, Will Bratton and Sharyn Felder, Avis Brown, Jim Ed Brown, Monty and Marsha Brown, Tony Brown, James Burton, Sheila Caan, Trevor Cajiao, Louis Cantor, Jerry Carrigan, Martha Carson, Johnny Cash, Anne Cassidy, Marshall Chess, Gene Chrisman, Galen Christy, Dr. Charles L. Clarke, Quinton Claunch, Rose Clayton, Jack Clement, Jackie Lee Cochran, Jim Cole, Biff Collie, L. C. Cooke, Al Cooley, Daniel Cooper, X. Cosse, the Country Music Foundation, Floyd Cramer, Jack Cristil, Peter Cronin, Mike Crowley, T. Tommy Cutrer, Bill Dahl, Pete Daniel, Sherry Daniel, Fred Danzig, Fred Davis, Hank Davis, Richard Davis, Joan Deary, Bill Denny, Jesse Lee Denson, Jimmy Denson, Howard DeWitt, Jim and Mary Lindsay Dickinson, Duff Dorrough, Carole Drexler, Vince Edwards, Leroy Elmore, Sam Esgro, David Evans, Eddie Fadal, Charles Farrar, Charlie Feathers, Robert Ferguson, Lamar Fike, D. J. Fontana, Buzzy Forbess, Trude Forsher, Alan Fortas, Lillian Fortenberry, Fred Foster, Ted Fox, Andy Franklin, Ann Freer, Donnie Fritts, Anne Fulchino, Lowell Fulson, Ray Funk, Marty Garbus, Honeymoon Garner, Galen Gart, Gregg Geller, Larry Geller, Gary Giddins, Homer Gilliland, Cliff Gleaves, Glen Glenn, Billy Goldenberg, Stuart Goldman, John Goldrosen, Kay Gove, Betty Grant, Sid Graves, Tom Graves, Alan Greenberg, Bob Groom, Jimmy Guterman, Joe Haertel, Rick Hall, Jim Hannaford, Glenn D. Hardin, Gary Hardy, Sandy Harmon, Dottie Harmony, Phyllis Harper, Homer Ray Harris, Randy Haspel, Dot Hawkins, Martin Hawkins, Rick Hawks, Joseph Hazen, Skip Henderson, Curley Herndon, Lamar Herrin, Jake Hess, Charlie Hodge, Lester and Sterling Hofman, Bones Howe, Eliot Hubbard, Tom Hulett, Maylon Humphries, Nick Hunter, Bill Ivey, Mark James, Roland Janes, Jim Jaworowicz, Jimmy Johnson, Sandi Kallenberg, Hal Kanter, Jerry

Kennedy, Stan Kesler, Merle Kilgore, Buddy Killen, Paul Kingsbury, Millie Kirkham, Pete Kuykendall, Sleepy LaBeef, Charlie Lamb, Guy Lansky, Dickey Lee, Mike Leech, Ed Leek, Lance LeGault, Jerry Leiber, Barbara Leigh, Ed Leimbacher, David Leonard, Stan Lewis, Horace Logan, Mary Logan, Larrie Londin, Lorene Lortie, Bill Lowery, Archie Mackey, Kenneth Mann, Brad McCuen, Judy McCulloh, Charlie McGovern, Gerry McLafferty, Andy McLenon, John and Pat McMurray, Scott McQuaid, Sandi Miller, Bill Mitchell, Bill Monroe, Sputnik Monroe, Bob Moore, Bobbie Moore, Steve Morley, John Morthland, Joe Moscheo, Alanna Nash, David Naylor, Jimmy "C" Newman, Thorne Nogar, John Novarese, Herbie O'Mell, Jim O'Neal, Sean O'Neal, Michael Ochs, Bob Oermann, Jay Orr, Terry Pace, Frank Page, Colonel Tom Parker, Ed Parker, Pat Parry, Judy Peiser, Carl Perkins, Millie Perkins, Tom Perryman, Brian Petersen, Pallas Pidgeon, Bob Pinson, Barbara and Willie Pittman, Randy Poe, Gail Pollock, Doc Pomus, Steve Popovich, Bill Porter, John Andrew Prime, Mark Pucci, Ronnie Pugh, Norbert Putnam, Pat Rainer, Charles Raiteri, Jerry Reed, Eleanor Richman, JillEllyn Riley, Fran Roberts, Don Robertson, Jeffrey Rodgers, Steve Rosen, Neil Rosenberg, John Rumble, Wayne Russell, Ben Sandmel, Johnny Saulovich, Jerry Scheff, Tony Scherman, Tom Schultheiss, Joel Selvin, Jan Shepard, Barbara Sims, John and Shelby Singleton, the Reverend and Mrs. Frank Smith, Myrna Smith, Ronald Smith, Hank Snow, the Reverend Jimmy Snow, Jessica St. John, Kevin Stein, Jim Stewart, Alan Stoker, Gordon Stoker, Mike Stoller, Dave Stone, Billy Strange, Peter Stromberg, Marty Stuart, J. D. Sumner, Billy Swan, Russ Tamblyn, Corinne Tate, Bob Terrell, Rufus and Carla Thomas, Linda Thompson, Sam Thompson, Roland Tindall, Nick Tosches, Ruth Trussell, Ernest Tubb, Justin Tubb, Gabe Tucker, Cindy Underwood, Billy Walker, Slim Wallace, Jan Walner, Dick Waterman, Monte Weiner, Ben Weisman, Alfred Wertheimer, Kathy Westmoreland, Jerry Wexler, Jonny Whiteside, Tex Whitson, Willie Wileman, Jimmy Wiles, Charles Wolfe, Gloria Wolper, Terry Wood, Eve Yohalem, Chip Young, Jimmy Young, Reggie Young, and Mrs. W. A. Zuber.

Once again Bill Millar generously provided tapes, clippings, insights, and information, as did Ger Rijff, Karen Loper, Poul Madsen, Stephen Stathis, Rich Kienzle, and Diana Magrann. Robert Gordon energetically uncovered all kinds of arcane Memphis information and lore (and accompanied me to Riverside Park, the site of Rocky's Lakeside refreshment stand); I'm looking forward to reading Robert's take on some of this same material in his forthcoming book, *It Came from Memphis*. Other gracious Memphis hosts and guides were Bill Burk, Shelley Ritter, David and Angela Less, Jackson Baker, Ronny Trout, and the South Memphis gang to whom Ronnie Smith introduced me. In Nashville, too, I couldn't begin to name all my unflagging guides and personal sponsors, but Mary Jarvis and David Briggs in particular went out of their way to vouch for me and set me off in the right direction on my travels. Elaine Dundy, whom I first met when I began work on the book, soon became a fast friend and introduced me to all of *her* friends in Tupelo (whom she had met in the course of writing her own book, *Elvis and Gladys*). Those she didn't introduce me to personally, local historian and genealogist Roy Turner, who helped Elaine with her research and is Tupelo's resident expert on Marilyn Monroe, did. In Shreveport, Alton and Margaret Warwick and Tillman Franks fulfilled much the same function, doing everything in their power to provide me with all the background on the Hayride that I could absorb and introducing me cheerfully to many of its key figures.

I am greatly indebted to John Bakke, chairman of the Department of Theatre and Communication Arts, for making available to me both the resources of the Mississippi Valley Collection at Memphis State University and the tapes of the annual memorial service program, which was cosponsored by Dean Richard Ranta of the College of Communication and Fine Arts each August for ten years after Elvis' death. Andrew Solt and Malcolm Leo each helped immeasurably in opening up to me the resources, contacts, and files (not to mention knowledge, insights, and goodwill) that they developed initially in making *This Is Elvis* and in their subsequent work both together and individually over the years.

Both Dixie Locke and June Juanico were more than generous in their sharing of personal memories and thoughtful insights. Jerry Schilling, George Klein, and Joe Esposito gave freely of their time, reflection, and good offices. Chick Crumpacker and Grelun Landon were my unfailing guides and friends, taking me down various obscure and pleasurable paths, generally in the way of reminiscence but, in Chick's case, in semi-corporeal reality, too, when we revisited the old RCA building, studio, and environs with Ernst Jorgensen.

Scotty Moore patiently submitted to interview after interview (over the passage of more than fifteen years), finally played me his Josh White records, and said "Ouch, that hurts!" only often enough to point out what painful brain twisters the past can inevitably present. The late Marion Keisker, too, was the best of friends, always kept me abreast of the latest Memphis news, and was quick to share her views on everything from theater and film (in which she was an active participant) to feminism (ditto) to the Memphis Pyramid. I can't overstate my thanks to Sam Phillips, Knox Phillips, and the entire Phillips family, for their unstinting friendship and dedication to helping in this project in every way, down to the last, most infinitesimal detail. Sam, Marion, and Scotty all came together at a moment in history, and while their recollection of that moment has sometimes differed sharply, their commitment to its unblinking portrayal, whether presenting them in a flattering or unflattering light, and their sense of its significance independent of their own role in it have remained unswerving.

Kit Rachlis once again provided the most helpful (not to mention annoyingly perceptive) editorial suggestions and advice, and Alexandra Guralnick patiently read, transcribed, debated, and imagined the details of the story every step of the way. Colin Escott read the manuscript for accuracy and supplied clippings, information, and advice toward that end, while Ernst Jorgensen, co-compiler of Elvis' *Complete 50's* and *Essential 60's Masters*, RCA's two definitive five-CD sets, proved even more obsessive than I in running down obscure facts, upsetting theoretical applecarts, and refusing to allow a dream scenario to get in the way of the real one. My thanks to past and present editors Jim Landis and Michael Pietsch; to Dick

McDonough; to Debbie Jacobs for her tireless, sympathetic, and cheerfully stringent copyediting; and, once again, to Susan Marsh, not just for her fifteen-year partnership in design but for all her help, encouragement, perspective, and unflaggingly professional passion for the work.

Thanks to all, and to all those not named, from whom I drew encouragement, sustenance, and inspiration, not to mention the courage (and enthusiasm) to begin Volume II!

Index

Page numbers in *italic* type refer to illustrations.